Lecture Notes in Computer Science 10824

Commenced Publication in 1973
Founding and Former Series Editors:
Gerhard Goos, Juris Hartmanis, and Jan van Leeuwen

T0222942

More information about this series at http://www.springer.com/series/7407

Nikolaos Voros · Michael Huebner
Georgios Keramidas · Diana Goehringer
Christos Antonopoulos · Pedro C. Diniz (Eds.)

Applied Reconfigurable Computing

Architectures, Tools, and Applications

14th International Symposium, ARC 2018
Santorini, Greece, May 2–4, 2018
Proceedings

 Springer

Editors

Nikolaos Voros
Technological Educational Institute
  of Western Greece
Antirrio
Greece

Michael Huebner
Ruhr-Universität Bochum
Bochum
Germany

Georgios Keramidas
Technological Educational Institute
  of Western Greece
Antirrio
Greece

Diana Goehringer
Technische Universität Dresden
Dresden
Germany

Christos Antonopoulos
Technological Educational Institute
  of Western Greece
Antirrio
Greece

Pedro C. Diniz
INESC-ID
Lisbon
Portugal

ISSN 0302-9743   ISSN 1611-3349   (electronic)
Lecture Notes in Computer Science
ISBN 978-3-319-78889-0   ISBN 978-3-319-78890-6   (eBook)
https://doi.org/10.1007/978-3-319-78890-6

Library of Congress Control Number: 2018937393

LNCS Sublibrary: SL1 – Theoretical Computer Science and General Issues

Printed on acid-free paper

This Springer imprint is published by the registered company Springer International Publishing AG
part of Springer Nature
The registered company address is: Gewerbestrasse 11, 6330 Cham, Switzerland

Preface

Reconfigurable computing platforms offer increased performance gains and energy efficiency through coarse-grained and fine-grained parallelism coupled with their ability to implement custom functional, storage, and interconnect structures. As such, they have been gaining wide acceptance in recent years, spanning the spectrum from highly specialized custom controllers to general-purpose high-end programmable computing systems. The flexibility and configurability of these platforms, coupled with increasing technology integration, have enabled sophisticated platforms that facilitate both static and dynamic reconfiguration, rapid system prototyping, and early design verification. Configurability is emerging as a key technology for substantial product life-cycle savings in the presence of evolving product requirements, standards, and interface specifications.

The growth of the capacity of reconfigurable devices, such as FPGAs, has created a wealth of new research opportunities and intricate engineering challenges. Within the past decade, reconfigurable architectures have evolved from a uniform sea of programmable logic elements to fully reconfigurable systems-on-chip (SoCs) with integrate multipliers, memory elements, processors, and standard I/O interfaces. One of the foremost challenges facing reconfigurable application developers today is how to best exploit these novel and innovative resources to achieve the highest possible performance and energy efficiency; additional challenges include the design and implementation of next-generation architectures, along with languages, compilers, synthesis technologies, and physical design tools to enable highly productive design methodologies.

The International Applied Reconfigurable Computing (ARC) symposium series provides a forum for dissemination and discussion of ongoing research efforts in this transformative research area. The series of editions started in 2005 in Algarve, Portugal. The second edition of the symposium (ARC 2006) took place in Delft, The Netherlands, and was the first edition of the symposium to have selected papers published as a Springer LNCS (*Lecture Notes in Computer Science*) volume. Subsequent editions of the symposium have been held in Rio de Janeiro, Brazil (ARC 2007), London, UK (ARC 2008), Karlsruhe, Germany (ARC 2009), Bangkok, Thailand (ARC 2010), Belfast, UK (ARC 2011), Hong Kong, SAR China (ARC 2012), California, USA (ARC 2013), Algarve, Portugal (ARC 2014), Bochum, Germany (ARC 2015), Rio de Janeiro, Brazil (ARC 2016), and Delft, The Netherlands (ARC 2017).

This LNCS volume includes the papers selected for the 14th edition of the symposium (ARC 2018), held in Santorini, Greece, during May 2–4, 2018. The symposium attracted a large number of very good papers, describing interesting work on reconfigurable computing-related subjects. A total of 78 papers were submitted to the symposium from 28 countries. In particular, the authors of the submitted papers are from the following countries: Australia (3), Belgium (5), Bosnia and Herzegovina (4), Brazil (24), China (22), Colombia (1), France (3), Germany (40), Greece (44),

India (10), Iran (4), Ireland (4), Italy (5), Japan (22), Malaysia (2), The Netherlands (5), New Zealand (1), Norway (2), Poland (3), Portugal (3), Russia (8), Singapore (7), South Korea (2), Spain (4), Sweden (3), Switzerland (1), UK (18), and USA (11).

Submitted papers were evaluated by at least three members of the Program Committee. The average number of reviews per submission was 3.7. After careful selection, 29 papers were accepted as full papers (acceptance rate of 37.2%) and 22 as short papers. These accepted papers led to a very interesting symposium program, which we consider to constitute a representative overview of ongoing research efforts in reconfigurable computing, a rapidly evolving and maturing field. In addition, the symposium included a special session dedicated to funded research projects. The purpose of this session was to present the recent accomplishments, preliminary ideas, or work-in-progress scenarios of on-going research projects. Nine EU- and national-funded projects were selected for presentation in this session.

Several people contributed to the success of the 2018 edition of the symposium. We would like to acknowledge the support of all the members of this year's symposium Steering and Program Committees in reviewing papers, in helping the paper selection, and in giving valuable suggestions. Special thanks also to the additional researchers who contributed to the reviewing process, to all the authors who submitted papers to the symposium, and to all the symposium attendees. In addition, special thanks to Dr. Christos Antonopoulos from the Technological Educational Institute of Western Greece for organizing the research project special session. Last but not least, we are especially indebted to Anna Kramer from Springer for her support and work in publishing this book and to Pedro C. Diniz from INESC-ID, Lisbon, Portugal, for his strong support regarding the publication of the proceedings as part of the LNCS series.

February 2018

Nikolaos Voros
Michael Huebner
Georgios Keramidas
Diana Goehringer

Organization

The 2018 Applied Reconfigurable Computing Symposium (ARC2018) was organized by the Technological Educational Institute of Western Greece, by the Ruhr-Universität, Germany, and by the Technische Universität Dresden, Germany. The symposium took place at Bellonio Conference Center in Fira, the capital of Santorini in Greece.

General Chairs

Nikolaos Voros   Technological Educational Institute of Western Greece
Michael Huebner   Ruhr-Universität, Bochum, Germany

Program Chairs

Georgios Keramidas   Technological Educational Institute of Western Greece
Diana Goehringer   TU Dresden, Germany

Publicity Chairs

Luigi Carro   UFRGS, Brazil
Chao Wang   USTC, China
Dimitrios Soudris   NTUA, Greece
Stephan Wong   TU Delft, The Netherlands

EU Projects Track Chair

Christos Antonopoulos   Technological Educational Institute of Western Greece

Proceedings Chair

Pedro C. Diniz   INESC-ID, Lisbon, Portugal

Web Chair

Christos Antonopoulos   Technological Educational Institute of Western Greece

Steering Committee

Hideharu Amano   Keio University, Japan
Jürgen Becker   Universität Karlsruhe (TH), Germany
Mladen Berekovic   Braunschweig University of Technology, Germany
Koen Bertels   Delft University of Technology, The Netherlands
João M. P. Cardoso   University of Porto, Portugal

Krzysztof Kepa	GE Global Research, USA
Andreas Koch	TU Darmstadt, Germany
Stavros Koubias	University of Patras, Greece
Dimitrios Kritharidis	Intracom Telecom, Greece
Vianney Lapotre	Universit de Bretagne-Sud - Lab-STICC, France
Eduardo Marques	University of São Paulo, Brazil
Konstantinos Masselos	University of Peloponnese, Greece
Cathal Mccabe	Xilinx, Ireland
Antonio Miele	Politecnico di Milano, Italy
Takefumi Miyoshi	e-trees.Japan, Inc., Japan
Walid Najjar	University of California Riverside, USA
Horácio Neto	INESC-ID/IST/U Lisboa, Portugal
Dimitris Nikolos	University of Patras, Greece
Roman Obermeisser	University of Siegen, Germany
Kyprianos Papadimitriou	Technical University of Crete, Greece
Monica Pereira	Universidade Federal do Rio Grande do Norte, Brazil
Thilo Pionteck	Otto-von-Guericke Universität Magdeburg, Germany
Marco Platzner	University of Paderborn, Germany
Mihalis Psarakis	University of Piraeus, Greece
Kyle Rupnow	Advanced Digital Sciences Center, USA
Marco Domenico Santambrogio	Politecnico di Milano, Italy
Kentaro Sano	Tohoku University, Japan
Yukinori Sato	Tokyo Institute of Technology, Japan
António Beck Filho	Universidade Federal do Rio Grande do Sul, Brazil
Yuichiro Shibata	Nagasaki University, Japan
Cristina Silvano	Politecnico di Milano, Italy
Dimitrios Soudris	NTUA, Greece
Theocharis Theocharides	University of Cyprus, Cyprus
George Theodoridis	University of Patras, Greece
David Thomas	Imperial College, UK
Chao Wang	USTC, China
Markus Weinhardt	Osnabrück University of Applied Sciences, Germany
Theerayod Wiangtong	KMITL, Thailand
Roger Woods	Queens University Belfast, UK
Yoshiki Yamaguchi	University of Tsukuba, Japan

Additional Reviewers

Dimitris Bakalis	University of Patras, Greece
Guilherme Bileki	University of São Paulo, Brazil
Ahmet Erdem	Politecnico di Milano, Italy
Panagiotis Georgiou	University of Ioannina, Greece
Adele Maleki	University of Siegen, Germany
Farnam Khalili Maybodi	University of Siena, Italy
André B. Perina	University of São Paulo, Brazil

Marco Procaccini	University of Siena, Italy
Jose Rodriguez	University of California Riverside, USA
Bashar Romanous	University of California Riverside, USA
Leandro Rosa	University of São Paulo, Brazil
Skyler Windh	University of California Riverside, USA
Vasileios Zois	University of California Riverside, USA

Sponsors

The 2018 Applied Reconfigurable Computing Symposium (ARC2018) is sponsored by:

Contents

Applications and Surveys

Fault-Tolerance, Security and Communication Architectures

Reconfigurable and Adaptive Architectures

Design Methods and Fast Prototyping

FPGA-Based Design and Applications

Special Session: Research Projects

Machine Learning and Neural Networks

Approximate FPGA-Based LSTMs Under Computation Time Constraints

Michalis Rizakis[✉], Stylianos I. Venieris[iD], Alexandros Kouris[iD], and Christos-Savvas Bouganis[iD]

Department of Electrical and Electronic Engineering,
Imperial College London, London, UK
{michail.rizakis14,stylianos.venieris10,a.kouris16,
christos-savvas.bouganis}@imperial.ac.uk

Abstract. Recurrent Neural Networks, with the prominence of Long Short-Term Memory (LSTM) networks, have demonstrated state-of-the-art accuracy in several emerging Artificial Intelligence tasks. Nevertheless, the highest performing LSTM models are becoming increasingly demanding in terms of computational and memory load. At the same time, emerging latency-sensitive applications including mobile robots and autonomous vehicles often operate under stringent computation time constraints. In this paper, we address the challenge of deploying computationally demanding LSTMs at a constrained time budget by introducing an approximate computing scheme that combines iterative low-rank compression and pruning, along with a novel FPGA-based LSTM architecture. Combined in an end-to-end framework, the approximation method parameters are optimised and the architecture is configured to address the problem of high-performance LSTM execution in time-constrained applications. Quantitative evaluation on a real-life image captioning application indicates that the proposed system required up to 6.5× less time to achieve the same application-level accuracy compared to a baseline method, while achieving an average of 25× higher accuracy under the same computation time constraints.

Keywords: LSTM · Low-rank approximation · Pruning · FPGAs

1 Introduction

Recurrent Neural Networks (RNNs) is a machine learning model which offers the capability of recognising long-range dependencies in sequential and temporal data. RNN models, with the prevalence of Long Short-Term Memory (LSTMs) networks, have demonstrated state-of-the-art performance in various AI applications including scene labelling [1] and image generation [2]. Moreover, LSTMs have been successfully employed for AI tasks in complex environments including human trajectory prediction [3] and ground classification [4] on mobile robots, with more recent systems combining language and image processing in tasks such as image captioning [5] and video understanding [6].

© Springer International Publishing AG, part of Springer Nature 2018
N. Voros et al. (Eds.): ARC 2018, LNCS 10824, pp. 3–15, 2018.
https://doi.org/10.1007/978-3-319-78890-6_1

Despite the high predictive power of LSTMs, their computational and memory demands pose a challenge with respect to deployment in latency-sensitive and power-constrained environments. Modern intelligent systems such as mobile robots and drones that employ LSTMs to perceive their surroundings often operate under time-constrained, latency-critical settings. In such scenarios, retrieving the best possible output from an LSTM given a constraint in computation time may be necessary to ensure the timely operation of the system. Moreover, the requirements of such applications for low absolute power consumption, which would enable a longer battery life, prohibit the deployment of high-performance, but power-hungry platforms, such as multi-core CPUs and GPUs. In this context, FPGAs constitute a promising target device that can combine customisation and reconfigurability to achieve high performance at a low power envelope.

In this work, an approximate computing scheme along with a novel hardware architecture for LSTMs are proposed as an end-to-end framework to address the problem of high-performance LSTM deployment in time-constrained settings. Our approach comprises an iterative approximation method that applies simultaneously low-rank compression and pruning of the LSTM model with a tunable number of refinement iterations. This iterative process enables our framework to (i) exploit the resilience of the target application to approximations, (ii) explore the trade-off between computational and memory load and application-level accuracy and (iii) execute the LSTM under a time constraint with increasing accuracy as a function of computation time budget. At the hardware level, our system consists of a novel FPGA-based architecture which exploits the inherent parallelism of the LSTM, parametrised with respect to the level of compression and pruning. By optimising the parameters of the approximation method, the proposed framework generates a system tailored to the target application, the available FPGA resources and the computation time constraints. To the best of our knowledge, this is the first work in the literature to address the deployment of LSTMs under computation time constraints.

2   Background

2.1   LSTM Networks

A vanilla RNN typically processes an input and generates an output at each time step. Internally, the network has recurrent connections from the output at one time step to the hidden units at the next time step which enables it to capture sequential patterns. The LSTM model differs from vanilla RNNs in that it comprises control units named gates, instead of layers. A typical LSTM has four gates. The *input* gate (Eq. (1)), along with the *cell* gate (Eq. (4)) are responsible for determining how much of the current input will propagate to the output. The *forget* gate (Eq. (2)) is responsible for determining whether the previous state of the LSTM will be forgotten or not, while the *output* gate (Eq. (3)) determines how much of the current state will be allowed to propagate to the final output of the LSTM at the current time step. Computationally, the gates are matrix-vector multiplication blocks, followed by a nonlinear elementwise activation function. The equations for the LSTM model are shown below:

$$\boldsymbol{i}^{(t)} = \sigma(\boldsymbol{W}_{ix}\boldsymbol{x}^{(t)} + \boldsymbol{W}_{ih}\boldsymbol{h}^{(t-1)}) \tag{1}$$

$$\boldsymbol{f}^{(t)} = \sigma(\boldsymbol{W}_{fx}\boldsymbol{x}^{(t)} + \boldsymbol{W}_{fh}\boldsymbol{h}^{(t-1)}) \tag{2}$$

$$\boldsymbol{o}^{(t)} = \sigma(\boldsymbol{W}_{ox}\boldsymbol{x}^{(t)} + \boldsymbol{W}_{oh}\boldsymbol{h}^{(t-1)}) \tag{3}$$

$$\boldsymbol{c}^{(t)} = \boldsymbol{f}^{(t)} \odot \boldsymbol{c}^{(t-1)} + \boldsymbol{i}^{(t)} \odot tanh(\boldsymbol{W}_{cx}\boldsymbol{x}^{(t)} + \boldsymbol{W}_{ch}\boldsymbol{h}^{(t-1)}) \tag{4}$$

$$\boldsymbol{h}^{(t)} = \boldsymbol{c}^{(t)} \odot \boldsymbol{o}^{(t)} \tag{5}$$

$\boldsymbol{i}^{(t)}, \boldsymbol{f}^{(t)}$ and $\boldsymbol{o}^{(t)}$ are the *input, forget* and *output* gates respectively, $\boldsymbol{c}^{(t)}$ is the current state of the LSTM, $\boldsymbol{h}^{(t-1)}$ is the previous output, $\boldsymbol{x}^{(t)}$ is the current input at time t and $\sigma(\cdot)$ represents the sigmoid function. Equation (5) is frequently found in the literature as $\boldsymbol{h}^{(t)} = \boldsymbol{c}^{(t)} \odot tanh(\boldsymbol{o}^{(t)})$ with $tanh(\cdot)$ applied to the *output* gate. In this work, we follow the image captioning LSTM proposed in [5] which removes the $tanh(\cdot)$ from the *output* gate and therefore we end up with Eq. (5). Finally, all the $\boldsymbol{W}$ matrices denote the weight matrices that contain the trainable parameters of the model, which are assumed to be provided.

3   Related Work

The effectiveness of RNNs has attracted the attention of the architecture and reconfigurable computing communities. Li et al. [7] proposed an FPGA-based accelerator for the training of an RNN language model. In [8], the authors focus on the optimised deployment of the Gated Recurrent Unit (GRU) model [9] in data centres with server-grade FPGAs, ASICs, GPUs and CPUs and propose an algorithmic memoisation-based method to reduce the computational load at the expense of increased memory footprint. The authors of [10] present an empirical study of the effect of different architectural designs on the computational resources, on-chip memory capacity and off-chip memory bandwidth requirements of an LSTM model. Finally, Guan et al. [11] proposed an FPGA-based LSTM accelerator optimised for speech recognition on a Xilinx VC707 FPGA platform.

From an algorithmic perspective, recent works have followed a model-hardware co-design approach. Han et al. [12] proposed an FPGA-based speech recognition engine that employs a load-balance-aware compression scheme in order to compress the LSTM model size. Wang et al. [13] presented a method that addresses compression at several levels including the use of circulant matrices for three of the LSTM gates and the quantisation of the trained parameters, together with the corresponding ASIC-based hardware architecture. Zhang et al. [14] presented an FPGA-based accelerator for a Long-Term Recurrent Convolutional Network (LRCN) for video footage description that consists of a CNN followed by an LSTM. Their design focuses on balancing the resource allocation between the layers of the LRCN and pruning the fully-connected and LSTM layers to minimise the off-chip memory accesses. [12–14] deviate from the faithful LSTM mapping of previous works but also require a retraining step in order to compensate for the introduced error of each proposed method. Finally, He and Sun [15] focused on CNNs and investigated algorithmic strategies for model selection under computation time constraints for both training and testing.

Our work differs from the majority of existing efforts by proposing a hardware architecture together with an approximate computing method for LSTMs that is application-aware and tunable with respect to the required computation time and application-level error. Our framework follows the same spirit as [12–14] by proposing an approximation to the model, but in contrast to these methods does not require a retraining phase and assumes no access to the full training set. Instead, with a limited subset of labelled data, our scheme compensates for the induced error by means of iterative refinement, making it suitable for applications where the dataset is privacy-critical and the quality of the approximation improves as the time availability increases.

4   Methodology

In this section, the main components of the proposed framework are presented (Fig. 1). Given an LSTM model with its set of weight matrices and a small application evaluation set, the proposed system searches for an appropriate approximation scheme that meets the application's needs, by applying low-rank compression and pruning on the model. The design space is traversed by means of a roofline model to determine the highest performing configuration of the proposed architecture on the target FPGA. In this manner, the trade-off between computation time and application-level error is explored for different approximation schemes. The design point to be implemented on the device is selected based on user-specified requirements for the maximum computation time or application-level error tolerance.

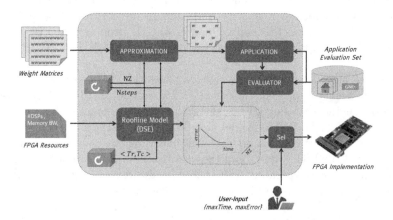

Fig. 1. Design flow of the proposed framework

4.1   Approximations for LSTMs

At the core of an LSTM's computational workload lie the matrix-vector multiplications in each of the four gates. Neural networks have been extensively studied to have redundancy in terms of their trained parameters [16]. To reduce the computational demands of the LSTM, we propose an approximate computing scheme that enables the tuning between computational cost and application-level accuracy. The proposed approach exploits the statistical redundancy of the LSTM by acting at two levels: (i) approximating the weight matrices with a low-rank, SVD-based decomposition and (ii) pruning the network by sparsifying the weight matrices based on an importance criterion of their elements.

Low-rank approximation. Based on the set of LSTM Eqs. (1)–(4), each gate consists of two weight matrices corresponding to the current input and previous output vectors respectively. In our scheme, we construct an augmented matrix by concatenating the input and output weight matrices as shown in Eq. (7). Similarly, we concatenate the input and previous output vectors (Eq. (6)) and thus the overall gate computation is given by Eq. (8).

$$\tilde{\boldsymbol{x}}^{(t)} = \left[\boldsymbol{x}^{(t)T} \boldsymbol{h}^{(t-1)T} \right]^T \tag{6}$$

$$\boldsymbol{W}_i = \left[\boldsymbol{W}_{ix} \boldsymbol{W}_{ih} \right], \forall i \in [1,4] \tag{7}$$

$$\boldsymbol{y}_i = nonlin(\boldsymbol{W}_i \tilde{\boldsymbol{x}}^{(t)}), \forall i \in [1,4] \tag{8}$$

where $nonlin(\cdot)$ is either the sigmoid function $\sigma(\cdot)$ or $tanh(\cdot)$. In this way, a single weight matrix is formed for each gate, denoted by $\boldsymbol{W}_i \in \mathbb{R}^{R \times C}$ for the i_{th} gate. We perform a full SVD decomposition on the four augmented matrices independently as $\boldsymbol{W}_i = \boldsymbol{U}_i \boldsymbol{\Sigma}_i \boldsymbol{V}_i^T, \forall i \in [1,4]$, where $\boldsymbol{U}_i \in \mathbb{R}^{R \times R}$, $\boldsymbol{\Sigma}_i \in \mathbb{R}^{R \times C}$ and $\boldsymbol{V}_i \in \mathbb{R}^{C \times C}$ and employ a rank-1 approximation to obtain $\widetilde{\boldsymbol{W}}_i = \sigma_1^i \boldsymbol{u}_1^i \boldsymbol{v}_1^{iT}$ by keeping the singular vectors that correspond to the largest singular value.

Pruning by means of network sparsification. The second level of approximation on the LSTM comprises the structured pruning of the connectivity between neurons. With each neural connection being captured as an element of the weight matrices, we express network pruning as sparsification applied on the augmented weight matrices (Eq. (7)). To represent a sparse LSTM, we introduce four binary mask matrices $\boldsymbol{F}_i \in \{0,1\}^{R \times C}$, $\forall i \in [1,4]$, with each entry representing whether a connection is pruned or not. Overall, we employ the following notation for a (weight, mask) matrix pair $\{\boldsymbol{W}_i, \boldsymbol{F}_i | i \in [1,4]\}$.

In the proposed scheme, we explore sparsity with respect to the connections per output neuron and constrain each output to have the same number of inputs. We cast LSTM pruning as an optimisation problem of the following form.

$$\min_{\boldsymbol{F}_i} || \boldsymbol{W}_i - \boldsymbol{F}_i \odot \boldsymbol{W}_i ||_2^2, \text{s.t.} || \boldsymbol{f}_j^i ||_0 = \text{NZ}, \ \forall i \in [1,4], \forall j \in [1,R] \tag{9}$$

where $\boldsymbol{f}_j^i$ is the j_{th} row of $\boldsymbol{F}_i$ and NZ is the number of non-zero elements on each row of $\boldsymbol{F}_i$. $|| \cdot ||_0$ is the l_0 pseudo-norm denoting the number of non-zero entries in a vector. The solution to the optimisation problem in Eq. (9) is given by keeping the NZ elements on each row of $\boldsymbol{W}_i$ with the highest absolute value and setting their indices to 1 in $\boldsymbol{F}_i$.

In contrast to the existing approaches, the proposed pruning method does not employ retraining and hence removes the computationally expensive step of retraining and the requirement for the training set, which is important for privacy-critical applications. Even though our sparsification method does not explicitly capture the impact of pruning on the application-level accuracy, our design space exploration, detailed in Sect. 5, searches over different levels of sparsity and as a result it explores the effect of pruning on the application.

Hybrid compression and pruning. By applying both low-rank approximation and pruning, we end up with the following weight matrix approximation:

$$\widetilde{\boldsymbol{W}}_i = \boldsymbol{F}_i \odot (\sigma_1^i \boldsymbol{u}_1^i \boldsymbol{v}_1^{iT}) \tag{10}$$

In this setting, for the i_{th} gate the ranking of the absolute values in each row of the rank-1 approximation $\sigma_1^i \boldsymbol{u}_1^i \boldsymbol{v}_1^{iT}$ depends only on $\boldsymbol{v}_1^i$, with each element of $\sigma_1^i \boldsymbol{u}_1^i$ operating as a shared scaling factor for all elements of a row. Therefore, for the i_{th} gate all the rows of $\boldsymbol{F}_i$ become identical and hence can be represented by a single mask vector $\boldsymbol{f}^i \in \{0,1\}^C$. This leads to a weight matrix with zeros along $(C-\text{NZ})$ of its columns, which is described by the following expression:

$$\widetilde{\boldsymbol{W}}_i = \sigma_1^i \boldsymbol{u}_1^i (\boldsymbol{f}^i \odot \boldsymbol{v}_1^i)^T \tag{11}$$

$$\tilde{\boldsymbol{y}}_i = \sum_{n=1}^{N_{steps}} \left\{ \sigma_1^{i(n)} \boldsymbol{u}_1^{i(n)} \left((\boldsymbol{f}^{i(n)} \odot \boldsymbol{v}_1^{i(n)})^T \tilde{\boldsymbol{x}}^{(t)} \right) \right\} \tag{12}$$

In order to obtain a refinement mechanism, we propose an iterative algorithm, presented in Algorithm 1, that employs both the low-rank approximation and pruning methods to progressively update the weight matrix. On lines 4–6 the first approximation of the weight matrix is constructed by obtaining the rank-1 approximation of the original matrix and applying pruning in order to have NZ non-zero elements on each row, as in Eq. (11). Next, the weight matrix is refined for N_{steps} iterations, by computing the error matrix $\boldsymbol{E}$ (line 10) and employing its pruned rank-1 approximation as an update (line 15).

Different combinations of levels of sparsity and refinement iterations correspond to different design points in the computation-accuracy space. In this respect, the number of non-zero elements in each binary mask vector and the number of iterations are exposed to the design space exploration as tunable parameters (NZ, N_{steps}) to explore the LSTM computation-accuracy trade-off.

4.2   Architecture

The proposed FPGA architecture for LSTMs is illustrated in Fig. 2. The main strategy of the architecture includes the exploitation of the coarse-grained parallelism between the four LSTM gates and is parametrised with respect to the

Algorithm 1. Iterative LSTM Model Approximation

Inputs:

1: Weight matrices $\boldsymbol{W}_i \in \mathbb{R}^{R \times C}$, $\forall i \in [1, 4]$

2: Number of non-zero elements, NZ

3: Number of refinement iterations, N_{steps}

Steps:

1: - - For all gates - -

2: **for** $i = 1$ to 4 **do**

3:     - - Initialise weight matrix approximation - -

4:     $\left[\boldsymbol{u}_1^{i(0)}, \sigma_1^{i(0)}, \boldsymbol{v}_1^{i(0)}\right] = \text{SVD}(\boldsymbol{W}_i)_1$

5:     $\boldsymbol{f}^{i(0)} \leftarrow$ solution to Eq. (9) for vector $\boldsymbol{v}_1^{i(0)}$

6:     $\widetilde{\boldsymbol{W}}_i^{(0)} = \sigma_1^{i(0)} \boldsymbol{u}_1^{i(0)} \left(\boldsymbol{f}^{i(0)} \odot \boldsymbol{v}_1^{i(0)}\right)^T$

7:     - - Apply refinements - -

8:     **for** $n = 1$ to N_{steps} **do**

9:         - - Compute error matrix - -

10:       $\boldsymbol{E} = \boldsymbol{W}_i - \widetilde{\boldsymbol{W}}_i^{(n-1)}$

11:       - - Compute refinement - -

12:       $\left[\boldsymbol{u}_1^{i(n)}, \sigma_1^{i(n)}, \boldsymbol{v}_1^{i(n)}\right] = \text{SVD}(\boldsymbol{E})_1$

13:       $\boldsymbol{f}^{i(n)} \leftarrow$ solution to optimisation problem (9) for vector $\boldsymbol{v}_1^{i(n)}$

14:       - - Update weight matrix approximation - -

15:       $\widetilde{\boldsymbol{W}}_i^{(n)} = \widetilde{\boldsymbol{W}}_i^{(n-1)} + \sigma_1^{i(n)} \boldsymbol{u}_1^{i(n)} \left(\boldsymbol{f}^{i(n)} \odot \boldsymbol{v}_1^{i(n)}\right)^T$

16:     **end for**

17: **end for**

Notes: $\text{SVD}(\boldsymbol{X})_1$ returns the rank-1 SVD-based approximation of $\boldsymbol{X}$.

---

fine-grained parallelism in the dot-product and elementwise operations of the LSTM, allowing for a compile-time tunable performance-resource trade-off.

SVD and Binary Masks Precomputation. In Algorithm 1, the number of refinement iterations (N_{steps}), the level of sparsity (NZ) and the trained weight matrices are data-independent and known at compile time. As such, the required SVD decompositions along with the corresponding binary masks are precomputed for all N_{steps} iterations at compile time. As a result, the singular values $\sigma_1^{i(n)}$, the vectors $\boldsymbol{u}_1^{i(n)}$ and only the non-zero elements of the sparse $\boldsymbol{f}^{i(n)} \odot \boldsymbol{v}_1^{i(n)}$ are stored in the off-chip memory, so that they can be looked-up at run time.

Inter-gate and Intra-gate Parallelism. In the proposed architecture, each gate is allocated a dedicated *hardware gate unit* with all gates operating in parallel. At each LSTM time-step t, a hardware gate unit computes its output by performing N_{steps} refinement iterations as in Eq. (12). At the beginning of the time-step, the current vector $\tilde{\boldsymbol{x}}^{(t)}$ is stored on-chip as it will be reused in each iteration by all four gates. The vectors $\boldsymbol{u}_1^{i(n)}$ and $\boldsymbol{v}_1^{i(n)}$ for each gate, along with their singular values $\sigma_1^{i(n)}$, are streamed in the architecture from the off-chip

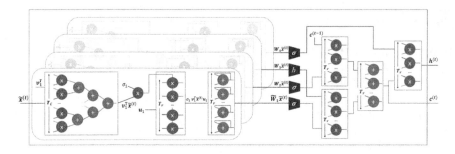

Fig. 2. Diagram of proposed hardware architecture

memory in a tiled manner. $\boldsymbol{u}_1^{i(n)}$ and $\boldsymbol{v}_1^{i(n)}$ are tiled with tile sizes of T_r and T_c respectively, leading to $\frac{R}{T_r}$ and $\frac{C}{T_c}$ tiles sequentially streamed in the architecture.

At each gate, a dot-product unit is responsible for computing the dot product of the current tile of $\boldsymbol{v}_1^{i(n)}$ with the corresponding elements of the input $\tilde{\boldsymbol{x}}^{(t)}$. The dot-product unit is unrolled by a factor of T_c in order to process one tile of $\boldsymbol{v}_1^{i(n)}$ per cycle. After accumulating the partial results of all the $\frac{C}{T_c}$ tiles, the result is produced and multiplied with the scalar $\sigma_1^{i(n)}$. The multiplication result is passed as a constant operand to a multiplier array, with $\boldsymbol{u}_1^{i(n)}$ as the other operand. The multiplier array has a size of T_r in order to match the tiling of $\boldsymbol{u}_1^{i(n)}$. As a final stage, an array of T_r accumulators performs the summation across the N_{steps} iterations as expressed in Eq. (12), to produce the final gate output.

The outputs from the *input*, *forget* and *output* gates are passed through a sigmoid unit while the output of the *cell* gate is passed through a *tanh* unit. After the nonlinearities stage, the produced outputs are multiplied element-by-element as dictated by the LSTM equations to produce the cell state $\boldsymbol{c}^{(t)}$ (Eq. (4)) and the current output vector $\boldsymbol{h}^{(t)}$ (Eq. (5)). The three multiplier arrays and the one adder array all have a size of T_r to match the tile size of the incoming vectors and exploit the available parallelism.

5   Design Space Exploration

Having parametrised the proposed approximation method over NZ and N_{steps} and its underlying architecture over NZ and tile sizes (T_r, T_c), corresponding metrics need to be employed for exploring the effects of each parameter on performance and accuracy. The approximation method parameters are studied based on an application-level evaluation metric (discussed in Sect. 5.2), that measures the impact of each applied approximation on the accuracy of the target application. In terms of the hardware architecture, roofline performance modelling is employed for exhaustively exploring the design space formed by all possible tile size combinations, to obtain the highest performing design point (discussed in Sect. 5.1). Based on those two metrics, the computation time-accuracy trade-off is explored.

5.1   Roofline Model

The design space of architectural configurations for all tile size combinations of T_r and T_c is explored exhaustively by performance modelling. The roofline model [17] is used to develop a performance model for the proposed architecture by relating the peak attainable performance (in terms of throughput), for each configuration on a particular FPGA device, with its operational intensity, which relates the ratio of computational load to off-chip memory traffic. Based on this model, each design point's performance can be bounded either by the peak platform throughput or by the maximum performance that the platform's memory system can support. In this context, roofline models are developed for predicting the maximum attainable performance for varying levels of pruning (NZ).

Given a tile size pair, the performance of the architecture is calculated as:

$$Perf(ops/s) = \frac{workload(ops/input)}{II(cycles/input)} clk = \frac{4N_{steps}(2NZ+2R+1)+37R}{max(N_{steps}max(\frac{R}{T_r},\frac{NZ}{T_c}),37\frac{R}{T_r})} clk \quad (13)$$

where each gate performs $2NZ+2R+1$ operations per iteration and $37R$ accounts for the rest of the operations to produce the final outputs. The initiation interval (II) is determined based on the slowest between the gate stage and the rest of the computations. Similarly, a gate's initiation interval depends on the slowest between the dot-product unit and the multiplier array (Fig. 2).

Respectively, the operational intensity of the architecture, also referred to in the literature as Computation-to-Communication ratio (CTC), is formulated as:

$$CTC(ops/byte) = \frac{operations(ops)}{mem\ access(bytes)} = \frac{4N_{steps}(2NZ+2R+1)+37R}{4(4N_{steps}(NZ+R+1)+2R)} \quad (14)$$

where the memory transfers include the singular vectors and the singular value for each iteration of each gate and the write-back of the output and the cell state vectors to the off-chip memory. The augmented input vector $\tilde{x}^{(t)}$ is stored on-chip in order to be reused across the N_{steps} iterations. All data are represented with a single-precision floating-point format and require four bytes.

The number of design points allows enumerating all possible tile size combinations for each number of non-zero elements and obtaining the performance and CTC values for the complete design space. Based on the target platform's peak performance, memory bandwidth and on-chip memory capacity, the subspace containing the platform-supported design points is determined. The proposed architecture is implemented by selecting the tile sizes (T_r, T_c) that correspond to the highest performing design point within that subspace.

5.2   Evaluating the Impact of Approximations on the Application

The proposed framework requires a metric that would enable measuring the impact of the applied approximations on the application-level accuracy for different (NZ, N_{steps}) pairs. In our methodology, the error induced by our approximation methods is measured by running the target application end-to-end over an evaluation set with both the approximated weight matrices given a selected (NZ, N_{steps}) pair and with the original pretrained LSTM, acting as a reference model. By treating the output of the reference model as the ground truth, an application-specific metric is employed that assesses the quality of the output that was generated by the approximate model, exploring in this way the relationship between the level of approximation and the application-level accuracy.

6   Evaluation

The image captioning system presented by Vinyals et al. [5] (winner of the 2015 MSCOCO challenge) is examined as a case study for evaluating the proposed framework. Input images are encoded by a CNN and fed to a trained LSTM model to predict corresponding captions. In the proposed LSTM, each gate consists of two $R \times R$ weight matrices, leading to a $(R \times C)$ augmented weight matrix per gate with $R = 512$ and $C = 2R$, for a total of 2.1 M parameters. To determine the most suitable approximation scheme, we use a subset of the validation set of the Common Objects in Context (COCO) dataset[1], consisting of 35 images. To obtain image captions that will act as ground truth for the evaluation of the proposed approximation method, the reference image captioning application is executed end-to-end over the evaluation set, using TensorFlow[2]. As a metric of the effect of low-rank approximation and pruning on the LSTM model, we select Bilingual Evaluation Understudy (BLEU) [18], which is commonly employed for the evaluation of machine translation's quality by measuring the number of matching words, or "blocks of words", between a reference and a candidate translation. Due to space limitations, more information about adopting BLEU as a quality metric for image captioning can be found in [5].

Experimental Setup. In our experiments, we target the Xilinx Zynq ZC706 board. All hardware designs were synthesised and placed-and-routed with Xilinx Vivado HLS and Vivado Design Suite (v17.1) with a clock frequency of 100 MHz. Single-precision floating-point representation was used in order to comply with the typical precision requirements of LSTMs as used by the deep learning community. Existing work [7,12] has studied precision optimisation in specific LSTM applications, which constitutes a complementary method to our framework as an additional tunable parameter for the performance-accuracy trade-off.

Baseline Architecture. A hardware architecture of a faithful implementation of the LSTM model is implemented to act as a baseline for the proposed system's evaluation. This baseline architecture consists of four gate units, implemented in parallel hardware, that perform matrix-vector multiplication in a tiled manner. Parametrisation with respect to the tiling along the rows (T_r) and columns (T_c) of the weight matrices is applied to this architecture and roofline modelling is used to obtain the highest performing configuration (T_r, T_c), similarly to the proposed system's architecture (Fig. 3). The maximum platform-supported

---

[1]   http://cocodataset.org.
[2]   https://www.tensorflow.org.

attainable performance was obtained for $T_r = 2$ and $T_c = 1$, utilising 308 DSPs (34%), 69 kLUTs (31%), 437 kFFs (21%) and 26 18 kbit BRAMs (2%). As Fig. 3 demonstrates, the designs are mainly memory bounded and as a result not all the FPGA resources are utilised. To obtain the application-level accuracy of the baseline design under time constrained scenarios, the BLEU of the intermediate LSTM output at each tile step of T_r is examined (Fig. 4).

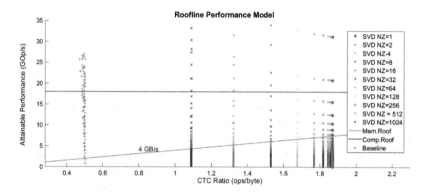

Fig. 3. Roofline model of the proposed and baseline architectures on the ZC706 board

6.1 Comparisons at Constrained Computation Time

This section presents the gains of using the proposed methodology compared to the baseline design under computation time constraints. This is investigated by exploring the design space, defined by (NZ, T_r, T_c), in terms of (i) performance (Fig. 3) and (ii) the relationship between accuracy and computation time (Fig. 4). As shown in Fig. 3, as the level of pruning increases and NZ becomes smaller, the computational and memory load per refinement iteration becomes smaller and the elementwise operations gradually dominate the computational intensity (Eq. (14)), with the corresponding designs moving to the right of the roofline graph. With respect to the architectural parameters, as the tiling parameters T_r and T_c increase, the hardware design becomes increasingly unrolled and moves towards the top of the roofline graph. In all cases, the proposed architecture demonstrates a higher performance compared to the baseline design reaching up to 3.72× for a single non-zero element with an average of 3.35× (3.31× geo. mean) across the sparsity levels shown in Fig. 3.

To evaluate our methodology in time-constrained scenarios, for each sparsity level the highest performing design of the roofline model is implemented. Figure 4 shows the achieved BLEU score of each design over the evaluation set with respect to runtime, where higher runtime translates to higher number of refinements. In this context, for the target application the design with 512 non-zero elements (50% sparsity) achieves the best trade-off between performance per refinement iteration and additional information obtained at each iteration. The highest performing architecture with NZ of 512 has a tiling pair of (32, 1)

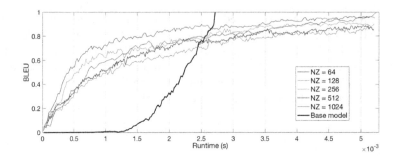

Fig. 4. BLEU scores over time for all methods

and the implemented design consumes 862 DSPs (95%), 209 kLUTs (95%), 437 kFFs (40%) and 34 18kbit BRAMs (3%). In the BLEU range between 0.4 and 0.8, our proposed system reaches the corresponding BLEU decile up to 6.51× faster with an average speedup of 4.19× (3.78× geo. mean) across the deciles.

As demonstrated in Fig. 4, the highest performing design of the proposed method (NZ = 512) constantly outperforms the baseline architecture in terms of BLEU score at every time instant up to 2.7 ms, at which a maximum BLEU value of 0.9 has been achieved by both methods. As a result, given a specific time budget below 2.7 ms, the proposed architecture achieves a 24.88× higher BLEU score (geo. mean) compared to the baseline. Moreover, the proposed method demonstrates significantly higher application accuracy during the first 1.5 ms of the computation, reaching up to 31232× higher BLEU. In this respect, our framework treats a BLEU of 0.9 and a time budget of 2.7 ms as switching points to select between the baseline and the architecture that employs the proposed approximation method and deploys the highest performing design for each case.

7   Conclusion

The high-performance deployment of LSTMs under stringent computation time constraints poses a challenge in several latency-critical applications. This paper presents a framework for mapping LSTMs on FPGAs in such scenarios. The proposed methodology applies an iterative approximate computing scheme in order to compress and prune the target network and explores the computation time-accuracy trade-off. A novel FPGA architecture is proposed that is tailored to the degree of approximation and optimised for the target device. This formulation enables the co-optimisation of the LSTM approximation and the architecture in order to satisfy the application-level computation time constraints. Future work includes the extension of the proposed methodology to scenarios where the training data are available to perform retraining, leading to even higher gains.

Acknowledgements. The support of the EPSRC Centre for Doctoral Training in High Performance Embedded and Distributed Systems (HiPEDS, Grant Reference EP/L016796/1) is gratefully acknowledged. This work is also supported by EPSRC grant 1507723.

References

1. Byeon, W., Breuel, T.M., Raue, F., Liwicki, M.: Scene labeling with LSTM recurrent neural networks. In: CVPR, pp. 3547–3555 (2015)
2. Gregor, K., Danihelka, I., Graves, A., Rezende, D., Wierstra, D.: DRAW: a recurrent neural network for image generation. In: ICML, pp. 1462–1471 (2015)
3. Alahi, A., Goel, K., Ramanathan, V., Robicquet, A., Fei-Fei, L., Savarese, S.: Social LSTM: human trajectory prediction in crowded spaces. In: CVPR (2016)
4. Otte, S., et al.: Recurrent neural networks for fast and robust vibration-based ground classification on mobile robots. In: ICRA, pp. 5603–5608 (2016)
5. Vinyals, O., Toshev, A., Bengio, S., Erhan, D.: Show and tell: lessons learned from the 2015 MSCOCO image captioning challenge. TPAMI **39**, 652–663 (2017)
6. Donahue, J., et al.: Long-term recurrent convolutional networks for visual recognition and description. TPAMI **39**(4), 677–691 (2017)
7. Li, S., Wu, C., Li, H., Li, B., Wang, Y., Qiu, Q.: FPGA acceleration of recurrent neural network based language model. In: FCCM, pp. 111–118 (2015)
8. Nurvitadhi, E., et al.: Accelerating recurrent neural networks in analytics servers: comparison of FPGA, CPU, GPU, and ASIC. In: FPL, pp. 1–4 (2016)
9. Chung, J., et al.: Empirical evaluation of gated recurrent neural networks on sequence modeling. In: NIPS Workshop on Deep Learning (2014)
10. Chang, A.X.M., Culurciello, E.: Hardware accelerators for recurrent neural networks on FPGA. In: ISCAS, pp. 1–4 (2017)
11. Guan, Y., Yuan, Z., Sun, G., Cong, J.: FPGA-based accelerator for long short-term memory recurrent neural networks. In: ASP-DAC, pp. 629–634 (2017)
12. Han, S., et al.: ESE: efficient speech recognition engine with sparse LSTM on FPGA. In: FPGA, pp. 75–84 (2017)
13. Wang, Z., Lin, J., Wang, Z.: Accelerating recurrent neural networks: a memory-efficient approach. TVLSI **25**(10), 2763–2775 (2017)
14. Zhang, X., et al.: High-performance video content recognition with long-term recurrent convolutional network for FPGA. In: FPL, pp. 1–4 (2017)
15. He, K., Sun, J.: Convolutional neural networks at constrained time cost. In: CVPR (2015)
16. Denil, M., Shakibi, B., Dinh, L., Ranzato, M.A., de Freitas, N.: Predicting parameters in deep learning. In: NIPS, pp. 2148–2156 (2013)
17. Williams, S., et al.: Roofline: an insightful visual performance model for multicore architectures. Commun. ACM **52**(4), 65–76 (2009)
18. Papineni, K., Roukos, S., Ward, T., Zhu, W.-J.: BLEU: a method for automatic evaluation of machine translation. In: ACL, pp. 311–318 (2002)

Redundancy-Reduced MobileNet Acceleration on Reconfigurable Logic for ImageNet Classification

Jiang Su[1,2]([✉]), Julian Faraone[1,2], Junyi Liu[1,2], Yiren Zhao[1,2], David B. Thomas[1,2], Philip H. W. Leong[1,2], and Peter Y. K. Cheung[1,2]

[1] Imperial College London, London, UK
j.su13@ic.ac.uk
[2] University of Sydney, Sydney, Australia

Abstract. Modern Convolutional Neural Networks (CNNs) excel in image classification and recognition applications on large-scale datasets such as ImageNet, compared to many conventional feature-based computer vision algorithms. However, the high computational complexity of CNN models can lead to low system performance in power-efficient applications. In this work, we firstly highlight two levels of model redundancy which widely exist in modern CNNs. Additionally, we use MobileNet as a design example and propose an efficient system design for a Redundancy-Reduced MobileNet (RR-MobileNet) in which off-chip memory traffic is only used for inputs/outputs transfer while parameters and intermediate values are saved in on-chip BRAM blocks. Compared to AlexNet, our RR-mobileNet has 25× less parameters, 3.2× less operations per image inference but 9%/5.2% higher Top1/Top5 classification accuracy on ImageNet classification task. The latency of a single image inference is only 7.85 ms.

Keywords: Pruning · Quantization · CNN · FPGA
Algorithm acceleration

1 Introduction

Modern CNNs have achieved unprecedented success in large-scale image recognition tasks. In order to obtain higher classification accuracy, researchers proposed CNN models with increasing complexity. The high computational complexity present challenges for power-efficient hardware platforms like FPGAs mainly due to the high memory bandwidth requirement. On one hand, the large amount of parameters leads to an inevitably off-chip memory storage. Together with inputs/outputs and intermediate computation results, current FPGA devices struggle to provide enough memory bandwidth for sufficient system parallelism. On the other hand, the advantages of the large amount of flexible on-chip memory blocks are not sufficiently explored as they are mostly used as data buffers

© Springer International Publishing AG, part of Springer Nature 2018
N. Voros et al. (Eds.): ARC 2018, LNCS 10824, pp. 16–28, 2018.
https://doi.org/10.1007/978-3-319-78890-6_2

which have to match with off-chip memory bandwidth. In this work, we address this problem by reducing CNN redundancy so that the model is small enough to fit on-chip and our hardware system can benefit from the high bandwidth of FPGA on-chip memory blocks.

There are existing works that have explored redundancy in CNNs on model-level and data-level separately. Model-level redundancy leads to redundant parameters which barely contribute to model computation. For example, a trained AlexNet may have 20% to 80% kernels with very low values and the computation can be removed with very limited effect to the final classification accuracy [1]. Data-level redundancy, on the other hand, refers to unnecessarily high precision for data representation to parameters. However, there are very limited work that quantitatively consider both redundancy at the same time, especially in a perspective of their impacts to a hardware system design. The contributions of this work is as follows:

- We consider both model-level and data-level redundancy, which widely exist in CNNs, in hardware system design. A quantitative analysis is conducted to show the hardware impacts of both types of redundancy and their cooperative effects.
- We demonstrate the validity of the proposed redundancy reduction analysis by applying it to a recent CNN model called MobileNet. Compared to a baseline AlexNet model, our RR-MobileNet has $25\times$ less parameters, $3.2\times$ less operations per image computation but 9% and 5.2% higher Top1/Top5 accuracy on ImageNet classification.
- An FPGA based system architecture is designed for our RR-MobileNet model where all parameters and intermediate numbers can be stored with on-chip BRAM blocks. Therefore, the peak memory bandwidth within the system can achieve 1.56 Tb/s. As a result, our system costs only 7.85 ms on each image inference computation.

About this topic, several works have explored in one perspective or another. In terms of data-level redundancy, [2–4] and several other works explores FPGA based acceleration system for CNN models with fixed point parameters and activation values. But model-level redundancy is not considered for further throughput improvement. On the other side, works like [1,5] explored model-level redundancy in CNN hardware system design, but these works are presented without quantitative discussion about hardware impacts of reduced-precision parameters used in CNN models. In this work, we consider both types of redundancy and report our quantitative consideration for a MobileNet acceleration system design.

The two-level redundancy in neural networks and its impacts to hardware system design are introduced in Sect. 2. Section 3 introduces an FPGA system design for our Redundancy-Reduced MobileNet for ImageNet classification tasks. The experimental results are discussed in Sects. 4 and 5 finally concludes the paper.

2   Accelerating Redundancy-Reduced Neural Networks on FPGA

In this section, we firstly give a brief introduction to MobileNet [6]. Then, our redundancy reduction strategy is introduced with an explanation of how redundancy affects the hardware resource requirements. Next, we show a system architecture design for accelerating our Redundancy-Reduced MobileNet (RR-MobileNet).

2.1   MobileNet Complexity Analysis

MobileNet [6] is a recent CNN model that aims to present decent classification accuracy with reduced amount of parameters compared to CNN models with conventional convolutional (Conv) layers. Figure 1 shows the building blocks of MobileNet called depthwise separable convolutional (DSC) layer, which consist of a depthwise convolutional (DW_Conv) layer and a pointwise convolutional (PW_Conv) layer. A DW_Conv layer has a $K \times K \times N$ kernel which is essentially consist of a $K \times K$ kernel for each Input Feature Map (IFM) channel. So 2 dimensional convolutions are conducted independently in a channel-wise manner. Differently, PW_Conv layer is a special case of a general Conv layer and it has kernel size of $1 \times 1 \times N \times M$ while a general Conv layer may have kernels with a more general size of $K \times K \times N \times M$. MobileNet models, as shown in Table 2, can be formed by several general Conv layers and mostly DSC layers.

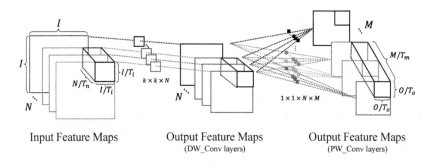

Input Feature Maps   Output Feature Maps   Output Feature Maps
                              (DW_Conv layers)   (PW_Conv layers)

Fig. 1. Tilling in depthwise separable layer for MobileNet

For a general Conv layer, below equations show the resulting operation count C_{Conv} and parameter amount P_{Conv} given that a IFM is $I \times I \times N$ and an Output Feature Map (OFM) size is $O \times O \times M$:

$$C_{Conv} = 2 \times K^2 \times O^2 \times N \times M, P_{Conv} = K \times K \times N \times M, \qquad (1)$$

where 2 in Eq. 1 indicates that we consider either a single multiplication or an addition as a fundamental operation in this work. On the other side, the operation count and parameter amount of a DSC layer are as listed below:

$$C_{DSC} = 2 \times (K^2 \times O^2 \times N + O^2 \times N \times M), P_{DSC} \quad = K \times K \times N + N \times M. \tag{2}$$

As shown in Eq. 2, the amount of parameters in a DSC layer is an addition of the parameters in both DW_Conv and PW_Conv layers. In practice, a DSC layer has a parameter complexity of $O(n^3)$ while a Conv layer has $O(n^4)$ and this leads to a much smaller model for MobileNet compared to conventional CNNs [6].

2.2   Model-Level Redundancy Analysis

As mentioned in Sect. 1, there are several works that address model-level redundancy, we use an iterative pruning strategy. Firstly, a quantization training process, which will be shortly described in Algorithm 1, is conducted on the baseline MobileNet model (Table 2). Then, an iterative pruning and re-training process is conducted. In each iteration of such process, $Prune(*)$ is applied to remove the model kernels according to β by layer-wisely thresholding the kernels values. Noticeably, our iterative pruning process is similar to strategy in [7]. However, in our strategy, a kernel is either removed or kept as a whole according to the summation of its values rather than turning it into a sparse kernel. This is called kernel-level pruning in [8]. By doing such structured pruning, we avoid using extra hardware resources to build sparse matrix formatting modules as needed in unstructured pruning strategies [5]. Finally, each pruning step inevitably leads to model accuracy loss although only less important kernels are removed. So we conduct re-training to compensate the lost model accuracy.

What pruning essentially does is changing M in Eqs. 1 and 2 to $\beta \times M$. Correspondingly, such kernel pruning leads to a reduction of sizes of the OFM and kernels, which results in a smaller memory requirement to hardware. For example, β_l is the pruning rate of l-th layer. Kernel parameters are represented by DW_p-bit numbers while feature maps are represented by DW_a-bit numbers. For a pruned Conv layer, the memory footprint required to store kernel parameters Mem_l^p is as below:

$$Mem_l^p = K \times K \times N \times M \times DW_p \times \beta_l. \tag{3}$$

While to an SDC layer, the memory footprint is changed to following:

$$Mem_l^p = (K_l \times K_l \times N_l \times \beta_{l-1} + N_l \times M_l \times \beta_l) \times DW_p. \tag{4}$$

Equation 4 implies that the reduced parameters in the DW_Conv of a DSC layer is determined by the pruning rate of its preceding layer β_{l-1} while the PW_Conv layer memory saving is from β_l. Specially, β_0 is 1 for the input layer.

Meanwhile, the memory footprint for storing IFMs Mem_l^I and OFMs Mem_l^O for both types of layers are as following:

$$Mem_l^I = I_l \times I_l \times N_l \times DW_a \times \beta_{l-1}, Mem_l^O = O_l \times O_l \times M_l \times DW_a \times \beta_l, \tag{5}$$

Additionally, kernel pruning also reduces computational complexity in a proportion of β. The reduced operation counts can be illustrated by Eqs. 1 and 2 with M displaced by its discounted value $M * \beta$ when calculating C_{Conv} and C_{DSC} separately for Conv and DSC layers.

In the next part, we will show the relationship between data-level redundancy and above-mentioned model-level redundancy as well as their cooperative effects to the hardware resources.

2.3   Data-Level Redundancy Analysis

Data-level redundancy studied in this work, mainly aims to use reduced-precision parameters to replace their high-precision alternatives such as single/double-precision floating numbers that are widely used in CPU/GPU computing platforms. Instead, we explore fixed point representations with arbitrary bitwidth for parameters and activation values and quantitatively analyse their hardware impacts. Firstly, we introduce our quantization training strategy in Algorithm 2, which is used in this work for training reduced-precision neural networks.

Specially, the training procedure is completed off-line with GPU platforms. Only the trained model with reduced-precision parameters is loaded to our FPGA system for inference computation, which is the focus of this work.

Algorithm 1. Quantization Training Process for A L-layer neural network

---

Require: Inputs a_0, labels a^*, kernel parameters W, batch normalization parameters θ, maximum iteration number $MaxIter$, lower bound value min, upper bound value max.

Ensure: W and θ at $MaxIter$ iteration.

    for $iter = 1$ to $MaxIter$ **do**
        // Forward Propagation
        $a_0^Q \leftarrow Quantize(a_0)$
        for $l = 1$ to L **do**
            $W_l^Q \leftarrow Quantize(W_l)$
            $a_l \leftarrow layer\_forward(a_{l-1}^Q, W_l^Q);$
            $a_l^Q \leftarrow Quantize(a_l);$
        end for

        // Backward Propagation
        for $l = L$ to 1 **do**
            $g_{a_{l-1}}, g_{W_l^Q} \leftarrow layer\_backward(g_{a_l}, W_l^Q)$
            $\theta_l \leftarrow Update(\theta_l, g_{\theta_l})$
            $W_l \leftarrow Clip(Update(W_l, g_{W_l^Q}), min, max)$
        end for
    end for

Based on the quantization training strategies proposed in [9], we extend their training strategy to support arbitrary parameter precision as shown in Algorithm 1. In forward pass, both model parameters, or weights, W and feature map values, or activations, a are quantized before actual computations during inference. The $Quantize(*)$ function converts real values to the nearest pre-defined fixed point representation. $layer\_forward(*)$ conducts the inference computation we described in Sect. 2.1.

In backward propagation, parameters are updated with the gradient in terms of the quantized weights g_{W^Q} so that the network learns to do classification with the quantized parameters. However, the updating is applied to the real-valued weights W rather than their quantized alternatives W^Q so that the training error can be reserved in higher precision during training. Additionally, $Clip(*)$ helps the training to provide the quantized parameters within a particular range where values can be presented by a pre-defined fixed point representation. Concrete data representation will be introduced in Sect. 4. At last, we use the same hyperparameters for training provided by [9].

Particularly, our iterative pruning and quantization training strategy (Algorithm 1) is different from the pruning and weight sharing method proposed in [7] in several ways. Their method highlights weight sharing rather than changing the data representation. Their iterative training for pruning purposes is a separate process before weight sharing while in our approach, we do iterative pruning together with quantization training process so that model-level and data-level redundancy are both considered during training.

Above training process eventually generates a model with fixed point representations for parameters and feature map values represented with DW'_p and DW'_a bits separately. So the memory ratio between a pruned value and the its high-precision alternative are $\alpha_p = DW'_p/DW_p$ and $\alpha_a = DW'_a/DW_a$. Based on Eqs. 3–4, the memory requirement for parameters after removing both model-level and data-level redundancy is shown below for Conv layers:

$$Mem_l^p = K \times K \times N \times M \times DW_p \times \beta_l \times \alpha_p. \tag{6}$$

For DSC it is:

$$Mem_l^p = (K_l \times K_l \times N_l \times \beta_{l-1} + N_l \times M_l \times \beta_l) \times DW_p \times \alpha_p, \tag{7}$$

and for feature maps:

$$Mem_l^I = I_l \times I_l \times N_l \times DW_a \times \beta_{l-1} \times \alpha_a, Mem_l^O = O_l \times O_l \times M_l \times DW_a \times \beta_l \times \alpha_a. \tag{8}$$

We refer α as data-level memory saving factor and β as model-level memory saving factor. These two factors affects memory requirement for parameters in a multiplication way (Eqs. 6–8). This effect can be represented as a final saving factor of $\alpha_p \times \beta_{l-1}$ for DW_Conv and $\alpha_p \times \beta_l$ for PW_Conv and general Conv layers as shown in Eqs. 6 and 7. Similarly, feature map values are affected by a factor of $\alpha_a \times \beta_{l-1}$ for IFMs and $\alpha_a \times \beta_l$ for OFMs as shown in Eq. 8. In Sect. 4, we will further show that the cooperative effects of α and β are vital to our FPGA hardware architecture implementation on FPGA that provides high system performance.

3   RR-MobileNet FPGA Acceleration System Design

Based on the model-level and data-level redundancy analysis in the preceding sections, we introduce in this part what values of α and β can lead to a high-performance architecture design. In this work, we aim to achieve On-Chip Memory (OCM) storage for both parameters and feature map values. This can be achieved only with careful memory system design which is supported by a corresponding redundancy removal strategy. Firstly, we introduce the building block module design. Next, we show the conditions its memory system design should satisfy in order to implement the architecture within given FPGA resources.

3.1   System Architecture

We design a loop-back architecture, which processes our RR-MobileNet model layer by layer. Only neural network inputs, such as images, and the classification results are transferred to external of the programmable logic. So all parameters, feature maps and intermediate values are stored on FPGA OCM resources. The overall system architecture is shown in Fig. 2.

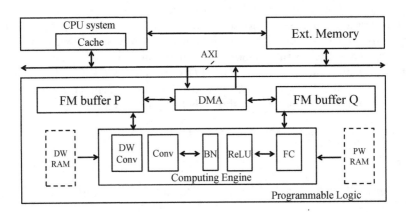

Fig. 2. System architecture design for RR-MobileNet

Network inputs are stored in external memory and streamed into our acceleration system by DMA through AXI bus. After Computation, the classification results are transferred back to the external memory for further usage. Within the system on the programmable logic, there are two on-chip buffers for storing feature map values. They are Feature Map (FM) buffer P and Q. Initially, the inputs from external memory are transferred to the FM buffer P and the computation can be started from this point. The computing engine module is the computational core that can process one layer at a time. Once the computing engine completes the computation of the first layer, the OFMs of the first layer will be stored in FM buffer Q. Noticeably, FM buffer P and Q are used for storage of IFMs and OFMs in an alternating manner for consecutive layers due to the fact that the OFMs of a layer are the IFMs of its following layer.

DW and PW RAMs are for parameter storage. As the module names suggested, DW RAM is for DW_Conv layer parameters while PW RAM is for ones in PW_Conv layers. There are also non-DSC layers in MobileNet structure, whose parameters are also stored in these two memory blocks. Due to the fact that DW_Conv layers have much smaller amount of parameters compared to PW_Conv layers, the DW RAM is hence used for Conv layer parameters as well as batch normalization parameters. More details about OCM utilization will be intruduced in Sect. 4.

The computing engine consists of DW Conv, Conv, BN and ReLU modules, which conduct the computation of either a Conv or a DSC layer. For DSC layers, its DW_Conv layer is computed by the DW Conv module followed by a BN module for batch normalization and ReLU for activation function computations. Meanwhile, its PW_Conv layer is computed in the Conv module and its following BN and ReLU modules. Due to the fact that PW_Conv layer is a special case of a Conv layer with all $1 \times 1 \times M$ kernels, the Conv module is also used for general Conv layer computation.

The DW module and its following BN/ReLU blocks are an array of Processing Elements (PE) as shown in Fig. 3. Each PE has 32 parallel dataflow paths that are capable of processing 32 channels in parallel. As we use pre-trained batch normalization parameters, each BN module essentially takes inputs and apply a multiplication and an addition for scaling operations defined in batch normalization [10]. ReLU simply caps negative input values with 0. The Conv module is designed by conducting loop unrolling based on output feature channels M, i.e. M dataflow paths can produce outputs for the output channels in parallel. Similarly, Conv module is also consist of an array of PEs as shown in Fig. 4. Each PE can produce values for 32 OFM channels in parallel. The patch buffers are used for loading the feature map numbers involved in each kernel window step and broadcasting these numbers to all computational units within the PE for OFM computations. Finally, FC modules are designed for the

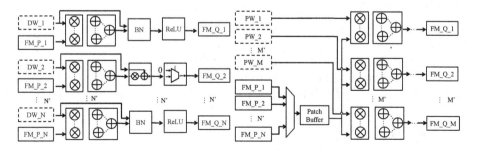

Fig. 3. PE of DW module   **Fig. 4.** PE of Conv module

output layer, which essentially are parallel multiplier and adder trees for efficient computation of the last Conv layer that behaves as a Fully-connected (FC) layer.

In the next section, we specially introduce our design principles for FM buffers and parameter OCM storage mentioned in above system description.

3.2   Memory Usage

In order to avoid the time spent on off-chip memory traffic for parameters and feature map values, we aim to map both data onto the available OCMs given an FPGA device. Based on the layer-wise memory requirement analysis in Eqs. 6 and 7, the overall memory requirement for our Redundancy-reduced MobileNet (RR-Mobi), which contains I Conv layers and J DSC layers, is shown below:

$$
\begin{aligned}
Mem^p_{RR-Mobi} = &\sum_{i=1}^{I} K_i \times K_i \times N_i \times M_i \times \beta_i \times \alpha_p \times DW_p \\
&+ \sum_{j=1}^{J} (K_j \times K_j \times N_j \times \beta_{j-1} + N_j \times M_j \times \beta_j) \times DW_p \times \alpha_p.
\end{aligned}
\tag{9}
$$

This indicates that the memory reuse is impossible among for parameter storage among all layers in a MobileNet and the overall requirement is a summation of individual layers. Differently, the memory for feature map storage can be reused among layers because of the fact that the OFMs of layer i are only used to compute IFMs of layer $i+1$. Therefore, the memory accolated for OFM_i can be reused for storing the feature maps of the following layers. So the memory requirement for feature map storage is capped by the layer with the largest feature map values:

$$
Mem^a_{RR-Mobi} = \bigcup_{l=1}^{l=I+J} (I_l^2 \times N_l \times \beta_{l-1} \times DW_a \times \alpha_a + O_l^2 \times M_l \times DW_a \times \beta_l \times \alpha_a),
\tag{10}
$$

where $\bigcup_{l=1}^{l=I+J}$ returns the maximum memory requirement for feature maps of any single layer among all $I+J$ layers. If Mem_{OCM} represent the OCM resources available on a particular FPGA device, below condition should be valid in a memory system design:

$$
Mem^a_{RR-Mobi} + Mem^p_{RR-Mobi} < Mem_{OCM}.
\tag{11}
$$

So our redundancy removal strategy should ideally provide values of α and β for each layer that satisfies Eq. 11. In the experiments in Sect. 4, we will show our resulting strategy of redundancy removal for above-mentioned purposes.

3.3   Layer Tilling

As introduced in Sect. 3.1, feature maps are organized based on channels for parallel access. However, some layers have just a few channels but with large amount of numbers in each channel or the other way around, which lead to an efficient storage. For example, the IFMs of the first Conv layer in MobileNet can be images in the ImageNet dataset and the size can be $224 \times 224 \times 3$. However, our proposed system architecture would have higher efficiency if the feature maps have many channels but only reasonably small amount of numbers in each, like the DSC hidden layers in the middle part of the MobileNet topology. So we do tilling to balance the memory for layers like the first Conv layer by divide the IFMs along the channel direction and break them down to smaller blocks that can fit the memory system more efficiently.

An example of applying tilling to a DSC layer is shown in Fig. 1. $I \times I \times N$ IFMs are tilled into $T_i \times T_i \times T_n$ components, which can be computed in parallel in the computing engine. Similarly, for the PW_Conv layer, OFMs can be divided into $T_o \times T_o \times T_m$ parallel tiles. In the Sect. 4, we will show our tilling strategy for our RR-MobileNet system.

4   Experimental Evaluation

4.1   Experimental Results

In this section, we report implementation details of our RR-MobileNet redundancy removal strategy and acceleration system. Meanwhile, we compare our restuls with several other works to demonstrate the validity of our proposed method.

4.2   Experimental Settings

The system is implemented with Vivado HLS complied in Xilinx SDx v2016.3 version. The working clock frequency is 150 MHz. We use Xilinx Zynq UltraScale+ MPSoC as our design hardware platform. Its quad-core ARM Cortex-A53 and a XCZU9EG FPGA chip are separately corresponding to the CPU and programmable logic in Fig. 2. We train and predict our RR-MobileNet model on ImageNet dataset and report the results from predicting on the validation set for the Top1/Top5 classification accuracy. The overall system resource utilization is shown in Table 1. Our system is mainly limited by on-chip memory resources which are used for storing all quantized parameters and feature maps. Considering the data access based on Eq. 11, the resulting number of PEs in DW_conv and Conv moduls are 9. Therefore, up to $9 \times 32 = 288$ kernel channels can be computed in parallel. According to this information, the final RR-MobileNet topology and our redundancy removal strategy are described in Table 2. Meanwhile, a resulting layer-wise memory requirement before and after pruning is shown in Fig. 5. It is shown in the figure that the layers towards the input and output layers are both memory-heavy layers but for different reasons. The input side layers are because of massive feature maps numbers while the output side layers are due to the large amount of parameters. In order to handle this, we apply tilling especially with higher factors to these layers as shown in Table 2. Meanwhile, we apply β to the hidden layers in the middle to further bring down

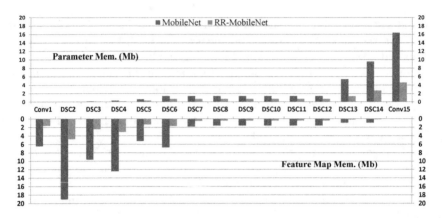

Fig. 5. Per-layer memory requirement with/without redundancy removal

the memory requirements. Specially, our design finally uses a α_a of 0.25 and α_w of 0.5 for data representation. we found this α and β combination gives us fittable design with reasonable model accuracy presented. So the determined data representations for parameters and feature maps are Q2.6 and Q2.2 fixed point values with setting min and max in Algorithm 2 to -1 and 1 separately. We adopt TensorFlow implementation running on an Nvidia Titan X GPU for iterative pruning and quantization training. Only inference is accelerated on FPGA. The final classification accuracy is shown in Table 3.

Table 1. Resource utilization

	BRAM_18K	DSP	FF	LUT
Usage	1729	1452	55K	139K
Total	1824	2520	548K	274K
Util.	95%	58%	11%	51%

As shown in Table 3, we compare our RR-MobileNet with several other CNN hardware accelerators as well as the baseline MobileNet without any redundancy reduction. It shows that our re-training strategy can reserve the original model accuracy to some extend while reducing redundancy from the neural network. Our RR-MobileNet removes 42% of the original MobileNet parameters. Specially, compared to the baseline AlexNet design, our model requires 25× less parameters and 3.2× less operations per image computation to achieve about 9% and 5.2% higher Top1/Top5 accuracy.

We also compare our results with several other state-of-the-art works as shown in Table 3. Because our work is the first one that maps MobileNet on FPGA platforms, we can only compare with existing works that focus on different CNN models. Our system can achieve lower latency than other works mainly

Table 2. Redundancy reduction and tilling

	Conv1	DSC2	DSC3	DSC4	DSC5	DSC6	DSC7-12	DSC13	DSC14	Conv15
M	32	64	128	128	256	256	512	1024	1024	1000
Pruned M	32	64	128	128	256	256	288	576	768	1000
β	0	0	0	0	0	0	0.56	0.56	0.75	0
Tilling (Ti/Tj/Tn/Tm)	4/4/1/1	2/2/1/1	2/2/1/1	1/1/1/1				1/1/1/2	1/1/1/3	1/1/1/4

Table 3. Comparison with other works

Work	Model	Params (M)	GOps/F	FPGA	Freq. (MHz)	Prec. (W/a)	#ms per Inf. (ms)	GOPS	Top1 Acc.	Top5 Acc.
[2]	AlexNet	62.4	2.27	Stratix-V	100	8/10	∼13	114.5	55.6	79.3
[4]	VGG-16	132	30.94	Zynq XC7Z045	150	16/16	224.6	136.97	68	87.9
[6]	MobileNet	4.2	1.13	-/-	-/-	16/16 (FP)	-/-	-/-	0.71	0.90
Ours	RR-MobileNet	2.5	0.72	XCZU9EG	150	8/4	7.85	91.2	64.6	84.5

because of the high on-chip memory bandwidth access, which can achieve a top 15.6 Tb/s. However, current memory system design also limits the PE parallelism due to fixed data access pattern. So the throughput is relatively lower than other works. This will be studied in our future works.

5 Summary and Conclusion

In this work, we present our quantitative analysis of both model-level and data-level redundancy in MobileNet and implement an FPGA acceleration system for our RR-MobileNet. Although we only focus on MobileNet model in this work, our redundancy removal methods are general to a broad range of neural networks. In the future work, we will focus on improving our system throughpout using orthogonal CNN loop manipulation techniques. We will also extend our study to other types of neural networks.

References

1. Parashar, A., et al.: SCNN: an accelerator for compressed-sparse convolutional neural networks. CoRR, vol. abs/1708.04485 (2017)
2. Ma, Y., et al.: Scalable and modularized RTL compilation of convolutional neural networks onto FPGA. In: FPL (2016)
3. Umuroglu, Y., Fraser, N.J., Gambardella, G., Blott, M., Leong, P.H.W., Jahre, M., Vissers, K.A.: FINN: a framework for fast, scalable binarized neural network inference. CoRR, vol. abs/1612.07119 (2016)
4. Qiu, J., et al.: Going deeper with embedded FPGA platform for convolutional neural network. In: Proceedings of ACM/SIGDA ISFPGA, pp. 26–35 (2016)
5. Han, S., et al.: EIE: efficient inference engine on compressed deep neural network (2016)

6. Howard, A., et al.: Mobilenets: efficient convolutional neural networks for mobile vision applications. CoRR, vol. abs/1704.04861 (2017)
7. Han, S., Mao, H., Dally, W.J.: Deep compression: compressing deep neural network with pruning, trained quantization and huffman coding. CoRR, vol. abs/1510.00149 (2015)
8. Anwar, S., et al.: Structured pruning of deep convolutional neural networks. CoRR, vol. abs/1512.08571 (2015)
9. Zhou, S., Ni, Z., Zhou, X., Wen, H., Wu, Y., Zou, Y.: DoReFa-Net: training low bitwidth convolutional neural networks with low bitwidth gradients. CoRR, vol. abs/1606.06160 (2016)
10. Ioffe, S., Szegedy, C.: Batch normalization: accelerating deep network training by reducing internal covariate shift. In: Proceedings of ICML, pp. 448–456 (2015)

Accuracy to Throughput Trade-Offs
for Reduced Precision Neural Networks
on Reconfigurable Logic

Jiang Su[1,2]([✉]), Nicholas J. Fraser[1,2], Giulio Gambardella[1,2], Michaela Blott[1,2], Gianluca Durelli[1,2], David B. Thomas[1,2], Philip H. W. Leong[1,2], and Peter Y. K. Cheung[1,2]

[1] Xilinx Research Labs, Imperial College London, London, UK
j.su13@ic.ac.uk, {nfraser,giulio,mblott}@xilinx.com
[2] University of Sydney, Sydney, Australia

Abstract. Modern Convolutional Neural Networks (CNNs) are typically based on floating point linear algebra based implementations. Recently, reduced precision Neural Networks (NNs) have been gaining popularity as they require significantly less memory and computational resources compared to floating point. This is particularly important in power constrained compute environments. However, in many cases a reduction in precision comes at a small cost to the accuracy of the resultant network. In this work, we investigate the accuracy-throughput trade-off for various parameter precision applied to different types of NN models. We firstly propose a quantization training strategy that allows reduced precision NN inference with a lower memory footprint and competitive model accuracy. Then, we quantitatively formulate the relationship between data representation and hardware efficiency. Our experiments finally provide insightful observation. For example, one of our tests show 32-bit floating point is more hardware efficient than 1-bit parameters to achieve 99% MNIST accuracy. In general, 2-bit and 4-bit fixed point parameters show better hardware trade-off on small-scale datasets like MNIST and CIFAR-10 while 4-bit provide the best trade-off in large-scale tasks like AlexNet on ImageNet dataset within our tested problem domain.

Keywords: Reduced precision · Neural Networks · FPGA
Algorithm acceleration

1 Introduction

Modern CNNs may contain millions of floating-point parameters and require billions of floating-point operations to recognize a single image. These requirements tend to increase as researchers explore deeper networks. On the other hand, the integration of computing resources on hardware platforms is hampered by the

© Springer International Publishing AG, part of Springer Nature 2018
N. Voros et al. (Eds.): ARC 2018, LNCS 10824, pp. 29–42, 2018.
https://doi.org/10.1007/978-3-319-78890-6_3

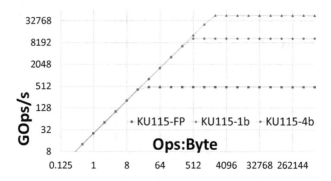

Fig. 1. Roofline model for Xilinx KU115 FPGA

slowing down of Moore's law. Therefore, it is meaningful to study efficient model designs with customized data paths and effective data representations.

Previous work showed that using reduced precision for NN parameters provide massive improvements on system performance such as throughput, computational resource usage and memory footprint [1–3]. For example, Fig. 1 shows the roofline for Xilinx KU115 device in terms of its arithmetic intensity and peak board performance. It shows that higher performance "ceiling" can be achieved if using lower precision data in operations. However, as mentioned in [1,4], reduced-precision parameters need more operations and parameters to achieve the same accuracy provided by high precision alternatives. Additionally, the "operation" as for the y axis in Fig. 1 can be different to various data types. For example, instead of expensive Multiply Accumulate (MAC) operations for floating point (FP) or fixed point (FIX) representations, XNOR and popcount logic can be used for Binary Neural Networks (BNNs). Therefore, compared to FP, binary number operations may lead to a system with higher throughput (GOps/s), but does this higher throughput provide as good NN accuracy? Another way to ask the question is that if a target classification accuracy is given to a particular dataset, can binary parameter based NN still allow more efficient hardware systems than floating point parameters? We found many questions like this remain unanswered. For example, how does parameter precision in NNs affect the hardware throughput given a particular system architecture? Which data type provides the best trade-off between model accuracy and hardware performance?

In order to address above questions, we focus on an exploration space for various data representations in NN computation in order to study their impacts to hardware system efficiency and model accuracy. In contrast to previously published work, which focuses either on hardware-wise efficiency [1,2,5] or model performance [6–8], we consider both perspectives and tentatively provide a more comprehensive view of using reduced-precision for NN system design. The contributions of this work is as follows:

– We report our quantization training strategy for NN inference with quantized weights and activations in arbitrary precision types. Without any compression

techniques, our training strategy requires less memory footprint and achieves
competitive accuracy compared to several state-of-the-art compression techniques on the same task.

– We propose quantitative estimation models to show how parameter precision
  affects hardware cost and system throughput for a NN hardware system.
– We publish systematic experimental results for different types of NNs with
  weights and activations represented separately in 1-bit (Binary), 2-bit (INT2),
  4-bit (INT4), 8-bit(INT8), 16-bit (INT16) fixed point values and 32-bit floating point values (FP32) and show their impacts to classification accuracy,
  hardware cost and inference throughput.
– Finally, our exploration space provides useful insights and a more comprehensive view of using reduced-precision values in NN acceleration. For example, in
  our MNIST experiments, a networks with FP32 parameters is more memory
  efficient than 1-bit parameters for achieving 99% accuracy due to the smaller
  topology required. In general, 2-bit and 4-bit fixed point parameters show
  better hardware trade-off on small-scale datasets like MNIST and CIFAR-
  10 while 4-bit provide the best trade-off in large-scale tasks like AlexNet on
  ImageNet dataset within our tested problem domain.

In the next section, we introduce our training strategy for reduced precision parameters. Next, Sect. 3 introduces the proposed estimation models for
hardware cost and system throughput. The experimental results are discussed
in Sect. 4 and Sect. 5 finally concludes the paper.

2   Training Strategies

In this work, weights and activation values are quantized before used in the
feedforward and backward propagation. For fixed-point representations, values
are represented with WL bits, in which the Most Significant Bit (MSB) indicates
the sign while FL and $(WL - FL - 1)$ bits are used for expressing the fractional
and the integer parts separately.

Specifically, for binary representation, we adopted the deterministic binariza-
tion function used in [2] as our quantization method:

$$x^Q = Sign(x) = \begin{cases} +1 & \text{if } x \geq 0 \\ -1 & \text{otherwise.} \end{cases} \qquad (1)$$

For fixed point values, the quantization function converts real values to nearest pre-defined fixed point representations.

As mentioned in [1,2], for training binary parameters, batch normalization
is generally conducted before the activation function while for other representations, it's the other way around. For activation functions, we use both of the Hard
Hyperbolic Tangent Function (hard-tanh) $\sigma(x) = Min(1, Max(-1, x))$ and the
Rectified Linear Unit (ReLU) $\sigma(x) = Max(0, x)$. Both of the activations are
used in our experiments and the one that delivers a higher model accuracy is
selected.

Algorithm 1. Quantization training strategy for an L-layer neural network

---

Require: At time step t, a batch of inputs a_0 and their labels a^*, network weights W, Batch Normalization parameter θ, learning rate η and its decay factor λ.

Ensure: At time step $t + 1$, the updated weights W^{t+1}, the updated Batch Normalization parameter θ^{t+1} and the updated learning rate η^{t+1}.

{1. Propagations with Limited Precision Parameters}

{1.a Feedforward Propagation:}

1: **for** $i = 1$ to L **do**
2:     $W_i^Q \leftarrow Quantize(W_i)$
3:     $s_i \leftarrow a_{i-1}^Q * W_i^Q$
4:     **if** $i < L$ **then**
5:        $a_i \leftarrow ActFunc(\hat{s}_i)$
6:        $\hat{s}_i \leftarrow BatchNorm(s_i, \theta_i)$
7:        $a_i^Q \leftarrow Quantize(a_i)$
8:     **end if**
9: **end for**

{1.b Backward Propagation:}

Compute $g_{a_L} = \frac{\partial C}{\partial a_L}$ knowing a_L and a^*

10: **for** $i = L$ to 1 **do**
11:     **if** $i < L$ **then**
12:        $(g_{s_i}, g_{\theta_i}) \leftarrow BackBatchNorm(\hat{g}_{a_i}, s_i, \theta_i)$
13:        $\hat{g}_{a_i} \leftarrow BackActFunc(g_{a_i})$
14:     **end if**
15:     $g_{a_{i-1}^Q} \leftarrow g_{s_i} * W_i^Q$
16:     $g_{W_i^Q} \leftarrow g_{s_i}^T * a_{i-1}^Q$
17: **end for**

{2. Weight Updating with High Precision Parameters}

18: **for** $i = 1$ to L **do**
19:     $\theta_i^{t+1} \leftarrow Update(\theta_i, \eta, g_{\theta_i})$
20:     $W_i^{t+1} \leftarrow Clip(Update(W_i, \gamma_i \eta, g_{W_i^Q}), -1, 1)$
21:     $\eta^{t+1} \leftarrow \lambda \eta$
22: **end for**

Globally, quantized low-precision weights and activations are used for feedforward and backpropagation passes. After this process, the floating point parameters are updated accordingly (line 20, Algorithm 1). High-precision values are used for updating because they can accumulate tiny value changes while lower-precision values can improve the computational efficiency during inference due to the low design complexity [9].

Our quantization training process is shown in Algorithm 1. $Quantize(*)$ is the quantization function. $BatchNorm(*)$ and $BackBatchNorm(*)$ are functions that propagate neuron-generated values and gradients separately in feedforward and backpropagations. Similarly, $ActFunc(*)$ and $BackActFunc(*)$ are activation passes in above-mentioned bidirectional propagations. $Update(*)$ specifies the parameter updating strategy, ADAM Updating is used in this work [10]. Network weights are initialized based on [11]. Finally, C is the cost function.

Table 1. The expected cost per operation for each precision type

Datatype	LUTs Min	LUTs Max	LUTs Avg	DSPs Min	DSPs Max	DSPs Avg	C_{avg} $\times 10^{-6}$	C_{rel}
Binary	4.24	8.00	5.58	0	0	0	12.02	1
INT2	10.98	18.74	13.52	0	0	0	29.12	2.42
INT4	27.18	35.56	30.06	0	0	0	64.76	5.39
INT8	83.28	91.92	86.38	0	0	0	186.02	15.48
INT16	21.64	38.36	28.66	1	1	1	181.16	15.07
FP32	356	-	-	4	-	-	766.6	63.79
KU115	-	663,360	-	-	5,520	-	-	-

In the feedforward process, real-valued weights W are firstly quantized into low-precision weights W^Q as shown in line 2. After batch normalization and activation function, neuron activations are also quantized to low precision (line 7). Above steps form a layer-wise process until the training error g_{a_L} is calculated in the last layer according to the outputs in the output layer a_L and the corresponding data label $a*$. Then backward propagation starts with the error calculated through above feedforward pass. After going through backward passes for the activation function and batch normalization function, the quantized weights W^Q are used for the calculation of gradients of both neurons and connections. Noticeably, this is the key point that the model is "aware" of the quantized parameters. This process is a layer-wise process from the output layer to input layer (line 10–17). Finally, parameters are updated with the gradients following the ADAM rule. Specifically, the updated values are clipped between -1 and $+1$ for regularization. The ADAM parameter θ and learning rate η are also updated accordingly. If the $ActFunc(*)$ is hard-tanh and $Quantize(*)$ is Eq. 1, the Algorithm 1 depicts the training strategy proposed in [2] for 1 bit binary parameters.

The quantization training process is done offline and we only deploy the inference process online with the trained parameters. In the next section, a hardware cost model is introduced for a specific system architecture on FPGAs.

3   Hardware Cost Model for Different Precision Types

In this work, we build up our hardware impact analysis based on a hardware system architecture that is introduced in this section. Firstly, processing elements are introduced as the basic building blocks of conducting above operations. Then a hardware cost model is proposed to theoretically formulate the relationship between parameter precision and system throughput, which is then later applied to our studied trade-offs.

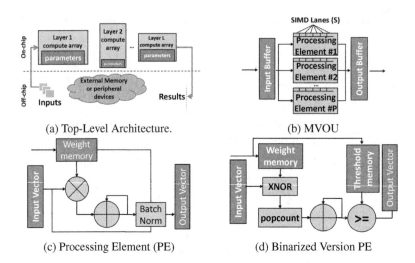

(a) Top-Level Architecture.   (b) MVOU

(c) Processing Element (PE)   (d) Binarized Version PE

Fig. 2. Hardware system components for neural network computation

3.1   System Architecture

As shown in Fig. 2a, the overall system architecture used in this work is based
on a data-flow framework for CNN inference called FINN [1]. Network inputs
are loaded from off-chip memory to layer-wise on-chip processing modules. After
completing the feedforward computation, the classification outputs are finally
transferred back to off-chip memory storage. As shown in Fig. 2a, each layer is
mapped with an array of Matrix-Vector Operation Unit (MVOU) modules as
shown in Fig. 2b.

Internally, the MVTU consists of an input and output buffer, and an array
of Processing Elements (PEs) each with a number of SIMD lanes. The number
of PEs (P) and SIMD lanes (S) are configurable to control the throughout. A
PE can be thought of as a hardware neuron capable of processing S synapses
per clock cycle. Each PE receives exactly the same control signals and input
vector data, but multiply-accumulates the input with a different part of the
matrix. Figure 2c shows the PE data-path for FIX/FP numbers and Fig. 2d
shows its counterpart for 1 bit binary numbers, which is used in [1]. Noticeably,
the Multiplier-ACcumulate (MAC) structures (Fig. 2c) for FIX/FP are replaced
with XNOR and popcount structure for binary numbers. **Either MAC or
XNOR/popcount is referred as "operation" or "fundamental operation" for its corresponding data type throughout this paper.** Please
note, for higher precision parameters, the dataflow model is not necessarily feasible when the chips are not sufficiently large. These situations are beyond the
assumption of this work and the related analysis is only for theoretical reference.

3.2   Hardware Cost Estimation Model

Based on the architecture described in last section, we propose our hardware cost estimation model for arbitrary parameter precision type and theoretically formulate the relationship between hardware cost and parameter precision type for the given architecture. Table 1 shows the average hardware cost per fundamental operation for each precision type. In order to get this table, different levels of parallelism for the MVOU has been tried in each data representation and we report an average value for fair comparisons. Because of the sharing of control logic, the average hardware cost for the basic operations can be different depending on the level of parallelism. So we mark the minimum and maximum cost of resources as "min" and "max" in the table and eventually use the average value of them for a more precise estimation. Look-Up-Tables (LUTs) and DSP blocks are both considered as hardware cost in this work. The average cost per operation, C_{avg} is calculated as follows:

$$C_{avg} = \max(\frac{LUTs/MAC}{LUT_{usage} * LUTs_{TOTAL}}, \tag{2}$$
$$\frac{DSPs/MAC}{DSP_{usage} * DSPs_{TOTAL}}),$$

where $LUTs_{TOTAL}$ and $DSPs_{TOTAL}$ are separately the total available LUTs and DSPs on the target device and LUT_{usage} and DSP_{usage} are separately the proportion of LUTs and DSPs that can be used for arithmetic on the target device. We've estimated $LUT_{usage} = 0.7$ and $DSP_{usage} = 1.0$ in this work. C_{avg} is the fraction of the target device resources that are used in average by a fundamental operation for each type and as such is a measure of scarcity of resource. Relative cost, C_{rel}, is used to compare the arithmetic cost of binarized networks against other precision types directly. For example, if a Binary and an INT4 network have been trained to achieve the same level of accuracy, the INT4 network must have 5.38 less operations to have the same accuracy/computation trade-off as the binarized one.[1]

Interestingly, modelling computational cost this way means that INT16 has a *lower* hardware cost than INT8, because it uses less LUTs/Op than INT8 and the proportion of DSPs that it uses per Op with respect to the total on the target device, a Xilinx Kintex UltraScale 115, is less than the proportion of LUTs/Op used by INT8. These resource usage data are calculated based on Vivado HLS 2016.3 synthesis reports. In this work, we only consider the default synthesis results from the compiler. Optimization to INT8 can be applied to recent Xilinx DSP blocks. This will improve INT8 performance but will not affect the correctness of our estimation model and hence not specially applied in our work. In essence, we assume a custom dataflow architecture generated for each specific network topology (different sizes for the compute arrays in different layers as shown in Fig. 2a), meaning that the "one-size-fits-all" inefficiencies of

---

[1] This assumes that both networks have the same memory footprint for their parameters.

loopback accelerators are avoided. As such, peak performance of a particular device is almost achievable in practice.

3.3 Throughput Estimation Model

Hardware cost is highly related to the system performance and computation efficiency. Theoretically, we formulate the relationship between inference throughput and hardware cost as follows:

$$Throughput \approx \frac{Freq.}{\#OP \times C_{avg} + \Delta},\tag{3}$$

where $Freq.$ is the working clock frequency, $\#OP$ is the number of operations required to compute a single NN input frame, which is a fixed value once network topology is determined. Δ stands for extra resource overhead used for control logic and C_{avg} is defined in Eq. 2 as average hardware cost per operation. Because C_{avg} in our estimation model is a ratio between required resource and the overall resource budget, C_{avg} implies resource folding factor in order to get all computations done with available resource. We migrate and apply this folding effect to timing and interpret it as folding of clock cycles in unit time so that throughput can be estimated. As shown in Table 1, from binary values to 32-bit floating point values, the C_{avg} is roughly getting higher due to the increasing hardware complexity except for the case where INT16 is more efficient than INT8 due to the explanation in Sect. 3.2. Meanwhile, according to Eq. 3, higher C_{avg} brings down the throughput for the same network implementation on a specific device. This will be demonstrated in Sect. 4.1.

According to our observation in real systems, as resource usage of the target device increase, the models become more accurate. For concrete examples, we compare results from our estimation model to real implementation from Fraser et al. [12]. The measured GOps/s for their cnn(1/2) and cnn(1) models are 1856 and 7407. According to our estimation model, the estimated minimum performance for the corresponding models are 2051 and 8596, which are 35% and 16% difference. The discrepancy between estimated and measured performance could be due to the following factors: 1. Difference in clock frequency between estimated and measured models. 2. An underestimation of the control logic overhead when a small portion of the target device is used. 3. the model doesn't take into account that the first layer has 8-bit pixel images as inputs.

4   Experimental Evaluation

We tested on 6 precision types: 1-bit binary values (Binary), fixed point representations with 2-bit (INT2), 4-bit (INT4), 8-bit (INT8), 16-bit (INT16) and single-precision floating point values (FP32). 2 bits are reserved for the integer part and rest for fractional part (FL). The fully-connected NNs are tested on the MNIST dataset. CNNs are tested on CIFAR-10 [13] and ImageNet [14] datasets. All input images are expressed in 8-bit fixed point numbers.

We used Fully-Connected (FC) and CNN models in our experiments. FC is a reference network topology with 3 hidden layers with each containing 4096 hidden neurons fully connected to its proceeding layer. For CNN, the reference topology is the VGG-16 inspired model [15], which contains a succession of $(3 \times 3$ convolution, 3×3 convolution, 2×2 maxpool) layers repeated three times with 128-256-512 channels, followed by two fully-connected layers with 1024 neurons in each. For ImageNet tasks, we use AlexNet [14] as baseline model. In terms of activation function, all the precision options are trained with ReLU and hard-tanh and the best accuracy results are used to report the performance. Additionally, 5 values for scaling factor s are applied to the reference networks in order to expand or shrink the reference topology in a specific ratio. The values are 0.03125, 0.0625, 0.125, 0.25, 0.5, 1. For example, all tested FC networks have the same number of hidden layers, but with $1024 * s$ neurons correspondingly. Similarly to CNNs, scaling factors are multiplied with the number of filters in each conv layer, but they do not change the depth of the topology. For ImageNet tasks, smaller models provide unacceptably low accuracy, so we only report the results of 0.25, 0.5 and 1.

In this work, we use Xilinx Kintex UltraScale 115 as the target FPGA device. The working clock frequency is 250 MHz. In terms of metrics, **throughput** is measured in this work as frames per second and a frame is an image fed to a neural network. **Hardware Cost** is studied through computational resources and block ram (BRAM) usage. Since we are not competing for the best model accuracy, better classification results can be achieved if using other optimization techniques, which can be orthogonal to the training strategy used in this work. To make fair comparison, we train all experiments for each dataset/topology with the same hyper-parameters including number of epochs, learning rate decay strategy etc.

4.1   Experimental Results

The results shown in this section are based on our estimation models. Figures 3 and 4 show the trade-off curves for different dataset and network combinations. Each curve indicates a data representation for both weight and activation. Each marker on the curve shows the result for a network with a specific scaling factor. In Fig. 3, the areas highlighted in red colour are emphasized in an attached zoom-in view in order to show more information about regions for high classification accuracy regions, which may deliver more insights that global trends cannot display.

MNIST on FC Layers. From Fig. 3, we can see that FP32 delivers the highest accuracy in 3 of its topology options and Binary provides best options in terms of hardware efficiency with a much higher accuracy drop (6.24%) compared to the best FP32 results. In general, INT2, FP32 and INT4 dominate the Pareto Frontier. From the zoom-in views, a noticeable observation is that among solutions that give no higher than 1.2% classification error, which is the best achievable result for binary, INT2, INT4 and even FP32 can all provide more efficient solutions than Binary in terms of memory usage. The reason for this is that Binary

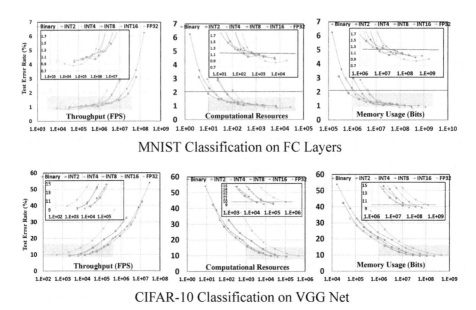

MNIST Classification on FC Layers

CIFAR-10 Classification on VGG Net

Fig. 3. Experimental results for CIFAR10 and MNIST classification (Color figure online)

requires a larger topology and more computation to achieve the same model accuracy. For example, only $4096 * 0.125 = 512$ neurons are needed in each hidden layer for FP32 to achieve 1.02% error while 4096 neurons per hidden layer are needed for Binary to achieve a similar error of 1.2%. Required memory for Binary is 37.0 Mb and 29.8 Mb for FP32.

Noticeably, with a relatively small budget of BRAM smaller than 1Mb, only Binary, INT2 and INT4 are feasible options for hardware implementations while INT2 can achieve the highest accuracy (98.1%). If comparing the representability of Binary and FP32 by looking at the solutions with best accuracy for each, Binary requires only 27 Mb memory for an accuracy of 98.8% while FP32 needs 1.2 GB for only a 0.25% higher accuracy. Additionally, if setting the accuracy goal as 98% on MNIST task (red dotted line on the global figure), INT2 provides the most efficient option in terms of computational resource and memory usage. Meanwhile, Binary at least requires 6.2× more computational resources and 7.8× more memory compared to the optimal INT2 option. Besides, INT4 also provides more resource/memory efficient options than Binary.

Moreover, our low-precision training strategy allows memory saving when conducting inference, which achieves a very similar effect of network compression. We compare our results with several state-of-the-art compression works on the same dataset (MNIST) and the same network topology. Table 2 shows that without using any compression techniques, our INT4, INT8, INT16 results can

Table 2. Memory saving and model accuracy comparison between our work and RER [16], LRD [6], DK [17], HashNet [18], Q-CNN [8] and Q-CNN(EC)[8] on MNIST classification task with 784-1000-1000-1000-10 FC networks

	Ours					RER	LRD	DK	HashNet	Q-CNN	Q-CNN(EC)
	Binary	INT2	INT4	INT8	INT16						
Mem. saving	32×	**16×**	8×	4×	2×	8×	8×	8×	8×	12.1×	12.1×
Error	1.5	1.25	**1.16**	1.13	1.13	1.24	1.77	1.26	1.22	1.34	1.19

achieve higher model accuracy than the other methods[2]. Meanwhile, INT2 and Binary achieve higher memory saving rate and still keep competitive accuracy. As highlighted in red colour, our results either achieve best compression rate or highest accuracy on the exactly same network topology compared to the other state-of-art results.

CIFAR10 on VGGNet. Second row in Fig. 3 shows trade-offs for CIFAR10 classification with VGGNets. Noticeably, INT4, INT8 and INT16 provide very close best accuracy and all higher then FP32 alternative. The rounding noise introduced in parameter quantization may help to improve the classification accuracy in this particular case. Similarly, Binary provides the most efficient solution among all precision types but with much higher error (54%). INT2 and INT4 provide high accuracy options with relatively higher throughput, lower resource and memory usage, as shown in the zoom-in views. They are considered as optimal parameter data type as they contribute most of the Pareto-efficient options. FP32 options are not advantageous on either model accuracy or hardware cost because of the high complexity. As shown by the red dotted lines in the zoom-in views, for the range where accuracy is higher than 90%, it is INT2, rather than Binary, that provides the most efficient options in terms of computational resource and memory usage. Specifically, for 91% accuracy, INT2 provide 13.9K FPS which is 26× higher than FP32, 6× higher than INT8 and INT16 alternatives. On the other hand, Binary requires a larger topology to achieve the same level of accuracy compared to the other alternatives by 1 scaling factor. But it presents only 1.7% accuracy degradation with 32× less memory and 63.8× less computational resource requirement if we compare the most accurate options provided by Binary and FP32.

ImageNet on AlexNet. ImageNet tasks show clearer relative positions among curves in Fig. 4. This can be caused by the higher complexity in the classification tasks compared to MNIST and CIFAR10. Noticeably, Binary and INT2 solutions cannot achieve comparable model accuracy to other data types as they are in MNIST and CIFAR10 tasks. As shown in all figures, there is an accuracy gap between these two types and the others. Some very recent works like [19] try to target on this accuracy gap by optimizing the quantization function

---

[2] The reason that the particular 784–1000 × 3–10 structure is selected in Table 2 is that it is the only structure that is reported in all mentioned works. We compare different methods on the same structure in the same classification task for fair comparisons on memory and accuracy.

for parameters with extremely low bitwidth. This topic is very interesting and definitely deserves more efforts, but it is beyond the scope of this paper. In particular, INT4, compared to FP32, provide solution with 8× memory saving and 11.8× higher throughput with only less than 1% accuracy drop. Similarly, INT8 can provide a 4.3× higher throughput solution with no accuracy loss compared to FP32. Therefore, FP32 again loses its advantage on either model accuracy or hardware efficiency. In general, INT4, INT8 and INT16 and FP32 present accuracy with negligible difference. However, INT4 has the best trade-off due its less memory and computational resource requirements as well as higher system throughput possibly provided.

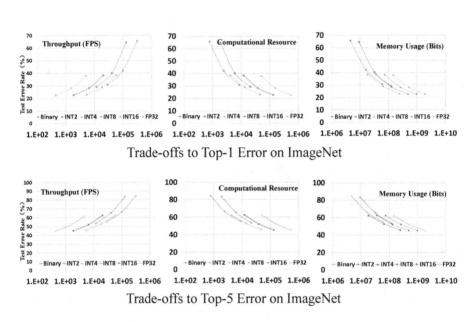

Fig. 4. Experimental results for ImageNet classification on AlexNet

5 Summary and Conclusion

In this work, we firstly introduce our quantization training strategy that allows training NNs with arbitrary parameter precision. Then, we propose our hardware cost and throughput estimation models. Finally, we conduct our experiments in the exploration space consist of 6 different data types, 3 different NN models and 3 different benchmarks. We found that Binary does not necessarily provide hardware solutions with highest efficiency due to larger amount of parameters required for Binary to achieve the same level of model accuracy with its high precision alternatives. Within our studied cases, INT2 and INT4 generally provide better trade-offs in small image classification tasks, MNIST and CIFAR10, while INT4 provide the best trade-offs among all other types in ImageNet tasks. More insightful observations have been pointed out in Sect. 4, which hopefully can be helpful to reduced-precision NN system design on reconfigurable hardware.

Acknowledgments. The authors from Imperial College London would like to acknowledge the support of UK's research council (RCUK) with the following grants: EP/K034448, P010040 and N031768. The authors from The University of Sydney acknowledge support from the Australian Research Council Linkage Project LP130101034.

References

1. Umuroglu, Y., Fraser, N.J., Gambardella, G., Blott, M., Leong, P.H.W., Jahre, M., Vissers, K.A.: FINN: a framework for fast, scalable binarized neural network inference, CoRR (2016)
2. Courbariaux, M., Hubara, I., Soudry, D., El-Yaniv, R., Bengio, Y.: Binarized neural networks: training deep neural networks with weights and activations constrained to +1 or −1, CoRR abs/1602.02830 (2016)
3. Rastegari, M., Ordonez, V., Redmon, J., Farhadi, A.: XNOR-Net: imagenet classification using binary convolutional neural networks. In: ECCV (2016)
4. Sung, W., Shin, S., Hwang, K.: Resiliency of deep neural networks under quantization, CoRR abs/1511.06488 (2015)
5. Zhou, S., Ni, Z., Zhou, X., Wen, H., Wu, Y., Zou, Y.: DoReFa-Net: training low bitwidth convolutional neural networks with low bitwidth gradients, CoRR abs/1606.06160 (2016)
6. Denil, M., Shakibi, B., Dinh, L., Ranzato, M., de Freitas, N.: Predicting parameters in deep learning, CoRR abs/1306.0543 (2013)
7. Hwang, K., Sung, W.: Fixed-point feedforward deep neural network design using weights +1, 0, and −1. In: Proceedings of IEEE ICASSP, pp. 1–6. IEEE (2014)
8. Wu, J., Leng, C., Wang, Y., Hu, Q., Cheng, J.: Quantized convolutional neural networks for mobile devices, CoRR abs/1512.06473 (2015)
9. Courbariaux, M., Bengio, Y., David, J.: Low precision arithmetic for deep learning, CoRR abs/1412.7024 (2014)
10. Kingma, D.P., Ba, J.: Adam: a method for stochastic optimization, CoRR abs/1412.6980 (2014)
11. Glorot, X., Bengio, Y.: Understanding the difficulty of training deep feedforward neural networks. In: Proceedings of AISTATS 2010 (2010)
12. Fraser, N.J., et al.: Scaling binarized neural networks on reconfigurable logic, CoRR abs/1701.03400 (2017)
13. Krizhevsky, A., Hinton, G.: Learning multiple layers of features from tiny images, Technical report (2009)
14. Krizhevsky, A., Sutskever, I., Hinton, G.E.: Imagenet classification with deep convolutional neural networks. In: Proceedings of NIPS, pp. 1097–1105 (2012)
15. Simonyan, K., Zisserman, A.: Very deep convolutional networks for large-scale image recognition, CoRR abs/1409.1556 (2014)
16. Ciresan, D.C., Meier, U., Masci, J., Gambardella, L.M., Schmidhuber, J.: High-performance neural networks for visual object classification, CoRR abs/1102.0183 (2011)

17. Hinton, G., Vinyals, O., Dean, J.: Distilling the knowledge in a neural network abs/1503.02531 (2015)
18. Chen, W., Wilson, J.T., Tyree, S., Weinberger, K.Q., Chen, Y.: Compressing neural networks with the hashing trick, CoRR abs/1504.04788 (2015)
19. Cai, Z., He, X., Sun, J., Vasconcelos, N.: Deep learning with low precision by half-wave Gaussian quantization, CoRR abs/1702.00953 (2017)

Deep Learning on High Performance FPGA Switching Boards: Flow-in-Cloud

Kazusa Musha[1]([✉])[iD], Tomohiro Kudoh[2], and Hideharu Amano[1]

[1] Keio University, Yokohama 223-8522, Japan
mushak@am.ics.keio.ac.jp
[2] The University of Tokyo, Tokyo 113-8654, Japan
fic@am.ics.keio.ac.jp

Abstract. FiC (Flow-in-Cloud)-SW is an FPGA-based switching node for an efficient AI computing system. It is equipped with a number of serial links directly connected to other nodes. Unlike other multi-FPGA systems, the circuit switching fabric with the STDM (Static Time Division Multiplexing) is implemented on the FPGA for predictable communication and cost-efficient data broadcasting. Parallel convolution modules for AlexNet are implemented on FiC-SW1 prototype boards consisting of Kintex Ultrascale FPGA, and evaluation results show that the parallel execution with 20 boards achieved 4.6 times better performance than the state of art implementation on a single Virtex 7 FPGA board.

1 Introduction

Cost and energy efficient AI computing is one of the major goals of recent studies on computer architectures. FiC (Flow-in-Cloud) project aim for it by combining many heterogeneous computing nodes, such as energy efficient GPUs and FPGAs, which are directly connected by a wide bandwidth network. No host processors are involved in the communication between the FiC computing nodes.

As shown in Fig. 1, the first prototype of the FiC platform will consist of FPGA switching nodes with an FPGA and low power GPUs. The FPGA switching nodes will be used as network switches as well as data processing accelerators. In this earliest prototype, GPU is not used and it is designed as a system only for customized FPGA boards. These FPGA switching boards are connected by high-speed serial links. In the future, links will be replaced with optical interconnects.

Here, we focus on the FPGA switching node of the FiC platform called FiC-SW. It is equipped with a number of serial links directly connected to other boards. Unlike other multi-FPGA systems, the circuit switching fabric with the STDM (Static Time Division Multiplexing) is implemented on the FPGA to reduce the overhead in the communication. The FiC-SW supports accelerator functions adopting the concept of Accelerator in Switch (AiS) [1], in which an accelerator and a switching fabric are tightly coupled on a large scale FPGA. Since the latency of communication is completely predictable in the STDM network, the application program can communicate data almost without any synchronization. Therefore, the flow-control which tends to make switching fabrics

© Springer International Publishing AG, part of Springer Nature 2018
N. Voros et al. (Eds.): ARC 2018, LNCS 10824, pp. 43–54, 2018.
https://doi.org/10.1007/978-3-319-78890-6_4

complicated is not required. Also, the data broadcasting can be easily and efficiently implemented.

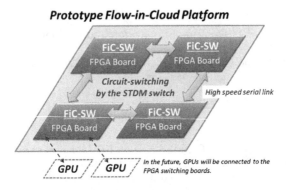

Fig. 1. A FiC system

In this paper, first, the FiC-SW and its prototype board are introduced. Then as an example, an implementation of a CNN using multiple FiC-SW boards is shown with its performance estimation.

2   FiC-SW

2.1   STDM Switching

FiC is designed considering the use of optical interconnect technologies to connect the computing nodes in the system. In the future, interconnects with tens-Tbps bandwidth can be used for connecting nodes by using the wavelength division multiplexing (WDM) and advanced modulation technologies which are currently used in the broadband wide area network.

Currently, communication between computers is realized as a copy between memories of the sender and the receiver nodes. Also, packet switching is commonly used, which stores communicating data in memory when the output port is not available. However, tens of Tbps is wider than the bandwidth of the top-end memory modules, and thus communication architecture itself should not depend on the use of memory. In addition, for switching such a high bandwidth communication with WDM efficiently, the use of optical switches which do not require OE/EO conversions is essential, and circuit switching is far more advantageous compared with the packet switching, in terms of complexity, cost and energy consumption. Multiple number of circuits can be provisioned on a fiber using WDM and wavelength based optical switches. Although the prototype FiC-SW treated here uses electric interconnects, we adopted a circuit switching network using STDM considering the future possibility to use such wide bandwidth interconnects.

Here, we introduce the STDM switch implemented on a prototype board FiC-SW1. The data from other boards come in to high speed serial inputs. A FiC-SW1 FPGA has 32 pairs of high speed serial input and output, each of which has a physical transfer rate of 9.9 Gbps. After de-serialization with 64b/66b coding, the input data are translated into 150 MHz 64-bit signals. This 64-bit signal is handed off to the FPGA internal 100 MHz clock domain, and after ECC decoding, an 85-bit payload is obtained in every 100 MHz clock cycle. The FiC system uses the same clock source for the communicating nodes in the entire system. Therefore, there are no clock frequency difference between a sender and a receiver, and the flow control to compensate possible slight frequency difference between the sender and the receiver is not required.

Each of four pairs of input and output are grouped to connect to the same counter part node. Here, we call the 9.9 Gbps high speed serial connection a *lane*, and the group of four lanes which connects a pair of nodes a *link*. As for payload, each lane has 8.5 Gbps data rate and each link has a total of 34 Gbps data rate.

In a circuit switched system, every pair of nodes which needs to communicate each other has to provide a path between them. Therefore, a lot of paths are required to support a complicated communication pattern. Since each link has four lanes, up to four simultaneous paths can go through a link, if each a path uses a lane. To support more than a path on a lane, we introduced clock-by-clock time division multiplexing. Each lane can have multiple time slots, and each slot at an input lane is associated to a slot at an output lane by a routing table. The number of slots and the routing table is statically set before a job or a part of a job is executed, and so it is basically not changed on the fly.

Figure 2 shows the case with six input lanes each of which has six time slots. Here, for simplicity, we assumed only one lane is on a link (i.e. port). The 85-bit data come in to a port appear to the input slots (S0 to S5) in order. As soon as a data flit appears at a slot at the left, it is transferred to an output slot at the right according to the routing table. The arrows between the left slots and right slots are decided according to the routing table. The data written to the output slots are read out cyclically and sent to the destination node through the ECC encoder, clock domain hand-off and a serializer. The routing table should be properly set so as to avoid associating multiple inputs to the same output. On the other hand, by associating multiple output slots to an input slot, multicast can be easily realized as shown in the dotted line in Fig. 2. Therefore, broadcasting, which is often required in CNN applications, can be easily and efficiently supported by the FiC-SW.

In this way, a path from a source node to a destination node is established by setting the routing table in each switch. Depending on the number of the slots at a lane and the alignment of the receiving slots and sending slots, the latency to go thorough this switching fabric will vary. We can minimize the number of time slots by using an algorithm like [2].

When an accelerator function is implemented on a FiC-SW FPGA, the input/output interface of the function can be implemented as an extension of the STDM switch. Each function can have multiple lanes/slots as input and output. By setting the routing table, a path between functions on different

FiC-SW FPGAs can be also established, and because of the nature of the circuit switching, the communication latency between the functions is predictable.

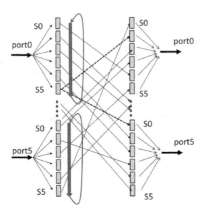

Fig. 2. A STDM switch fabric

The number of the time slots per lane can be determined depending on the target system and applications. A routing table generator for a given set of required circuits for a FiC system with arbitrary network topologies is now under development. By minimizing the number of the slots for each application, we can reduce the communication latency.

2.2 Dragonfly Network for Connecting Boards

Although the FiC system can use any type of networks suitable for its application, we adopted Dragonfly [3], a high-radix network proposed for large scale clusters. In Dragonfly, nodes are classified into several groups, and by using complete connection for both inner-group network and inter-group network, diameter becomes only 3. It achieves high degree of total performance per cost in large scale systems.

For example, in a Dragonfly network which connects 20 FiC-SW boards, Each board uses four links to connect three group members and one for another group. Since each group has four links to other groups, five groups make fully coupled network. It can broadcast the data also with three steps. For building a large scale system, Flatten Butterfly can be used instead of complete interconnection for inner-group connection to keep the required number of links low. In that case, the diameter will become 5 or more. The drawback of Dragonfly is its long inter-group links. However, in FiC systems, optical interconnects will be used for long inter-group links, while short inner-group links can be implemented using economical electric coaxial cables.

2.3 Prototype Board: FiC-SW1

We developed a prototype FiC-SW board called FiC-SW1. It provides 32 high speed serial lanes with 9.9 Gbps bandwidth at maximum. There are 8 full-duplex links by using four lanes for each direction. It is equipped with two 16 GB DRAM modules each can be accessed with 72-bit data width to store streaming data or weight data for CNN. In order to provide a large number of lanes and DRAM modules, we used a high-end FPGA in the middle rank family, Xilinx's Kintex Ultrascale XCKU095. It is one of the most cost-efficient FPGAs available in the current market. For configuration data management, Raspberry Pi 3 card is mounted as a daughter board which can be connected with Ethernet. Figure 3 shows the photo of the prototype board.

Fig. 3. A photo of FiC-SW1

3 CNN Implementation on the FiC-SW1 Boards

3.1 Convolutional Neural Network

Convolutional Neural Network (CNN) is one of the core algorithm of machine learning technology used for image identification, object recognition and natural language processing. It has a Fully-Connected Layer in which the input layer and the output layer are fully combined with learning weights. In the CNN, a convolution layer is introduced for giving locality to weight, reducing the total calculation amount and improving the accuracy.

Image identification CNN: AlexNet. In this paper, we implemented three 3×3 convolution layers of AlexNet [4] on the prototype FiC system. It is the CNN of the winner at ImageNet2012 and has been used as a basis of recent sophisticated CNNs. The CNN, consisting of 5 convolution layers, 3 pooling layers, 2 normalization layers and 3 fully-connected layers, can classify 227×227 color images into 1000 categories.

3.2   CNN Parallel Computation

In order to compute the convolution layer of CNN at multiple nodes, we must consider a method for distributing application to be executed in parallel. In our implementation, we adopted a method of distributing weight data on each node and exchanging input/output feature map by broadcast, to make full use of the broadcast function provided by the STDM switch. Figure 4 shows its state. The weight data used in the convolutional operation are divided and stored in the local storage of each node, and an output feature map is obtained by transmitting the input feature map thereto. The output feature map is re-broadcasted for computation of the next layer as necessary.

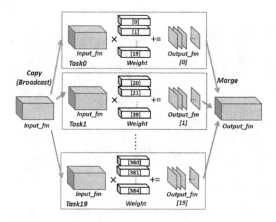

Fig. 4. CNN parallel computation by 20 nodes

3.3   Design of the Parallel Convolution Calculator

Figure 5 shows the diagram of the parallel convolution calculator which is implemented to each node. The calculator has multiply-add processing element (PE), input/output buffer and the streaming ports. The input/output buffer is for exchanging feature maps. In order to overlap the communication with the computation, the double buffer structure is adopted. The streaming port uses Xilinx's AXIStream IP which provides 6.4 Gbps bandwidth at 100 MHz clock.

The feature map, weight and bias data are all represented with 32bit floating point numbers, as same as the original AlexNet, since the main purpose of the implementation is the evaluation of the FiC-SW1 system. As in the common implementation in FPGAs, we can reduce the data width to improve performance.

Processing Element. Processing elements (PEs) calculate N-channel output feature map from M-channel input feature map. Thus, the weights used in the calculation becomes $N \times M$ matrix. For enhancing the performance, the PE is pipelined to generate an output value in a clock cycle. N and M are used for representing the scale of the calculator.

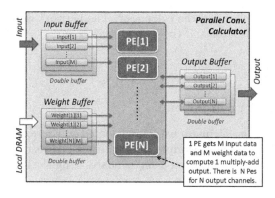

Fig. 5. The diagram of the parallel convolution calculator

Double Buffer. The data for input port are stored into the input buffer in the FPGA. In order to perform convolution as fast as possible, a PE needs to access the input feature map at a wider bandwidth as possible. Thus, the input buffer is divided into a channel of the feature map and can be accessed in parallel. That is, a map datum can be fetched in a clock cycle. The similar structure is used in the output buffers and weight buffers. It allows to perform the data transfer during the computation.

The size of calculator. The size of the calculator is set as shown in Fig. 8 according to the limitation of the FPGA resource. If the number of FiC-SW1 boards is small, N should be set to a large value because the output feature maps which one node must process increases.

3.4 Implementation

The parallel convolution calculator is implemented on FiC-SW1's FPGA as shown in Fig. 6. The total system is consisting of the layered modules: STDM

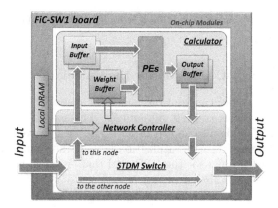

Fig. 6. Implementation

switch, network controller and the calculator. The network controller interfaces AXIStream of the calculator and the STDM switch.

4 Evaluation

4.1 Experimental Environment

The parallel convolution calculator was implemented on Kintex UltraScale FPGA on the FiC-SW1 board. The performance of multiple boards comes from simulation based on an implementation on a single board using the testing module.

4.2 STDM Switch

The STDM switch generator, which can generate Verilog HDL description from the physical topology and circuit switching network topology on it, was developed. It also generates slot assignment table according to the algorithm shown in [2]. Here, the broadcast network used in the CNN is generated for Dragonfly physical topologies, and the hardware resource is evaluated. Note that the number of slot is the same as the number of nodes for broadcasting. In all Dragonfly topologies, the latency for the broadcast is three. The STDM switch is designed to work at 100 MHz clock. Figure 7 shows the required resource for the STDM switch. It shows that even with Dragonfly with 72 nodes, the required LUT is 13% of those in XCKU095 FPGA. Other resource utilization is less than 5%.

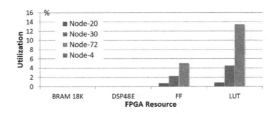

Fig. 7. Resource utilization for the STDM switch fabric

4.3 FPGA Resource Utilization for the Calculator

Figure 8 shows the parallel convolution calculator resource usage in an FPGA when the number of nodes is 4, 20, 30, and 72. The size of the calculator represented with N and M is also shown in it. It can be observed that even with a small number of nodes, resource utilization is moderately increased. Resource usage is less than 50% except for the DSP, and there is enough margin for combining the switch fabric as shown in Fig. 7.

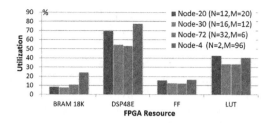

Fig. 8. Resource utilization for the parallel convolution calculator

4.4 Total Execution Time of 3 × 3 Convolution Layer

We designed a test module that mimics the communication quality guaranteed by the STDM switch. And we measured the execution speed of 3 × 3 convolution layer of AlexNet in the parallel convolution calculator on the FiC-SW1 boards by the simulation.

The total execution time from AlexNet-CONV3 to AlexNet-CONV5, which are convolution layers with a deep feature map channel, is summarized in Fig. 9. For example, when the number of nodes is 20, three layers of the convolution can be calculated in 1.9 ms. When the number of nodes is large as the case of 72, the number of input channels that the calculator can process in a clock cycle increases, and the input data receiving throughput becomes the bottleneck, so that the performance is not improved. If the number of nodes is small as the case of 4, the number of output channels that must be processed per node increases and it taked 40 ms over for the three layers. In this case, the output data transfer throughput becomes the bottleneck, and the performance tends to decline sharply. When the number of nodes is 20 or 30, the time for calculation and communication will be almost same. Thus, a system with 20 nodes is the best for the current implementation.

On the other hand, the speed of the system with a small number of nodes may be enhanced by reviewing the parallel work distribution and adjusting the size of the calculator (N, M).

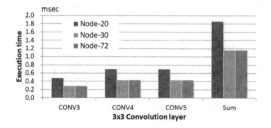

Fig. 9. Performance of our implementation

The comparison of the performance between the previous works and our implementation is shown in Table 1. The UCLA design [5] is the one of the state of the art design of the CNN acceleration. Intel Xeon CPU E5-2430 (@2.20 GHz) was used for the CPU baseline in UCLA works, and the data are also listed in Table 1 for reference.

Our implementation using 20 FiC-SW1 boards is 4.62 times faster than a single Virtex-7 FPGA implementation and nearly 70 times the performance of the software execution by Intel Xeon CPU. Kintex Ultrascale uses more advanced process technology than that of Virtex-7, and the result is with the parallel processing of 20 boards. So, the performance improvement is not surprising. However, this evaluation result demonstrates that the parallel processing with multi-FPGA system with middle range FPGAs can overcome the execution on a single high-end FPGA.

Table 1. Comparison to other implementations

(ms)	CPU 16 threads [5]	Virtex7 [5]	Our implementation 20 FiC-SW1
CONV3	24.30	3.79	0.48
CONV4	65.58	2.88	0.69
CONV5	40.70	1.93	0.69
Sum	130.58	8.60	1.86

5   Related Work

5.1   Multi-board FPGA Systems

Most of recent multi-board FPGA systems use a standard bus or network. Imperial College's Axel uses PCIe, Ethernet and Infiniband to connect CPU, FPGA, and GPUs [6]. Berkeley's BEE3 [7] and Zedwulf [8] use Ethernet to connect between boards. Tohoku Univ's tightly coupled FPGA clusters use PCIe and Ethernet with original light weight protocol [9]. Microsoft's Catapult [10] exceptionally uses an original 10 Gbps serial link. All of them are based on packet switching, to the best of our knowledge, FiC is the first large scale multi-FPGA systems with circuit switching network using STDM.

5.2   Switch-In Accelerator with FPGA

Packet filtering, encryption and decryption on an FPGA network interface have been commonly investigated. Recently, off-loading jobs to network interface or switches has been researched especially for big data processing. Some of the functions for database processing or learning have been off-loaded to network interface FPGAs [11,12]. Also, collective operations are popular off-loading target into an FPGA for a network interface or a switching hub.

These accelerators are designed for an unused area of FPGA for switching fabrics. In the FiC, switching fabric specialized for the applications can be generated and implemented together.

5.3   CNN Implementation on FPGA

In recent years, CNN implementation on FPGAs has received much attention. [5, 13] proposed methods to optimize the implementation analytically using the roof line model. [14] suggests implementation on FPGAs used in data centers. [15] proposed the OpenCL base design, improving the power performance compared to TitanX GPU. There are also many other CNN implementation studies.

Our work focuses on implementing the CNN accelerator on a multi-FPGA system rather than a single high-end FPGA.

6   Conclusion

FiC (Flow-in-Cloud)-SW, an FPGA switching board for AI computing system is proposed. The parallel convolution calculator for AlexNet is implemented on prototype FPGA switching board, FiC-SW1, consisting of Kintex Ultrascale FPGA. The evaluation using a single board showed that each 3×3 convolution layer can be calculated with less than 1 msec in the FiC system using 20 FiC-SW1 boards.

Acknowledgements. This paper is based on results obtained from a project commissioned by the New Energy and Industrial Technology Development Organization (NEDO).

References

1. Tsuruta, C., Miki, Y., Kuhara, T., Amano, H., Umemura, M.: Off-loading LET generation to PEACH2: a switching hub for high performance GPU clusters. In: ACM SIGARCH Computer Architecture News-HEART15, vol. 43, no. 4, April 2016
2. Koibuchi, M., Anjo, K., Yamada, Y., Jouraku, A., Amano, H.: A simple data transfer technique using local address for netowrks-on-chips. IEEE Trans. Parallel Distrib. Syst. **17**(12), 1425–1437 (2006)
3. Kim, J., Dally, W.J., Scott, S., Abts, D.: Technology-driven, highly-scalable dragonfly topology. In: 2008 35th International Symposium on Computer Architecture. ISCA 2008, pp. 77–88, June 2008
4. Krizhevsky, A., Sutskever, I., Hinton, G.E.: Imagenet classification with deep convolutional neural networks. In: Advances in Neural Information Processing Systems 25 (2012)
5. Zhang, C., Li, P., Sun, G., Guan, Y., Xiao, B., Cong, J.: Optimizing FPGA-based accelerator design for deep convolutional neural networks. In: FPGA 2015 Proceedings of the 2015 ACM/SIGDA International Symposium on Field-Programmable Gate Arrays (2015)
6. Niu, X.Y., Tsoi, K.H., Luk, W.: Reconfiguring distributed applications in FPGA accelerated cluster with wireless networking. In: The 21st International Conference on Field Programmable Logic ADN Application (FPL), pp. 545–550, September 2011
7. Muehlbach, S., Koch, A.: A scalable multi-FPGA platform for complex networking applications. In: IEEE Annual International Symposium on Field-Programmable Custom Computing Machines (FCCM), pp. 81–84, May 2011

8. Moorthy, P., Kapre, N., Zedwulf: power-performance tradeoffs of a 32-node zynq soc cluster. In: IEEE 23rd Annual International Symposium on Field-Programmable Custom Computing Machines (FCCM), pp. 68–75, May 2015

9. Sano, K., Hatsuda, Y., Yamamoto, S.: Multi-FPGA accelerator for scalable stencil computation with constant memory bandwidth. IEEE Trans. Parallel Distrib. Syst. **25**(3), 695–705 (2013)

10. Putnum, A., et al.: A reconfigurable fabric for accelerating large-scale datacenter services. In: IEEE/ACM The 41st Annual International Symposium on Computer Architecture (ISCA), pp. 81–84, May 2014

11. Fukuda, E.S., Inoue, H., Takenaka, T., Kim, D., Sadahira, T., Asai, T., Motomura, M.: Caching memcached at reconfigurable network interface. In: Proceedings of the International Conference on Field Programmable Logic and Application (FPL 2014), September 2014

12. Hayashi, A., Matsutani, H.: An FPGA-based In-NIC cache approach for lazy learning outlier filtering. In: 25th Euromicro International Conference on Parallel, Distributed and Network-based Processing (PDP), March 2017

13. Zhang, C., Fang, Z., Zhou, P., Pan, P., Cong, J.: Caffeine: towards uniformed representation and acceleration for deep convolutional neural networks. In: 2016 IEEE/ACM International Conference on Computer-Aided Design (ICCAD) (2017)

14. Ovtcharov, K., Ruwase, O., Kim, J.-Y., Fowers, J., Strauss, K., Chung, E.: Accelerating deep convolutional neural networks using specialized hardware, February 2015

15. Aydonat, U., O'Connell, S., Capalija, D., Ling, A.C., Chiu, G.R.: An OpenCL(TM) deep learning accelerator on Arria 10. CoRR, abs/1701.03534 (2017)

SqueezeJet: High-Level Synthesis Accelerator Design for Deep Convolutional Neural Networks

Panagiotis G. Mousouliotis$^{(\boxtimes)}$ and Loukas P. Petrou

Division of Electronics and Computer Engineering,
Department of Electrical and Computer Engineering, Faculty of Engineering,
Aristotle University of Thessaloniki, 54124 Thessaloniki, Greece
pmousoul@ece.auth.gr, loukas@eng.auth.gr

Abstract. Deep convolutional neural networks have dominated the pattern recognition scene by providing much more accurate solutions in computer vision problems such as object recognition and object detection. Most of these solutions come at a huge computational cost, requiring billions of multiply-accumulate operations and, thus, making their use quite challenging in real-time applications that run on embedded mobile (resource-power constrained) hardware. This work presents the architecture, the high-level synthesis design, and the implementation of SqueezeJet, an FPGA accelerator for the inference phase of the SqueezeNet DCNN architecture, which is designed specifically for use in embedded systems. Results show that SqueezeJet can achieve 15.16 times speed-up compared to the software implementation of SqueezeNet running on an embedded mobile processor with less than 1% drop in top-5 accuracy.

Keywords: DCNN accelerator · FPGA · High-level synthesis

1 Introduction

Since the impressive results of AlexNet deep convolutional neural network (DCNN) in the Image-Net Large-Scale Vision Recognition Challenge (ILSVRC) in [1], DCNN research activity has seen exponential growth with the trend being deeper architectures accompanied by higher accuracies [2,3]. Following this trend, research in DCNN FPGA accelerators provides solutions that use high-end costly FPGA devices and aim at the datacenter rather than the mobile applications [4–6]. An exception to the-most-accurate-network trend in the DCNN architecture research, is SqueezeNet[1] (SqN) [7,12], an AlexNet-level accuracy architecture which reduces dramatically the number of MACs and network parameters, requiring half of the MACs and fifty times less parameters compared to AlexNet. Even though the SqN DCNN architecture is more suitable than others for use in embedded mobile applications, it is still computationally

---

[1] In this work, SqueezeNet refers to SqueezeNet v1.1.

© Springer International Publishing AG, part of Springer Nature 2018
N. Voros et al. (Eds.): ARC 2018, LNCS 10824, pp. 55–66, 2018.
https://doi.org/10.1007/978-3-319-78890-6_5

very demanding and cannot be used in applications running on an embedded mobile processor.

The contribution of this work is the design of SqueezeJet (SqJ), a small FPGA convolutional (conv) layer accelerator for SqN, that can be used as a coprocessor to an embedded mobile processor and enable the development of mobile computer vision (CV) applications. Specifically, the SqJ design: (1) deals with the challenge of the implementation of a single accelerator for multiple conv layers with variable input arguments, (2) implements streaming input/output (I/O) interfaces which, after the initialization phase, consume and produce data pixel-by-pixel[2], (3) uses a sophisticated hardware (HW) mechanism, which mimics software (SW) pointers to the rows of a two-dimensional array, taking advantage of the spatial locality of data and minimizing unnecessary data movement, (4) presents the possibilities of high-level synthesis (HLS) design by using the Xilinx Vivado HLS (VHLS) tool, (5) is implemented on a low-end FPGA system on chip (SoC) device, the Xilinx XC7Z020, using the Xilinx SDSoC tool, and (6) it achieves 80.29% ILSVRC12 top-5 accuracy when it is used for the inference phase of SqN. To the best of the authors' knowledge, the current work presents the first low-end FPGA SoC (XC7Z020) DCNN implementation which achieves 80.29% ILSVRC12 top-5 accuracy.

The rest of this paper is organized as follows: Sect. 2 presents related work. Section 3 is an introduction to the conv layer's operation. Section 4 presents the architecture, the HLS design, and the implementation of the SqJ accelerator. Section 5 shows results related to the performance, the accuracy, and the power consumption of SqJ. Finally, Sect. 6 concludes the paper and proposes future work.

2   Related Work

Works related to DCNN FPGA accelerators can be classified into two main categories; those which accelerate only the conv layer and those which accelerate two or more layer types of a DCNN.

Conv layer accelerators: *Zhang et al.* [4] designed an architecture template for the conv layer using loop tiling, loop arrangement based on data dependencies, computation optimizations (loop unrolling and pipelining), and optimizations for efficient data reuse. Using the parameters of the template and the roofline model, they performed design space exploration (DSE) and found the optimal solution which defined the parameters of their accelerator. A similar approach is followed by *Motamedi et al.* [5] starting with a completely different architectural template. Specifically, they designed their template to take advantage of all the possible forms of parallelism; intra/inter-kernel and inter-output. They eventually used the design parameters and proceeded as in the aforementioned work. Both of these works use DSE to minimize the execution time of the accelerator and 32-bit floating-point arithmetic.

---

[2] A pixel is comprised by all the channels at a specific (x, y) location in the future map volume (see Fig. 1).

Multi-layer accelerators: *Qiu et al.* [8] developed a dynamic-precision data quantization flow and designed a dynamic-precision 16-bit fixed-point accelerator which is capable of accelerating conv, fully connected (FC), and pooling layers. Their implementation is used to accelerate the VGG16-SVD DCNN, which is the VGG16 DCNN with reduced weight matrices for the FC layers; SVD is used for the weight matrix reduction. This accelerator also uses a huge amount of FPGA resources to accelerate one of the most computational demanding DCNNs, requiring 15470 million MACs for a single forward pass. *Gschwend* [9] converted all the layers, except the last global pooling layer, of the SqueezeNet v1.0 DCNN architecture to conv layers and accelerated, using floating-point arithmetic, the new DCNN, called ZynqNet, using VHLS. *Gokhale et al.* [10] designed and implemented nn-X, a complete low-power system for DCNN acceleration composed from a host processor, a coprocessor, and external memory. The coprocessor consists of an array of processing elements which can perform convolution, sub-sampling, and non-linear functions. *Ma et al.* [11] designed an accelerator that supports conv, pooling and fully-connected layers by following a strategy that minimizes computing latency, partial sum storage, access of on-chip buffer, access of external memory, and uses loop optimization techniques. Their accelerator uses 8–16 bit dynamic fixed point arithmetic and it is evaluated by accelerating the VGG-16 DCNN.

SqJ is a conv layer accelerator and it uses fixed-point arithmetic for both parameters (8 bits) and activations (16 bits), which results in considerable savings in both the resources and the power consumption compared to floating-point implementations [4,5,9]. Furthermore, even though works in [8,10,11] use fixed-point arithmetic, they require large costly FPGA devices for their implementation.

3   Convolutional Layer Basics

The conv layer of a DCNN can be described by:

$$FM_o(y_o, x_o, c_o) =$$

$$\sum_{k_h=0}^{K_h-1} \sum_{k_w=0}^{K_w-1} \sum_{c_i=0}^{C_i-1} FM_i((y_o \cdot S + k_h), (x_o \cdot S + k_w), c_i) \cdot W(c_o, k_h, k_w, c_i) \quad (1)$$

$$+B(c_o),$$

where FM_o, FM_i are the output and the input future maps (fmaps) respectively, and W, B are the weight and bias parameters respectively. The y, x, c, represent the vertical, the horizontal, and the channel dimensions of the fmaps, S is the stride, and k_h, k_w are the vertical and horizontal dimensions of the kernel[3].

The second line in Eq. 1 represents a 3D convolution between FM_i, and C_o number of 3D kernels, the weight parameters. To calculate the first output

---

[3] In this work, kernel has the same meaning as filter.

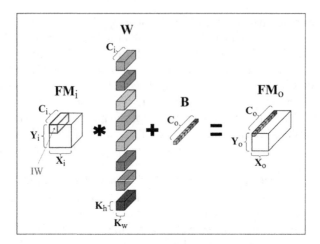

Fig. 1. Calculation of the channels of the first pixel of FM_o. The number of 3D kernels is equal to C_o, the number of output channels.

channel of the first output pixel of FM_o, an input window IW of the FM_i, of size $IW[K_h][K_w][C_i]$ is multiplied element-wise with kernel $W[0][K_h][K_w][C_i]$ and all partial results are accumulated to a single value. This value is then added to the respective bias term, $B(0)$, to produce the first output channel of the first output pixel of FM_o. This procedure is depicted in Fig. 1, which shows the calculation of all the channels of the first pixel of FM_o. To calculate all the elements of FM_o, the IW is moved vertically and horizontally by $y_o \cdot S$ and $x_o \cdot S$ respectively, and the above procedure is repeated. The resulted size of each Y, X dimension of the FM_o is calculated by:

$$Y_o = (Y_i - K_h + 2 \cdot P)/S + 1$$
$$X_o = (X_i - K_w + 2 \cdot P)/S + 1, \tag{2}$$

where P denotes the number of pixels added for padding the FM_i. In all the practical cases $Y_i = X_i$ and $K_h = K_w$.

An activation function always follows a conv layer. Thus, it is convenient, from an implementation point of view, to include the activation layer in the conv layer. In this case, the output of the conv layer becomes:

$$FM_{o,a}(y_o, x_o, c_o) = f(FM_o(y_o, x_o, c_o)), \tag{3}$$

where $f()$ is the activation function used in the specific DCNN, e.g. the Rectified linear unit (ReLU) described by:

$$f(x) = max(0, x) \tag{4}$$

The accelerator described in the next section, accelerates this fused convolution-activation layer with output given by Eq. 3.

4   The SqueezeJet Accelerator

SqN is a DCNN architecture focused in reducing the network parameter count for a given accuracy. Specifically, SqN achieves AlexNet-level accuracy with fifty times less parameters, making its model sufficiently small to be stored in on-chip FPGA memories and removing the need for off-chip memory access. For an FPGA accelerator, such as SqJ, implemented on a device with a few Mbits of block RAM (BRAM) resources, this means that the parameters (weight and bias values) of a single layer can fit in the BRAMs. Thus, for the calculation of the FM_o of a specific conv layer by an accelerator, the following procedure is required: the parameters are brought from off-chip memory and stored to BRAMs, the FM_i is streamed from off-chip memory in the accelerator, the calculation of FM_o pixel(s) takes place, and the resulting FM_o pixel(s) are streamed back to the off-chip memory. Having the layer's parameters stored on-chip is a big advantage as they will be reused for the calculation of each pixel of FM_o.

Following the architecture principle "make the common case fast", SqJ is designed to accelerate conv layers described by Eq. 3 with stride limited to one; it can be used for the acceleration of all the SqN conv layers except the first one, which can be implemented as a distinct module. All SqN conv layers, except the first one, share the following common characteristics: (1) a stride equal to 1, (2) an input channel dimension with a greatest common divisor (GCD) equal to 16 and (3) an output channel dimension which is divisible by a power of 2. SqJ uses all these three characteristics to accelerate a conv layer; the first SqN conv layer does not have characteristics (1) and (2). Implementing SqJ to support the first SqN conv layer would significantly degrade the acceleration of the other 17 conv layers (25 conv modules) of SqN.

This section describes the architecture, the high-level synthesis design, and the implementation of SqJ.

4.1   Architecture

Data organization: The data organization of all the convolution array arguments is shown in Eq. 1. This data organization is imposed by the 3D convolution operation; it is necessary to read all the input channels of the IW pixels in order to be able to calculate a single output channel. Because SqJ accelerates 3D convolutions, the design of a streaming architecture is not possible, but it is possible to design the accelerator to use streaming I/O interfaces.

Buffering: The implementation of the 3×3 convolution introduces an input data access pattern which requires multiple lines of the input. Because FM_i data is streamed in the accelerator, FM_i data lines must be buffered. In the general case, the size of the input tile buffer ITB is:

$$ITB = K \cdot Y_i \cdot C_i, \tag{5}$$

where K denotes the kernel size (considering that $K = K_h = K_w$, see Fig. 1), and Y_i and C_i denote the width and the channels of FM_i respectively. In the

SqJ case, where support for up to $3 \times 3 \times C_i$ 3D kernels is required, $K = 3$ and $ITB_{3 \times 3}$ is implemented as a set of 3 line buffers whose access is determined by a pointer array. In this way, $ITB_{3 \times 3}$ shifts down the FM_i without the need for any data shift to take place; only the lowest, as defined by the pointer array, line buffer gets updated. This shift mechanism is also used by the input tile window buffer $ITWB$ (depicted as IW in Fig. 1) to update only one of its columns as it shifts horizontally on the ITB, taking advantage of the spatial locality of the input data. Figure 2 shows the internal organization of ITB and the operation of pointer array for $ITB_{3 \times 3}$. Apart from the ITB and $ITWB$, buffers are used to store the weights, the bias, and one pixel of FM_o. The buffer used to store the FM_o pixel could be omitted if each output channel was calculated serially, but buffering is required to calculate multiple output channels in parallel and to stream them out of the accelerator in order.

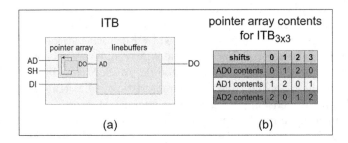

Fig. 2. ITB: (a) schematic and (b) pointer array content of $ITB_{3 \times 3}$ after a number of shifts. AD denotes memory address, SH denotes a shift signal, and DI, DO denote data input and output respectively.

Parallelism exploitation: SqJ takes advantage of the fact that SqN increases in the input channel dimension and, with the exception of the first conv layer, all conv layers' input channels have a GCD equal to $CI_{min} = 16$. The accelerator is designed to perform CI_{min} multiplications concurrently. These CI_{min} products are then fed to an accumulator unit which outputs a CI_{min} MAC result. The combination of the CI_{min} concurrent multiplications plus the accumulator unit forms a MAC-CI_{min} unit which is pipelined. CI_{min} is a design parameter and can be easily modified according to the architecture of a different DCNN. This intra-kernel parallelism has the advantage that it exploits parallelism in the input channel dimension and it is independent from the kernel size K. Thus, SqJ can be easily modified to support kernel sizes larger than 3×3. Another form of parallelism that is used is the concurrent calculation of multiple output channels for a specific output pixel. This is achieved by splitting the weights buffer in 2^n $(n = 1, 2, 3, ...)$ equal groups of 3D kernels and assigning them to 2^n MAC-CI_{min} units.

Operation: First step in the operation of SqJ is the initialization of the input buffers. Weights and bias are brought from off-chip memory and, only in the case where kernel $K = 3$, the ITB is initialized. After the initialization step, the convolution begins:

- For each row of FM_o: (1) only if $K = 3$, the ITB is shifted down (in FM_i) and two FM_i pixels are written in the empty line buffer, and (2) only if $K = 3$, the $ITWB$ is initialized with ITB data.
- For each column of each row of FM_o: (1) ITB is updated with a new FM_i pixel and $ITWB$ is updated with a new ITB column, (2) the weight buffers and the $ITWB$ are used to calculate one pixel of FM_o, and (3) the computed pixel is written back to off-chip memory.

4.2   Implementation

FPGA algorithm acceleration is not as trivial as implementing an algorithm in SW using a general purpose programming language such as C/C++. Even though HLS tools advertise the automatic generation of FPGA IP cores from C/C++ code, this process requires knowledge of the architecture of the FPGA device, knowledge of the internals of the HLS compiler [13], and use of a C/C++ coding style compatible with the HLS capabilities. This paragraph describes the process of generating an IP core for SqJ using the Xilinx VHLS tool and implementing it as a real application using the SDSoC tool.

Coding style: Hardware description languages (HDL) books warn the reader that if the designer cannot understand what logic circuit is described by the HDL code, then the design tool is not likely to synthesize the circuit that the designer is trying to model [14]. The same applies for the C/C++ code used as input to VHLS. A result of this coding style is the implementation of ITB shown in Fig. 2, which uses the HW model of pointers to the rows of a two-dimensional array. Even though VHLS simplifies the HW design of an algorithm, it doesn't provide a straightforward way for making a design scalable as it is the case with the combination of generate constructs and generics/parameters used in HDLs.

Interfaces: The SqJ IP core requires buffers for the weights, the bias, the ITB (FM_i), and the FM_o buffer for storing the output pixel. Three FIFO interfaces are used to stream data in and out of the IP core; one for streaming in the parameter (weights, bias) data, one for the FM_i data, and one for the output (FM_o) data. In addition, an AXI-Lite interface is used for acquiring the rest of the required HW function arguments. The SDSoC tool is used for interface synthesis.

Optimizations: VHLS provides many optimization possibilities both in terms of performance and resource usage [15].

- **Parallelism:** SqJ exploits parallelism in: (a) the input channel dimension (intra-kernel parallelism), by calculating the result of CI_{min} MACs every clock cycle of the operation of the pipelined MAC-CI_{min} unit, and (b) the output channel dimension, by calculating 2^n ($n = 1, 2, 3, ...$) output channels concurrently. Parallelism in (a) requires a CI_{min}-wide data register and partitioning the operand buffers (array partitioning) in a way which makes them able to provide CI_{min} outputs concurrently. Parallelism in (b) requires 2^n $ITWB$ buffers and the same number of MAC-CI units.

- **Arbitrary precision types:** To further decrease the model size of SqN and reduce the amount of logic required by SqJ, fixed-point quantization in both the parameters and the FM_i is used. Specifically, Ristretto [16] is used to specify the proper quantization of the parameters (weights and bias) and the FM_i. Parameters are quantized at 8 bits (1 bit integer + 7 bits fractional) and FM_i at 16 bits (13 bits integer + 3 bits fractional), achieving 0.88% top-5 accuracy loss without performing any fine-tuning.

In Fig. 3, the block diagram of SqJ, implemented (for simplicity) with 4 MAC-CI_{min} units, is shown. Since the parallelization factor is equal to 4, the sizes of the buffers are: (1.179648/4) Mbits for the weights$_i$, (2048/4) bits for the bias$_i$, 344.064 Kbits for the ITB, 73.728 Kbits for each ITWB$_i$, and (4096/4) bits for the fmap_o$_i$. Table 1 presents the FPGA resources required for the implementation of **conv_l0**, the accelerator of the first SqN conv layer, and **SqJ**, in an 8 MAC-16 unit configuration, on the XC7Z020 FPGA SoC. The **conv_l0 + SqJ** implementation is the one used in the results of the next Section.

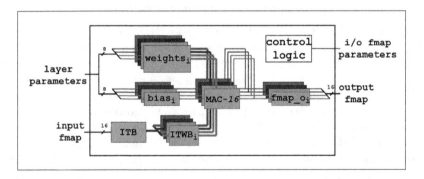

Fig. 3. SqJ block diagram implemented with 4 MAC-CI_{min} units. Bold lines denote $CI_{min} = 16$ times the data size shown at the left side of the figure.

Table 1. Resource utilization of conv_l0 and SqJ on the XC7Z020 FPGA SoC

Resource	Available	conv_l0 Util.	Util. %	SqJ Util.	Util. %	conv_l0 + SqJ Util.	Util. %
LUT	53200	9405	17.678	12692	23.857	20631	38.780
LUTRAM	17400	707	4.063	726	4.172	1273	7.316
FF	106400	15459	14.529	18114	17.024	30554	28.716
BRAM	140	13	9.285	124	88.571	134.5	96.071
DSP	220	37	16.818	149	67.727	186	84.545

5   Performance Evaluation

Table 2 presents the per-layer execution times, the accuracy, and the chip power consumption[4] of SqN implemented on 4 different processing unit configurations, an Intel Core i3-7100U@2.4 GHz core (Intel NUC), an ARM Cortex-A53@1.2 GHz core (Raspberry Pi 3 (RPI3) Model B V1.2), an ARM Cortex-A9@667 MHz core (Xilinx ZC702), and an ARM Cortex-A9@667 MHz core with the SqJ@100 MHz accelerator in an 8 MAC-16 unit configuration (Xilinx ZC702).

Table 2. SqN application execution time/accuracy/power results

Processing Unit	NUC Intel i3@2.4GHz	RPI3 ARM A53@1.2GHz	ZC702 ARM A9@667MHz	ZC702 ARM A9@667MHz conv_l0@100MHz SqJ@100MHz
SqN Implementation Accuracy (bits)				
Activations	32			16
Weights, Bias	32			8
SqN Application Per-Layer Execution Time Results (ms)				
Load Image	0.1761	1.2137	21.3210	54.4263
0:Conv	25.3118	131.5186	297.2426	26.2756
1:Maxpool	2.0531	18.2868	28.7206	22.7574
2:Fire	16.1473	142.7623	446.1214	32.6526
3:Fire	17.0744	150.7194	474.7981	34.7981
4:Maxpool	1.3333	13.4446	27.3646	18.0916
5:Fire	13.5606	124.2315	450.0168	17.7738
6:Fire	14.5805	135.3108	482.2875	18.9882
7:Maxpool	0.6023	7.1370	14.4114	9.4158
8:Fire	7.4712	69.1218	257.9832	8.6426
9:Fire	7.8755	72.4013	273.4599	8.8704
10:Fire	13.1197	125.8514	497.6390	12.2322
11:Fire	13.6331	132.5349	517.09514	12.7946
12:Conv	34.7681	324.9181	1257.4682	33.9618
13:Fixed2float	0.0001	0.0004	0.0003	15.4479
13:Avgpool	1.5295	4.3149	5.7796	5.7085
14:Softmax	0.0260	0.1528	0.2212	0.2220
Total Conv	162.4322	1395.4275	4892.9386	174.9867
Total Merge	13.74	13.89	60.43	31.97
Total Maxpool	3.99	38.87	70.49	50.26
Total	169.2627	1453.9202	5051.2337	333.0595
FPS	5.907	0.687	0.198	3.002
SqN ILSVRC12 Accuracy Results (%)				
Top-1	58.38			57.46
Top-5	81.01			80.29
SqN Application CPU/SoC Power Consumption Results (Watts)				
Technology	14nm	n/a	28nm	28nm
Chip Power	5.3253	2.9	1.569	2.275
FPS/W	1.109	0.237	0.126	1.319

SqN is a single floating point precision C/C++ Linux application accelerated with single-instruction multiple-data (SIMD) instruction set extensions (Intel AVX, ARM NEON) and executed on a single core of the target CPU-only processing systems. In the case where the SqJ accelerator is used, the implementation uses 16 bits for the activations and 8 bits for the weights and bias. GCC

---

[4] In the case of the ARM Cortex-A53, we measure RPI3 board power consumption, because there is no way to acquire power consumption measurements or estimations for the Broadcom 2837 SoC.

(version 6.3.0 for the Intel (64-bit) and RPI3 (32-bit) configurations, and version 6.2.1 for the ZC702 (32-bit) configuration) with the -O3 flag is used to build the SqN Linux application. Execution times are an average of 1000 inference iterations. Power consumption is acquired: (1) using Intel PCM[5] while the processing system executes 1000 SqN iterations, in the case of the Intel i3 CPU, (2) using a power plug and measuring board power consumption, in the case of RPI3, and (3) using Xilinx XPE[6] in the case of Xilinx ZC702. Accuracy is evaluated using the Ristretto[7] tool.

Results show that the SqJ configuration achieves an 15.16x execution time speedup in SqN inference when compared to the ARM A9 core configuration, 4.36x execution time speedup in SqN inference when compared to the ARM A53 core, and similar convolution performance (see **Total Conv** in Table 2) to the Intel i3 core configuration, with less than 1% top-5 accuracy loss. In terms of performance per Watt, frames per second per Watt (FPS/W), the SqJ implementation is 10.46 times better than the ARM A9 core configuration; again, with less than 1% accuracy loss. The **Load Image** execution time in the SqJ implementation includes the conversion of the image from 32-bit floating point to 16-bit fixed point; that's why it takes more than double of the ARM A9 corresponding time. Because of the use of lower precision for the activations, **Total Merge** (merge operations are included in the Fire layers) and **Total Maxpool** operations require much less time than the ARM A9 implementation. Furthermore, the Maxpool layers require 15% of the **Total** SqJ implementation time and could be incorporated in a future SqJ implementation. Table 3 summarizes the characteristics of the SqJ implementation.

Table 3. SqJ (conv_l0+SqJ) implementation summary

	SqueezeNet v1.1
FPGA	Zynq XC7Z020
Frequency (MHz)	100
Design Tool	Vivado HLS
DCNN Ops (GOPs)	0.7755
Precision	8-16 bits
DSP (Util.)	186 (84.5%)
BRAM (Util.)	134.5 (96%)
LUT (Util.)	20631 (38.8%)
LUTRAM (Util.)	1273 (7.3%)
FF (Util.)	30554 (28.7%)
Conv Latency/Image (ms)	175
Throughput (GOPs)	4.43
Top-5 ILSVRC12 Accuracy	80.29%

---

[5] https://www.intel.com/software/pcm.

[6] https://www.xilinx.com/products/technology/power/xpe.html.

[7] https://github.com/pmgysel/caffe.

6   Conclusion

In this paper, we present the design and the implementation of SqJ, an FPGA-based convolution layer accelerator which can be used to boost the performance of an embedded mobile processor running a CV task. The accelerator, consisting of a buffering architecture and multiple computational units, is designed using the Xilinx Vivado HLS tool. The Ristretto tool is used to squeeze the SqN DCNN in the Xilinx XC7Z020 FPGA SoC, and the Xilinx SDSoC tool is used to deploy SqJ accelerated SqN to the XC7Z020 device. To the best of our knowledge, our work is the first one which implements the SqN DCNN in a small FPGA SoC device, such as the XC7Z020, and achieves 80.29% top-5 ILSVRC12 accuracy (using XC7Z020). Results show that SqJ accelerates by 15.16 times the SqN inference execution time of an embedded mobile processor while being 10.46 times more power efficient with less than 1% top-5 accuracy drop. Improvements to the HLS SqJ design could include: (1) Maxpool layer support, since they require considerable amount (15%) of the total inference time on a mobile ARM core, and (2) streaming execution, to avoid memory accesses for fmaps (requires additional BRAM resources). Future work could use an enhanced version of SqJ as a template and perform multiobjective optimization for finding the best solution in terms of performance, resources, accuracy, power, and cost.

References

1. Krizhevsky, A., Sutskever, I., Hinton, G.E.: Imagenet classification with deep convolutional neural networks. In: Advances in Neural Information Processing Systems, pp. 1097–1105 (2012)
2. Szegedy, C., Liu, W., Jia, Y., Sermanet, P., Reed, S., Anguelov, D., Erhan, D., Vanhoucke, V., Rabinovich, A.: Going deeper with convolutions. In: Proceedings of the IEEE Conference on Computer Vision and Pattern Recognition, pp. 1–9 (2015)
3. He, K., Zhang, X., Ren, S., Sun, J.: Deep residual learning for image recognition. In: Proceedings of the IEEE Conference on Computer Vision and Pattern Recognition, pp. 770–778 (2016)
4. Zhang, C., Li, P., Sun, G., Guan, Y., Xiao, B., Cong, J.: Optimizing FPGA-based accelerator design for deep convolutional neural networks. In: Proceedings of the 2015 ACM/SIGDA International Symposium on Field-Programmable Gate Arrays, pp. 161–170. ACM, 2015 February
5. Motamedi, M., Gysel, P., Akella, V., Ghiasi, S.: Design space exploration of FPGA-based deep convolutional neural networks. In: 2016 21st Asia and South Pacific, Design Automation Conference (ASP-DAC), pp. 575–580. IEEE, January 2016
6. Ovtcharov, K., Ruwase, O., Kim, J.Y., Fowers, J., Strauss, K., Chung, E.S.: Accelerating deep convolutional neural networks using specialized hardware. Microsoft Res. Whitepaper **2**(11) (2015)
7. Iandola, F.N., Han, S., Moskewicz, M.W., Ashraf, K., Dally, W.J., Keutzer, K.: SqueezeNet: AlexNet-level accuracy with 50x fewer parameters and <0.5 MB model size. arXiv preprint (2016). arXiv:1602.07360

8. Qiu, J., Wang, J., Yao, S., Guo, K., Li, B., Zhou, E., Yu, J., Tang, T., Xu, N., Song, S., Wang, Y.: Going deeper with embedded FPGA platform for convolutional neural network. In: Proceedings of the 2016 ACM/SIGDA International Symposium on Field-Programmable Gate Arrays, pp. 26–35. ACM, February 2016

9. Gschwend, D.: Zynqnet: an FPGA-accelerated embedded convolutional neural network. Masters thesis, Swiss Federal Institute of Technology Zurich (ETH-Zurich) (2016)

10. Gokhale, V., Jin, J., Dundar, A., Martini, B., Culurciello, E.: A 240 G-ops/s mobile coprocessor for deep neural networks. In: Proceedings of the IEEE Conference on Computer Vision and Pattern Recognition Workshops, pp. 682–687 (2014)

11. Ma, Y., Cao, Y., Vrudhula, S., Seo, J.S.: Optimizing loop operation and dataflow in FPGA acceleration of deep convolutional neural networks. In: Proceedings of the 2017 ACM/SIGDA International Symposium on Field-Programmable Gate Arrays, pp. 45–54. ACM, February 2017

12. Iandola, F.: SqueezeNet/SqueezeNet_v1.1 at master. DeepScale/SqueezeNet (2017). https://github.com/DeepScale/SqueezeNet/tree/master/SqueezeNet_v1.1

13. Xilinx Inc.: High-Level Synthesis. Vivado Design Suite User Guide. UG902 (2017). https://www.xilinx.com/support/documentation/sw_manuals/xilinx2017_2/ug902-vivado-high-level-synthesis.pdf

14. Vranesic, Z., Brown, S.: Fundamentals of Digital Logic with Verilog Design, 3rd edn. McGraw-Hill Education, New York (2014)

15. Ali, K.M.A., Ben Atitallah, R., Fakhfakh, N., Dekeyser, J.-L.: Exploring HLS optimizations for efficient stereo matching hardware implementation. In: Wong, S., Beck, A.C., Bertels, K., Carro, L. (eds.) ARC 2017. LNCS, vol. 10216, pp. 168–176. Springer, Cham (2017). https://doi.org/10.1007/978-3-319-56258-2_15

16. Gysel, P., Motamedi, M., Ghiasi, S.: Hardware-oriented approximation of convolutional neural networks. arXiv preprint (2016). arXiv:1604.03168

Efficient Hardware Acceleration of Recommendation Engines: A Use Case on Collaborative Filtering

Konstantinos Katsantonis[1,2], Christoforos Kachris[1,2(✉)],
and Dimitrios Soudris[1,2]

[1] National Technical University of Athens (NTUA), Athens, Greece
kachris@gmail.com
[2] Institute of Computer and Communications Systems (ICCS), Athens, Greece

Abstract. Recommendation engines are widely used in order to predict the rating that a user would give to an item based on the user's past behavior. Modern recommendation engines are based on computational intensive algorithms like collaborative filtering that needs to process huge sparse matrices in order to provide efficient results. This paper presents a novel scheme for the acceleration of Alternating Least Squares-based (ALS) collaborative filtering for recommendation engines that can be used to speedup significantly the processing time and also reduce the energy consumption of computing platforms. The proposed scheme is implemented in reconfigurable logic and is mapped to the Pynq platform that is based on an all-programmable MPSoC Zynq system. The hardware acceleration is integrated with the Spark framework and evaluated on real benchmarks from movielens. The performance evaluation shows that the proposed scheme can achieve up to $120x$ kernel speedup and up to $12x$ energy-efficiency compared to the embedded ARM processor of Zynq.

Keywords: Reconfigurable logic · Recommendation systems
Cloud computing

1 Introduction

The need for large scale and energy efficient computation has evolved to unprecedented levels. Huge amounts of data are being gathered from multiple sources [1] such as social networks, IoT devices and web pages in general, while simultaneously we are deploying more sophisticated algorithms to process this data in order to perform various AI and machine-learning tasks. Big organizations offering such services, like Google, Amazon and Microsoft are constantly expanding their data-center infrastructures to meet the processing demands. However traditional semiconductor technologies are reaching their physical limits [2] and the Moore's Law seems unable to back up this challenge. Moreover energy consumption is becoming the dominant limiting factor in datacenters. In order to meet

© Springer International Publishing AG, part of Springer Nature 2018
N. Voros et al. (Eds.): ARC 2018, LNCS 10824, pp. 67–78, 2018.
https://doi.org/10.1007/978-3-319-78890-6_6

the needs for huge processing power and energy efficiency, novel architectures based on reconfigurable logic are adopted by data center operators.

This paper presents a novel scheme for the acceleration on recommendation engines that are based on collaborative filtering. The proposed system is evaluated using the Pynq boards built around the Zynq-7000 platforms. Zynq is an Heterogeneous SoC that incorporates both an ARM CPU and a FPGA [3].

The main contributions of this paper are the following:

– Design Space Exploration of a Recommendation System using Matrix Factorization trained by Alternating Least Squares.
– Efficient mapping in reconfigurable computing using High-Level Synthesis (HLS).
– Performance and power evaluation.
– Creation of a python interface for the accelerator.
– Integration with the Spark framework through python.

2   Related Work

On 2009 Yang et al. presented an FPGA Implementation for Solving Least Square Problem [11]. However, at the time the urge for low energy consumption was not as intense as today and as a result there was no reference to power metrics. Moreover the design took place on a an FPGA and not on SoC embedded heterogeneous platform.

In this paper we present a novel approach focusing both on performance and power consumption of the recently released Zynq device, for alternating least squares learning algorithm which is an extension of least squares algorithm, with the second one having somewhat more applications in modern computing. Our prototype cluster is almost identical with the one presented here [14] and here [15], except from the fact that we used the Pynq Boards instead of ZedBoards and Apache Spark, instead of Hadoop. Furthermore in our case the bitstream can be downloaded at runtime, as long as it is stored in the boards SD card, using a module that comes with Pynq's image. A very nice proposal concerning the integration of FPGAs in data centers is presented here [16], but emphasis is given in the aspect of partial reconfiguration which is not considered at all in this paper. A more related work to this paper is [12] on Neighborhood based Collaborative Filtering on Zynq (2015), however in this paper we also present an attempt to integrate the kernel with a high level language on cluster running Apache Spark. Work related to accelerators running in parallel on a cluster has taken place in from Muhuan Huang at UCLA [13].

3   Algorithm Overview

For this study we developed a recommendation system in software, which uses collaborative filtering with matrix factorization and is trained with the Alternating Least Squares (ALS) learning algorithm. Without Loss of Generality we assume that the items to be recommended are movies.

3.1   Brief Algorithm Description

Let $R = [r_{ij}]_{n_u \times n_m}$ denote the input user-movie matrix, where each element r_{ij} represents the rating score of user i to movie j with each value being either a real number or missing, n_m and n_u denotes the number of movies and number of users respectively. Our task is to fill the missing values of R with values as close to reality as possible, based on the known values.

Both movies and users are modeled with a feature vector and each rating (either known or unknown) as the inner product of the corresponding movie and user Vector. Let $U = [u_i]$ be the user feature matrix where $u_i \in \mathbb{R}^{n_f}$ for $i = 1...n_u$, and let $M = [m_j]$ be the movie feature matrix, where $m_j \in \mathbb{R}^{n_f}$ for all $j = 1...n_m$. The dimension of the feature space in n_f, it is the number of features/latent-factors the algorithm will have to learn for each user and each movie. Determining the best possible n_f as well as some other model regularization parameters, which will be presented later on, can be achieved by cross-validation or other popular techniques used in machine learning, but at this study we won't focus at all on the methods used to find the optimal values for the mentioned variables.

Ideally we would like to achieve $r_{ij} = <u_i, m_j> \forall i, j$. In practice however we try to minimize a loss function of U and M to obtain them. In this algorithm we examined the Mean-Squared-Error however our purpose is not to tune the model-parameters as best as possible to minimize RMSE but to accelerate the algorithm. The loss function due to a single rating is as follows.

$$L^2(r, u, m) = (r - <u, m>)^2 \tag{1}$$

Then the total loss function, given the whole matrices U, M can be defined as the average loss on all known ratings

$$L^{total}(R, U, M) = \frac{1}{n} \sum_{(i,j) \in I} L^2(r_{ij}, u_i, m_j) \tag{2}$$

where I is the index set of all known ratings and n is the number of elements inside I.

Our algorithm's task is as follows

$$(U, M) = min_{(U,M)} L^{total}(R, U, M)$$

where $U \in \mathbb{R}^{n_u \times n_f}$ and $M \in \mathbb{R}^{n_m \times n_f}$.

Hence, we have totally $(n_u + n_m) \times n_f$ free parameters that are used for the learning process. We avoid over-fitting by using Ttkhonov regularization [5] term to the total cost function.

The algorithm we used for acceleration [5] can be summarized in the following steps

1. Initialize matrix M by assigning small random numbers to the movie vector elements.

Table 1. Execution time as deducted by 10 iterations on the movielens-1m dataset.

Operation	Execution time (%)
Matrix_Op	92.35
Cholesky	7.02
Rest	1.63

2. Fix M, Solve U by minimizing the objective function (the sum of squared errors);
3. Fix U, solve M by minimizing the objective function similarly;
4. Repeat Steps 2 and 3 until a stopping criterion is satisfied.

Let I_i denote the set of movies j user i has rated and I_j denote the users that have rated movie j.($\mathbf{card}(I_i) = n_{u_i}$ and $\mathbf{card}(I_j) = n_{u_j}$)

$$u_i = A_i^{-1}V_i \forall i \tag{3}$$

where $A_i = M_{I_i}M_{I_i}^T + \lambda n_{u_i}E, V_i = M_{I_i}R(i, I_i)$ and E is the $n_f \times n_f$ identity matrix. Once again M_{I_i} is the sub-matrix of M where the columns $j \in I_i$ are chosen, and $R(i, I_i)$ is the i'th row of R from which only the columns $j \in I_i$ are chosen.

Similarly, in case we want to update the elements of M each m_j is calculated by using the feature vectors of the users who have rated the corresponding movie j and of course the ratings themselves:

$$m_j = A_j^{-1}V_j, \forall j \tag{4}$$

in this case, $A_j = U_{I_j}U_{I_j}^T + \lambda n_{m_j}E$ and $V_j = U_{I_j}R(I_j, j)$. U_{I_j} is the sub-matrix U where only rows $i \in I_j$ are chosen, and $R(I_j, j)$ is the sub-vector of R where only rows $i \in I_j$ of the j'th column are chosen.

4 Profiling Execution Time

The first step of our design methodology was to profile the algorithm in order to indicate the most computational intensive part. We executed the algorithm with input movielens_1m [9] and number of features ranging form 10 to 100 with a step of 10, with ten iterations executed for each latent factor we found out that the execution profile converges approximately to that presented in Table 1. With the matrix operations occupying approximately 92% of the execution time we proceeded with the design of such a kernel.

5 Prototyping on Zedboard Using SDSoC

5.1 Data Mapping

To achieve an efficient hardware implementation, the memory access pattern was studied, in order to map input and output data in a way that prevents

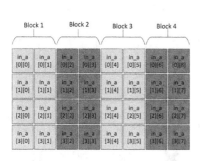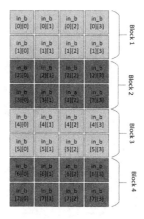

Fig. 1. Input data mapping on Brams. With this type of mapping we can fetch whole columns or whole rows in a clock cycle.

bottlenecks. Zynq's programming logic features dual port BRAMs meaning that we can fetch two elements per cycle from each. Hence, we partitioned the data in pairs of rows or columns, depending on the memory access pattern of each calculation type (Fig. 1).

5.2 Computational Part of the Kernel

For the implementation of the kernel, we developed two similar computational units that work in parallel in order to simultaneously perform operations on four matrices. Each computational unit consists of a DSP48 row that is fed with raw input data. The DSP48 row performs multiplications in parallel and feeds the result in a tree adder. The whole unit is pipelined in order to maximize the throughput (Fig. 2).

5.3 Software - Kernel Interface Version 1

In the first version of the kernel we used AXI4-Stream to transfer the data between the DMAs and the hardware function. For this version we designed the protocol's interface directly on the accelerator. In this version a software driver was used for sending data windows of size 20 × 80 to the kernel. Although this implementation achieved great speedup against the ARM-only execution, it had many drawbacks like the need for two-dimensional zero-padding of the input data, and the need to transfer multiple arrays used as intermediate accumulators for the storage of the partial results.

5.4 Software - Kernel Interface Version 2

In an attempt to increase the performance we used Xilinx's IP FIFO Accelerator Adapter. This IP is responsible for managing efficiently the AXI4_STREAM protocol exposing to the hardware kernel a simple FIFO interface. This IP relieved

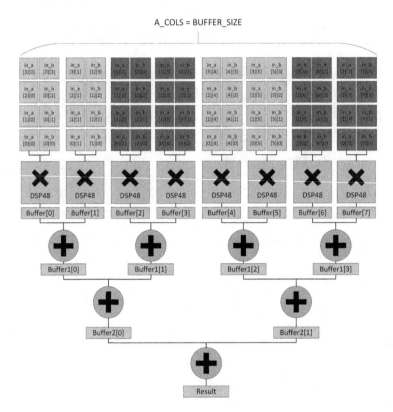

Fig. 2. Abstract representation of the main computational unit. The DSP48 row is longer in the actual implementation.

us from the need to design our own AXI4-stream interface and increased even more the performance, but didn't solve the problems emerged from the first version of the interface.

5.5　Software - Kernel Interface Version 3

In the final version we took advantage of the Accelerator Adapter's programming capabilities to boost up the performance. More specifically we configured the adapter in a way that allows passing arrays, from software to hardware, whose one dimension is determined at runtime from the processing system, and as a result we reduced the amount of padding needed to the data transferred, leading to less unnecessary operations which in turn leads to greater performance and energy efficiency.

6　Python Integration on Pynq

To leverage the use of the hardware acceleration unit and make easy the utilization from high-level programming framework, we developed the required APIs that allow the transparent deployment of the accelerators. Specifically, we developed the required libraries that allow the instantiation of the kernel from a high-level language like python, which is widely used in Machine Learning Tasks. The whole process took place by using the Pynq Board, which is a prototype board from Digilent that comes with a Linux image containing python libraries that help designers use kernel's from python scripts. The whole process is described below:

1. We created a bitstream for our IP matching the new Device (PYNQ), using Vivado.
2. Then we wrote the software Part of the algorithm in Python, using efficient libraries (numpy, scipy).
3. Finally by using the libraries coming with the Linux image of PYNQ, we created the appropriate software driver responsible for the software-hardware communication.

At the final step of the mentioned process we had to perform manually the operations that are performed by SDSOC framework automatically. The Python Libraries are wrappers of C language that are used for the interprocess communication. This wrap is accomplished with the use of a library called *cffi*, which allows python scripts to execute C code coming either precompiled either in source-code form. This means that this integration can happen in any platform rather than Pynq. Moreover with the use of *cffi* we can hide low level implementation details from the developer under python hood.

7   Apache Spark Integration

Apache Spark [6] is a framework designed for fast large-scale data processing. Spark stores data in a structure called resilient distributed datasets (RDD) [7], that is a read only (for ease of coherency purposes) collection of the data. Spark data operations are scheduled in a DAG scheme. Each task consists of a series of **transformations** that generate new RDDs and an **action** which corresponds to the reduce step of the map-reduce programming model. Spark performs lazy evaluation, in order to perform as much tranformations as possible in one step so that it can achieve more efficient task scheduling. In a glance it is an improved version of Hadoop MapReduce [8]. At the moment, Spark is one of the most popular big-data frameworks.

On this step we made a prototype Cluster consisting of four Pynq boards in order to run the algorithm both in parallel using Apache Spark and accelerated using the programming logic of each PYNQ [10]. The idea is that every worker of the cluster, each PYNQ board in our case, contains the bitstreams of the accelerator and the Apache driver program commands the workers to configure their FPGAs appropriate for the computation that is about to happen. This happens by calling a dummy *map*() function, before the actual computational *map*() operation, whose purpose is to instruct the workers to overlay the appropriate bitstream.

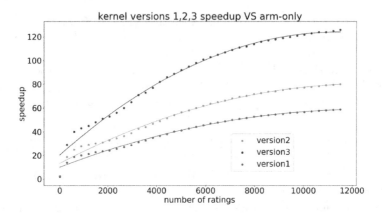

Fig. 3. Accelerator speedup against arm only execution. Points represent our measurements for different input sizes. $n_f = 80$

8   Performance Evaluation

8.1   Kernel-Only Performance Evaluation on Zedboard

The first implementation created on SDSoC framework, achieved speedup of up to 120× for input matrices of size 12000 × 80, against the arm-only execution. As the input matrix size increased, the speedup was also increased. It is important to notice that Fig. 3 refers only to the speedup of the accelerated part (kernel) and not the speedup of the whole ALS algorithm.

8.2   ALS Performance Evaluation Zedboard

Embedding the Version 3 kernel in ALS algorithm and running iterations using the datasets movielens_1m and movielens_100k we get the speed_up shown in Table 2. Notice that the column presenting the average number of ratings per movie/user is present, because this is a good metric indicating the average size of the matrices that will be produced at runtime. As a result, from this metric combined with Fig. 3 and Amdahl's law, we can estimate the anticipated speedup for the specific dataset, this observation is actually verified by the actual speedup measurements which happen to be very similar to the ones anticipated.

We also compared this implementation against a software only implementation on two other platforms, an Intel(R) Core(TM) i7-7500U CPU @ 2.70 GHz, and Intel(R) Xeon(R) CPU E5-2650 v2 @ 2.60 GHz. For this comparison we used as input the movielens_1m dataset and the result was that the implementation on the accelerated embedded system outperformed the i7 processor by a factor of 1.7× and the Xeon processor by a factor of 2.7×. It is important to notice that such small datasets like movielens_1m are unable to demonstrate the kernel's full potential which is presented in Fig. 3, because the small number of ratings per user/movie leads to matrix operations of very limited size.

Table 2. Execution time speedup as deducted of the ALS algorithm on datasets movielens-1m and movielens_100k with $n_f = 80$.

Dataset	Speed-up vs arm-only	Average ratings per movie/user
movielens_100k	18.8×	76.2
movielens_1m	36×	205.2

8.3   Power Consumption

In Figs. 4 and 5 we show the power consumption of the algorithm for one iteration on two different datasets. Although the accelerated version consumes more power momentarily in the beginning of the execution the fact that it runs for much less duration leads to a great improvement to the Performance per Watt metric versus the arm only execution. Specifically one iteration on movielens_100k dataset consumed 12× less energy while an iteration on movielens_1m consumed 27× less energy. We can notice both in performance and energy consumption evaluation that the kernel scales very well, meaning that as the input size increases the performance speedup and the energy savings increase too (Table 3).

Table 3. Energy savings as deducted of the ALS algorithm on datasets movielens-1m and movielens_100k.

Dataset	Energy savings	Average ratings per movie/user
movielens_100k	12×	76.2
movielens_1m	27×	205.2

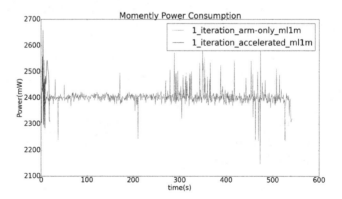

Fig. 4. Power consumption profiling of the system for 1m dataset (from one iteration)

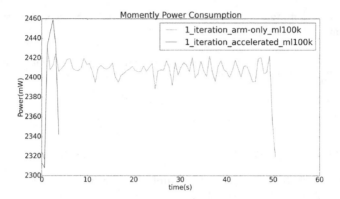

Fig. 5. Power consumption profiling of the system for 100k dataset (from one iteration)

8.4   Python on Pynq

This implementation showed-up great results in performance but the speedup achieved compared to an arm only execution was quite reduced compared to the one achieved on the previous implementations. The reason is that a high level language like python and its corresponding libraries were not created having in mind integration with hardware accelerators and as a result specific data conversions are needed that consume great percent of the execution time.

8.5   Apache Spark Integration

Four Pynqs accelerated and coordinated by spark managed to run 4–5× faster than an arm only execution. On this case there are many software parts added to the algorithm by spark. Spark adds serialization and deserialization tasks data broadcasts over Ethernet and more. As a result the part which is accelerated is smaller compared to the total execution time and as a direct impact of Amdahl's law we expected a smaller speedup (Table 4).

Table 4. Execution time speedup as deducted of the ALS algorithm with $n_f = 80$ on datasets movielens-1m and movielens_100k.

Dataset	Speed-up of python implementation
movielens_100k	5.8×
movielens_1m	13.8×

9   Conclusion and Future Work

In this paper we discussed the path of reconfigurable architectures as an computational alternative path, and we attempted to sum a performance and energy evaluation of that path on embedded boards. Moreover we attempted to test this technology with a popular scripting language like python in order to make it more accessible and easy to use by software developers. The results are definitely promising from both power consumption and performance perspectives.

However in order to make these architectures a common case, we must expand the library so that it contains multiple accelerators, for many computational intensive tasks. Moreover it is great need to make these accelerators easy to use by constructing a fine tuned and efficient python library that allowed smooth transitions from software execution to hardware and vice versa. Except from python, apache spark could be extended in order to natively support accelerated execution more efficiently, by integrating specific instructions for configuring the slave's programming logic instead of forcing us to use "map()" calls that don't have computational intentions but were just written for FPGA configuration purposes.

Acknowledgment. This project has received funding from the European Union's Horizon 2020 research and innovation programme under grant agreement No. 687628 - VINEYARD: Versatile Integrated Heterogeneous Accelerator-based Data Centers.

References

1. Gupta, P.K.: Director of Intel Cloud Platform Technology, Xeon+FPGA Platform for the Data Center (2015)
2. Esmaeilzadeh, H.: Dark Silicon and the End of Multicore Scaling. In: ISCA (2011)
3. Rajagopalan, V.: Xilinx Zynq-7000 EPP: An Extensible Processing Platform Family (2011)
4. Koren, Y.: Matrix Factorization Techniques for Recommender Systems. IEEE Computer Society (2009)
5. Zhou, Y.: Large-Scale Parallel Collaborative Filtering for the Netflix Prize (2008)
6. Zaharia, M.: Spark: cluster computing with working sets. In: Proceedings of the 2nd USENIX Conference on Hot Topics in Cloud Computing (2010)
7. Zaharia, M.: Resilient distributed datasets: a fault-tolerant abstraction for in-memory cluster computing. In: Proceedings of the 9th USENIX Conference on Networked Systems Design and Implementation (2012)
8. Shi, J.: Clash of the titans: MapReduce vs. spark for large scale data analytics. In: Proceedings of the 41st International Conference on Very Large Data Bases, Kohala Coast, Hawaii (2015)
9. Ma, X., Wang, C., Yu, Q., Li, X., Zhou, X.: An FPGA-based accelerator for neighborhood-based collaborative filtering recommendation algorithms. In: 2015 IEEE International Conference on Cluster Computing (CLUSTER), September 2015
10. Kachris, C., Koromilas, E., Stamelos, I., Soudris, D.: FPGA acceleration of Spark applications in a Pynq cluster. In: IEEE International Conference on Field-Programmable Logic and Applications, Ghent, Belgium, September 2017
11. Yang, D.: An FPGA Implementation for Solving Least Square Problem. IEEE (2009)
12. Ma, X.: An FPGA-based accelerator for neighborhood-based collaborative filtering recommendation algorithms. In: IEEE International Conference on Cluster Computing (CLUSTER) (2015)

13. Huang, M.: Programming and runtime support to blaze FPGA accelerator deployment at datacenter scale. In: SoCC Proceedings of the Seventh ACM Symposium on Cloud Computing (2016)

14. Lin, Z., Chow, P.: ZCluster: A Zynq-Based Hadoop Cluster, pp. 450–453. IEEE (2014)

15. Neshatpour, K., Malik, M., Ghodrat, M.A., Sasan, A., Homayoun, H.: Energy-efficient acceleration of big data analytics applications using FPGAs. In: IEEE International Conference on Big Data, pp. 115–123 (2015)

16. Fahmy, S.A., Vipin, K., Shreejith, S.: Virtualized FPGA accelerators for efficient cloud computing. In: IEEE International Conference on Cloud Computing Technology and Science (CloudCom), Vancouver, Canada, 30 November–3 December, pp. 430–435 (2015)

FPGA-based Design and CGRA Optimizations

VerCoLib: Fast and Versatile Communication for FPGAs via PCI Express

Oğuzhan Sezenlik$^{(\boxtimes)}$ ⓘ, Sebastian Schüller ⓘ, and Joachim K. Anlauf ⓘ

Technical Computer Science, Institute of Computer Science VI, University of Bonn,
Endenicher Allee 19 A, 53115 Bonn, Germany
{sezenlik,anlauf}@cs.uni-bonn.de, schueller@ti.uni-bonn.de

Abstract. PCI Express plays a vital role in including FPGA accelerators into high-performance computing systems. This also includes direct communication between multiple FPGAs, without any involvement of the main memory of the host. We present a highly configurable hardware interface that supports DMA-based connections to a host system as well as direct communication between multiple FPGAs. Our implementation offers unidirectional channels to connect FPGAs, allowing for precise adaptation to all kinds of use cases. Multiple channels to the same endpoint can be used to realise independent data transmissions. While the main focus of this work is flexibility, we are able to show maximum throughput for connections between two FPGAs and up to 88% saturation of the available bandwidth for connections between the FPGA and the host system.

Keywords: VerCoLib · PCI Express · FPGA
Communication library · Transceiver

1 Introduction

FPGAs are widely used to accelerate state-of-the-art algorithms or as co-processors in heterogeneous high performance computer systems. FPGA vendors offer affordable evaluation boards with high-end FPGAs, especially popular in academic research. Through the development of high level synthesis tools like Xilinx Vivado HLS or intelFPGA OpenCL, FPGAs became a more accessible and viable platform. While writing code for the FPGA accelerator itself is one part of a design another important factor is to utilise its full performance by transferring data reliably and with sufficient throughput. Here a common high-bandwidth interface like PCI Express (PCIe in the following) is essential, the use of which requires fundamental knowledge about its protocol, underlying computer hardware as well as kernel driver programming. Therefore developers often face the problem to implement the required complex logic to interface the

---

O. Sezenlik and S. Schüller—These authors contributed equally to this work.

© Springer International Publishing AG, part of Springer Nature 2018
N. Voros et al. (Eds.): ARC 2018, LNCS 10824, pp. 81–92, 2018.
https://doi.org/10.1007/978-3-319-78890-6_7

PCIe IP core provided by the vendor and integrate access to the accelerator into their software. Furthermore modern mainboards allow devices to communicate directly via PCIe, completely bypassing the main memory, a feature heavily used to connect multiple GPUs and build low-cost supercomputers for various scientific applications. The same idea also applies to FPGAs: one could simply plug several off-the-shelf FPGA boards into one standard desktop computer to improve the computational power. Such a feature is especially useful, since combining several smaller FPGAs is more cost efficient than using high-end variants.

Our goal is to provide a highly configurable and easy to use open-source communication library (VERsatile COmmunication LIBrary) that allows FPGA-programmers to focus on their primary objective, namely implementing their algorithms. With our interface it is very easy to build affordable multi-FPGA computers, where communication is performed between Host and FPGA as well as directly between FPGAs via PCIe. This includes configurable and generic modules used on the FPGA as well as a Linux kernel driver to set up communication channels and performing the host part of the data transmission. After setting up the channels between FPGAs, the host system is not involved into FPGA-FPGA communication at all.

This paper is structured as follows: In Sect. 2 we give an overview about existing commercial and open-source PCIe solutions and our motivation for the development of VerCoLib. Then the hardware architecture and features of our transceiver are described in Sect. 3, followed by the software interface and driver in Sect. 4. Finally the resource consumption and performance are evaluated in Sect. 5.

2   Related Work

There are already several other systems that provide a PCIe interface for FPGA accelerators. In general the different solutions can be categorised based on the PCIe configurations they support and the resulting theoretical maximum bandwidth. This bandwidth depends on the generation of the PCIe standard as well as the number of PCIe lanes a device is connected to. For reference, the maximum bandwidth for a Gen2 device with 8 lanes is 4 GB/s. This also applies to Gen3 devices with 4 lanes. Gen3 devices with 8 lanes theoretically reach a bandwidth of 8 GB/s.

Out of the available commercial solutions, the interfaces provided by Xillybus [1] and Northwest Logic [2] are the most notable ones. The designs from Northwest are limited to Xilinx devices and are used in the reference design Xilinx offers, supporting PCIe Gen3 with 8 lanes. Xillybus is available for both Xilinx and intelFPGA FPGAs and provides host software for Linux and Windows operating systems.

Academic solutions include RIFFA 2.2 [3], JetStream [4], ffLink [5], EPEE [6] and DyRact [7]. Out of these solutions, PCIe Gen2 is supported by EPEE (8 lanes), DyRact (4 lanes) and RIFFA (8 lanes), Gen3 is supported by RIFFA (4 lanes), JetStream and ffLink (8 lanes).

RIFFA offers a host-FPGA interface for a wide range of devices and PCIe configurations with drivers for both Linux and Windows as well as APIs for a variety of programming languages. Their transceiver reaches a throughput of up to 3.64 GB/s (upstream) and 3.43 GB/s (downstream).

EPEE is designed around the concept of a general purpose PCIe interface including DMA communications with up to 3.28 GB/s, a set of IO registers reachable from both hardware and software as well as user defined interrupts. They support Xilinx Virtex-5, 6 and 7 series FPGAs on Linux systems. While multiple independent DMA channels are supported as a plugin, there are no measurements of the performance impact in terms of resource usage or throughput.

DyRact implements an interface for dynamic partial reconfiguration within its PCIe solution, allowing for convenient and efficient reconfiguration of user designs with PCIe connections. Since they only support Gen2 devices with up to 4 lanes, their bandwidth peaks at 1.54 GB/s.

The ffLink interface is created mainly out of IP-Cores supplied by Xilinx and relies heavily on the AXI-4 [8] infrastructure. Strongly relying on IP-Cores has the advantage of low development times and bug fixes from the IP-Core developer. On the flip side, this also means a comparatively high resource usage and makes it impossible to adapt the design to other vendors. The ffLink system achieves a maximum throughput of 7.04 GB/s.

JetStream is the only other solution we have found that supports direct PCIe FPGA-FPGA communication. They demonstrate the effectiveness of direct FPGA-FPGA communication with a large FIR filter that spans multiple FPGAs. They were able to show that distributing the data directly between FPGAs can result in a reduction of memory bandwidth by up to 75%. Their host-FPGA solution supports only Gen3 devices with 8 lanes with a maximum throughput of 7.09 GB/s. However, the missing support for Gen2 devices effectively limits the use of JetStream to high-end devices.

3   FPGA Transceiver Design

The central concept of VerCoLib deals with unidirectional, independent channels. A channel is the user interface to send or receive data, translating between raw data and PCIe packets.

Every configuration of the transceiver has the same structure, consisting of one endpoint module, an arbiter and an arbitrary number of channels, all of them using the same handshake interface, equivalent to AXI4-Stream [8]. An example is shown in Fig. 1.

The function of the endpoint is to handle global resources which need to be shared among the channels. This includes interfacing the Xilinx specific hard IP-Core [9] and handling internal communication with the software driver as well as managing the interrupts from all channel modules and providing dynamic tag mapping for downstream DMA transfers.

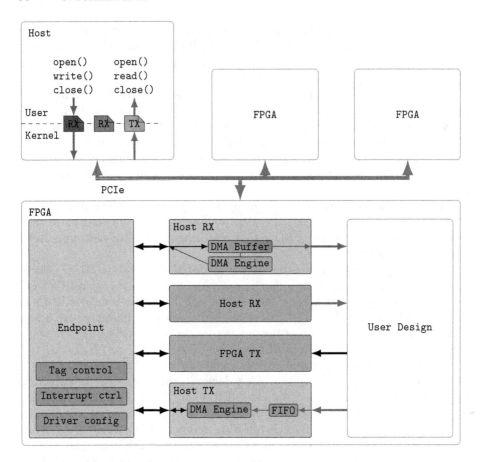

Fig. 1. System overview of example configuration. Best viewed in color. The colors indicate independent data streams. Black and gray connections may contain data from all streams and fading colors displays the data being filtered. Note that a user can instantiate channel modules as necessary.

We are using MSI-X interrupts that allow devices to allocate up to 2048 interrupt vectors instead of only 32 vectors allowed by MSI. This makes it possible to map every channel uniquely to a MSI-X vector. Thereby the driver is able to immediately identify the channel that issued an interrupt without further communication, which in turn reduces communication overhead and latency.

In a multi-channel PCIe transceiver design special consideration is required when handling DMA transfers from host to FPGA. According to the PCIe specification [10], the receiver has to request data from the main memory of the host system with memory read request packets. These are answered by the host via memory completion packets with the requested data as payload. PCIe provides a tag field with at most 256 different values in the packet header which is used to determine the affiliation of each completion with a request. To reach optimal utilization of the PCIe-bandwidth the transceiver has to keep several requests in flight. The easiest solution to identify the channel a completion belongs to would be to use a fixed range of tag values per channel, but in this case the number of available tag values per channel depends on the total number on instantiated channels. This could reduce the bandwidth a single channel can reach, which contradicts our goal to provide a flexible and high-performance interface, without making assumptions about the detailed requirements of the attached user design. In our solution the endpoint assigns unused tags dynamically to requests. Note that no demultiplexing is done anywhere in the design. Instead all channels receive the same data, filter out all packets not belonging to them and ignore the rest. As a result the design allows for multiple independent data streams by simply attaching more channel modules to the same endpoint with a simple arbiter module. Channels may be arbitrarily mixed to optimally fit the requirements of the application, while using as little as possible of the resources of the FPGA.

Everything else is handled by the channel modules. They are designed individually for specialised tasks, translating between raw data and PCIe packets, as shown in Fig. 1. At this point we have implemented four different channel types (host-rx/tx, FPGA-rx/tx). Each channel takes complete care of a unidirectional transfer to or from the host or the FPGA.

3.1   Host Communication Channel

All data transfers between host and FPGA are initiated by the software driver. The host-rx channel implements the downstream direction of the host communication, i.e. the transmission of data from host to FPGA. First the driver sends the address and size of the data buffer to be transmitted to the host-rx channel with the desired id. Then the DMA-Engine will check the available free memory in the DMA-Buffer and starts requesting data from the main memory of the host. Note that PCIe permits the host to answer requests in a different order than originally issued. The DMA-Buffer is capable of reordering incoming completion packets in order to extract and forward the raw data to the user design attached to it. After the transfer is finished the DMA-Engine issues an interrupt, which is finally handled by the MSI-X-interrupt handler in the endpoint and waits for the next buffer information.

The host-rx channel is capable of processing incoming packets every clock cycle, therefore it never stops the endpoint from sending data. Since it requests only as much data as it can store in its memory, it will never create back-pressure to the endpoint. This guarantees that deadlocks from data transmissions are avoided in all cases. The throughput depends on the rate the user design pulls data from the channel and the available bandwidth provided by the PCIe bus.

The host-tx channel works similar in the upstream direction. As before the DMA-Engine waits for the buffer information from the driver and checks if the FIFO has gathered enough data from the user design to generate at least one memory write request packet. While the DMA-Engine always tries to maximise the size of a packet to ensure high transfer rates, the user design has the option to force a transmission prematurely by tagging the last valid data word it presents to the host-tx channel. This is necessary in cases where the user design does not produce enough data to fill a PCIe packet completely. Furthermore the channel is able to generate and transmit PCIe packets at every clock cycle, as long as the vendor-ip-endpoint is capable of accepting data.

3.2   Direct FPGA-FPGA Communication

To realise direct FPGA to FPGA communication it was sufficient for us to develop a variation of the host communication channels. In order to send data unidirectionally from one device to the other, a pair of FPGA-FPGA channel modules is necessary: one receiver channel on the receiving FPGA to request data and buffer incoming packets and one sender channel on the sending FPGA to pack the PCIe packets and send them off.

These pairs are connected by the software on the host system which sends the necessary address information to each channel during initialisation of the system. The addresses are global on the complete system and consist of the FPGA PCIe bus- and device number as well as a local channel number which needs to be unique on its FPGA design. Pairs can be re-assigned by the software at any point in time. For the sake of simplicity, we have not implemented a mechanism that blocks re-assignment during a transfer, meaning that the user should check that all communication ceased before changing the pair configurations.

Since all channel modules are designed never to create back-pressure to the endpoint, the receiving channels contain a FIFO storing incoming packets. To ensure that this FIFO never overflows, the receiver actively requests an amount of data from the sender that is guaranteed to be free in the FIFO. If the user design consumes enough data from the FIFO, the receiver can safely post a new request even if not all data from the last request arrived yet. The sender combines all requests it receives into a single one.

To minimise the overhead produced by PCIe packet headers, the sender channel tries to create PCIe packets of maximum size. Smaller packets will only be created if the user design indicates the end of the data stream or the amount of requested data is too small.

In contrast to the JetStream design in [4] which employs memory read request and completions to realise direct FPGA to FPGA communication, we chose to use a protocol solely based on memory write requests. Vesper et al. advocate their decision with the ability to reuse the already existing host communication for direct FPGA-FPGA transmissions. On the other hand, creating special modules allows to save a lot of FPGA resources since there are fewer cases to take care of when transferring data between FPGAs. The issue of memory reordering is one example of a fairly complex and resource intensive operation that can be ignored, since we are in control of both endpoints.

Although the presented channels are sufficient for most FPGA-accelerators, some designs might require special functionality and therefore modifications to the transceiver. In order to add features, understanding existing open-source transceivers is often very difficult, hence modifying them is an error prone task. The modularity of our transceiver allows the user to develop and integrate their own channels without the necessity to alter the already existing infrastructure. The developer only has to make sure, that the new channel implements the handshake-protocol to the endpoint and arbiters correctly.

In fact, the first version of the transceiver only allowed host to FPGA communication, channels, enabling direct FPGA to FPGA connections were added later, without changing the overall architecture.

Another benefit of our design can be shown with the following use case. Imagine a developer wants to prioritise transfers higher for one particular core he has implemented. This is simply possible by replacing the arbiter with a weighted version. The arbiter itself is a very simple module, agnostic to the PCIe interface and therefore it contains no special logic to process PCIe packets.

4 Software Interface

The Linux kernel driver for VerCoLib focuses on simplicity and tries to adhere to standard Unix syscalls.

The driver presents each hardware channel as its own device which can be interacted with using standard calls like open, close, read, and write. On initialization the driver gets the number and directions of instantiated buffers automatically from the FPGA transceiver. Note that hardware receiver channels only support the 'write' call and analogue to this hardware sending channels only support the 'read' call.

Aside from that the behaviour of the channel interfaces is comparable to communication through a POSIX network socket. After opening a channel device the user only needs to supply a pointer to the buffer that should be read from/written to, as well as the number of bytes that should be transferred.

Internally the driver manages up to eight buffers per channel to realise multi buffering for enhanced performance. If the user issues a transfer consisting of more bytes than the buffers can hold, the driver will copy as many data as possible into the buffers and informs the user of the amount of copied data. The write/read calls return immediately after copying and remember used buffers internally. If the user wants to transmit data on a channel that has no free buffer available the call will block until the current transmission is finished. The driver supports the poll/select calls on channel devices to allow the user to find a channel ready for transmissions. For transmissions from the FPGA to the host, the driver continuously requests data from the host-sender channel as soon as the channel device is opened by the user. This allows for data transmissions before the user reads from the channel device and thus reducing the latency of this operation.

Since each channel has an individual set of buffers, the channel devices are inherently thread-safe. Thus the user is allowed to handle different channel devices in individual threads/processes.

Figure 2 shows a simple but representative use of the software API. Since the API follows the POSIX standard it automatically supports all languages (additional to C/C++) that allow for direct write/read calls, e.g. python or rust.

The driver creates one additional device per FPGA in order to allow the user to communicate directly with the hardware PCIe transceiver. This interface offers the user the ability to set up and control direct FPGA-FPGA communication between channels on different FPGAs. This is also very useful during development to debug the state of the hardware.

```
unsigned long size = data_transfer_size();
void* buffer = create_data_to_transfer();

int fd = open("/dev/fpga_0_downstream_0", O_WRONLY);

while(size) {
    unsigned long written = write(fd, buffer, size);
    if(written < 0) handle_error();
    buffer += written;
    size    -= written;
}

close(fd);
```

Fig. 2. API of the software interface

5   Evaluation

For all experiments in this section, we used two Xilinx VC707 development boards (containing the Virtex-7 XC7VX485T) which are communicating with 8 PCIe Gen2 lanes. The host system features a Intel Core i5-3300 CPU and 16 GB of RAM. DyRact and RIFFA also took their measurements on the XC7VX485T board while ffLink and JetStream used the Xilinx VC709 development board with the Virtex-7 XC7VX690T chip. It should be noted that the VC709 supports the PCIe Gen3 standard, leading to the expectation of higher throughput and a higher absolute resource usage.

In a typical scenario with one data connection from the host to the FPGA and one connection in the opposite direction, the VerCoLib PCIe transceiver uses very few FPGA resources as shown in Table 1. Only DyRact used fewer resources than VerCoLib and they only implement a Gen2 solution with up to 4 lanes which is implemented internally with a 64 b interface in contrast to the 128 b interface used by Gen2 solutions with 8 lanes. If we additionally consider having direct FPGA to FPGA communication only, our solution uses the fewest resources overall.

In Table 2 we compare configurations with multiple independent data channels. The notation VerCoLib (x,y) should be read as a PCIe configuration with x host downstream and y host upstream channels. The resource consumption of the RIFFA configurations were calculated from the costs of adding a single channel to the configuration, reported in [3]. It can be seen that our solution uses significantly fewer resources than a comparable configuration of RIFFA.

Especially configurations which use an asymmetrical amount of channels such as VerCoLib (6,1) show the benefit of uni-directional channel designs. A RIFFA configuration that allows for six independent connections uses significantly more resources since it only allows for bi-directional connections.

Table 1. Comparison of resources of different PCIe solutions. [*] ffLink provided measurements given in percent only. The absolute numbers were calculated based on the data-sheet of the VC7VX690T.

	LUT	FF	BRAM
DyRact	5181	6971	26
RIFFA 2.1	7396	7489	16
VerCoLib Host	6410	7817	11
VerCoLib FPGA	5086	6559	8
ffLink*	12996	43320	132
JetStream	8571	6955	17

Table 2. Resource comparison of configurations with multiple channels.

	LUT	FF	BRAM
RIFFA 2 channel	11767	12710	28
RIFFA 6 channel	29251	33594	76
VerCoLib (2,2)	8524	10007	17
VerCoLib (6,6)	18276	21021	41
VerCoLib (6,1)	12778	15602	31

For all tests the maximum payload size was set to 128 bytes. A larger maximum payload size would have been preferable, however the available host system did not allow for 256 or more bytes.

With a maximum of 128 B payload and 16 B header we can reach up to $128/(128+14) \approx 0.888$ times of the bandwidth the wire can handle. Since PCIe Gen2 with 8 lanes can reach a throughput of 4 GB/s, the maximum throughput we can achieve in practice is ≈ 3.555 GB/s.

Bandwidths for host to FPGA data transmission with different channel configurations are shown in Table 3. We measured the time a test software takes to stream 1 GB of data in each direction. In half-duplex mode our transceiver achieves transfer rates of about 3.13 GB/s for downstream (host to FPGA) and 3.11 GB/s for upstream transfers, thus utilizing about 88% of the theoretical maximum in both directions. In full duplex mode VerCoLib achieves a throughput of 2.79 GB/s, or 79% of the theoretical maximum in both directions. Different channel configurations, including asymmetric designs have no noteworthy impact to the performance.

Table 3. Maximum transfer rates in GB/s for host - FPGA communication. Omitted half duplex measurements in asymmetric configurations are equal to the respective symmetric ones. ([*] downstream/upstream)

Configuration	Half duplex downstream	Half duplex upstream	Full duplex
DyRact	1.54	1.51	N/A
VerCoLib (1/1)	3.13	3.11	2.78
VerCoLib (4/4)	3.13	3.18	2.79
VerCoLib (4/1)			2.8
VerCoLib (1/4)			2.79
RIFFA 2.1	3.32	3.56	N/A
EPEE	3.2	3.28	2.76/2.62*
ffLink	7.1	6.3	N/A
JetStream	6.4	6.4	N/A

While RIFFAs implementation achieves about up to 11.4% higher throughput than VerCoLib in half duplex mode - at the cost of considerable more resource consumption as shown before - they did not publish comparable values for full duplex transfers. EPEE shows very similar results in terms of throughput, whereas the former is slightly faster in half-duplex mode, VerCoLib has an advantage in full duplex transfers. Although the performance of our design is not directly comparable to DyRact, ffLink and Jetstream, all show similar transfer rates with respect to the theoretical maximum given by the different hardware they are using.

For direct communication between FPGAs we performed measurements of the time it takes to transfer 16 GB data sequences. The measurements were taken by counting the cycles between the first and last data word on the target FPGA. This kind of measurement implies that the initial latency between sending the first request for data and the arrival of the data is not taken into account. For a sufficiently large amount of transferred data, the influence of this latency is not significant. The measurements were performed over different amounts of transferred data, ranging from 4096 kbyte to 16 GB. The measured mean transfer rate was 3351.45 MB/s, which is roughly 204.1 MB/s less than the estimated theoretical throughput.

Additional measurements were obtained on a transceiver-configuration using two and four channel pairs. The setup for these were taken analogue to the first measurement, each channel transferred a 16 GB long data sequence to the target FPGA. This resulted in a mean transfer rate of ≈1675 MB/s per channel for the configuration with two channel pairs and ≈837 MB/s per channel for the configuration with four pairs. The total transfer rate per configuration adds up to ≈3351 MB/s in both cases, implying that using multiple channel pairs has no negative effect on the bandwidth. Since all channel pairs show similar results in every configuration, it can be further argued that the channels indeed work independently from each other.

A separate experiment was conducted to measure the round trip time of a single packet from one FPGA to another and back again. For this a special module was written which sends a packet of length one to the other FPGA and counts the number of cycles it takes until the packet returns. These counts are summed up over a series of 2000 sent packets, resulting in a mean round trip time of ≈176.5 cycles or ≈705 ns with a standard deviation of less then 0.15 cycles or 0.6 ns.

6   Conclusion

VerCoLib is a versatile, fast, and resource saving framework for communication from FPGA to FPGA, from host to FPGA, and FPGA to host via PCIe. The flexibility mainly originates from the fact that the logic for generating PCIe packets and reacting on responses from the PCIe bus is handled individually by the channel modules. Nevertheless the resource consumption in typical situations is not higher than in other solutions since the configuration can be adapted to the requirement of the applications in a very flexible way, using absolutely needed resources only. Standardised interfaces allow for straightforward extensions of functionalities and reduce the effort necessary for maintenance.

Part of the framework is a Linux kernel driver that is responsible for setting up the communication channels and performing the communication between host and the FPGAs, whereas the communication between FPGAs is handled completely by the hardware itself without any interaction with the driver or the application software, except for the initial setup of the channels. VerCoLib was tested on the Xilinx Virtex-7 VC707 development board and the Linux kernel version 4.4.

7   Future Work

We plan to release the VerCoLib framework under a permissive open-source license in the near future. Without changing the general philosophy of VerCoLib it will be possible to integrate other communication channels into the same framework, e.g. Ethernet or USB channels. Thanks to the modular design, we are confident that VerCoLib is easy to adapt to other hardware, e.g. an FPGA using the PCIe v3.0 standard. Another topic for future work is extending VerCoLib to support scatter/gather DMA transmissions.

References

1. Billauer, E.: Xillybus. http://xillybus.com
2. Northwest Logic: PCI Express Solution (2017). http://nwlogic.com/products/pci-express-solution/
3. Jacobsen, M., Richmond, D., Hogains, M., Kastner, R.: RIFFA 2.1: A reusable integration framework for FPGA accelerators. ACM Trans. Reconfigurable Technol. Syst. 8(4), 22:1–22:23 (2015). https://doi.org/10.1145/2815631

4. Vesper, M., Koch, D., Vipin, K., Fahmy, S.A.: JetStream: an open-source high-performance PCI express 3 streaming library for FPGA-to-host and FPGA-to-FPGA communication. In: 2016 26th International Conference on Field Programmable Logic and Applications (FPL), pp. 1–9 (2016). https://doi.org/10.1109/FPL.2016.7577334

5. de la Chevallerie, D., Korinth, J., Koch, A.: ffLink: a lightweight high-performance open-source PCI express Gen3 interface for reconfigurable accelerators. SIGARCH Comput. Archit. News **43**(4), 34–39 (2016). https://doi.org/10.1145/2927964.2927971

6. Gong, J., Wang, T., Chen, J., Wu, H., Ye, F., Lu, S., Cong, J.: An efficient and flexible host-FPGA PCIe communication library. In: 2014 24th International Conference on Field Programmable Logic and Applications (FPL), pp. 1–6 (2014). https://doi.org/10.1109/FPL.2014.6927459

7. Vipin, K., Fahmy, S.A.: DyRACT: a partial reconfiguration enabled accelerator and test platform. In: 2014 24th International Conference on Field Programmable Logic and Applications (FPL), pp. 1–7 (2014). https://doi.org/10.1109/FPL.2014.6927507

8. ARM Ltd.: AMBA AXI4-Stream Protocol Specification v1.0 (2010). http://infocenter.arm.com/help/index.jsp?topic=/com.arm.doc.ihi0051a/index.html

9. Xilinx Inc.: 7 Series FPGAs Integrated Block for PCI Express v2.2 Product Guide for Vivado Design Suite (2016)

10. PCI-SIG: PCI Express Base Specification Revision 2.1 (2009)

Lookahead Memory Prefetching for CGRAs Using Partial Loop Unrolling

Lukas Johannes Jung[(✉)] and Christian Hochberger

Department of Electrical Engineering and Information Technology,
Computer Systems Group, TU Darmstadt, Darmstadt, Germany
{jung,hochberger}@rs.tu-darmstadt.de

Abstract. Coarse Grained Reconfigurable Arrays have become an established approach to provide high computational performance in various environments. Several researchers have found that the achievable performance highly depends on the interface between memory and CGRA. In this contribution we show that a smart prefetching mechanism can increase the performance of the CGRA. At the same time it consumes less hardware resources and energy as state of the art prefetching mechanisms.

Keywords: Prefetching · Loop unrolling · CGRA

1 Introduction

Coarse Grained Reconfigurable Arrays (CGRA) have been invented as an alternative to Field Programmable Gate Arrays (FPGA) on the one hand and Very Large Instruction Word (VLIW) processors on the other hand. They consist of an array of tightly coupled Processing Elements (PE) that can execute many word level operations in parallel. Typically, PEs also contain local register files and routing elements to access the neighbours. Thus, CGRAs provide a much better scalability than VLIW processors. PEs are controlled by context memories that require orders of magnitude less configuration information than FPGAs.

Early experiments with CGRAs have shown that only CGRAs with an autonomous memory access can provide high performance. Thus, the memory interface of a CGRA is of utmost importance for the CGRA microarchitecture. Multiple PEs should be equipped with a facility to access the memory independent of the host processor and the other PEs. Typically, a cache is used to decouple the PEs from the main memory or secondary cache levels.

Nevertheless, even in such a system, the total time spent waiting for the memory can be a major part of the overall execution time. Thus, it is helpful to reduce this waiting time. Prefetching of memory addresses has shown its usefulness for this purpose in multicore processors. In this contribution, we present our new smart prefetching approach and compare it with the state of the art prefetching. We show that our smart prefetch provides good speedup, while minimizing the additional energy and hardware required by the prefetching mechanism.

© Springer International Publishing AG, part of Springer Nature 2018
N. Voros et al. (Eds.): ARC 2018, LNCS 10824, pp. 93–104, 2018.
https://doi.org/10.1007/978-3-319-78890-6_8

The following section discusses related work. Section 3 describes the technical background of this work, while Sect. 4 explains how applications are mapped to the CGRA. Our prefetching algorithm is shown in the next section. It is thoroughly evaluated against a standard prefetching mechanism in Sect. 6. Finally, a conclusion and an outlook onto future work is given.

2   Related Work

Many current memory prefetchers use historical data to predict the memory accesses in the future. This will lead to good results for streaming applications or other applications with regular execution. For applications with irregular execution it is harder to predict the future memory accesses.

To overcome this issue the authors of [7] proposed a Continuous Runahead Engine which is part of the memory controller in a multi-core system. This engine calculates memory addresses continuously ahead of time to be able to prefetch data from the memory.

In [4] the authors propose a loop aware prefetcher for conventional processor systems. Here, the program flow is taken into account to predict the memory accesses for the next loop iteration. For this purpose they define the Cache Block Working Set (CBWS) which is the ordered vector of all accessed cache lines in one loop. The difference of CBWS from two consecutive loop iterations gives a good prediction. The compiler marks the relevant code blocks with special instructions. These instructions control the calculation of CBWS differentials using dedicated hardware.

The authors of [16] implemented a prefetcher for CGRAs using a similar principle. They precalculate access patterns for kernels that are mapped onto the CGRA. When that kernel is executed, the prefetcher loads the corresponding pattern from a cache (*Context Directed Pattern Matching*). It is then continuously executed, evaluated and updated if necessary. While this leads to good results, it comes at the cost of additional hardware effort.

Plasticine is a reconfigurable architecture for parallel patterns [12]. Here the accesses to the main memory are minimized by coalescing and linear prefetching. WARP [14] uses an FPGA as reconfigurable accelerator. Dedicated address generators are used to stream data from the memory to the FPGA. In DySer [8] as well as in ADRES [15] there are no particular prefetching algorithms for the reconfigurable accelerator, as the memory access component is part of the coupled processor. Many other CGRAs like [2,11] concentrate mainly on the optimization of sequential memory accesses.

In this work we combine the approaches of [4,7] with partial loop unrolling and apply it to CGRAs. For the innermost loops we calculate the addresses of future memory accesses using partial loop unrolling in order to request prefetches. Instead of a dedicated engine, the processing elements (PE) on the CGRA will perform the lookahead execution in parallel to the normal execution. Thus, no additional hardware is needed to find memory access patterns like in [16].

3   System Architecture

In this work an AMIDAR-Java Processor will be used as a host processor for the CGRA based accelerator. AMIDAR stands for *Adaptive Microinstruction Driven Architecture* and describes a reconfigurable class of processors [5]. AMIDAR processors consist of a set of *Functional Units* (FU) that operate independently and potentially in parallel. FUs can for example be an ALU, Local Variable Memory or the Heap-Memory as shown in Fig. 1. The Token Machine loads the machine instructions from the instruction memory and translates each instruction into the Tokens for all FUs. Tokens are sent via the Token Distribution Network (TDN) and data is exchanged via multiple data busses.

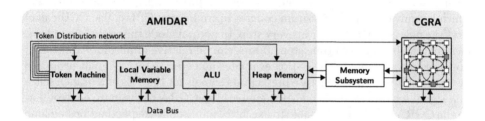

Fig. 1. Structure of an AMIDAR processor coupled with a CGRA

3.1   CGRA Architecture

The CGRA is included in AMIDAR as an FU. Figure 2 shows an overview of the CGRA [13]. The four main components are the Array of Processing elements (green), Context Control Unit (red), Condition Box (yellow) and the Context Memories (blue).

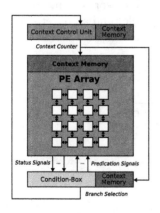

Fig. 2. Structure of the CGRA (Color figure online)

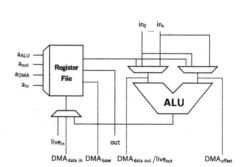

Fig. 3. Structure of a PE with optional live-in, live-out and memory connections

The Processing Element (PE) Array executes the actual computation on the CGRA. Figure 3 shows the structure of a single PE. In order to exchange local variables (Live-In and Live-Out Variables [10]) between the CGRA and the host processor on the Data Bus, live-in and live-out connections are provided as shown in Fig. 3. Optional DMA connections enable the CGRA to access the main memory via caches. In this work the memory is addressed virtually with handle and offset.

Each PE needs to be provided with control signals like for example the register file addresses. The set of all those control signals is called context and defines the operation of the PE in one time step. A particular Kernel normally consists of several contexts which are stored in the Context Memories. Both Context Control Unit (CCU) and Condition-Box (C-Box) also have context memories. All context memories are always addressed with the same address called the *context counter* which is equivalent to the program counter in traditional CPUs. The CCU calculates the new context counter in every step. In normal mode the context counter is incremented by one each time step. Jumps can be relative or absolute and conditional or unconditional. The C-Box evaluates and stores status signals produced by the PEs. It is used to generate predication signals for the PEs or a branch selection signal for the CCU. The C-Box enables the CGRA to evaluate control flow on the CGRA. Thus, it is possible to execute complex data dependant nested loop structures directly on the CGRA autonomously. No interaction with the host processor is necessary which is a unique characteristic of our CGRA.

The actual verilog description of a CGRA instance can be generated fully automatically from a textual description in JSON format [13] with user defined PE operations and interconnect. Preliminary tests showed that the CGRA ASICs can run at more than 1 GHz on 45 nm TSMC technology.

3.2   Memory Subsystem

Each PE with DMA-connections is provided with a dedicated L1-Cache. In order to simplify Garbage Collection in the AMIDAR processor, the memory is addressed virtually with an object reference (called handle) and an offset. All L1 Caches in the CGRA and the L1 Cache in the AMIDAR Heap FU access the L2 Cache via the Coherence Controller shown in Fig. 4.

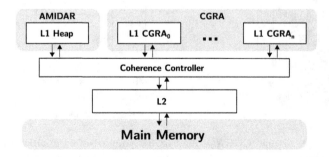

Fig. 4. Structure of the cache hierarchy

The Coherence Controller uses the Dragon Protocol [1] to guarantee coherence. This protocol ensures that when a shared cache line is modified in one cache, it is immediately updated in the other caches holding that line. Experiments have shown that this protocol results in a better performance than MOESI or MESI in this setup. In those protocols the cache lines are only invalidated in all other caches. This leads to delays because the new version of that invalid cache line is only loaded on demand. In this work the different caches connected to the PEs need access the same memory regions more often than the caches in conventional multiprocessor systems. Thus, the usage of the more expensive dragon protocol is appropriate. The properties of the cache system can be found in Table 1[1].

Note that when no L1 Cache holds the desired data, the virtual address consisting of handle and offset has to be resolved. This can result in additional cycles when accessing the L2 Cache or the main memory. In the L1 Cache the cache lines are aligned to objects whereas in the L2 Cache the cache lines are aligned to the physical addresses. Thus, it is likely that the cache lines are not aligned and two lines have to be read when the L2 cache is accessed.

Table 1. Cache properties

L1 Cache Amidar Heap	64 kB, 4-Way, 32 Byte per Line, virtually addressed
L1 Cache CGRA (each)	16 KB, 4-Way, 32 Byte per Line, virtually addressed
L2 Cache	256 KB, 4-Way, 32 Byte per Line, physically addressed
L1 miss Latency	
Read from another L1 Cache	4 Cycles
Read from L2 Cache	9+ Cycles
Read from main memory	49+ Cycles

4   Kernel Mapping Algorithm

The AMIDAR processor contains a hardware profiler [6] which can identify compute intensive loops called kernels. When the profiler identifies a candidate kernel, the mapping[2] process is started. First, method inlining and partial loop unrolling are performed. From the resulting bytecode sequence a control and data flow graph (CDFG) is created. This step includes common subexpression elimination, instruction folding and constant folding. The graph is then subject to scheduling and binding [13]. Afterwards the CGRA contexts are generated and the bytecode is patched so that the kernel will now be executed on the CGRA instead of the AMIDAR processor [10]. In the following section partial loop unrolling is described in detail as this is the foundation for the proposed prefetching mechanism.

---

[1] Values are based on our FPGA implementation of the System (work in progress).

[2] Also called *synthesis* in previous publications.

4.1   Partial Loop Unrolling

In order to increase the utilization of the PEs and the memory ports partial loop unrolling of the innermost loops was implemented [9]. The unrolling is done on bytecode level by copying the loop body u-times into the loop. Algorithm 2 shows the resulting code when Algorithm 1 is unrolled three times. The Figs. 5 and 6 show the resulting dependency graphs, respectively. It can be seen that when simply copying the loop body, all three loop iterations (marked in yellow, green and blue) are still executed sequentially because each iteration depends on the increment of the loop variable i in the previous iteration. Optimizations described in [9] lead to an improved dependency graph (Fig. 7) which leads to a significantly shorter schedule on the CGRA.

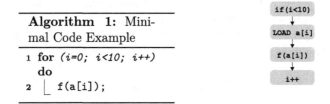

Algorithm 1: Minimal Code Example

---

1 **for** *(i=0; i<10; i++)* do
2 | f(a[i]);

Fig. 5. Dependency graph of Algorithm 1 (Color figure online)

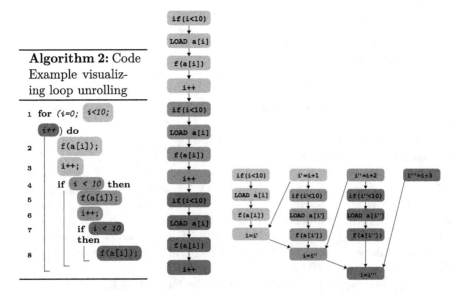

Algorithm 2: Code Example visualizing loop unrolling

---

1 **for** *(i=0; i<10;* *i++)* **do**
2 | f(a[i]);
3 | i++;
4 | **if** *i < 10* **then**
5 | | f(a[i]);
6 | | i++;
7 | | **if** *i < 10* **then**
8 | | | f(a[i]);

Fig. 6. Dependency graph of Algorithm 2 (Color figure online)

Fig. 7. Improved dependency graph of Algorithm 2 (Color figure online)

5   Prefetching

Experiments have shown that on average 20.6% of the execution time (see Fig. 8) of the CGRA is spent waiting on at least one of the caches (called *cache wait time*). This shows the need to implement a prefetching algorithm. This section describes our prefetching mechanism in two parts. First, the generation of prefetch requests is described and then how the coherence controller handles these requests.

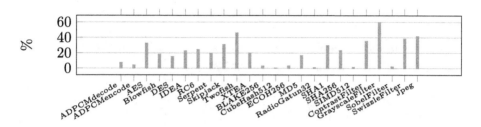

Fig. 8. Cache wait time in percent of CGRA execution time (Color figure online)

5.1   Generation of Prefetch Requests

The first idea for prefetching is to request the subsequent cache line (if it is not already in the cache) when a cache hit occurs [3]. This mechanism is called Linear Prefetching during this work (in some publications it is also called sequential prefetching). It is particularly suited for streaming applications. While Linear Prefetching reduces the cache wait time to 12.2%, many unnecessary prefetch requests are issued. Thus, we invented the unroll-based Lookahead Prefetching to improve the performance further.

The idea is to look f loop iterations (*fill iterations*) into the future, and prefetch all data needed for the next p iterations (*prefetch iterations*). As described above, the innermost loops are unrolled u-times on bytecode level to increase parallelism. Now the loop is unrolled $u + f + p$-times. Then the CDFG for this code sequence is generated and the last p iterations (prefetch iterations) are modified as follows:

- All memory instructions (both store and load) are transformed to prefetch instructions.
- Find groups of prefetches that access a similar memory region assuming that all of them map to the same cache line. Delete all but one of those prefetches. (The groups are found by looking for prefetches with the same handle and similar offsets like $i+1$ and $i+2$.)
- All instructions that do not produce data which is relevant for the prefetch instruction are removed.
- All original conditions are removed.

- All prefetch instructions that need data from another prefetch get a new condition: The dependent prefetch is only executed when the previous prefetch is unnecessary because the data is already present in the cache and can be used directly. This is done using the C-Box.

The previous f iterations (fill iterations) are not needed on their own. Thus, all nodes from the fill iterations that are not needed in the prefetch iterations are deleted. Figure 9 shows the CDFG for Algorithm 2 with prefetching (marked instruction) before and after the modifications.

Before modification:

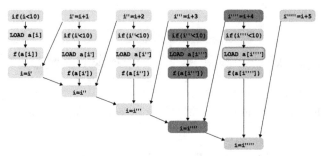

After modification:

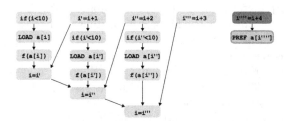

Fig. 9. Dependency graph of Algorithm 2 with one fill iteration (blue) and one prefetch iteration (green) (Color figure online)

It is obvious that including the prefetch instructions increases the workload that has to be performed on the CGRA as more instructions have to be executed. At the same time the prefetch instructions reduce the cache wait time. The higher the values of f and p, the higher is the overhead. The following heuristic is used to determine values for f and p:

- $p = 0, f = 0$, if more than 40% of all bytecodes in the innermost loop are memory instructions. Such loops will probably already use the whole memory bandwidth and prefetches bring no benefit.
- $p = 1, f = 4$, if less than 7% of all bytecodes in the innermost loop are memory instructions. In such loops the overhead for the prefetches is relatively small, so it is beneficial to request prefetches that are further in the future.

– $p = 1, f = 0$, otherwise

All values above were found empirically and lead to good results for our benchmark set[3].

Experiments have shown that some prefetch instructions need complex offset calculations even if $f = 0$ and $p = 1$. In those cases the increased workload on the CGRA outweighs the benefit of prefetching which leads to a decreased performance. Thus, we defined a metric for prefetch instructions called longest prefetch path. This is the highest number of hops in the CDFG from an instruction that is not part of the prefetch or fill iteration to the prefetch instruction (via instructions of fill or prefetch iterations). All prefetch instructions with a longest prefetch path longer than a threshold are also removed (and all the instruction producing data for this prefetch). For our benchmark set a threshold of 2 gives good results.

5.2   Handling Prefetch Requests

Each cache has a ring buffer of length 8 to store prefetch requests. Each ring buffer has a write and a read pointer. The pointers are updated as follows:

- PE requests a new prefetch:
  1. Store the request at position *write pointer*
  2. Set *read pointer = write pointer*
  3. Set *write pointer = write pointer + 1*
     (If the ring buffer ist full, the oldest value is overwritten)
- Coherence controller is idle, round robin arbiter chooses the cache and the request at position *read pointer* is valid:
  1. Execute the request at position *read pointer*
  2. Mark request at position *read pointer* as invalid
  3. Set *read pointer = read pointer − 1*

This results in the following properties: 1. The newest requests are handled first. 2. If the Coherence controller already handled a request in the buffer and a new request is inserted, all older requests will never be executed, because the handled request is now invalid and blocks the decrement of the read pointer.

This behaviour is desired, as prefetches are most efficient when the actual access to that memory position is far in the future so that the memory access time can be masked. The older the prefetch request is, the closer is the actual memory access. So it is beneficial to favour the newer prefetch requests.

6   Evaluation

The proposed prefetching mechanism is evaluated using the cycle accurate AMIDAR simulator with a CGRA with 16 PEs shown in Fig. 1. All PEs support

---

[3] Simply setting $f = p = 0$ and increasing u will result in a worse performance because high u decrease performance as shown in [9].

the same operations. Only the four grey PEs have a memory access. The performance will be evaluated with 23 different applications from the application domains cryptography, hash functions, filters and compression algorithms.

We compare Lookahead Prefetch to the Linear Prefetch. Other approaches are not considered for direct comparison as they target different hardware architectures like conventional CPUs [4,7] or CGRAs which allow only one context per kernel [16], while our CGRA supports multiple contexts per kernel.

The experiments showed that the insertion of prefetch instructions increases the number of contexts by 1.1% on average[4].

Figure 10 shows that for linear prefetching the memory access time increases in some cases when the access patterns are not linear. In Lookahead Prefetching this case never occurs. The memory access time is at most the same but decreased in most cases. On average Linear Prefetching reduces the memory access time by 38.3% while Lookahead Prefetching reduces it by 42.9%.

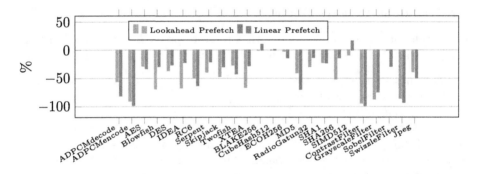

Fig. 10. Improvement of average memory access time (in percent)

Figure 11 shows the resulting improvement in runtime relative to CGRA execution without prefetching for all applications. It can be seen that in five cases (ADPCM encode, ECOH, Radio Gatun, SIMD and Sobel Filter) the proposed method results in a slowdown. This is because the inserted prefetch nodes only increase the number of contexts but have no effect on the cache hit rate. For example in the Sobel Filter only the access to the 9 filter coefficients is prefetched. This has no benefit as those values are used frequently and are always present in the cache. The access to the array storing the image is not prefetched as the offset calculation is more complex and the longest prefetch path is 10 so the corresponding prefetch instructions are removed.

Linear Prefetching also results in a slowdown for some of the hash functions because many of the access patterns are not linear. For some cases like SIMD512 prefetching has no impact on the runtime because the cache wait time is only a small fraction of the total execution time as shown in Fig. 8.

---

[4] Note that the number of contexts does not directly correlate to the runtime, because some contexts are executed more often as they are part of inner loops or even different kernels.

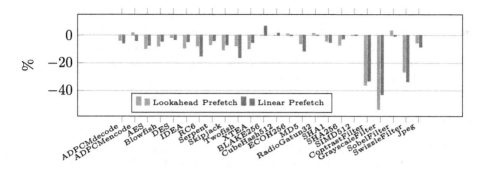

Fig. 11. Improved runtime relative to execution without prefetching (in percent)

Both Linear and Lookahead Prefetching result in a similar performance and reduce the runtime by about 8.5%. Linear Prefetching achieves this with significantly more prefetch requests that have to be handled by the Coherence Controller. Figure 12 shows the number of cache line fills. On average Lookahead Prefetching results in 15.1% less cache line fills than Linear Prefetching (no prefetching has 19.7% less cache line fills). Thus, energy consumption will be lower with Lookahead Prefetching while the same performance is achieved.

Additionally, the hardware effort is lower, as the PEs that are already present on the CGRA execute the lookahead and prefetching.

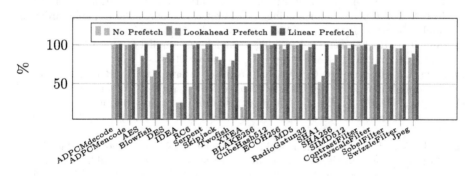

Fig. 12. Number of cache line fills relative to linear prefetching

7   Conclusion

In this contribution, we have shown that prefetching can be implemented under control of the CGRA. Using techniques to partially unroll loops, we can precompute future memory addresses and prefetch them in a lookahead fashion. This improves the overall runtime by 8.5% on average. At the same time, the number of additional memory accesses is much smaller than with Linear Prefetching. Thus, our PE controlled prefetching technique is more efficient than Linear Prefetching with respect to the HW resources and the energy consumption.

In the future, we want to give the scheduler more freedom to choose prefetch operations. Prefetches and the instructions required for address computation will thus be marked as optional before scheduling. Then, the scheduler can decide upon resource availability which prefetch operations can be executed without affecting the overall schedule length.

References

1. Archibald, J., Baer, J.L.: Cache coherence protocols: evaluation using a multiprocessor simulation model. ACM Trans. Comput. Syst. **4**(4), 273–298 (1986)
2. Cong, J., Huang, H., Ma, C., Xiao, B., Zhou, P.: A fully pipelined and dynamically composable architecture of CGRA. In: 2014 FCCM, pp. 9–16, May 2014
3. Dahlgren, F., Stenstrom, P.: Evaluation of hardware-based stride and sequential prefetching in shared-memory multiprocessors. TPDS **7**(4), 385–398 (1996)
4. Fuchs, A., Mannor, S., Weiser, U., Etsion, Y.: Loop-aware memory prefetching using code block working sets. In: 2014 MICRO, pp. 533–544, December 2014
5. Gatzka, S., Hochberger, C.: The AMIDAR class of reconfigurable processors. J. Supercomput. **32**(2), 163–181 (2005)
6. Gatzka, S., Hochberger, C.: Hardware based online profiling in AMIDAR processors. In: IPDPS, p. 144b (2005)
7. Hashemi, M., Mutlu, O., Patt, Y.N.: Continuous runahead: transparent hardware acceleration for memory intensive workloads. In: 2016 MICRO, pp. 1–12, October 2016
8. Hoy, C.H., Govindarajuz, V., Nowatzki, T., Nagaraju, R., Marzec, Z., Agarwal, P., Frericks, C., Cofell, R., Sankaralingam, K.: Performance evaluation of a DySER FPGA prototype system spanning the compiler, microarchitecture, and hardware implementation. In: 2015 ISPASS, pp. 203–214, March 2015
9. Jung, L.J., Hochberger, C.: Feasibility of high level compiler optimizations in online synthesis. In: 2015 ReConFig, pp. 1–7, December 2015
10. Jung, L.J., Hochberger, C.: Optimal processor interface for CGRA-based accelerators implemented on FPGAs. In: 2016 ReConFig, pp. 1–7, November 2016
11. Lee, H., Nguyen, D., Lee, J.: Optimizing stream program performance on CGRA-based systems. In: Proceedings of the 52nd DAC, DAC 2015, pp. 110:1–110:6. ACM, New York (2015)
12. Prabhakar, R., Zhang, Y., Koeplinger, D., Feldman, M., Zhao, T., Hadjis, S., Pedram, A., Kozyrakis, C., Olukotun, K.: Plasticine: a reconfigurable architecture for parallel paterns. In: Proceedings of the 44th ISCA, ISCA 2017, pp. 389–402. ACM, New York (2017)
13. Ruschke, T., Jung, L.J., Wolf, D., Hochberger, C.: Scheduler for inhomogeneous and irregular CGRAs with support for complex control flow. In: 2016 IPDPSW, pp. 198–207, May 2016
14. Vahid, F., Stitt, G., Lysecky, R.: Warp processing: dynamic translation of binaries to FPGA circuits. Computer **41**(7), 40–46 (2008)
15. Veredas, F.J., Scheppler, M., Moffat, W., Mei, B.: Custom implementation of the coarse-grained reconfigurable ADRES architecture for multimedia purposes. In: FPL 2005, pp. 106–111, August 2005
16. Yang, C., Liu, L., Yin, S., Wei, S.: Data cache prefetching via context directed pattern matching for coarse-grained reconfigurable arrays. In: 2016 53nd DAC, pp. 1–6, June 2016

Performance Estimation of FPGA Modules for Modular Design Methodology Using Artificial Neural Network

Kalindu Herath$^{(\boxtimes)}$, Alok Prakash, and Thambipillai Srikanthan

Nanyang Technological University, Singapore, Singapore
kalindub001@e.ntu.edu.sg, {alok,astsrikan}@ntu.edu.sg

Abstract. Modern FPGAs consist of millions of logic resources allowing hardware designers to map increasingly large designs. However, the design productivity of mapping large designs is greatly affected by the long runtime of FPGA CAD flow. To mitigate it, modular design methodology has been introduced in the past that allows designers to partition large designs into smaller modules and compile & test the modules individually before assembling them together to complete the compilation process. Automated decision making on placing these modules on FPGA, however, is a slow and tedious process that requires large database of precompiled modules, which are compiled on a large number of placement positions. To accelerate this placement process during modular designing, in this paper we propose an ANN based performance estimation technique that can rapidly suggest the best shape and location for a given module. Experimental results on legacy as well as state-of-the-art FPGA devices show that the proposed technique can accurately estimate the F_{max} of modules with an average error of less than 4%.

Keywords: FPGA · Floorplaning · Modular design methodology
Computer-aided designing

1 Introduction

The rapid scaling of transistors over the past decade has allowed commercial Field Programmable Gate Array (FPGA) giants like Altera [1] and Xilinx [7] to realize FPGAs with tens of millions of logic gates alongside useful ready-to-use hard Intellectual Property (IP) cores such as Block-RAMs (BRAMs) of different size and Digital Signal Processors (DSPs). Such resource-rich modern FPGAs permit system designers to use FPGAs for application specific implementation as well as to map increasingly complex applications. At the same time, the increasingly strict non-recurring engineering (NRE) costs and time-to-market (TTM) constraints are also pushing FPGAs favourably when compared to ASICs [24].

However, while FPGA devices are becoming more sophisticated, the computer-aided design (CAD) tools used for FPGA-based designs have not yet

© Springer International Publishing AG, part of Springer Nature 2018
N. Voros et al. (Eds.): ARC 2018, LNCS 10824, pp. 105–118, 2018.
https://doi.org/10.1007/978-3-319-78890-6_9

matured sufficiently to efficiently map large-scale applications into such FPGAs [26]. It is observed that typical CAD flow can take tens of minutes to hours or even days [8] for such applications, thereby significantly limiting design productivity. Such mapping with existing CAD can also result in poor placement and routing decisions, which can lead to degradation in the quality of result (QoR), i.e. performance and power consumption of the final design. Placement step of current CAD flow has also been identified as the most time consuming step, contributing to almost 50% of total CAD runtime [20]. Traditional Simulated Annealing (SA) based placement algorithms are known to produce superior quality placement results for small and medium scale designs. However, SA does not scale well for larger designs, and hence resulting in longer runtime [9].

There have been attempts in developing scalable CAD to reduce the runtime. Altera improves their proprietary CAD tool, Quartus, by introducing parallelism in their SA based Q2P placer [18]. Similarly, Xilinx introduces an analytical placement strategy in their CAD [11], inspired by ASIC placement strategies.

However, the runtime of these CAD tools are still considerably high, especially for large and complex designs. To address the design productivity inefficiencies while compiling large applications [16], existing research work in FPGA CAD has proposed a new CAD flow, called *modular design methodology (MDM)*. This technique breaks a large system into smaller modules. Some of the modules, for example, board support packages or external memory interfaces, do not change frequently in a development cycle. Hence, these modules can be placed and routed individually and stored in a library and therefore can be excluded from subsequent compilations. The reuse of pre-compiled library modules significantly decrease the runtime of the flow [14]. Commercial FPGA vendors have also introduced augmented modular compile flow support to their CAD flow. Altera uses Quartus Incremental Compilation Flow [3] and Xilinx has integrated Hierarchical Design Suite [6] in PlanAhead Design and Analysis Tool [5]. However, this design technique is not sensitive to the connection information between modules. It avoids optimization of those connections that is possible in usual compilation flow. As a result, QoR of modular design methodology is typically degraded [12].

Modular design workflows use a large database of pre-compiled modules. Modules are placed and routed at large number of possible locations on FPGA during offline *module creation phase*. During *design assembly phase*, best set of pre-compiled modules are searched and mapped to get the final design. Large heterogeneous FPGAs offer greater possible ways a module to be placed on FPGA space, making large solution space for the module assembly stage. However, due to availability of different types of resources on these FPGAs, selecting a place and a shape for a given module from the library becomes more critical. Wrong selection either could lead to resource wastage [16] or could affect the performance of the module [15]. In addition, pre-compiling large number of variations per each module becoming increasingly time consuming. During our experiments, each module took about 3 h to compile all possible placement variations. Therefore, it is apparent that module creation phase has become less feasible, especially if the module library changes frequently [19].

In this paper, we propose an artificial neural network (ANN) based approach to estimate the shape and placement of a given module in order to achieve the best performance. Aim of this estimation is to make swift placement decisions during module based development, eliminating the need of having frequently changing pre-compiled module database. In the next section we discuss the existing modular design workflows, followed by a motivational example in Sect. 3. In Sect. 4, we explain the proposed methodology that estimates performance of modules in detail. Section 5 evaluates the proposed method and discusses the experimental results. Section 6 concludes this paper.

2   Related Workflows

MDM is an extensively explored design paradigm. Frontier [23] is a module based hierarchical placement framework. It uses a library of pre-placed modules to identify similar patterns in a given application. Identified patterns are clustered, and placed on FPGA by using library information. However, Frontier does not preserve routing information of the modules. HMFlow [14], on the other hand, maintains a library with pre-routed modules. It also creates new library modules for application logic which does not match with any library Module. BPR [8] uses coarser pre-compiled modules as compared to HMFlow to improve compilation time. In addition, its module library keeps different variations of each module by placing and routing for all possible locations on FPGA. During full compilation, only one version of each module is selected. qFlow [9] divides a given design into evolving (frequently changes) and invariant portions. Evolving portion is compiled as modules and is combined with invariant section. TFlow [17] extends qFlow methodology and uses bitstream level modules during design assembly phase. However, placement of bitstream level modules is less flexible due to restriction in bitstream configuration boundaries.

The effect of module size on QoR has been explored in [10]. Authors analysed QoR in their module based placement approach by varying the granularity of the modules. Analysis has been done in terms of runtime of the placement tool, and the Half Perimeter Wire Length of the placement solution. The impact of shapes of modules to overall FPGA resource utilization and placement flexibility is greatly discussed in [16]. They have shown multi shape pre-compiled modules can lead to better resource utilization and additional placement flexibility, which ultimately results more packing of modules on FPGA. Module shape exploration has been used in FPGA floorplanning techniques such as [22,25] but they considered shapes with single resource type. On the other hand, [19] argues pre-synthesising each module for different shape ratios is a tedious process. They suggest a method to change the shapes of modules during the placement stage using a pre-placed library of modules with a single size.

Most of the modular design workflows aim on turnaround time of a design cycle, rather than achieving both high performance while improving runtime. Large pre-compiled libraries involve in most workflows, while having a single shape for each pre-compiled module. Shape exploration for library modules with heterogeneous resources has been done, but it targets resource utilization on FPGA as a measurement of QoR. Previous work lacks a shape exploration framework to achieve better performance in each module.

3   Motivation

Modern FPGA architectures, including Altera and Xilinx FPGAs, are typically categorized as island-style FPGA architecture where resources such as BRAMs and DSPs are arranged in columns and interleaved between a sea of Configurable Logic Blocks (CLBs) columns. Interconnect wires are provided in copious amounts to provide for high bandwidth connectivity between these resources. It has also been observed that these resources are arranged homogeneously along the vertical axis such that most of the rows look identical in an FPGA.

However, as FPGAs continue to become more heterogeneous, incorporating different types and location of resources, it is important to identify the optimum placement and shape for a design module implemented in such FPGAs. The shape of a module refers to the rectangular space in the FPGA within which the module can be placed and routed. The optimum placement and shape ensures that the most widely used resources are available at a physically closer distance, thereby potentially reducing length of the interconnecting wires, ultimately leading to better performance and lower power consumption [13].

Figure 1 shows two different shapes and placement locations for a single module. The module is isolated from the rest of the design, so that it is independent from the connections for module to the rest of the design. We have observed that the shape given in Fig. 1(b) produces 12% greater maximum allowable clock frequency (F_{max}) as compared to (a). While similar number of resources are consumed in both cases, the main difference is the arrangement of resource columns. Depending on how the CLBs BRAMs and DSPs are connected within a module, an arrangement of columns in a rectangular region can be more preferable for the module. Hence, in this paper we propose a methodology, which is able to predict the F_{max} of given module on a FPGA device, when shape and application parameters given. As discussed in the previous section, existing module based designing techniques have not explored the relationship between module performance and its shape as well as the location in the FPGA fabric.

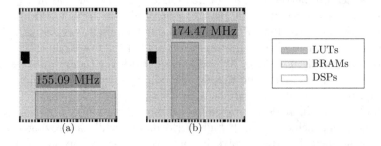

Fig. 1. Performance (F_{max}) of a module in two location and shapes

4   Methodology

In this section, we first provide some background information before explaining our approach. We use the Altera's Quartus CAD tools to explain the proposed methodology as well as for our experiments. It should be noted that the proposed methodology does not depend on vendor specific CAD tools. It is also noteworthy that Xilinx offers equivalent functionalities in their PlanAhead tool flow [5].

4.1   Background

Quartus Incremental Compilation (QIC). In the default Quartus compilation flow, also referred to as 'flat compilation', all the RTL code files are processed simultaneously in the Analysis and Synthesis step and the entire post-synthesis netlist is placed and routed subsequently by the fitter. If any changes need to be made after a flat compilation, one needs to perform a fresh re-compilation.

Altera includes a toolset for modular design methodology (MDM) in Quartus, called Incremental Compilation Design Flow. It allows hardware designers to follow a divide and conquer strategy, by partitioning a large design into relatively smaller modules and develop each module separately. In the rest of the paper, we use the term *module* and *partition* interchangeably. Some modules in a design might require frequent revisions than some other modules. For such situations, incremental compilation technique allows designers to change the code segments of only some modules and compile them separately without having to compile the whole project or alter the rest of the design.

Partitioning a large design into relatively smaller modules is typically performed using a bottom-up approach, where one or more VHDL entities or Verilog modules in the RTL code are defined as a design partition by the designer. Performing an incremental compilation after defining partitions creates separate netlist for each partition after each stage. For instance, after the 'Analysis and Synthesis' step a *post-synthesis netlist* or after 'Fitter' step *post-fit netlist* is generated. A single full post-fit netlist is created by merging netlists from each partition at the end of the incremental compilation flow. Quartus allows us to preserve the generated netlist of each partition at any stage by setting a parameter called *preservation level*. A partition with post-fit netlist preservation will not be processed during both synthesis and fitter steps, and its post-fit netlist generated in previous compilation is used for producing the full post-fit netlist.

LogicLock. The atomic components (CLBs, BRAMs and DSPs) of a partition might be placed anywhere in the FPGA space during the fitter step. However, Quartus LogicLock feature allows designer to restrict the placement of these components to a rectangular region in the FPGA space. Designers can define such regions by providing the shape information (width and height), placement information (bottom left coordinate) and VHDL entities/Verilog modules belonging to the partition which needs to be in the region. Such rectangular regions with shape and placement information are called *footprint* of a partition.

4.2   Footprint Generation for Design Partitions

Footprint of a Design Partition. A design partition P_i is characterized by a resource requirement, which we express as a tuple $A_i = \{l, m, d\}$ where l, m, d are the minimum requirement of CLBs, BRAMs and DSPs on the FPGA space in order to successfully map the partition into FPGA. During the incremental compilation flow, designers have to ensure that the final compilation of the overall design at least provides for A_i resources for each partition P_i. Therefore, during the early stages, we reserve a FPGA region with A_i resources for P_i by defining a LogicLock region LL_i. This LogicLock region is referred to as the footprint of the design partition. The shape and location properties of footprint LL_i can be expressed as a tuple $S_i = \{x, y, w, h\}$ where x and y are the bottom left corner of the rectangle in FPGA space, and w, h is width and height of the rectangle. In a typical island style FPGA, the bottom left corner block is marked as the origin of the coordinate plane which is $\{1, 1\}$.

For example, consider two different footprints $LL_{1,1}$, $LL_{1,2}$ for partition P_1 with $A_1 = \{421, 20, 0\}$ on Altera EP2C35 FPGA [2] as shown in Fig. 2. The shape parameters of two footprints are $S_{1,1} = \{1, 1, 56, 8\}$ and $S_{1,2} = \{1, 1, 52, 9\}$. Here, the second variable (k) in the notations, $LL_{i,k}$ & $S_{i,k}$, denotes the different footprints and shape parameters respectively of a single design partition (i). Both footprints consist of 3 BRAM columns and 1 DSP column but contain 52 CLB columns in the former case and 48 CLB columns in the latter. $LL_{1,1}$ offers FPGA resources $\{432, 24, 8\}$ which satisfies the requirement A_1. If we reduce the width of $LL_{1,1}$ to 52 without adjusting the height, the resultant resource coverage on FPGA will be only $\{384, 24, 8\}$ which does not satisfy the CLB requirement hence it is an invalid footprint. However, by increasing the height to 9 while reducing width to 52, we can achieve $LL_{1,2}$ which offers FPGA resources $\{432, 27, 9\}$. Note that both $LL_{1,1}$ and $LL_{1,2}$ cause resource wastage. However, if we select a region with height of 7 for P_1, the CLB requirements cannot be satisfied even if its width is set to the entire device width of this FPGA (i.e. 64). The subsequent sections uses the proposed ANN based performance estimation technique to identify the best footprint for each module in a modular design methodology.

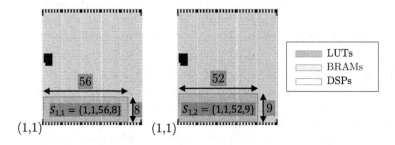

Fig. 2. Footprint variation for a given subsystem

4.3   Methodology for Training an Artificial Neural-Network

Now, we present our artificial neural-network (ANN) based approach to estimate the performance of a given design partition. We train the ANN using application and architecture parameters through supervised training technique by providing the expected output performance (F_{max}) for the respective input data.

Training Dataset. In order to generate a large dataset for a better ANN training, we use the RTL design of a benchmark application and treat it as a design partition p_1. For this p_1, we exhaustively generate many footprints $LL_{1,x}$, where each $LL_{1,x}$ has different values for the parameters as explained below, and is compiled using Altera Incremental Compilation to get the respective F_{max}. We generated the footprints in this exhaustive manner for several benchmark as well as handwritten applications in order to create a large training data for the ANN.

Modelling Parameters. The following are the input parameters we use to model the performance of a given footprint. These parameters are analogous to independent variables in typical regression.

1. Architecture features: Starting horizontal coordinate (x), width (w) and height (h) of the rectangular region on FPGA space.
   Note that we ignore the vertical coordinate (y), as a feature due to uniformity of the FPGA architecture along vertical direction. In other words, if we move any rectangular region along vertical axis on FPGA space, it does not change the number of resources within that region. The FPGA architectural features in a region, such as the number and position of resource columns of each resource type, are captured by the (x), (w) and (h) parameters.
2. Application Area: Area requirement A_i, as discussed in Sect. 4.2, signifies the minimum resources needed to implement the application partition p_i.
3. Application internal links (c_i): Performance (F_{max}) of a design partition depends on number of available routing resources in the respective region. High routing resource utilization within the region typically results in longer routing paths for some routes, which could lower the performance.
4. Application default critical path (cp_i): Critical path of a design is the longest path between two registers. Some applications may contain critical paths along the combinational logic while others may have paths along memory and DSP I/O. To have this differentiation in our dataset, we include a parameter as an estimation of the critical path for each application. However, this estimated critical path is same for all the footprints of a single application, and should not be mistaken with the output of the model.

Problem Statement. Given a design/application partition p_i with an area requirement A_i, with c_i internal links and a default critical path cp_i, what is the expected F_{max} if it is compiled to a footprint of $S_i = \{x, w, h\}$.

Training Procedure. As shown in Fig. 3, we use a benchmark or handwritten application in entirety for the training step. The application is treated as an isolated module and is defined as a design partition in Quartus tool. We first extract the application specific parameters 2, 3 and 4 defined above by performing a one-time incremental compilation for the defined designed partition. This compilation is done without footprints information.

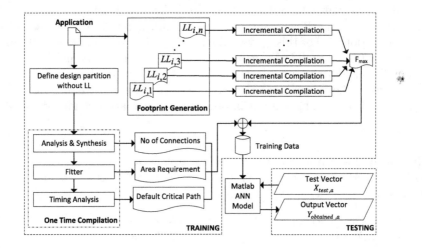

Fig. 3. ANN training methodology

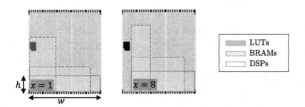

Fig. 4. Generating footprints for training

Next, we generate a series of footprints $LL_{i,k}$ by setting different shape properties $S_{i,k}$ using LogicLock for set of i applications. Figure 4 shows the way we set $S_{i,k}$. For $LL_{i,k}$ we set $x = 1$ and w to the device maximum width (i.e. 64 for our case). The height h of the footprint is calculated using A_i, which is known from onetime-compilation discussed above. For instance, if $A_i = \{421, 20, 0\}$ then for a rectangular region on an EP2C35 FPGA device, with starting coordinate $x = 1$ and $w = 64$, the height should be at least 8 to satisfy the area constraint

A_i. Therefore, we set $S_{i,1} = \{1, 64, 8\}$. For the next footprint $LL_{i,2}$, w is set to 63, reduced by one compared to $LL_{i,1}$, while keeping $x = 1$. Similar to previous case, h is calculated according to A_i, resulting $S_{i,2} = \{1, 63, 8\}$. Likewise, set of footprints are generated by reducing w and calculating respective h while $x = 1$, until w cannot be reduced further to generate a valid footprint. This footprint generation process can be repeated by shifting the starting position $x = 2, 3, \ldots$ until there are no more valid footprints. We obtained the training data by changing x and w with an interval of 2.

We used separate Quartus project to compile each footprint using Quartus Incremental Compilation. The application code is included into a single VHDL entity and kept within project's top level entity. During the incremental compilation, we set the netlist preservation level of the application to *Source Code Level* while the top level entity is kept as *Empty* preservation level in order to treat the application as an isolated module. After each compilation, we note the performance (F_{max}) of the application located at the respective footprint. This (F_{max}) is used as the output of training data set. Note that, all these footprints carry same application specific modelling parameters. An example for a training dataset entry k of application i can be notified as $\{S_{i,k}, A_i, c_i, cp_i, F_{max_{i,k}}\}$. Once the training dataset is created using all the benchmark and handwritten applications, we train a standard MatLab deep learning ANN model [4]. ANN model is trained with 8 hidden layers and using standard Resilient Backpropagation training algorithm. Appropriate number of hidden layers and the training function were found empirically.

5   Results and Discussion

5.1   Benchmarks Applications and Target Platforms

We use a total of 26 applications, 16 from Polybench benchmark suite [21] and 10 handwritten, in this work. Out of these 26 applications, 23 were used during the training phase, while the remaining 3 were used to evaluate the proposed methods. Application parameters of these applications are shown in Table 1. As discussed in Sect. 4.3, Table 1 presents the modelling parameters for each application, i.e. Application area ($A_i(l, m, d)$), Application internal connections (c_i) and Application default critical path (cp_i).

For an extensive evaluation, we experimented using four FPGA devices; (a) Cyclone II, EP2C35 - a smaller device with homogeneous floorplan (b) Cyclone V, 5CGXBC4 - one of the latest device with heterogeneous floorplan which includes number of BRAM and DSP columns (c) Cyclone V, 5CGTFD9 - largest FPGA of Altera Cyclone FPGAs (d) Cyclone 10LP, 10C025 - very recently released FPGA. Characteristics of these devices are listed in Table 2.

Table 1. Benchmark applications used for modelling and testing

	Application	CLB(l)	BRAM(m)	DSP(d)	Connections(c_i)	Default critical path(cp_i)
1	2 mm	36	40	3	128	98.01
2	3 mm	51	56	9	384	234.96
3	bicg	25	12	3	256	235.07
4	conv2d	19	16	2	64	108.31
5	conv3d	25	64	2	64	101.55
6	doitgen	22	72	3	160	167.95
7	fdtd2d	56	25	2	384	91.93
8	gemm	26	24	3	128	197.75
9	gemver	72	16	9	544	163.23
10	gesummv	34	19	6	224	189.54
11	mvt	29	12	6	256	209.47
12	symm	26	24	3	128	212.76
13	syrk	33	16	6	160	194.59
14	syr2k	37	24	6	192	211.73
15	atax	25	11	3	224	239.29
16	trmm	21	16	3	96	234.58
17	subsys1	421	20	0	3200	163.91
18	subsys2	360	18	0	2688	167.5
19	subsys3	349	20	0	2688	165.7
20	subsys4	357	22	0	3008	168.92
21	subsys5	325	21	0	2496	170.39
22	subsys6	121	16	0	960	183.82
23	subsys7	61	14	0	480	191.75
24	subsys8	91	21	0	800	168.63
25	subsys9	523	30	0	4512	157.8
26	subsys10	523	36	0	4704	164.8

Table 2. Target FPGA architecture characteristics

Family	Device	Logic elements	BRAM columns	DSP columns
Cyclone II	EP2C35	35k	3	2
Cyclone V	5CGXBC4	50k	8	5
Cyclone V	5CGTFD9	301k	11	6
Cyclone 10LP	10CL025	25k	2	2

5.2   Training Error and Testing Error

Training the ANN Based Model. The training data set contains data points from 23 applications as described above. These applications are compiled at various footprints as described in Sect. 4.3 to generate the large training dataset.

We calculate the training error for each application for every footprint as a percentage difference between the actual performance (F_{max}) and the predicted performance from the model. The average training error across all applications at every footprint for each device is shown in Table 3.

Table 3. Training error

Device	No. of data points	Average training error(%)
EP2C35	6818	3.5
5CGXBC4	7059	3.27
5CGTFD9	19738	2.65
10CL025	3471	2.58

Testing the Model. To evaluate the effectiveness of the model, we use three applications, where the expected output (ground truth) was first obtained by compiling these applications using Quartus at every footprint. We use the *atax* and *2* mm applications from Polybench [21] and a handwritten *subsys10* application for the testing phase.

We calculate the test error similar to the training error above. Table 4 shows the individual test error for the 3 test applications, average across all footprint, for each device. Overall, the maximum average error across all applications and devices is less than **4%**.

To evaluate the error values in a greater detail, we also plot the histogram of errors at the various footprints for each of the test applications on the EP2C35 device. Figure 5 shows these histogram plots. It can be clearly observed that at the majority of footprints, the error stays at the lower end of the histogram, showing the overall effectiveness in predicting the performance (F_{max}) using the proposed ANN based technique. Error histograms for the other devices are similar to Fig. 5 hence are not shown in the paper due to the space constraints.

5.3   Discussion

While the above results confirm the accurate prediction of F_{max} using the proposed ANN based technique for a given design partition in a footprint, a more interesting application of our approach is to identify the best footprint that provides the highest F_{max} for a given design partition.

It is indeed possible to obtain this using the proposed methodology by rapidly predicting the performance at all footprints using our model and then identifying

Table 4. Test error percentages

Device	atax	2 mm	subsys10
	Average error(%)	Average error(%)	Average error(%)
EP2C35	2.56	1.36	2.30
5CGXBC4	3.76	2.43	2.99
5CGTFD9	3.79	1.76	3.63
10CL025	3.35	1.68	3.08

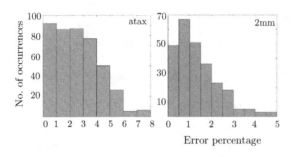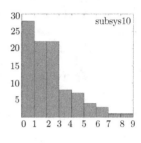

Fig. 5. Test error percentage histogram

the footprint with the highest F_{max}. This is immensely useful in a modular design methodology, where, instead of storing a pre-placed and routed database for all the partitions for all possible locations, a smaller database could be maintained during full design incremental compilation by setting preservation level of the best footprint set of *post-fit*. Though we explain the proposed work using Quartus specific terminology, similar toolset is available in Xilinx environments as well [5]. Hence the proposed methodology is also applicable Xilinx based designs.

It should also be noted that, the model is architecture specific and needs to be trained for each device. However, this requirement is common for all the module based FPGA designing approaches since the post-fit netlists are indeed architecture specific.

6   Conclusion

In this paper, we presented our artificial neural-network based methodology to estimate F_{max} of a design partition at any footprint on a FPGA device. We have used Altera Quartus incremental compilation tools for implementing the design partitions and used MatLab to train the ANN model. The proposed methodology accurately estimates F_{max} with less than 4% average error across the test applications and 4 widely used latest state-of-the-art FPGA devices. The proposed technique can be of immense benefit in a modular design methodology to reduce module library sizes by keeping only the best footprints set for a given partition while discarding the other footprints.

While in this work, we can accurately estimate the best footprint for a partition in isolation, in future, we propose to find the best footprints for all the partitions in a design in order to obtain a globally optimal footprint for the entire design that achieves the highest F_{max} performance.

References

1. Altera. https://www.altera.com/
2. CycloneII FPGAs. https://www.altera.com/products/fpga/cyclone-series/cyclone-ii/support.html
3. Increasing Productivity with Quartus II Incremental Compilation. https://goo.gl/uy225f
4. Neural Network Toolbox. https://www.mathworks.com/products/neural-network.html
5. PlanAhead Design and Analysis Tool. https://www.xilinx.com/products/design-tools/planahead.html
6. Vivado Design Suite User Guide-Hierarchical Design. https://goo.gl/6bUqqD
7. Xilinx. https://www.xilinx.com/
8. Coole, J., et al.: BPR: fast FPGA placement and routing using macroblocks. In: CODES+ISSS (2012)
9. Frangieh, T., et al.: A design assembly framework for FPGA back-end acceleration. Microprocess. Microsyst. **38**, 889–898 (2014)
10. Gort, M., et al.: Design re-use for compile time reduction in FPGA high-level synthesis flows. In: FPT (2014)
11. Gupta, S., et al.: CAD techniques for power optimization in Virtex-5 FPGAs. In: Custom Integrated Circuits Conference, CICC 2007. IEEE (2007)
12. Haroldsen, T., et al.: Rapid FPGA design prototyping through preservation of system logic: a case study. In: FPL (2013)
13. Herath, K., et al.: Communication-aware partitioning for energy optimization of large FPGA designs. In: GLSVLSI (2017)
14. Lavin, C., et al.: HMFlow: accelerating FPGA compilation with hard macros for rapid prototyping. In: FCCM (2011)
15. Lavin, C., et al.: Impact of hard macro size on FPGA clock rate and place/route time. In: FPL (2013)
16. Lee, K., et al.: Shape exploration for modules in rapid assembly workflows. In: ReConFig (2015)
17. Love, A., et al.: In pursuit of instant gratification for FPGA design. In: FPL (2013)
18. Ludwin, A., et al.: Efficient and deterministic parallel placement for FPGAs. ACM Trans. Des. Autom. Electron. Syst. (TODAES) **16**, 1–23 (2011)
19. Mao, F., et al.: Dynamic module partitioning for library based placement on heterogeneous FPGAs. In: RTCSA (2017)
20. Murray, K.E., et al.: Titan: enabling large and complex benchmarks in academic CAD. In: 2013 23rd International Conference on Field Programmable Logic and Applications (FPL) (2013)
21. Pouchet, L.N.: Polybench: the polyhedral benchmark suite (2012). http://web.cs.ucla.edu/~pouchet/software/polybench/ (2012)
22. Rabozzi, M., et al.: Floorplanning for partially-reconfigurable FPGA systems via mixed-integer linear programming. In: FCCM (2014)
23. Tessier, R.: Fast placement approaches for FPGAs. TODAES **7**, 284–305 (2002)

24. Trimberger, S.M.: Three ages of FPGAs: a retrospective on the first thirty years of FPGA technology. Proc. IEEE. **103**, 3108–331 (2015)
25. Vipin, K., Fahmy, S.A.: Architecture-aware reconfiguration-centric floorplanning for partial reconfiguration. In: Choy, O.C.S., Cheung, R.C.C., Athanas, P., Sano, K. (eds.) ARC 2012. LNCS, vol. 7199, pp. 13–25. Springer, Heidelberg (2012). https://doi.org/10.1007/978-3-642-28365-9_2
26. Wirthlin, M., et al.: Future field programmable gate array (FPGA) design methodologies and tool flows. Technical report (2008)

Achieving Efficient Realization of Kalman Filter on CGRA Through Algorithm-Architecture Co-design

Farhad Merchant[1(✉)], Tarun Vatwani[2], Anupam Chattopadhyay[2],
Soumyendu Raha[3], S. K. Nandy[4], and Ranjani Narayan[5]

[1] Institute for Communication Technologies and Embedded Systems,
RWTH Aachen University, Aachen, Germany
`farhad.merchant@ice.rwth-aachen.de`
[2] Hardware and Embedded Systems Lab, Nanyang Technological University,
Singapore, Singapore
[3] Scientific Computation Laboratory, Indian Institute of Science, Bangalore, India
[4] Computer Aided Design Laboratory, Indian Institute of Science, Bangalore, India
[5] Morphing Machines Pvt. Ltd., Bangalore, India

Abstract. In this paper, we present efficient realization of Kalman Filter (KF) that can achieve up to 65% of the theoretical peak performance of underlying architecture platform. KF is realized using Modified Faddeeva Algorithm (MFA) as a basic building block due to its versatility and REDEFINE Coarse Grained Reconfigurable Architecture (CGRA) is used as a platform for experiments since REDEFINE is capable of supporting realization of a set algorithmic compute structures at run-time on a Reconfigurable Data-path (RDP). We perform several hardware and software based optimizations in the realization of KF to achieve 116% improvement in terms of Gflops over the first realization of KF. Overall, with the presented approach for KF, 4-105x performance improvement in terms of Gflops/watt over several academically and commercially available realizations of KF is attained. In REDEFINE, we show that our implementation is scalable and the performance attained is commensurate with the underlying hardware resources.

Keywords: Kalman Filter · Reconfigurable architectures
Computation · Parallelism

1 Introduction

Coarse Grained Reconfigurable Architectures (CGRAs) have been active topic of research due to their power performance and flexibility [9]. CGRAs are capable of domain customization and they are targeted to achieve performance of Application Specific Integrated Circuits (ASICs) and flexibility of Field Programmable Gate Arrays (FPGAs) through presence of ASIC-like structures [8,14]. Typically, CGRAs occupy middle ground between ASICs and FPGAs [16,17]. Furthermore, CGRAs are preferred as a platform in the application domains like

© Springer International Publishing AG, part of Springer Nature 2018
N. Voros et al. (Eds.): ARC 2018, LNCS 10824, pp. 119–131, 2018.
https://doi.org/10.1007/978-3-319-78890-6_10

signal processing and automotive that are embedded in nature [9]. Acceleration of scientific code on CGRA with high precision floating point arithmetic is yet to be fully explored. There exist very few attempts in the literature where computations like double precision General Matrix Multiplication (dgemm), QR factorization (dgeqrf), and LU factorization (dgetrf) are accelerated on CGRAs. Scientific application like Kalman Filter (KF) is rich in these matrix operations and has wide range of applications from trajectory optimization, and navigation to econometric [1]. Here we see an opportunity to accelerate KF using a highly efficient Dense Linear Algebra (DLA) accelerator. Since, KF can be transformed as a series of matrix operations, we use Modified Faddeeva Algorithm (MFA) as a basic building block for our realization of KF [15]. We take an approach of algorithm-architecture co-design where we identify several macro operations in the routines required for MFA and realize them on a specialized data path that leads to significant performance improvement in KF. Major Contributions in this paper are as follows:

- We adopt a library based approach and realize KF using MFA where MFA is realized using dgemm, dgetrf, and dgeqrf routines. The first realization is capable of achieving 30% of the theoretical peak performance of the underlying platform. We call this implementation as a base realization of KF
- A set of macro operations identified in dgemm, dgeqrf, and dgetrf are realized on a tightly coupled Reconfigurable Data-path (RDP) and the implementation results in 66% of performance improvement over base realization at minimal area and energy cost. We call this implementation as hardware optimized KF
- A scheduling optimization is presented for KF that results in 30% performance improvement over the hardware optimized realization and 116% improvement over base realization. We also show that the final implementation is able to achieve 4-105x performance improvement over several academic and commercial realizations of KF. We call this implementation as software optimized KF
- Parallel realization of KF is presented on REDEFINE and it is shown that REDEFINE scales well with increasing size of co-variance matrix.

For our experiments, we use Processing Element (PE) design presented in [9]. We optimize Floating Point Unit (FPU) design presented in [13] with recommendations presented in [12] for optimum Instructions Per Cycle (IPC). The paper is organized as follows: In Sect. 2, MFA, KF and REDEFINE are discussed. In Sect. 3, we present case studies on multicore and General Purpose Graphics Processing Unit (GPGPU) and show that the performance attained on these platforms even with highly tuned software packages is not satisfactory. KF implementation is discussed in Sect. 4. Parallel realization of KF and results are discussed in Sect. 5. We conclude our work in Sect. 6.

2   Background and Related Work

In this section, we first discuss MFA and KF briefly and show connection between MFA and KF. In Sect. 2.1, we introduce REDEFINE and discuss unique features of REDEFINE CGRA. We focus on some of the recent realizations of KF in Sect. 2.2.

2.1   Background

Modified Faddeeva Algorithm and Kalman Filter. MFA was originally presented in [15] that is an enhancement over the original Faddeeva algorithm. QR factorization was incorporated instead of Gaussian elimination process to improve stability of Faddeeva algorithm. For rectangular matrices $A_{m \times n}, B_{m \times p}, C_{k \times n}$, and $D_{k \times p}$, compound matrix is shown in Eq. 1.

$$M = \begin{bmatrix} A & B \\ -C & D \end{bmatrix} \tag{1}$$

Applying MFA on compound matrix M incorporates following two steps.

- **Step 1:** Upper triangularization of matrix A using QR factorization and update matrix B
- **Step 2:** Annihilate matrix C using diagonal elements of upper traingularized matrix A.

At the end of an MFA operation, the matrix D is of the form $D + CA^{-1}B$ that is also known as the Schur complement. Versatility of MFA is described in Fig. 1(a) where it is shown that based on different initial input matrices, several operations like matrix multiplication, matrix addition, and linear system solution can be obtained. Due to versatility in MFA, it is desirable to write applications in terms of matrix operation that can translate into series of calls of MFA. One such application is KF. A simplistic multi-dimensional KF is shown in the Fig. 1(b).

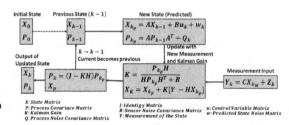

(a) Several Operations that can be Performed Using MFA based on Different Initial Values of Matrices A, B, C, and D

(b) Multi Dimensional Kalman Filter

Fig. 1. MFA and KF

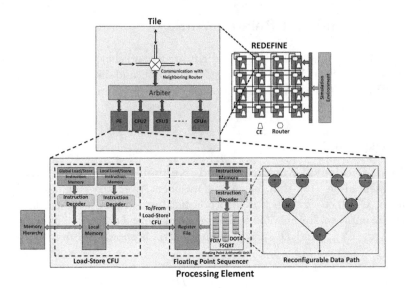

Fig. 2. REDEFINE CGRA and design of PE (with RDP)

An iteration of KF requires complex matrix operations ranging from matrix multiplication to computation of numerical stable matrix inverse. One such classical GR based numerical stable approach is presented in [20]. From Fig. 1(b), matrix inverse being the most complex operation in KF, and computation of inverse using QR factorization being a numerical stable process, proposed library based approach is the most suitable for such applications.

REDEFINE. REDEFINE is a CGRA that can be domain customized for variety application domains [10]. In REDEFINE, several Tiles are connected through a packet switched Network-on-Chip (NoC) [10,11]. Each Tile consists of a Compute Element (CE) and a Router. CEs in REDEFINE can be enhanced with a Custom Function Units (CFUs) that can be tailored for a desired application domain. For our implementation, we use a Processing Element (PE) that is highly customized for Dense Linear Algebra (DLA) computations [9]. REDEFINE micro-architecture along with PE is shown in Fig. 2. It can be observed in the Fig. 2 that the PE consists of a RDP as an arithmetic unit that can be reconfigured at run-time through instruction to realize identified macro operations in the Directed Acyclic Graph (DAG) of DLA computations. It is well established in the literature that such an approach yields significant improvement in energy efficiency in the overall system [3].

2.2 Related Work

Due to wide range of applications of KF, there are several implementations of KF in the literature. We present brief summary of some of the recent realizations of KF. Early realizations of KF are based on systolic array since systolic arrays are highly suitable for matrix computations [4]. One of the recent realization of KF presented in [22] is targeted for advanced driver assistance system. The implementation presented in [22] does not focus on the acceleration of matrix operations encountered in KF and hence leaves opportunities for further performance improvements. Similarly, KF implementation presented in [2] focuses on parallel implementation using OpenMP and FPGA based implementation presented in [18] focuses on optimizations in arithmetic operations in KF for performance improvement. MFA based KF presented in [7] focuses on denoising of images with additive white Gaussian noise. Although the work presented in [7] realized KF using MFA, the implementation is not scalable and can operate only on the images of size 512×512. Furthermore, focus of the work presented in [7] is not on acceleration of KF through acceleration of matrix operations in MFA. In this paper, we focus on energy efficient fast realization of KF by accelerating gemm, QR factorization, and LU factorization.

3 Case Studies

In this section we present case studies on the operation encountered in MFA. Since, we implement KF using double precision FPU, we present case studies on dgeqrf, dgetrf, and dgemm. We discuss performance of dgemm, dgeqrf, and dgetrf in highly optimized software libraries like Parallel Linear Algebra Software for Multicore Architectures (PLASMA) and Matrix Algebra for GPU and Multicore Architectures (MAGMA).

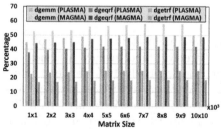
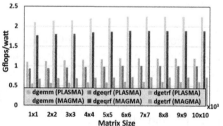

(a) Percentage of Theoretical Peak Performance Attained in dgemm, dgeqrf, and dgetrf in Intel Core i7 (PLASMA) and Nvidia Tesla C2075 (MAGMA)

(b) Performance Attained in terms of Gflops/watt in dgemm, dgeqrf, and dgetrf in Intel Core i7 (PLASMA) and Nvidia Tesla C2075 (MAGMA)

Fig. 3. Performance of dgemm, dgeqrf, dgetrf, and KF in multicore and GPGPU

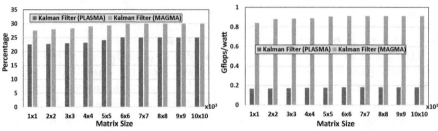

(a) Percentage of Theoretical Peak Performance Attained in KF in Intel Core i7 (PLASMA) and Nvidia Tesla C2075 (MAGMA)

(b) Performance Attained in terms of Gflops/watt in KF in Intel Core i7 (PLASMA) and Nvidia Tesla C2075 (MAGMA)

Fig. 4. Performance of dgemm, dgeqrf, dgetrf, and KF in multicore and GPGPU

3.1   dgeqrf

Routine dgeqrf computes QR factorization of an input matrix A and returns uppter triangular matrix R and Q where $QQ^T = Q^TQ = I$. Householder Transform (HT) based QR factorization routine in Linear Algebra Package (LAPACK) is shown in Algorithm 1.

Input: Matrix $A_{m \times n}$
Output: Upper triangle matrix R
for $i = 1$ *to* n **do**
    Compute Householder vector v
    Compute P where $P = I - 2vv^T$
    Update trailing matrix using *dgemv*
end

Algorithm 1. dgeqr2 in LAPACK (dgemv is double precision matrix-vector multiplication)

In Algorithm 1, majority of the computations are performed in terms of double precision matrix vector multiplication (dgemv). Since dgemv is a memory bound operation, the realization of dgeqr2 yields hardly 10% of the theoretical peak performance in GPGPU and 2–3% of the theoretical peak performance in multicores. In the dense linear algebra software packages like LAPACK, PLASMA, and MGAMA, the software routines are tiled/blocked and written in terms of dgemm for efficient exploitation of memory hierarchy of the underlying platform where dgemm is compute bound operation [19]. dgeqrf routine that uses dgeqr2 and dgemm as subroutines is shown in Algorithm 2.

Input: Matrix $A_{m \times n}$
Output: Upper triangle matrix R
for $i = 1$ *to* n **do**
    Compute Householder vectors for block column $m \times k$
    Compute P where P is multiplication of Householder vectors
    Update trailing matrix using *dgemm*
end

Algorithm 2. dgeqrf in LAPACK

3.2 dgetrf

dgetrf routine computes LU factorization of a general $m \times n$ matrix, so $A = PLU$ where L is unit lower triangular, U is upper triangular matrix, and P is permutation matrix. dgetrf2 routine is shown in Algorithm 3.

Input: Matrix $A_{m \times n}$
Output: Unit lower triangular matrix L and upper triangular matrix U
for $i = 1$ *to* n **do**
    Find pivot
    Interchange pivot rows
    Compute elements of L matrix
    Update the trailing matrix using dgemv
end

Algorithm 3. dgetrf2 in LAPACK

Input: Matrix $A_{m \times n}$
Output: Unit lower triangular matrix L and upper triangular matrix U
for $i = 1$ *to* n **do**
    Find pivot
    Interchange pivot rows
    Compute elements of L matrix
    Update the trailing matrix using dgemm
end

Algorithm 4. dgetrf in LAPACK

A similar approach to QR factorization is adopted for LU factorization in LAPACK where a blocked routine shown in the Algorithm 4 is developed to exploit the memory hierarchy of cache based platforms. For our implementation, since we do not require pivoting, we remove pivoting related routine from dgetrf2 and adopt the routine to support realization of MFA.

3.3 dgemm

Due to prevalent in the literature, we do not reproduce pseudo code of dgemm. Typically, dgemm is part of Level-3 Basic Linear Algebra Subprograms (BLAS) and used as a subroutine in the operations like LU and QR factorizations since dgemm is compute bound operation and theoretically dgemm is capable of attaining $O(n)$ computations to communication ratio for the matrices of size $n \times n$ [5].

3.4 Performance Evaluation of dgeqrf, dgetrf and dgemm on Multicore and GPGPU

We evaluate performance of dgeqrf, dgetrf, and dgemm on multicore and GPGPU. Performance in terms of percentage of theoretical peak performance in Intel Core i7 for dgeqrf, dgetrf, and dgemm is shown in Fig. 3(a). It can be observed in the Fig. 3(a) that in Intel Core i7, performance attained by dgeqrf is 42% (21 Gflops), performance attained by dgetrf is 25% (12 Gflops) and performance attained by dgemm is 50% (24 Gflops). Similarly, percentage of theoretical peak performance attained in GPGPU for dgeqrf is 48% (247.2 Gflops), for dgemm it is 58% (298 Gflops), and for dgetrf it is 20% (103 Gflops). We ensure to compile PLASMA and MAGMA with OpenBLAS [21]. Performance attained in terms of Gflops/watt ranges between 0.6 to 2.1 for GPGPU and 0.6 to 1.1 for multicore as shown in Fig. 3(b). It can be observed that the performance attained by dgeqrf is 84.2% of the performance attained by dgemm and performance attained by dgetrf is 50% of the performance attained by dgemm. This is mainly due to presence of non-parallelizable computations in dgeqrf and dgetrf that limits the performance considering Amdahl's law [6].

Similarly, for KF the performance attained in terms of percentage of theoretical peak performance is 25% for multicore and 30% for GPGPU as shown in Fig. 4(a). Performance attained in terms of Gflops/watt for KF is 0.15 in multicore and 0.9 in GPGPU. Based on our case studies in dgemm, dgeqrf, and dgetrf it can be inferred that the performance attained in the latest multicore and GPGPU is hardly 50–52% even for highly parallel operations like dgemm. Due to this shortcoming of multicore and GPGPU, we choose a customizable platform for our implementation presented in [9] that is capable of achieving up to 74% of the theoretical peak in dgemm [9,14].

4   Kalman Filter Realization in Processing Element

We present realization of KF on PE depicted in the Fig. 2. Three different implementations of KF are presented here: (1) base implementation of KF, (2) hardware optimized KF, and (3) software optimized KF.

4.1   Base Implementation of KF

In base implementation of KF, we realize matrix operation of in the MFA using scalar multiplier and adder in the PE. In base realization of KF, we are able to achieve up to 30% of the theoretical peak performance of the PE. Here, since we are using only one multiplier and adder for our implementation, the theoretical peak performance of the PE is 1.4 Gflops at 700 MHz.

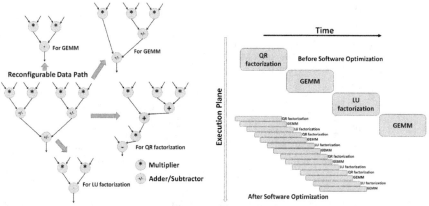

(a) Different Configurations of RDP Corresponding to Identified Macro Operations in dgemm, dgeqrf, and dgetrf

(b) Software Optimization in KF Resulting in Reduction in the Run-time (logical diagram)

Fig. 5. RDP configurations for KF and scheduling of different routines in KF

4.2   Hardware Optimized KF

In hardware optimized KF, we revisit the basic operations required to be performed in MFA like dgemm, dgeqrf, and dgetrf and identify several macro operations in these basic operations. We realize these macro operations in RDP depicted in the Fig. 2. Configurations of RDP corresponding to the identified macro operations in dgemm, dgeqrf and dgetrf are shown in Fig. 5(a). With these configurations, we achieve up to 50% of the theoretical peak of the PE where theoretical peak of the PE is 4.9 Gflops at 700 MHz. Here theoretical peak of the PE is increased since we are using RDP that consists of 4 multipliers and 3 adders.

We perform a software optimization in MFA by analysis of the DAG of MFA. We overlap dgeqrf, dgemm, and dgetrf routines as shown in Fig. 5(b). Optimization diagram shown in the Fig. 5(b) is logical flow of computations post software optimization. To overlap these routines, we identify pipeline stalls in the PE while execution and insert independent instructions while also maintaining operation correctness. Overlapping dgeqrf, dgemm, and dgetrf results in significant reduction in the run-time of MFA that directly translates to performance improvement in KF. After software optimization, we are able to attain 65% of the theoretical peak in PE which is 30% improvement. Performance improvement after each optimization is shown in Fig. 6. In the Fig. 6, we have also incorporated the performance attained in multicore and GPGPU.

It can be observed in the Fig. 6 that the performance of KF in multicore and GPGPU is hardly 20–30% of the theoretical peak of these platforms, while we achieve up to 65% of the theoretical peak of PE in KF which is 2.15x higher.

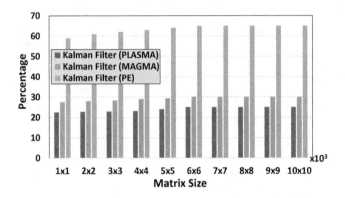

Fig. 6. Performance of KF in PE, multicore, and GPGPU

5   Parallel Realization and Results

For parallel realization of KF, we use three different configurations of REDE-
FINE. Two configurations are shown in Fig. 7. In configuration 1 we use 2×2
Tile array, in configuration 2 we use 3×3 Tile array, and in configuration 3, we
use 4×4 Tile array. In our simulations, for configuration 1 and configuration 2,
we use last column of the Tile array as a memory where we attach memories as
a PE.

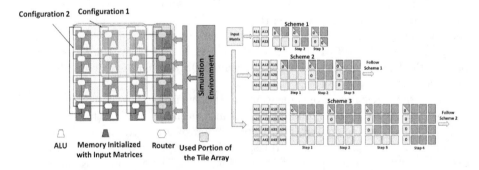

Fig. 7. Different configurations of REDEFINE for KF realization and scheduling

In configuration 3, we use entire Tile array for computations and hence we
attach another memory PE to the Router along side the compute PE. Memory
PE is divided into to segments and the second half of the segment in memory PE
acts as a global memory that is accessible by all other Tiles while the first half of
the memory segment is private to the compute PE that is used for computations
on local data. Typically, we have 256 K bytes of memory per Tile and compute PE
consists of 256 registers of width 64 bits. Scheduling technique for REDEFINE

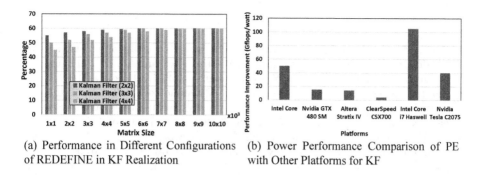

(a) Performance in Different Configurations   (b) Power Performance Comparison of PE
of REDEFINE in KF Realization   with Other Platforms for KF

Fig. 8. RDP configurations for KF and scheduling of different routines in KF

is shown in the right side of the Fig. 7. We use a technique where we divide input
matrix into $k \times k$ blocks where k is size of row/column of the Tile array. These
blocks are further divided into the sub-blocks where size of the sub-blocks depend
on the number of local registers available and size of the local memory available
to a PE. Blocks of the matrices are loaded and computation is performed and the
result is stored to the global memory. Percentage of theoretical peak performance
attained for each configuration is shown in Fig. 8(a). It can be observed in the
Fig. 8(a) that the performance attained for each configuration saturates at 60%
of the theoretical peak performance which is 2x higher than the performance
attained in multicore and GPGPU.

We evaluate power performance of PE based on technique presented in [10].
We compare PE with other platform for KF as shown in Fig. 8(b). It can be
observed that the PE is capable of achieving 4–105x higher performance improvement over platforms like ClearSpeed CSX700, Intel Core i7, and Nvidia GPGPU.

6   Conclusion

In this paper, we presented efficient realization of KF. We used versatile MFA
as a tool for efficient realization of KF. Based on the case studies presented on
dgemm, dgetrf, and dgeqrf, it was identified that the performance of these operations on multiore and GPGPU is not satisfactory even with hightly optimized
software packages like PLASMA and MAGMA. It was also shown that the performance attained in KF on multicore and GPGPU is 20–30% of the theoretical
peak performance of underlying platform. To accelerate KF on customizable
platform like REDEFINE, we identify macro operations in the routines of MFA
and realized them on RDP. Our approach resulted in 67% improvement in the
performance of KF. A software tuning in MFA was also presented that resulted
in 30% performance improvement over the hardware optimized KF. Overall, our
approach of algorithm-architecture co-design resulted in 116% of performance
improvement over the base realization of KF. In terms of Gflops/watt, KF is
2-105x better than multicore and GPGPU platforms.

References

1. Baluni, A., Merchant, F., Nandy, S.K., Balakrishnan, S.: A fully pipelined modular multiple precision floating point multiplier with vector support. In: 2011 International Symposium on Electronic System Design, pp. 45–50, December 2011
2. Cerati, G., Elmer, P., Lantz, S., MacNeill, I., McDermott, K., Riley, D., Tadel, M., Wittich, P., Würthwein, F., Yagil, A.: Traditional tracking with kalman filter on parallel architectures. J. Phys.: Conf. Ser. **608**(1), 012057 (2015)
3. Das, S., Madhu, K.T., Madhu, K., Krishna, M., Sivanandan, N., Merchant, F., Natarajan, S., Biswas, I., Pulli, A., Nandy, S.K., Narayan, R.: A framework for post-silicon realization of arbitrary instruction extensions on reconfigurable datapaths. J. Syst. Archit. - Embed. Syst. Des. **60**(7), 592–614 (2014)
4. Gentleman, W.M., Kung, H.T.: Matrix triangularization by systolic arrays. In: SPIE Proceedings, vol. 298, pp. 19–26 (1982)
5. Higham, N.J.: Exploiting fast matrix multiplication within the level 3 BLAS. ACM Trans. Math. Softw. **16**(4), 352–368 (1990)
6. Hill, M.D., Marty, M.R.: Amdahl's law in the multicore era. Computer **41**(7), 33–38 (2008)
7. Johnson, B., Thomas, N., Rani, J.S.: An FPGA based high throughput discrete Kalman filter architecture for real-time image denoising. In: 2017 30th International Conference on VLSI Design and 2017 16th International Conference on Embedded Systems (VLSID), January 2017
8. Mahadurkar, M., Merchant, F., Maity, A., Vatwani, K., Munje, I., Gopalan, N., Nandy, S.K., Narayan, R.: Co-exploration of NLA kernels and specification of compute elements in distributed memory CGRAs. In: XIVth International Conference on Embedded Computer Systems: Architectures, Modeling, and Simulation, SAMOS 2014, Agios Konstantinos, Samos, Greece, 14–17 July 2014, pp. 225–232 (2014)
9. Merchant, F., Maity, A., Mahadurkar, M., Vatwani, K., Munje, I., Krishna, M., Nalesh, S., Gopalan, N., Raha, S., Nandy, S.K., Narayan, R.: Micro-architectural enhancements in distributed memory CGRAs for LU and QR factorizations. In: 2015 28th International Conference on VLSI Design (VLSID), pp. 153–158, January 2015
10. Merchant, F.A., Vatwani, T., Chattopadhyay, A., Raha, S., Nandy, S.K., Narayan, R.: Efficient realization of householder transform through algorithm-architecture co-design for acceleration of QR factorization. IEEE Trans. Parallel Distrib. Syst. **PP**(99), 1 (2018)
11. Merchant, F., Chattopadhyay, A., Garga, G., Nandy, S.K., Narayan, R., Gopalan, N.: Efficient QR decomposition using low complexity column-wise givens rotation (CGR). In: 2014 27th International Conference on VLSI Design and 2014 13th International Conference on Embedded Systems, Mumbai, India, 5–9 January 2014, pp. 258–263 (2014)
12. Merchant, F., Chattopadhyay, A., Raha, S., Nandy, S.K., Narayan, R.: Accelerating BLAS and LAPACK via efficient floating point architecture design. Parallel Process. Lett. **27**(3–4), 1–17 (2017)
13. Merchant, F., Choudhary, N., Nandy, S.K., Narayan, R.: Efficient realization of table look-up based double precision floating point arithmetic. In: 29th International Conference on VLSI Design and 15th International Conference on Embedded Systems, VLSID 2016, Kolkata, India, 4–8 January 2016, pp. 415–420 (2016)

14. Merchant, F., Vatwani, T., Chattopadhyay, A., Raha, S., Nandy, S.K., Narayan, R.: Achieving efficient QR factorization by algorithm-architecture co-design of house-holder transformation. In: 29th International Conference on VLSI Design and 15th International Conference on Embedded Systems, VLSID 2016, Kolkata, India, 4–8 January 2016, pp. 98–103 (2016)
15. Nash, J.G., Hansen, S.: Modified Faddeeva algorithm for concurrent execution of linear algebraic operations. IEEE Trans. Comput. **37**(2), 129–137 (1988)
16. Rákossy, Z.E., Merchant, F., Acosta Aponte, A., Nandy, S.K., Chattopadhyay, A.: Efficient and scalable CGRA-based implementation of column-wise givens rotation. In: ASAP, pp. 188–189 (2014)
17. Rákossy, Z.E., Merchant, F., Acosta Aponte, A., Nandy, S.K., Chattopadhyay, A.: Scalable and energy-efficient reconfigurable accelerator for column-wise givens rotation. In: 22nd International Conference on Very Large Scale Integration, VLSI-SoC, Playa del Carmen, Mexico, 6–8 October 2014, pp. 1–6 (2014)
18. Sandhu, F., Selamat, H., Alavi, S.E., Behtaji Siahkal Mahalleh, V.: FPGA-based implementation of kalman filter for real-time estimation of tire velocity and accel-eration. IEEE Sens. J. **17**(17), 5749–5758 (2017)
19. Smith, B.J.: R package magma: matrix algebra on GPU and multicore architec-tures, version 0.2.2, 3 September 2010. http://cran.r-project.org/package=magma
20. Thornton, C.L., Bierman, G.J.: Givens transformation techniques for kalman fil-tering. Acta Astronaut. **4**(7–8), 847–863 (1977)
21. Wang, Q., Zhang, X., Zhang, Y., Yi, Q.: AUGEM: automatically generate high performance dense linear algebra kernels on x86 CPUs. In: Proceedings of the International Conference on High Performance Computing, Networking, Storage and Analysis, SC 2013, pp. 25:1–25:12. ACM, New York (2013)
22. Zhong, G., Niar, S., Prakash, A., Mitra, T.: Design of multiple-target tracking system on heterogeneous system-on-chip devices. IEEE Trans. Veh. Technol. **65**(6), 4802–4812 (2016)

FPGA-Based Memory Efficient Shift-And Algorithm for Regular Expression Matching

Junsik Kim and Jaehyun Park$^{(\boxtimes)}$ ⓘD

Department of Information and Communication Engineering,
Inha University, Incheon 22212, Korea
jskim@emcl.org, jhyun@inha.ac.kr

Abstract. This paper proposes a FPGA-based reconfigurable regular expression matching engine for a network intrusion detection system (NIDS). In the proposed system, the Shift-And algorithm was used to process a regular expression matching. To improve the memory efficiency of the algorithm especially used for the Non-deterministic Finite Automata (NFA) with large number of states, this paper proposes a parallel matching module with a counter module and a priority encoder. In addition, in the proposed system, a large NFA can be divided into several NFAs and process separately by parallel matching module. The proposed architecture with 265 regular expression matching modules is implemented using Xilinx Zynq-7030 FPGA, that shows 1.066 Gbps throughput and uses 54.81% LUT.

1 Introduction

Recently, the importance of network security has increased as the damage caused by DDos attack or Ransomware increases. To reduce this network security risk, Network Intrusion Detection System (NIDS) that protects the computer system by analyzing network packets is widely adopted. NIDS distinguishes the malicious packets among the received network packets based on the predefined rules that is usually written in Perl-compatible regular expression. Snort [1] and Suricata [2] are the most widely used intrusion detection softwares that provide user-defined detection rules in Perl-compatible regular expression for deep packet inspection. In spite of its flexibility and expandability, the software-based NIDS has some disadvantages. First of all, since Snort is not an intrusion prevention system but a pure intrusion detection system, NIDS software itself can be infected and altered by other virus-software [3]. In that case, normal intrusion detection function may be stumbled. Secondly, since the network pattern matching is performed by software, the processing speed depends on the performance of the CPU core. This means the detection speed may be slower as the complexity of the rules grows.

To overcome these shortcomings of software-based NIDS, several hardware-based NIDS systems that are normally designed using high performance FPGA

© Springer International Publishing AG, part of Springer Nature 2018
N. Voros et al. (Eds.): ARC 2018, LNCS 10824, pp. 132–141, 2018.
https://doi.org/10.1007/978-3-319-78890-6_11

have been proposed during the past decades. Clark proposed a parallel decoder to process multiple input characters [4]. Sidhu suggested a way to convert regular expressions to Non-deterministic Finite Automata (NFA) and binary logic expression [5]. Yamagaki proposed an efficient character set comparison logic and a NFA configuration algorithm for parallel character processing [6]. However, these architecture should modify the internal logic when the regular expressions changes, and in turn, the logic blocks should be reconfigured.

Another approach to design a FPGA-based NIDS is using the memory-based pattern matching scheme. To implement an ordinary Deterministic Finite Automata (DFA) to search ASCII strings represented in regular expression with N possible states, $256 \times N$ state transition tables are necessary in all memory, which is very inefficient in memory usage and almost impossible to handle a large regular expression in a practical NIDS system. To improve the efficiency in memory usage, Hieu proposed a structure that combines redundant states into one [7] and Freire proposed a method using Huffman coding [8]. Huffman coding analyzes user-defined rules and assigns short codes to frequently occurred characters to increase overall memory efficiency. Also, Harwayne-Gidansky and Meghana proposed NIDS using the data structure of the counting bloom filter [9,10]. The counting bloom filter is suitable for the black or white list method because there is no false error but the probability of positive error occurs. The string matching algorithm using hash function is also proposed. [11–14]. Bando proposed a way to avoid overlapping by specifying a character set as a symbol set in range hash, and to transmit only the packets included in the range to the main module, thereby reducing the overall throughput [11]. Lee proposed a structure that dynamically reconfigure regular expressions [15]. However, since it uses Xilinx's shift register LUT (SRL), it has limitations that can not be applied to the other FPGA architecture. Divyasree proposed a structure based on Shift-OR algorithm and bit-map with Glushkov-NFA that showed an outstanding throughput more than 4 Gbps [16]. Cronin proposed a structure using countable Bit-Parallel Glushkov-NFA (BPG-NFA)[17].

Meanwhile, the Extended Shift-And algorithm is useful for dynamically reconfiguring patterns such as DNA and text searching efficiently because with which the NFA can be updated at once with bit-parallelism [18]. To achieve high throughput in the NIDS system, Kaneta implemented the Extended Shift-And algorithm using an FPGA [19]. However, in their architecture, the maximum number of states depends on the length of the register, so it is hard to apply a regular expression having many states. In addition, the number of states in the NFA can quickly increase due to constrained repetition. In practical NIDS system, thousands of repetition expression of the detection rules are easily used, which results in a very large number of states. Therefore, in this paper, a memory efficient architecture that can be applied to the Extended Shift-And algorithm is proposed to solve this problem.

This paper consists of five sections. Section 2 introduces the extended regular expression and the Shift-And algorithm using Bit-parallelism. In Sect. 3, the

overall system design and implementation details are described. Section 4 shows
the implementation results and Sect. 5 concludes this paper.

2   Pattern Matching Method

2.1   Background

The regular expressions are often used to specify a set of strings to match multiple strings in a single pattern. They are primarily used for character searches,
DNA pattern detection, and deep packet inspection in NIDS software. In this
paper, the regular expression is used to define the packet detection rules used
by FPGA-based NIDS engine. Table 1 summarized the regular expressions supported by the proposed scheme.

Table 1. Regular expression description

Symbol	Description
.	Matches any one character
[,]	It is the same as selecting one of several characters and using multiple |. A range can be specified with the "-" symbol
(,)	Multiple expressions can be bound together
*	Zero or more characters
{m, n}	m times or more, and n times or less
?	0 or 1 occurrence
+	More than once
|	Including one of the two

To apply the Extended Shift-And algorithm, regular expressions should be
converted to Non-deterministic Finite Automata defined like Eq. (1).

$$A = (Q, \Sigma, I, F, \Delta) \tag{1}$$

where Q is the entire state set, Σ is all characters in the regular expression, I is
the start state, F is the end state, and Δ is the transition function. Transition
function Δ determines the next state. When a new character α is received to
the NFA, the next state is determined according to the Eq. (2). D is a specific
function that determines the next state depending on the input character and
the current state.

$$\Delta = \{(q, \alpha, q'), q \in Q, \alpha \in \Sigma \cup \{\epsilon\}, q' \in D(q, \alpha)\} \tag{2}$$

Thompson [20] and Glushkov [21] NFA can move from one state to several states,
so multiple states can be active at the same time. However, to apply the Shift-
And algorithm, the NFA should have a property of moving only in one direction.
Figure 1 shows the NFA with that property.

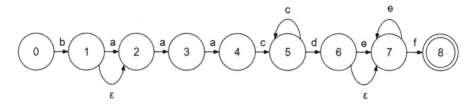

Fig. 1. NFA of $R = ba\{2,3\}c + de*f$

2.2   Shift-And Algorithm

In this paper, the Extended Shift-And algorithm is used to process the regular expression [18]. Since the active state is expressed in bits, state transitions can be performed through a shift operation. Thus, if the register length is w bits, w consecutive strings can be detected.

The NFA of the algorithm is linear and the state transition proceeds step by step. When B has the transition conditions of all characters Σ in table form, the input character α is used as the address of the table. If the current state of the NFA is D, and a new character arrives, the next state D_n is updated by Eq. (3).

$$D_n \leftarrow ((D << 1) \mid 0^{m-1}1)\&B[\alpha] \tag{3}$$

In Eq. (3), the current state D is compared with $B(q, \alpha)$ after the shift operation to determine the next state. Pattern matching is determined whether $D'\&10^{m-1} \neq 0$ or not. It is determined that pattern matching has occurred. Since Eq. (3) is an exact pattern matching, it can not be applied to extended regular expressions. Therefore, R, F, I, and A are added for extend regular expression and the next state D_n is calculated by the following equations.

$$D' \leftarrow (((D << 1) \mid 0^{m-1}1)\&B[\alpha]) \mid (D\&R[\alpha]) \tag{4}$$

$$D_f \leftarrow D' \mid F \tag{5}$$

$$D_n \leftarrow D' \mid (A\&((\sim (D_f - I)) \oplus D_f)) \tag{6}$$

Equation (4) is used for exact pattern matching and iteration expressions. Equations (5) and (6) are used where ϵ can occur, such as $?, +, \{m, n\}$. R has a table of repetition conditions for all characters Σ, and F, I, and A are used to indicate the location of ϵ occurrence in that regular expression. However, since $R = \alpha\{m, n\}$ is replaced by $R = \alpha?^{n-m}\alpha^m, (n \geq m)$, the number of states increases.

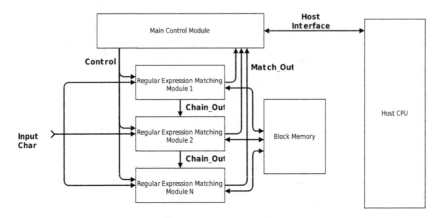

Fig. 2. Overall system block diagram

3   Countable Pattern Matching Structure

3.1   Overall System Structure

Figure 2 shows the overall system architecture with parallel Regular Expression Matching Module (REMM). A host interface is required to exchange the detection rules written in regular expression generated by the host CPU. The main control module controls each REMM by generating a module enable signals and a chain enable signals. REMM has a 32-bits length, so it can represent a regular expression with maximum 32 NFA states. If there are more states than this limitation, the remaining states are processed by the next REMM module with indicating by the `Chain_Out` signal. For example, if the number of NFA states of any regular expression is 120, the number of modules N required is $(120 >> 5) + 1 = 4$, and the last module would use only 24 bits ($120 \bmod 32$). Therefore, a host needs to create a transition table for multi-matching in preprocessing for modules with two regular expressions overlapping. Each REMM reads the bit patterns stored in the FPGA's block memory and performs comparison operations. The matching signal of each module is encoded in the main control module and transmitted to the host. The main control module performs register and memory update of REMM and controls the connection state of each module through the `Chain_Enable` signal.

3.2   Regular Expression Matching Module

Figure 3 shows the structure of the regular expression matching module that is similar to the original form of the Extended Shift-And structure proposed in [19]. To solve unrolling issue, signals for counter module and daisy chain signals were added. `Chain_In` is the signal from the previous module and `Chain_Out` is the signal to activate the next module. `En` and `Chain_En` signals of the main control module control activation of the next module. The `Match_Out` signal

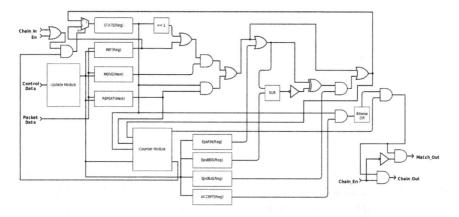

Fig. 3. Regular expression matching module

passes the pattern matching result to the main control module. The STATE, MOVE and REPEAT in Fig. 3 correspond to D, B and R in Eq. (1), respectively. EpsBEG, EpsEND, and EpsBLK represent I, F and A, respectively, as well. MOVE and REPEAT are block memory and use the input packet as an address. Therefore, when a new packet arrives, the operation is performed in the combinational circuit within one clock. And the REMM includes one counter module for supporting constrained repetition expression. The update module updates the contents of the block memory when the main control module receives a new regular expression from the host.

3.3 Counter Module

Figure 4 shows the structure of the counter module. The counter module has a Constrained-repetition Register(CR) indicating the position of the constrained

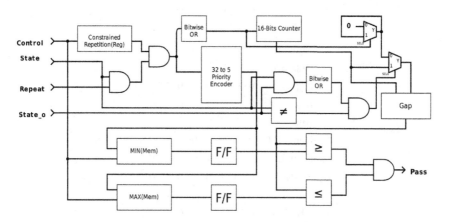

Fig. 4. Counter module

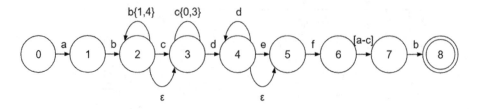

Fig. 5. NFA of $R = ab\{1, 4\}\, c\{0, 3\}\, d + e?f\,[a - c]\, b$

repetition expression and a memory storing a range of counts. If the current state of the NFA indicates a repetition expression, the CR bit is activated to 1. Then, the current NFA state is used as an input and the counter is incremented by bitwise-OR operation after performing the &-operation with the CR and REPEAT registers. And &-operation result is used as the input of 32 to 5 priority encoder to find the most significant bit position among the activated bits and read the range value of the corresponding position from the memory. As a result, two clocks are consumed in the memory operation and the counter comparison operation. If the state of the constrained repetition is consecutive, the counter module is one, so it continues to operate without initialization. For

Table 2. Example of transition table: $R = ab\{1, 4\}\, c\{0, 3\}\, d + e?f\,[a - c]\, b$

Position	1	2	3	4	5	6	7	8
Init	1	0	0	0	0	0	0	0
Accept	0	0	0	0	0	0	0	1
Move[a]	1	0	0	0	0	0	1	0
Move[b]	0	1	0	0	0	0	1	0
Move[c]	0	0	1	0	0	0	1	0
Move[d]	0	0	0	1	0	0	0	0
Move[e]	0	0	0	0	1	0	0	0
Move[f]	0	0	0	0	0	1	0	0
Repeat[a]	0	0	0	0	0	0	0	0
Repeat[b]	0	1	0	0	0	0	0	0
Repeat[c]	0	0	1	0	0	0	0	0
Repeat[d]	0	0	0	1	0	0	0	0
Repeat[e]	0	0	0	0	0	0	0	0
Repeat[f]	0	0	0	0	0	0	0	0
EpsBEG	0	1	0	1	0	0	0	0
EpsEND	0	0	1	0	1	0	0	0
EpsBLK	0	0	1	0	1	0	0	0
CR	0	1	1	0	0	0	0	0

example, if a state transition occurs at the B in $R = A\{1, 3\} B \{2, 4\} C$, the count value of A is temporarily stored in register. Then, the difference value between two states is used to determine whether the condition of B is satisfied. In the figure, a GAP block performs the corresponding operation. Due to this operation, table construction conditions are added as follows.

- The bit in the REPEAT register must be activated as well as the constrained repetition.
- If m is zero in $\{m, n\}$, the corresponding bit in EpsBEG, EpsEND, and EpsBLK must be activated.

Table 2 shows example transitions table when the regular expression is $R = ab\{1, 4\} c\{0, 3\} d+e?f[a-c]b$. In the case of $R_1 = c\{0, 3\}$, the bit for ϵ processing is activated as $R_2 = e?$. Figure 5 is the NFA for Table 2.

4   Implementation Results

The proposed architecture was implemented to prove the concept. For implementation, Xilinx Vivado 2017.1 was used and target FPGA was Zynq-7030 SoC. The entire system uses 43080 LUTs, accounting for 54.81% of the total. Since MOVE and REPEAT each use 0.5 BRAM, one REMM uses one BRAM. The implemented prototype contains 265 REMMs because of the size of BRAM in Zynq-7030, 265 BRAMs. MAX and MIN of the counter module are composed of distributed RAM, so they consume LUTs. The implementation result shows that the proposed structure can compare 137 more regular expressions compare to the original extended Shift-And architecture proposed by Kaneta [19]. The maximum operating clock of the implementation prototype is 133.35 MHz and it can be applied to networks up to 1.066 Gbps.

5   Conclusion

This paper proposes a FPGA-based reconfigurable regular expression matching engine for a network intrusion detection system (NIDS). The proposed structure extends the existing Shift-And algorithm structure to solve the memory inefficiency caused by the constrained repetition. In the proposed system, the unrolled states are replaced to one state by adding a constrained repetition register and a priority encoder can detect activated state for count operation. In addition, in the proposed system, a large NFA can be divided into several NFAs and processed separately by parallel matching module. The proposed architecture with 265 regular expression matching modules is implemented using Xilinx Zynq-7030 FPGA, that shows 1.066 Gbps throughput and uses 54.81% LUT.

Acknowledgment. This work was supported by the Korea Institute of Energy Technology Evaluation and Planning (KETEP) and the Ministry of Trade, Industry & Energy (MOTIE) of the Republic of Korea (No. 20161510101820).

References

1. Cisco: Snort user manual, April 2017. http://www.snort.org. Accessed 1 July 2017
2. OISF: Suricata user guide (2016). http://www.suricata-ids.org. Accessed 1 July 2017
3. Kacha, C.C., Shevade, K.A., Raghuwanshi, K.S.: Improved Snort intrusion detection system using modified pattern matching technique. Int. J. Emerg. Technol. Adv. Eng. **3**(7), 81–88 (2013)
4. Clark, C.R., Schimmel, D.E.: Scalable pattern matching for high speed networks. In: 12th Annual IEEE Symposium on Field-Programmable Custom Computing Machines (FCCM), pp. 249–257, April 2004
5. Sidhu, R., Prasanna, V.K.: Fast regular expression matching using FPGAs. In: 9th Annual IEEE Symposium on Field-Programmable Custom Computing Machines (FCCM), pp. 227–238, March 2001
6. Yamagaki, N., Sidhu, R., Kamiya, S.: High-speed regular expression matching engine using multi-character NFA. In: 2008 International Conference on Field Programmable Logic and Applications, pp. 131–136, September 2008
7. Hieu, T.T., Tran, N.T.: A memory efficient FPGA-based pattern matching engine for stateful NIDS. In: Fifth International Conference on Ubiquitous and Future Networks (ICUFN), pp. 252–257, July 2013
8. Freire, E., Schnitman, L., Oliveira, W., Duarte, A.: Evaluation of the huffman encoding for memory optimization on hardware network intrusion detection. In: III Brazilian Symposium on Computing Systems Engineering, pp. 131–136, December 2013
9. Harwayne-Gidansky, J., Stefan, D., Dalal, I.: FPGA-based SOC for real-time network intrusion detection using counting bloom filters. In: IEEE Southeastcon 2009, pp. 452–458, March 2009
10. Meghana, V., Suresh, M., Sandhya, S., Aparna, R., Gururaj, C.: SoC implementation of network intrusion detection using counting bloom filter. In: 2016 IEEE International Conference on Recent Trends in Electronics, Information Communication Technology (RTEICT), pp. 1846–1850, May 2016
11. Bando, M., Artan, N.S., Wei, R., Guo, X., Chao, H.J.: Range hash for regular expression pre-filtering. In: ACM/IEEE Symposium on Architectures for Networking and Communications Systems (ANCS), pp. 1–12, October 2010
12. Kastil, J., Korenek, J.: Hardware accelerated pattern matching based on deterministic finite automata with perfect hashing. In: 13th IEEE Symposium on Design and Diagnostics of Electronic Circuits and Systems, pp. 149–152, April 2010
13. Thinh, T.N., Kittitornkun, S.: Massively parallel cuckoo pattern matching applied for NIDS/NIPS. In: 2010 Fifth IEEE International Symposium on Electronic Design, Test Applications, pp. 217–221, January 2010
14. Thinh, T.N., Hieu, T.T., Dung, V.Q., Kittitornkun, S.: A FPGA-based deep packet inspection engine for network intrusion detection system. In: 2012 9th International Conference on Electrical Engineering/Electronics, Computer, Telecommunications and Information Technology, pp. 1–4, May 2012
15. Lee, T.H.: Hardware architecture for high-performance regular expression matching. IEEE Trans. Comput. **58**(7), 984–993 (2009)
16. Divyasree, J., Rajashekar, H., Varghese, K.: Dynamically reconfigurable regular expression matching architecture. In: 2008 International Conference on Application-Specific Systems, Architectures and Processors, pp. 120–125, July 2008

17. Cronin, B., Wang, X.: Hardware acceleration of regular expression repetitions in deep packet inspection. IET Inf. Secur. **7**(4), 327–335 (2013)
18. Navarro, G., Raffinot, M.: Flexible Pattern Matching in Strings: Practical On-Line Search Algorithms for Texts and Biological Sequences. Cambridge University Press, Cambridge (2002)
19. Kaneta, Y., Yoshizawa, S., Minato, S., Arimura, H., Miyanaga, Y.: Dynamic reconfigurable bit-parallel architecture for large-scale regular expression matching. In: International Conference on Field-Programmable Technology, pp. 21–28, December 2010
20. Thompson, K.: Regular expression search algorithm. Commun. ACM **11**(6), 419–422 (1968)
21. Glushkov, V.M.: The abstract theory of automata. Russ. Math. Surv. **16**(5), 1–53 (1961)

Towards an Optimized Multi FPGA Architecture with STDM Network: A Preliminary Study

Kazuei Hironaka$^{(\boxtimes)}$, Ng. Anh Vu Doan, and Hideharu Amano

Department of Information and Computer Science, Keio University, 3-14-1 Hiyoshi,
Kohoku-ku, Yokohama, Kanagawa 223-8522, Japan
nyacom@am.ics.keio.ac.jp

Abstract. In this work, we propose a multi FPGA architecture with STDM network that aims to tackle compute-intensive applications such as neural networks training or pattern recognition in artificial intelligence while realizing high cost-performance and energy efficiency. To achieve this goal, optimizing different aspects of the system communication is a key challenge. In order to do this, a preliminary study on the application mapping for both the execution time and the number of slots for the STDM is carried out. An optimization based on a multi-criteria paradigm is implemented and the preliminary results show the possibility to optimize several parameters of the communication simultaneously alongside quantitative analyses of different architecture choices.

1 Introduction

Along with artificial intelligence (AI) technology generalization, energy efficient and scalable computing platform has drawn a certain attention. The FiC (Flow in Cloud) project [1] is aiming to realize a high cost-performance and energy efficient computing platforms to accelerate AI computing such as neural networks, collective computation, and pattern recognition.

The FiC architecture is a heterogeneous clustered computing platform which combines multiple FPGAs and GPUs with flexible and high-speed serial interconnect network. Figure 1 shows an example of a FiC platform prototype. It consists of multiple FPGAs, GPUs, and storage (memory) nodes. Every FPGA node can be used as a computational accelerator and as a communication switch to other nodes, acting like a hub on the modern Ethernet. The serial links use high-speed optical fibre to consider network scalability and low latency.

In this work, we consider a FiC platform prototype called *FiC-SW*. In this system, each FPGA can be used for computational purposes and communication switching with other FPGA boards. This design is based on the *Accelerator in Switch* (AiS) concept [2], where switching fabric and computing accelerator are tightly coupled on the same FPGA.

Unlike other multi FPGA systems, *FiC-SW* implements the STDM (Static Time-Division Multiplexing) technique to share the fabric communications

© Springer International Publishing AG, part of Springer Nature 2018
N. Voros et al. (Eds.): ARC 2018, LNCS 10824, pp. 142–150, 2018.
https://doi.org/10.1007/978-3-319-78890-6_12

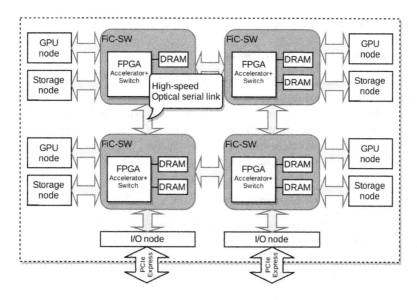

Fig. 1. Example of Flow-in-Cloud system with 4 FPGAs

resources between different FPGAs, as it is a commonly-used method with optical links and to avoid buses between all FPGAs. Since communication latency in
STDM is predictable, the execution time of an application for *FiC-SW* can be
easily computed without any complex data flow-control. Thanks to this characteristic, STDM adds support to the *FiC-SW* efficiency by making the switching
fabric simple, small, and fast.

However, since STDM shares the link bandwidth between multiple channels,
the communication between nodes can be limited. To achieve high application
performance on the *FiC-SW* system, optimizing among others the configuration
of the switches, the number of shared channels on the same link, and the network
topology is a key challenge to maximize the network usage and the application
performance.

In this work, we focus on how to allow such developments by presenting
a model that will allow to optimize and simulate the communication in the
FiC-SW platform. As a preliminary study, we tackle the application mapping
to optimize the number of shared channels and the execution time. This will
enable the possibility to fully configure the communication parameters within
the system as future developments.

This paper is organized as follows. First, we introduce the *FiC-SW* platform
and detail our model which will enable the optimization of the system communication. Then, we present preliminary results of the application mapping where a
multi-objective paradigm is used before concluding and discussing future works.

2 Related Work

2.1 Multi-board FPGA Systems

Most of recent multi-board FPGA systems embed standard buses or networks. For instance, the platforms proposed in [3–6] use a combination of PCIe, Ethernet, and Infiniband to ensure the communication, whereas Microsoft's Catapult [7] notably integrates an original 10 Gbps serial link. All of them are based on packet switching, and to the best of our knowledge, FiC is the first large scale multi-FPGA systems with circuit switching network using STDM.

2.2 STDM Network Optimization

In [8–11], several problems related to STDM network such as slots assignment, scheduling, routing, mapping, etc. have been studied. However, they all focus on network-on-chip systems, and as far as we know, developments considering multi FPGA platforms requirements have yet to be carried out.

3 FiC-SW Architecture

3.1 STDM Fabric

In the FiC-SW architecture implementation, STDM switches are implemented in the FPGA. Each switch is connected with a *lane* consisting of 9.9 Gbps serial I/O with 64b/66b coding. Each lane has a configurable number of slots for the multiplexing. Each four *lanes* connecting nodes is called a *link*. At a frequency of 100 MHz on the FPGA, 85-bit payload with ECC can be transmitted per *link* each clock cycle. Therefore, each *lane* has a bandwidth of 8.5 Gbps so a *link* has 34 Gbps of bandwidth in total. To make the switch simple and avoid complex flow control in the STDM communication, we use a single clock source for all STDM switches to ensure complete synchronization.

3.2 Communication with an STDM Network

STDM is a technique for time division multiplexing on a single communication line with several communications. In our implementation, STDM is realized as time slots on the individual lanes. In each slot, data from an input slot is associated to its destination slot by a routing table in the switch. The number of slots on a lane and the routing table on the switch are configurable before execution.

Figure 2 shows an example for slot communication on the STDM switch, which each lane containing 4 slots. In this switch implementation, each slot can buffer incoming data and transfer it to its destination on the next cycle. In this manner, it is possible to predict the data transfer latency as the sum of the number of network hops and the slot waiting time at every switch. Therefore, if several communications are using the same switch simultaneously, the required number of slots on the switch is increased.

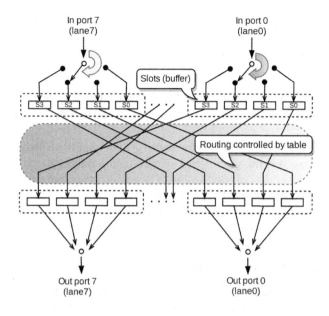

Fig. 2. STDM switch communication

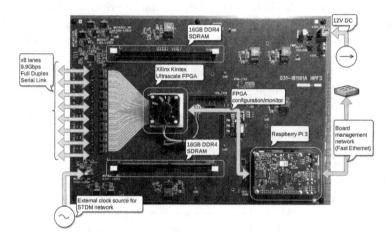

Fig. 3. FiC-SW1 prototype

3.3 FiC-SW1 Prototype

Figure 3 shows our prototype system FiC-SW1. The FiC-SW1 consists of a Xilinx Kintex Ultrasacle XCKU095 FPGA with two 16 GB DDR4 SDRAM for SDTM network switch and accelerator, and a Raspberry Pi 3 for board management (e.g., FPGA programming via the Ethernet, configuring the STDM switches, and monitoring the system). The FPGA provides 9.9 Gbps high speed serial links by Xilinx Aurora IP core. In the current status, the prototype is using ordinary copper wire for the physical communication, but optical links will ultimately be used in future. The synchronization clock for the STDM network is provided from an off-board clock generator.

4   Multi-objective Optimization for Application Mapping Considering Execution Time and Number of Slots

To achieve an efficient and high performance STDM implementation, it is necessary to optimize several parameters of the communication within the network. Therefore, after describing the *FiC-SW* architecture, we present as a first approach a multi-criteria based methodology to tackle the application mapping problem so that it is possible to consider simultaneously the execution time and the number of slots, and apply a multi-objective optimization (MOO).

4.1   The Multi-criteria Paradigm

Since our aim is to optimize several aspects of the communication in the *FiC-SW* platform, we choose to adopt a multi-criteria paradigm. In this approach, the first step is generally to identify the Pareto optimal frontier which is the set of the efficient solutions. This is based on the dominance principle which is defined as follows: a solution A dominates a solution B if A is at least as good as B for all criteria, and A is strictly better than B for at least one criterion [12].

The problem of optimizing the application mapping is a constrained quadratic assignment problem which is an NP-hard problem [13], and has a huge solution space. The optimal solution is unknown and an exhaustive search would take a prohibitive time. Also, we aim to also consider the number of slots for the STDM, which adds more complexity. For those reasons, we have few hopes to be able to develop an exact method and therefore choose to use an approximate approach with a multi-objective metaheuristic. Several MOO algorithms have been developed and interested readers can find more information about them in reference books such as [12].

Since our aim is to optimize sets of solutions, we choose to use a genetic algorithm (GA) for the MOO. In this work, we will use one of the most known approaches in EAs called NSGA-II (Non-dominated Sorting Genetic Algorithm-II) which is an extension of (the original) NSGA [14]. Let us note that the main objective of this work is on the work flow to optimize and simulate the communication in a multi FPGA system with STDM network, rather than pure algorithmic performance. Therefore, the choice of NSGA-II has essentially been made because of its flexibility and its wide-use as a prototyping algorithm [15].

4.2   Optimization Model

In this work, we aim to tackle the application mapping on a multi FPGA platform with STDM network, with consideration of the execution time and the maximum number of required slots.

As a first approach, we choose to represent the multi FPGA platform topology and the data flow graph (DFG) of an application as directed graphs. The general flowchart of NSGA-II can be summarized as follows:

1. an initial population is randomly generated;
2. the population to treat is selected depending on the Pareto rank principle;
3. the selected population generate offspring with crossover and mutation operations;
4. the new population to treat comes from the merging of the previous one and the generated offspring;
5. steps 2 to 4 are repeated until one or several stopping conditions are met (e.g., maximum number of iterations, unchanged population, duration, etc.).

A mapping is coded as a list specifying which node a task is assigned to (the tasks are identified by their index in the list). The mapping is then routed in the network using a shortest path approach and evaluated. The genetic operations are as follows: single-point crossover, and mutation where two tasks swap their node. The parameters are set following commonly-used values [16] (crossover and mutation probabilities respectively at 0.7 and 0.3).

5   Implementation and Evaluation

The optimization is performed using the Python programming language, with the DEAP framework [17] for the NSGA-II algorithm. The simulation have been performed on randomly-generated irregular DFG, which is assumed to be a CNN application running on multiple FPGAs. The DFG can be defined as $G = (T, E)$ where each task $T = \{t1, t2, \ldots, tn\}$ to be executed is a node in the graph, and $E = \{e_{ij}; i = 1, 2, \ldots, n; j = 1, 2, \ldots, n\}$ is a set of directed edges corresponding to the data flow dependency in the DFG. Each edge $e_{ij} \in E$ denotes a edge connecting the tasks ti and tj. If m CNN layers are considered, a random number of tasks is assigned to each layer L_k $(k = 1, 2, \ldots, m - 1)$ (e.g. $L_1 = \{t1\}, L_2 = \{t2, t3, t4\}, L_3 = \{t5, t6, \ldots, t8\}, \ldots$). The last level (L_m) can only contain one task, because it is assumed in our DFG model that it gathers and returns the results obtained from the previous layers, acting as the output layer. Therefore, each layer besides the input $(k = 1)$ and the output $(k = m)$ can be interpreted as a hidden layer of random size.

In this evaluation, each task in the DFG is assumed to require 1 cycle of execution time, and the DFG is mapped on mesh, torus, and dragonfly topologies. As a first approach, we consider a number of tasks equal to the number of nodes on the topologies, and carried out simulations for:

- 16 tasks on 4×4 mesh, 4×4 torus, 4 groups of 4 nodes dragonfly;
- 64 tasks on 8×8 mesh, 8×8 torus, 8 groups of 8 nodes dragonfly;
- 256 tasks on 16×16 mesh, 16×16 torus, 16 groups of 16 nodes dragonfly.

The results are shown in Table 1. These values are the non-dominated solutions provided by five independent simulations.

Table 1. Simulation results

Topology	Evaluation (execution time, number of slots)		
	16 tasks	64 tasks	256 tasks
Mesh	(13, 8)	(128, 5)	(3759, 18)
			(4024, 15)
			(3793, 14)
			(4012, 13)
			(4110, 12)
Torus	(11, 8)	(86, 5)	(2176, 10)
			(2177, 9)
			(2297, 8)
Dragonfly	(10, 8)	(57, 5)	(415, 5)

As we can observe, the results are rather similar for all mesh, torus, and dragonfly topologies for a low number of tasks (16). However, for a larger number of tasks (64 and 256), torus is better than mesh, but both are outperformed by dragonfly, which confirms its high scalability property. Besides, it is possible to quantify the comparison between different choices. These preliminary results show that with the proposed model, it is possible to optimize the application mapping for both the execution time and the number of slots, and to compare different topologies.

6   Conclusion and Future Works

In this work, we have introduced a multi FPGA architecture with STDM network, *FiC-SW*, whose aim is to accelerate computate-intensive applications such as the ones found in AI, while realizing high cost-performance and energy efficiency. In such platforms, optimizing the communication is a key challenge to achieve high application performance. Therefore, we have studied, as a first approach, the application mapping to minimize both the execution time and the maximum number of slots. We have implemented a MOO algorithm and our preliminary results show that adopting a multi-criteria paradigm not only allows to optimize several parameters simultaneously, but also enables quantitative analyses of different possibilities.

Currently, only simulations for randomly-generated applications have been carried out. Real applications such as neural networks have yet to be tested. Besides, even if the current optimization deals with the application mapping and the number of slots, it still has to consider the energy consumption for which a model has to be developed. Finally, hardware evaluations also constitute a major future work.

Acknowledgments. This paper is based on results obtained from a project commissioned by the New Energy and Industrial Technology Development Organization (NEDO).

References

1. National Institute of Advanced Industrial Science and Technology (AIST): Flow-centric computing (2017). https://www.itri.aist.go.jp/cpc/research/Flow-centricComputing.html
2. Tsuruta, C., Miki, Y., Kuhara, T., Amano, H., Umemura, M.: Off-loading LET generation to PEACH2: a switching hub for high performance GPU clusters. In: ACM SIGARCH Computer Architecture News - HEART15, vol. 43, no. 4, April 2016
3. Niu, X.Y., Tsoi, K.H., Luk, W.: Reconfiguring distributed applications in FPGA accelerated cluster with wireless networking. In: The 21st International Conference on Field Programmable Logic and Application (FPL), pp. 545–550, September 2011
4. Muehlbach, S., Koch, A.: A scalable multi-FPGA platform for complex networking applications. In: IEEE Annual International Symposium on Field-Programmable Custom Computing Machines (FCCM), pp. 81–84, May 2011
5. Moorthy, P., Kapre, N.: Zedwulf: power-performance tradeoffs of a 32-node Zynq SoC cluster. In: IEEE 23rd Annual International Symposium on Field-Programmable Custom Computing Machines (FCCM), pp. 68–75, May 2015
6. Sano, K., Hatsuda, Y., Yamamoto, S.: Multi-FPGA accelerator for scalable stencil computation with constant memory bandwidth. IEEE Trans. Parallel Distrib. Syst. **25**(3), 695–705 (2013)
7. Putnum, A., et al.: A reconfigurable fabric for accelerating large-scale datacenter services. In: IEEE/ACM the 41st Annual International Symposium on Computer Architecture (ISCA), pp. 81–84, May 2014
8. Stefan, R., Goossens, K.: A TDM slot allocation flow based on multipath routing in NoCs. Microprocess. Microsyst. **35**(2), 130–138 (2011). Special Issue on Network-on-Chip Architectures and Design Methodologies
9. Stefan, R.: Resource allocation in time-division-multiplexed networks on chip. Ph.D. thesis, Technische Universiteit Delft, April 2012
10. Schoeberl, M., Brandner, F., Sparsø, J., Kasapaki, E.: A statically scheduled time-division-multiplexed network-on-chip for real-time systems. In: 2012 IEEE/ACM Sixth International Symposium on Networks-on-Chip, pp. 152–160, May 2012
11. Mirza, U.M., Gruian, F., Kuchcinski, K.: Mapping streaming applications on multiprocessors with time-division-multiplexed network-on-chip. Comput. Electr. Eng. **40**(8), 276–291 (2014)
12. Talbi, E.G.: Metaheuristics: From Design to Implementation. Wiley, Hoboken (2009)
13. Sahni, S., Gonzalez, T.: P-complete approximation problems. J. ACM **23**(3), 555–565 (1976)
14. Deb, K., Pratap, A., Agarwal, S., Meyarivan, T.: A fast and elitist multi-objective genetic algorithm: NSGA-II. IEEE Trans. Evol. Comput. **6**, 182–197 (2000)

15. Padhye, N., Kalia, S.: Rapid prototyping using evolutionary approaches: part 1. In: Proceedings of the 11th Annual Conference Companion on Genetic and Evolutionary Computation Conference: Late Breaking Papers. GECCO 2009, pp. 2725–2728. ACM, New York (2009)
16. Davis, L.: Adapting operator probabilities in genetic algorithms. In: Proceedings of the Third International Conference on Genetic Algorithms, San Francisco, CA, USA, pp. 61–69. Morgan Kaufmann Publishers Inc. (1989)
17. Fortin, F.A., De Rainville, F.M., Gardner, M.A., Parizeau, M., Gagné, C.: DEAP: evolutionary algorithms made easy. J. Mach. Learn. Res. **13**, 2171–2175 (2012)

Applications and Surveys

An FPGA/HMC-Based Accelerator for Resolution Proof Checking

Tim Hansmeier[1]([⊠]) [iD], Marco Platzner[1] [iD], and David Andrews[2] [iD]

[1] Paderborn University, Paderborn, Germany
tiha@mail.upb.de, platzner@upb.de
[2] University of Arkansas, Fayetteville, USA
dandrews@uark.edu

Abstract. Modern Boolean satisfiability solvers can emit proofs of unsatisfiability. There is substantial interest in being able to verify such proofs and also in using them for further computations. In this paper, we present an FPGA accelerator for checking resolution proofs, a popular proof format. Our accelerator exploits parallelism at the low level by implementing the basic resolution step in hardware, and at the high level by instantiating a number of parallel modules for proof checking. Since proof checking involves highly irregular memory accesses, we employ Hybrid Memory Cube technology for accelerator memory. The results show that while the accelerator is scalable and achieves speedups for all benchmark proofs, performance improvements are currently limited by the overhead of transitioning the proof into the accelerator memory.

1 Introduction

Boolean satisfiability (SAT) is a prominent problem in complexity theory, since it was the first problem for which NP-completeness was proven [4]. Additionally, it is practically highly relevant with many applications in areas such as, for example, computer-aided design, combinatorial optimization, and artificial intelligence. SAT solvers take a Boolean expression as input, typically in conjunctive normal form (CNF), and either determine a variable assignment that satisfies the Boolean expression or prove that the expression is unsatisfiable (UNSAT).

Over the last several decades, SAT solvers have been greatly improved by incorporating advanced algorithmic techniques. Modern SAT solvers are thus quite extensive software packages for which a formal correctness proof is out of reach. What is possible, however, is to verify the SAT solver's answer to a concrete CNF input instance. In case a SAT solver returns a satisfying variable assignment, correctness can be easily verified by instantiating the variable values into the CNF. In case of UNSAT, modern SAT solvers are able to emit a proof of unsatisfiability. Despite the fact that in terms of complexity verifying a proof is

This work was partially supported by the German Research Foundation (DFG) within the Collaborative Research Centre "On-The-Fly Computing" (SFB 901).

much simpler than determining UNSAT in the first place, such proofs can grow very large in size and incur considerable runtimes for checking them. The need for checking UNSAT proofs also arises in combinational equivalence checking [3], in model checking [8], and for the extraction of clausal cores, e.g. minimal unsatisfiable subsets of CNF clauses [5]. Furthermore, a fast validation of an UNSAT proof is a key component in the approach of proof-carrying hardware [7].

The novel contribution of this work is the presentation of a scalable FPGA-based accelerator for checking resolution proofs, a popular proof format for SAT solvers. To the best of our knowledge, no accelerator for resolution proof checking has been proposed before. Checking resolution proofs is a combinatorial problem and thus our work slightly resembles earlier accelerator work on SAT or graph algorithms, e.g., in [1,11]. Two key characteristics of combinatorial problems are (i) plenty of low-level parallelism, which leads to efficient implementations of custom data types and operators in reconfigurable logic, and (ii) highly irregular access to a huge amount of data, which impedes or even prevents streaming approaches. Our accelerator design emphasizes the memory architecture and employs a reconfigurable computing platform with Hybrid Memory Cube (HMC) [10] technology.

The remainder of this paper is structured as follows: In Sect. 2 we provide background about resolution proofs and the HMC technology, Sect. 3 presents the design of our accelerator for resolution proof checking, and Sect. 4 details our implementation and experimental results. Finally, Sect. 5 concludes the paper.

2   Background

In this section we first briefly describe resolution proofs and the software resolution checker TraceCheck, based on [5], followed by a short introduction to HMC technology.

2.1   Resolution Proofs

A resolution proof contains the original clauses of the CNF and a list of clausal resolutions, which derive new clauses from the given clauses. New clauses are derived by applying a sequence of basic *resolution steps*. When two given clauses contain the same variable occurring as positive literal in one clause and as negative literal in the other, they can be resolved to a new clause encompassing all remaining literals of the two given clauses. The given clauses are denoted as *antecedents* and the new clause is denoted as *resolvent*. As an example, the two antecedents $C_1 = (x_1 + x_2 + \bar{x}_3)$ and $C_2 = (\bar{x}_2 + \bar{x}_3 + x_4)$ can be resolved to the resolvent $C = (x_1 + \bar{x}_3 + x_4)$. A sequence of such resolution steps, where resolvents can become antecedents in subsequent steps, is called a *resolution chain*. Any resolvent that is obtained through resolution of clauses belonging to the same CNF is logically implied by the CNF, meaning that the resolvent can be included in the original Boolean expression without changing the set of satisfying assignments.

A resolution proof of UNSAT consists of resolution chains which lead to the resolution of the empty clause ϵ, which is unsatisfiable by definition and thus proves the unsatisfiability of the original Boolean expression. Resolution proofs can be visualized as directed acyclic graphs (DAGs), with the original clauses of the CNF as leaf nodes and the empty clause ϵ as root node. Figure 1 shows a resolution graph proving the unsatisfiability of the CNF $(x_1 + \bar{x}_2 + \bar{x}_3) \cdot (x_1 + x_3) \cdot (\bar{x}_1) \cdot (x_2 + \bar{x}_3)$. Checking the correctness of a resolution proof encompasses the validation of every derived clause stated in the proof. In Fig. 1, the antecedents $(x_1 + x_3)$ and $\bar{x}_1$ are resolved to x_3, and the antecedents x_3 and $(x_2 + \bar{x}_3)$ are resolved to x_2, where both resolution chains require one basic resolution step. The final resolution chain resolves the empty clause from the antecedents $(x_1 + \bar{x}_2 + \bar{x}_3)$, x_3, $\bar{x}_1$, and x_2 and involves three basic resolution steps.

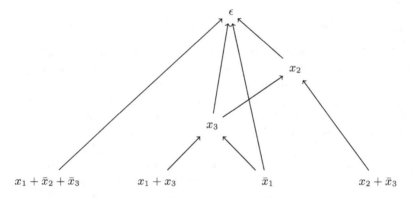

Fig. 1. Representation of the resolution proof for $(x_1 + \bar{x}_2 + \bar{x}_3) \cdot (x_1 + x_3) \cdot (\bar{x}_1) \cdot (x_2 + \bar{x}_3)$ in form of a directed acyclic graph

A popular resolution proof checker is TraceCheck[1], which serves as the software reference in this work. TraceCheck uses a textual representation of a resolution proof in which each line represents a clause, either a original clause of the CNF or a derived clause. Each clause is assigned an index, stated at the start of the line. The index is followed by the zero-terminated list of literals belonging to the clause and a zero-terminated list of antecedents, representing the resolution chain used to obtain the clause. The literals are represented by numbers, with the negative sign denoting a negative literal.

Figure 2 shows the proof from Fig. 1 in the TraceCheck format, with indices and delimiters in bold face. The first four clauses are original clauses from the CNF and thus have no resolution chains associated with them. Clauses with indices 5, 6 and 7 are derived clauses. To verify the proof, we have to check whether in each of these lines the resolution steps are actually correct. Since

---

[1] http://fmv.jku.at/tracecheck/.

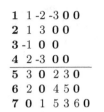

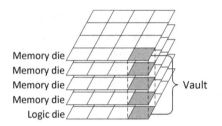

Fig. 2. TraceCheck format of the example proof from Fig. 1

Fig. 3. Conceptual HMC architecture [6]

every derived clause requires an independent set of antecedents for resolution, checking imposes memory accesses with an irregular address pattern.

2.2 Hybrid Memory Cube (HMC)

The Hybrid Memory Cube (HMC) is a 3-D stacked memory technology which unifies multiple memory dies and a single logic die at the bottom in one package [10]. Both logic and memory layers are divided into equally sized partitions. A *vault* denotes the cuboid formed by one logic partition at the bottom and all memory partitions located above it, as shown in Fig. 3. The logic partition manages the requests to the memory partitions above it and thus serves as their memory controller. Since vaults can work independently, the HMC offers a high level of memory parallelism. Hence, HMC technology is advertised to be well-suited for random memory access patterns [10]. HMC technology is already being deployed in high-performance computing systems. An example for a reconfigurable computing system employing HMC as memory technology is Pico Computing's (now Micron) AC-510 PCIe accelerator card[2] used in this work. Future HMC generations will extend the logic partitions to additionally support atomic operations on data [6], which is a relevant feature for processing-in-memory (PIM) approaches, e.g. PIM-accelerated graph computing [9].

3 Accelerator Design

Figure 4 displays the top-level architecture of our accelerator. We employ a Pico Computing AC-510 card holding a Xilinx Kintex Ultrascale FPGA connected to a 4 GB HMC module. For PCIe communication between the host and the FPGA, we use Micron's Pico PCIe Framework. In combination with the 10-port HMC Controller IP from Micron, the framework allows for direct memory access (DMA) into the HMC. The host executes preprocessing steps on the resolution proof trace, constructs a proof representation suited for the HMC, and then writes this representation into the HMC using DMA.

---

[2] http://picocomputing.com/ac-510-superprocessor-module/.

Our accelerator performs the resolution checking step of TraceCheck in hardware and comprises a control logic and a scalable number of resolution proof checkers (RPC) modules. Figure 4 shows an accelerator with eight RPC modules. Each RPC reads a set of lines from the resolution proof in the HMC, i.e., derived clauses and their resolution chains, and determines their correctness. An RPC either signals the control logic that it was able to successfully verify its assigned clauses or that it detected an error in some resolution step. In case an error is detected, the control logic immediately stops all computations. In case all RPCs successfully verify their derived clauses, the resolution proof is shown to be correct. Our parallelization scheme assumes that we can check all derived clauses independently, i.e., in a arbitrary order. This assumption is valid since we are only interested in whether a resolution proof is correct or not, which requires us to check all derived clauses. Pinpointing the exact location of erroneous resolutions within the proof would require a different strategy.

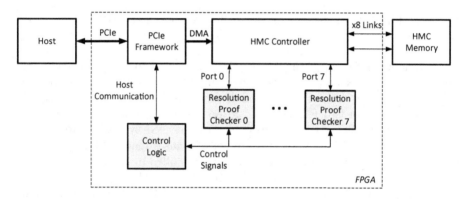

Fig. 4. Accelerator architecture on the Pico Computing AC-510 with eight resolution proof checker modules (gray boxes denote accelerator modules)

Figure 5 shows a block diagram for the RPC, comprising a request module, a reordering module, five resolution chain checkers (RCCs), and a number of FIFOs. The request module issues memory read requests to the HMC using one of its controller ports. To hide the latency of the HMC and to achieve the maximum bandwidth, requests are pipelined with a maximum of 64 requests being on-flight. To be able to map the HMC responses to the requests, we need to add a tag to each request. The `tags_available` FIFO holds the tags that are currently available, and the request module feeds the `tags_used` FIFO whenever a request is issued. Requests are always issued with the maximum possible size, because this is a critical aspect for getting the maximum read bandwidth (see Sect. 4 for more details). Limitations on the request size are imposed by the proof, e.g., when mainly short clauses are accessed, and by the HMC itself, since requests are not allowed to cross a 128 byte boundary.

Since the HMC can deliver responses out of order, the RPC contains a reordering module that buffers the responses and uses the information from

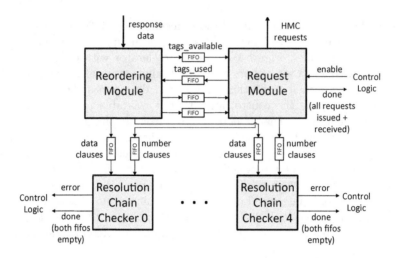

Fig. 5. Block diagram for the resolution proof checker (RPC)

the `tags_used` FIFO to put the data back in order and to forward it correctly. Some responses may contain information about other clauses to be read from the HMC, in which case the reordering module forwards the response to the request module by means of two FIFOs. Most responses will contain clauses that are forwarded to the RCC. Each resolution chain is checked by a single RCC. The RCC receives information about the number of clauses required for the resolution chain from the `number clauses` FIFO, that is filled by the request module, and the clauses from the `data clauses` FIFO, that is filled by the reordering module. The resolution chains are assigned to the RCCs with a round-robin scheme.

The RCC implements the resolution chain checker logic. The core of this customized operator is a bit vector used to store intermediate resolvents. Each bit of the bit vector represents a literal, defining the length of the bit vector to two times the number of variables in the CNF. When the first clause of a resolution chain is processed, all its literals are added to the resolvent by setting the corresponding fields to 1 in the bit vector. For all following clauses, we compare their literals with the literals set in the bit vector. If both literals of a variable are set, the resolution rule states that this variable has to be removed from the resolvent and we clear both literal bits in the bit vector. When the end of a resolution chain is reached, the resolvent has to be compared to the derived clause stated in the proof. This is done by flipping the bits representing the literals of the derived clause and subsequently checking whether the resolvent is now an all-zero bit vector. To illustrate this process, Fig. 6 shows the steps for resolving the clause $(\bar{x}_1 + x_3)$ with the clause $(x_1 + x_2)$ to the derived clause $(x_2 + x_3)$.

Erroneous resolutions manifest in the following situations: (a) Either none or multiple variables can be removed from the resolvent while processing a clause.

Step 1: Add first clause $(\bar{x}_1 + x_3)$

x_1	$\bar{x}_1$	x_2	$\bar{x}_2$	x_3	$\bar{x}_3$
0	1	0	0	1	0

Step 2: Add second clause $(x_1 + x_2)$: clear $\bar{x}_1$ and x_1

x_1	$\bar{x}_1$	x_2	$\bar{x}_2$	x_3	$\bar{x}_3$
0	0	1	0	1	0

Step 3: Flip literal bits of derived clause $(x_2 + x_3)$: correct if vector is all-zero

x_1	$\bar{x}_1$	x_2	$\bar{x}_2$	x_3	$\bar{x}_3$
0	0	0	0	0	0

Fig. 6. Checking the resolution of $(\bar{x}_1 + x_3)$ with $(x_1 + x_2)$ to $(x_2 + x_3)$ using a bit vector for storing the intermediate resolvent

These situations indicate an invalid resolution step. (b) The resulting bit vector is not all-zero, which indicates that the resolvent claimed in the proof can not be derived from the antecedents.

4   Experimental Results

This section first presents our accelerator implementation, followed by the experimental setup used for its evaluation and experimental results with respect to functionality and performance, scalability, and the HMC's bandwidth utilization.

4.1   Implementation

We have implemented the accelerator for TraceCheck on a Pico Computing (Micron) AC-510 card. On this system, the HMC controller IP offers 10 ports which can be used independently of each other to access the HMC. One port is reserved for the DMA functionality of the Pico framework. Our implementation employs eight RPC modules (see Fig. 4) and distributes the clauses of the proof to be checked equally among these modules. Each of the eight RPCs comprises five RCC modules (see Fig. 5), which we found sufficient to fully utilize the bandwidth provided by one port of the HMC controller during the checking of our benchmark proofs (cmp. Sect. 4.5). The resolvent bit vectors are implemented in Block-RAM (BRAM) and have a length of 16,384 bit, allowing the accelerator to verify proofs with up to 8,191 variables (with zero not being a valid variable). All modules are running at a frequency of 187.5 MHz, since this is the frequency at which the HMC controller achieves its maximum memory performance.

Table 1 shows the resource utilization of our accelerator as reported by Xilinx Vivado. With approximately 46% of the lookup tables (LUTs) and 58% of the BRAM used, the design leaves some resources available to extend the accelerator's functionalities, for example to increase the length of the resolvent bit vector and thus the number of variables a proof can use. DSP blocks are not used by our accelerator. About 20% of the LUTs and 25% of the BRAM accounts for the instantiation of the framework and the HMC controller.

Table 1. LUT and BRAM utilization of the FPGA

Xilinx Kintex Ultrascale XCKU060	LUTs	BRAM
Available	331,680	1080 Tiles
Used	151,125	627 Tiles
Utilization	45.56%	58.06%
— Used by HMC controller + Pico framework	19.62%	25.46%
— Used by accelerator modules	25.94%	32.59%

4.2 Experimental Setup

For evaluation of the accelerator, we have created resolution proofs for a set of 38 benchmarks from the random track of the SAT competition 2007[3] using the SAT solver PicoSAT [2]. The CNFs have between 45 and 4,500 variables and 1,491 to 12,014 clauses, leading to resolution proofs with a size between 66 MB and 2,203 MB. The experiments were conducted on a system with a six-core Intel i7-5930K CPU running at 3.50 GHz and 32 GB RAM, running under Ubuntu 14.04 with the proofs stored on the internal SSD. We have measured wall-clock runtimes using the *gettimeofday()* Unix utility.

4.3 Functionality and Runtime

We have tested the functionality of the accelerator by comparing its results with the results of TraceCheck's resolution for all benchmark proofs and for proofs that we have manually modified to become incorrect.

Figure 7 compares the processing flows of the TraceCheck software reference and the accelerator and visualizes the speedup metrics reported on in Table 2. Both the software reference and the accelerator require a preprocessing step running on the host. The software reference then performs the resolution in software. In contrast, for the accelerator we need to construct the proof data structure and DMA it into the HMC before we can start the hardware resolution. These two steps are considered as overhead. We have measured runtimes for all steps for both the software reference and the accelerator and averaged the resulting speedups over all benchmark proofs. We achieve an end-to-end speedup greater than one for each single benchmark proof, comparing the total runtimes of the accelerator with the reference. The speedups are obviously limited due to Amdahl's law. The maximum end-to-end speedup over all benchmarks is 1.59X, and the average end-to-end speedup amounts to 1.27X. Looking only at the resolution step, we observe a raw resolution speedup of 2.56X including the

---

[3] www.satcompetition.org.

overhead for the accelerator and 10.06X excluding the overhead. The 10.06X is the potential we can approach (for the given benchmark set) by reducing the overhead and the preprocessing. The overhead, which currently is 74.5% of the resolution time on average, could be reduced by, for example, (a) modifying TraceCheck to use an accelerator-friendly proof representation in memory and by (b) using a machine with shared memory between the host and the accelerator.

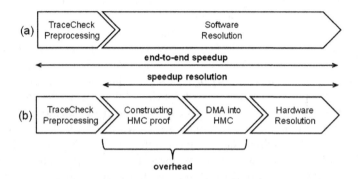

Fig. 7. TraceCheck processing steps without (a) and with the accelerator (b)

Table 2. Geometrically averaged runtime evaluation results

Maximum end-to-end speedup	1.59X
Achieved end-to-end speedup	1.27X
Speedup resolution (incl. overhead)	2.56X
Speedup resolution (excl. overhead)	10.06X
Percentage of overhead for resolution	74.5%

4.4 Scalability

Our accelerator design is scalable in the number of RPCs. The current implementation employs eight RPCs, which allows us to check 40 resolution chains in parallel since each RPC comprises five RCCs. Larger proofs exhibit potential for higher speedups. To realize this potential we need to instantiate more RPCs, which possibly requires HMCs with higher bandwidth or systems with more HMC modules.

An important question regarding scalability is how to distribute the derived clauses to be checked among the RPCs. Our implementation distributes the clauses equally, but since the time required to check one derived clause can greatly vary, other distribution schemes might be superior. To study this aspect of scalability, we define a balance metric λ as:

$$\lambda = \frac{D}{T \cdot B}$$

where D, given in MiB, is the overall amount of data read from the HMC during checking a proof, T is the resolution runtime of the accelerator in seconds (without overhead), and B, given in MiB/s, is the sum of the bandwidths achieved by the eight used ports of the HMC controller during checking of the resolution chains. If the load is perfectly balanced among the RPCs, the HMC ports are busy for the whole runtime, which results in $\lambda = 1$.

Figure 8(a) shows the accelerator's resolution runtimes for the proof with the lowest metric ($\lambda = 0.863$) and Fig. 8(b) the resolution runtimes for the proof with the highest metric ($\lambda = 0.967$) among our benchmark set. Both figures display the runtimes over a varying number of RPCs. The dashed curves show the optimal runtimes for a perfectly balanced distribution of derived clauses to RPCs, i.e., the runtime is inversely proportional to the number of instantiated RPCs. The solid curves show the measured runtimes. As shown in Fig. 8(b), the proof with the highest λ scales nearly perfectly with the number of RPCs, while the scalability for the proof with the lowest λ is less distinct, as expected. This experiment underlines that the actual proof to be checked has a non-negligible influence on scalability. Future work should thus devise a load balancing mechanism to distribute the derived clauses among the RPCs based on the load they impose.

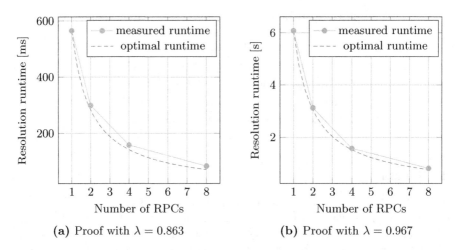

(a) Proof with $\lambda = 0.863$ **(b)** Proof with $\lambda = 0.967$

Fig. 8. Hardware resolution runtimes for a varying number of resolution proof checkers (RPCs) and for proofs with the lowest and highest balance metric λ

4.5   HMC Utilization

To evaluate the memory performance of our accelerator, i.e., to what extent the accelerator is able to utilize the HMC's bandwidth, we have used the GUPS (Giga-UPdates per Second) benchmark provided by Micron. We have configured

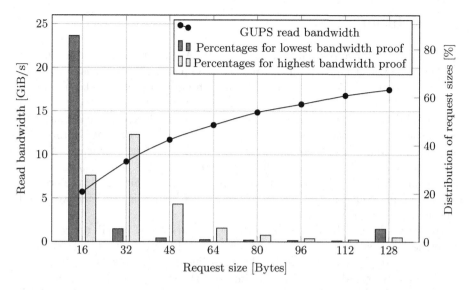

Fig. 9. Read bandwidth for the GUPS benchmark as a function of the request size (solid curve) and the distribution of request sizes used during the checking

GUPS to perform random read accesses to the HMC using eight HMC controller ports to mimic our accelerator's architecture. Figure 9 shows the achieved bandwidth for the eight possible request sizes. The maximum bandwidth of approximately 17.5 GiB/s is only reached for the largest request size of 128 bytes; for the smallest request size of 16 bytes the read bandwidth reduces to 5.7 GiB/s.

In our accelerator, the achieved bandwidth depends on the proof that is checked. For our benchmark set we have observed bandwidths between 6.93 GiB/s and 8.89 GiB/s, which clearly stays below the maximum bandwidth of 17.5 GiB/s achieved by GUPS. The main reason for the lower HMC utilization is that our benchmark proofs lead to requests with rather small sizes. In Fig. 9 we present the distribution of request sizes for the proof achieving the lowest and the highest HMC bandwidth. The majority of the requests have sizes between 16 and 48 bytes. For the proof with the lowest bandwidth, approximately 85% of the requests are of the smallest possible size. The proof with the highest bandwidth leads to larger requests, but even there the majority of the requests have only 32 bytes. Apart from the proof composition, another reason for small request sizes is imposed by the HMC architecture, which limits requests to a 128 byte address range. Requests that cross this boundary need to be split into several, smaller requests. Furthermore, in contrast to the GUPS benchmark our accelerator has to reorder responses from the HMC which also might contribute to the decreased memory performance.

5   Conclusion

In this paper, we have presented a scalable FPGA accelerator for the resolution proof checker TraceCheck which exploits low-level parallelism by a custom resolution operator and high-level parallelism through parallel proof checker modules. We have implemented a prototype on a Micron reconfigurable system with an HMC module and evaluated it under a set of benchmark resolution proofs. The results show that the accelerator achieves speedups for all evaluated proofs, on average 1.27X out of the theoretically achievable 1.59X. The overhead of transitioning the resolution proof from the host into the HMC's address space limits performance, with the result that a speedup of 2.56X is achieved for the accelerated processing step and the evaluated proofs. Without this overhead we would achieve a speedup of 10.06X.

Future work will thus focus on reducing the overhead by (i) restructuring TraceCheck's host code or by improving the DMA functionality of the used framework and (ii) moving additional processing steps from software to reconfigurable hardware. Moreover, we will improve the scalability of the accelerator by devising a load balancing technique to distribute clauses among RPCs which will facilitate the use of larger reconfigurable platforms. Since our RPC's performance is memory-bound, we will also investigate ways to re-use clauses occuring in multiple resolution chains. Currently, such clauses are read from memory multiple times. Finally, a quantitative comparison between HMC and other memory technologies is of interest.

References

1. Babb, J., Frank, M., Agarwal, A.: Solving graph problems with dynamic computation structures. In: Proceedings of SPIE: High-Speed Computing, Digital Signal Processing, and Filtering Using Reconfigurable Logic, vol. 2914, pp. 225–236 (1996)
2. Biere, A.: Picosat essentials. J. Satisf. Boolean Model. Comput. (JSAT) **4**, 75–97 (2008)
3. Chatterjee, S., Mishchenko, A., Brayton, R., Kuehlmann, A.: On resolution proofs for combinational equivalence. In: 2007 44th ACM/IEEE Design Automation Conference, pp. 600–605, June 2007
4. Cook, S.A.: The complexity of theorem-proving procedures. In: Proceedings of the Third Annual ACM Symposium on Theory of Computing, STOC 1971, pp. 151–158. ACM, New York (1971)
5. Heule, M., Biere, A.: Proofs for satisfiability problems, vol. 55, pp. 1–22. College Publications (2015)
6. Hybrid Memory Cube Consortium: Hybrid memory cube specification 2.0 (2014)
7. Isenberg, T., Platzner, M., Wehrheim, H., Wiersema, T.: Proof-carrying hardware via inductive invariants. ACM Trans. Des. Autom. Electron. Syst. **22**(4), 61:1–61:23 (2017)
8. McMillan, K.L.: Interpolation and SAT-based model checking. In: Hunt, W.A., Somenzi, F. (eds.) CAV 2003. LNCS, vol. 2725, pp. 1–13. Springer, Heidelberg (2003). https://doi.org/10.1007/978-3-540-45069-6_1

9. Nai, L., Hadidi, R., Sim, J., Kim, H., Kumar, P., Kim, H.: GraphPIM: enabling instruction-level PIM offloading in graph computing frameworks. In: 2017 IEEE International Symposium on High Performance Computer Architecture (HPCA), pp. 457–468, February 2017
10. Pawlowski, J.T.: Hybrid memory cube (HMC). In: 2011 IEEE Hot Chips 23 Symposium (HCS), pp. 1–24, August 2011
11. Skliarova, I., de Brito Ferrari, A.: Reconfigurable hardware SAT solvers: a survey of systems. IEEE Trans. Comput. **53**(11), 1449–1461 (2004)

An Efficient FPGA Implementation of the Big Bang-Big Crunch Optimization Algorithm

Almabrok Abdoalnasir[1], Mihalis Psarakis[1(✉)] 📵,
and Anastasios Dounis[2] 📵

[1] Department of Informatics, University of Piraeus, Piraeus, Greece
{nass,mpsarak}@unipi.gr
[2] Department of Automation Engineering,
Piraeus University of Applied Sciences, Aigaleo, Greece
aidounis@puas.gr

Abstract. Big Bang-Big Crunch (BB-BC) is an optimization method inspired by the corresponding evolutionary theory of the universe [1]. The BB-BC method is performed in two phases: in the Bing Bang phase, similarly to other Genetic Algorithms (GAs) it generates a random population of candidate solutions, while in the Big Crunch phase it shrinks these candidates around an optimal point via a center-of-mass or minimal cost approach. It has been shown that the BB-BC method outperforms classical GA algorithms for several optimization problems in terms of convergence speed. In this paper, we study the FPGA implementation of the BB-BC algorithm. We show that the BB-BC algorithm does not suffer from the design limitations of the classical GAs that impede the performance of their hardware-based accelerators. We propose an efficient fully pipelined design of both BB-BC phases that achieves significant speedup compared to the software counterpart. We also present a parallel scheme which integrates several BB-BC pipelined engines to improve system performance. The proposed FPGA architecture has been demonstrated for a typical optimization problem and implemented on a Xilinx Virtex-5 device.

Keywords: FPGA-based acceleration · Genetic algorithm
Big Bang-Big Crunch optimization algorithm

1 Introduction

Genetic algorithms (GAs) have been proved effective in solving complex optimization and search problems. However, due to their large exploration space and heuristic nature, GAs typically suffer from long execution time. Hardware platforms, such as GPUs and FPGAs have been used in the past to accelerate the execution of GAs. Due to their high-performance and reconfigurability, modern FPGAs provide a flexible and effective platform to speedup the evolution process. Exploiting the hardware parallelism to perform complex computation tasks and the inherent parallelism of these algorithms yields significant speedup. Since the first FPGA-based GA system proposed in [2], several researchers have presented efficient FPGA implementations of both

© Springer International Publishing AG, part of Springer Nature 2018
N. Voros et al. (Eds.): ARC 2018, LNCS 10824, pp. 166–177, 2018.
https://doi.org/10.1007/978-3-319-78890-6_14

application-specific [3, 4] and general-purpose GAs [5, 6]. According to [6], FPGA-based GAs may achieve an average speedup of around 5x compared to their software counterparts.

Moreover, hardware acceleration techniques, such as pipelining [7, 8] and parallel execution [9], have been applied to the FPGA designs to further improve GA performance. Pipelined and parallel GA architectures aim at eliminating the pipeline stalls and increasing the execution parallelism during the various stages of the evolution process (e.g. random population generation, fitness calculation, genetic operations). However, some features of the evolutionary process, such as the inherent data dependency between successive generations and the large shared population memory [8], do not map efficiently to hardware accelerators. In other words, these features introduce some design bottlenecks in the FPGA architecture that limit the maximum achievable speedup. To overcome these limitations, recent approaches study the implementation of "hardware-friendly" GA approaches, such as pipelined genetic propagation (PGN) [8] and parallel (pGA) or distributed (dGA) algorithms [9].

In this paper, we address, for first time in the literature, the FPGA-based acceleration of the *Big Bang-Big Crunch* (BB-BC) optimization algorithm [1]. This optimization algorithm is based on one of the evolutionary theories of the universe, namely the Big Bang and Big Crunch theory. It consists of two phases: the Big Bang phase, where randomness is the main feature and a population of random, disordered candidates is produced within the allowable search space, followed by the Big Crunch phase, where candidates are evaluated and ordered according to some quality metrics. After the Big Crunch phase, the algorithm generates new candidates to be used as the target population of the next iteration. The new population is created based on information obtained in the previous iteration: the new candidates are spread randomly around the center of mass calculated by the previous Big Crunch. As the number of successive explosions and contractions increases, the distribution deviation of the candidates around the center of mass becomes smaller and the algorithm converges to an optimal solution.

It has been shown that the BB-BC algorithm outperforms the classical GAs for many test functions [1] in terms of convergence speed and computational cost. The BB-BC method has been used in several optimization problems, for example the optimal design of truss structures [10], Schwedler and ribbed domes [11], concrete retaining walls [12], fuzzy inverse controllers [13] and fuzzy PID controllers [14]. In some cases, where the optimization task is adaptive and the application has hard real-time constraints [13, 14], the BB-BC algorithm has been adopted due to its low computational time and high global convergence speed. These features of the BB-BC algorithm mainly motivated our work, since an FPGA-based BB-BC accelerator can greatly reduce the computational time providing an ideal platform for large-scale adaptive or latency-sensitive optimization problems.

Towards this end, we propose a *novel pipelined FPGA design* of the BB-BC algorithm. All the stages of the algorithm are implemented in a fully pipelined fashion to reduce pipeline stalls. This is feasible because the BB-BC algorithm does not suffer from the design bottlenecks of the GAs and provides higher flexibility in its hardware implementation. We present a parameterized FPGA BB-BC architecture to provide tradeoff between algorithm accuracy, circuit area and clock frequency: (i) the calculation of center of mass can be driven either by a light minimal cost function or a complex equation (inverse of fitness function), (ii) the arithmetic circuits can be built using synthesized HDL operators or highly optimized IP cores (Core Generator), (iii) the length of integer and fractional parts of fixed point arithmetic can be configured, (iv) other configurable parameters of the BB-BC algorithm are: number of iterations, population size, candidate length, LFSR seeds for the random candidate generators.

We also present a *parallel scheme* of the FPGA accelerator that integrates several pipelined BB-BC engines. These engines generate and process concurrently different parts of the population but during the Bing Crunch phase they are synchronized and collaborate to produce a merged center of mass. The parallel scheme reduces further the execution time of the algorithm at the expense of extra reconfigurable resources. We have demonstrated the FPGA BB-BC accelerator for a typical optimization problem (Rosenbrock function) and implemented it on a Xilinx Virtex-5 device. The experimental results proved that the proposed FPGA accelerator achieves an average speedup of around 165x and 101x against custom GA s/w and BB-BC s/w programs running on an ARM Cortex-A9 embedded processor.

The outline of the paper is as follows. Section 2 introduces the BB-BC algorithm and explains why it favors a pipelined hardware implementation. Section 3 presents the architecture of the proposed FPGA accelerator while Sect. 4 provides the experimental results. Finally, Sect. 5 concludes the paper.

2   Big Bang-Bing Crunch (BB-BC) Algorithm

2.1   Description of the Algorithm

The Bing Bang-Bing Crunch algorithm was introduced by Erol and Eksin in [1]. It is a nature-inspired optimization method which has similarities with classical GAs in respect to the random generation of the initial population. The generation of the population is called Big Bang. In this phase, the candidate solutions are spread all over the search space in a uniform manner. If there are problem-dependent boundaries for the values of the candidate features (i.e. chromosomes) and the random generators produce feature values that exceed these boundaries, it is required to saturate the values to the adjacent boundaries. The Big Bang is followed by the Big Crunch phase. The Big Crunch is a convergence operator that has many inputs but only one output, which can be named as the center of "mass", since the only output has been derived by calculating the center of mass. Here, the term "mass" refers to the inverse of the fitness function value. The point representing the Center of Mass (CoM) is denoted by $\vec{x}^c$ and calculated according to:

$$\vec{x}^c = \frac{\sum_{i=1}^{N} \frac{1}{f^i} \vec{x}^i}{\sum_{i=1}^{N} \frac{1}{f^i}} \tag{1}$$

where $\vec{x}^i$ a point within an L-dimensional search space, f^i is a fitness function value of this point, and N is the size of the population generated in the Big Bang phase. After the

Big Crunch, the algorithm creates new members to be used as the Big Bang of the next iteration according to the following formula:

$$x^{new} = x^c + r * l/k \tag{2}$$

where r is a random number with normal distribution, k is the number of Big Bang iterations and l is a problem-dependent constant, $l = a * (x_{max} - x_{min})$; parameter α limits the search space, while x_{max} and x_{min} are the upper and lower values of the optimization function variables. After the second explosion, the CoM is recalculated. These successive explosion and contraction steps are carried out repeatedly until a stopping criterion has been met. Since normally distributed numbers can be exceeding ± 1, it is necessary to keep the candidate values within the predefined search space bounds.

The steps of the BB-BC algorithm are summarized as follows:

1. Form an initial generation of N candidates in a random manner.
2. Calculate the fitness function values of all the candidate solutions. This step depends on the target optimization problem.
3. Find the CoM according to Eq. (1). Best fitness individual of each generation can be also chosen as the CoM instead of using Eq. (1) reducing the computation time.
4. Calculate new candidates around the CoM using Eq. (2). Notice that the random value added or subtracted to the CoM decreases as the iterations elapse.
5. Return to Step 2 until stopping criteria has been met.

2.2 Hardware Design Bottlenecks

As stated above, the BB-BC algorithm does not suffer from the design bottlenecks of the typical GAs which restrict the parallelization efficiency of the FPGA accelerators, and consequently the maximum achievable speedup. More specifically:

Data dependencies between the Big Bang and Big Crunch phases do not cause pipeline stalls. In the case of GAs, the selection and reproduction operations of the evolution process are actually two-by-two combination calculations. Thus, in order the evolution process proceeds, the algorithms needs to wait the generation of the entire population. These data dependencies between the population generation stage and the parent selection/reproduction stage cause stalls in the pipelined execution of these two stages slowing down the system performance. Whereas in the case of the BB-BC algorithm, the calculations performed during the Big Crunch phase can commence before the completion of the Big Bang phase. This is because the center of mass can be calculated on-the-fly by processing every newly generated candidate. This is valid for both the center of mass calculation alternatives. In the case of the best fitness candidate, a reduction operation (comparison) is performed in the series of sequentially generated candidates. Similarly, in the case of Eq. (1), the numerator and denominator of the equation can be separately calculated by a reduction operation (accumulation) in the sequentially generated candidates and their fitness values. Thus, the operations performed during both the Big Bang and Big Crunch phases can be fully pipelined to improve speedup.

Buffering of the population is not required. Typical GAs require a large amount of memory to store the population in each generation. The selection and reproduction operators can run in parallel but require access in the shared population memory. This introduces a memory-access bottleneck in the FPGA implementations which limits the level of execution parallelism. In the case of BB-BC algorithm, the calculation of the center of mass can be performed on-the-fly as explained in the above paragraph, and thus it does not require any buffering of the population. Only in the case, that the reduction operation (comparison or accumulation) has a long latency (i.e. data reduction is slower than the data generation), the reduction circuit requires a small buffer for rate compensation.

3   Proposed FPGA Architecture

3.1   Pipelined BB-BC Engine

In this section, we describe the proposed FPGA architecture of the BB-BC algorithm. The main building block of the FPGA architecture is the BB-BC engine shown in Fig. 1. BB-BC engine implements the three processing stages (i.e. random generation, fitness function, center-of-mass calculation) of each iteration of the algorithm in a fully pipelined fashion.

Figure 2 presents the pipelined execution of two consecutive BB-BC iterations. Each BB-BC iteration includes three stages: Generation of candidate (Cand), Calculation of fitness function (Fit) and Calculation of Center of Mass (CoM). Notice that in order an iteration cycle commences, the previous one must have been completed (i.e. pipelined execution is not feasible at iteration level). This is due to the fact that the Big Bang phase (random generation) requires the value of the CoM obtained by the Big Crunch phase of the previous iteration.

The description of the pipeline stages of the BB-BC engine follows.

- *Generation of candidate*: The RandGen module generates a candidate ($\vec{x}^i$), either to form an initial population (iteration 0) or to form new candidates around the CoM (iteration > 0). The candidate value is stored in a pipelined register. A typical linear feedback shift register (LFSR) is used to generate random numbers based on a configurable seed. The random number r is multiplied by the value l/k, as depicted in Eq. (1). The value l/k is calculated statically and stored in a ROM with M entries, where M is the number of iterations. Thus, its calculation does not impose delay in the generation of candidates. The stage delay is actually dominated by the multiplier latency. In each cycle, the RandGen module generates L random numbers, where L is the number of features of each candidate. In each iteration, the module generates N candidates sequentially.
- *Calculation of fitness function*: The Fitness module calculates the fitness function (f^i) for each candidate. The fitness function is application dependent. The stage latency depends on the fitness function complexity. For complex fitness function, the stage should be pipelined to achieve high clock frequency.

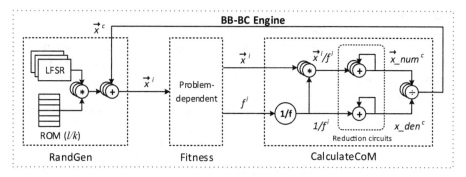

Fig. 1. Block diagram of BB-BC engine

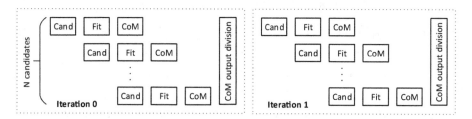

Fig. 2. Pipelined execution of BB-BC engine

- *Calculation of CoM*: The CalculateCoM module calculates the CoM ($\vec{x}^c$) for each iteration. The module runs N consecutive cycles to sample and process the N candidates of the current iteration. The calculation of CoM is finished since the last candidate has been processed. The module supports two alternatives for the calculation of CoM (in Fig. 1 only the second option is depicted):

  a. *minimal cost function*: $\vec{x}^c = \vec{x}^i \ni \min_{i=1..N} f^i$ which chooses the candidate of the generation with the best (smaller) fitness function value. In this case the CalculateCoM module integrates a simple reduction (comparison) circuit to perform this function. The stage delay depends on the comparator latency.

  b. *complex inverse fitness function* (see Eq. (1)): $\vec{x}^c = \vec{x}\_num^c / x\_den^c$. The module calculates separately the numerator ($\vec{x}\_num^c$) and the denominator (x_den^c) of the CoM. It integrates a divider to calculate the reciprocal of f^i and L multipliers for the products $x^i * 1/f^i$. Also, $L + 1$ reduction (accumulation) circuits are used to calculate the numerator (L points) and the denominator and L dividers to calculate the final result. The output dividers are activated when the last candidate has been processed. The module has been designed in a fully pipelined fashion (assuming that the arithmetic circuits are also pipelined) and its total delay depends on the latency of the arithmetic circuits (i.e. divider, multiplier, accumulator). Note that the design of reduction circuits requires special attention when the reduction operation has a long latency. For more information about the design of high-speed reduction circuits see Subsect. 3.2.

Our FPGA BB-BC architecture is parameterized to support various alternatives regarding the function for the calculation of center of mass, the implementation of the arithmetic operators (multipliers), the number representation (fixed point arithmetic) and the parameters of the BB-BC algorithm. The main parameters of the FPGA BB-BC architecture are presented in Table 1.

The latency and the arithmetic operators of the pipeline stages of the BB-BC engine are presented in Table 2. Note that the output divider for the calculation of complex CoM is activated only for the last candidate of every iteration (see asterisk in the last row of the Table). Assuming population size N and number of iterations M, the total execution time (ET) of the proposed FPGA architecture for the minimal cost function (ET-MCF$_{total}$) and the complex CoM equation (ET-CCE$_{total}$) are (T_A, T_M, T_D, T_R and T_c are the Adder, Multiplier, Divider, Reciprocal and Comparator latencies):

$$\text{ET-MCF}_{total} = M \times ((1 + T_M + T_A) + T_F + T_C + N) \tag{3}$$

$$\text{ET-CCE}_{total} = M \times ((1 + T_M + T_A) + T_F + (T_R + T_M + T_A) + N + T_D) \tag{4}$$

Table 1. FPGA BB-BC architecture parameters

Parameter	Values	Comments
CoM calculation function	(a) minimal cost function (b) complex inverse fitness function	Option (a) reduces system complexity, while option (b) improves convergence speed/accuracy
Arithmetic circuits	(a) simple non-pipelined HDL operators (b) use of highly optimized IP blocks	Option (b) is selected for speed optimization
Number representation	Fixed point arithmetic (variable length of integer and fractional parts)	Future versions will support floating-point arithmetic
BB-BC fitness function	Problem-dependent	Future versions will support dynamic reconfiguration of fitness function
BB-BC algorithm parameters	(a) number of iterations (M) (b) population size (N) (c) number of candidate features (L) (d) LFSR seeds	Algorithm parameters are configured statically. Future versions will support dynamic reconfiguration of all parameters

Table 2. BB-BC engine latency and arithmetic operations

Pipeline stage	CoM function	Latency	Arithmetic operations
Candidate generation	–	$1 + T_M + T_A$	L LFSR, L Multipliers, L Adders
Fitness calculation	–	T_F Problem-dependent	Problem-dependent
CoM calculation	Minimal cost	T_C	1 Comparator
	Complex CoM	$(T_R + T_M + T_A) + T_D^{(*)}$	1 Reciprocal, L Multipliers, $L + 1$ Adders, L Dividers

3.2   High-Speed Reduction Circuits for the Calculation of CoM

Reduction method refers to reducing a series of sequentially generated input values (in our case the candidate values and their inverse fitness functions) to one value (the numerator and the denominator of the complex CoM equation) using one type of binary operator (in our case $\sum d_i$, where d_i equals $\frac{1}{f^i}x^i$ and $\frac{1}{f^i}$ for the numerator and the denominator, respectively). If the latency of the primitive operation (comparison or accumulation) is 1 clock cycle, then the design of the reduction circuit is straightforward. However, in the case of multiple-clock-cycle latency (e.g. due to the use of high-speed pipelined operators or floating-point arithmetic), the design of the reduction circuit requires special attention. For example, if a simple accumulator is employed to perform the reduction for an operator with t-cycle latency, then the circuit must wait for t clock cycles before feeds the next value to the accumulator introducing pipeline stalls in the reduction process.

The CoM reduction could be implemented using a full binary tree with P leaf operators. A pipelined implementation of the tree provides a high-speed reduction circuit, which may input up to P candidate values in every clock cycle. However, this solution requires a large amount of hardware resources (i.e. $P - 1$ operators) and it is practically infeasible even for moderate values of P. Instead, high-speed reduction circuits such as those proposed in [15, 16] can be utilized. These circuits reduce multiple sets of sequentially generated input data without stalling the pipeline or imposing large buffer requirements. In this paper, one-cycle latency reduction operations (comparison, accumulation) are assumed and thus no sophisticated reduction circuits are required. We aim at integrating a high-speed reduction scheme in future versions of the FPGA accelerator in order to support long-latency operators.

3.3   Parallel FPGA BB-BC Architecture

To improve performance, several BB-BC engines can be integrated in our hardware accelerator. Figure 3d shows four BB-BC engines running in parallel. Each engine encapsulates a RandGen module to generate random candidates $\vec{x}^i$, a Fitness module to calculate the fitness function f^i and a CalcCoM module (Fig. 3a) which calculates the reciprocal of f^i and the product $\vec{x}^i * 1/f^i$. The values produced by all parallel engines are processed by a full binary tree of 2-cand-add operators. Each 2-cand-add module (Fig. 3b) produces the sum of the values ($\vec{x}^i/f^i$ and $1/f^i$) of two candidates. The final output of the binary tree is the sum of the values $\sum_{i=1}^{4} \vec{x}^i/f^i$ and $\sum_{i=1}^{4} 1/f^i$ of all four engines. The output of the tree is fed to the CoM-reduction module (Fig. 3c) which reduces the sequentially generated values of the partial sums of four candidates to calculate the numerator ($\vec{x}\_num^c$) and the denominator (x_den^c) of the Eq. (1) and finally the CoM of the generation.

The latency and the arithmetic operators of the extra modules used in the parallel scheme are presented in Table 3. Assuming G parallel engines, the full binary tree includes $G - 1$ 2-cand-add modules. The total execution time (ET) of the parallel FPGA architecture for the minimal cost function (ET-MCF$_{total}$) and the complex CoM equation (ET-CCE$_{total}$) are

$$\text{ET-MCF}_{\text{total}} = M \times ((1 + T_M + T_A) + T_F + T_C + N/G) \tag{5}$$

$$\text{ET-CCE}_{\text{total}} = M \times ((1 + T_M + T_A) + T_F + (T_R + T_M) + (\log_2 G \times T_A) + T_A + N/G + T_D)) \tag{6}$$

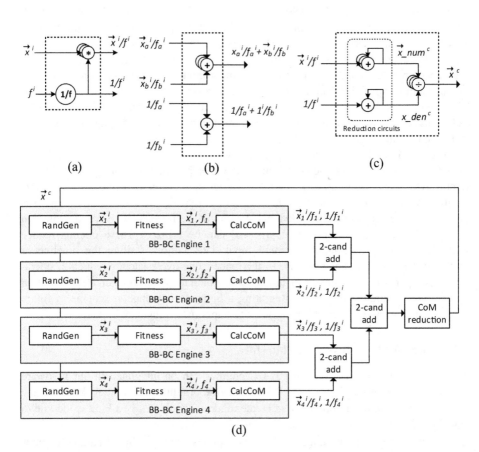

(a)   (b)   (c)

(d)

Fig. 3. Parallel BB-BC architecture: (a) CalcCoM module, (b) 2-cand-add module, (c) CoM-reduction module, (d) Four parallel BB-BC engines

Table 3. Parallel BB-BC scheme latency and operations ($T_{A/M/D/R/C}$: Adder/Multiplier/Divider/Reciprocal/Comparator latency)

Module	CoM function	Latency	Arithmetic operations
CalcCoM	Minimal cost	–	–
	Complex CoM	$T_R + T_M$	1 Reciprocal, L Multipliers
2-cand-add tree	Minimal cost	$\log_2 G * T_C$	$G - 1$ Comparators
	Complex CoM	$\log_2 G * T_A$	$(G - 1) * (L + 1)$ Adders
CoM-reduction	Minimal cost	T_C	1 Comparator
	Complex CoM	$T_A + T_D^{(*)}$	$L + 1$ Adders, L Dividers

4 Experimental Results

The proposed FPGA BB-BC architecture has been implemented for a typical benchmark problem in the Xilinx Virtex-5 XC5VLX10T device (Xilinx XUPV505 development board). The adopted benchmark is the two-variable Rosenbrock function $f(x_1, x_2) = (a - x_1)^2 + b(x_2 - x_1^2)^2$. Different versions of the BB-BC architecture have been implemented and compared in terms of device utilization, operating frequency and performance (i.e. total execution time). Table 4 presents the device utilization and operating frequency of several BB-BC versions: (i) single engine vs. dual (parallel) engine, (ii) function for the calculation of CoM: minimal cost function (MCF) vs. complex CoM equation (CCE), (iii) arithmetic circuits (multipliers): non-pipelined HDL operators vs. highly optimized IP cores (Core Generator).

Table 4. Reconfigurable resources and maximum operating frequency

CoM function	Scheme	Arithmetic circuits	LUTs	Registers	DSP48Es	Clock freq (MHz)
MCF	Single engine	HDL	1115	952	22	70.7
		CoreGen	1371	1193	24	215
	Dual engine	HDL	1986	1798	44	58.8
		CoreGen	2725	2267	48	183.6
CCE	Single engine	HDL	3422	5207	30	70.7
		CoreGen	3820	5437	32	215
	Dual engine	HDL	4787	6870	60	58.8
		CoreGen	5543	7392	64	183.6

Figure 4a presents the execution time (in μs) of the single and dual engines (using the CCE function and CoreGen building blocks) versus: (a) the number of iterations (M) assuming population size (N) is 256 and (b) the population size (N) assuming the number of iterations (M) is 256 (arithmetic circuits latencies are $T_A = 1$, $T_M = 6$, $T_D = 32$, $T_R = 22$, $T_c = 1$ and $T_F = 17$). The curves clearly demonstrate the performance improvement achieved by the parallel scheme (dual engine) compared to the single engine which increases with the number of iterations and population size. Figure 4b presents the product "area × execution time" of the single and dual engines (using the CCE function) with HDL or CoreGen multiplier circuits versus the population size (N) assuming the number of iterations (M) is 256. For the area calculation, an 644-LUT equivalent area for the DSP48E has been assumed [17]. Thus, the product "area × execution time" is (LUTs + Regs + 644 × DSP48E) × ET (in μs). The curves show that: (a) the highly optimized multipliers improve significantly the max operating frequency and consequently the system performance and (b) the single engine achieves a better tradeoff between area and execution time compared to the dual engine. It should be noted that results for more parallel engines are not presented because they exceed the available number of DSP48Es of the target Virtex-5 device.

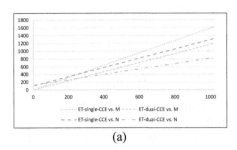 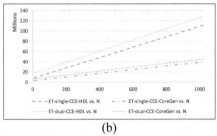

(a)   (b)

Fig. 4. Comparison between single and dual engine: (a) execution time, (b) execution time × area

To demonstrate the speedup achieved by the proposed FPGA accelerator, we developed single-threaded C software programs for the BB-BC algorithm and a typical GA algorithm. In order to emulate an embedded real-time platform, we run the GA and BB-BC programs as baremetal applications in an ARM Cortex-A9 processor running at 866 MHz. Table 5 compares the execution time between the proposed FPGA BB-BC accelerator (single-CCE engine and dual-CCE engine with CoreGen building blocks) and the GA and BB-BC s/w programs for various numbers of generations (M) and population size (N) equal to 256. The single engine achieves an average speedup of 121x and 74x, while the dual engine achieves an average speedup of 165x and 101x against the GA and BB-BC s/w programs, respectively. The results prove both the superiority of the proposed BB-BC algorithm against the GAs for real-time optimization problems and the efficiency of the proposed FPGA accelerator.

Table 5. Execution time of GA s/w, BB-BC s/w and FPGA BB-BC (in ms)

M	GA s/w	BB-BC s/w	FPGA: Single-CCE			FPGA: Dual-CCE		
			Exec. time	Speedup vs GA	Speedup vs BB-BC	Exec. time	Speedup vs GA	Speedup vs BB-BC
100	21.33	12.25	0.16	133	77	0.12	178	102
200	39.17	23.50	0.32	122	73	0.23	170	102
500	92.00	58.75	0.80	115	73	0.59	156	100
1000	181.00	116.63	1.59	114	73	1.17	155	100

5 Conclusion

In this paper, we studied the FPGA-based acceleration of a low-complexity optimization algorithm, namely *Big Bang-Big Crunch* (BB-BC). We proposed a novel, parameterized, pipelined FPGA design of the BB-BC algorithm that achieves significant speedup compared to its software counterpart. We also presented a parallel scheme which integrates several BB-BC engines to improve performance. Given the high-convergence speed of the BB-BC compared to typical genetic algorithms, the proposed FPGA accelerator greatly reduces the computational time providing an ideal platform for large-scale adaptive or latency-sensitive optimization problems.

Acknowledgement. This work has been partly supported by the University of Piraeus Research Center.

References

1. Erol, O.K., Eksin, I.: A new optimization method: Big Bang-Big Crunch. Adv. Eng. Softw. **37**(2), 106–111 (2006)
2. Scott, S.D., Samal, A., Seth, S.: HGA: a hardware-based genetic algorithm. In: Proceedings of the 1995 ACM Third International Symposium on Field-Programmable Gate Arrays, pp. 53–59. ACM, February 1995
3. Tang, W., Yip, L.: Hardware implementation of genetic algorithms using FPGA. In: The 2004 47th Midwest Symposium on Circuits and Systems, MWSCAS 2004, vol. 1, pp. I-549. IEEE, July 2004
4. dos Santos, P.V., Alves, J.C., Ferreira, J.C.: A framework for hardware cellular genetic algorithms: an application to spectrum allocation in cognitive radio. In: 2013 23rd International Conference on Field Programmable Logic and Applications (FPL), pp. 1–4. IEEE, September 2013
5. Tachibana, T., Murata, Y., Shibata, N., Yasumoto, K., Ito, M.: General architecture for hardware implementation of genetic algorithm. In: Annual IEEE Symposium on Field-Programmable Custom Computing Machines, FCCM 2006, pp. 291–292, April 2006
6. Fernando, P.R., Katkoori, S., Keymeulen, D., Zebulum, R., Stoica, A.: Customizable FPGA IP core implementation of a general-purpose genetic algorithm engine. IEEE Trans. Evol. Comput. **14**(1), 133–149 (2010)
7. Shackleford, B., Snider, G., Carter, R.J., Okushi, E., Yasuda, M., Seo, K., Yasuura, H.: A high-performance, pipelined, FPGA-based genetic algorithm machine. Genet. Program Evolvable Mach. **2**(1), 33–60 (2001)
8. Guo, L., Guo, C., Thomas, D.B., Luk, W.: Pipelined genetic propagation. In: 2015 IEEE 23rd Annual International Symposium on Field-Programmable Custom Computing Machines (FCCM), pp. 103–110. IEEE, May 2015
9. Guo, L., Funie, A.I., Thomas, D.B., Fu, H., Luk, W.: Parallel genetic algorithms on multiple FPGAs. ACM SIGARCH Comput. Archit. News **43**(4), 86–93 (2016)
10. Kaveh, A., Talatahari, S.: Size optimization of space trusses using Big Bang-Big Crunch algorithm. Comput. Struct. **87**(17), 1129–1140 (2009)
11. Kaveh, A., Talatahari, S.: Optimal design of Schwedler and ribbed domes via hybrid Big Bang-Big Crunch algorithm. J. Constr. Steel Res. **66**(3), 412–419 (2010)
12. Camp, C.V., Akin, A.: Design of retaining walls using Big Bang-Big Crunch optimization. J. Struct. Eng. **138**(3), 438–448 (2011)
13. Kumbasar, T., Eksin, I., Guzelkaya, M., Yesil, E.: Adaptive fuzzy model based inverse controller design using BB-BC optimization algorithm. Expert Syst. Appl. **38**(10), 12356–12364 (2011)
14. Yesil, E.: Interval type-2 fuzzy PID load frequency controller using Big Bang-Big Crunch optimization. Appl. Soft Comput. **15**, 100–112 (2014)
15. Zhuo, L., Morris, G.R., Prasanna, V.K.: High-performance reduction circuits using deeply pipelined operators on FPGAs. IEEE Trans. Parallel Distrib. Syst. **18**(10), 1377–1392 (2007)
16. Huang, M., Andrews, D.: Modular design of fully pipelined reduction circuits on FPGAs. IEEE Trans. Parallel Distrib. Syst. **24**(9), 1818–1826 (2013)
17. Jaiswal, M.K., So, H.K.H.: DSP48E efficient floating point multiplier architectures on FPGA. In: 2017 30th International Conference on VLSI Design and 2017 16th International Conference on Embedded Systems (VLSID), pp. 1–6. IEEE, January 2017

ReneGENE-GI: Empowering Precision Genomics with FPGAs on HPCs

Santhi Natarajan$^{(\boxtimes)}$, N. KrishnaKumar , Debnath Pal, and S. K. Nandy

Indian Institute of Science, Bangalore 560012, India
santhi@cadl.iisc.ernet.in

Abstract. Genome Informatics (GI) serves to be a holistic and inter-disciplinary approach in understanding genomic big data from a computational perspective. In another decade, the omics data production rate is expected to be approaching one zettabase per year, at very low cost. There is dire need to bridge the gap between the capabilities of Next Generation Sequencing (NGS) technology in churning out omics big data and our computational capabilities in omics data management, processing, analytics and interpretation. The High Performance Computing platforms seem to be the choice for bio-computing, offering high degrees of parallelism and scalability, while accelerating the multi-stage GI computational pipeline. Amidst such high computing power, it is the choice of algorithms and implementations in the entirety of the GI pipeline that decides the precision of bio-computing in revealing biologically relevant information. Through this paper, we present ReneGENE-GI, an innovatively engineered GI pipeline. We also present the performance analysis of ReneGENE-GI's Comparative Genomics Module (CGM), prototyped on a reconfigurable bio-computing accelerator platform. Alignment time for this prototype is about one-tenth the time taken by the single GPU OpenCL implementation of ReneGENE-GI's CGM, which itself is 2.62x faster than CUSHAW2-GPU (the GPU CUDA implementation of CUSHAW). With the single-GPU implementation demonstrating a speed up of 150+ x over standard heuristic aligners in the market like BFAST, the reconfigurable accelerator version of ReneGENE-GI's CGM is several orders faster than the competitors, offering precision over heuristics.

1 Introduction

Embedded in a long string spanning several billion characters, drawn from a set of genetic alphabets, the genomic big data encompasses a well authored genetic literary work that narrates the story of evolution over billions of years. Genome Informatics (GI), the study of genomes, integrates the big data of genomes with a ubiquitous base of interoperable medical and engineering disciplines. GI has evolved to be a discovery-driven approach to analyse the unstructured genomic big data, which takes inferences from an organism's genetic code to

© Springer International Publishing AG, part of Springer Nature 2018
N. Voros et al. (Eds.): ARC 2018, LNCS 10824, pp. 178–191, 2018.
https://doi.org/10.1007/978-3-319-78890-6_15

arrive at translationally important interpretations. Upcoming and widely popular GI applications cater to numerous domains including targeted personalized diagnostics and therapeutics, thereby improving the effectiveness of healthcare.

Understanding the genome through GI involves determining the order of the genetic alphabets or bases, namely adenine (A), cytosine (C), guanine (G) and thymine (T), within the genomic sequence, and the process is widely known as sequencing. Next Generation Sequencing (NGS) involves massively parallel sequencing of genetic data with high throughput, while offering an unparalleled interrogation of the genome, throwing deeper insight into the functional and structural investigation of genetic data [1,2]. By the year 2025, genomic data acquisition through NGS, being highly geographically distributed across multiple species, is predicted to reach the rate of one zettabase per year [3].

To perform associated complex computational data analytics on such large data volumes, GI adopts a multi-stage pipeline. The deployment of the GI pipeline exploits the best practices in High Performance Computing (HPC) on platforms like clouds, grids, accelerators and clusters, while strictly following bio-computational principles in classical genetics, molecular and cell biology. All such efforts are predominantly directed towards prospecting the unexploited scope of parallelism and scalability of the HPC platforms [4,5].

However, the bio-computing within the GI pipeline is irregular and combinatorial in nature. It is heavily data dependent, lacking sense of temporal and spatial locality of data. This severely curbs the performance of modern processor architectures built on deep memory hierarchies meant for pertinent data structures. The runtime computational irregularities are perfectly complemented by the non-contiguous file accesses, making an optimal parallelization of GI pipeline on a multi-core environment more difficult. The big data along with an all-to-all computation contributes to the time and computational complexity of the combinatorial algorithms. This makes fine-grain synchronization an utmost necessity to exploit data-level and process-level parallelism in a multi-node and multi-core HPC environment. In presence of a variety of accelerator platforms to conceive the parallel versions of the various computational algorithms, a substantial engineering effort is required in optimizing bio-computing on the available HPC hardware for concurrency, time, cost, and coverage [6–9].

Through this paper, we present ReneGENE-GI, an innovatively engineered GI pipeline. It performs mapping of raw genomic data from the NGS platforms with high precision. The pipeline hosts a unique blend of highly dynamic multi-dimensional data structures and parallel algorithms designed for executing the irregular genomic computing on accelerator based hardware and HPC platforms. ReneGENE-GI exploits the inherent parallelism and scalability of the hardware at the level of micro and system architecture to offer a reliable mapping for any NGS read data, regardless of the size. This allows for optimizing time, cost, and affordability without unduly penalizing biological fidelity of the results. It exploits a substantial degree of latent parallelism by engaging fine-grain synchronization, while allowing the application to scale up on HPC platforms.

The principal novelty of our solution involves engineering of the pipeline using existing algorithms on platforms using a data streaming approach that minimizes heap memory footprint and input/output bottlenecks. It is also supplemented by compiler-level and architecture-specific optimizations to improve the performance in a reconfigurable HPC environment. We also present the performance analysis for ReneGENE-GI's Comparative Genomics Module (CGM), implemented on a reconfigurable bio-computing accelerator platform.

2   The ReneGENE-GI Pipeline

The ReneGENE-GI pipeline, illustrated in Fig. 1, performs Short Read Mapping (SRM). The small fragments of genome from the NGS platforms, generally known as short reads, are mapped or aligned against a reference genome string through SRM. SRM works on the massive input data set of short reads, typically of the order of petabytes, and aims to find the region of origin of each short read string with respect to the reference, and hence find regions of similarity or dissimilarity. Eventually, SRM builds the longer genome from the short reads, by putting short reads together as in a jig-saw puzzle, with respect to a reference genome. SRM is interpreted as a classic Approximate String Matching (ASM) problem, to find occurrences of a smaller short read in a much larger reference [11–13].

The novelty of the ReneGENE-GI pipeline lies in the fact that it offers a unique blend of comparative genomics and *de novo* sequence assembly, offering the most precise SRM. The CGM exploits parallel dynamic programming methodology to accurately map the short reads against the reference genome. The alignment is backed by an exhaustive indexing and lookup of reads against the reference using the parallel implementation of dynamic Monotonic Minimal Perfect Hashing (MMPH) method [14]. This is a complete index of the reference, where the k-mer seeds fully cover the entire span of the reference, inclusive of the repeat regions. As compared to other indexing techniques that employ heuristics

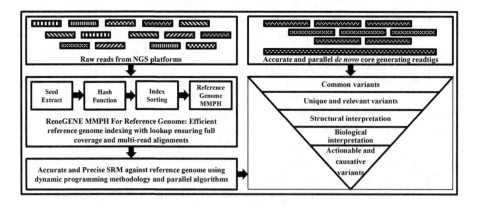

Fig. 1. The ReneGENE-GI pipeline

of purging repeat region hits, ReneGENE-GI pipeline reports those hits as well, throwing light on many anomalies embedded in these repeats.

The *de novo* module is implemented as a parallel map-reduce based readtig generation technique. The readtigs are extended short reads, based on a novel read extension algorithm, prototyped and verified for precision on HPC platforms with reconfigurable accelerator support. The readtigs are further mapped on to the reference genome to encompass the possible insertions and deletions of genetic alphabets at certain locations, thereby widening the map space and coverage.

The final SRM alignment results are then subjected to variant calling or preliminary tertiary analysis.

2.1   Read Extension Module of ReneGENE-GI

The *de novo* read extension module of the pipeline, deals with the problem of grouping the short reads based on an overlap relationship among the reads, in the absence of a reference genome. Related reads are grouped together and they grow to form longer sequences called readtigs. Here again, a single read can share a similar overlap relationship with several of its sequence neighbours, resulting in a single seed growing into many readtigs. This is decided on run time and hence the computations are clearly irregular due to the irregularity in the relationships among the input data sets. To accommodate the readtigs or extended reads that grow on the fly, this module implements dynamically growing data structures cast in the map-reduce framework, allowing a parallel deployment. The *de novo* module processing is shown in Algorithm 1.

Algorithm 1. RENEGENE_NOVO_READTIG()

// **Purpose:** *de novo* read extension function to generate readtigs
// **Input:** Input short reads R in fastq format
// **Output:** Assembled Readtigs C in fastq format
- -
Partition the short reads R into S_n read sets
for each read set S_i in S_n **do**
    Load each M_i in M_n readtig maps with reads from S_i to form readtig seeds
end for
for each readtig map M_i in M_n parallel maps **do**
    for each read r in R in the forward direction **do**
        if r overlaps with a readtig seed from M_i **then**
            Assemble r with the seed
        end if
    end for
    for each read r in R in reverse direction **do**
        if r overlaps with a readtig seed from M_i **then**
            Assemble r with the seed
        end if
    end for
end for
for each readtig map M_i in M_n **do**
    Merge contents to form readtig set C
end for

2.2   Variant Calling in ReneGENE-GI

Variants or mutations in a genome sequence represent the unique changes in genomic alphabets along the length of the target genome, with respect to a reference genome at specific locations. Variant calling is the process of identifying such variants for the sample under consideration. These variants can eventually throw light on many structural and functional anomalies embedded in the genomes and its repeat regions, manifesting in the form of structural and Copy Number Variations (CNVs), Single Nucleotide Polymorphisms (SNPs) etc. A precise alignment achieved through ReneGENE-GI's SRM enables a variant calling of high quality and confidence levels, allowing a more precise genotyping and phenotyping in presence of fusion genes and translocations within repeat regions in a genome. The SRM output from ReneGENE-GI is presented to variant calling tools like GATK, SAMTOOLS, FreeBayes etc which provide the resultant variant calls in the standard VCF format.

Amidst a wide variety of state-of-the art GI solutions [17,18], the genomic computing community faces a lack of consensus or standards in brewing a flawless elucidation of biologically relevant information. In addition, the choices of algorithms and implementations in intermediate stages of GI have been subjective enough to snub out the useful information for downstream analyses, in the process of optimizing and accelerating the pipeline. As a result, downstream analyses continue to suffer due to the sufficiently large heuristics-driven errors that creep into the pipeline and subsequent biologically relevant inferences. In this context, the ReneGENE-GI pipeline stands out in offering the optimal choice for performing GI, over a fully accelerated pipeline, with an underlying confidence in the biologically significant and causative inferences made downstream.

3   ReneGENE AccuRA - The Comparative Genomics Module (CGM) of ReneGENE-GI

3.1   AccuRA: The SRM Pipeline

ReneGENE-GI's CGM is implemented on a reconfigurable accelerator platform as ReneGENE-AccuRA. This is an extended version of AccuRA, published in our earlier work [19], which presents AccuRA's architecture, algorithms, mathematical model and scalability analysis. The AccuRA hardware archetype is presented in Fig. 2.

The SRM performed by the CGM, when applied to very long genomic sequences, is interpreted as an Approximate String Matching (ASM) problem. SRM algorithmically analyses the structural, functional and evolutionary relationship between the two input strings. SRM attempts to search the specific short read string q of length $|q|$ (ranging from about 25 to a few hundred bases), over a much longer reference genome string G of length $|G|$ (a human reference genome is typically 3 billion bases long). The aim is to find the regions of origin of each short read string with respect to the reference, and hence find regions of similarity or dissimilarity, over the character set $\Sigma = \{A, C, G, T\}$.

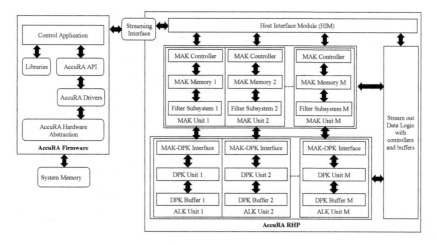

Fig. 2. AccuRA SRM pipeline architecture: the RHP hosts Mapper Kernel (MAK) units embedded with filter subsystem and Aligner Kernel (ALK) Units embedded with Dynamic Programming Kernel (DPK) units.

Algorithm 2. SRM_DP()

// **Purpose:** Approximate String Matching for pairwise sequence alignment with DP algorithms
// **Input:** short reads q, reference genome sub string g, DP algorithm parameters
// **Output:** Final optimal alignment score
- -
for Each Read in Read Set **do**
   Load Read q
   Load Reference genome substrings set, post lookup
   for Each g in reference substrings set **do**
      Initialize Alignment Matrix D
      Align q to gaps $D[0][j] = 0$ //$0 < j < N$
      Align g to gaps $D[i][0] = 0$ //$0 < i < M$
      $Score_{opt} \leftarrow 0$ //Initialize optimal score to 0
      Intialize Insertion Matrix I;
      for $i = 1$ to M **do**
         for $j = 1$ to N **do**   //recursive scoring model with affine gap penalty
            DP_SRM_Recursive_Function()
            Update $Score_{opt}$
         end for
      end for
      $Score_{opt} \leftarrow \displaystyle\max_{i=1, j=1}^{M,N} (D[i][j])$
      Call_Traceback()
   end for
end for

The SRM, based on a Dynamic Programming (DP) [20] method, with preprocessing, is shown in Algorithm 2. While handling genome sequences, the DP technique is proven to be the most sensitive in performing ASM. The DP method comes with a quadratic time and space complexity of $O\ (LN)$. The DP based algorithms employ a recursive scoring or cost function model, with an appropriate linear or affine penalty model (for the dissimilarities and string errors), to assign scores for mapping. The algorithm adopts a matrix space, called the alignment matrix, D.

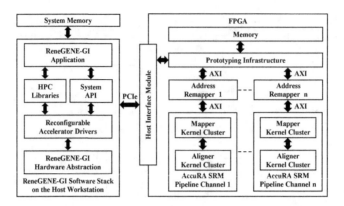

Fig. 3. ReneGENE-AccuRA: the multi-channel architecture based on AccuRA SRM pipeline

The Dynamic Programming Kernel (DPK) units in AccuRA's hardware host a highly efficient and parallel DPK kernel to achieve traceback in hardware, based on a DP alignment algorithm. The hardware performs alignment, in the shortest deterministic time, agnostic to short read length. AccuRA achieves a significant improvement in performance over conventional RHP models for SRM, with adequate sequence partitioning and scheduling schemes in the SRM workflow. By performing traceback in hardware overlapped with the forward scan during alignment, AccuRA eliminates the memory bottleneck issues and reduces the compute intensive tasks on the host significantly. The AccuRA prototype, configured on a reconfigurable hardware like FPGA, scaled well towards accommodating the big data of short reads of varying lengths, from smaller prokaryotic genomes to the larger mammalian genome, with a fine-grained single nucleotide resolution.

3.2 ReneGENE-AccuRA: A Multichannel Implementation of AccuRA SRM Pipeline

The scalability analysis and results from various prototypes in our earlier work proved to substantiate the scalability and performance of the parallel AccuRA SRM pipeline, making it a promising target to accelerate the SRM process in the NGS pipeline. Here, we present ReneGENE-AccuRA, a multi-channel, scalable and massively parallel computing pipeline that performs ultra-fast alignment of DNA short reads, presented in Fig. 3. Each channel of ReneGENE-AccuRA is composed of one AccuRA SRM pipeline, hosting several DPK and mapper units. A single reconfigurable hardware like FPGA can host multiple such AccuRA SRM pipelines. Supplemented with multi-threaded firmware architecture, ReneGENE-AccuRA precisely aligns short reads, at a fine-grained single nucleotide resolution, and offers full alignment coverage of the genome including repeat regions. ReneGENE-AccuRA is a fully streaming solution that eliminates memory bottleneck and storage issues, thus reducing the computing and I/O burden on the host significantly. With an appropriate data streaming pipeline, we provide an affordable solution, customizable according to scalability needs and capital availability. It is also pluggable to any genome analysis pipeline for use across multiple domains from research to clinical environment.

4 ReneGENE-AccuRA: Prototype and Results

4.1 Prototype Model for ReneGENE-AccuRA

ReneGENE-AccuRA was prototyped on an HPC platform supported with a reconfigurable accelerator card built on multiple Xilinx Virtex 7 XC7V2000T devices, that is scalable upto 633 million ASIC gates. The host interface is through a Kintex-7 XC7K325T-FBG900 FPGA. The host processor is interfaced to the Kintex-7 FPGA via the high speed interface of PCI-E x8 gen3. The embarassingly parallel bio-computing in AccuRA's SRM is further favoured by the inherent reprogrammability of FPGAs, massively parallel compute resources, extreme data path parallelism and fine grained control mechanisms offered by the FPGAs.

4.2 ReneGENE-AccuRA Software

The software stack comprises of the preprocessing and post-processing modules of the ReneGENE-GI pipeline. This includes: (i) the reference index hashing step based on the MMPH algorithm, (ii) the read-lookup algorithm against the indexed reference for candidate genomic locations for a probable alignment, (iii) the HPC platform specific libraries and middleware, (iv) the hardware abstraction layer with the corresponding device drivers and platform drivers, (v) the post-processing module that makes decisions for the best alignment, secondary alignments, the corresponding computations for alignment/map qualities and (vi) a subsequent formatting of the output data in the Sequence Alignment (SAM) format. The pipeline also allows conversion of the SAM file to its compressed Binary Alignment (BAM) file and its verification towards fitness for downstream NGS data analytics. The software runs on a multi-core host (Intel core i7 8-core processor) with 32 GB system RAM.

4.3 ReneGENE-AccuRA Hardware

The multi-channel ReneGENE-AccuRA is represented as DUT within each FPGA. It is interfaced with the prototyping infrastructure on the FPGA through the standard AXI4 interface with 256 bit-wide data bus, running at a frequency of 125 MHz. The Address Remapper unit allows an automatic remapping of the address spaces of DUT for transactions, allowing an ease of scalability in adding more AccuRA SRM channels to the DUT. The implementation is done using VHDL and Verilog.

4.4   Scalability Analysis for ReneGENE-AccuRA

The parameters in scalability analysis for ReneGENE-AccuRA are given in Table 1. Consider the multi-channel AccuRA SRM pipeline model, where the reads are streamed in at the rate R_{in} (measured as Giga Reads/second or GR/s) over an input streaming bandwidth of BW_{in} (measured as Giga Bytes/second

Table 1. Scalability analysis parameters

Symbols	Description
BW_{in}	Streaming input bandwidth
L	Short read length
B	Streaming buffer depth
l	Subsequence length for short read
m	Number of partitions for input short read, with overlapping
b	Number of bits for encoding each bp of input short read
bl	Streaming buffer width
τ_{MAK}	MAK unit clock period
τ_{DPK}	DPK unit clock period
x	MAK unit operating cycles
y	DPK unit operating cycles
P	Total number of pairs launched on MAK-DPK units for SRM
N	Number of MAK-DPK units deployed on a single AccuRA SRM pipeline channel
$p = \frac{P}{N}$	Number of pairs allotted for SRM, per MAK-DPK unit
C	No. of cell updates per DPK unit
K	No. of filter kernel operations per MAK unit
R_{in}	No. of filter kernel operations per MAK unit $R_{in} = \frac{8 \times BW_{in}}{b \times m \times l}$
T_{MAK}	Total MAK unit time to cover P pairs $T_{MAK} = x \times \tau_{MAK}$
T_{DPK}	Total DPK unit time to cover P pairs $T_{DPK} = y \times \tau_{DPK}$
R_{RHP}	Read Processing Rate of a single AccuRA SRM pipeline channel $R_{RHP} = \frac{N}{T_{MAK}+T_{DPK}}$
T_{RHP}	Alignment Time of a single AccuRA SRM pipeline channel $T_{RHP} = p \times (T_{MAK} + T_{DPK})$
$T_{single\_channel\_AccuRA}$	The total time invested in performing SRM in a single AccuRA SRM pipeline channel $T_{single\_channel\_AccuRA} \approx T_{Load} + T_{RHP} + T_{Unload}$
P_{MAK}	Performance of MAK units within a single AccuRA SRM pipeline, measured in terms of Giga Maps Per Second (GMPS) $P_{MAK} = \frac{N \times K}{x \times T_{MAK}}$
P_{DPK}	Performance of DPK units within a single AccuRA SRM pipeline, measured in terms of Giga Cell Updates Per Second (GCUPS) $P_{DPK} = \frac{N \times C}{y \times T_{DPK}}$

or GB/s). The m subsequences of short reads, each of length l, are streamed through a streaming buffer of depth B, which holds one subsequence in each word of storage.

Each MAK unit performs filtering in time T_{MAK}, over x cycles of the MAK unit clock, with period τ_{MAK}. Each DPK unit performs alignment in time T_{DPK}, over y cycles of the DPK unit clock, with period τ_{DPK}. If N MAK-DPK units are configured within a single AccuRA SRM pipeline channel, then each unit gets its share of p pairs for performing SRM. The single AccuRA SRM pipeline channel thus performs N SRMs in a total time of $T_{MAK} + T_{DPK}$, with N MAK-DPK units running in parallel. The single channel hence processes reads at a rate of R_{RHP} measured in GR/s. At this rate, the hardware aligns all the P reads, with p reads aligned in parallel over N MAK-DPK units, over a total time of T_{RHP}.

For scaling up the performance, let us include C such channels of AccuRA SRM pipelines within a single FPGA. Here, each channel will take the same amount of time to process the same number of reads.

Now, the overall performance from all the MAK units from C channels, measured in terms of Giga Maps Per Second (GMPS), is given by:

$$P_{MAK} = \frac{C \times N \times K}{x \times T_{MAK}} \tag{1}$$

The overall performance of DPK unit, measured in terms of Giga Cell Updates Per Second (GCUPS), is given by:

$$P_{DPK} = \frac{C \times N \times C}{y \times T_{DPK}} \tag{2}$$

Thus, we see that by scaling up the single AccuRA SRM pipeline channel, by increasing N, the ReneGENE-AccuRA hardware gains a better throughput, as it can handle more pairs in parallel. The scalability is complemented by further scaling up the number of such channels, C, within a single FPGA. The number of such channels within an FPGA is limited only by the allowed reconfigurable hardware space for the DUT within the FPGA. The input data is then fairly divided among the channels, so that the SRM process is complete in approximately $1/C$ times the total time taken for SRM by a single channel.

4.5   Results from Large Genome Benchmarks for ReneGENE-AccuRA

The ReneGENE-AccuRA prototype was tested by running SRM for very large data sets of the order of several Giga Bytes, for the mammalian human genome. The details of the input data set is provided in Table 2. We have used the GrCh38 reference genome assembly, which is around 3 billion bases long, consisting of all the 23 chromosomes and the mitochondrial DNA. We have considered the alignment of three human genomes, each of which correspond to a family of father (SRR1559289, SRR1559290, SRR1559291, SRR1559292, SRR1559293), mother (SRR1559294, SRR1559295, SRR1559296, SRR1559297, SRR1559298) and their

Table 2. Human genome experiment details

ID	SRR read	No. of reads	No. of bases	Buffer contents for SRM	No. of streamed batches
1	SRR1559289	27594045	5.5G	1545583696	82
2	SRR1559290	28019239	5.6G	1567102768	84
3	SRR1559291	169777482	34G	9616084216	510
4	SRR1559292	168278483	33.7G	9031420804	479
5	SRR1559293	168484341	33.7G	9194814968	488
6	SRR1559294	180827103	36.2G	10449482200	554
7	SRR1559295	96741850	19.3G	5716247292	303
8	SRR1559296	148849161	29.8G	8719041172	462
9	SRR1559297	33028205	6.6G	1872052764	100
10	SRR1559298	33621893	6.7G	1899810824	101
11	SRR1559281	146929886	29.4G	8661172200	459
12	SRR1559282	143848074	28.8G	8348191016	443
13	SRR1559283	144871968	29G	8415342112	446
14	SRR1559284	142831237	28.6G	8303472652	440

child (SRR1559281, SRR1559282, SRR1559283, SRR1559284). Here, each read is 200 bp long. The reads are subjected to lookup against the reference genome index. Subsequently, they are sent for alignment on the FPGA by streaming over the PCIe link through buffers that are configured to hold up to 18874368 words of data in one batch.

The ReneGENE-AccuRA prototype was tested with single and dual channel AccuRA SRM pipelines within a single FPGA while aligning the human short read sets. Each channel hosted 16 MAK units and 16 DPK units. With this configuration, to align 500 million reads (100 bases long) against the reference genome (3 billion bases long), with each read reporting a mapping at five locations on the reference, ReneGENE-AccuRA performs 4.65 Tera map operations and 10.24 Tera cell updates at the rate of 21.14 GMPS and 46.56 GCUPS in about 3.68 min. The implementation results for the dual-channel ReneGENE-AccuRA are provided in Table 3.

Table 3. ReneGENE-AccuRA utilization report, with single and dual channel AccuRA SRM pipeline single Xilinx Virtex 7 XC7V2000T device

Feature	Single channel	Percentage utilization: single channel	Dual channel	Percentage utilization: dual channel
Number of slice registers	128708 out of 2443200	5.26	213366 out of 2443200	8.73
Number of slice LUTs	170177 out of 1221600	13.93	310045 out of 1221600	25.35
Number of bonded IOBs	166 out of 850	19.52	96 out of 850	19.52
Number of block RAM/FIFO	203 out of 1292	15.71	374 out of 1292	28.90

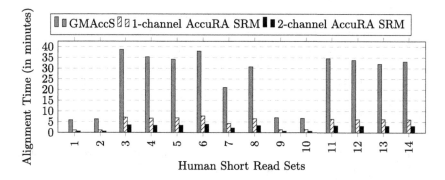

Fig. 4. Performance comparison of FPGA versus GPU for human short read sets.

For the human genome read sets in Table 2, the alignment times for various configurations are shown in Fig. 4. Here, we can see that the time taken by ReneGENE-AccuRA is about one-fifth (with single channel AccuRA SRM pipeline) and about one-tenth (with dual channel AccuRA SRM pipeline), the time taken by the single GPU OpenCL implementation of ReneGENE-GI's CGM. This single GPU implementation is itself 2.62x faster than CUSHAW2-GPU (the GPU CUDA implementation of CUSHAW) [21,22]. With the single-GPU implementation demonstrating a speedup of 150x over standard heuristic aligners in the market like BFAST [23], the reconfigurable accelerator version of ReneGENE-AccuRA is several orders faster than the competitors, offering precision over heuristics. By extending the implementation to four and six channels within a single FPGA, there is a definite increase expected in the performance as evident from the scalability analysis. With multiple FPGAs available on the platform, the scope for further improvement in performance increases with increase in number of FPGAs and number of channels supported within the FPGAs.

5   Conclusion

Through this paper, we have presented ReneGENE-GI, an innovatively engineered GI pipeline. The pipeline strikes the right balance between comparative genomics and *de novo* read extension, to run an irregular application like GI. With parallel algorithms executed on reconfigurable accelerator hardware, ReneGENE-GI exploits the inherent parallelism and scalability of the hardware at the level of micro and system architecture, amidst fine-grain synchronization.

Supplemented with a multi-threaded firmware architecture, the Comparative Genomics Module (CGM) in ReneGENE-GI precisely aligns short reads, at a fine-grained single nucleotide resolution, and offers full alignment coverage of the genome including repeat regions. The parallel dynamic programming kernels on multiple channels of CGM seamlessly perform traceback process in hardware simultaneously along with forward scan, thus achieving short read mapping in minimum deterministic time. ReneGENE-GI is a fully streaming solution that eliminates memory bottleneck and storage issues, thus reducing the computing and I/O burden on the host significantly. With an appropriate data streaming pipeline, we provide an affordable solution, customizable according to scalability needs and capital availability. It is also pluggable to any genome analysis pipeline for use across multiple domains from research to clinical environment.

References

1. Frese, K.S., Katus, H.A., Meder, B.: Next-generation sequencing: from understanding biology to personalized medicine. Biology **2**(4), 378–398 (2013)
2. Mardis, E.R.: A decade's perspective on DNA sequencing technology. Nat. Perspect. **470**, 198–203 (2011)
3. Stephens, Z.D., Lee, S.Y., Faghri, F., Campbell, R.H., Zhai, C., Efron, M.J., et al.: Big data: astronomical or genomical? PLOS Biol. **13**(7), e1002195 (2015)
4. Lee, C.Y., Chiu, Y.C., Wang, L.B., et al.: Common applications of next-generation sequencing technologies in genomic research. Transl. Cancer Res. **2**(1), 33–45 (2013)
5. Alyass, A., Turcotte, M., Meyre, D.: From big data analysis to personalized medicine for all: challenges and opportunities. BMC Med. Genom. **8**, 33 (2015)
6. Costa, F.F.: Big data in genomics: challenges and solutions. G.I.T. Lab. J. **11**(12), 2–4 (2012)
7. Baker, M.: Next-generation sequencing: adjusting to data overload. Nat. Methods **7**, 495–499 (2010)
8. Chen, C., Schmidt, B.: Performance analysis of computational biology applications on hierarchical grid systems. In: Proceedings of IEEE International Symposium on Cluster Computing and the Grid, CCGrid 2004, Chicago, IL, pp. 426–433 (2004)
9. Bader, D.A.: High-performance algorithm engineering for large-scale graph problems and computational biology. In: Nikoletseas, S.E. (ed.) WEA 2005. LNCS, vol. 3503, pp. 16–21. Springer, Heidelberg (2005). https://doi.org/10.1007/11427186_3
10. SERC: Indian Institute of Science, Bangalore. Sahasrat (Cray XC40). http://www.serc.iisc.in/facilities/cray-xc40-named-as-sahasrat/
11. Navarro, G.: A guided tour to approximate string matching. ACM Comput. Surv. **33**(1), 31–88 (2001)
12. Smith, T.F., Waterman, M.S.: Identification of common molecular subsequences. J. Mol. Biol. **147**, 195–197 (1981)
13. Altschul, S.F., Bundschuh, R., Olsen, R., Hwa, T.: The estimation of statistical parameters for local alignment score distributions. Nucl. Acids Res. **29**, 351–361 (2001)
14. Myers, E.: A sublinear algorithm for approximate keyword searching. Algorithmica **12**, 345–374 (1994)
15. Treangen, T.J., Salzberg, S.L.: Repetitive DNA and next-generation sequencing: computational challenges and solutions. Nat. Rev. **13**, 36–46 (2012)
16. Flicek, P., Birney, E.: Sense from sequence reads: methods for alignment and assembly. Nat. Methods **6**, S6–S12 (2009)
17. Li, H., Homer, N.: A survey of sequence alignment algorithms for next-generation sequencing. Briefings Bioinform. **2**, 473–483 (2010)
18. Hatem, A., Bozdag, D., Toland, A.E., Catalyurek, U.V.: Benchmarking short sequence mapping tools. BMC Bioinform. **14**, 184 (2013)

19. Natarajan, S., KrishnaKumar, N., Pal, D., Nandy, S.K.: AccuRA: accurate alignment of short reads on scalable reconfigurable accelerators. In: Proceedings of IEEE International Conference on Embedded Computer Systems: Architectures, Modeling and Simulation (SAMOS XVI), pp. 79–87, July 2016

20. Natarajan, S., KrishnaKumar, N., Pavan, M., Pal, D., Nandy, S.K.: ReneGENE-DP: accelerated parallel dynamic programming for genome informatics. In: Accepted at the 2018 International Conference on Electronics, Computing and Communication Technologies (IEEE CONECCT), March 2018

21. Liu, Y., Schmidt, B., Maskell, D.L.: CUSHAW: a CUDA compatible short read aligner to large genomes based on the Burrows-Wheeler transform. Bioinformatics **28**(14), 1830–1837 (2012)

22. Liu, Y., Schmidt, B.: CUSHAW2-GPU: empowering faster gapped short-read alignment using GPU computing. IEEE Des. Test Comput. **31**(1), 31–39 (2014)

23. Homer, N., Merriman, B., Nelson, S.F.: BFAST: an alignment tool for large scale genome resequencing. PLoS ONE **4**, e7767 (2009)

FPGA-Based Parallel Pattern Matching

Masahiro Fukuda[1,2(✉)] ⓘ and Yasushi Inoguchi[1]

[1] Japan Advanced Institute of Science and Technology, Ishikawa, Japan
fukuda-masahiro@jaist.ac.jp
[2] National Institute of Technology, Ishikawa College, Ishikawa, Japan

Abstract. To protect IoT (Internet of Things) nodes against cyber attacks, NIDS (Network-based Intrusion Detection System) is becoming important. On future high-speed networks, NIDS needs to be high-speed hardware and parallelization is inevitable. The pattern matching of PCRE (Perl Compatible Regular Expressions) is one of the most complex parts in NIDS. We tried to improve the parallelization of PCRE pattern matching in Snort, implementing it on an FPGA. The essence of our method is eliminating memory from STEs (State Transition Elements), which is the bottleneck of parallelization. Our evaluation shows the proposed method is 8.37 times faster than a previous method.

Keywords: Field-Programmable Gate Array
Perl Compatible Regular Expressions · State Transition Element

1 Introduction

Recently, IoT (Internet of Things) is becoming prevalent. Household appliances and office supplies, even such as cameras, printers and digital video recorders as well as personal computers and smartphones are on the Internet. Currently these embedded equipments are often vulnerable mainly because of unchanged initial passwords. However, there is another near future problem that they generally do not have the computing power to execute antivirus software or anomaly analysis software to deal with cyber attacks.

Therefore, we think that NIDS (Network-based Intrusion Detection System) or NIPS (Network-based Intrusion Prevention System) will become important for such systems. NIDS is put on a computer network and monitors packets to detect intrusions. They detect attacks on the network rather than the host. Their main difficulty is executing complicated pattern matching of PCRE (Perl Compatible Regular Expressions) at high-speed. For example, Snort [1] is a famous open-source software of NIDS/NIPS and now developed by Sourcefire Inc owned by Cisco Systems. It can analyze traffic on IP (Internet Protocol) network and contains thousand kinds of PCREs such as /buy\x2f\?code\=\d/, /or[\s\x2f\x2A]+1=1/ or so on.

The network speed is increasing from 1 Gbps to 400 Gbps. Table 1 shows examples of the most famous MAC (Media Access Control) sublayer interfaces

© Springer International Publishing AG, part of Springer Nature 2018
N. Voros et al. (Eds.): ARC 2018, LNCS 10824, pp. 192–203, 2018.
https://doi.org/10.1007/978-3-319-78890-6_16

standardized by IEEE [2]. It is obvious that the parallelization of pattern matching is inevitable for dealing with multiple 8-bit input symbols without increasing the clock frequency more than now.

Table 1. Examples of MAC sublayer interfaces

	Speed [Gbps]	Clock freq. [MHz]	Clock period [ns]	Bus width [bits]
GMII	1	125.00	8.00	8
XGMII	10	156.25	6.40	64
XLGMII	40	625.00	1.60	64
CGMII	100	1,562.50	0.64	64

Our research purpose is accelerating pattern matching of PCRE in NIDS without interfering high-speed networks. Software implementation is not suitable for 100 Gbps because the delay of memory or input/output is generally longer than 0.64 ns and fine-grained control of on-chip memory is difficult. Hence our choice is a hardware implementation, especially FPGA. We also aimed for high parallelization instead of increasing the clock frequency.

The rest of this paper is organized as follows. Section 2 reviews related works. Section 3 describes a previous research. Section 4 introduces our method without memory and how to parallelize the circuit. Section 5 evaluates our method. Section 6 concludes the work.

2   PCRE and Related Works

2.1   PCRE

A PCRE (Perl Compatible Regular Expressions) is a regular expression in Perl language. It is used in Snort to define and detect strings included in complicated cyber attacks.

For example, /or[\s\x2f\x2A]+1 = 1/ is a PCRE. [\s\x2f\x2A] is called a character class and it matches \s, x2f or x2A. \s means white space characters, including SP (SPace) LF (Line Feed), HT (Horizontal Tab.) and so on. \x2f and \x2A means slash and asterisk in ASCII character table, respectively. Other characters (o, r, +, 1, = and 1) are not character classes (single characters). Totally, /or[\s\x2f\x2A]+1 = 1/ matches "or 1 = 1", "or[HT]1 = 1" or so on, where [HT] means a horizontal tab.

There are some processes in Snort, such as detecting HTTP requests and responses, extracting Cookies and so on, but processing PCRE is the most difficult part because of the increase of the dataset 3.

2.2 Software-Based Approaches

Fast software implementations tend to be DFA (Deterministic Finite Automaton) based and need memory of large capacity, because NFA (Non-deterministic Finite Automaton) based methods have to read the state transition table from memory many times. Pu et al. developed a software tool to translate regular expressions and the execution time is reduced by 66%, but is still 10.7 ms [4]. Another research by Yi et al. presents SFA (Semi-deterministic Finite Automaton) and it is between DFA and NFA in terms of computational and memory complexities, but it did not reach even 1 Gbps throughput [5]. Such software implementations take advantage of an off-chip large memory and it cannot provide a fast access of one clock cycle.

There are also several researches on GPU-based approach. It can be faster than CPU and implemented by software, but the power consumption is high. For example, Zu et al. achieved 10 Gbps and more with NVIDIA GTX-460 [6], but such a GPU consumes 100 W at least. Considering embedding it into network equipments, typical GPUs are not the best choice.

2.3 Hardware-Based Approaches

FPGA (Field-Programmable Gate Array) is used in or near network equipments for various applications [7] and many efficient implementations of regular expression matching on FPGA are proposed in recent years 3. Furthermore, in terms of power consumption, FPGAs are a few watts to tens of watts, even relatively high-end devices such as Virtex-7.

As one of the most recent researches, Dlugosch et al. presented a semiconductor implementation of AP (Automata Processor) corresponding to many functions of PCRE [8]. In this research, it aimed to general-purpose pattern matching and used much memory.

Roy's research is a case where Dlugosch's AP was applied to Snort and so on [9]. It reports an estimate that 10.3 Gbps can be realized, but it is the ideal performance when 48 chips are used and communication breakdown is a certain balance.

As another research, Cronin et al. proposed an efficient FPGA implementation for quantifications of PCRE [10]. However, this method needs BRAM (Block RAM) for quantifications and can be a bottleneck of parallelism even here.

In this paper, we will compare our method with Dlugosch's research as a previous study. Our method eliminates memory, which was the bottleneck of high parallelization to be realized.

3 Full-STE

3.1 Full-STE's Architecture

Automata Processor (AP) [8] presented by Dlugosch can perform pattern matching when PCRE or ANML (Automata Network Markup Language), both of which are languages capable of describing NFA, is compiled and loaded. ANML is beyond the scope of this paper, but in both cases, STE (State Transition Element) is one of the basic elements of this AP, and one STE corresponds to one state transition. Each STE determines whether or not its state transition is done per input symbol.

Figure 1 shows Full-STEs, which are simplified from Dlugosch's ones by omitting an OR-gates. A Full-STE is composed of a D-FF, an AND-gate and 256-bit memory. More specifically, when an input symbol s is inputted, Decoder recognizes s and asserts only the corresponding $RE(s)$, Recognition Enable. Memory reads the $Mb(s)$ bit corresponding to $RE(s)$. This $Mb(s)$ represents whether or not the condition of state transition is satisfied. On the other hand, a D-FF in the bottom of the Fig. 1 represents whether or not the source state is active. D-FF is always 1 if it is the initial state. If the source state is currently active and the condition of state transition is satisfied, then the destination state becomes active. Match signal is the output signal and represents that a match of one of PCREs at least is detected.

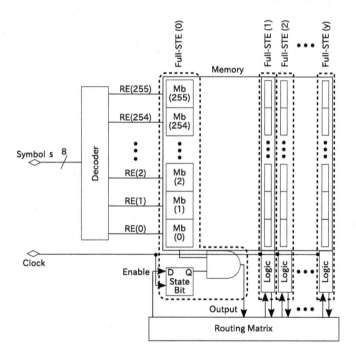

Fig. 1. Full-STE's architecture

Let y be the number of Full-STEs and it depends on the size of the rule set. They are connected by Routing Matrix, which determines the order of state transitions. In Dlugosch's paper, the maximum number of available Full-STEs was $y = 49,152$ and the size of memory was $256 \times 49,152 = 12,582,912$ bits, or

12 Mibit. But our research uses FPGA and y is variable depending on the rule set. Also, the wiring of Routing Matrix was hierarchical in order to suppress the propagation delay among 49,152 Full-STEs. In our research, the hierarchical architecture was not used and the estimation of propagation delay was left to the development tool by FPGA vendors.

A strength of Full-STE is that it can support arbitrary character class only by rewriting the content of Memory. This feature appears to be convenient for semiconductor implementation. And the condition of the state transition of each Full-STE is implemented as 256 bits of memory, so state transition by any character class can be realized as long as input symbol s is 1 byte.

For example, a PCRE, /or[\s\x2f\x2A]+1 = 1/, known as SQL injection, is converted into 7 Full-STEs. The content of memory in Full-STEs are shown in Table 2. The only 1 of memory in Full-STE(0) is 112th bit and it means o in ASCII character table. In Full-STE(1), only the 115th bit (r) is set. In Full-STE(2), several bits are set and they are corresponding to [\s\x2f\x2A]. Full-STE(3), Full-STE(4), Full-STE(5) and Full-STE(6) are almost the same as Full-STE(0) and Full-STE(1).

When o comes as an input symbol, the both inputs of AND-gate in Full-STE(0) become 1s and then the D-FF in Full-STE(1) also becomes 1. If the next input symbols are r, SP, +, 1, = and 1, then D-FFs in Full-STE(2), Full-STE(3), ⋯, Full-STE(6) become 1s in this order and finally Match signal becomes 1.

Table 2. An example of memory in Full-STEs

Full-STE	Content of memory as hexadecimal
Full-STE(0)	0000000000000000000000000001000000000000000000000000000000000000
Full-STE(1)	0000000000000000000000000002000000000000000000000000000000000000
Full-STE(2)	007C0000802100000000000000000000000000000000000000000000000000000
Full-STE(3)	0000000001000000000000000000000000000000000000000000000000000000
Full-STE(4)	0000000000040000000000000000000000000000000000000000000000000000
Full-STE(5)	0000000000000040000000000000000000000000000000000000000000000000
Full-STE(6)	0000000000040000000000000000000000000000000000000000000000000000

3.2   Full-STE's Problem in Snort Case

However, Full-STE needs a lot of memory and prevents further parallelization. In our estimation, the number of Full-STEs for 1 PCRE in the Snort rule set is about 10, and there are 7,898 PCREs. Simple calculation shows that $10 \times 7,898 \times 256 = 20,218,880$ bits are required for full support of the Snort rule set, although an FPGA device with such big BRAMs is limited. For example, Virtex-7 VX690T, one of Xilinx's high-end devices, has BRAMs of 52,920 Kbits and FFs of 866 Kbits, so the degree of parallelism is 2 at the maximum. If the processing speed is 1 Gbps without parallelization, it just becomes 2 Gbps with parallelization. VC709 has two external DRAMs (8 GB in total, DDR3) and they can be read by more than 10 Gbps, but it takes more than 1 clock cycle per read and is not useful in the case of random accesses.

According to a further analysis below, Full-STE is wasteful of memory when the state transition condition is not a character class but a single character. For example, considering a Full-STE that makes a state transition with the letter A, only the bit in the address 41 h is 1 according to the ASCII code. All other 255 bits of memory are 0s. Even character classes are often wasteful. For example, a character class \d means 0, 1, $\cdots$, 9, and it turns only 10 bits out of 256 bits to 1.

We examined how much single characters and character classes are in the snort rule set. The result was Table 3 63.7% was a single character. In other words, if we apply Dlugosch's AP to the Snort rule set, the Full-STE that only 1 bit is 1 occupies 63.7%. We think that Dlugosch's research aimed to create a general-purpose AP, but when trying to apply it to the Snort rule set, memory usage is inefficient. That is the cause of prevention of parallelization.

Table 3. Statistics about characters in Snort PCRE

	# of appearences (percentage)	# of kinds (percentage)
Single character	78,544 (63.7)	123 (42.7)
Character class	44,666 (36.3)	165 (57.3)
Total	123,210 (100.0)	288 (100.0)

If we can eliminate such big memory of Full-STEs, the bottleneck might be removed and further parallelization be achieved. Actually, combinatorial circuits to recognize all single characters and character classes in the Snort rule set can be implemented.

4   Proposed Methods

4.1   Single-STE

Our method, Single-STEs, shown in Fig. 2, upgrade Decoder to Character Class Recognizer instead of using memory. Character Class Recognizer is a combination circuit that judges whether an input symbol s corresponds to various characters or character classes and outputs it as RE. When an input symbol s is inputted, Character Class Recognizer outputs RE(s) and it goes into the Logic part (AND gate) of Single-STE through wiring like a matrix switch in the top right of the figure. The other, including Routing Matrix, is the same as Full-STEs.

Character Class Recognizer lets multiple REs be 1 at the same time unlike Decoder. In order not to interfere with them, only one RE for each Single-STE enter the lower side AND gate.

The strength of Single-STE is to eliminate memory. The weakness is that changing the rule set has to reconfigure Character Class Recognizer. If it is

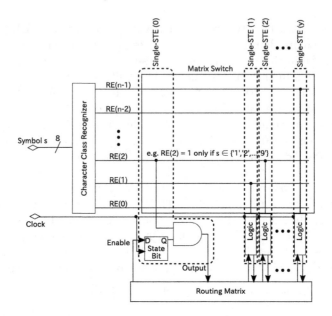

Fig. 2. Single-STE's architecture

premised to implement as semiconductor, it is advantageous that Full-STE can cope with change rule set simply by rewriting memory. But Single-STE can eliminate BRAM and can be highly parallelized in case of FPGA implementation.

About the example of /or[\s\x2f\x2A]+1 = 1/, 7 Single-STEs are needed just like Full-STEs. The conditions that D-FFs and Match signal are activated are also the same as Full-STEs. In the Single-STEs case, there is Character Class Recognizer instead of the memory in Full-STEs. In this case, Character Class Recognizer outputs RE(0), RE(1), $\cdots$, RE(5) and each means that the input symbol is o, r, [\s\x2f\x2A], +, 1 and =. The final 1 of the PCRE is represented as RE(4).

Above all, Single-STEs do not need any BRAM and the bottleneck of parallelization is eliminated. Furthermore, a duplication of 1 in this PCRE has been removed and the resource usage of LUTs is saved. They contribute a high parallelization.

4.2 Parallelization

Parallelization is done like Fig. 3. It is an example of two parallelization case. The left half circuit is exactly the same as Single-STEs shown in Fig. 2, but the wiring is changed in Routing Matrix. The circuit of the right half is also almost same as Fig. 2, but a D-FF in each Single-STE is removed and the circuit does not hold the current states. The role is to inform the left half circuit of only the result of state transition.

The wiring of Routing Matrix is as follows. The output of Single-STE(0), Single-STE(1), Single-STE(2) in the left half is connected to the input of Single-STE'(1), Single-STE'(2), Single-STE'(3) in the right half, respectively. On the other hand, the output of Single-STE'(0), Single-STE'(1), Single-STE'(2) in the right half is connected to the input of Single-STE(1), Single-STE(2), Single-STE(3) in the left half, respectively. These wirings let the left half process s_1 and the right half process s_2 just after s_1. Finally, Match signal is OR of the output of Single-STE(3) in the left half and Single-STE'(3) in the right half.

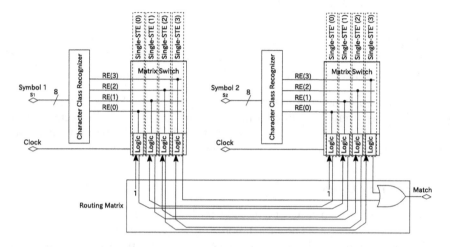

Fig. 3. Parallelization of Single-STEs

More specifically, when a stream $s = s_1 s_2 s_3 \cdots$ is inputted, the first two symbols s_1 and s_2 come into Fig. 3 in a clock cycle. The first symbol s_1 comes to the Character Class Recognizer of the left half in the figure, and the second symbol s_2 comes to the right half. Then REs (Recognition Enables) corresponding to s_1 and s_2 are asserted and they go to logic parts of STEs. The outputs of STEs in the left half represent the next states by inputting s_1. Then, the outputs of STEs in the right half represent the next states by inputting s_2 after s_1. They go to the left half and update the states of D-FFs. The above is done in one clock cycle because Single-STE'(0), Single-STE'(1), $\cdots$ in the right half do not include D-FFs.

By doing the same thing, it is theoretically possible to have parallel degree 3 or more. When trying to parallelize with Full-STE, BRAM doubles and triples, and it puts pressure on resources.

4.3   Automatical Conversion from PCRE to Verilog HDL

We developed a tool to automatically convert PCREs to Verilog HDL source files. The outlined way to generate them is as follows. Since this is not the subject of this paper, we will not go into details.

1. Remove PCREs including unsupported functions
2. Generate Character Class Recognizer
3. Generate Matrix Switch and Routing Matrix

In this way, disjunctions, quantifiers, etc. are not yet supported at the moment, so PCREs including them are eliminated. At this point, there were 7,898 rules and reduced to only 47. After that, we generate Verilog HDL of Character Class Recognizer, Matrix Switch and Routing Matrix. In the case of Full-STE, a COE file representing memory data is generated instead of a Character Class Recognizer. Then Routing Matrix is generated.

5   Simulation

5.1   Experimental Conditions

Synthesis and Implementation have been performed using Xilinx Vivado 2017.3. Their strategies were Vivado Synthesis Default and Vivado Implementation Default. The board was VC709 Connectivity Kit. In the constraint file, I set the clock cycle to 8 ns. The Snort rule set is a Registered edition, 2.9.9.0.

5.2   Resource Usage

The report on resource usage by Vivado is shown in the Tables 4 and 5. p is the degree of parallelism. The target board is VC709 Connectivity Kit and the numbers of available LUTs, FFs and BRAMs are 433,200, 866,400 and 1,470, respectively.

Table 4. Resource usage of Full-STEs

Type	$p = 1$	$p = 2$	$p = 4$	$p = 8$	$p = 16$	$p = 32$
LUT	521	526	639	1,277	2,453	4,380
FF	548	548	548	548	548	548
BRAMs	8.5	17	34	68	136	272

Table 5. Resource usage of Single-STEs

Type	$p = 1$	$p = 2$	$p = 4$	$p = 8$	$p = 16$	$p = 32$
LUT	287	837	1,328	2,508	4,920	9,625
FF	495	515	515	515	515	515
BRAMs	0	0	0	0	0	0

Figures 4 and 5 shows the resource utilizations ratio of Full-STE and Single-STE. BRAM is obviously the bottleneck of parallelization in Full-STE and there is no BRAM used in Single-STE. Single-STEs appears to be parallelized up to

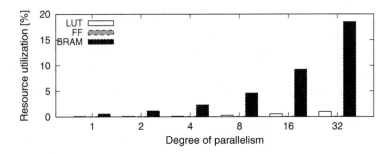

Fig. 4. Resource utilizations ratio of Full-STE

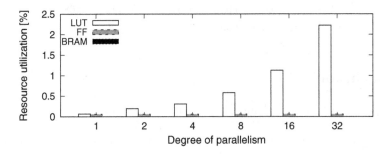

Fig. 5. Resource utilizations ratio of Single-STE

1,440 with the bottleneck of LUTs, while Full-STEs can be parallelized up to 172 with the bottleneck of BRAMs.

This simulation tells that it is expected that the degree of parallelism of Single-STEs can be greatly improved compared to Full-STEs. With Full-STEs for 47 PCREs, the degree of parallelism appears to be 172 at the maximum. In the case of Single-STEs, it is about 1,440, or 8.37 times of Full-STEs.

5.3 Timing Requirements

The report of timing analysis by Vivado is shown in the Tables 6 and 7. WNS (Worst Negative Slack), WHS (Worst Hold Stack) and WPWS (Worst Pulse Width Slack) represent the margins to meet the timing requirements. The WNS, WHS and WPWS are to meet the setup time, the hold time and the clock period of 8 ns, respectively. Obviously, parallelization decreases these slacks because the critical path becomes longer by the delay of wiring of Routing Matrix. But there is still plenty of slack even if the degree of parallelism is 32. When non-parallel circuit can process 8-bit input symbols per 8 ns and the degree of parallelism becomes 32, the throughput of the total circuit is 32 Gbps.

Table 6. Slack of Full-STE

Type	$p = 1$	$p = 2$	$p = 4$	$p = 8$	$p = 16$	$p = 32$
WNS [ns]	5.479	6.006	5.512	3.654	3.095	1.215
WHS [ns]	0.103	0.085	0.027	0.233	0.118	0.168
WPWS [ns]	3.600	3.600	3.600	3.600	3.600	3.600

Table 7. Slack of Single-STEs

Type	$p = 1$	$p = 2$	$p = 4$	$p = 8$	$p = 16$	$p = 32$
WNS [ns]	6.823	5.911	5.884	4.209	4,759	3,537
WHS [ns]	0.090	0.084	0.085	0.111	0.111	0.168
WPWS [ns]	3.358	3.600	3.600	3.600	3.600	3.600

6   Conclusion

In this paper, we presented an FPGA implementation to accelerate pattern matching of PCRE used in Snort (NIDS). In Full-STE method, how to use the on-chip memory was wasteful and it was the bottleneck of parallelization. As an improved method, Single-STE was proposed and it uses Character Class Recognizer instead of the memory. Single-STE eliminates the bottleneck of parallelization by using no memory for conditions of state transitions. Although Character Class Recognizer in Single-STE requires more LUTs than Full-STE, the potential degree of parallelism is still higher for a high-end device such as Virtex-7. Our evaluation shows that the degree of parallelism of Full-STE was $1,470/(272/32) = 172$ at most with 47 PCREs. On the other hand, that of Single-STE could be $433,200/(9,625/32) = 1,440$, or 8.37 times than Full-STE.

Future work will support more Snort rules and evaluate them. Like a previous work [8], disjunction and quantifier should be supported and back reference is also desired.

References

1. Snort. http://www.snort.org/
2. LAN/MAN Standards Committee of the IEEE Computer Society: IEEE Standard for Ethernet (2015)
3. Hieu, T.T., Thinh, T.N., Vu, T.H.: Optimization of regular expression processing circuits for NIDS on FPGA. In: Proceedings of Second International Conference on Networking and Computing, pp. 105–112 (2011)
4. Pu, S., Tan, C.-C., Liu, J.-C.: SA2PX: a tool to translate SpamAssassin regular expression rules to POSIX. In: Proceedings of 6th Conferences on Email and Anti-Spam, pp. 1–10 (2009)
5. Yang, Y.-H., Prasanna, V.K.: Space-time tradeoff in regular expression matching with semi-deterministic finite automata. In: Proceedings of IEEE INFOCOM, pp. 1853–1861 (2011)

6. Zu, Y., Yang, M., Xu, Z., Wang, L., Tian, X., Peng, K., Dong, Q.: GPU-based NFA implementation for memory efficient high speed regular expression matching. ACM SIGPLAN Not. **47**(8), 129–140 (2012)
7. Fukuda, M., Inoguchi, Y.: Probabilistic strategies based on staged LSH for speedup of audio fingerprint searching with ten million scale database. In: Proceedings of International Symposium on Highly-Efficient Accelerators and Reconfigurable Technologies (2017)
8. Dlugosch, P., Brown, D., Glendenning, P., Leventhal, M., Noyes, H.: An efficient and scalable semiconductor architecture for parallel automata processing. IEEE Trans. Parallel Distrib. Syst. **25**(12), 3088–3098 (2014)
9. Roy, I., Srivastava, A., Nourian, M., Becchi, M., Aluru, S.: High performance pattern matching using the automata processor. In: IEEE Parallel and Distributed Processing Symposium, pp. 1123–1132 (2016)
10. Cronin, B., Wang, X.: Hardware acceleration of regular expression repetitions in deep packet inspection. Inst. Eng. Technol. Inf. Secur. **7**(4), 327–335 (2013)

Embedded Vision Systems:
A Review of the Literature

Deepayan Bhowmik$^{(\boxtimes)}$ and Kofi Appiah

Department of Computing, Sheffield Hallam University, Sheffield S1 1WB, UK
{deepayan.bhowmik,k.e.appiah}@shu.ac.uk

Abstract. Over the past two decades, the use of low power Field Programmable Gate Arrays (FPGA) for the acceleration of various vision systems mainly on embedded devices have become widespread. The reconfigurable and parallel nature of the FPGA opens up new opportunities to speed-up computationally intensive vision and neural algorithms on embedded and portable devices. This paper presents a comprehensive review of embedded vision algorithms and applications over the past decade. The review will discuss vision based systems and approaches, and how they have been implemented on embedded devices. Topics covered include image acquisition, preprocessing, object detection and tracking, recognition as well as high-level classification. This is followed by an outline of the advantages and disadvantages of the various embedded implementations. Finally, an overview of the challenges in the field and future research trends are presented. This review is expected to serve as a tutorial and reference source for embedded computer vision systems.

1 Introduction

Scene understanding and prompt reaction to an event is a critical feature for any time critical computer vision system. The deployment scenarios include a range of applications such as mobile robotics, autonomous cars, mobile and wearable devices or public space surveillance (airport/railway station). Modern vision systems which play a significant role in such interaction process require higher level scene understanding with ultra-fast processing capabilities operating at extremely low power. Currently, such systems rely on traditional computer vision techniques which often follow compute intensive brute-force approaches (slower response time) and prone to fail in environments with limited power, bandwidth and computing resources. The aim of this paper is to review state-of-the-art embedded vision systems available from the literature and in the industry; and therefore to aid researchers for future development.

Research into computer vision has made steady and significant progress in the past two decades. The tremendous progress, coupled with cheap computational power has enabled many portable and embedded devices to operate with vision capabilities. Digital Signal Processing and for that matter Digital Image Processing (DIP) is an exciting area to be involved in today. Having been around for over two decades, it is typically used in application areas where cost and

© Springer International Publishing AG, part of Springer Nature 2018
N. Voros et al. (Eds.): ARC 2018, LNCS 10824, pp. 204–216, 2018.
https://doi.org/10.1007/978-3-319-78890-6_17

performance are key [7], including the entertainment industry, security surveillance systems, medical systems, automotive industry and defence. DIP systems are often implemented using the ubiquitous general purpose processors (GPPs). The increasing demand for high-speed has resulted in the use of dedicated Digital Signal Processors (DSPs) and General Purpose Graphics Processing Units (GPGPU); special types of GPP optimised for signal processing algorithms. However, power dissipation is important in almost all DSP-based consumer electronic devices; hence the high-speed, power-hungry GPPs become unattractive. Battery-powered products are highly sensitive to energy consumption, and even line-powered products are often sensitive to power consumption [41]. For hardware acceleration and low power consumption, DIP designers have opted for alternatives like the Field Programmable Gate Array (FPGA) and Application Specific Integrated Circuits (ASIC).

The use of FPGAs in application areas like communication, image processing and control engineering has increased significantly over the past decade [54]. Computer vision and image processing algorithms often perform a large number of inherently parallel operations, and are not good candidates for implementation on machines designed around the von Neumann architecture. Some image processing algorithms have successfully been implemented on embedded system architectures running in real-time on portable devices [35,45], and relatively small literature has been dedicated to the development of high-level algorithms for embedded hardware [39,63]. The demand for real-time processing in the design of any practical imaging system has led to the development of the Intel Open source Computer Vision library (OpenCV) for the acceleration of various image processing tasks on GPPs [46]. Many imaging systems rely heavily on the increasing processing speed of today's GPPs to run in real-time.

2 Application Specific Vision Systems

Every embedded vision systems follows a common pipeline of image processing functional blocks as depicted in Fig. 1. The image sensor or camera is the starting

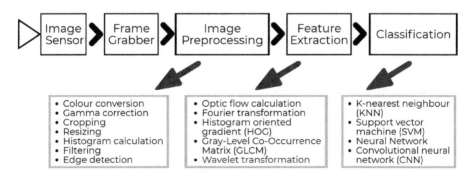

Fig. 1. Vision system pipeline.

point of this pipeline followed by a frame grabber that controls the frame synchronization and frame rate. The raw pixels are then passed for further processing which includes image pre-processing, feature extraction and classification. Within this higher level abstraction various vision systems implemented required functionalities as shown in the figure. Image preprocessing functions are often pixel processing and offer stream computations. However features extraction and classification tasks are complex in nature and usually involves non-deterministic loop conditions. Analysis and optimisations [59] of such complexity with respect to performance and power [13] is an emerging topic of interest and often seen as a trade-off including the choice of the hardware.

Embedded vision systems are usually developed either to accelerate complex algorithms that handles large stream of image data, *e.g.*, stereo matching, video compression etc.; or to minimize power at resource constraint systems including unmanned aerial vehicle (UAV) or autonomous driver assistant systems. While a large number of applications of embedded vision systems can be found in the literature, they can be grouped to major application areas including robotics, face detection applications, multimedia compression, autonomous driving and assisted living as shown in Table 1. Various implementation techniques are proposed in the literature that considers a range of image processing algorithms. Efforts were made either to parallelize the algorithms, or to approximate computing to reduce computational complexities.

While the first approach has implications in performance improvement, the latter ones are more suitable for low power applications. Popular higher level complex image processing algorithms that are used in embedded computer vision

Table 1. Embedded vision application areas. UAV: unmanned aerial vehicle; AUV: autonomous underwater vehicle.

	Robotics			Face detection	Media compression	Autonomous driving	Assisted living
	UAV	Mobile robot	AUV				
Cesetti et al. [15]	X						
Humenberger et al. [31]							X
Yang et al. [70]			X				
Chen et al. [17]						X	
Velez et al. [65]						X	
Yang et al. [69]				X			
Lin et al. [42]	X						
Oleynikova et al. [50]	X						
Flores et al. [22]	X			X			
Xu and Shen [68]		X					
Wang and Yu [67]			X				
Abeydeera et al. [1]					X		
He et al. [28]					X		
Basha and Kannan [10]					X		

literature includes stereo vision, feature extraction and tracking, motion estimation, object detection, scene segmentation and more recent convolutional neural network (CNN). These categories and corresponding literature are captured in Table 2.

Table 2. Common high level algorithms used in embedded vision systems.

	Feature point extraction	Stereo vision	Motion estimation	Object detection	Scene segmentation	CNN
Park *et al.* [51]	X					
Jin *et al.* [36]		X				
Chen *et al.* [17]	X				X	
Belbachir *et al.* [11]				X		
Banz *et al.* [8]		X				
Cesetti *et al.* [15]	X					
Humenberger *et al.* [32]		X				
Lin *et al.* [42]	X			X	X	
Oleynikova *et al.* [50]		X				
Flores *et al.* [22]	X					
Ttofis *et al.* [64]		X				
He *et al.* [28]			X			
Basha and Kannan [10]			X			
Liu *et al.* [43]				X		X
Zhao *et al.* [74]				X		X

3   Embedded Vision Systems

3.1   Central Processing Unit (CPU)

The widespread adoption of imaging and vision applications in industrial automation, robotics and surveillance calls for a better way of implementing such techniques for real-time purposes. The need to address the gap in knowledge for students who have either studied computer vision or microelectronics to fill positions in the industry requiring both expertise has been address with the introduction of various CPU based platforms like Beagleboard [47] and Raspberry-Pi [48]. Hashmi *et al.* [27] used a beagleboard-xM low-power open-source hardware to prototype a real-time copyright protection algorithm. A human tracking system which reliably detect and track human motion has been implemented on a beagleboard-xM [24]. In [5], a LeopardBoard has been used to implement an efficient edge-detection algorithm for tracking activity level in an indoor environment. Similarly, Sharma and Kumar [56] presented an image enhancement algorithm on a beagleboard, mainly for monitoring the health condition of an individual. To demonstrate the efficiency of embedded image processing Sahani and Mohanty [55] showcased various computer vision applications developed on Raspberry-Pi. The system uses a camera powered by the raspberry-pi with a resolution of 1280×720 to detect text and images in real-time. Various other computer vision algorithm have been implemented on small dedicated platforms using Raspberry-Pi. In [30], a robot with on-board camera for carrying lightweight objects is presented and uses raspberry-pi to process the camera data in aid of navigation. Other robotic systems like [37, 44] have all implemented some vision based algorithms on a Raspberry-Pi because of its portability and ease of programmability.

3.2   Graphic Processing Unit (GPU)

The parallel nature of GPUs have made them a choice for the acceleration of many computer vision algorithms [66]. Coupled with the emerging heterogeneous programming models like OpenCL, GPGPU has been enabled on mobile devices. To explore the capabilities of mobile GPU for the acceleration of computer vision algorithms, Wang et al. [66] presented and exemplar-based inpainting algorithm for object removal. Rister et al. [53] presented an implementation of the Scale-Invariant Feature Transform feature detection algorithm on a mobile based GPU to achieved $7\times$ speed-up over optimised GPP implementation. A face detection and recognition system implementation on two GPU architectures are presented in [71] with reported speed-up of approximately $3.7\times$. A mobile GPU based object detection algorithm with twofold speed-up compared to a similar implementation on a mobile GPP is presented in [3]. The implementation also reported energy savings of up to 84% compared to a smartphone GPP. A GPU enabled architecture for scaling up convolutional networks have been presented in [62]. The explored networks [62] are trained with stochastic gradient distributed machine learning system using 50 replicas on a NVidia Kepler GPU. Deep learning or Convolutional Neural Network (CNN) has become popular in the fields of machine learning and computer vision, because of it's high performance in object detection [33]. Using only GPP, a complex CNN may require more than one month to train [19]. GPUs offer approximately ten fold speed-up compared to GPP, which is demonstrated in [33] for faster training and testing. A number of other computer vision and image processing algorithms [9, 34, 57] have been implemented on GPU mainly to accelerate them for real time needs.

3.3   Field Programmable Gate Array (FPGA)

FPGAs are successfully used in many application areas, including embedded computer vision and image processing. The key advantage of FPGAs over conventional CPUs or GPUs is configurability. Resource allocation and memory hierarchy on general purpose processors must perform well across a range of applications, whereas FPGA designs leave many of those decisions to the application designer to optimally use logic gates to implement one specific application. Moreover, they can be significantly faster as their nature supports fine-grained, massively parallel and pipelined execution. FPGAs allows stream processing from camera input and offers parallel execution of processing blocks that resembles the vision system pipeline as depicted in Fig. 1. Various forms of parallelism, *e.g.*, pipeline, task or data parallelism were exploited in FPGA based vision systems [59]. Additionally FPGAs are known for low power execution and vision system designers often exploit this characteristics by using multi-clock domain design paradigm [13]. However on the downside, FPGAs are blamed on programmability aspect as FPGAs are most often specified directly in low level less expressive hardware description languages such as Verilog or VHDL.

The intrinsic parallel architecture of FPGAs have also been exploited in a number of application areas including high level feature classification with conventional neural networks [29,60], convolutional neural networks [12,18,52] and architecture specific neural networks [4,49]. A variant of self-organising map designed specifically for FPGA is presented in [4] and tested on two computer vision applications; character recognition and appearance-based object identification. The implementation in [4] was achieved using Xilinx Virtex-4 XC4VLX160 and capable being trained with approximately 25,000 patterns every second. Embedded vision systems, implemented on FPGAs are usually evaluated on a few objective measurements including (1) performance measured in throughput (*e.g.*, frames per second or fps); (2) clock frequency; (3) input image frame size; (4) FPGA resource usage (*e.g.*, DSP, BRAM, FF/LUTs) and (5) power consumption. Power consumption on FPGAs consists of *(a) static power*, which is directly proportional to the amount of used logic; and *(b) dynamic power*, which is a weighted sum of several components (these include clock signal propagation power, proportional to clock frequency; signals power, proportional to signal switching rates, among others). The implementation relies on available programmable logic gates available on different FPGA boards from handful of manufacturers, including Xilinx and Altera (now Intel). Table 3 provides a comparative overview of these measurements metrics reported in the literature that are referred earlier in Sect. 2.

3.4   ASIC

Vision based applications and systems are typically associated with high computational cost, slow when implemented on general purpose processors and not very useful in real-time applications. To address some of theses problems, mainly the real-time requirements, most researchers have resulted to the use of dedicated and application specific systems. In [61], Sugiura *et al.* used an application specific instruction-set processor to execute a lossless data compression method as part of a visual prosthesis systems. Deep networks, models for understanding the content of images, videos and audio have been used successfully in various application [40] with relatively high computational cost. Gokhale *et al.* [26] presented a scalable, low-power co-processor for enabling real-time execution of deep neural networks on mobile devices. This was implemented using a large number of parallel operators, optimised to process multiple streams of information. The implementation presented in [26] shows that image understanding with deep networks can be accelerated on custom hardware to achieve better performance per

Table 3. A comparative overview of the FPGA metrics used in embedded computer vision.

	Frame size	Frame rate	Max. clock frequency	Target devices
Jin *et al.* [36]	640 × 480	230 fps	93 MHz	Xilinx Virtex-4
Appiah *et al.* [6]	640 × 480	35 fps	65 MHz	Xilinx Virtex-4
Banz *et al.* [8]	640 × 480	30 fps	39 MHz	Xilinx Virtex-5
Oleynikova *et al.* [50]	640 × 480	60 fps	-	Xilinx Artix-7
Ttofis *et al.* [64]	1280 × 720	60 fps	103 MHz	Xilinx Kintex-7
He *et al.* [28]	7680 × 4320	30 fps	188 MHz	Altera Stratix II
Abeydeera *et al.* [1]	4096 × 2160	30 fps	150 MHz	Xilinx Zynq 7045
Tanabe and Maruyama [63]	640 × 480	349 fps	228 MHz	Xilinx Virtex-6
Albo-Canals *et al.* [2]	177 × 144	1562 fps	30 MHz	Actel IGLOO
Bhowmik *et al.* [13]	320 × 240	52 fps	85 MHz	Xilinx Zynq 7020

watt. Chen *et al.* [16] presented an application specific integrated circuit accelerator on a 65 nm scale technology, for large-scale convolutional and deep neural networks capable of performing 452 GOP/s of key neural network operations in a small footprint. A convolution chip built on 0.35 μm CMOS technology for event-driven vision sensing and processing is presented in [14].

4   Future Trends and Conclusions

In this paper we made a modest effort to review embedded computer vision systems that satisfy application specific constraints *e.g.*, performance or power. The literature is scattered and covers a range of application areas, vision algorithms and target hardware. This paper made an effort to categorize them in an orderly fashion. We identified two emerging trends (described below) in this domain namely, heterogeneous computing and bi-inspired computing for efficient vision systems.

4.1   Heterogeneous Computing for Vision Systems

Current computer vision algorithms are highly complex and consist of different functional blocks that are suitable for a variety of targets *i.e.*, CPUs, GPUs or FPGAs. Therefore, designing computer vision systems for single target hardware platform is inefficient and does not necessarily meet performance and power budgets especially for embedded and remote operations. A heterogeneous architecture is a natural alternative but manifests new challenges:

- design choices to dissect the algorithm according to their suitability for the target hardware,
- interoperability and data flow synchronisations between functional units as different blocks may have different timing constraints.

– programmability and coordination between different hardware platforms. There is a need for unified programming environment.

Although recently hardware manufacturers launched new heterogeneous products, e.g., Xilinx Zynq Ultrascale+ MPSoC[1] (CPU, GPU and FPGA) and Altera SoC products[2] (CPU and FPGA), these are not fully exploited in computer vision domain (except handful of recent work, e.g., Zhang et al. [73]) as majority of the existing algorithms are not designed to target heterogeneous platforms. Consideration of target hardware during the algorithmic development cycle is not always necessary and the domain experts often prototype new algorithms using library-rich languages such as MATLAB. However, efficient deployment of these prototypes on a heterogeneous hardware is challenging. Asynchronous data process network [20] may provide a plausible solution to this problem, however requires further research.

4.2 Biologically Inspired Vision Systems

The ability to detect moving objects in a scene is a fundamental problem in computer vision. This is a baseline problem that requires detection accuracy as well as computational efficiency to guarantee a successful high level processing in behavioural or event analysis [72]. Various background subtraction methods [25] have been proposed and proven to be successful for detecting moving objects with the use of stationary cameras. These methods build statistical background models and extract moving objects by finding regions which do not have similar characteristics to the background model. Human visual systems processes a very high volume of data and hence it is often selective and activity driven (responsive to the scene event).

The high volume data problem is also faced by many modern technical systems like computer vision systems which need to deal with a multitude of image pixels at any point in time. Physiological research has illustrated that biological vision systems use neuronal circuits to extract movement in the visual scenes [38]. Biological visual systems are intrinsically complex hierarchical processing systems with diverse specialised neurons, displaying very powerful specific biological processing functionalities that traditional computer vision techniques have not yet fully emulated [38]. Another important finding during the last decades, that most neuromorphic designers may overlook is the fact that processing of the visual information is not serial but rather highly parallel [23] and hence such implementations should target parallel architectures.

A concept proposed and implemented in [21], shows that motion information can be capture with the use of one retina sheet and two LGN sheets (one ON and one OFF). Orientation preference has successfully been modelled using a Gain Control, Adaptation, Laterally (GCAL) model consisting of four two-dimensional sheets. Solari et al. [58], presented a feed-forward model based on

[1] https://www.xilinx.com/products/silicon-devices/soc/zynq-ultrascale-mpsoc.html.
[2] https://www.altera.com/products/soc/overview.html.

the biological visual system to solve motion estimation problem. The model integrates media temporal (MT) neurons for estimation of optical flow by extending it into a scalable framework. What is missing from their model is the feedback capabilities as perceived in the visual pathway, but the results are very promising and acts as a good starting point for building bio-inspired scalable computer vision algorithms.

Acknowledgement. We acknowledge the support of two HEIF Impact fellowships at Sheffield Hallam University.

References

1. Abeydeera, M., Karunaratne, M., Karunaratne, G., De Silva, K., Pasqual, A.: 4K real-time HEVC decoder on an FPGA. IEEE Trans. Circuit Systems Video Technol. **26**(1), 236–249 (2016)
2. Albo-Canals, J., Ortega, S., Perdices, S., Badalov, A., Vilasis-Cardona, X.: Embedded low-power low-cost camera sensor based on FPGA and its applications in mobile robots. In: 19th IEEE International Conference on Electronics, Circuits, and Systems, pp. 336–339 (2012)
3. Andargie, F.A., Rose, J., Austin, T., Bertacco, V.: Energy efficient object detection on the mobile GP-GPU. In: 2017 IEEE AFRICON, pp. 945–950, September 2017
4. Appiah, K., Hunter, A., Dickinson, P., Meng, H.: Implementation and applications of tri-state self-organizing maps on FPGA. IEEE Trans. Circuits Syst. Video Technol. **22**(8), 1150–1160 (2012)
5. Appiah, K., Hunter, A., Lotfi, A., Waltham, C., Dickinson, P.: Human behavioural analysis with self-organizing map for ambient assisted living. In: 2014 IEEE International Conference on Fuzzy Systems (FUZZ-IEEE), pp. 2430–2437, July 2014
6. Appiah, K., Hunter, A., Dickinson, P., Meng, H.: Accelerated hardware video object segmentation: from foreground detection to connected components labelling. Comput. Vis. Image Underst. **114**(11), 1282–1291 (2010)
7. Athi, M.V., Zekavat, S.R., Struthers, A.A.: Real-time signal processing of massive sensor arrays via a parallel fast converging SVD algorithm: latency, throughput, and resource analysis. IEEE Sens. J. **16**(8), 2519–2526 (2016)
8. Banz, C., Hesselbarth, S., Flatt, H., Blume, H., Pirsch, P.: Real-time stereo vision system using semi-global matching disparity estimation: architecture and FPGA-implementation. In: International Conference on Embedded Computer Systems (SAMOS), pp. 93–101 (2010)
9. Barbu, A., She, Y., Ding, L., Gramajo, G.: Feature selection with annealing for computer vision and big data learning. IEEE Trans. Pattern Anal. Mach. Intell. **39**(2), 272–286 (2017)
10. Basha, S.M., Kannan, M.: Design and implementation of low-power motion estimation based on modified full-search block motion estimation. J. Comput. Sci. **21**, 327–332 (2017)
11. Belbachir, A.N., Hofstatter, M., Litzenberger, M., Schon, P.: High-speed embedded-object analysis using a dual-line timed-address-event temporal-contrast vision sensor. IEEE Trans. Ind. Electron. **58**(3), 770–783 (2011)
12. Bettoni, M., Urgese, G., Kobayashi, Y., Macii, E., Acquaviva, A.: A convolutional neural network fully implemented on FPGA for embeded platforms. In: 2017 New Generation of CAS (NGCAS), pp. 49–52, September 2017

13. Bhowmik, D., Garcia, P., Wallace, A., Stewart, R., Michaelson, G.: Power efficient dataflow design for a heterogeneous smart camera architecture. In: Conference on Design and Architectures for Signal and Image Processing (DASIP 2017), August 2017

14. Camunas-Mesa, L., Acosta-Jimenez, A., Zamarreno-Ramos, C., Serrano-Gotarredona, T., Linares-Barranco, B.: A 32x32 pixel convolution processor chip for address event vision sensors with 155 ns event latency and 20 meps throughput. IEEE Trans. Circuits Syst. I: Regular Papers **58**(4), 777–790 (2011)

15. Cesetti, A., Frontoni, E., Mancini, A., Zingaretti, P., Longhi, S.: A vision-based guidance system for UAV navigation and safe landing using natural landmarks. J. Intell. Robot. Syst. **57**(1–4), 233 (2010)

16. Chen, T., Du, Z., Sun, N., Wang, J., Wu, C., Chen, Y., Temam, O.: Diannao: a small-footprint high-throughput accelerator for ubiquitous machine-learning. In: Proceedings of 19th International Conference on Architectural Support for Programming Languages and Operating Systems, ASPLOS 2014, pp. 269–284. ACM, New York (2014)

17. Chen, Y.L., Wu, B.F., Huang, H.Y., Fan, C.J.: A real-time vision system for night-time vehicle detection and traffic surveillance. IEEE Trans. Ind. Electron. **58**(5), 2030–2044 (2011)

18. Colangelo, P., Luebbers, E., Huang, R., Margala, M., Nealis, K.: Application of convolutional neural networks on Intel; Xeon; processor with integrated FPGA. In: 2017 IEEE High Performance Extreme Computing Conference (HPEC), pp. 1–7, September 2017

19. Courbariaux, M., Bengio, Y.: BinaryNet: training deep neural networks with weights and activations constrained to +1 or −1. CoRR abs/1602.02830 (2016)

20. Eker, J., Janneck, J.: CAL language report: specification of the CAL actor language (2003)

21. Fischer, T.: Model of all known spatial maps in primary visual cortex. Master's thesis, University of Edinburghs (2014)

22. Flores-Delgado, J., Martínez-Santos, L., Lozano, R., Gonzalez-Hernandez, I., Mercado, D.: Embedded control using monocular vision: Face tracking. In: 2017 International Conference on Unmanned Aircraft Systems (ICUAS), pp. 1285–1291. IEEE (2017)

23. Frintrop, S., Rome, E., Christensen, H.I.: Computational visual attention systems and their cognitive foundations: a survey. ACM Trans. Appl. Percept. **7**(1), 6:1–6:39 (2010)

24. Gantala, A., Nehru, K., Telagam, N., Anjaneyulu, P., Swathi, D.: Human tracking system using beagle board-xM. Int. J. Appl. Eng. Res. **12**(16), 5665–5669 (2017)

25. Ge, W., Guo, Z., Dong, Y., Chen, Y.: Dynamic background estimation and complementary learning for pixel-wise foreground/background segmentation. Pattern Recogn. **59**(Suppl. C), 112–125 (2016)

26. Gokhale, V., Jin, J., Dundar, A., Martini, B., Culurciello, E.: A 240 g-ops/s mobile coprocessor for deep neural networks. In: The IEEE Conference on Computer Vision and Pattern Recognition (CVPR) Workshops, June 2014

27. Hashmi, M.F., Shukla, R.J., Keskar, A.G.: Platform independent real time copyright protection embedding and extraction algorithms on android and embedded framework. In: International Symposium on Signal Processing and Information Technology (ISSPIT), pp. 000189–000194 (2014)

28. He, G., Zhou, D., Li, Y., Chen, Z., Zhang, T., Goto, S.: High-throughput power-efficient VLSI architecture of fractional motion estimation for ultra-HD HEVC video encoding. IEEE Trans. Very Large Scale Integr. VLSI Syst. **23**(12), 3138–3142 (2015)

29. Ho, S.M.H., Hung, C.H.D., Ng, H.C., Wang, M., So, H.K.H.: A parameteriz-able activation function generator for FPGA-based neural network applications. In: IEEE 25th Annual International Symposium on Field-Programmable Custom Computing Machines (FCCM) (2017)

30. Horak, K., Zalud, L.: Image processing on raspberry PI for mobile robotics. Int. J. Sig. Process. Syst. 4(2), 1–5 (2016)

31. Humenberger, M., Schraml, S., Sulzbachner, C., Belbachir, A.N., Srp, A., Vajda, F.: Embedded fall detection with a neural network and bio-inspired stereo vision. In: IEEE Computer Society Conference on Computer Vision and Pattern Recognition Workshops (2012)

32. Humenberger, M., Zinner, C., Weber, M., Kubinger, W., Vincze, M.: A fast stereo matching algorithm suitable for embedded real-time systems. Comput. Vis. Image Underst. 114(11), 1180–1202 (2010)

33. Islam, S.M.S., Rahman, S., Rahman, M.M., Dey, E.K., Shoyaib, M.: Application of deep learning to computer vision: a comprehensive study. In: 2016 5th International Conference on Informatics, Electronics and Vision (ICIEV), pp. 592–597, May 2016

34. Jain, V., Patel, D.: A GPU based implementation of robust face detection system. Procedia Comput. Sci. 87(Suppl. 1), 156–163 (2016). Fourth International Confer-ence on Recent Trends in Computer Science & Engineering (ICRTCSE 2016)

35. Jasani, B.A., Lam, S.K., Meher, P.K., Wu, M.: Threshold-guided design and opti-mization for Harris corner detector architecture. IEEE TCSVT **PP**(99), 1 (2017)

36. Jin, S., Cho, J., Dai Pham, X., Lee, K.M., Park, S.K., Kim, M., Jeon, J.W.: FPGA design and implementation of a real-time stereo vision system. IEEE Trans. Cir-cuits Syst. Video Technol. 20(1), 15–26 (2010)

37. Jing, X., Gong, C., Wang, Z., Li, X., Ma, Z.: Remote live-video security surveillance via mobile robot with raspberry Pi IP camera. In: Huang, Y.A., Wu, H., Liu, H., Yin, Z. (eds.) ICIRA 2017. LNCS (LNAI), vol. 10463, pp. 776–788. Springer, Cham (2017). https://doi.org/10.1007/978-3-319-65292-4_67

38. Kerr, D., McGinnity, T., Coleman, S., Clogenson, M.: A biologically inspired spiking model of visual processing for image feature detection. Neurocomputing 158(C), 268–280 (2015)

39. Khan, M.U.K., Khan, A., Kyung, C.M.: EBSCAM: background subtraction for ubiquitous computing. IEEE Trans. Very Large Scale Integr. Syst. 25(1), 35–47 (2017)

40. Krizhevsky, A., Sutskever, I., Hinton, G.E.: Imagenet classification with deep con-volutional neural networks. Commun. ACM 60(6), 84–90 (2017)

41. Li, Y., Chen, L., Benson, B., Kastner, R.: Determining the suitability of FPGAs for a low-cost, low-power underwater acoustic modem. In: Deng, W. (ed.) Future Con-trol and Automation. LNEE, vol. 173, pp. 509–517. Springer, Heidelberg (2012). https://doi.org/10.1007/978-3-642-31003-4_65

42. Lin, F., Dong, X., Chen, B.M., Lum, K.Y., Lee, T.H.: A robust real-time embedded vision system on an unmanned rotorcraft for ground target following. IEEE Trans. Ind. Electron. 59(2), 1038–1049 (2012)

43. Liu, Z., Dou, Y., Jiang, J., Xu, J., Li, S., Zhou, Y., Xu, Y.: Throughput-optimized FPGA accelerator for deep convolutional neural networks. ACM Trans. Reconf. Technol. Syst. (TRETS) 10(3), 17 (2017)

44. Loureiro, R., Lopes, A., Carona, C., Almeida, D., Faria, F., Garrote, L., Premebida, C., Nunes, U.J.: ISR-RobotHead: robotic head with LCD-based emotional expres-siveness. In: 2017 IEEE 5th Portuguese Meeting on Bioengineering (ENBENG), pp. 1–4, February 2017

45. Ma, X., Borbon, J.R., Najjar, W., Roy-Chowdhury, A.K.: Optimizing hardware design for human action recognition. In: 2016 26th International Conference on Field Programmable Logic and Applications (FPL), pp. 1–11, August 2016

46. Mazumdar, A., Moreau, T., Kim, S., Cowan, M., Alaghi, A., Ceze, L., Oskin, M., Sathe, V.: Exploring computation-communication tradeoffs in camera systems. In: 2017 IEEE International Symposium on Workload Characterization (IISWC) (2017)

47. Morison, G., Jenkins, M.D., Buggy, T., Barrie, P.: An implementation focused approach to teaching image processing and machine vision - from theory to beagleboard. In: European Embedded Design in Education and Research Conference (EDERC), pp. 274–277 (2014)

48. Nguyen, H.Q., Loan, T.T.K., Mao, B.D., Huh, E.N.: Low cost real-time system monitoring using raspberry PI. In: 2015 7th International Conference on Ubiquitous and Future Networks, pp. 857–859, July 2015

49. Nurvitadhi, E., Sheffield, D., Sim, J., Mishra, A., Venkatesh, G., Marr, D.: Accelerating binarized neural networks: comparison of FPGA, CPU, GPU, and ASIC. In: 2016 International Conference on Field-Programmable Technology (FPT), pp. 77–84, December 2016

50. Oleynikova, H., Honegger, D., Pollefeys, M.: Reactive avoidance using embedded stereo vision for MAV flight. In: International Conference on Robotics and Automation (ICRA), pp. 50–56 (2015)

51. Park, J.S., Kim, H.E., Kim, L.S.: A 182 mW 94.3 f/s in full HD pattern-matching based image recognition accelerator for an embedded vision system in 0.13-mm CMOS technology. IEEE Trans. Circuit Syst. Video Technol. 23(5), 832–845 (2013)

52. Qiu, J., Wang, J., Yao, S., Guo, K., Li, B., Zhou, E., Yu, J., Tang, T., Xu, N., Song, S., Wang, Y., Yang, H.: Going deeper with embedded FPGA platform for convolutional neural network. In: Proceedings of 2016 ACM/SIGDA International Symposium on Field-Programmable Gate Arrays, FPGA 2016, pp. 26–35. ACM, New York (2016)

53. Rister, B., Wang, G., Wu, M., Cavallaro, J.R.: A fast and efficient sift detector using the mobile GPU. In: Proceedings of IEEE ICASSP, pp. 2674–2678 (2013)

54. Romoth, J., Porrmann, M., Ruckertr, U.: Survey of FPGA applications in the period 2000–2015. Technical report, Bielefeld University, Germany, March 2017

55. Sahani, M., Mohanty, M.N.: Realization of different algorithms using raspberry Pi for real-time image processing application. In: Jain, L.C., Patnaik, S., Ichalkaranje, N. (eds.) Intelligent Computing, Communication and Devices. AISC, vol. 309, pp. 473–479. Springer, New Delhi (2015). https://doi.org/10.1007/978-81-322-2009-1_53

56. Sharma, G., Kumar, K.: Prototyping of image enhancement algorithms using beagle board for rural health monitoring. In: International Conference on Recent innovations in Science, Management, Education and Technology, pp. 346–358, August 2016

57. Singh, R., Ranasinghe, L.: Accelerating computer vision on mobile embedded platforms. In: 2016 IEEE Region 10 Conference (TENCON), pp. 3131–3134, November 2016

58. Solari, F., Chessa, M., Medathati, K., Kornprobst, P.: What can we expect from a classical V1-MT feedforward architecture for optical flow estimation? Sig. Process. Image Commun. 49(1), 250–257 (2015)

59. Stewart, R.J., Bhowmik, D., Wallace, A.M., Michaelson, G.: Profile guided dataflow transformation for FPGAs and CPUs. Sig. Process. Syst. 87(1), 3–20 (2017)

60. Su, J., Liu, J., Thomas, D.B., Cheung, P.Y.: Neural network based reinforcement learning acceleration on FPGA platforms. SIGARCH Comput. Arch. News **44**(4), 68–73 (2017)

61. Sugiura, T., Yu, J., Takeuchi, Y., Imai, M.: A low-energy ASIP with flexible exponential Golomb codec for lossless data compression toward artificial vision systems. In: 2015 IEEE Biomedical Circuits and Systems Conference (BioCAS), pp. 1–4, October 2015

62. Szegedy, C., Vanhoucke, V., Ioffe, S., Shlens, J., Wojna, Z.: Rethinking the inception architecture for computer vision. In: IEEE Conference on Computer Vision and Pattern Recognition (CVPR), June 2016

63. Tanabe, Y., Maruyama, T.: Fast and accurate optical flow estimation using FPGA. SIGARCH Comput. Arch. News **42**(4), 27–32 (2014)

64. Ttofis, C., Kyrkou, C., Theocharides, T.: A low-cost real-time embedded stereo vision system for accurate disparity estimation based on guided image filtering. IEEE Trans. Comput. **65**(9), 2678–2693 (2016)

65. Velez, G., Cortés, A., Nieto, M., Vélez, I., Otaegui, O.: A reconfigurable embedded vision system for advanced driver assistance. J. Real-Time Image Process. **10**(4), 725–739 (2015)

66. Wang, G., Xiong, Y., Yun, J., Cavallaro, J.R.: Accelerating computer vision algorithms using OpenCL framework on the mobile GPU - a case study. In: 2013 IEEE International Conference on Acoustics, Speech and Signal Processing, pp. 2629–2633, May 2013

67. Wang, K., Yu, J.: An embedded vision system for robotic fish navigation. In: International Conference on Computer Application and System Modeling (ICCASM), vol. 4, pp. V4–333. IEEE (2010)

68. Xu, H., Shen, Y.: Target tracking control of mobile robot in diversified manoeuvre modes with a low cost embedded vision system. J. Ind. Robot **40**(3), 275–287 (2013)

69. Yang, M., Crenshaw, J., Augustine, B., Mareachen, R., Wu, Y.: AdaBoost-based face detection for embedded systems. Comput. Vis. Image Underst. **114**(11), 1116–1125 (2010)

70. Yang, X., Wu, Z., Yu, J.: Design and implementation of a robotic shark with a novel embedded vision system. In: 2016 IEEE International Conference on Robotics and Biomimetics (ROBIO), pp. 841–846. IEEE (2016)

71. Yi, S., Yoon, I., Oh, C., Yi, Y.: Real-time integrated face detection and recognition on embedded GPGPUs. In: 2014 IEEE 12th Symposium on Embedded Systems for Real-Time Multimedia (ESTIMedia), pp. 98–107, October 2014

72. Yun, K., Choi, J.Y.: Robust and fast moving object detection in a non-stationary camera via foreground probability based sampling. In: 2015 IEEE International Conference on Image Processing (ICIP), pp. 4897–4901, September 2015

73. Zhang, B., Zhao, C., Mei, K., Zheng, N., et al.: Hierarchical and parallel pipelined heterogeneous SoC for embedded vision processing. IEEE Trans. Circuit Syst. Video Technol. (2017)

74. Zhao, R., Niu, X., Wu, Y., Luk, W., Liu, Q.: Optimizing CNN-based object detection algorithms on embedded FPGA platforms. In: Wong, S., Beck, A.C., Bertels, K., Carro, L. (eds.) ARC 2017. LNCS, vol. 10216, pp. 255–267. Springer, Cham (2017). https://doi.org/10.1007/978-3-319-56258-2_22

A Survey of Low Power Design
Techniques for Last Level Caches

Emmanuel Ofori-Attah[1], Xiaohang Wang[2], and Michael Opoku Agyeman[1(✉)]

[1] Faculty of Art, Science and Technology, University of Northampton,
Northampton, UK
Michael.OpokuAgyeman@northampton.ac.uk
[2] South China University of Technology, Guangzhou, China

Abstract. The end of Dennard scaling has shifted the focus of performance enhancement in technology to power budgeting techniques, specifically in the nano-meter domain because, leakage power depletes the total chip budget. Therefore, to meet the power budget, the number of resources per die could be limited. With this emerging factor, power consumption of on-chip components is detrimental to the future of transistor scaling. Fortunately, earlier research has identified the Last Level Cache (LLC) as one of the major power consuming element. Consequently, there have been several efforts towards reducing power consumption in LLCs. This paper presents a survey of recent contribution towards reducing power consumption in the LLC.

1 Introduction

Multi-level Cache Architectures (MCA) have become increasingly popular for mitigating the disparity between memory and processors trading-off power consumption. MCA (Fig. 1) consumes a significant amount of power and affects the chip's total power ($P_{total} = P_{dynamic} + P_{leakage}$). Particularly, the Last Level Cache (LLC) is said to consume most of the power and occupies 50% of the chip area due to its large size [1,2]. With leakage power set to dominate power consumption in the near future, a reduction in LLC power and area can increase the number of components which can be activated through the Dark-Silicon solution. Particularly, in a many-core system comprising of a MCA and the Network-on-Chip (NoC) interconnect [3–5].

Figure 1 a depicts a multi-level cache architecture in a typical heterogeneous many-core system incorporating the Network-on-Chip (NoC) interconnect. The L1 cache is the closest to the processor, small in size and thus, it is the fastest. In contrast, the L3 cache (LLC) is the furthest away from the processor and thus, is slower. However, it is much bigger, holds a large amount of data and thus, consumes most of the cache power.

In modern technology, on-chip caches are made up of Static Random-Access Memory (SRAM) technology, which has improved performance, but is expensive and suffers excessively from leakage power as technology scales down below

© Springer International Publishing AG, part of Springer Nature 2018
N. Voros et al. (Eds.): ARC 2018, LNCS 10824, pp. 217–228, 2018.
https://doi.org/10.1007/978-3-319-78890-6_18

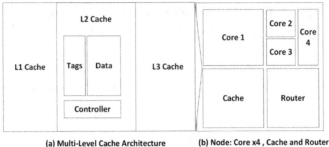

(a) Multi-Level Cache Architecture   (b) Node: Core x4 , Cache and Router

Fig. 1. Cache architecture

40 nm [6,7]. Previously, Dynamic Random-Access Memory (DRAM) was used to design caches but have been overlooked due to the desirable properties (Low Access Latency and very high write endurance) of SRAM (Table 1). DRAM is slower and thus cannot respond quickly to the demands of the cores (Fig. 1). With the number of core integration per chip escalating above its 100's, large and fast caches capable of handling large data will be required. Therefore, to avoid high access latency, the capacity of SRAM LLCs have to be increased proportionate to the number of the cores in System-on-Chip (SoC) for an assured Quality of Service (QoS). However, increase of SRAM LLCs multiplies the power consumption making it an undesirable technology for future embedded systems [8]. What this entails is an increase in the cost of implementation as well as the leakage power consumption in cache architectures. Therefore, efficient alternative design for SRAM technology is highly demanded for the scaling trend in transistors to continue.

Alternatively, to reduce the power consumption in caches, power-gating techniques are used to power-off idle parts of the cache during run-time since not all workloads require full access to the cache. However, these techniques degrade the performance of the system and therefore, minimizing cache power and finding a balance between power efficiency and high performance have become an interesting research area. Nonetheless, several architectural design techniques have been proposed to overcome this challenge.

This paper presents a survey of recent contributions towards reducing power consumption in cache architectures. Particularly, to reduce a significant amount of power, we target LLCs since it consumes majority of on-chip power. The rest of the paper is organised as follows, Sect. 2 presents surveys that also look into low power design techniques for caches. Section 3 presents an overview of Non-Volatile memory technologies while Sect. 4 introduces monitoring cache behaviour as a technique for reducing power consumption in caches. Section 5 presents cache resizing techniques. Section 6 summarises the techniques presented and finally, Sect. 7 concludes the paper.

2   Related Work

Cache power consumption is increasingly becoming a constraint for SoC. Although performance is enhanced by the introduction of MCA, high power consumption and chip temperature becomes a problem [9–13]. To overcome this issue, several surveys [14–16] have presented low power consumption design techniques for caches. Ofori-Attah et al. [16] conducted a survey on recent techniques for reducing the power consumption in Network-on-Chip (NoC) and Caches. In their work, techniques for leakage and dynamic power of caches have been addressed. Aside the Cache, NoC is also identified as a power consuming component. Consequently, existing efforts [17,18] have presented a survey of techniques on how to improve the power efficiency of the crossbar and buffers. However, to the best of our knowledge, LLCs have not received much attention. Artes et al. [19] presented techniques for instruction memory organisations. Wei Zang et al. [14] evaluated the pros and cons of offline static and online dynamic cache tuning techniques. Mittal et al. [15] presented architecture level techniques on improving cache power management during run-time. They focussed on optimizing power efficiency. In [20], Mittal et al. also presented a comprehensive study of memory technologies and techniques to overcome the challenges in caches. Indumathi et al. [21] presented design techniques for optimizing SRAM technology. Contrary to the work above, this work emphasises on reducing power consumption in LLCs.

3   Hybrid Architectures

One possible solution to this issue is the emerging Non-Volatile Memory (NVM) technologies (Spin-Transfer Torque RAM (STT-RAM) [22], Phase Change Memory (PCM), Resistive RAM (R-RAM) and Magnetic RAM (MRAM)). Memory itself can either be volatile or non-volatile. Volatile Memory (VM) requires power for it to function, and loses its content when the memory is powered-off. NVM on the other hand does not require power to store data. In addition to this, data is retained when the memory is shutdown. Although VM is faster, NVM are desirable because of their low cost of implementation, high speed, high density, scalability and ability to hold data under low power [23,24].

Unfortunately, NVM technologies suffer from low write endurance (RRAM $(10\ \lambda^{11})$, PCM $(10\ \lambda^{8})$, STT-RAM $(10\ \lambda^{15})$) and incur high energy during write operations which degrades their performance and use, due data being stored in the form of change in physical state [20]. Especially, during write intensive workloads. Therefore, implementing NVM trades-off leakage power for dynamic power. Furthermore, although MRAM implementation provides larger memory for the same die of footprint as SRAM, its write latency and energy are higher [25].

Table 1 presents a comparative evaluation of SRAM and NVM technologies. From the table, we can conclude that, STT-RAM mirrors characteristics (high data storage, fast speed) close to the properties of SRAM in terms of performance and power even though it suffers from dynamic power. However, in comparison to other technologies such as DRAM and PRAM, the cost is affordable. For example, although DRAM does not consume a lot of power, its high read and write latency can have a negative impact on the performance of the system as more cores are integrated. This even gets worse as workload increases. PRAM is also a good alternative for SRAM, however, its write latency is too high to consider implementing the LLC with.

Table 1. Memory technology comparison [20]

Characteristics	SRAM	STT-RAM	DRAM	PRAM
Read latency	Very low	Low	High	High
Write latency	Very low	High	High	Very high
Read power	Low	Low	Average	Average
Write power	Low	High	Average	Low
Leakage power	High	Low	Average	Low
Dynamic power	Low	High	Average	High

However, as identified by [26], the high write energy of STT-RAM as a standalone technology in LLC makes it difficult to implement. For this purpose, hybrid memories have been proposed to exploit the low leakage power of STT-RAM and high performance of SRAM. In such an architecture, SRAM is used for write-intensive workloads while the STT-RAM is used for read-intensive workloads.

3.1   SRAM and STT-RAM Architectures

In this section, we discuss the techniques which have been employed in STT-RAM and SRAM hybrid architectures.

Li et al. [26] proposed a scheme for a hybrid architecture comprised of STT-RAM and SRAM. Firstly, a Neighbourhood Group Caching (NCU) technique is used for neighbouring cores to share their private STT-RAM groups with each other. This allows data to be shared among each core reducing latency and power consumption. During write misses, target blocks are loaded in the SRAM banks since it consumes less power and it is quicker. Furthermore, during a cache read, a request hit will be made available to the neighbouring groups or a copy of the target block will be made available for a future read. Compared to state-of-art architectures, the proposed architecture reduces power consumption by 40%.

Kim et al. [27] proposed a hybrid exclusive LLC cache architecture. Exclusive caches behave, perform, and operate differently from inclusive caches. In an exclusive cache architecture, cache blocks are inserted into the LLC after it has been evicted from the lower-level caches which is contrary to inclusive caches where, data is duplicated in each of the memory hierarchy. The proposed architecture has been implemented with many STT-RAM blocks and a few SRAM blocks. To reduce high write energy latency, a reuse distance predictor is used to determine which data needs to be placed in the SRAM or STT-RAM region of the LLC. The main idea is to eliminate the use of writing data that is less likely to be used again in the caches. By utilizing this technique, the power consumption in the LLC is reduced by 55%.

Similarly, Cheng et al. [28] proposed LAP, a technique which combines both non-inclusive and exclusive designs to manage the way the caches are handled in the LLCs. By using exclusive properties in the cache policy, the LAP is able to cache only the required data of the upper-level data in the LLC to reduce redundant writes. This technique reduces unnecessary writes in NVM memory technology reducing high energy writes. The characteristics of LAP are: only write non-duplicate data, duplicate only useful clean data and no redundant LLC data-fill in the LLC.

Fanfan et al. [29] propose a technique called Feedback Learning Based Dead Write Termination (FLDWT) for eliminating dead blocks from inclusive STT-RAM LLCs. The proposed architecture works by classifying blocks into two categories (dead and live) based on access behaviour. Dead blocks are blocks which are have not been referenced for a long time. The technique works by discarding the dead blocks from being written to LLC before they are evicted to save power. The proposed technique reduces power consumption by 44.6%.

Safayenikoo et al. [30] proposed a hybrid cache memory for 3D CMPs comprised of STT-RAM and SRAM banks. To reduce the power consumption of high energy writes in STT-RAM cache banks, the number of writes to STT-RAM is monitored. Data is migrated to SRAM banks when the number of writes to the STT-RAM increases. This is done by employing a counter to count the number of accesses and writes for each bank. Mittal et al. [31] propose AYUSH, a technique which swaps an STT-RAM block to an SRAM block if the data stored in the SRAM block is old. This is done by using a least recently used parameter to determine if the data-item stored in the SRAM is likely to be used. If it is likely to be used, a NVM block data which just got inserted will be swapped for that SRAM block since it is likely to be used in the future to prevent high energy writes. Sukarn et al. [32] deals with high energy writes in STT-RAM based hybrid caches by restricting the number of writes associated with private blocks.

Aluru et al. [33] reduces the high current write in STT-RAM by splitting the cache line into many parts and writes them in different locations in the cache. The proposed solution reduces power consumption and reduces the errors that occur. Sato et al. [34] on other hand reduces power consumption by merging two adjacent lines and then writes them back to the STT-RAM LLC as one line instead of two writes and minimizes latency.

3.2 Data Compression Schemes

Safayenikoo et al. proposed a compression method to reduce the number of write count which in turns reduces the power consumption in the LLCs by 78%. The proposed compression scheme reduces the number of repetitive words (zero) (Table 2).

Table 2. LLC SRAM and STT-RAM technology comparisons

Characteristics	SRAM	STT-RAM	Hybrid
Read latency	Low	Low	Low
Write latency	Low	High	Average
Read power	Low	Low	Low
Write power	Low	High	Average
Leakage power	High	Low	Average
Dynamic power	Low	High	Average

Similarly, Liu et al. [35] proposed two compression schemes to reduce the power consumption in Multi-Level Cell (MLC) STT-RAM. MLC STT-RAM stores soft-bits and hard-bits but takes longer during read and write operations even though they offer better performances than single-level STT-RAMs. Unfortunately, during hard-bit accesses, it takes longer and consumes power and therefore downgrades the performance of the system. To overcome this, the first data compression technique reduces the size of the cache lines and reduces the time it takes to access it. The second technique allows an additional line to be stored in the hard-bit region. The proposed architecture reduces power consumption by 19%.

4 Monitoring Cache Behaviour

One of the most effective ways to reduce power consumption in on-chip caches is by monitoring cache blocks. Along these lines, two different approaches can be implemented (bypass predictions and dead blocks). Although the principal of locality is used to make decisions about data exchange in caches, majority of cache blocks in the LLCs are never referenced again and thus, useless/dead blocks dominate the LLC. For an LLC architecture which incorporates STT-RAM technology, bypassing writes to its bank could reduce the high write energy.

4.1 Bypass Predictions

Park et al. [36] proposed a Bypass First Policy (BFP) which reduces the number of blocks which are less likely to be used. This is done by bypassing blocks that are less likely to be used by default thus reducing useless blocks in the LLC which consumes a lot of power and space. The proposed solution reduces power consumption by 57%.

Hameed et al. [37] proposed a shared Row Buffer (RB) Organisation in an STT-RAM cache architecture which exploits the Row Buffer Locality (RBL) to reduce row buffer power consumption. In STT-RAM, each bank consists of a RB which stores the row that was recently accessed. If a data is required in the same row in the near future, this data is fetched from the row buffer instead of accessing the STT-RAM bit cell. This saves time and power. Unfortunately, RB conflict occurs when a current row in the RB is evicted and replaced with a new one. This increases the access latency. To reduce the RB conflict and misses, a shared RB organisation is proposed. Each bank is divided into different groups. Each group share the RB resources available to that group. This increases the RB hit rate because each group now has an RB assigned to it. In addition to this, a write-back bypass policy is proposed to reduce low RBL insertions into the RB and to also bypass the RB for write-back requests.

Azad et al. [7] proposed an Error-Correcting Code (ECC) protection technique which protects cache blocks by partitioning them into different groups. Instead of using worst-case protection for all cache blocks, the proposed technique categorises blocks into groups with different level of protection depending on the write requests. In comparison with conventional non-uniform ECC, the proposed algorithm reduces power consumption by 50% and guarantees the same level protection.

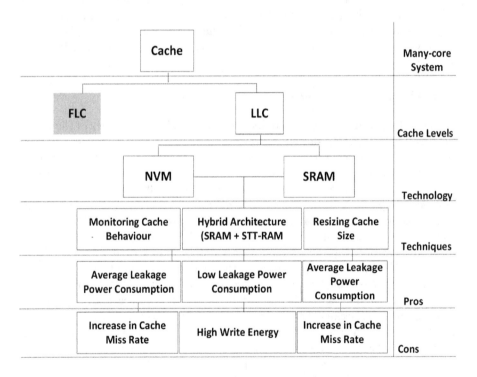

Fig. 2. Summary of LLC design techniques

4.2 Dead Blocks

Mnivannan et al. [38] proposed RADAR, a technique which eliminates dead blocks from the LLCs. RADAR works by using a Look-ahead and Look-back scheme to predict the regions that will be accessed. Based on the information gathered, RADAR evicts cache blocks in dead regions.

Das et al. [39] proposed a Sub-Level Insertion Policy (SLIP) to manage the movement of cache lines from one location to the other. SLIP is used to place cache lines into groups with similar cache access energy. This technique reduces power consumption in the LLCs by 22%.

Kurian et al. [40] proposed a technique that only replicates the high locality cache lines in the LLC slice and bypasses replicating low locality cache lines. The number of times a cache line is accessed is tracked and depending on the number of times it has been accessed, a replica will be made in the LLC. Similarly, Chaturvedi et al. [41] propose a technique that dynamically replicate high usage cache lines in the local banks close to the requesting core in non-uniform cache architectures.

Agawal et al. [32] on the hand proposed a hybrid architecture that reduces the number of writes by only storing the tags and directory entry of private blocks in the LLC. Private blocks are blocks that have exclusive permission to only one core and thus, they are different from the copies in the LLC. Therefore, these copies are useless and are only useful when a write-back occurs. To reduce this, only tags and directory entries are stored instead of data to reduce the write energy.

5   Resizing Cache Size

Another widely used technique to reduce power is to shutdown parts of the cache which are idle. However, shutting down idle parts of the cache affects performance. Particularly, when there is a sudden overshoot in the workloads. Therefore, power-gating techniques should consider performance degradation when resizing the cache (cache banks and ways are powered-off) [42].

Chakraborty et al. [42] proposed a bank shutdown technique to reduce the power consumption in the LLCs. The banks that are less likely to be used are powered-off and their future requests redirected to neighbouring banks with average utilization. High active banks will not be selected to respond to the requests of the shutdown banks because they will not be able to handle it and will have a negative impact on the performance of the system. Furthermore, there is a limit to the number of banks that can be powered-off to prevent performance loss. Consequently, because not all banks can be powered-off, lightly used banks will have some of their ways turned off. To choose which bank to shutdown, a counter is attached to monitor accesses.

Park et al. [43] proposed a technique which improves the performance of LLCs when some cache ways are powered-off to reduce the power consumption by 34%. In the proposed architecture, all tag ways can be accessed in parallel. Additionally, a partial tag-based way filter is proposed and attached to each cache way. The proposed algorithm dynamically activates the number of ways that is required.

Cheng et al. [44] proposed a mechanism for turning off cache slices. To turn off a cache slice, a power management unit is employed to store information about the cache access from the previous epoch. This information is then used to decide the capacity required by the workload.

Choi et al. [45] proposed a cache way allocation scheme which effectively allocates SRAM and NVM ways by considering the impact of NVM writes by the landfill operation. Unlike other schemes which allocates write-intensive blocks to the SRAM ways, this scheme reduces the NVM write counts through a two-step approach. The proposed approach reduces power consumption with approximate range of 28.6%–37%.

Figure 2 presents an overview of the techniques presented in this paper where the grey rectangle represents the First Level Cache (FLC) and the white rectangle represents the LLC[1]. The techniques discussed so far can be categorised into three main parts (Monitoring cache behaviour, hybrid architecture and resizing the cache size. Although all the techniques reduce leakage power consumption, the hybrid architecture reduces a large amount.

6 Summary

There is no doubt that the LLC consumes power and therefore needs to be addressed. For this purpose, we have categorised existing techniques into three different groups with a view of discussing the advantages and disadvantages. In terms of the category of techniques presented, adopting hybrid architectures is the most efficient way of saving power because SRAM technology consumes a lot of power and with the number of powered-off cores increasing with each technology node as a result of leakage power which cannot be controlled, STT-RAM switches the focus from leakage power to dynamic power which in some way can be controlled. By combining these materials, there is a balance and a trade-off between each material. Power consumption is however reduced at the expense of a slight degrade in performance.

In contrary, Monitoring Cache Behaviour and Resizing cache sizes focuses solely on reducing power consumption through efficient performing of the cache through software procedures hence why hybrid architectures reduces more power consumption. Preventing cache misses and increasing the chance of cache hits to effectively improve the performance of the cache. Additionally powering-off cache slices also saves power, however the impact on leakage saving is minimum. Charabotey et al. [42] proposed technique of shutting down cache slices and redirecting future request to neighbouring banks have the ability to improve the performance of under average utilization. However, in a many-core system, it is unlikely that this technique will be adopted.

7 Conclusion

To address the power challenges in Multi-Level Caches, various solutions have been proposed over the past years. However, comprehensive work that evaluates

---

[1] Though FLC power consumption is important, we focus on the LLC because they have not received much attention and consumes more power and area.

low power techniques for LLC design is limited. In this paper, we presented low power design techniques for LLCs. Our findings demonstrate that, integrating caches with STT-RAM and SRAM provides an effective solution to the leakage power consumption dominating modern technology. By creating a hybrid memory, STT-RAM banks can be used for read-intensive data while SRAM is used for write-intensive workloads. In addition to this, LLC power consumption can also be reduced by data compression schemes, eliminating dead blocks, and resizing cache size.

References

1. Wendel, D., Kalla, R., Cargoni, R., Clables, J., Friedrich, J., Frech, R., Kahle, J., Sinharoy, B., Starke, W., Taylor, S., Weitzel, S., Chu, S.G., Islam, S., Zyuban, V.: The implementation of POWER7TM: a highly parallel and scalable multi-core high-end server processor. In: SSCC (2010)
2. Gammie, G., Wang, A., Mair, H., Lagerquist, R., Chau, M., Royannez, P., Gururajarao, S., Ko, U.: SmartReflex power and performance management technologies for 90 nm, 65 nm, and 45 nm mobile application processors. Proc. IEEE **98**, 144–159 (2010)
3. Agyeman, M.O., Zong, W.: An efficient 2D router architecture for extending the performance of inhomogeneous 3D NoC-based multi-core architectures. In: International Symposium on Computer Architecture and High Performance Computing Workshops, SBAC-PAD 2016, pp. 79–84 (2016)
4. Agyeman, M.O., Vien, Q.T., Ahmadinia, A., Yakovlev, A., Tong, K.F., Mak, T.S.T.: A resilient 2-D waveguide communication fabric for hybrid wired-wireless NoC design. IEEE Trans. Parallel Distrib. Syst. **28**, 359–373 (2017)
5. Agyeman, M.O.: Optimizing heterogeneous 3D networks-on-chip architectures for low power and high performance applications. Ph.D. dissertation, Glasgow Caledonian University, UK (2014)
6. Bi, X., Mao, M., Wang, D., Li, H.H.: Cross-layer optimization for multilevel cell STT-RAM caches. IEEE Trans. Very Large Scale Integr. (VLSI) Syst. **25**, 1807–1820 (2017)
7. Azad, Z., Farbeh, H., Monazzah, A.M.H., Miremadi, S.G.: An efficient protection technique for last level STT-RAM caches in multi-core processors. IEEE Trans. Parallel Distrib. Syst. **28**, 1564–1577 (2017)
8. Kurd, N.A., Bhamidipati, S., Mozak, C., Miller, J.L., Wilson, T.M., Nemani, M., Chowdhury, M.: Westmere: A family of 32nm IA processors. In: ISSCC (2010)
9. Awan, M.A., Petters, S.M.: Enhanced race-to-halt: a leakage-aware energy management approach for dynamic priority systems. In: 23rd Euromicro Conference on Real-Time Systems (2011)
10. Ofori-Attah, W.B.E., Agyeman, M.O.: Architectural techniques for improving the power consumption of NoC-based CMPS: a case study of cache and network layer. In: Emerging Network-on-Chip Architectures for Low Power Embedded Systems (2017)
11. Dai, J., Guan, M., Wang, L.: Exploiting early tag access for reducing L1 data cache energy in embedded processors. IEEE Trans. Very Large Scale Integr. (VLSI) Syst. **22**, 396–407 (2014)

12. Ranjan, A., Venkataramani, S., Pajouhi, Z., Venkatesan, R., Roy, K., Raghunathan, A.: STAxCache: An approximate, energy efficient STT-MRAM cache. In: DATE Conference Exhibition (2017)

13. Gan, Z., Zhang, M., Gu, Z., Zhang, J.: Minimizing energy consumption for embedded multicore systems using cache configuration and task mapping. In: CyberC (2016)

14. Zang, W., Gordon-Ross, A.: A survey on cache tuning from a power/energy perspective. ACM Comput. Surv. **45**, 32 (2013)

15. Mittal, S.: A survey of architectural techniques for improving cache power efficiency. sustainable computing: Informatics and systems. Sustain. Comput.: Inform. Syst. (SUSCOM) **4**, 33–43 (2014)

16. Ofori-Attah, E., Bhebhe, W., Agyeman, M.O.: Architectural techniques for improving the power consumption of NoC-based CMPS: a case study of cache and network layer. J. Low Power Electron. Appl. **7**, 14 (2017)

17. Ofori-Attah, E., Agyeman, M.O.: A survey of low power NoC design techniques. In: AISTECS 2017 (2017)

18. Ofori-Attah, E., Agyeman, M.O.: A survey of recent contributions on low power NoC architectures. In: Computing Conference (2017)

19. Artes, J.A., Ayala, J., Catthoor, F.: Survey of low-energy techniques for instruction memory organisations in embedded systems. J. Signal Process syst. **70**(1), 1–19 (2013)

20. Mittal, S., Vetter, J.S., Li, D.: A survey of architectural approaches for managing embedded DRAM and non-volatile on-chip caches. IEEE Trans. Parallel Distrib. Syst. **26**, 1524–1537 (2015)

21. Indumathi, G., Aarthi, V.P.M.B.: Energy optimization techniques on SRAM: a survey. In: International Conference on Communication and Network Technologies (2014)

22. Apalkov, D., Khvalkovskiy, A., Watts, S., Nikitin, V., Tang, X., Lottis, D., Moon, K., Luo, X., Chen, E., Ong, A., Driskill-Smith, A., Krounbi, M.: Spin-transfer torque magnetic random access memory (STT-MRAM). J. Emerg. Technol. Comput. Syst. **9**, 23 (2013)

23. Noguchi, H., Kushida, K., Ikegami, K., Abe, K., Kitagawa, E., Kashiwada, S., Kamata, C., Kawasumi, A., Hara, H., Fujita, S.: A 250-mhz 256b-i/o 1-mb STT-MRAM with advanced perpendicular MTJ based dual cell for nonvolatile magnetic caches to reduce active power of processors. In: Symposium on VLSI Circuits (2013)

24. Noguchi, H., Ikegami, K., Shimomura, N., Tetsufumi, T., Ito, J., Fujita, S.: Highly reliable and low-power nonvolatile cache memory with advanced perpendicular STT-MRAM for high-performance CPU. In: Symposium on VLSI Circuits Digest of Technical Papers (2014)

25. Senni, S., Torres, L., Sassatelli, G., Bukto, A., Mussard, B.: Exploration of magnetic RAM based memory hierarchy for multicore architecture. In: IEEE Computer Society Annual Symposium on VLSI (2014)

26. Li, J., Xue, C.J., Xu, Y.: STT-RAM based energy-efficiency hybrid cache for CMPs. In: IEEE/IFIP 19th International Conference on VLSI and System-on-Chip (2011)

27. Kim, N., Ahn, J., Seo, W., Choi, K.: Energy-efficient exclusive last-level hybrid caches consisting of SRAM and STT-RAM. In: IFIP/IEEE International Conference on Very Large Scale Integration (VLSI-SoC) (2015)

28. Cheng, H.Y., Zhao, J., Sampson, J., Irwin, M.J., Jaleel, A., Lu, Y., Xie, Y.: Lap: Loop-block aware inclusion properties for energy-efficient asymmetric last level caches. In: ACM/IEEE 43rd Annual International ISCA (2016)

29. Shen, F., He, Y., Zhang, J., Jiang, N., Li, Q., Li, J.: Feedback learning based dead write termination for energy efficient STT-RAM caches. Chin. J. Electron. **26**, 460–467 (2017)

30. Safayenikoo, P., Asad, A., Fathy, M., Mohammadi, F.: Exploiting non-uniformity of write accesses for designing a high-endurance hybrid last level cache in 3D CMPs. In: IEEE 30th Canadian Conference on Electrical and Computer Engineering (CCECE) (2017)

31. Mittal, S., Vetter, J.S.: AYUSH: Extending lifetime of SRAM-NVM way-based hybrid caches using wear-leveling. In: IEEE 23rd International Symposium on Modeling, Analysis, and Simulation of Computer and Telecommunication Systems (2015)

32. Agarwal, S., Kapoor, H.K.: Restricting writes for energy-efficient hybrid cache in multi-core architectures. In: IFIP/IEEE International Conference on Very Large Scale Integration (VLSI-SoC) (2016)

33. Aluru, R.K., Ghosh, S.: Droop mitigating last level cache architecture for STTRAM. In: DATE (2017)

34. Sato, M., Sakai, Z., Egawa, R., Kobayashi, H.: An adjacent-line-merging writeback scheme for STT-RAM last-level caches. In: IEEE Symposium in Low-Power and High-Speed Chips (COOL CHIPS) (2017)

35. Liu, L., Chi, P., Li, S., Cheng, Y., Xie, Y.: Building energy-efficient multi-level cell STT-RAM caches with data compression. In: 22nd ASP-DAC (2017)

36. Park, J.J.K., Park, Y., Mahlke, S.: A bypass first policy for energy-efficient last level caches. In: International Conference on Embedded Computer Systems: Architectures, Modeling and Simulation (SAMOS) (2016)

37. Hameed, F., Tahoori, M.B.: Architecting STT last-level-cache for performance and energy improvement. In: 17th ISQED (2016)

38. Manivannan, M., Papaefstathiou, V., Pericas, M., Stenstrom, P.: RADAR: Runtime-assisted dead region management for last-level caches. In: IEEE International Symposium on HPCA (2016)

39. Das, S., Aamodt, T.M., Dally, W.J.: SLIP: Reducing wire energy in the memory hierarchy. In: ACM/IEEE 42nd Annual on ISCA (2015)

40. Kurian, G., Devadas, S., Khan, O.: Locality-aware data replication in the last-level cache. In: IEEE 20th International Symposium on High Performance Computer Architecture (HPCA) (2014)

41. Chaturvedi, N., Subramaniyan, A., Gurunarayanan, S.: Selective cache line replication scheme in shared last level cache. Proced. Comput. Sci. **46**, 1095–1107 (2015)

42. Chakraborty, S., Kapoor, H.K.: Static energy reduction by performance linked dynamic cache resizing. In: IFIP/IEEE International Conference on Very Large Scale Integration (VLSI-SoC) (2016)

43. Park, J., Lee, J., Kim, S.: A way-filtering-based dynamic logicalassociative cache architecture for low-energy consumption. IEEE Trans. Very Large Scale Integr. (VLSI) Syst. **25**, 793–805 (2017)

44. Cheng, H.Y., Poremba, M., Shahidi, N., Stalev, I., Irwin, M.J., Kandemir, M., Sampson, J., Xie, Y.: EECache: Exploiting design choices in energy-efficient last-level caches for chip multiprocessors. In: IEEE/ACM ISLPED (2014)

45. Choi, J., Park, G.H.: NVM way allocation scheme to reduce NVM writes for hybrid cache architecture in chip-multiprocessors. IEEE Trans. Parallel Distrib. Syst. **28**, 2896–2910 (2017)

Fault-Tolerance, Security and Communication Architectures

ISA-DTMR: Selective Protection in Configurable Heterogeneous Multicores

Augusto G. Erichsen[1]([✉])(iD), Anderson L. Sartor[1](iD), Jeckson D. Souza[1](iD),
Monica M. Pereira[2](iD), Stephan Wong[3], and Antonio C. S. Beck[1](iD)

[1] Institute of Informatics, Universidade Federal do Rio Grande do Sul (UFRGS),
Porto Alegre, Brazil
{agerichsen,alsartor,jeckson.souza,caco}@inf.ufrgs.br
[2] Department of Computer Science and Applied Mathematics,
Universidade Federal do Rio Grande do Norte (UFRN), Natal, Brazil
monicapereira@dimap.ufrn.br
[3] Computer Engineering Laboratory, Faculty of EEMCS,
Delft University of Technology, Delft, The Netherlands
j.s.s.m.wong@tudelft.nl

Abstract. The well-known Triple Modular Redundancy (TMR), when applied to processors to mitigate the occurrence of faults, implies that all applications have the same level of criticality (since they are all equally protected) and are executed in a homogeneous environment, which naturally would waste precious resources in terms of area and energy. However, many current systems are composed of heterogeneous cores that implement the same ISA (e.g., ARM's big.LITTLE or DynamIQ), executing some applications that may be more critical than others and that would require different levels of protection. With that in mind, we propose ISA-DTMR, a non-intrusive approach that, taking advantage of heterogeneous systems, can protect applications at different levels in a totally transparent fashion. By using heterogeneous multicore configurations composed of configurable processors that implement the same Instruction Set Architecture (ISA), we will show that it is possible to adapt the level of protection for each application according to its reliability requirements. When compared to homogeneous processors, ISA-DTMR reduces area by up to 54.9%, and energy consumption by 30.35%, with negligible overhead on performance, for a configuration that balances performance and energy consumption. ISA-DTMR is able to provide the same level of protection for critical applications and even improve the reliability for non-critical applications.

Keywords: Fault tolerance · Heterogeneous architecture · TMR
DMR

1 Introduction

The evolution of integrated circuit manufacturing technology has also increased its susceptibility to failure, which can be caused by many factors such as variability, aging, and radiation effects [4]. Many fault tolerance techniques have

© Springer International Publishing AG, part of Springer Nature 2018
N. Voros et al. (Eds.): ARC 2018, LNCS 10824, pp. 231–242, 2018.
https://doi.org/10.1007/978-3-319-78890-6_19

been developed to enable correct execution or detection of errors, and all of them present some sort of overhead when compared to the unprotected version: area, performance, or energy consumption. TMR is one of the most popular, and works by replicating the circuit that needs protection, checking correctness using a majority voter so the faults can be masked. While it presents a high fault tolerance to Single Event Effects (SEE), it results in a huge area and power dissipation overhead. Most importantly, in the case of an environment composed of General Purpose Processor (GPPs) executing multiple processes, it usually assumes that all processors are the same and that all the applications are critical (thus they all should be protected). On the other hand, the advantage of TMR is that it is completely non-intrusive: it can be implemented without any changes in the underlying microarchitecture, so potentially any Commercial Off-The-Shelf (COTS) GPP can be used.

ARM big.LITTLE and, more recently, DynamIQ [1] brought to mainstream market systems that are composed of different microarchitectures but implement the same ISA so that the same binary can transparently execute on different microarchitectures. To save energy, applications that do not need full performance can migrate from one (big) core to another (LITTLE), which indirectly enables the fabrication of integrated circuits with decreased transistor count and die size. Borrowing from this same idea, one could consider that instead of performance, an application would not need to be fully protected: in a very common scenario where many applications are executing, each of them may have its own requirements when it comes to reliability (some being more critical than others). Therefore, if a non-critical application (i.e., can present errors or will not lead to a system failure even if it is not executed until completion) is executed in a completely protected circuit (e.g., TMR), resources (performance, area, and energy) would be wasted in the same way as applications that would not need full performance executing in a homogeneous multicore environment.

Considering the discussion above, this work proposes ISA-DTMR, which is a new design capable of providing protection only to critical applications, taking advantage of current systems with a homogeneous ISA and heterogeneous microarchitectures, lowering the overheads presented by the original TMR. It keeps the software transparency, since no changes in the source code are necessary; and to the hardware, since no changes in the processor are needed. ISA-DTMR uses a similar idea (but for a different end) as the Design Diversity Redundancy (DDR) methodology [3], in which different designs for the same application are available and work together, increasing fault tolerance.

The general architecture of ISA-DTMR is implemented using configurable processors, following the same concept as the ARM big.LITTLE or DynamIQ: it comprises different processors of the same (ISA) that require different amounts of resources to be implemented and have different trade-offs considering performance, energy and fault tolerance. To better illustrate the approach, Fig. 1 depicts a scenario in which four applications are executed in a heterogeneous quad-core processor. In this example, *App #1* is protected with TMR, *App #2* and *App #4* with Dual Modular Redundancy (DMR), and *App #3* is executed without any fault tolerance technique.

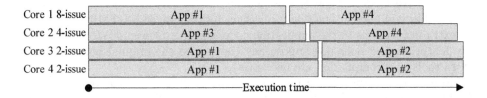

Fig. 1. Applications running in heterogeneous cores

We developed the proposed technique in the VEX ISA, using different designs of the ρ-VEX configurable VLIW processor [27]. The ρ-VEX can be easily configured to have a different number of issue slots (e.g., 2, 4, or 8). Each configuration brings changes to the optimization axes. The 8-issue usually has the best performance for the benchmarks, but greater area occupation and power consumption. The 2-issue, on the other hand, has lower performance in exchange of its reduced power consumption and area occupation. Finally, the 4-issue has better balance between both. We take advantage of these features to build heterogeneous multicore processors, which can have different optimization axes.

The design was synthesized for both ASIC and FPGA. We have compared nine different processor configurations (three homogeneous and six heterogeneous), with two benchmark sets. By applying the proposed approach to a heterogeneous quad-core in the most energy-oriented configuration, it is possible to reduce the area and power dissipation by 54.9% and 57.7%, respectively, when compared to its homogeneous counterpart comprised of 8-issue processors. Considering a particular set of applications, we show that energy is reduced by up to 35.06% with 12.08% of performance overhead. By using a configuration that weighs performance and energy, it is possible to reduce the energy consumption by 30.35% while maintaining almost the same performance. Moreover, all ISA-DTMR designs maintain the same level of protection to critical applications as the conventional TMR when applied to homogeneous processors. Therefore, ISA-DTMR can be used to execute applications with different priorities in terms of protection and, at the same time, save area and energy consumption.

This article is organized as follows. We discuss the state-of-art in Sect. 2. In Sect. 3, the proposed approach is presented and its implementation details are discussed. In Sect. 4, the results are presented in terms of area, power dissipation, energy consumption, performance, and error/failure rates. Section 5 concludes this paper and presents future directions.

2   Related Work

Several works have been proposed for the detection and correction of transient faults in multicore processors. These works aim to improve the fault tolerance of the target system, typically based on redundancy, which may be implemented in software, hardware, or both. Next, some of these techniques will be discussed.

Software-based techniques that use the compiler to replicate instructions are common both for VLIW processors [5,12,16,24] and for superscalar processors [13]. Unlike compiler instruction replication techniques, ISA-DTMR introduces no extra instructions to the application code, keeping its original size and memory footprint; and does not impose any changes to the original binary (so no extra tools or recompilation are necessary).

Nonetheless, software solutions can also be applied at thread-/process-level. In [14], the authors exploit the parallel capacities of SMT processors to duplicate threads and detect faults via DMR, while in [11] this technique was improved and tested in a dual core, SMT enabled processor, using a higher workload (multiple applications). The authors of [23] take advantage of spare or idle cores in multi-core systems to triplicate application processes and apply TMR to detect and correct faults. On the other hand, [6] propose a generic approach for many-core systems, in which a dedicated hardened core controller is responsible for replicating and synchronizing threads for fault detection and recovery by either Duplication With Comparison (DWC) or TMR techniques. Although most of these software-based techniques rely on replicating threads similarly as ISA-DTMR, they do not consider a heterogeneous environment with different levels of criticality for the applications (including the possibility of no protection at all for some of them).

Among the many hardware-based solutions, the authors of [8,9] propose a framework that creates sets of single-ISA cores with different strategies for fault tolerance (fully TMR cores, pipeline, register file and cache TMR). The sets are generated to maximize reliability for different applications, while keeping a power budget, considering future restrictions brought by dark silicon. Then, during runtime, depending on the running application's requirement, a core that gives the necessary protection level is selected, while all the others are kept dark. The authors in [18] trade-off the axes of fault tolerance, energy consumption, and performance by using techniques to duplicate and re-execute faulty instructions, reduce energy consumption by using power gating and control the Instruction-level Parallelism (ILP) of the application so more duplication or energy savings can be achieved. The following works look into these techniques in different granularities [19–21]. In contrast to all those hardware-based solutions, ISA-DTMR requires no modifications inside the processor (i.e., it is not intrusive), so it can be totally based on COTS GPPs. Comparators and voters can be included in many non-intrusive ways, such as in a separate ASIC, in a MPSoC or even by software. Therefore, ISA-DTMR can use existing cores of heterogeneous GPPs to increase reliability, considering individual application criticality to minimize resource usage. Moreover, if the cores are not used for redundancy, they can be used for regular application execution or turned off. This contrasts to typical DMR/TMR solutions, in which all the redundant hardware is permanently used for reliability; or, in the specific case of [9], to the impossibility of using the extra transistors added for fault tolerance to accelerate execution.

Still related to hardware, to reduce the probability of Common Mode Failures (CMF) occurrence, one solution is to provide TMR using different technologies or architectures. This technique is called Diversity TMR (DTMR), or TMR based on DDR [10]. The authors in [25] propose DTMR to investigate protection against CMF in an 8×8 matrix implemented in FPGA. [2] uses DTMR to improve fault tolerance in FPGAs. [26] presents a reliability analysis using design diversity as metric using RISC, VLIW and CGRA architectures to generate the results. Differently from other works in DTMR, ISA-DTMR exploits the binary compatibility between cores in heterogeneous single-ISA multicores. Having the same ISA between cores eases the software development process, since no special compilers or toolchains are necessary to deploy the system.

Therefore, by considering that applications may have different levels of criticality, ISA-DTMR uses the same idea of design diversity as DTMR, but taking advantage of configurable processors to build heterogeneous multicore environments that implement a single ISA. So, in cases some applications do not demand high reliability, it is possible to use the extra cores for parallel execution of other applications or even turn them off to save energy. In this work we reassemble a big.LITTLE-based environment by using different designs of the ρ-VEX family, considering a great number of scenarios. We show how such environment can be employed for fault tolerance and, at same time, balance energy and performance, when criticality is not necessary for all applications.

3   ISA-DTMR Implementation

As already discussed, ISA-DTMR considers the fact that different applications have different needs when it comes to reliability: some are critical and need to be protected against soft errors, while non-critical ones may tolerate erroneous results. ISA-DTMR exploits this difference of criticality by protecting some applications with TMR, others with DMR, and by executing non-critical applications without any fault tolerance mechanism, all concurrently, thus reducing energy and area. Application criticality can be decided at design time, or through dynamic strategies, such as shown in [6].

In this work, the configurable ρ-VEX softcore VLIW processor [27] is used as case study, which is implemented in VHDL and we have full access to its low level description. The ρ-VEX core has a five-stage pipeline, and it can be easily configured to have a different number of issue slots (e.g., 2, 4, or 8). Each pipelane (issue-slot) may contain different functional units from the following set: ALU (always present), multiplier, memory, and branch units. The ISA-DTMR implementation of the ρ-VEX is done by combining processors with different issue widths, as can be seen in Fig. 2.

When using TMR with a common diverse processor strategy, the correct execution verification is always dependent of the slowest processor (i.e., faster processors would have to wait for the slowest one). However, in the case of the ISA-DTMR, the fastest processors can execute different applications while waiting for the slowest processor to finish, using this spare time to perform actual

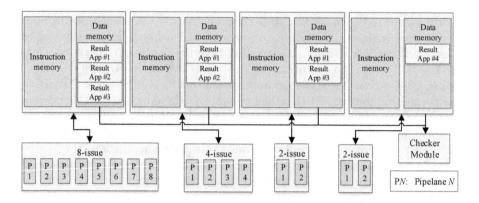

Fig. 2. Example of an ISA-DTMR implementation. A quad-core with one 8-issue core, one 4-issue and two 2-issue

computation [7]. If a processor executing an application with DMR protection fails, the voter module will flag the execution as faulty and trigger its re-execution so the fault can be corrected.

To keep the transparency as high as possible, the applications are only checked at the end of the execution by a specific hardware (Checker Module in Fig. 2). The Checker Module is responsible for verifying the correctness of the result, based on the reliability requirement of the given application. In case of a protected application, it compares the resulting memories to check the execution correctness. The Checker module implements a Finite-State Machine (FSM), which reads the application result from the memory in a burst, and the results are compared to detect errors. If there is a mismatch in a memory position, an error bit will flag the faulty result.

4   Results

In this section, we evaluate the proposed approach and analyze the results for fault tolerance, area, performance, power, and energy consumption.

4.1   Methodology

A total of nine designs were evaluated in this work: three homogeneous quad-core processors with issue-widths of 8 (baseline), 4, and 2 (i.e., 8-8-8-8, 4-4-4-4, 2-2-2-2); and six heterogeneous with the following configurations: 8-8-8-4, 8-8-4-4, 8-4-4-4, 8-4-4-2, 8-4-2-2, 8-2-2-2.

In order to analyze the reliability of the circuit, we have used a variation of the Mean Work to Failure metric, proposed in [15], as defined below.

$$MWTF = \frac{amount\ of\ work\ completed}{number\ of\ errors\ encountered} = \frac{core\ occupation}{(failure\ rate) \times (execution\ time)}$$

Where the core occupation is the ratio between the number of program instructions and the total number of instructions (program instructions plus NOPs). With that, it is possible to capture the trade-off between performance and fault tolerance and allows one to evaluate the reliability of different issue-widths removing the influence of the NOPs (free slots that the compiler was not able fill to exploit the instruction-level parallelism from the program) and the difference in execution time when the issue-width is reduced or increased.

To obtain the failure rate, a fault injection campaign was conducted and faults were injected at the gate-level signals of the design, using the Simbah-FI framework [17]. In this work, we consider that the memory and register file of the processors are protected with Error-Correcting Code (ECC). Our fault injection method simulates the occurrence of Single Event Transient (SET) faults, like the ones caused by radiation effects. The faults are injected at any internal and low-level signal of the target module. The injection instant follows a uniform probability function in the range between *zero* and t equal to the expected execution time from the application without faults, and to increase the likelihood of the SET to be captured by a flip-flop, the signal is forced for the duration of one clock cycle.

The fault injection campaign resulted in more than 500 thousand faults, injected at gate-level signals. For instance, the 8-issue homogeneous quad-core has 147,140 gate-level signals. To obtain accurate area and power measurements for ASICs, the designs were synthesized with the Cadence Encounter with a 65 nm CMOS cell library from STMicroelectronics. For the dynamic power consumption, the switching activity is considered to be of 30%, which is the traditionally assumed value for system level analysis of microprocessors [7]. When there is no switching activity in a given pipelane, only the static power dissipation is considered. For FPGAs, the design was synthesized to a Virtex-6 XC6VLX240T with the Xilinx ISE tool.

The applications used to evaluate our technique were selected from the ρ-VEX and the Powerstone benchmark suites [22] and they were divided into two scenarios that were tested in the nine different multicore designs:

- Scenario 1: FIR (TMR), POCSAG (DMR), LUDCMP (DMR), and CRC (unprotected execution).
- Scenario 2: Matrix multiplication (TMR), DFT (DMR), x264 (DMR), and Qurt (unprotected execution).

Even though the level of criticality of the selected applications may not reflect the same requirements they would have in a real system, they serve as examples for how ISA-DTMR behaves and to show the trade-offs when comparing it to conventional fault tolerance techniques. The applications were statically scheduled to the cores, aiming to minimize the total execution time as much as possible, for both the homogeneous and heterogeneous (ISA-DTMR) designs. In the heterogeneous designs, heavier applications are scheduled to the most powerful cores, following the same strategy as the schedulers used in ARM's big.LITTLE environments.

4.2   Fault Injection Campaign and MWTF Evaluation

As the FIR (*scenario 1*) and Matrix Multiplication (*scenario 2*) benchmarks are protected with TMR, they can mask all single faults in the design. By using ISA-DTMR, the replicates of these applications may be executed on cores with different configurations, exploiting heterogeneity with its advantages. The DMR applications (POCSAG and LUDCMP for *scenario 1*, and DFT and x264 for *scenario 2*) will result in re-execution when an error is detected, while the unprotected applications (CRC and Qurt) are considered non-critical and will remain with an incorrect result in case of a failure. Figure 3 presents the relative MWTF when compared to the 8-issue homogeneous quad-core processor (8-8-8-8), for the DMR-protected and unprotected applications. The applications with TMR have all their faults masked, thus it is not possible to evaluate their MWTF as the failure rate will be zero.

The amount of work that each application can perform until a failure occurs depends on the application's behavior and on which core configuration it is running on. For instance, when running the POCSAG application, the reduction in performance outweighs the reduction in the sensitive area, resulting in less work until a failure, compared to the 8-issue. On the other hand, for the x264 application (*scenario 2*), the 2-issue is able to improve the MWTF when compared to all other configurations. In this case, performance proportionally decreases less than the sensitive area, which means that even though the application takes longer to execute on the 2-issue processor, the processor is less exposed to radiation sources as its area is smaller.

This discussion highlights an important observation. By correctly choosing the core's issue-width in a heterogeneous processor, it is possible to improve the amount of work that an application can perform until a failure is detected in the system, even for those applications that are not critical.

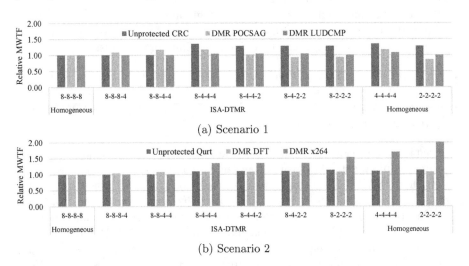

(a) Scenario 1

(b) Scenario 2

Fig. 3. MWTF rate results for each scenario normalized to the 8-8-8-8 processor

4.3   Area Occupation and Power Dissipation

Table 1 presents the area (for both FPGA and ASIC) and power comparison (for ASICs) for the homogeneous designs and the proposed ISA-DTMR designs. The Checker Module occupies 1,581 cells and dissipates 0.89 mW of power for ASICs, and 426 LUTs (look-up tables) and 165 FF (flip-flop registers) for FPGAs. As expected, the ISA-DTMR implementation occupies less area compared to the homogeneous baseline implementation. In our designs, a 2-issue core occupies 40% less area compared to a 4-issue, and a 4-issue occupies 57% less area compared to an 8-issue. The proposed approach occupies considerably less area than the homogeneous 8-issue quad-core baseline design: the area reduction varies from 13.6% to 58.3% for FPGAs and from 14.2% to 54.9% for ASICs as the processor configuration is changed from 8-8-8-4 to 8-2-2-2. The power dissipation is also reduced from 14% (8-4-4-4) to 57.7% (8-2-2-2) when compared to the baseline. This will impact on energy consumption, as discussed next.

4.4   Energy Consumption and Performance

Figure 4 shows the results for energy consumption, area, and performance normalized to the homogeneous 8-issue processor. In scenario 1, by using ISA-DTMR with the 8-4-4-4 configuration, it is possible to reduce the energy consumption and area in 27.75% and 42.78%, respectively, while maintaining negligible performance overhead (less than 1%) when compared to the homogeneous 8-issue. In the 8-2-2-2 configuration, it is possible to reduce the energy and area by 29.86% and 55.21%, while having a performance overhead of 43.7%.

4.5   Combining Reliability, Energy Consumption, and Performance

As one could observe in the previous subsections, with ISA-DTMR, it is possible to trade-off the axes of performance, energy consumption, power dissipation,

Table 1. Power dissipation and area occupation

Design		ASIC		FPGA		
		Power (mW)	Cells	LUT	FF
Heterogeneous	2-2-2-2	34.4	70,493	31,262	10,773
	4-4-4-4	65.5	113,777	64,150	12,353
	8-8-8-8	149.6	262,705	140,362	15,853
ISA-DTMR	8-8-8-4	128.6	225,473	121,309	14,978
	8-8-4-4	107.5	188,241	102,256	14,103
	8-4-4-4	86.5	151,009	83,203	13,228
	8-4-4-2	78.8	140,188	74,981	12,833
	8-4-2-2	71.0	129,367	66,759	12,438
	8-2-2-2	63.2	118,546	58,537	12,043

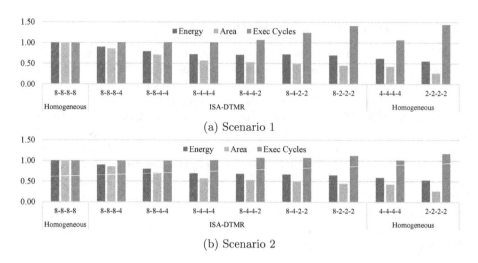

(a) Scenario 1

(b) Scenario 2

Fig. 4. Energy, area, and performance for each scenario normalized to the 8-8-8-8 processor

and area, providing expressive energy and area reductions at a low performance cost, and even improving the MWTF with the aforementioned savings in some cases. In this subsection, we summarize the benefits of applying the ISA-DTMR technique to improve fault tolerance in multicore systems.

Protecting applications with TMR, ISA-DTMR provides a fault tolerance mechanism to mask all single faults in the processor for critical applications and it still is able to reduce the area and energy consumption by executing the replicas on heterogeneous cores. Protecting applications with DMR, by using the proposed approach, it is also possible to improve the MWTF of the DMR-protected applications for almost all processor configurations, with the exception of the POCSAG application in the 8-4-2-2 and 8-2-2-2 processors, as discussed in Sect. 4.2. In the most significant case the MWTF is improved by more than 50% (x264 in the 8-2-2-2). This means that such applications will be able to perform more work until an error is detected and the re-execution of the application is performed, resulting in less re-executions. Therefore, the total energy consumption will be reduced as well as the performance overhead for all the re-executions. Executing Unprotected applications, even though these applications are not critical for the system, when the proposed technique is used, such applications are able to perform more work until a failure (up to 35%), when compared to the homogeneous 8-issue quad-core processor, which also means that these applications will fail less times. Thus, improving reliability just by choosing a core configuration that best fits the application behavior, instead of running all applications on homogeneous cores. In addition, the energy consumption can be reduced when choosing a smaller core without highly affecting performance for some applications, such as in the big.LITTLE approach.

5   Conclusion and Future Work

In this work, the ISA-DTMR is proposed, exploiting the fact that a number of different microarchitectures that implement the same ISA are available. The results showed that this technique can improve the fault tolerance consuming fewer resources, compared to the baseline, on both scenarios, with the exception of the 8-4-2-2 and 8-2-2-2 designs. The 8-4-4-2 exhibit the most balanced configuration, improving fault tolerance with more than 28% of reduction in energy consumption and half area occupation, compared to the baseline.

This work also shows that it is possible to improve the applications reliability by correctly choosing the core's issue-width. As future work, this technique will be applied to other processor architectures and more scenarios with different applications will be assessed. In addition, a dynamic scheduler and dynamic application criticality assessment mechanism will be implemented, and a software-based checker will be assessed and compared to the hardware approach.

Acknowledgement. This work was supported in part by CNPq, FAPERGS, and CAPES.

References

1. Arm Limited: Arm DynamIQ technology framework to design and build Cortex-A CPU systems (2017). https://developer.arm.com/technologies/dynamiq
2. Ashraf, R.A., Mouri, O., Jadaa, R., Demara, R.F.: Design-for-diversity for improved fault-tolerance of TMR systems on FPGAs. In: 2011 International Conference on Reconfigurable Computing and FPGAs, pp. 99–104, November 2011
3. Avizienis, A., Kelly, J.P.J.: Fault tolerance by design diversity: concepts and experiments. Computer **17**(8), 67–80 (1984)
4. Beck, A.C.S., Lisbôa, C.A.L., Carro, L.: Adaptable Embedded Systems. Springer Science & Business Media, Heidelberg (2012). https://doi.org/10.1007/978-1-4614-1746-0
5. Bolchini, C.: A software methodology for detecting hardware faults in VLIW data paths. IEEE Trans. Reliab. **52**(4), 458–468 (2003)
6. Bolchini, C., Carminati, M., Miele, A.: Self-adaptive fault tolerance in multi-/many-core systems. J. Electron. Test. **29**(2), 159–175 (2013)
7. Geuskens, B., Rose, K.: Modeling Microprocessor Performance. Springer Science & Business Media, Heidelberg (2012). https://doi.org/10.1007/978-1-4615-5561-2
8. Kriebel, F., Rehman, S., Sun, D., Shafique, M., Henkel, J.: ASER: adaptive soft error resilience for reliability-heterogeneous processors in the dark silicon era. In: ACM/EDAC/IEEE Design Automation Conference (DAC), pp. 1–6, June 2014
9. Kriebel, F., Shafique, M., Rehman, S., Henkel, J., Garg, S.: Variability and reliability awareness in the age of dark silicon. IEEE Des. Test **33**(2), 59–67 (2016)
10. Littlewood, B.: The impact of diversity upon common mode failures. Reliab. Eng. Syst. Saf. **51**(1), 101–113 (1996)
11. Mukherjee, S.S., Kontz, M., Reinhardt, S.K.: Detailed design and evaluation of redundant multi-threading alternatives. In: Proceedings 29th Annual International Symposium on Computer Architecture, pp. 99–110 (2002)

12. Pillai, A., Zhang, W., Kagaris, D.: Detecting VLIW hard errors cost-effectively through a software-based approach. In: 21st International Conference on Advanced Information Networking and Applications Workshops, AINAW 2007, vol. 1, pp. 811–815, May 2007
13. Ray, J., Hoe, J.C., Falsafi, B.: Dual use of superscalar datapath for transient-fault detection and recovery. In: MICRO-34 Proceedings of the 34th ACM/IEEE International Symposium on Microarchitecture, pp. 214–224, December 2001
14. Reinhardt, S.K., Mukherjee, S.S.: Transient fault detection via simultaneous multithreading. In: Proceedings of 27th International Symposium on Computer Architecture (IEEE Cat. No. RS00201), pp. 25–36, June 2000
15. Reis, G.A., Chang, J., Vachharajani, N., Mukherjee, S.S., Rangan, R., August, D.I.: Design and evaluation of hybrid fault-detection systems. In: 32nd International Symposium on Computer Architecture (ISCA 2005), pp. 148–159, June 2005
16. Sabena, D., Reorda, M.S., Sterpone, L.: On the development of software-based self-test methods for VLIW processors. In: IEEE Symposium on Defect and Fault Tolerance in VLSI and Nanotechnology Systems (DFT), pp. 25–30, October 2012
17. Sartor, A.L., Becker, P.H.E., Beck, A.C.S.: Simbah-FI: simulation-based hybrid fault injector. In: 2017 VII Brazilian Symposium on Computing Systems Engineering (SBESC), pp. 94–101, November 2017
18. Sartor, A.L., Becker, P.H.E., Hoozemans, J., Wong, S., Beck, A.C.S.: Dynamic trade-off among fault tolerance, energy consumption, and performance on a multiple-issue VLIW processor. IEEE Trans. Multi-scale Comput. Syst. **55**(99), 1 (2017)
19. Sartor, A.L., Lorenzon, A.F., Carro, L., Kastensmidt, F., Wong, S., Beck, A.C.S.: A novel phase-based low overhead fault tolerance approach for VLIW processors. In: Computer Society Annual Symposium on VLSI, pp. 485–490, July 2015
20. Sartor, A.L., Wong, S., Beck, A.C.S.: Adaptive ILP control to increase fault tolerance for VLIW processors. In: Conference on Application-Specific Systems, Architectures and Processors (ASAP), pp. 9–16, July 2016
21. Sartor, A.L., Lorenzon, A.F., Carro, L., Kastensmidt, F., Wong, S., Beck, A.C.S.: Exploiting idle hardware to provide low overhead fault tolerance for VLIW processors. J. Emerg. Technol. Comput. Syst. **13**(2), 13:1–13:21 (2017)
22. Scott, J., et al.: Designing the low-power m* core architecture. In: IEEE Power Driven Microarchitecture Workshop. Citeseer (1998)
23. Shye, A., Moseley, T., Reddi, V.J., Blomstedt, J., Connors, D.A.: Using process-level redundancy to exploit multiple cores for transient fault tolerance. In: IEEE/IFIP Conference on Dependable Systems and Networks, pp. 297–306, June 2007
24. Sterpone, L., Sabena, D., Campagna, S., Reorda, M.S.: Fault injection analysis of transient faults in clustered VLIW processors. In: IEEE Symposium on Design and Diagnostics of Electronic Circuits and Systems, pp. 207–212, April 2011
25. Tambara, L.A., Kastensmidt, F.L., Azambuja, J.R., Chielle, E., Almeida, F., Nazar, G., Rech, P., Frost, C., Lubaszewski, M.S.: Evaluating the effectiveness of a diversity TMR scheme under neutrons. In: European Conference on Radiation and its Effects on Components and Systems (RADECS), pp. 1–5, September 2013
26. Wang, Z., Yang, L., Chattopadhyay, A.: Architectural reliability estimation using design diversity. In: Symposium on Quality Electronic Design, pp. 112–117, March 2015
27. Wong, S., van As, T., Brown, G.: ρ-VEX: A reconfigurable and extensible softcore VLIW processor. In: Conference on Field-Programmable Technology, pp. 369–372, December 2008

Analyzing AXI Streaming Interface for Hardware Acceleration in AP-SoC Under Soft Errors

Fabio Benevenuti$^{(\boxtimes)}$ and Fernanda Lima Kastensmidt

Instituto de Informática – PGMICRO,
Universidade Federal do Rio Grande do Sul (UFRGS), Porto Alegre, Brazil
{fbenevenuti,fglima}@inf.ufrgs.br
http://www.ufrgs.br/pgmicro

Abstract. The focus of this work lies on Xilinx's SRAM-based FPGAs and All Programmable System-on-Chip (AP-SoC) devices that combines FPGAs and ARM processors having the AMBA Advanced eXtensible Interface (AXI) as one of its main interfaces. The use of commercial off-the-shelf SRAM-based FPGA devices integrating multi-core processors and custom IP blocks through general purpose interfaces can help in coping with performance requirements and time-to-market constraints. On the other hand, when considering its application in critical cyber-physical systems, there are reliability issues that must be dealt with. SRAM-based FPGAs are susceptible to soft-errors causing persistent changes on configuration memory that will accumulate until reconfiguration is performed. Mitigation techniques inside the user-designed IP blocks allow to delay this reconfiguration but choices on the interface between those blocks have impact on the effectiveness of the mitigations. This work consisted in evaluating an IP block generated by Xilinx's High-level Synthesis (HLS) tools and designed to use the AXI Streaming interface available. The results obtained from fault injection allowed to evaluate separately the reliability of the IP block core and the IP block AXI interface showing that, in this case, the IP block interface can undermine the efforts placed in the IP core hardening.

Keywords: Streaming interface · FPGA · Reliability
Fault injection · High-level synthesis

1 Introduction

As remarked in [1], state-of-art commercial off-the-shelf (COTS) SRAM-based FPGA devices have been used to leverage high-performance circuits in complex systems and heterogeneous hardware designs. A special case of those COTS devices is the Xilinx's All Programmable System-on-chip (AP-SoC) that profits from general purpose processing system (PS) combined with the custom programmable logic (PL).

© Springer International Publishing AG, part of Springer Nature 2018
N. Voros et al. (Eds.): ARC 2018, LNCS 10824, pp. 243–254, 2018.
https://doi.org/10.1007/978-3-319-78890-6_20

Being a COTS device, however, it brings some limitations on the choice of communication interfaces between the embedded processor and the programmable logic. In this sense, this work analyzes the case of Xilinx 7 Series FPGAs and AP-SoCs, such as the Xilinx Zynq-7000 which is based on a dual-core ARM Cortex-A9, and, ultimately, have the ARM Advanced Microcontroller Bus Architecture (AMBA) Advanced eXtensible Interface (AXI) as one of its major communication interface.

Further, in a scenario of always shortening time-to-market, we consider the case of new development methodologies such as high-level synthesis (HLS) and the use of general purpose COTS reusable blocks for AXI bus interconnects and direct memory access (DMA), provided by the AP-SoC manufacturer to be implemented on the programmable logic, supporting the interconnection between the user designed custom IP blocks and the processing system.

The manufacturer provides a series of soft IP blocks implementing different aspects of the AXI interface to be used at the FPGA, including several types of interconnects, arbiters, crossbars, protocol converters, stream routers and clock rate converters. Some of these functions are also available as hard IP blocks at the processor system in parts such as Zynq-7000.

The aspect of reliability is arisen when those high performance applications on AP-SoC and its SRAM-based FPGA are also critical systems, as discussed on the following sections.

The main novelty of this work is on decomposing the reliability of a HLS generated module in its processing core and its interface components allowing deeper analysis of its reliability behavior. The case-study is a serial stream system composed of processor and accelerator module. The reliability behavior is analyzed according to the number of accumulated upsets, performed by bitstream fault injection and modeled by a Weibull distribution.

Results show the impact of architectural decisions about interface types and better assessment of reliability improvements due to mitigation techniques implemented in C language level, previously partially masked by the interface component reliability.

2   Reliability in SRAM-Based FPGA

2.1   Soft Errors

High performance computing, aerospace and critical cyberphysical systems (CPS) in general must consider the effect that glitches, electromagnetic interference and radiation can have on electronic components.

FPGAs are reconfigurable systems with its functionality programmed by the user on a configuration memory. In SRAM-based FPGAs, specifically, this configuration memory is implemented as millions of SRAM cells. In the case of combinational logic circuits, for instance, truth tables can be stored in look-up tables (LUT) as part of the configuration memory of the FPGA. Several other resources of the FPGA also make use of this configuration memory, including all the interconnection point switches that route the signals throughout the FPGA fabric.

Single event upsets (SEU), also called bit-flips, may change the content of the SRAM configuration memory, changing, effectively, the used-defined combinational logic or any other relevant configuration causing errors, failures and occasionally severe losses. Single event upsets and single event transients (SET) also have impact on other storage elements besides the FPGAs configuration memory, such as flip-flops (FF) used to implement sequential logic, but in SRAM-based FPGAs, due to the huge amount of configuration memory, its susceptibility is a continuous research subject.

Also, when those upsets occur in user data flip-flops (FF) it may have a temporary effect, limited on how often those registers will be captured or updated and how far the erroneous data will propagate on the processing pipeline. On the other hand, when those upsets occur on configuration memory cells, the effect is persistent, cumulative and, unless some type of reprogramming is applied [2], it will lead eventually to a functional failure.

However, a single upset alone does not necessarily create a soft error [3] as, for each specific application of the SRAM-based FPGA, only a relatively small portion of the millions of configuration memory bits will convey useful user-programmed configuration. In general, it is expected that only 5% to 10% of the upsets will cause a functional error [3], being characterized as critical configuration bits [2].

Aside the critical bits, it is the persistence and accumulation of bit-flips along the time that will lead to errors and failures. Thus, given a specific application of SRAM-based FPGA, it is useful to determine what is the reliability of that application, in terms both of critical bit-flips that will lead to immediate failure and accumulated bit-flips, which modules are more sensitive, which mitigation techniques can be applied and how long the FPGA reprogramming can be delayed.

2.2 Fault Injection

We use fault injection on the SRAM-based FPGA configuration memory to evaluate the overall reliability and also the relative reliability of different modules or IP blocks implemented on the programmable logic.

Compared to radiation exposition experiments, this approach has a lower cost and allows for a finer analysis of how each component contributes to the reliability to the whole system and yet, when fault injection is applied to the whole system, its results can be related to the radiation exposition experiments as seen on Velazco et al. [4] and Tambara et al. [1].

The fault injection engine for Xilinx SRAM-based FPGA is described by Tonfat et al. [5] and consists of instantiation of the Xilinx Internal Configuration Access Port (ICAPE2) hard IP and instrumentation of the FPGA with additional design modules of the fault injection platform.

On Xilinx 7 Series FPGA and AP-SoC the configuration memory is segmented in frames of 3232 bits, or 101 words of 32 bits, grouped in rows, columns and subcolumns. The frame of 3232 bits is the minimum unit to read or write through the ICAPE2 configuration port.

A same configuration frame may convey both configuration for DSP resources or combinational logic look-up tables and other logic resources as configuration for signal routing through interconnect point switches and multiplexers.

In this setup, injecting a fault consists of reading a frame, inverting a single bit value in a given position and writing the frame back into the configuration memory. The frame address and bit position where a fault will be injected is defined at the fault injection campaign control station which runs a script according to the test plan.

When searching for critical bits, such script will scan sequentially and exhaustively the whole region of interest, injecting one fault, verifying the design proper functioning, cleaning the fault injected and repeating all steps on the next position.

When evaluating the design reliability, the script injects faults randomly over the region of interest, accumulating instead of cleaning each fault, and repeats the process until a design malfunction is detected. All the accumulated faults are then cleaned and a new sequence is started. This is repeated until a sufficient number of failures is collected.

As the upsets on configuration memory are, by nature, persistent, it is not required that faults be injected on every possible state or clock cycle of the whole processing cycle of the design under evaluation. Since persistent faults will still be present on the next and all the following processing cycles, it suffices that the design under evaluation executes only a single complete processing cycle between each fault injected.

The total number of faults accumulated, or bit-flips, is then equal to the number of design processing cycles. The duration of each design processing cycle, in clock cycles or any other time unit, can be related to the exposition time and vulnerability factor while, together with the total number of faults accumulated and number of errors detected, can be related to radiation fluence and known hardware device cross section. These relationships are further discussed by Velazco et al. [4].

3   Hardware Accelerator Interface and Analysis Methodology

3.1   Benchmark Application

This work explores as benchmark application an out-of-core accelerator for matrix multiplication generated by high-level synthesis (HLS) from C language source code, as presented by dos Santos et al. [6].

Matrix multiplication represents a good benchmark because it is based on the multiply-accumulate (MAC) pattern that is present on several current applications of digital signal processing (DSP), pattern recognition, machine learning and neural networks. Also it mixes both programmable logic and mathematical resources (DSP) available at the FPGA and is a real opportunity to contribute with processing power and acceleration to the processor system in scenarios of reconfigurable computing.

This matrix multiplication out-of-core accelerator was originally conceived using an AXI-S data streaming interface. This interface allows for chaining several user designed blocks in a processing pipeline. Since this architecture leads to a serial subsystem whose reliability depends on the product of the reliability of each component block, it motivates a deeper study on the reliability of each component and how it compromises the whole subsystem reliability.

3.2 Interface Choice at High Level Synthesis Tool

The Xilinx's HLS tool can generate different interface adapters for the hardware IP blocks generated from C language code. Among the interface styles we find the AXI bus and the AXI-S streaming. The choice of interface to be generated also is done by the use of specific #pragma directives provided by the HLS tool.

The first interface to be evaluated in this work is the AXI-S streaming interface with data transfer assisted by an AXI direct memory access (DMA) IP, also provided by Xilinx, as seen at dos Santos et al. [6] and simplified at Fig. 1. The only difference between the unhardened and hardened data transfer is that in the unhardened there is only one AXI DMA block while in the hardened there are three.

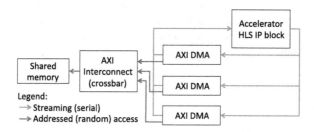

Fig. 1. Data transfer interfaces (control signals omitted for clarity).

3.3 Design Hardening Approaches

The benchmark application adopted in this work consists of an out-of core matrix multiplication accelerator written in C language from which an IP block is generated using Xilinx's high-level synthesis (HLS) tool.

As this IP block is to be implemented in a SRAM-based FPGA it becomes more susceptible to radiation-induced upsets as described previously.

With the use of mitigation techniques one can postpone the correction of those persistent failures until the moment when it is safe or more economic to correct. Carmichael [7] proposes the use of triple modular redundancy as such mitigation technique.

In this work, we compare the unmitigated design with data transfer throughout a single input and a single output channel and a mitigated designs, for instance with the matrix multiplication core mitigated with TMR at the C language level and with redundant data transfer throughout triple input and triple output AXI-S channels.

This approach presents both advantages and challenges. Since the high-level specification is in C language, as advantage we have the possibility of applying to the design several classes of mitigation techniques originally conceived to be used on software. The study and reuse of such applicable techniques is one of the motivations for hardening at high-level synthesis. Meanwhile, a great challenge is how to add mitigations at the C language level that will be preserved by high-level synthesis.

Much of mitigations based on error detection codes, redundancy and algorithm specific properties are prone to be removed from the final implemented circuit through by the high-level synthesis optimizations and further HDL synthesis optimizations.

3.4   TMR at High Level Synthesis Tool

The use of TMR in matrix multiplication is discussed in more details by dos Santos et al. [6] but we can summarize that in its implementation at the C language level, as seen by the HLS tool, the modular redundancy and voting are simply additional function calls as seen on Fig. 2. The difference between the unhardened and the TMR mitigated matrix multiplication core is only the triplication of the multiply and accumulate instruction and the presence of the voter before transferring accumulated value to the result matrix.

```
void mxm_tmr3cgp_core_3ch() {
#pragma HLS INLINE off
    for(int i=0; i<DIM; i++) {
        for(int j=0; j<DIM; j++) {
            accum1 = accum2 = accum3 = 0;
            for(int k=0; k<DIM; k++) {
                accum1 += mat_a1[i][k] * mat_b1[k][j];
                accum2 += mat_a2[i][k] * mat_b2[k][j];
                accum3 += mat_a3[i][k] * mat_b3[k][j];
            }
            mat_c1[i][j]=voter1(accum1, accum2, accum3);
            mat_c2[i][j]=voter2(accum1, accum2, accum3);
            mat_c3[i][j]=voter3(accum1, accum2, accum3);
        }
    }
}
```

Fig. 2. Pseudo code for TMR matrix multiplication.

Special care must be taken in C language coding, including the use of specific #pragma directives provided by the HLS tool, to avoid any undesired code simplification that would eliminate the modular redundancy. Special coding is also required to avoid undesired simplification and merge at the hardware description language (HDL) synthesis level that can be done by proper directives placed as design constraints.

During the fault injection stage it was found that the design reliability is highly sensitive to the design area, thus the simpler the better. So, to this work, the C language code for the matrix multiplication core, seen on, is even simpler than that presented by dos Santos et al. [6].

3.5   IP Block Decomposition for Fault Injection

At the current stage of this work the accelerator IP block depicted at Fig. 1 is where the mitigation technique is being applied and is also the region of interest for fault injection. This block is exactly the IP block as generated by the HLS tool, which is further detailed at Fig. 3.

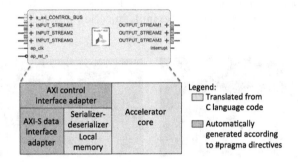

Fig. 3. Simplified internal view of the generated HLS IP block.

To evaluate separately the reliability of the matrix multiplication accelerator core, which is mitigated by TMR, and the other parts of the IP block the HLS was directed to keep the function body hierarchy and generate separate HDL specifications for each C language function of interest. It was achieved by the use of the `#pragma HLS INLINE off` directive as seen on Fig. 2.

Since each function of interest is a distinct HDL entity, when the IP block is instantiated at the design those HDL entities can be placed arbitrarily at the SRAM-based FPGA floorplan using HDL synthesis constraints.

3.6   Floorplanning and Experimental Procedure

The unhardened and the TMR mitigated IP blocks generated with the HLS tool were implemented in a Xilinx 7 Series Artix-7 SRAM-based FPGA. This device is fabricated in technology of 28 nm and reliability metrics, such as the static cross section per bit for neutron upsets, are provided by its manufacturer [3].

Three physical blocks were defined on the device floorplan for placement of the design components. The first one is the region of interest for fault injection, shown at the left side of the floorplans at Fig. 4, the second one, shown at the right side of the floorplans at Fig. 4, will contain other parts of the IP block that are kept safe away from fault injection and the third and last physical block, not shown at Fig. 4, contains all the other components of the design not related to the experiment.

While moving the modules on the device physical floorplan shall lead to a different set of critical bits, it has no significant impact on the shape or scale of the reliability curve. On the other hand, using the same physical block for fault injection has the advantage of promoting that all modules are analyzed under exactly the same fault intensity.

For fault injection, first only the matrix multiplication accelerator core, as indicated at Fig. 3 and described at Fig. 2, is placed inside the fault injection physical block (Fig. 4a) while other components are kept safe and a fault injection campaign is executed. Then all the other components of the IP block, such as AXI interface adapters and local memory, are placed at the fault injection while the matrix multiplication accelerator core is kept safe (Fig. 4b). Finally all the IP block components are placed at the fault injection physical block (Fig. 4c).

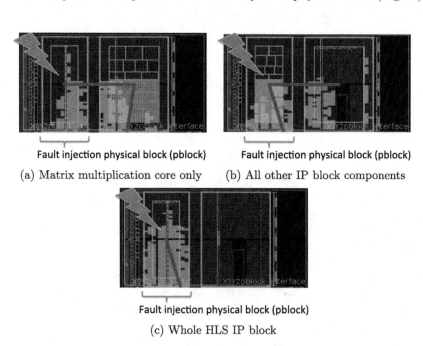

(a) Matrix multiplication core only   (b) All other IP block components

(c) Whole HLS IP block

Fig. 4. Fault injection targets

Fault injection was executed with the help of the fault injection engine presented by Tonfat et al. [5] accumulating faults until a functional failure was observed. Each fault injected consisted of a single bit flip at the configuration memory of the SRAM-based FPGA. The fault injection control station randomized the locus of the fault uniformly over the configuration memory address space of the fault injection physical block. The matrix multiplication was executed after each fault injected. Before each multiplication the input matrices were filled with random values using a diversity value also randomized by the fault injection control station.

A functional failure was defined as the case when any value of the computed result matrix was different from the expected gold result. The matrix contents are integer values and no distance metric or approximation tolerance was adopted. Once a functional failure was detected, the configuration memory of the SRAM-based FPGA was corrected by reprogramming the configuration memory and a new cycle was started. Each fault injection campaign consisted of at least 2,000 reconfiguration cycles.

Finally, no other mitigation strategy was active during fault injection or, more specifically, no configuration memory scrubbing was active. This approach is important to distinguish the influence of the redundancy introduced inside the IP block under analysis and also because it may be the results of this analysis that will determine which type of memory scrubbing shall be applied and how that scrubbing will be scheduled to fulfill requirements such as power consumption and mission time.

4   Experimental Results

4.1   Extraction of Reliability Metrics

For generality and results comparison the reliability observations from fault injection was fitted to a Weibull distribution and the mean time between failure (MTBF) was taken as the Weibull mean life, using one processing cycle as time unit, as summarized at Table 1.

This is done under the assumption that the time to repair is insignificant for the design under evaluation, what means no reposition time, and so we can approximate the mean time to failure (MTTF) as equal to the MTBF and, accordingly, the failure intensity can the considered equal to the failure rate. Also, the number of accumulated faults is significantly lower than the number of bits at the configuration memory and the likelihood of the same bit be flipped more then once can be considered as very low.

Additional fault injection campaigns over the voters alone indicated that the susceptibility of the voter is negligible in this context. In fact, a voter is a simple combinational logic and occupies only 16 look-up tables at the FPGA, or 4 configurable logic block (CLB) slices, while the whole hardened IP block under evaluation occupies over 8000 look-up tables and over 2000 slices.

4.2   Comparative Analysis of Fault Injection Results

The cumulative failure distribution $F(t)$ was obtained from fault injection for each experimental setup, taking one processing cycle as the time unit, which also corresponds to a persistent fault injected on configuration memory, as described

Table 1. Reliability metrics extracted from fault injection (time unit is processing cycle)

Experimental setup	MTBF	Weibull fitting		
		β	α	Error (SSE)
Unhardened core	643.4	0.9998	643.4	5.3%
Unhardened interface	122.7	1.0044	122.9	1.5%
Whole unhardened IP block	103.5	0.9927	103.1	0.6%
TMR mitigated core	484.0	1.3367	526.8	2.0%
Triplicated interface	116.7	1.3291	126.9	1.4%
Whole TMR mitigated IP block	95.1	1.3530	103.8	1.7%

earlier. The reliability computed as the complement of the cumulative failure distribution $(R(t) = 1 - F(t))$ is presented in Fig. 5. The thinner continuous lines at the plot from Fig. 5 were obtained from fault injection over the matrix multiplication core only, as presented in Fig. 4a. The dashed lines at the plot were obtained from fault injection over the other IP block components as presented in Fig. 4b. Finally, the thicker lines were obtained from fault injection over the whole IP block, as seen in Fig. 4c.

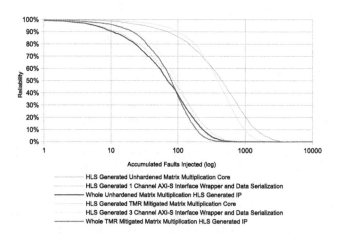

Fig. 5. Reliability obtained from fault injection.

A few points worth noting in these results:

- The behavior of the reliability for the whole IP block is consistent with the reliability obtained for the separate components since, as an eminently serial composition, the reliability of this subsystem is given by the product of the reliability of its components;
- The mitigation effort on the matrix multiplication core has limited impact as the weak link in this subsystem is outside the matrix multiplication core;

– Finally, even if its impact will be limited by the reliability of other components, the reliability obtained by TMR at the core is lower then the expected for an ideal TMR that can be estimated from the unhardened design reliability.

This last point deserves further consideration. Given the reliability $R_M(t)$ of the simplex module, the reliability of triple modular redundancy (TMR) system is well known and is described as

$$R_{TMR}(t) = 3[R_M(t)]^2 - 2[R_M(t)]^3. \tag{1}$$

As seen in Table 1, the scale parameter β obtained on Weibull fitting of failures observations can can be rounded to 1 for the unhardened matrix multiplication IP core, what is consistent with the expectation that it be modeled by an exponential distribution. On the same time, also as expected, the scale parameter $\beta > 1$ for TMR system.

However, when we consider only the matrix multiplication core, that is where TMR as applied, and we compare $R_M(t)$ and $R_{TMR}(t)$ observations from fault injection (Fig. 5) with Eq. 1 for the TMR core, we see that there is an offset at the expected TMR reliability, depicted at Fig. 6.

Considering it as an additive failure rate also modeled by an exponential distribution, this offset was estimated, for this experiment, as equivalent to a component with MTBF around 2600 accumulated faults.

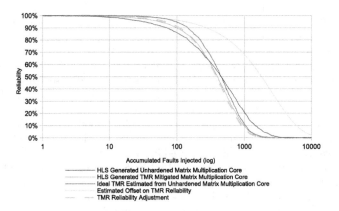

Fig. 6. Observed and ideal TMR reliability.

The offset at the $R_{TMR}(t)$ suggests that some control sequences at C language source code, such as the `for` loops seen on Fig. 2 that are not protected by the voters, still have relevant impact over the IP block reliability. Also, despite the efforts in marking the C language source code with `#pragma HLS` directives and further use of constraints at the HDL synthesis tool, the overall synthesis flow may not be completely hardening preserving.

5   Final Notes

This paper presented the evaluation of an IP block designed to interconnect through the AXI interface. Reliability results evidences how the choice of data communication interface can impact and limit the profit given by mitigation techniques. These results were obtained from fault injection on configuration memory of a Xilinx 7 Series FPGA.

While other evaluation techniques, such as accelerated irradiation, also allow estimation of reliability for the whole system, this fault injection approach allow for a fine grained estimation of reliability for each module implemented at the SRAM-based FPGA while still allowing comparison and crosschecking with irradiation results at the system level.

Further studies under development include the generation of the same IP block by the HLS tool using other interfaces available at the same platform, either allowing the processor to access directly the local data inside the IP block or allowing the IP block to access directly the processor memory and, thus, avoiding both data streaming and data storage at the programmable logic.

References

1. Tambara, L.A., Tonfat, J., Santos, A., Kastensmidt, F.L., Medina, N.H., Added, N., Aguiar, V.A.P., Aguirre, F., Silveira, M.A.G.: Analyzing reliability and performance trade-offs of HLS-based designs in SRAM-based FPGAs under soft errors. IEEE Trans. Nucl. Sci. **64**(2), 874–881 (2017)
2. Le, R.: Soft error mitigation using prioritized essential bits, April 2012. https://www.xilinx.com/support/documentation/application_notes/xapp538-soft-error-mitigation-essential-bits.pdf. Application Note XAPP538
3. Xilinx Inc.: Device reliability report: first half 2017, November 2017. https://www.xilinx.com/support/documentation/user_guides/ug116.pdf. User Guide UG116
4. Velazco, R., Foucard, G., Peronnard, P.: Combining results of accelerated radiation tests and fault injections to predict the error rate of an application implemented in SRAM-based FPGAs. IEEE Trans. Nucl. Sci. **57**(6), 3500–3505 (2010)
5. Tonfat, J., Tambara, L., Santos, A., Kastensmidt, F.: Method to analyze the susceptibility of HLS designs in SRAM-based FPGAs under soft errors. In: Bonato, V., Bouganis, C., Gorgon, M. (eds.) ARC 2016. LNCS, vol. 9625, pp. 132–143. Springer, Cham (2016). https://doi.org/10.1007/978-3-319-30481-6_11
6. dos Santos, A.F., Tambara, L.A., Benevenuti, F., Tonfat, J., Kastensmidt, F.L.: Applying TMR in hardware accelerators generated by high-level synthesis design flow for mitigating multiple bit upsets in SRAM-based FPGAs. In: Wong, S., Beck, A.C., Bertels, K., Carro, L. (eds.) ARC 2017. LNCS, vol. 10216, pp. 202–213. Springer, Cham (2017). https://doi.org/10.1007/978-3-319-56258-2_18
7. Carmichael, C.: Triple module redundancy design techniques for Virtex FPGAs (2006). https://www.xilinx.com/support/documentation/application_notes/xapp197.pdf. Application Note XAPP197

High Performance UDP/IP 40Gb Ethernet Stack for FPGAs

Milind Parelkar$^{(\boxtimes)}$ and Darshan Jetly

Qualcomm Technologies Inc., San Diego, CA 92121, USA
{milindp,djetly}@qti.qualcomm.com

Abstract. As Ethernet bandwidths continue to increase, the challenge of meeting these increased throughput requirements remains a non-trivial problem, especially when the underlying IP is implemented on a reconfigurable fabric like an FPGA. In order to meet the higher throughput rates, it becomes necessary to have wider data paths, operating at much higher frequencies - both of which add complexity to a Network Stack design implemented on an FPGA. Wider data paths necessitate routing a larger number of wires across the underlying fabric, while higher operating frequencies make it more difficult to attain timing closure. Apart from the above mentioned challenges, it is important to keep the footprint for such an infrastructural module as small as possible, in order to guarantee that maximum amount of resources are available for the rest of the user logic. This paper puts forth a resource optimized 40Gb Ethernet Network Stack design, with support for UDP/IP, along with support for ARP and ICMP protocols, and a host of other features. Timing closure is targeted at 250 MHz, with Xilinx UltraScale family of devices.

Keywords: 40Gb Ethernet · Network Stack · FPGA
Xilinx UltraScale · UDP/IP · ICMP · ARP

1 Introduction

FPGA based Network stacks for UDP/IP [1,2] have been in existence for quite some time, but most of the implementations are targeted towards Gigabit Ethernet or 10Gb Ethernet. Implementing a network stack for 40Gb Ethernet has additional challenges of having to deal with wider data paths and higher clock frequencies. Implementation of a UDP/IP stack on an FPGA enables point-to-point connectivity as well as high speed communication over a Local Area Network (LAN). Typical applications involve transferring a large amount of data among multiple FPGA/Host end-points, as well as offloading packet encapsulation tasks to hardware. The underlying Ethernet framework, along with off-the-shelf NIC cards and switches, makes it very easy and convenient to come up with a variety of network configurations.

[3] introduces communication over Gigabit Ethernet from a host PC to an FPGA. Another implementation of a Gigabit Ethernet UDP/IP stack is presented in [4]. Most of the concepts presented in [4] hold true for a 40GbE stack.

© Springer International Publishing AG, part of Springer Nature 2018
N. Voros et al. (Eds.): ARC 2018, LNCS 10824, pp. 255–268, 2018.
https://doi.org/10.1007/978-3-319-78890-6_21

The proposed implementation forgoes UDP header checksum computation and validation and relies on the Ethernet Frame Check Sequence (FCS) to catch bit and framing errors. Other implementations of Gigabit Ethernet Stack, one of which, is presented in [5], puts forth a full featured UDP/IP stack, but without support for ICMP Echo Request/Response *(ping)* packets and Address Resolution Protocol (ARP) packets [6,7].

Xilinx, in collaboration with their IP design partner, Cast Inc., has started licensing a 40G UDP/IP Hardware Protocol Stack [8], with comparable functionality to the 40G Network Stack (herein after referred to as the *Netstack*), described in this paper.

This paper presents a resource optimized version of a Xilinx UltraScale [9] FPGA-based 40GbE UDP/IP Netstack, operating at frequencies upwards of 250 MHz.

2   Xilinx 40GbE IP Core

The 40GbE Netstack is designed to interface to the Xilinx 40GbE IP Core [10]. The Xilinx IP core is available in various configurations. The options include a choice of [128 256 512 1024] bit wide data path and a segmented or a non-segmented version of the local bus (LBUS).

The selected configuration was based on implementation feasibility for a networking application on a Xilinx UltraScale XCVU190 FPGA [9]. Wider data paths allow the user to clock the IP core at a lower clock frequency, thereby making it easier to achieve timing closure. The main drawback of a wider data path is an increase in resource utilization with the addition of extra pipeline stages. Typical FIFO primitives for Xilinx UltraScale and 7-Series devices are 72 bits wide and 512 locations deep [11]. A wider data path results in a linear increase in the number of BlockRAM resources required. For example, a 512-bit wide data path requires twice the number of BlockRAMs as a 256-bit wide data path for an implementation with a similar FIFO depth.

Taking into consideration all the above factors, we decided to opt for a narrower data path, running at a comparatively higher clock frequency. The chosen configuration includes a 256-bit wide non-segmented LBUS, running at a *minimum* clock frequency of 216 MHz. The minimum clock speed is mandated by Xilinx and is necessary to maintain a throughput of 40 Gbps, including the overhead for 64*b*/66*b* encoding. Our design goal was to enable timing closure at a clock frequency of 250 MHz.

3   Netstack Architecture

This section explains the overall architecture of the 40GbE Netstack and some design choices along with the reasons for making those. Please refer to Fig. 1 for the top-level block diagram of the Netstack.

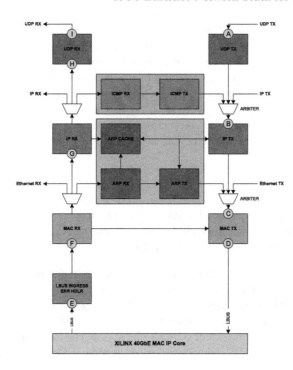

Fig. 1. 40GbE Netstack block diagram

The Netstack architecture consists of the following major blocks -

1. Receive data path
   (a) MAC Receive Processing (MAC Rx)
   (b) IP Receive Processing (IP Rx)
   (c) UDP Receive Processing (UDP Rx)
2. Transmit data path
   (a) MAC Transmit Processing (MAC Tx)
   (b) IP Transmit Processing (IP Tx)
   (c) UDP Transmit Processing (UDP Tx)
3. ICMP Processing
4. ARP Processing and ARP Cache
5. LBUS Ingress Error Handler
6. Register File
7. Statistics Computation Module

The register file and the statistics computation module are not shown in Fig. 1.

The internal dataflow is from bottom to the top on the ingress or the receive data path and from top to the bottom on the egress or the transmit data path. Within the Netstack, the connections between various blocks consist of two separate interfaces, a 256-bit wide data path and the required sideband bus. The

256-bit wide data path follows the same format as the Xilinx LBUS, with the exception of the *error* signal. Each processing block on the receive data path strips off the header and passes the header fields to upstream blocks over the sideband interface. Similarly, processing blocks on the transmit side, receive relevant sideband information necessary for header construction from the upstream blocks along with in-band data.

The data path and sideband connections are specified as SystemVerilog interfaces for ease of connection at the top-level.

4   Design Details

Before going into the design details of the Netstack sub-blocks, we want to present the rules and guidelines that were followed while coming with with the architecture for the stack and coding up the blocks [12].

1. All sub-blocks shall have their inputs/outputs registered. This shall aid in floorplanning the blocks at the sub-block level.
2. The design shall be pipelined to achieve timing closure at 250 MHz.
3. Reset propagation shall be limited to essential control logic and state machines. Data pipelines shall typically have only the first stage reset through a global reset signal. This aids in reducing routing congestion, caused by reset propagation.
4. The design shall have hooks to make it easily expandable beyond the currently supported packet formats.

In addition to the receive and the transmit data paths, the Netstack also allows MAC-level loopback for debugging.

The Netstack also features a fully optimized statistics gathering module, which provides packet counts at various points in the data path. The statistics module can be programmed to continuously update the count registers, or to update only on a user command.

5   Receive Data Path (Ingress)

As mentioned earlier, the Xilinx 40GbE IP core does not allow the user logic to exert back-pressure on the receive side. Design details of the sub-blocks in the receive chain are described in this section.

5.1   LBUS Error Handler

On the Rx LBUS interface, the packet error indicator, *rx_errout*, is valid only with EOP. This implies that the Netstack will not be able to figure out if a received packet has an error, till the entire packet has been received. Passing an erroneous packet up the stack could cause unpredictable behavior and possible lock-ups in the upstream state machines. The LBUS Error Handler is a *store-and-forward* module implemented using a dual-port memory rather than a synchronous FIFO. With a dual-port memory, the read address pointer can skip over an erroneous packet, instead of having to flush the entire bad packet, as would have been necessary with a FIFO implementation. Having to flush a bad packet from the FIFO would result in an added latency before subsequent packets can be processed.

5.2   MAC Receive Processing (MAC Rx)

The MAC Rx module strips off the MAC header from the ingress packets, re-aligns the packet payload to the 256-bit boundary, and forwards it to the IP Rx or the ARP module. The MAC Rx module also re-computes the number of *empty* (MTY) bytes, based on the re-aligned version of the data stream.

The size of the MAC header is either 12 bytes (when VLAN tagging is disabled) or 16 bytes, with VLAN enabled. MAC Rx module figures out if VLAN is enabled or not from the MAC header and re-aligns the outgoing data accordingly.

EtherType field in the MAC header is parsed to determine if the ingress packet is an IP packet, an ARP packet or a packet of some other (unsupported) type. Depending on the packet type, a qualifying enable signal is asserted to the appropriate upstream block. Typical unsupported protocols include STP (Spanning Tree Protocol) packets, which ensure a loop-free network topology. All unsupported packets are sent out on the Ethernet Rx output port, shown in Fig. 1. This allows scope for expansion, without touching the existing design, if more packet types need to be supported in the future.

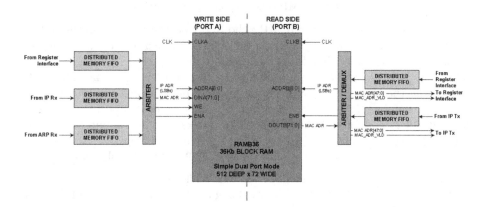

Fig. 2. ARP cache design

5.3   IP Receive Processing (IP Rx)

The IP Rx module processes the IP header and calculates the number of *empty* bytes, similar to MAC Rx. In addition, it takes the Source IP Address in the IP Header and the Source MAC Address received from MAC Rx, and forwards it to the ARP Cache. For every IP packet received, the ARP Cache gets updated with the MAC address/IP address information.

The IP Rx module determines if the packet is a UDP packet or an ICMP (ping) packet, and asserts the corresponding qualifying enable signal to the upstream blocks.

5.4   UDP Receive Processing (UDP Rx)

The UDP Rx module processes the UDP header and forwards the re-aligned payload along with the sideband information to the output of the Netstack. UDP checksum is an optional field in the header, and is not checked by the hardware.

6   ICMP Processing

The ICMP Processing module handles both ICMP Ping Requests and ICMP Ping Responses [1].

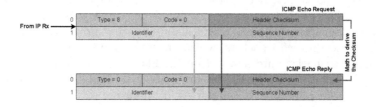

Fig. 3. ICMP ping response generation

As can be seen in Fig. 3, the ICMP Echo Reply packet differs from the ICMP Echo Response packet in only a single bit. The TYPE identifier in the incoming packet has a value of 8, while the ICMP Echo Reply packet has a TYPE identifier value of 0. All other fields remain unchanged, except the TYPE and the CHECKSUM. Computing the header checksum would typically be an expensive operation in hardware, but in this case, the checksum need not be computed from scratch. The CHECKSUM field for the ICMP Echo Reply packet can be computed from the CHECKSUM field in the received packet using a sequence of steps.

The sequence of steps to compute the CHECKSUM field is as follows -

1. Compute the one's complement of the CHECKSUM in the received ICMP Echo Request packet. This can be done by doing a bit-wise inversion of all the bits of the CHECKSUM.
2. Add one's complement of the 16-bit field consisting of TYPE and CODE, to the value generated in Step (1) above. The one's complement of $16'h0800$ is $16'hf7ff$. This number is added to the value generated in Step (1). The addition should generate a 17-bit one's complement number.
3. If a carry is generated after addition in Step (2), add it to the sum.
4. Compute the one's complement of the sum to get the value of the CHECKSUM for the ICMP Echo Reply packet.

7   ARP Cache Design

An ARP cache is a look-up table which maps the IP address of an Ethernet end-point to its MAC address. Upper layer modules typically only deal with IP addresses. It is the responsibility of the Netstack to maintain a look-up table with MAC addresses, in order to populate the Destination MAC address in the MAC Header, of egress Ethernet frames.

The Netstack implements a fully dynamic ARP cache with support for a single subnet with upto 512 end-points. Alternately, it can also be configured to support 2 subnets, each with upto 256 end-points.

A 32-bit IP address is typically structured to have a 24-bit routing prefix and an 8-bit subnet ID field, thereby allowing the user to address up to 256 end-points. The IP address definition is flexible enough to allow a smaller number of bits for the routing prefix, and more number of bits for the subnet ID, if more end-points per subnet are desired. The Netstack supports a single subnet with a 23-bit routing prefix, or 2 subnets with a 24-bit routing prefix.

The choice of subnet configuration is based on the size of a Xilinx Block-RAM primitive. The depth of a BlockRAM is 512 entries, thereby allowing us to store upto 512 MAC addresses in the memory. The index into the memory, or the addressing, is based on the IP address. As shown in Fig. 2, a Simple Dual Port memory based on the RAMB36 primitive is used. The width of the RAMB36 primitive is 72 bits. Only 49 bits are used per ARP cache entry; 48 bits to store the MAC address, and 1 bit to indicate if the entry is valid or not.

8   ARP Processing

The ARP processing module can respond to ARP requests (by generating ARP response packets), as well as originate ARP requests. The module also has the ability to send out Gratuitous ARPs, to let other end-points in the network know its MAC address [6].

ARP request and response packets have no payload, and are fixed-sized packets. The IP address and the MAC address of the sender are used to populate the Target Hardware Address and the Target Port Address, in the ARP response packet.

9   Transmit Data Path (Egress)

Modules in the transmit data path add appropriate headers on top of the payload, and pass the data on to the next stage for processing.

9.1   UDP Transmit Processing (UDP Tx)

The UDP Tx adds UDP headers to the payload, based on the sideband data provided to the module. Once the headers are added, data re-alignment is necessary, and the number of *empty* bytes on the last word need to be re-computed.

9.2   IP Transmit Processing (IP Tx)

Design of the IP Tx module is not trivial. In addition to the header insertion and calculation of *empty* bytes on the last word, the module also needs to compute the header checksum. Unlike, UDP header checksum, the IP header checksum is not an optional field.

The IP Tx module also performs an ARP cache look-up to figure out the MAC address of the packet's intended destination. The cache look-up takes 6 clock cycles; hence the data path pipeline needs to be deep enough to account for the additional delay. If the ARP cache look-up reveals an invalid entry for the IP address look-up, the packet is dropped, and an ARP request is *broadcast* to the network. Till an ARP response is received, and the ARP Cache is populated, all subsequent packets intended for the same IP address will be dropped.

One more thing to note in Fig. 1, is that a round-robin arbiter is required at the input of the IP Tx module in order to arbitrate between packets generated by UDP Tx and the ARP module, as well as generic IP packets coming in over the IP Rx interface.

9.3   MAC Transmit Processing (MAC Tx)

The MAC Tx module inserts MAC headers and re-aligns the payload to form MAC packets to be sent out to the Xilinx 40GbE IP Core. As per the Ethernet protocol specification, once the transmission of an Ethernet packet has started, there cannot be dead cycles on the bus till the transmission of the packet has been completed. In order to satisfy this requirement, an additional store-and-forward FIFO is required at the output of the MAC Tx module.

10   Implementation Results

The Netstack module was taken through synthesis and PAR using Xilinx Vivado tools (v2017.1), targeting Xilinx UltraScale XCVU190 part. Timing closure was attained on the Netstack at 250 MHz, on the main data path. The register file is clocked using a slower, 100 MHz clock.

10.1   Resource Utilization

Post-PAR resource utilization of the Netstack is presented in Table 1. As can be seen from the numbers, the block uses about 2% of CLBs and 1% of BlockRAM Tiles on Xilinx XCVU190 device.

Table 1. Resource utilization - Netstack on Xilinx XCVU190

Sub-module	LUTs	FFs	CLBs	BRAM tiles
MAC Rx	774	1885	466	0
IP Rx	396	1945	525	0
UDP Rx	51	51	29	0
MAC Tx	993	2799	630	10
IP Tx	730	2691	640	6
UDP Tx	98	1487	279	6
ICMP	92	1683	432	6
ARP	446	1371	374	6
ARP cache	608	1708	386	2
LBUS ErrHdlr	282	1215	247	4
Statistics	1522	3383	814	0
Register file	335	869	357	0
Total	**6327**	**21087**	**5179**	**40**
% of XCVU190	**0.58%**	**0.98%**	**2.2%**	**1.06%**

10.2 Performance Results - Throughput

The Netstack was designed to be able to provide an effective throughput as close to 40 Gbps, without the use of Jumbo Frames. Standard Ethernet frame sizes range from 64 bytes to 1500 bytes.

A UDP packet generator was designed in hardware, to allow transmission of various sized UDP packets. UDP payload length was varied between 64 bytes and 1450 bytes. For the chosen payload length, packets were transmitted out from the FPGA for a period of 5 s. Statistics were collected and translated into effective throughput values for specific payload sizes.

As can be seen from the plot in Fig. 4, the Netstack transmission approaches the maximum throughput of 40 Gbps as UDP payload size approaches the maximum size of 1450 bytes (1500 byte Ethernet Frame, including headers).

Performance results for packet reception also track the plot in Fig. 4.

10.3 Performance Results - Latency

Latency through the Netstack transmit and receive path was computed using a QSFP+ loopback connector inserted into the QSFP+ cage. The loopback connector loops the transmit data back to the receive path (between points D and E in Fig. 1). Latency through individual sub-modules was computed for selected packet sizes.

Latency numbers for the transmit data path latency are presented in Table 2. The latency through UDP Tx and IP Tx module are independent of the payload size. MAC Tx module implements a store-and-forward FIFO, thereby causing an increase in the latency as the payload size increases.

Table 2. Performance results - transmit data path latency

UDP payload size (Bytes)	Latency (clock cycles)					Total latency (ms) @250 MHz
	UDP Tx	IP Tx	MAC Tx	IP core	Total	
64	9	16	18	59	102	0.41
128	9	16	28	58	111	0.44
256	9	16	60	58	143	0.57
512	9	16	124	58	207	0.83
768	9	16	188	58	271	1.08
1024	9	16	252	58	335	1.34
1280	9	16	316	58	399	1.60
1450	9	16	361	58	444	1.78

Table 3. Performance results - receive data path latency

UDP payload size (Bytes)	Latency (clock cycles)						Total latency (ms) @250 MHz
	IP core	ErrHdlr	MAC Rx	IP Rx	UDP Rx	Total	
64	58	15	4	5	5	87	0.35
128	58	19	4	5	5	91	0.36
256	58	24	4	5	5	96	0.38
512	58	36	4	5	5	108	0.43
768	58	50	4	5	5	122	0.49
1024	58	63	4	5	5	135	0.54
1280	58	75	4	5	5	147	0.59
1450	58	84	4	5	5	156	0.62

Latency numbers for the receive data path are presented in Table 3. The latency through all blocks, except the Error Handler, is constant and independent of the packet size. The latency through the Error Handler module increases with increasing payload size, since the module has a store-and-forward mechanism, to prevent erroneous packets from propagating up the Netstack.

10.4   Performance Results - Ping Response Latency

DPDK drivers, specifically designed for fast packet processing, were used to flood the network with ping packets sent from a Linux host to the FPGA end-point. The largest sized ping packets, with 1500 bytes of data were used for the test. A million pings were sent out by the Linux host and there was no packet loss. The minimum round trip time (RTT) measured was 0.006 ms and the maximum RTT was 0.026 ms, with an average time of around 0.01 ms.

In comparison, 1500 byte pings sent out from one Linux host to another had a minimum RTT of 0.009 ms and a maximum of 0.034 ms, with an average of 0.025 ms.

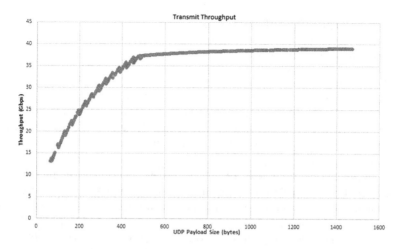

Fig. 4. Performance results - transmit throughput vs UDP payload size

11 Comparisons with Existing Work

The 40G UDP/IP Hardware Protocol Stack, licensed by Xilinx and Cast Inc., [8] seems to be the most feature compatible design, with the Netstack. Although design details are hard to come by in the openly available documentation, it is quite clear this IP core is not specifically designed to target Xilinx FPGA primitives. From the sparsely detailed documentation, an implementation targeting a Xilinx Kintex UltraScale device, XCKU115-2, consumes 1799 CLB Slices, 235 RAMB36 and 1 RAMB18 primitives. The Netstack stacks up comparably against this licensed IP, although, at first glance, it seems to consume a lot more CLBs. From Table 1, the utilization numbers for the Netstack indicate 6327 LUTs, 5179 CLBs and 40 BRAM tiles. In the case of the Netstack, no specific effort has been made to pack the design into as few CLBs as possible. Therefore, the tool has spread out the design as it deemed fit. A comparable number of CLBs (or CLB Slices) can be derived from the fact that each CLB has eight LUTs. Therefore the design can fit into $5179/8 = 790$ CLBs. Accounting for 20% overhead, the design can effectively be made to fit in, $1.2 * (5179/8) = 950$ CLBs, if smallest CLB footprint was the design goal.

Please note that in a Xilinx UltraScale device, a CLB consists of a single slice [13]. Hence, the terms CLB and CLB Slice can be used interchangeably.

Without access to more implementation details, it is difficult to do a more thorough comparison between the two designs. Form the available data, it seems that the designs are comparable in terms of CLB utilization, but the Netstack is a lot more optimal in terms of BlockRAM usage. When synthesized stand-alone, the Netstack $Fmax$ is around the specified $Fmax$ of 313 MHz, as mentioned in [8].

12   Design Optimizations

12.1   Sub-module Optimization

The Register File and the Statistics module, account for about 30% of the total LUTs in the design.

The Register File is just one of the ways of controlling run-time parameters on the Netstack. When integrated into a bigger design, the Register File can easily be pulled into the same scheme that is used to control the rest of the modules in the FPGA.

MAC loopback is a debug feature that aids in application development on the software side. The loopback feature swaps the source and the destination MAC addresses and turns the packets around. This facilitates early software development and provides an additional debug functionality. The MAC loopback block requires a FIFO and some pipelining in order to help timing closure. Removing the MAC loopback functionality will help reduce the CLB as well as the BRAM count.

12.2   ARP Cache

The Netstack ARP Cache is designed to handle ARP entries for up to 2 subnets. The ARP Cache has an entry for all possible IP addresses in the supported subnets. The cache is completely dynamic in the sense that the entries update in real-time, with an option for aging out the entries, if necessary.

A possible optimization would be to have only static entries in the cache, if the potential application of the Netstack can handle that. This would reduce the BlockRAM usage as well as the related logic that interfaces to the memories.

12.3   Choice of Xilinx FIFOs

All FIFOs used in the design are generated using the Vivado IP Generator [14]. The FIFOs utilize the "First Word Fall-Through" (FWFT) feature, which esentially adds an extra pipeline register at the output of the underlying BlockRAM.

Vivado provides the user a choice of 3 different base FIFO types -

1. Distributed RAM FIFO
2. BlockRAM based FIFO
3. Built-in FIFO

Distributed RAM FIFOs are typically optimal for small sizes and hence were ruled out for use in this design. Interestingly enough, BlockRAM based FIFOs seemed to provide better PAR results than Built-in FIFO based designs. This was even more apparent, when the register at the output of the FIFO was moved from the default setting of using the *Embedded Register* in the BlockRAM tile to a *Fabric Register*.

Using the Fabric Register gives the PAR tool more leeway in balancing the pipeline from the output of the FIFO to the next downstream sequential element.

12.4   Place and Route Directives

Xilinx synthesis and PAR tools have come a long way and generally do a good job with the default settings, in most cases. In the case of this particular design, it was necessary to turn off BlockRAM Power Optimization during the placement phase in order to mitigate timing closure issues. Vivado version 2017.1 was used for synthesis and PAR.

13   Conclusion and Future Work

This paper demonstrates that a fairly complex 40Gb Ethernet Network Stack, with a rich feature-set can be implemented in an FPGA, while utilizing relatively small amount of fabric resources. Timing closure at 250 MHz is fairly straightforward, as long as good design principles are followed and the module is pipelined enough to mitigate any synthesis and PAR issues. When implemented stand-alone, timing closure can be attained at frequencies higher than 300 MHz.

Further optimization to reduce resource usage are possible, with a reduced feature set, if necessary. A fully dynamic ARP Cache can be replaced with a reduced number of static IP/MAC address entries, if the network topology is pre-defined to have only a few end-points. Register File as well as the Statistics module also be optimized.

For lower latency applications, this Netstack implementation allows users to transmit pre-constructed IP packets or MAC packets, which reduced latency through the UDP Tx module and/or the ARP Cache look-up latency in IP Tx.

Future addendum to the Netstack could include a UDP packet router to distribute and aggregate UDP packets to/from multiple UDP end-points. Floorplanning would be a major consideration for such a Router since the common port would interface to the Netstack, but the individual UDP ports would interface to various blocks spread throughout the FPGA.

References

1. Postel, J.: RFC 791: Internet protocol (1981)
2. Postel, J.: RFC 768: User datagram protocol (1980)
3. Alachiotis, N., Berger, S.A., Stamatakis, A.: A versatile UDP/IP based PC FPGA communication platform. In: 2012 International Conference on Reconfigurable Computing and FPGAs, Cancun, pp. 1–6 (2012)
4. Mahmoodi, M.R., Sayedi, S.M., Mahmoodi, B.: Reconfigurable hardware implementation of gigabit UDP/IP stack based on Spartan-6 FPGA. In: 2014 6th International Conference on Information Technology and Electrical Engineering (ICITEE), Yogyakarta, pp. 1–6 (2014)
5. Herrmann, F.L., Perin, G., de Freitas, J.P.J., Bertagnolli, R., dos Santos Martins, J.B.: A Gigabit UDP/IP network stack in FPGA. In: 2009 16th IEEE International Conference on Electronics, Circuits and Systems - (ICECS 2009), Yasmine Hammamet, pp. 836–839 (2009)
6. Plummer, D.: RFC 826: Ethernet Address Resolution Protocol (1982)

7. Postel, J.: RFC 792: Internet Control Message Protocol (1981)
8. 40G UDP/IP Hardware Protocol Stack, Cast Inc
9. DS890: Xilinx UltraScale Architecture and Product Data Sheet
10. PG183: Xilinx High Speed Ethernet IP Core v4.2. LogiCORE IP Product Guide
11. UG974: Xilinx UltraScale Architecture Libraries Guide
12. UG949: Xilinx UltraFast Design Methodology Guide for Vivado Design Suite (2016)
13. UG574: Xilinx UltraScale Architecture CLB User Guide (2014)
14. PG057: Xilinx FIFO Generator v13.1. LogiCORE IP Product Guide (2017)

Tackling Wireless Sensor Network Heterogeneity Through Novel Reconfigurable Gateway Approach

Christos P. Antonopoulos[1(✉)], Konstantinos Antonopoulos[1],
Christos Panagiotou[2], and Nikolaos S. Voros[1]

[1] Computer and Informatics Engineering Department, TEI of Western Greece,
Antirio, Greece
cantonopoulos@teiwest.gr
[2] AVN Technologies, Limassol, Cyprus

Abstract. Without Gateways comprise critical cornerstones for a wide range of Cyber Physical Systems (CPS) and IoT application scenarios. In this context, the main objective of this paper is to present a novel Gateway able to effectively address all heterogeneity aspects. Additionally, a critical objective of the proposed Gateway is offering advanced features facilitating the dynamic, run time service management. Aiming to offer a comprehensive solution all important aspects are presented in detail while a real-world evaluation is provided. The latter, is achieved by integrating the implemented solution with a real CPS infrastructure enabling (i) hands on proof of concept concerning heterogeneity support and offered features and (ii) realistic performance evaluation.

Keywords: Wireless sensor networks · Gateway design
Cyber Physical Systems · Heterogeneous technologies
Message passing communication · Practical deployment implementation
Performance validation and verification

1 Introduction

The main objective of a Cyber Physical System (CPS) is to tightly integrate cyber and physical objects, which entails addressing a wide range of challenging heterogeneities [1]. Towards this objective the Gateway entity is of paramount importance since it comprises both the physical and architectural point where data from the physical domain are aggregated and effectively transported to the cyber domain and vise versa. The importance of an efficient Gateway is even more emphasized by the multiple scales a CPS system can be envisioned, as well as application scenarios ranging from smart houses to autonomous cars, and from advanced smart medical devices to emergency event detection and autonomous reaction [2]. Wireless Sensor Networks (WSNs) and embedded systems comprise the two main cornerstones of an effective and efficient Gateway design with respect to communication, processing and control, considering heterogeneous and diverse systems. In that context, messaging [3] represents a highly considered technology, enabling high-speed, asynchronous, highly reliable machine-to-machine or even program-to-program communication. Such communication is possible

© Springer International Publishing AG, part of Springer Nature 2018
N. Voros et al. (Eds.): ARC 2018, LNCS 10824, pp. 269–280, 2018.
https://doi.org/10.1007/978-3-319-78890-6_22

by exchanging data packets, called messages, to each other. Channels, also known as queues, are logical pathways that connect the programs and convey such messages. A channel behaves like a collection or array of messages shared across multiple Gateways and effectively any other component of the end-to-end CPS infrastructure [3].

Turning our attention to the physical domain respective sources of heterogeneity can be identified. On one hand, the diverse modalities and data types, imposed by versatile and flexible solutions, must be effectively handled by the Gateway architecture. This is important since at that point all different modalities and data are effectively homogenized and managed in a harmonized way. On the other hand, nowadays there is a wide range of heterogenous sensor communication technologies, each characterized by specific and distinct advantages and features. Consequently, an efficient CPS Gateway is required to handle data in a homogenous way aiming to offer common degree of robustness, QoS, synchronization and power efficiency [4].

Furthermore, during the last years due to advancements in areas such as embedded system and hardware design, Gateways are increasingly considered, not only for data aggregation and forwarding, but also to store, fuse and process data in real time. This demand opens us a whole new area of heterogeneities regarding processing capabilities, memory capabilities and data base integration requirements [5].

The heterogeneity reflects the necessity for reconfigurable solutions that could support high level of adaptability to domains with increased diversity like IoT and CPS. The gateway particularly, which is the link between the physical world and the cloud needs to bridge a plethora of communication technologies (with diverse requirements and constraints) with the fragmented world of IoT standards and protocols. A reconfigurable architecture for gateways in the IoT ecosystem will be a game changer towards the design and development of cost effective and efficient CPS and services under the IoT application domain.

Driven by the identified necessity for practical and reliable solutions, this paper presents a complete Gateway architecture yielding critical advantages, features and services able to effectively support a wide range of realistic application scenarios. Based on message passing communication technology and utilizing Commercial-Of-The-Shelf (COTS) technologies, the proposed Gateway is implemented offering an abstraction layer that effectively hides all technology heterogeneity and/or peculiarity. All design and implementation aspects of the involved entities are presented in detail in the following sections. Moreover, the overall performance of the proposed solution is demonstrated at system level by integrating the proposed Gateway to a real CPS infrastructure and focusing on two main aspects: (a) performance robustness and efficiency (in terms of being able to meet demanding application requirements), and (b) resource consumption, which is critical for incorporating the proposed architecture in real embedded systems. The high degree of reconfigurability, extendibility and scalability comprise the main directives that drive the design and implementation phases of the gateway.

The rest of the paper is structured as follows: The Sect. 2 discusses the main challenges that drove the design and implementation of the proposed Gateway. Section 3 offers detailed insight analysis of critical design aspects and decisions, while Sect. 4 presents the implementation of the proposed solution. Section 5 analyzes and presents performance evaluation and validation results pertaining to communication capabilities and resource expenditure. Finally, Sect. 6 concludes and summarizes the most important points of this paper.

2 Key Challenges Addressed

Driven by the requirements posed by, on one hand, nowadays and future CPS applications and, on the other hand, by the end users, the proposed Gateway focuses to address a wide range of emerging challenges.

Regarding the low power communication perspective of CPSs, although a plethora of different communication technologies (mainly originating from WSN research domain) are available, they offer diverse characteristics exhibiting high degree of incompatibility. In that respect, the proposed Gateway design supports all prominent short range wireless communication technologies such as IEEE 802.15.4 [6], ZigBee [7], Bluetooth [8], BLE [9], while currently, the support of Z-Wave [10] protocol is ongoing. Also, a critical goal of the design is to facilitate the continuous development and integration of new solutions.

To address the increased functional complexity, the presented Gateway design highlights the ability to support data acquisition by different modalities and using different communication technologies to be synchronized, homogenized and processed. In this way, sophisticated load balancing, data merging, QoS, prioritizing and many more mechanisms can be supported. This approach also facilitates real-time data processing and event detection which is of paramount importance in demanding applications such medical and industrial deployments.

A CPS platform is usually comprised by multiple, highly scattered nodes able to interact with the real world. Thus, controlling, optimizing, adjusting and enhancing a continuously expanding CPS platform by physically accessing each node or/and component is unpractical, cumbersome and in specific deployment practically impossible. Consequently, it is critical for an efficient Gateway to facilitate real-time remote control of all components as well as on-the-fly functional updates and service optimization. In the context of the proposed solution, remote monitoring, management and control is possible through message passing communication technologies via MQTT and MQTT-SN protocols [11]. However, the most important characteristic of the presented Gateway is the capability provided to the end user/service-provider to remotely reconfigure and seamlessly define a new service, deploy it and activate it throughout the network.

3 The Proposed Gateway Design

Aiming to offer a modular architecture Fig. 1 depicts the proposed design. The high-level design, of the Gateway architecture consists from three main components, namely the Kernel, Applications and the Messaging Bus. At the lower layer of the architecture lies the Kernel of the Gateway, where the core modules are deployed. On the contrary, at the top of the architecture, user-defined applications are commissioned, typically requiring a considerably higher degree of flexibility. Finally, in order to assure

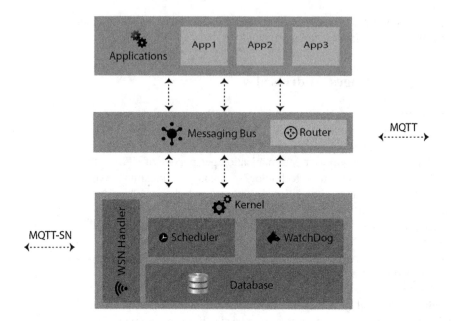

Fig. 1. The proposed Gateway design

efficient interconnection between the two aforementioned components, a dedicated intermediate layer, the Messaging Bus, is introduced providing intra Gateway modules communication capabilities and functionalities.

Starting with the internal communication requirements of a modular and reconfigurable design, the primary objective is to use a single communication protocol for all the communications among gateway entities, regardless if they physically reside in the Gateway or not. In that respect, the Message Queue Telemetry Transport (MQTT) [13] protocol utilized for all the communication between the gateway modules comprises a perfectly suiting solution.

The proposed design integrates wireless communication adapters in order to offer compatibility with a wide range of prominent wireless sensor networks, like Bluetooth, BLE, ZigBee, WI-FI, Z-wave etc. To effectively tackle the heterogeneity caused by the diverse wireless communication technologies, the MQTT-SN [14] protocol has been exploited. The main goal of the proposed WSN handler components is to handle all the heterogeneity and complexity, of the abovementioned communication technologies. An abstract view of the WSN Handler is depicted in Fig. 2.

As shown at the bottom level of the module, specific wireless communication adapters are developed, which forward all the WSN generated traffic to the Translator module. Then, the Translator receives the MQTT-SN messages and transforms them to valid MQTT messages. Finally, converted MQTT messages are forwarded to the connected MQTT Server, which in our proposed design is integrated into the Messaging Bus.

Device and Topics Registry comprise critical modules assuring the adequate operation of the WSN Handler. Specifically, topics registry contains the MQTT topics

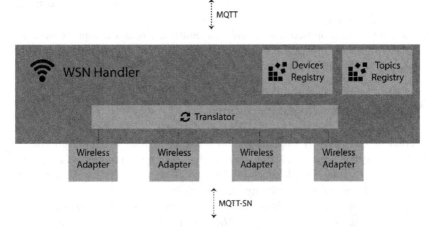

Fig. 2. WSN handler

and the corresponding MQTT-SN topics Identifiers. Devices Registry tackles the challenging heterogeneity caused by the incompatible WSN communication technologies regarding devices addresses.

The Messaging Bus, is the main aggregation point for all incoming and outgoing messages related to the Gateway. Internally, it offers local MQTT connections among the Gateway modules and applications. Externally, it maintains MQTT connections to IoT Back-end infrastructure, for the Gateway to communicate with the outside IP networks. Due to the existence of two different messaging systems, the internal Gateway messaging system (Modules, applications communication), and the external messaging system (Back-end IoT infrastructure communication), the need for a module was raised to bridge these two systems. To tackle this need, the Router plugin is added to the proposed design, inside the Messaging Bus. The plugin performs topic-based routing by intercepting messages from topics, analyzing them and finally forwarding them, to the appropriate, external or internal MQTT topics, without modifying the message content.

The Database module, as anticipated is responsible to provide storage capabilities to the Gateway entity. Every module or application that is connected or executed on the Gateway, can create its own database tables, and save, fetch or delete data using a generic and simplified API.

The Scheduler module, as the name implies is used for internal gateway tasks, concerning both modules and applications. Mainly there are two main type of tasks:

1. Repeatable tasks, repeatable fired tasks.
2. Future tasks, one time fired future tasks.

The watchdog module's main objective is to monitor all the hardware and software that the Gateway is running. It sends periodically status messages to an IoT Back-end infrastructure, which assist developers to effectively maintain the overall status of the deployed Gateways.

Finally, the Applications module is responsible for the deployment and management of user-defined applications.

Concluding, the proposed design offers a multifaceted and comprehensive architecture able to meet any demand or requirements posed by nowadays and future heterogenous WSN deployments.

4 Novel Gateway Implementation

The kernel of the Gateway implementation has been written in JAVA programming language, using the Spring [15] framework, thus providing component-based architecture and auto-wiring functionality to the core Gateway modules. As a prominent service-oriented framework the Spring framework is used for the development of the core Gateway. In this way, the implementation yields considerably lower complexity, compared to solutions such as the OSGI [16] framework leveraging the development of loosely coupled components that deliver their functionalities through MQTT topics. In the center of the application component nexus, exists a light and monolithic kernel that exposes the core gateway functionality. Consequently, respective implementation choice facilitates the development of a robust and reliable core, that will not change frequently. On top of this core all the functionalities will be exposed using APIs through messaging topics. Thus, allowing the development and dynamic customization of application components specifically tailored to the needs of the application scenario and in favor of modularity and reconfigurability.

The main implementation approach to structure the proposed Gateway is based on messaging patterns. In that respect, the implemented Gateway consists of modules exposing MQTT APIs. In order for the modules to expose such APIs, they must be connected to the Gateway Messaging Bus, as depicted in Fig. 1. The core implementation of the Messaging Bus, is based on ActiveMQ message broker [17]. ActiveMQ is a highly efficient JMS implementation product based on open sources of Apache protocol, with proven maturity and rich features. The default messaging protocol used by ActiveMQ is OpenWire [18]. The developed solution creates a duplex connection, allowing the Gateway to produce and consume messages from the IoT back-end infrastructure. However, such a connection type creates a critical point concerning how to distinguish which messages from the internal messaging system will be forwarded to the external messaging system and vice versa. In that respect, an ActiveMQ plugin has been developed comprising a topic-based interceptor, depicted as the Router in Fig. 1. Its main functionality it to examine MQTT topics names, and performing the bridging in case the corresponding topic bridge has been configured. Additionally, a flexible mechanism is implemented to add/remove bridges to/from the Router plugin. The router waits for messages in MQTT topic router/bridges in order to create or delete a bridge between the two messaging systems. The message payload used for all the MQTT APIs, is JSON [19]. JSON is used because it is a lightweight text-based protocol, with a human-readable format, which is capable to represent complex information, with minimum data.

The database module provides storage capabilities in the Gateway, for both Gateway modules and applications. We choose to utilize the SQLite [20] embedded database since it can be used in a zero-configuration mode and consume very little resources, which make it a valuable choice for an embedded system. Another significant advantage of SQLite is its ability to work in the two following modes, (i) In-memory where the data are stored to memory, and (ii) In-file, where the data are stored to disk files. In the context of the proposed Gateway, SQLite configured on In-memory mode is used. Again, the access of all the Gateway's modules to the database is accomplished through a MQTT API. In order to allow queries to be executed to the database authors define a simple Query Domain Specific Language (QDSL), using a JSON syntax.

The implemented Applications module is responsible to dynamically deploy and manage user-defined applications that run on the Gateway. Moreover, the APIs exposed by each module are used to monitor the health status of the applications and control their deployment cycle. The exposes a MQTT API that listens for incoming messages correlated with deployed applications, enabling to act on the application, such as start/stop an application.

The module is capable to deploy applications developed in any programming language. Due to this heterogeneity support, in applications, we need a unified way to structure applications, which at the same time will be simple, and allow the developers to structure their applications, in any way fitting their needs. In that respect authors choose to package our applications into compressed files like zip files, with the only requirement to contain a file, namely deploy.json, which will contain all the necessary instructing the module to deploy the application, and the executable file.

Facilitating the described functionality, an online repository has been developed and deployed on the IoT back-end infrastructure. This repository, aims to deliver to the gateway, applications that could modify or enhance its functionality.

The Scheduler module is a dynamic scheduling mechanism, exposing functionalities for the modules and applications that are running (or are connected) to the Gateway, enabling them to run repetitive or simple tasks. In order to avoid running sub-processes or multiple thread inside applications or modules, and given the fact that a messaging system can be used for triggering events, a simplified MQTT API is exposed to register future or repetitive tasks, using the following topic, scheduler/tasks.

5 Performance Evaluation

The main goal of this section is to demonstrate and evaluate the performance of the proposed Gateway implementation. Initially, aiming to evaluate time constrained behavior and performance robustness, the round-trip delay of a message sent by the Wireless Sensor Nodes until the respective response is received has been evaluated. Furthermore, in order to argue on the resource conservative design and scalability capabilities, CPU and memory usage are recorded on the Gateway during its full operation. Additionally, considering the efficient addressing of WSN heterogeneity challenge, both Bluetooth and IEEE 802.15.4 devices are utilized in the conducted experiments. The hardware platform hosting the proposed Gateway implementation is a typical Raspberry Pi device featuring 1 GB RAM memory and a 64-bit Quad-core ARMv8 1.2 GHz [21] running the Linux based Raspbian OS. For that purpose, the proposed Gateway is integrated in a real world Ambient Assisted Living House (AAL HOUSE) [12] controlled and monitored by a complete MQTT based infrastructure. AAL HOUSE is practically a smart home environment that is used for installing and evaluating the latest CPS technologies in real world scenarios.

Experimental Setup

Aiming to offer a useful, objective and multifaceted evaluation of the proposed Gateway design, the following network parameters have been taken into consideration:

1. Traffic data rate of 5 transmitted messages per second.
2. A data message size of 16 bytes, which is typical for WSNs in cyber-physical applications.
3. 1 up to 6 concurrently transmitting nodes.

The first and second parameter fulfill a typical use case scenario considered in the context of RADIO H2020 project [2] that requires the generation of 80 bytes per second. The values selected for the specific scenario, as well as the number of concurrently operational nodes, correspond to parameters required for a typical number of persons residing in realistic medium to large home environment. Regarding the measuring of the round-trip delay of a message, the following scenario has been implemented. In the context of real life home environment scenario a maximum round-trip delay requirement of 1 s is assumed.

Initially, a service is initiated in a back-end infrastructure designed and developed to support proposed GW design entitled ATLAS [24], that receives the measurement messages and, without performing any manipulation, sends them back to the Gateway. Sensors, before sending the message to the Gateway, they tag the transmission time. When the Gateway receives the message, it forwards it to the Messaging service, which in turn conveys it to the MQTT based network service. As mentioned before, when our service receives the message it sends it back to Message service, which forwards it again to the Gateway. At this point, the Gateway extracts the payload from the message in order to find the destination sensor mote towards which it will send it. Finally, when the sensor mote receives the message, it calculates the delay between the time of the message arrived and the time of message transmitted, that have been tagged when the message was initially transmitted.

The evaluation undertaken is conducted based on Shimmer platform [22], which offers both Bluetooth and 802.15.4, communication interfaces. Shimmer nodes' software stack is based on the open source TinyOS operating system. The Gateway is a standard x86 PC running Linux operating system.

Experimental Results

In order to expose the effect of heterogeneous communication technologies three different case are considered. On one hand, delay is measured considering solely devices transmitting messages using Bluetooth interfaces. On the other hand, delay performance with respect to solely IEEE 802.15.4 based wireless interfaces is considered. Finally, mixed network scenarios are formed, where half of the sensors send messages through Bluetooth and the rest through IEEE 802.15.4 interfaces.

Figure 3 depicts the time interval for a message to be sent from a sensor to the back infrastructure and get back the respective response. As shown, when only Bluetooth

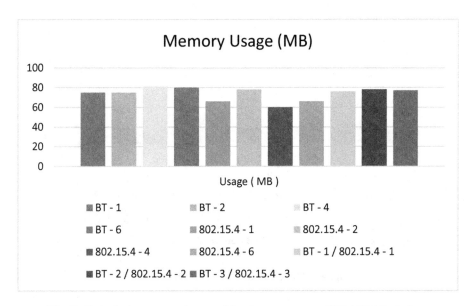

Fig. 3. Round trip messages' mean delay between sensor-GW-ATLAS platform

devices transmit messages, the mean delay ranges from 120 ms up to 150 ms, when 6 devices transmit concurrently.

Considering networks comprised by solely 802.15.4 based nodes, it is depicted that when there is no competition (i.e. single transmitting node), IEEE 802.15.4 mean delay is slightly reduced compared to Bluetooth cases. However, when there are concurrently competing nodes (i.e. 802.15.4-2/4/6), measurements indicate a steadily increasing delay overhead compared to Bluetooth graphs. Indicatively, considering six (6) concurrently transmitting nodes mean delay reaches up to 185 ms, corresponding to a 23% delay increased compared to Bluetooth respect case.

Finally, in the mixed networking scenario the results are approximately in the middle compared to cases based specifically on either IEEE 802.15.4 or Bluetooth. Consequently, the implemented Gateway effectively handled these two heterogenous communication technologies with no noticeable overhead. Additionally, it exhibits considerable stability with respect to heterogeneous technologies and varying number of sensors.

Moving on to resource consuming aspect of the evaluation, Fig. 4, depicts, the CPU usage of the Gateway, when sensors transmit data. As shown, the usage ranges mainly from 2% up 5% for all scenario, with few spikes, which reach up to 14%. Based on log file analysis, the latter originates from Bluetooth devices transmitting data.

Finally, Fig. 5 exhibits the memory usage of the Gateway when sensors transmit data. As shown, the usage ranges from 60 MB on low traffic scenarios, up to 80 MB when high traffic scenarios are imposed. Both memory and CPU utilization measurements appear to be quite low with respect to the demands which can be accommodated by nowadays embedded systems such as Raspberry PI [21] or Intel's Edison [23] based platforms.

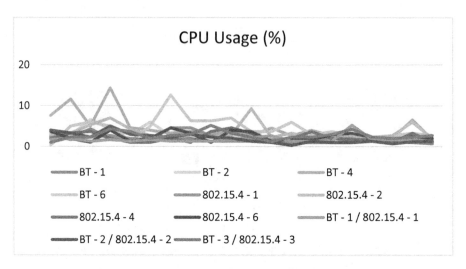

Fig. 4. CPU usage in ATLAS WSN devices

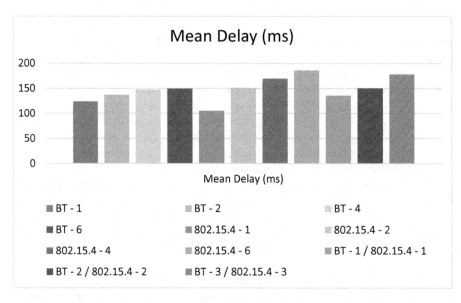

Fig. 5. Memory usage in ATLAS WSN devices

Summarizing, from a communication delay point of view it is shown that the number of concurrent transmitters comprises the most important factor affecting performance. Bluetooth is based on connection-oriented and highly robust behavior, exhibiting the smallest delay deviation with respect to competing nodes. However, in all cases, a time constrained behavior is observed, which is less than 200 ms for end-to-end round trip delay and advocates the use of the proposed platform both in conservative as well as relatively demanding smart home environments. From the processing power point of view, a quite reliable performance was also recorded which can be supported by nowadays single boards computer systems such as Raspberry Pi. Specifically, CPU utilization exceeded 8% only in isolated cases which can be attributed to a number of unpredictable processing situation of the Raspberry Pi processor. At the same time memory occupied ranged between 60 and 80 MB. Both aspects indicate a quite predictable and reliable behavior advocating the use of such solution in real life scenarios. This provides an objective proof-of-concept regarding the practical aspects of proposed GW with respect to heterogeneity support, flexibility and scalability.

6 Conclusions

Over the last few years, Cyber Physical Systems appear as one of the most prominent research areas able to unite the physical and cyber domains in the context of heterogeneous and diverse application scenarios. In this context, the impact of novel gateway architectures is critical since, they are assigned with the key role to provide interconnectivity and maximum application availability. Driven by this requirement, in this paper we present and analyze a novel, comprehensive, and reconfigurable Gateway architecture based on message passing communication paradigm. All aspects comprising a complete, efficient and versatile novel architecture effectively addressing respective requirements that are presented in detail. Additionally, the proposed architecture has been evaluated in the context of a real world smart home as undertake in RADIO project [2]. The reconfigurability of the gateway outshines when scenarios considering different WSN communication technologies and workload patterns are applied. At the same time, the gateway exhibits, in all cases, robust behavior and reliability with respect to time constraints and application requirements. Furthermore, resource requirements have been measured revealing rather conservative demands which can be easily met by most COTS embedded platforms.

As future directions, authors aim to explore ways where hardware acceleration components (e.g. FPGAs or GPUs) can be integrated to enhance processing capabilities in terms of data compression, security, feature extraction etc. by the next GW version. Additionally, specific QoS and data management mechanisms will be added to ensure time constrained behavior and data communication.

Acknowledgment. This study is part of the collaborative project RADIO which is funded by the European Commission under Horizon 2020 Research and Innovation Programme with Grant Agreement Number 643892.

References

1. Hu, F.: Cyber-Physical Systems - Integrated Computing and Engineering Design. CRC Press, Boca Raton (2014)
2. Antonopoulos, Ch., et al.: Robots in assisted living environments as an unobtrusive, efficient, reliable and modular solution for independent ageing: the RADIO perspective. In: Sano, K., Soudris, D., Hübner, M., Diniz, P.C. (eds.) ARC 2015. LNCS, vol. 9040, pp. 519–530. Springer, Cham (2015). https://doi.org/10.1007/978-3-319-16214-0_48
3. Hophe, G., Woolf, B.: Enterprise Integration Patterns: Designing, Building, and Deploying Messaging Solutions. The Addison Wesley Signature Series (2004). ISBN-13: 978-032120 0686, ISBN-10: 0321200683
4. Rajhans, A., et al.: Supporting heterogeneity in cyber-physical systems architectures. IEEE Trans. Autom. Control **59**(12), 3178–3193 (2014)
5. Kang, W., et al.: Design, implementation, and evaluation of a QoS-aware real-time embedded database. IEEE Trans. Comput. **61**(1), 45–59 (2012)
6. IEEE 802.15.4 Specification. http://standards.ieee.org/about/get/802/802.15.html
7. ZigBee Specification, January 2008
8. Bluetooth Specifications (SIG), Version 1.1 (2001)
9. Bluetooth SIG (Hrsg.): Specification of the Bluetooth System: Covered Core Package Version: 4.0, June 2010
10. OpenZwave: From OpenZwave Google code site (n.d.). https://code.google.com/p/ openzwave/. Accessed June 2013
11. Govindan, K., Azad, A.P.: End-to-end service assurance in IoT MQTT-SN. In: 2015 12th Annual IEEE Consumer Communications and Networking Conference (CCNC), Las Vegas, NV, pp. 290–296 (2015)
12. http://aalhouse.esda-lab.cied.teiwest.gr/index.php/en/
13. IBM MQTT Protocol Specification. http://public.dhe.ibm.com/software/dw/webservices/ws-mqtt/mqtt-v3r1.html. Accessed 22 Dec 2015
14. Stanford-Clark, A., Truong, H.L.: MQTT For Sensor Networks (MQTT-SN) Protocol Specification, Version 1.2, November 2013. http://mqtt.org/new/wp-content/uploads/2009/06/MQTT-SN_spec_v1.2.pdf
15. https://projects.spring.io/spring-boot/
16. Lai, C., et al.: OSGi-based services architecture for cyber-physical home control systems. J. Comput. Commun. **34**(2), 184–191 (2011)
17. Yin, J., et al.: Design and implementation of intelligent load-balancing heterogeneous data source middleware based on ActiveMQ and XML. In: 2015 ICIICII, Wuhan, China (2015)
18. http://activemq.apache.org/openwire.html
19. JSON. http://www.json.org/
20. Owens, M.: The Definitive Guide to Sqlite. Springer, New York (2005). https://doi.org/10.1007/978-1-4302-0172-4
21. Raspberry PI. https://www.raspberrypi.org/
22. Shimmer. http://www.shimmer-research.com/
23. Intel Edison. http://www.intel.com/content/www/us/en/do-it-yourself/edison.htm
24. ATLAS Backend Infrastructure. http://atlas.esda-lab.cied.teiwest.gr/

A Low-Power FPGA-Based Architecture for Microphone Arrays in Wireless Sensor Networks

Bruno da Silva$^{(\boxtimes)}$, Laurent Segers , An Braeken , Kris Steenhaut ,
and Abdellah Touhafi

INDI department, Vrije Universiteit Brussel (VUB), Brussels, Belgium
`bruno.da.silva@vub.be`

Abstract. Microphone arrays add an extra dimension to sensory information from Wireless Sensor Networks by determining the direction of the sound instead of only its intensity. Microphone arrays, however, need to be flexible enough to adapt their characteristics to realistic acoustic environments, while being power efficient, as they are battery-powered. Consequently, there is a clear need to design adaptable microphone array nodes enabling quality aware distributed sensing and prioritizing low power consumption. In this paper a novel dynamic, scalable and energy-efficient FPGA-based architecture is presented. The proposed architecture applies the Delay-and-Sum beamforming technique to the single-bit digital audio from the MEMS microphones to obtain the relative sound power in the time domain. As a result, the resource consumption is drastically reduced, making the proposed architecture suitable for low-power Flash-based FPGAs. In fact, the architecture's power consumption estimation can become as low as 649 μW per microphone.

1 Introduction

Microphone arrays composed of Micro-Electro Mechanical systems (MEMS) microphones are becoming popular as they are now also applied as nodes in Wireless Sensor Networks (WSNs). This is possible due to their relatively low cost and high level of integration. For instance, they have been used to automatically emphasize the speech coming from a particular direction [1] or for urban environmental monitoring [2,3]. Many applications benefit from the use of microphone arrays since they not only promise audio enhancement but also allow to determine the sound's Direction-of-Arrival (DoA). However, most of these applications need an accurate sound-source localization, which often can not be done with a standalone array. Existing solutions propose WSNs composed of microphone arrays for sensing the acoustic environment, locally processing the measured information and propagating it through a network to combine multiple captures. Despite the importance of power consumption in battery-based WSN nodes, it is often not considered.

Microphone arrays have been used as distributed acoustic sensing nodes for a broad range of applications. Sound-source detection using WSNs is usually

© Springer International Publishing AG, part of Springer Nature 2018
N. Voros et al. (Eds.): ARC 2018, LNCS 10824, pp. 281–293, 2018.
https://doi.org/10.1007/978-3-319-78890-6_23

related to surveillance, acoustic enhancement urban environmental monitoring or military applications. For instance, the authors in [6] and in [7] propose WSN counter-sniper systems composed of microphone arrays. Whereas the first one uses Wi-Fi as wireless communication, Bluetooth is proposed in the last one. None of the solutions, however, report their power consumption.

The authors in [8] propose a Wi-Fi based WSN composed of microphone arrays for deforestation detection. Their architecture computes the audio from an array composed of 8 microphones in an extremely low-power Flash-based FPGA, which allows to only consume 21.8 mW per node in the network. The same authors propose in [9] a larger microphone array composed of 16 microphones. Due to the additional computational operations, they consider a Xilinx Spartan6 FPGA. The power consumption, however, increases up to 61.71 mW for the 16 microphones' configuration. Our proposed architecture, instead, allows to compute more than 4 times the number of microphones with 6 times less power consumption thanks to a reduced resource requirements.

Other technologies also provide low the power solutions. A very interesting solution is proposed in [10], where the authors present a very low-power microphone array. Their architecture only consumes 1.8 mW per microphone thanks to exploiting the sleep modes of the microcontroller and microphones. The microphones are inactive 20% of the time and the microcontroller is only active during the I^2C communication.

An acoustic sensor called SoundCompass, capable of measuring sound intensity and directionality, has been developed in [3] to satisfy the requirements of sound-source localization applications. The SoundCompass is composed of digital MEMS microphone arrays, designed to function in a distributed manner as part of a WSN or as standalone node. A WSN composed of SoundCompasses is not only able to sample the sound field directionality, but also to fuse this information for applications such as sound-source localization or real-time noise maps. The original SoundCompass, however, lacks a good time response, is not power efficient, and does not offer a dynamic response to spontaneous acoustic events critical for many applications. New architectures have been recently proposed to increment the dynamism. For instance, the architecture in [4] is designed to perform a fast and power-efficient sound-source location by dynamically adapting both the number of beamed orientations and microphones. The architecture is based on a variant of the Filter-and-Sum beamforming, implementing a filter stage for each microphone before computing the beamforming operation. This architecture request many FPGA resources, leading to a relative high power consumption ranging from 122 to 138 mW [5]. In this paper we present an architecture prioritizing the power consumption by drastically reducing the resource consumption while maintaining the scalability and dynamism presented in previous architectures. A minimal resource-greedy architecture will require a totally different approach, which is presented in the following section. To the best of our knowledge, the new architecture achieves the lowest power per microphone ratio compared to existing solutions.

The low-power architecture is described and evaluated in Sect. 2 and in Sect. 3 respectively. The conclusions are drawn in Sect. 4.

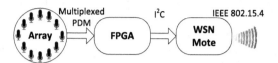

Fig. 1. Overview of the proposed WSN node. The proposed architecture computes the acquired audio signal to fully perform the sound source localization on the FPGA.

2   Architecture Description

Our proposed architecture for locating sound-sources in a 1 kHz to 15 kHz range is fully implemented in an FPGA, integrating the beamforming of the input signal, the filtering and audio conversion, and the sound's DoA. The architecture remains completely scalable and dynamic to adapt its response to the acoustic environment or to certain constraints such as extreme low-power conditions. The active configuration is received through the WSN mote. As a result, the architecture allows to activate or deactivate multiple microphones or to change the number of beamed orientations at runtime while continuing the processing as proposed in [4].

The following sections describe the sensor array, the FPGA's components and the WSN interface of a standalone device. The network analysis and considerations when combining multiple microphone arrays in a WSN are out of the scope of this paper and have been partially covered in [11].

2.1   Microphone Array

The proposed architecture for WSN relies on the same microphone array planar geometry as [3], where 52 MEMS microphones are placed on a 20 cm diameter planar geometry and grouped in four concentric sub-arrays of 4, 8, 16 and 24 MEMS microphones (Fig. 2). The circular distribution of the microphones

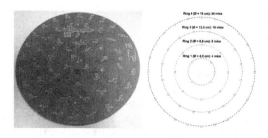

Fig. 2. The 52 digital MEMS microphones are distributed in 4 concentric circular MEMS microphone sub-arrays that can be activated or deactivated in runtime.

intends to maintain the array's response independent of the orientation. Each sub-array is differently positioned in order to facilitate the capture of the spatial acoustic information to be used by a beamforming technique for the localization of the sound source. The number of active microphones has a direct impact on the array's output signal-to-noise ratio (SNR) since it increases with the number of active microphones.

The microphones selected to compose the microphone array are digital MEMS microphones with a multiplexed pulse density modulation (PDM) output. Nowadays digital MEMS microphones such as the ICS-41350 from InvenSense [14] provide good omnidirectional polar response, a wide-band frequency response ranging from 100 Hz up to 15 kHz and offer a low-power sleep mode which drastically reduces the power consumption. The deactivation of the microphone's clock signal activates this low-power sleep mode. From the other side, the digital MEMS microphones need a clock in a 1 to 3 MHz range to oversample the audio signal by a factor of 64. The PDM signal needs to be filtered to remove the high-frequency noise and to be downsampled to retrieve the audio signal in a Pulse-Code Modulation (PCM) format.

2.2   FPGA

Figure 3 depicts the main components of the FPGA's implementation. The input rate is determined by the microphone's clock, which corresponds to the sampling frequency (F_s). The oversampled PDM signal coming from the microphones is multiplexed per microphone pair. A PDM splitter block demultiplexes this signal at every edge of the clock cycle and splits the sampled PDM into 2 PDM separate channels. The obtained PDM streams from each microphone of the array are properly delayed to perform the beamforming operation, called Delay-and-Sum.

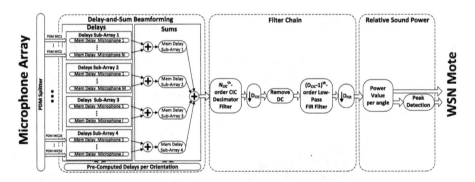

Fig. 3. Overview of the FPGA's components. The Delay-and-Sum beamforming is composed of several memories to properly delay the input signal. Our implementation groups the memories associated to each sub-array to disable those memories linked to deactivated microphones. The beamformed input signal is converted to audio in the cascade of filters. The DoA is finally obtained based on the relative sound power obtained per orientation.

This beamforming technique allows to amplify the sound coming from the set direction while suppressing the sound coming from other directions. Several cascaded filters remove the high-frequency noise and downsample the input signal to retrieve the audio signal. Finally, a *polar steering response map*, whose lobes are used to estimate the DoA for the localization of sound sources, is generated from the relative sound power.

To achieve the highest response time, this implementation is designed to operate in streaming mode, which warranties that each component is always computed after an initial latency.

Delay-and-Sum Beamforming. The beamforming stage is composed by a bank of memories, a pre-computed table of delays and cascaded additions (Fig. 1). The bank of memories is used to delay the different digital audio streams for the beamforming algorithm. Every microphone m is associated to a memory, which properly delays that particular audio stream with an amount Δ_m. The delay memories are grouped based on sub-arrays. Each delay memory belonging to a sub-array has the same width and length to support all the possible orientations. The width is determined by the PDM representation, which only needs one bit to represent the audio signal. The length is defined by the maximum delay $(max(\Delta_i))$ of that sub-array i, which is determined by the MEMS microphone planar distribution and F_s. In fact, the maximum $max(\Delta_i)$ determines the overall latency of the beamforming operation. Once the PDM input data is properly delayed for a particular orientation, the outputs of each memory are all added. This results in a summed PDM stream of the delayed PDM signals from the microphones.

Filters Description. The oversampled PDM signals from the digital MEMS microphones need to be downsampled and filtered to retrieve the original acquired audio signal. The downsampling is done by a cascade of a CIC decimator filter and a low-pass FIR filter. The CIC filter is an alteration on the FIR filter for which no multiplications are required, becoming less computationally intensive and less resource greedy [12]. Thus, a CIC filter with a N_{CIC} order, a decimation factor of D_{CIC} and a differential delay DD is chosen in our design based on the selected F_s. The CIC filter is followed by a signal averaging block to cancel out the effects caused by the microphones' DC offset output, improving the dynamic range and reducing the bit width required to represent the data after the CIC. The last cascaded filter is a low-pass compensation FIR filter designed in a serial fashion to reduce the resource consumption. Consequently, the maximum order (N_{FIR}) of the low-pass FIR filter is determined by D_{CIC}. The filtered signal is then further decimated by a factor of D_{FIR} to obtain the minimum bandwidth BW to satisfy the Nyquist theorem.

Relative Sound Power. The Delay-and-Sum beamforming technique allows to obtain the relative sound power of the retrieved audio stream for each steering

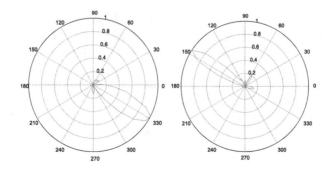

Fig. 4. Examples of *P-SRP* depicting the output power obtained under experimental conditions for sound sources of 3 kHz (left figure) and 5 kHz (right figure).

direction. The computation of the *Polar Steered Response Power* (*P-SRP*) in each steering direction provides information about the power response of the array. The power value per steering direction is obtained by accumulating all the individual power values measured for a certain time known as sensing time (t_s). This is a well-known parameter on radio frequency applications, which is known to increment the robustness against the noise. A higher t_s is needed to detect and locate sound sources under low signal-to-noise (SNR) conditions. All the power signals in one steering loop conform the *P-SRP* (Fig. 4). The peaks identified in the *P-SRP* point to the potential presence of sound sources.

The *P-SRP* is usually calculated in the frequency domain [3], using the Fourier transform, which increases the resource consumption and potentially enlarges the time the system focuses on a particular direction. In our architecture, the power of the signal is obtained in the time domain by applying the Parseval's theorem.

2.3   Wireless Sensor Network Mote

The proposed architecture includes a wireless communication capability. The calculation of *P-SRP* is performed in the FPGA, while the wireless communication is done externally by a low-power WSN mote. Figure 5 depicts the

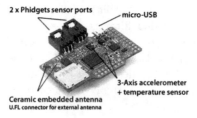

Fig. 5. The Zolertia WSN mote provides the wireless capability needed for our microphone array.

selected device, a Zoletia WSN platform Z1 based on the MSP430F2617 micro-controller [15]. This WSN mote is chosen due to its flexibility since it supports several wireless technologies such as IEEE 802.15.4 and 6LoWPAN. Another interesting feature of this mote is its low-power consumption, being on average 40 mW.

The communication between the FPGA and the Zolertia mote is done through an Inter-Integrated Circuit (I^2C), which is a serial communication bus system. I^2C uses a serial data line and a serial clock line to interconnect the FPGA and the Zolertia mote. It supports an extremely wide clock frequency range, reaching up to 400 Kb/s, enough to transmit the P-SRP values or to receive the configuration control signals to determine the number of active microphones or the number of orientations from the network.

Table 1. Configuration of the architecture under analysis.

Parameter	Definition	Value
F_s	Sampling Frequency	2.08 MHz
F_{min}	Minimum Frequency	1 kHz
F_{max}	Maximum Frequency	16.250 kHz
BW	Minimum bandwidth to satisfy Nyquist	32.5 kHz
DD	CIC Differential Delay	32
D_{CIC}	CIC Filter Decimation Factor	32
N_{CIC}	Order of the CIC Filter	4
D_{FIR}	FIR Filter Decimation Factor	2
N_{FIR}	Order of the FIR Filter	31

3   Design Analysis

In this section, the proposed architecture is firstly compared to the one presented in [5], discussing the frequency response, resource and power consumption and the time performance. The section concludes with a comparison with state-of-the-art related architectures.

The configurations of the architecture under evaluation are summarized in Table 1. The variation of the target F_{Max} and the F_s directly affects to the beam-forming stage by determining the length of the memories, and to the filter stage, by determining the decimation factor and the FIR Filter order. Although, the impact of the number of active microphones, which changes in runtime thanks to the sub-array distribution, is also analysed. The impact of the number of orientations is not evaluated here since it is partially discussed in [5]. For our evaluation, a complete steering loop is composed of 64 orientations, which represents an angular resolution of 5.625°.

3.1 Frequency Response

The frequency response of the microphone array is determined by the number of active microphones. Our experiments cover four configurations with 52, 28, 12 or 4 microphones determined by the number of active sub-arrays.

The proposed architecture is evaluated for three configurations (Table 1) by utilizing the directivity (D_P) to properly evaluate the quality of the array's response. The directivity reflects the ratio between the main lobe's surface and the total circle. Here we consider a threshold of 8 for D_P, which indicates that the main lobe's surface corresponds to at maximum half of a quadrant. The directivity is evaluated by placing a sound source at the 64 supported orientations. The average of all directivities along with the 95 % confidence interval is calculated for the supported orientations. Figure 6 (left) depicts the resulting directivities based on the active sub-arrays for the proposed architecture. In case the 4 inner microphones are enabled, the directivity in all directions does not reach the predefined ratio of 8. When 12 microphones are enabled the directivity increases, and reaches the value of 8 at 3.1 kHz. This value is reached at 2.1 kHz and 1.7 kHz when 28 and all microphones are enabled. One can also note that the 95 % confidence noticeably increases at 4 kHz, 6 kHz and 7 kHz for respectively the inner 4, 12 and 28, and all microphones.

The proposed architecture outperforms the frequency response of the architecture in [5], which is depicted in Fig. 6 (right). The variance of D_P of the architecture in [5] increases with the sound source frequency, becoming very sensitive to the beamed orientation. The proposed architecture has higher beamforming resolution thanks to beamforming before downsampling the input data. Instead, the architecture in [5] performs the beamforming after the filter stage, whose data has a lower rate. Nevertheless, as shown in Fig. 6, the capacity of properly

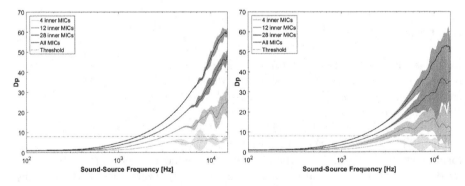

Fig. 6. Average D_P with a 95% confidence interval for the supported orientations when combining sub-arrays of the proposed architecture (left) and the architecture presented in [5] (right).

determining the DoA increases with the number of active microphones. The price to pay, however, is a higher resource and power consumption as detailed below.

3.2 Resource Consumption

The proposed architecture drastically reduces the resource consumption. Table 2 details the resource consumption when targeting a Zynq 7020 FPGA. Although the low resource consumption of this architecture allows to use a smaller and lower demanding power FPGA, the Zynq 7020 FPGA is used in order to fairly compare this new architecture with the one presented in [4] and accelerated in [5]. The amount of different types of resources demanded by the proposed architecture is significantly lower than the architecture presented in [4,5]. The reduction of the resource consumption is possible thanks to the reduction of the number of filter chains, leading to a more efficient beamforming operation in terms of resources.

Whereas in [4,5] each microphone has an individual filter chain, the proposed architecture only needs one. The percentage of resources dedicated to the filter chains represents around 91% of the registers and 89% for LUTs in [5]. This percentage decreases to 14.7% and 32.8% of the consumed registers and LUTs respectively in the proposed architecture. An efficient memory partition is possible thanks to the storage of PDM signals and to the use of LUTs as internal memory. The proposed architecture presents a lower LUTs' consumption, mostly used for the internal memory of the beamforming stage. As a result, the larger configuration of the proposed architecture demands up to 24 times less registers and 10 times less LUTs than the architecture in [5]. In fact, the available resources in the Zynq 7020 allow up to 10 instantiations of this architecture, which represents the computation of more than 500 microphones simultaneously.

Table 2. Zynq 7020 resource consumption after placement and routing when combining microphone sub-arrays.

Resource	Available Resource	Inner 4 MICs		Inner 12 MICs		Inner 28 MICs		Inner 52 MICs	
		[4,5]	Proposed	[4,5]	Proposed	[4,5]	Proposed	[4,5]	Proposed
Registers	106400	6144	1381	16882	1529	38183	1892	59093	2425
LUTs	53200	4732	1224	12299	1361	25032	2471	42319	4117
BRAM18k	140	2	1	6	1	14	1	22	1
DSP48	220	12	6	28	6	60	6	92	6

Table 3. Power consumption expressed in mW when combining microphone sub-arrays of a WSN node, including the microphones, FPGA and WSN mote power consumption. Values are obtained from the Libero SoC v.11.8 power report for the FPGA operating at $F_s = 2.08\,\mathrm{MHz}$, considering the low-power mode of the microphones [14,15]

Active Sub-Arrays	MEMS Microphones			Reported On-Chip Power			WSN	Total Power
	Active	Deactive	Total	Static	Dynamic	Total	Mote	
Inner 4 MICs	1.332	0.576	1.908	16.323	0	16.323	40	58.231
Inner 12 MICs	3.996	0.480	4.476	16.323	0	16.323	40	60.799
Inner 28 MICs	9.324	0.288	9.612	16.327	0.074	16.401	40	66.013
All 52 MICs	17.316	0	17.316	16.327	0.086	16.413	40	73.729

3.3 Power Analysis

The low resource requirements of the proposed architecture allows to target low-power FPGAs. Flash-based FPGAs like Microsemi's Igloo2, PolarFire or SmartFusion2 offer not only the lowest static power consumption, demanding only few tens of mW, but also support an interesting sleep mode called Flash-Freeze. The Flash-Freeze mode is a low power static mode that preserves the FPGA configuration while reducing the FPGA's power draw to just 1.92 mW for Igloo2 and SmartFusion2 FPGAs [13].

The proposed architecture has been evaluated for a SmartFusion2 M2S050 (Table 3). The reported power consumption rounds to 16.4 mW, which represents a significant reduction compared to the one reported in [5], ranging from 122 mW to 138 mW. Nevertheless, notice that the target FPGA in that case is a Zynq 7020. Our architecture presents a major reduction of the power consumption when compared to [5], achieving the lowest power per microphone ratio when all the sub-arrays are active.

3.4 Timing Analysis

The execution time (t_{P-SRP}) on the proposed architecture is the time needed to obtain the $P\text{-}SRP$. This time is distributed between the computation of three main operations: beamforming, filtering and reseting. The memories, which are composing the Delay-and-Sum beamforming implementation, need to be fetched with the input PDM samples before starting the filtering and the calculation of the $P\text{-}SRP$. This initial time (t_{Init}) is constant, since it depends on the microphones planar distribution, and rounds to 500 μs.

The time needed per orientation (t_o) is determined by the sensing time t_s, the group delay of the filter stage (t_g), and the time to reset the filters (t_r) at the end of the computation of each orientation. The time t_g groups the initiation interval (II) needed by the block in the filter stage before generating a valid output. This time depends on the filters characteristics, detailed in Table 1, and has a significant impact on the time performance.

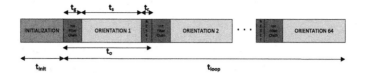

Fig. 7. Detailed schedule of the operations computed in serial.

Table 4. Definition of the architecture's parameter involved in the time analysis. N_s is the number of output samples and N_{am} is the number of active microphones.

Parameter	Definition	Equation	Value [cc/MHz]
t_{II}^{CIC}	II of the CIC Filter	$2 \cdot N_{CIC} + 1$	$9/F_s = 4.33\,\mu s$
t_{II}^{DC}	II of the Remove DC	$D_{CIC} + 2$	$34/F_s = 16.35\,\mu s$
t_{II}^{FIR}	II of the FIR Filter	$D_{CIC}^2/2 + 1$	$513/F_s = 246.6\,\mu s$
t_{II}^{Delay}	II of the delay memories at F_s	$max(\Delta)$	$1023/F_s = 491.18\,\mu s$
t_{II}^{Sum}	II of the cascaded sums	$2 \cdot \lceil log_2(N_{am}) \rceil$	$12/F_s = 5.77\,\mu s$
t_s	Sensing Time	$D_{CIC} \cdot D_{FIR} \cdot (N_s - 1)$	$4032/F_s = 1.94\,ms$
t_g	Group Delay	$t_{II}^{CIC} + t_{II}^{DC} + t_{II}^{FIR}$	$556/F_s = 267.31\,\mu s$
t_o	Time per Orientation	$t_g + t_s$	$4588/F_s = 2.2\,ms$
t_{init}	II of the Delay-and-Sum	$t_{II}^{Delay} + t_{II}^{Sum}$	$1035/F_s = 497.59\,\mu s$
t_{P-SRP}	Time to obtain a complete P-SRP	$t_{init} + N_o \cdot t_o$	$294667/F_s = 141.66\,ms$

The time t_o can be approximated to:

$$t_o = t_s + t_g + t_r \approx t_s + t_g \qquad (1)$$

because only few cc are needed to reset the filters. The execution time to obtain P-SRP (t_{P-SRP}) as detailed in Fig. 7 is:

$$t_{P-SRP} = t_{init} + N_o \times t_o = t_{init} + t_{loop} \qquad (2)$$

where N_o is the number of orientations, t_{init} is the initialization time of the beamforming operation, t_o is the time one orientation needs to be computed and t_{loop} is the time to compute N_o orientations. The t_{P-SRP} for the analyzed equals to 141 ms.

Table 4 provide further details about the timing analysis and includes the equations for the timing analysis, which are determined by the architecture design. Figure 8 shows a design space exploration similar to the one done in [5]. The architecture is evaluated for F_{max} ranging from 10 kHz to 16.5 kHz in steps of 125 Hz and F_s ranging from 1.25 MHz until 3.072 MHz. The order of the FIR filter (N_{FIR}) and the decimations factors D_{CIC} and D_{FIR} are obtained based on F_s and F_{max}. The equations in Table 4 are used to obtain t_{P-SRP} for each design. The frequency range of the target application determines F_{min} and F_{max}, which is used to select the F_s that offers the highest time performance in the proposed architecture. Unfortunately, due to the redesign of the architecture, the strategies like a faster clock proposed in [5] cannot be applied without a significant increment of the resource consumption.

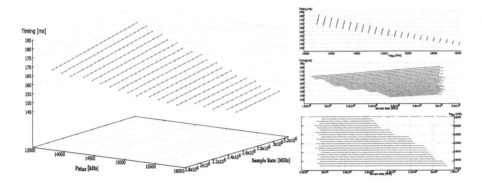

Fig. 8. Minimum t_{P-SRP} when evaluating values of F_{Max} and F_s. Different perspectives are displayed in the right side.

Table 5. Comparison of the time performance and the reported power consumption of the microphone array and the FPGA.

Reference	Device	Mic	Time [ms]	Time/Mic [ms/Mic]	Power [mW]	Power/Mic [mW/Mic]
[8]	Igloo 2	8	-	-	30.44	3.80
[9]	Spartan 6	16	18.85	1.18	78.99	4.94
[10]	EFM32	4	249	62.25	7.2	1.8
[5]	Zynq 7020	52	2	0.04	343.92	6.61
Proposed	**SmartFusion2**	**52**	**141.66**	**2.724**	**33.78**	**0.65**

3.5   Comparison

Table 5 summarizes the comparison of the proposed architecture and the related works from a timing and power consumption point of view. As a consequence of the lower resource consumption, not only larger microphone arrays can be processed in parallel but also more power-efficient FPGAs can be used to minimize the power consumption. Despite the proposed architecture is substantially slower than the one presented in [5], the time-per-microphone ratio is better than other related solutions.

4   Conclusions

The proposed architecture demonstrates that large MEMS microphone arrays are suitable for WSN, even when they are composed of tens of MEMS microphones. The drastic reduction of the resource requirements allows to consider more power efficient devices such as flash-based FPGAs. The price to pay is an acceptable degradation in the time response. Nevertheless, the new architecture not only offers a better frequency response but also an interesting balance between time performance and power consumption for applications on WSN.

Acknowledgments. This work was supported by the European Regional Development Fund (ERDF) and the Brussels-Capital Region-Innoviris within the framework of the Operational Programme 20142020 through the ERDF-2020 Project ICI-TYRDI.BRU.

References

1. Zwyssig, E., et al.: A digital microphone array for distant speech recognition. In: 2010 IEEE International Conference on Acoustics Speech and Signal Processing (ICASSP). IEEE (2010)
2. Zhang, X., et al.: Design of small MEMS microphone array systems for direction finding of outdoors moving vehicles. Sensors **14**(3), 4384–4398 (2014)
3. Tiete, J., et al.: SoundCompass: a distributed MEMS microphone array-based sensor for sound source localization. Sensors **14**(2), 1918–1949 (2014)
4. da Silva, B., et al.: Runtime reconfigurable beamforming architecture for real-time sound-source localization. In: 2016 26th International Conference on Field Programmable Logic and Applications (FPL). EPFL (2016)
5. da Silva, B., et al.: Design considerations when accelerating an FPGA-based digital microphone array for sound-source localization. J. Sens. **2017**, 1–20 (2017)
6. Ledeczi, A., et al.: Countersniper system for urban warfare. ACM Trans. Sens. Netw. (TOSN) **1**(2), 153–177 (2005)
7. Sallai, J., et al.: Weapon classification and shooter localization using distributed multichannel acoustic sensors. J. Syst. Archit. **57**(10), 869–885 (2011)
8. Petrica, L., et al.: Energy-efficient WSN architecture for illegal deforestation detection. Int. J. Sens. Sens. Netw. **3**(3), 24–30 (2015)
9. Petrica, L.: An evaluation of low-power microphone array sound source localization for deforestation detection. Appl. Acoust. **113**, 162–169 (2016)
10. Ottoy, G., et al.: A low-power MEMS microphone array for wireless acoustic sensors. In: 2016 IEEE Sensors Applications Symposium (SAS). IEEE (2016)
11. da Silva, B., et al.: A partial reconfiguration based microphone array network emulator. In: 2017 27th International Conference on Field Programmable Logic and Applications (FPL). IEEE (2017)
12. Hogenauer, E.: An economical class of digital filters for decimation and interpolation. IEEE Trans. Acoust. Speech Signal Process. **29**(2), 155–162 (1981)
13. Microsemi: User Guide 0444 V5 (UG0444), SmartFusion2 SoC and IGLOO2 FPGA Low-Power Design (2017)
14. InvenSens: ICS-41350 datasheet (2017)
15. Zolertia WSN platform: Z1 Datasheet, March 2010

A Hybrid FPGA Trojan Detection Technique Based-on Combinatorial Testing and On-chip Sensing

Lampros Pyrgas[2] and Paris Kitsos[1,2(✉)]

[1] Digital IC Design and Systems Laboratory (DICES Lab),
Computer and Informatics Engineering Department,
Technological Educational Institute of Western Greece, Antirrion, Greece
pkitsos@ieee.org
[2] Industrial Systems Institute of "Athena" RIC in ICT and Knowledge
Technologies, Patras, Greece
lpyrgas@hotmail.com

Abstract. A hybrid Hardware Trojan detection technique is proposed in this paper that combines Combinatorial Testing in order to consistently trigger the Hardware Trojan, if one is present, and a grid of compact on-chip sensors in order to detect differentiations in the circuit of the FPGA. Each sensor mainly consist of a three stage Ring Oscillator and a compact Residue Number System ring counter and requires just two FPGA slices, leading to a total overhead of less than 2% in hardware resources. The proposed technique was tested on a cryptographic module performing AES cipher. To emulate the effects of a Hardware Trojan, we used a 64-bit Linear Feedback Shift Register. The experimental results prove that the proposed hybrid technique can detect the presence of a Hardware Trojan.

Keywords: Chinese Remainder Theorem · Combinatorial Testing
FPGA security · Hardware Trojan horse detection · On-chip sensor
Ring counter · Ring Oscillator

1 Introduction

Hardware Trojans (HTs) have become a serious threat to the modern fabless semi-conductor industry because different manufacturing phases of an Integrated Circuit (IC) can be performed at different places. Therefore, a foe has enough room to design or insert a HT in the supply chain. For example, in the case of a FPGA IC, a HT could be introduced in the design flow by an untrusted FPGA foundry. Also, a malicious distributor can reduce the reliability of an FPGA in the supply chain, and even recycled FPGAs (with HTs) can be inserted into the FPGA supply chain. Finally, HTs can also enter through FPGA CAD tool flow. The effects of hardware Trojan insertion attacks range from monitoring and controlling of the processed data to observing secret information or downgrade the performance of the IC [1, 2]. A HT is a small modifi-cation in the design that consists of two part: First, the trigger that activate the HT in a rare input event. This means that the HT is inactive during most of the run-time and is

© Springer International Publishing AG, part of Springer Nature 2018
N. Voros et al. (Eds.): ARC 2018, LNCS 10824, pp. 294–303, 2018.
https://doi.org/10.1007/978-3-319-78890-6_24

very difficult to detect it using random or constraint random tests. Second, the payload that is the activity that the HT executes when it is activated.

The HT detection techniques are classified into two categories, destructive and non-destructive. The most important non-destructive techniques are test-time and run-time. In test-time techniques, special circuits are used in order to enhance the detection sensitivity of an IC under test. Comparisons of the side channels parameters (e.g. power, current etc.) with a golden IC can detect the presence of the HT. In run-time techniques, special monitoring circuits are used that can utilize pre-existing redundancy in the circuit and detour its infected parts. A major advantage in run-time techniques is that they do not require a golden IC. These special detection circuits typically contain some kind of on-chip sensor or a grid of sensors in order to capture any unexpected differentiation (in power, current etc.) in the IC. Many different types of on-chip digital sensors have been proposed in the literature as means for Trojan detection [3–6]. Most of those sensors are based on Ring Oscillators.

A Ring Oscillator (RO) [7] is a circuit composed of an odd number of NOT gates in a ring, whose output oscillates between two voltage levels. The NOT gates, are attached in a chain and the output of the last gate is fed back into the first. The oscillation frequency depends on the process variation, the environmental conditions (e.g., temperature) and the operating characteristics (e.g., signals' toggles around the RO, voltage). Therefore, minimal modifications of the circuit can result in an oscillation frequency change [8, 9]. Ring oscillators are widely used to detect changes in quantities of interest such as power, current etc. They can also be used as temperature sensors on FPGAs [10–13] in order to observe the health of the FPGA, and, consequently, as temperature sensors for Hardware Trojan detection [6, 14]. In [6] we used a detection technique based on a grid of RO-based thermal sensors. For our measurements, we used two distinctive groups of inputs: the first group contained ten inputs that did not activate the Trojan while the second group contained ten inputs that all activate the Trojan. In [14] the authors also proposed a RO based sensor in order to detect a temperature-triggered hardware Trojan.

In the HT triggering part, the proposed technique follows a different approach than [6]. We consider an IC-Under-Test (ICUT) and we want to specify whether a HT is present or not. The first step is to activate the HT by feeding test vectors into the HT's triggering logic. Typically, a large amount of test vectors is needed in order to ensure that the HT is going to be triggered (if a HT is inserted in the IC). Methods that reduce the required, random generated, number of test vectors have already been proposed. Automatic Test Pattern Generation (ATPG) [15–17], MERO [18] and MERS [19] are widely used for generating such test vectors. However, these methods still generate a large number of test vectors. In this paper, we opted for a method based on Combinatorial Testing (CT) [20–22]. This method, compared to the methods in [15–19], reduces the total number of test vectors that are needed for triggering the HT.

In conclusion, a hybrid detection approach is proposed in this paper that uses: first, combinatorial testing in order to trigger the HT which result higher levels of signals' toggles in the infected area and second, a grid of on-chip sensors in order to fully cover the implementation area and efficiently identify unexpected changes while keeping the hardware overhead to a minimum.

The rest of the paper is organized as follows. In Sect. 2, we discuss the sensor implementation in an FPGA and the attack model that we used. In Sect. 3, we describe the experimental setup and in Sect. 4, we discuss the results of our experiments and the detection efficiency. Finally, Sect. 5 concludes our paper.

2 Sensor Implementation and Attack Model

2.1 Sensor Implementation

The first step towards detecting a HT, in our experiment, is to cover the whole implementation area with a grid of sensors. In order to keep the grid's area overhead to a minimum, we opted for a very compact sensor design. Such a sensor has been proposed in [13], and has already been implemented by us in [6]. This compact sensor is composed of three parts: a RO, a compact Residue Number System (RNS) ring counter and a control multiplexer. The architecture of the proposed sensor is depicted in Fig. 1.

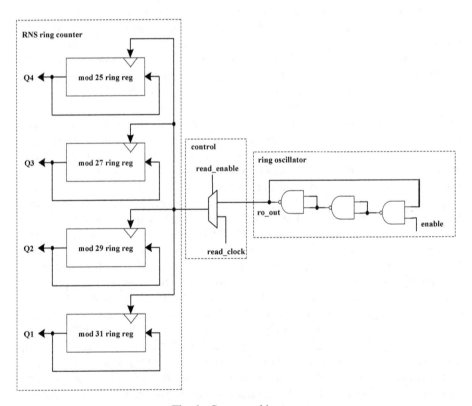

Fig. 1. Sensor architecture

After studying a variety of RO designs, we selected a standard three stage RO with an on/off (enable) control signal for our design due to being both compact and very sensitive. The three inversion stages are implemented by three NAND gates, each using a 6-input Look-Up-Table (LUT). The first gate has an enable signal as one of its input to control whether the RO oscillates or not. Initially, enable is set to '0', breaking the feedback path and there is no oscillation. When enable, is set to '1' the circuit oscillates.

In order to count how many times each RO oscillates we need to feed its output to a counter. In our design, we require a very compact counter that, at the same time, is very easy to decode and extract the count value. Luckily, such type of counter already exists; the Residue Number System (RNS) ring counter. It was initially proposed in [23] and then used in [13]. The RNS counter was implemented by using Xilinx's shift register LUTs (SRLs). Four 6-input LUT and four flip-flops were used for each RNS counter in our experiment. The RNS counter is composed of an array of ring counters (composed of a circular shift register) of varying lengths, specifically 31, 29, 27 and 25 supporting a counting period up to 606825. The total counting value is calculated by applying the Chinese Remainder Theorem (CRT) according to the Eq. 1:

$$counts = \sum_{i=1}^{k} r_i M_i y_i \mod M \tag{1}$$

where k is the number of moduli, r_i is a residue, $M_i = M/m_i$, where m_i is a modulus (and the shift register's length), M is the counting period $\left(M = \Pi_{i=1}^{k} m_i\right)$ and $y_i = M_i^{-1} \mod m_i$.

As already stated, the RO circuit's output is fed to the RNS counter. Therefore, when the RO circuit oscillates (measurement stage), the RNS counter captures the number of oscillations. When the RO finally stops, it is necessary to output the measurement. This is achieved by feeding the system clock (*read_clock*) to the counter's input and shift the counter's bits, one by one, to the output. The input to the RNS counter is controlled by the *read_enable* signal. The total area overhead for each sensor instance is only two slices, and in more detail, eight 6-input LUT and four flip-flops.

2.2   Attack Model

An attacker wants to be able to control the activation of the HT through some external input. The encryption/decryption key is a very good candidate for that purpose. Specific selected key bits are combined in order to form the triggering logic. When a specific pattern occurs in those key bits, the HT is activated. Design automation tools and established testing practices can reveal the presence of foreign logic, so the triggering logic has to be small but also not trivial, in order to escape detection.

The defender, on the other hand, must exhaustively test all possible inputs in order to detect the HT. This task is impossible in a realistic timeframe, due to the extremely large number of patterns that need to be covered. Therefore, the objective to reduce the size of the input test vectors rises. In this paper, we follow the approach first proposed in [20] and explored in detail in [21]. The approach utilizes the mathematical construct of covering arrays [24] and is based on the combinatorial testing (CT) principles. As shown in Table 1, the CT-based approach succeeds in greatly reducing the number of the input vectors that are needed in order to trigger the HT while at the same time is effectively covering all the possible input patterns.

Table 1. Number of test vectors needed to trigger the HT

Number of key bits used	Test vectors	Covered patterns
t = 2	11	32,512
t = 3	37	2,731,008
t = 4	112	170,688,000
t = 5	252	8,466,124,800
t = 6	720	347,111,116,800
t = 7	**2,462**	**12,099,301,785,600**
t = 8	17,544	366,003,879,014,400

In this paper we focused in the non-trivial and representative case where the triggering logic is formed from seven key bits (t = 7), thus we need 2,462 input test vectors to activate the HT. It is important to note that this group of test vectors (or test suite) activates the HT up to eleven times [21].

3   Experimental Setup

To test the proposed HT detection method, we designed and implemented an FPGA-based system on a Digilent Basys 3 FPGA development board [25]. The Basys 3 board features the Xilinx Artix-7-FPGA XC7A35T-1CPG236C. Its 5,200 slices provide 33,280 logic cells with each slice containing four 6-input LUTs and eight flip-flops.

First, for the implementation of the well-known AES cryptographic algorithm, we opted for the 128-bit plaintext and key open source AES implementation that is provided in [26]. Next, we placed 30 of the sensors on top of the previous implementation equidistant from each other, both vertically and horizontally, forming a 6×5 grid, in order to cover the whole implementation area. The total area overhead caused by the addition of our sensor grid and its supporting hardware is less than 2% of the FPGA resources.

Next, we implemented a 64-bit Linear Feedback Shift Register (LFSR) [27], to be used as a HT. The LFSR is enabled when the pattern '1111111' occurs in specific key bits (namely: 126, 99, 70, 57, 32, 18, 4). That way, we are able to only observe the impact of the LFSR when it is active (there is no signals' toggles of the LFSR when is inactive). Therefore, we can simulate the dynamic impact of any sequential HT (when it is active) as well as the static effect of any combinational or sequential HT. The LFSR was placed all around sensor 18 (Line 4, Column 3). The final layout with the 30 sensors (green color) and the 64-bit LFSR as HT (red color) is shown in Fig. 2.

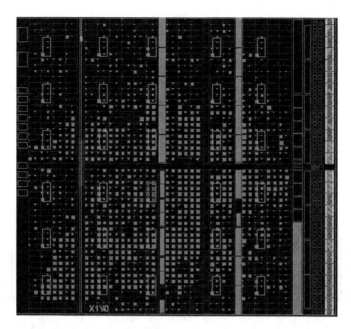

Fig. 2. Layout of AES, the 30 sensors, and the 64-bit LFSR (Color figure online)

Finally, we divided the 2,462 test vectors in 10 bins of 247 vectors each (padding with all-zero vectors where needed). As already stated, multiple test vectors activate the HT. These test vectors can be present in more than one bin, so we expect that we may observe that multiple bins activate the HT, if one exists, and multiple bins do not.

4 Results and Discussion

We began our experiment by executing the AES algorithm for each test vector in first bin. Communication with the board is achieved through a UART interface. All the sensors were activated before the first execution of the AES algorithm and they were deactivated after two AES executions for each vector. Each sensor's counter value was automatically received and stored for the estimation of the total counts through the Chinese Remainder Theorem (CRT) in MATLAB. We opted for an offline computation of the final value of the RNS counter in order to keep the used hardware resources to a minimum. Next, we repeated the same process for the remaining nine test vector bins. In order to obtain as accurate measurements as possible, we repeated our experiment 100 times and then we calculated a mean value of each sensor's counts for all ten test vector bins.

Twelve such descriptive mean count values, specifically for sensors 1, 3, 5, 8, 10, 13, 17, 18, 19, 23, 25, 29 are shown in Fig. 3. It is obvious that when the sensor is not close to the HT, the RO is not sensitive enough to detect the presence of the Trojan (count values have fractional differences). When the Trojan is close to the sensor, the count values between the bins are very different. Bins with test vectors that activate the

HT are easily distinguished from the other bins. That count difference is obvious for the sensor #18, the one sensitive to the presence of the Trojan.

Thus, it is proven from the results that a sensor placed close to the HT is sensitive enough to detect the HT. The CT-based approach, when it comes to the test vectors, ensures that the HT will be activated. Finally, the very compact sensor design allow us to fully cover the AES implementation area with very little overhead.

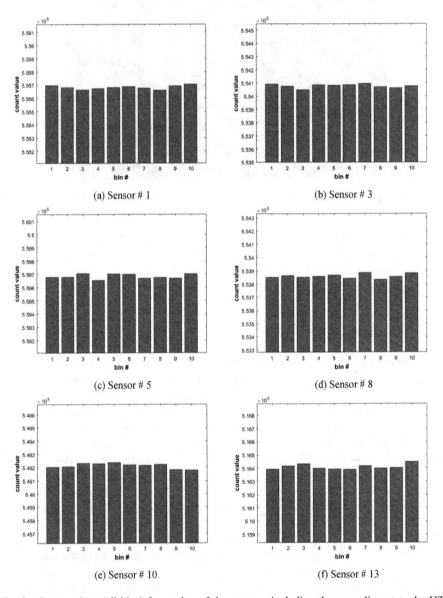

Fig. 3. Count values (all bins) for twelve of the sensors, including the one adjacent to the HT

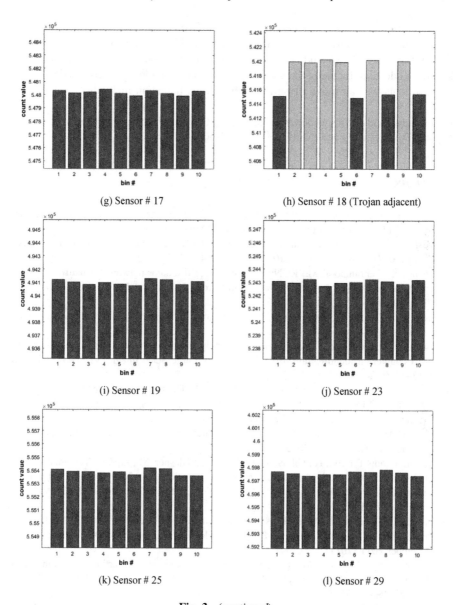

(g) Sensor # 17

(h) Sensor # 18 (Trojan adjacent)

(i) Sensor # 19

(j) Sensor # 23

(k) Sensor # 25

(l) Sensor # 29

Fig. 3. (*continued*)

5 Conclusions and Future Work

In this paper, a hybrid HT detection is proposed. The proposed methodology is based on two parts: First, a certain activation of the HT and second from the detection hardware. The first part is achieved by using the CT-based approach, when it comes to the test vectors. The second part is achieved by designing and implementing very compact sensors in order to achieve minimal hardware overhead. The total area overhead caused by the addition of our sensor grid is less than 2% of the FPGA resources, while the 6 × 5 grid structure covers the whole area of the FPGA implementation.

Future work includes study of advanced HT that incorporate state elements in their design. In addition, by using the CT-based approach and adding external side channel measurements we can move toward Golden-free IC detection methods.

Acknowledgements. This work was co-financed by Greece and the European Union - European Regional Development Fund (NSRF/EPAnEK I3T-5002434).

References

1. Tehranipoor, M., Wang, C.: Introduction to Hardware Security and Trust. Springer, New York (2011). https://doi.org/10.1007/978-1-4419-8080-9
2. Mishra, P., Bhunia, S., Tehranipoor, M. (eds.): Hardware IP Security and Trust. Springer, Cham (2017). https://doi.org/10.1007/978-3-319-49025-0
3. Zhang, X., Tehranipoor, M.: RON: an on-chip ring oscillator network for hardware Trojan detection. In: Design, Automation & Test in Europe 2011, Grenoble, France, 14–18 March 2011 (2011)
4. Kelly, S., Zhang, X., Tehranipoor, M., Ferraiuolo, A.: Detecting hardware trojans using on-chip sensors in an ASIC design. J. Electron. Test. **31**(1), 11–26 (2015)
5. Lecomte, M., Fournier, J., Maurine, P.: An on-chip technique to detect hardware Trojans and assist counterfeit identification. IEEE Trans. Very Large Scale Integr. (VLSI) Syst. **25**(12), 3317–3330 (2017)
6. Pyrgas, L., Pirpilidis, F., Panayiotarou, A., Kitsos, P.: Thermal sensor based hardware Trojan detection in FPGAs. In: 20th Euromicro Conference on Digital Systems (DSD 2017), Vienna, Austria, 30 August–1 September 2017 (2017)
7. Mandal, M.K., Sarkar, B.C.: Ring oscillators: characteristics and applications. Indian J. Pure Appl. Phys. **48**, 136–145 (2010)
8. Yu, H., Leong, P.H.W., Hinkelmann, H., Moller, L., Glesner, M., Zipf, P.: Towards a unique FPGA-based identification circuit using process variations. In: 2009 International Conference on Field Programmable Logic and Applications, Prague, Czech Republic, 31 August–2 September 2009 (2009)
9. Eiroa, S., Baturone, I.: An analysis of ring oscillator PUF behavior on FPGAs. In: 2011 International Conference on Field-Programmable Technology, New Delhi, India, 12–14 December 2011 (2011)
10. Lopez-Buedo, S., Garrido, J., Boemo, E.I.: Dynamically inserting, operating, and eliminating thermal sensors of FPGA-based systems. IEEE Trans. Compon. Packag. Technol. **25**(4), 561–566 (2002)
11. Velusamy, S., Huang, W., Lach, J., Stan, M., Skadron, K.: Monitoring temperature in FPGA based SoCs. In: International Conference on Computer Design (ICCD 2005), San Jose, California, pp. 634–640 (2005)
12. Sayed, M., Jones, P.: Characterizing non-ideal impacts of reconfigurable hardware workloads on ring oscillator-based thermometers. In: 2011 International Conference on ReConFig, pp. 92–98, December 2011
13. Zick, K.M., Hayes, J.P.: Low-cost sensing with ring oscillator arrays for healthier reconfigurable systems. ACM Trans. Reconfig. Technol. Syst. **5**(1), 1:1–1:26 (2012)

14. Li, X., Carrion Schafer, B.: Temperature-triggered behavioral IPs HW Trojan detection method with FPGAs. In: 25th International Conference on Field Programmable Logic and Applications (FPL 2015), London, United Kingdom, 2–4 September 2015 (2015)
15. Lesperance, N., Kulkarni, S., Cheng, K.-T.: Hardware Trojan detection using exhaustive testing of k-bit subspaces. In: 2015 20th Asia and South Pacific Design Automation Conference (ASP-DAC), Tokyo, Japan. IEEE, January 2015
16. Flottes, M.-L., Dupuis, S., Ba, P.-S., Rouzeyre, B.: On the limitations of logic testing for detecting hardware Trojans horses. In: 2015 10th IEEE International Conference on Design & Technology of Integrated Systems in Nanoscale Era (DTIS) (2015)
17. Cruz, J., Farahmand, F., Ahmed, A., Mishra, P.: Hardware Trojan detection using ATPG and model checking. In: International Conference on VLSI Design, Pune, India, 6–10 January 2018 (2018)
18. Chakraborty, R.S., Wolff, F., Paul, S., Papachristou, C., Bhunia, S.: *MERO*: A Statistical Approach for Hardware Trojan Detection. In: Clavier, C., Gaj, K. (eds.) CHES 2009. LNCS, vol. 5747, pp. 396–410. Springer, Heidelberg (2009). https://doi.org/10.1007/978-3-642-04138-9_28
19. Huang, Y., Bhunia, S., Mishra, P.: MERS: statistical test generation for side-channel analysis based Trojan detection. In: Proceedings of the 2016 ACM SIGSAC Conference on Computer and Communications Security, Vienna, Austria, 24–28 October 2016 (2016)
20. Kitsos, P., Simos, D.E., Torres-Jimenez, J., Voyiatzis, A.G.: Exciting FPGA cryptographic Trojans using combinatorial testing. In: 26th IEEE International Symposium on Software Reliability Engineering (ISSRE 2015), Gaithersburg, MD, USA, 2–5 November 2015 (2015)
21. Voyiatzis, A.G., Stefanidis, K.G., Kitsos, P.: Efficient triggering of Trojan hardware logic. In: 19th IEEE International Symposium on Design and Diagnostics of Electronic Circuits and Systems (DDECS 2016), Kosice, Slovakia, 20–22 April 2016 (2016)
22. Simos, D.E., Kuhn, R., Voyiatzis, A.G., Kacker, R.: Combinatorial methods in security testing. IEEE Comput. **49**(10), 80–83 (2016)
23. Zick, K.M., Hayes, J.P.: On-line sensing for healthier FPGA systems. In: 18th Annual ACM/SIGDA International Symposium on Field Programmable Gate Arrays, Monterey, California, USA, 21–23 February 2010 (2010)
24. Kuhn, D., Bryce, R., Duan F., Ghandehari, L., Lei, Y., Kacker, R.: Combinatorial testing: theory and practice. In: Advances in Computers, vol. 99. Academic Press (2015)
25. https://www.xilinx.com/products/boards-and-kits/1-54wqge.html
26. https://opencores.org/project,aes_core
27. Abramovici, M., Breuer, M.A., Friedman, A.D.: Digital Systems Testing and Testable Design. IEEE Press, New York (1990)

HoneyWiN: Novel Honeycomb-Based Wireless NoC Architecture in Many-Core Era

Raheel Afsharmazayejani[1]([✉]), Fahimeh Yazdanpanah[2], Amin Rezaei[3],
Mohammad Alaei[2], and Masoud Daneshtalab[4]

[1] Shahid Bahonar University of Kerman, Kerman, Iran
raheel_afshar@eng.uk.ac.ir
[2] Vali-e-Asr University, Rafsanjan, Iran
{yazdanpanahf,alaeim}@vru.ac.ir
[3] Northwestern University, Evanston, USA
me@aminrezaei.com
[4] Malardalen University, Vasteras, Sweden
masoud.daneshtalab@mdh.se

Abstract. Although NoC-based systems with many cores are commercially available, their multi-hop nature has become a bottleneck on scaling performance and energy consumption parameters. Alternatively, hybrid wireless NoC provides a postern by exploiting single-hop express links for long-distance communications. Also, there is a common wisdom that grid-like mesh is the most stable topology in conventional designs. That is why almost all of the emerging architectures had been relying on this topology as well. In this paper, first we challenge the efficiency of the grid-like mesh in emerging systems. Then, we propose HoneyWiN, a hybrid reconfigurable wireless NoC architecture that relies on the honeycomb topology. The simulation results show that on average HoneyWiN saves 17% of energy consumption while increases the network throughput by 10% compared to its wireless mesh counterpart.

Keywords: MCSoC · Wireless NoC · Honeycomb · Mesh
Energy efficiency

1 Introduction

Even though the communication infrastructure has been gradually changed from traditional bus to Network-on-Chip (NoC) [1] during the last decade, the focus of Multi-Processor and Many-Core System-on-Chips (MP & MCSoCs) have been still on the 2-D metal wire interconnects [2]. Nowadays, NoC-based systems capable of accommodating hundreds of Processing Elements (PEs) are commercially available [3], but the multi-hop nature of these architectures has become a bottleneck on improving both performance and energy consumption parameters with technology scaling [4]. This motivates the researchers to seek alternative

© Springer International Publishing AG, part of Springer Nature 2018
N. Voros et al. (Eds.): ARC 2018, LNCS 10824, pp. 304–316, 2018.
https://doi.org/10.1007/978-3-319-78890-6_25

architectures such as Hybrid Wireless NoC (HWNoC) [5–7] in which the key idea is to adopt express communication links in order to reduce transmission latency with a reasonable energy consumption while providing high bandwidth.

1.1 Background

In order to transmit data across the chip in HWNoC-based architectures, different approaches have been introduced. The metal zigzag antennas [8] utilize Millimeter Wave (mm-Wave) as part of the ElectroMagnetic (EM) spectrum to operate in tens of GHz frequency. By employing mm-Wave approach in 40 nm CMOS technology, the data rate of 11 Gbps at 56 GHz frequency with Bit Error Rate (BER) of 10^{-11} has been reported [9]. By designing an On-Off Keying (OOK) transmitter in 65 nm CMOS, the data rate of 16 Gbps at 60 GHz frequency has been achieved [10].

In RF-I approach, EM waves travel via transmission line to exchange data between long-distance on-chip cores. One of the first implementation of RF-I has been proposed in 90 nm CMOS technology with the data rate of 5 Gbps [12]. Although the propagation can happen in light speed, RF-I suffers from crosstalk and scalability issues [2].

On the other hand, Carbon NanoTube (CNT) technology operates in terahertz/optical frequency range while reduces the size of antennas. In [19], a fundamental property analysis of the CNT antennas including input impedance, current distribution, and radiation pattern has been provided. Also in [7], a CNT-based on-chip network with 24 different frequency channels and data rate of 10 Gbps per channel has been utilized.

Moreover, graphene antennas also operate in terahertz frequency and provide low energy dissipation and less area overhead [20]. But these miniaturized antennas suffer from different challenges during implementation. For example, in nanoscale communication of the terahertz band, molecular absorption causes path loss and high noise [21]. Although a recent work to address this issue has proposed a channel model [22], more efforts are required to fully design and measure physical properties of the graphene antennas.

Surface Wave Interconnect (SWI) is another approach in which a 2-D waveguide medium is used as the wireless communication layer to propagate surface

Table 1. Wireless on-chip transceivers comparison

Category	RF-I				mm-Wave				CNT	SWI
Technology (nm)	65	90	90	130	40	65	65	90	N/A	65
Data Rate (Gbps)	5	5	8	25	11	16	23	10.7	10	25
Frequency (GHz)	60	20	N/A	N/A	56	60	80	60	100-10k	140
Energy (pJ/b)	1.33	1.2	1.05	1.67	6.4	1.2	9.4	6.24	0.33	0.32
BER	$< 10^{-12}$	N/A	$< 10^{-12}$	$< 10^{-12}$	$< 10^{-11}$	10^{-15}	10^{-11}	10^{-12}	N/A	$< 10^{-14}$
Modulation	ASK	BPSK	N/A	N/A	ASK	OOK	ASK	OOK	OOK	ASK
Trans. Range (mm)	5.5	N/A	5	20	14	20	20	100	23	20
Area (mm²)	TX:0.0048	0.0107	0.002	TX:0.023	TX:0.06	TX: 0.077	TX:0.34	TX:0.15	N/A	0.408
	RX:0.034			RX:0.025	RX:0.07		RX:2.5	RX:0.29		
Reference	[11]	[12]	[13]	[14]	[9]	[10]	[15]	[16]	[7]	[17,18]

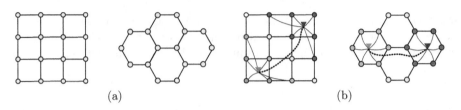

Fig. 1. Grid-like mesh and honeycomb topologies for 16-core system (a) Conventional (b) HWNoC

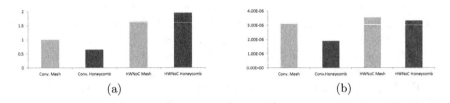

Fig. 2. Grid-like mesh and honeycomb topologies for 16-core system (a) Normalized network throughput (b) Total energy consumption (J)

wave signals. To physically implement this medium, a dielectric coated metal layer is used. Comparing with free space signal propagation environment, energy dissipation can be reduced substantially in SWI because of the signal propagation in 2-D communication fabric. The SWI-based architecture offers BER of less than 10^{-14} which is similar to BER of wired communication [17].

The comparison between different wireless on-chip transceivers are summarized in Table 1. The above efforts show how promising HWNoC is to be employed as the backbone of future MCSoCs. However, since Wireless Routers (WRs) are more energy hungry than Conventional Routers (CRs), new proposals are required to address the trade-off between energy and performance.

1.2   Motivation

There is a common wisdom that conventional grid-like mesh systems have better performance and reasonable energy consumption in comparison with other 2-D topologies. That is why almost all of the emerging HWNoC-based architectures also have been focused on grid-like mesh [23–26]. We run two sets of experiments to evaluate the correctness of this belief in conventional NoC and HWNoC.

Figure 1a shows a 16-core conventional grid-like mesh and a 16-core conventional honeycomb and Fig. 1b shows their hybrid wireless versions each equipped with two WRs. Figure 2a depicts the normalized throughput under Transpose1 traffic pattern for the mentioned topologies. Although the results confirm the superiority of the grid-like mesh over the honeycomb in conventional design, they show that this may not be the case for HWNoC-based systems. Moreover, the energy consumption comparison results in Fig. 2b reveal that although HWNoC-based architectures are by nature more energy hungry than conventional designs, the honeycomb topology can have less energy consumption compared to the well-known grid-like mesh.

These preliminary results not only challenge the efficiency of the mesh-based HWNoC, but also motivate us to seek alternative topologies in emerging MCSoCs. The contributions of this paper are as follows:

- Challenging the efficiency of the grid-like mesh topology in HWNoC-based architectures;
- Proposing an alternative Honeycomb-based Wireless NoC (HoneyWiN) architecture;
- Investigating the role of reconfigurable partitions (i.e. homogeneous/ heterogeneous and complete/partial partitionings) in HoneyWiN;
- Introducing a specific routing algorithm for HoneyWiN by utilizing a planar 3-axes coordinate system.

To the best of our knowledge, this paper is the first to study the possibility of using honeycomb topology in HWNoC-based MCSoCs.

2   HoneyWiN Architecture

HoneyWiN consists of a wired network in which each 5-port CR is connected to its corresponding core and at most three adjacent CRs via wireline communication. Also another port is forecasted for a possible connection to a WR. On top of the wired network, a wireless network is adopted by WRs. Each WR is a multi-port router equipped with a transceiver that is capable of both wired and wireless communications.

2.1   Partitioning

Different partitions may lead to different trade-offs in terms of performance, energy consumption, and even area overhead. Here, on-chip partitioning can be viewed and examined from different viewpoints. One way to see partitioning is based on the number of cores within each subnet that can be homogeneous (i.e. all the subnets have equal number of cores) or heterogeneous (i.e. each subnet can have different number of cores from the others.) Homogeneous partitioning is suitable for the networks with uniformly distributed communications. On the other hand, heterogeneous partitioning can be used in the networks with high communication demand for some specific cores.

Another way to see partitioning is based on the participant cores in the process of subdividing that can be complete (i.e. all the cores participate in partitioning) or partial (i.e. some of the cores are involved in the process.) Complete partitioning can be utilized in the networks with high traffic rates while partial partitioning is beneficial for medium and low traffic rates.

Figure 3a is a 24-core partially homogeneous HoneyWiN with three WRs while Fig. 3b and 3c show two completely homogeneous partitionings by dividing the network into four and six partitions respectively. Figure 4a depicts a completely homogeneous partitioning of a 54-core HoneyWiN. In this example,

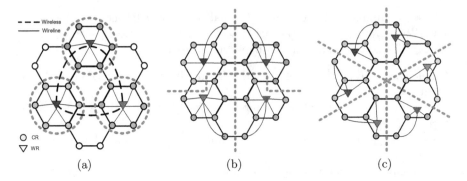

Fig. 3. 24-core HoneyWiN architecture (a) Partially homogeneous partitioning with three WRs (b) Completely homogeneous partitioning with four WRs (c) Completely homogeneous partitioning with six WRs

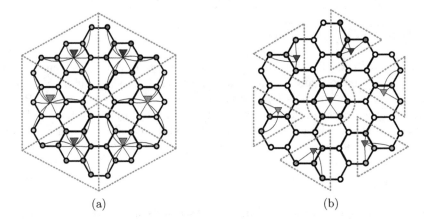

Fig. 4. 54-core HoneyWiN architecture (a) Completely homogeneous partitioning with six WRs (b) Partially heterogeneous partitioning with seven WRs

all the subnets are equipped with similar WRs. On the other hand, Fig. 4b illustrates a partially heterogeneous version of the same architecture. In this case, the middle subnet with more cores requires a stronger WR (i.e. a WR with more ports.)

Since in HoneyWiN, each CR has an additional port for wireless communication capabilities, multi-ports WR can be deployed to realize reconfigurable partitioning.

2.2 Routing

The proposed routing algorithm is based on a planar 3-axes coordinate system [27]. The X, Y and Z axes start from the center of the network and divide the topology into three regions. Packet traversal may happen via the wired network or the combination of wired and wireless networks. In each step, if the corresponding CRs of both source and destination cores are connected to two different WRs, express communication links are utilized to move the packet forward. In this case, long multi-hop wireline paths will be avoided. Otherwise, the algorithm adopts a turn model routing with wireline links [28]. In order to prevent deadlock in wired network, one out of six possible turns will be disabled in each clockwise and non-clockwise dependent cycles. Also, to prevent deadlock when packers are routed via both wired and wireless networks, in each input port of the routers two sets of Virtual Channels (VCs) are used [26]. One is for packet transmission from CR to WR while the other one is for packet transmission from WR/CR to CR. HoneyWiN routing algorithm is shown in Algorithm 1.

Algorithm 1. HoneyWiN routing algorithm

Input: Source router s and destination router d
Output: Routed packet
Initialization : n: Next router
$\qquad\qquad\qquad WR$: Set of wireless routers
$\qquad\qquad\qquad HC(a,b)$: Number of hops between routers a and b
while $s \neq d$ **do**
$\quad$ $\Delta X = d.X - s.X$;
$\quad$ $\Delta Y = d.Y - s.Y$;
$\quad$ $\Delta Z = d.Z - s.Z$;
$\quad$ $T = s.X + s.Y + s.Z$;
$\quad$ **if** $\exists i, j \in WR : HC(s,i) = 1 \wedge HC(d,j) = 1 \wedge i \neq j$ **then**
$\quad\quad$ Route packet from s to i via wired link ;
$\quad\quad$ Route packet from i to j via wireless link(s) ;
$\quad\quad$ Route packet from j to d via wired link ;
$\quad\quad$ break ;
$\quad$ **else if** $\Delta X < 0$ **then**
$\quad\quad$ $n = (s.X - 1, s.Y, s.Z)$;
$\quad$ **else if** $\Delta Z > 0$ **then**
$\quad\quad$ $n = (s.X, s.Y, s.Z + 1)$;
$\quad$ **else if** $T = 1 \wedge \Delta X > 0$ **then**
$\quad\quad$ $n = (s.X + 1, s.Y, s.Z)$;
$\quad$ **else if** $T = 1 \wedge \Delta Y > 0$ **then**
$\quad\quad$ $n = (s.X, s.Y + 1, s.Z)$;
$\quad$ **else if** $T = 1 \wedge \Delta Z > 0$ **then**
$\quad\quad$ $n = (s.X, s.Y, s.Z + 1)$;
$\quad$ **else if** $T = 2 \wedge \Delta X < 0$ **then**
$\quad\quad$ $n = (s.X - 1, s.Y, s.Z)$;
$\quad$ **else if** $T = 2 \wedge \Delta Y < 0$ **then**
$\quad\quad$ $n = (s.X, s.Y - 1, s.Z)$;
$\quad$ **else if** $T = 2 \wedge \Delta Z < 0$ **then**
$\quad\quad$ $n = (s.X, s.Y, s.Z - 1)$;
$\quad$ Route packet from s to n ;
$\quad$ $s = n$;

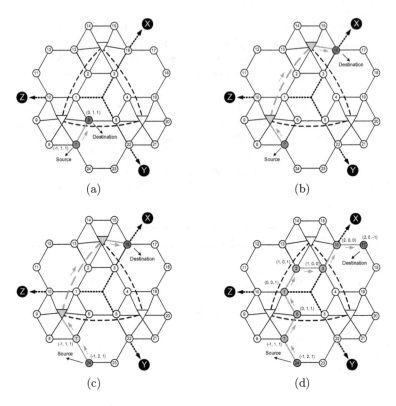

Fig. 5. Routing examples (a) 1-hop wireline (b) 3-hop wireline-wireless (c) 4-hop wireline-wireless (d) 7-hop wireline

Figure 5 shows different routing examples on the 24-core HoneyWiN architecture of Fig. 3a. As can be seen in Fig. 5a, the intra-partition communications will be done via wired links. On the other hand, for inter-partition communications, when the destination router is connected to a WR, the routing path will use both wired and wireless networks as shown in Figs. 5b and 5c. Otherwise, as depicted in Fig. 5d, only the wired network will be utilized. In other words, in order to prevent overutilization of WRs, only the packets in which their destination routers are connected to a WR are allowed to use the wireless network.

3   Experimental Results

For experiments, a SystemC-based cycle-accurate NoC simulator called Noxim [29] is used. Also, the energy analysis has been exploited by Orion 2.0 [30]. The comparisons are made between HoneyWiN and its mesh-based HWNoC counterpart for 24-core and 54-core networks. The simulation setup and traffics description are shown in Table 2.

Table 2. Simulation setup

(a) System configuration

Parameter	Value
Number of cores	24, 54
Number of WRs	2, 4, 6, 7, 8
Technology	65nm
Clock frequency	1 GHz
Switching mechanism	Wormhole
Radio access control	Token packet
Flit size	64 bits
Routing	XY, 3-axes
Wireless data rate	32 Gbps
Wireless communication	mm-Wave

(b) Traffic patterns

Pattern	Description
Uniform	Uniformly distributed traffic from source to destination
Transpose	Bit-permutation traffic using transpose matrix
Bit-reversal	Bit-permutation traffic from source to destination with reverse order address
Shuffle	Bit-permutation traffic from source to destination with shifted order address

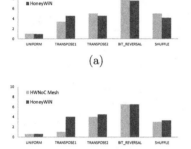

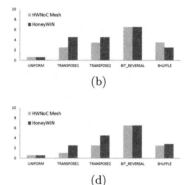

Fig. 6. Network throughput (flit/cycle) comparison for 24-core completely homogeneous system (a) Two WRs (b) Four WRs (c) Six WRs (d) Eight WRs

Network throughput comparisons for 24-core completely homogeneous system with two, four, six, and eight WRs with 0.1 injection rate are shown in Fig. 6. As can be seen, HoneyWiN has higher or equal network throughput in most of the benchmarks in comparison with mesh-based HWNoC.

In addition, Fig. 7 depicts the total energy consumption for the same architectures. As previously anticipated, HoneyWiN has less energy consumption than mesh-based HWNoC for all the benchmarks. Also according to Figs. 6 and 7, it seems that less number of WRs but stronger ones is more efficient in terms of both performance and energy consumption. However, the place and route stage for WRs with many ports is more challenging.

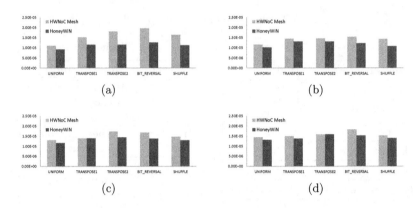

Fig. 7. Energy consumption (J) comparison for 24-core completely homogeneous system (a) Two WRs (b) Four WRs (c) Six WRs (d) Eight WRs

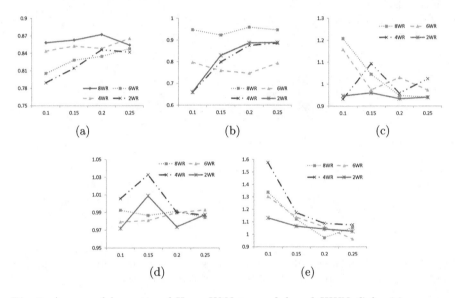

Fig. 8. Average delay ratio of HoneyWiN to mesh-based HWNoC for 24-core completely homogeneous system (a) Uniform (b) Transpose1 (c) Transpose2 (d) Bit-reversal (e) Shuffle

As another experiment, Fig. 8 shows the average delay ratio of HoneyWiN to mesh-based HWNoC by increasing injection rate. As can be seen, the delay ratio is less than one for most of the benchmarks. Also, generally HonwyWiN performs better than mesh-based HWNoC in high injection rates that makes this topology a suitable alternative for systems with frequent communications.

Moreover, throughput and energy consumption comparisons for 54-core completely homogeneous and partially heterogeneous systems are shown in Figs. 9 and 10 respectively. Although the average network throughput is almost the

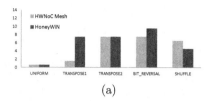
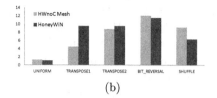

(a)   (b)

Fig. 9. Network throughput (flit/cycle) comparison for 54-core system (a) Completely homogeneous with six WRs (b) Partially heterogeneous with seven WRs

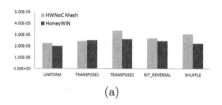
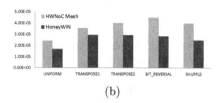

(a)   (b)

Fig. 10. Energy consumption (J) comparison for 54-core system (a) Completely homogeneous with six WRs (b) Partially heterogeneous with seven WRs

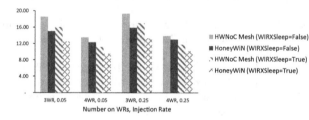

Fig. 11. Energy consumption (μJ) for 24-core system with/without power gating

same in both HoneyWiN and mesh-based HWNoC, more energy can be saved when HoneyWiN architecture is adopted. Besides, heterogeneous partitioning can provide more flexibility for application-specific architectures.

More energy can be saved by power-gating of WRs. In [31], a power gating method called WIRXSleep has been proposed to dynamically disable receiver modules and buffers of those WRs that will be not involved in any communication during the next forthcoming clock cycles. Figure 11 compares the energy saving for 24-core completely homogeneous systems with three (and four) WRs under 0.05 (and 0.25) injection rate for Transpose2 traffic pattern. As can be seen more energy can be saved when WIRXSleep is enabled.

4   Conclusion

In this paper, first we showed that mesh-based HWNoC does not always have the best performance and energy consumption in comparison with other 2-D topologies. Thus, it is a prejudice to assume that the grid-like mesh is the most stable network topology in emerging architectures. Then, we proposed a novel honeycomb-based HWNoC architecture called HoneyWiN along with its specific routing algorithm. The concepts of reconfigurable homogeneous/heterogeneous and complete/partial partitionings were also discussed. Finally, experimental results depicted that in comparison with mesh-based HWNoC, HoneyWiN saves more energy consumption (i.e. on average 17%) while still improves the network throughput (i.e. on average 10%). For future works, HoneyWiN-specific congestion-aware schemes [32] can be investigated.

References

1. Benini, L., De Micheli, G.: Networks on chips: a new SoC paradigm. Computer **35**(1), 70–78 (2002)
2. Karkar, A., Mak, T., Tong, K.F., Yakovlev, A.: A survey of emerging interconnects for on-chip efficient multicast and broadcast in many-cores. IEEE Circuits Syst. Mag. **16**(1), 58–72 (2016)
3. Rezaei, A., Zhao, D., Daneshtalab, M., Zhou, H.: Multi-objective task mapping approach for wireless NoC in dark silicon age. In: Euromicro International Conference on Parallel, Distributed and Network-based Processing (PDP), pp. 589–592 (2017)
4. Rezaei, A., Daneshtalab, M., Zhao, D., Modarressi, M.: SAMi: self-aware migration approach for congestion reduction in NoC-based MCSoC. In: IEEE International System-on-Chip Conference (SOCC), pp. 145–150 (2016)
5. Abadal, S., Cabellos-Aparicio, A., Alarcon, E., Torrellas, J.: WiSync: an architecture for fast synchronization through on-chip wireless communication. In: International Conference on Architectural Support for Programming Languages and Operating Systems (ASPLOS), pp. 3–17 (2016)
6. Gade, S.H., Deb, S.: HyWin: hybrid wireless NoC with sandboxed sub-networks for CPU/GPU architectures. IEEE Trans. Comput. **66**(7), 1145–1158 (2017)
7. Ganguly, A., Chang, K., Deb, S., Pande, P.P., Belzer, B., Teuscher, C.: Scalable hybrid wireless network-on-chip architectures for multicore systems. IEEE Trans. Comput. **60**(10), 1485–1502 (2011)
8. Mineo, A., Palesi, M., Ascia, G., Catania, V.: An adaptive transmitting power technique for energy efficient mm-wave wireless NoCs. In: Design, Automation and Test in Europe (DATE), p. 271 (2014)
9. Kawasaki, K., Akiyama, Y., Komori, K., Uno, M., Takeuchi, H., Itagaki, T., Hino, Y., Kawasaki, Y., Ito, K., Hajimiri, A.: A millimeter-wave intra-connect solution. IEEE J. Solid-State Circuits **45**(12), 2655–2666 (2010)
10. Yu, X., Sah, S.P., Rashtian, H., Mirabbasi, S., Pande, P.P., Heo, D.: A 1.2-pj/bit 16-gb/s 60-ghz ook transmitter in 65-nm cmos for wireless network-on-chip. IEEE Trans. Microw. Theory Tech. **62**(10), 2357–2369 (2014)
11. Wu, H., Nan, L., Tam, S.W., Hsieh, H.H., Jou, C., Reinman, G., Cong, J., Chang, M.C.F.: A 60GHz on-chip RF-interconnect with $\lambda/4$ coupler for 5Gbps bi-directional communication and multi-drop arbitration. In: IEEE Custom Integrated Circuits Conference (CICC), pp. 1–4 (2012)
12. Chang, M.F., Cong, J., Kaplan, A., Naik, M., Reinman, G., Socher, E., Tam, S.W.: CMP network-on-chip overlaid with multi-band RF-interconnect. In: International Symposium on High Performance Computer Architecture (HPCA), pp. 191–202 (2008)

13. Ito, H., Kimura, M., Miyashita, K., Ishii, T., Okada, K., Masu, K.: A bidirectional-and multi-drop-transmission-line interconnect for multipoint-to-multipoint on-chip communications. IEEE J. Solid-State Circuits **43**, 1020–1029 (2008)
14. Hu, J., Xu, J., Huang, M., Wu, H.: A 25-Gbps 8-ps/mm transmission line based interconnect for on-chip communications in multi-core chips. In: IEEE International Microwave Symposium Digest (IMS), pp. 1–4 (2013)
15. Nakajima, K., Maruyama, A., Kohtani, M., Sugiura, T., Otobe, E., Lee, J., Cho, S., Kwak, K., Lee, J., Yoshimasu, T., Fujishima, M.: 23Gbps 9.4pj/bit 80/100GHz band CMOS transceiver with on-board antenna for short-range communication. In: IEEE Asian Solid-State Circuits Conference (A-SSCC), pp. 173–176 (2014)
16. Byeon, C.W., Yoon, C.H., Park, C.S.: A 67-mw 10.7-Gb/s 60-GHz OOK CMOS transceiver for short-range wireless communications. IEEE Trans. Microw. Theory Tech. **61**, 3391–3401 (2013)
17. Karkar, A., Al-Dujaily, R., Yakovlev, A., Tong, K., Mak, T.: Surface wave communication system for on-chip and off-chip interconnects. In: International Workshop on Network on Chip Architectures (NoCArc), pp. 11–16 (2012)
18. Liang, Y., Yu, H., Zhao, J., Yang, W., Wang, Y.: An energy efficient and low cross-talk CMOS sub-THz i/o with surface-wave modulator and interconnect. In: IEEE/ACM International Symposium on Low Power Electronics and Design (ISLPED), pp. 110–115 (2015)
19. Hanson, G.W.: Fundamental transmitting properties of carbon nanotube antennas. IEEE Trans. Antennas Propag. **53**(11), 3426–3435 (2005)
20. Saxena, S., Manur, D.S., Shamim, M.S., Ganguly, A.: A folded wireless network-on-chip using graphene based THz-band antennas. In: International Conference on Nanoscale Computing and Communication (NanoCom), p. 29 (2017)
21. Balasubramaniam, S., Kangasharju, J,.: Realizing the internet of nano things: challenges, solutions, and applications. Computer **46**(2), 62–68 (2013)
22. Vien, Q.T., Agyeman, M.O., Le, T.A., Mak, T.: On the nanocommunications at THz band in Graphene-enabled wireless network-on-chip. In: Mathematical Problems in Engineering, Article ID 9768604 (2017)
23. Hu, W.H., Wang, C., Bagherzadeh, N.: Design and analysis of a mesh-based wireless network-on-chip. J. Supercomput. **71**(8), 2830–2846 (2015)
24. DiTomaso, D., Kodi, A., Kaya, S., Matolak, D.: iWISE: inter-router wireless scalable express channels for network-on-chips (NoCs) architecture. In: Annual Symposium on High Performance Interconnects (HOTI), pp. 11–18 (2011)
25. More, A., Taskin, B.: A unified design methodology for a hybrid wireless 2-D NoC. In: IEEE International Symposium on Circuits and Systems (ISCAS), pp. 640–643 (2012)
26. Rezaei, A., Daneshtalab, M., Safaei, F., Zhao, D.: Hierarchical approach for hybrid wireless network-on-chip in many-core era. Comput. Electr. Eng. **51**(C), 225–234 (2016)
27. Stojmenovic, I.: Honeycomb networks: topological properties and communication algorithms. IEEE Trans. Parallel Distrib. Syst. **8**(10), 1036–1042 (1997)
28. Yin, A.W., Xu, T.C., Liljeberg, P., Tenhunen, H.: Explorations of honeycomb topologies for network-on-chip. In: IFIP International Conference on Network and Parallel Computing (NPC), pp. 73–79 (2009)
29. Catania, V., Mineo, A., Monteleone, S., Palesi, M., Patti, D.: Cycle-accurate network on chip simulation with noxim. ACM Trans. Model. Comput. Simul. **27**(1), 4 (2016)

30. Kahng, A.B., Li, B., Peh, L.S., Samadi, K.: Orion 2.0: a power-area simulator for interconnection networks. IEEE Trans. Very Large Scale Integr. VLSI Syst. **20**(1), 191–196 (2012)
31. Catania, V., Mineo, A., Monteleone, S., Palesi, M., Patti, D.: Energy efficient transceiver in wireless network on chip architectures. In: Design, Automation and Test in Europe (DATE), pp. 1321–1326 (2016)
32. Rezaei, A., Daneshtalab, M., Palesi, M., Zhao, D.: Efficient congestion-aware scheme for wireless on-chip networks. In: Euromicro International Conference on Parallel, Distributed, and Network-Based Processing (PDP), pp. 742–749 (2016)

Reconfigurable and Adaptive Architectures

Fast Partial Reconfiguration on SRAM-Based FPGAs: A Frame-Driven Routing Approach

Luca Sterpone$^{(\boxtimes)}$ and Ludovica Bozzoli

Politecnico di Torino, Turin, Italy
{luca.sterpone,ludovica.bozzoli}@polito.it

Abstract. Reconfigurable SRAM-based FPGAs are increasingly attractive for high performance reconfigurable computing cores due to their flexibility, upgradability and computational capabilities. In general, Partial Reconfiguration (PR) improves the reconfigurable computing paradigm due to the possibility to modify only a portion of the FPGA's configuration memory, which results in reduced reconfiguration time. However, the speed-up gain SRAM-based FPGAs are able to achieve relies on the efficiency of the mechanism adopted to load frames in the FPGA's configuration memory. Despite the advantages of configuration memory Partial Reconfiguration, the lack of tools and design software to implement efficient frame-oriented configuration makes PR performance less powerful then expectation. In this work, we propose an approach to reduce the reconfiguration time of routing resources exploiting a frame-driven routing algorithm able to drastically reduce the number of configuration memory frames used in the design. The advantage of the proposed solution has been applied to several benchmark circuits implemented with our routing algorithm on a Xilinx Kintex-7 SRAM-based FPGA. Experimental results shown a reduction of the used configuration frames of more than 40% on the average and a measured reconfiguration time reduced of more than 35% with respect to traditional reconfiguration approaches.

Keywords: SRAM-based FPGAs · Partial reconfiguration
Reconfiguration time · Routing algorithm

1 Introduction

Nowadays Field Programmable Gate Arrays (FPGAs) using Static RAM (SRAM) configuration memory represent the most suitable devices used within High Performance Reconfigurable Computing (HPRC) systems [1]. In particular, their capability to be configured and remotely modified makes them flexible in the hardware design phases. Beside this, Reconfigurable FPGAs allow to make complex circuits for different application fields, ranging from video processing systems to fault tolerant self-reconfigurable hardware [2].

One of the key features provided by SRAM-based FPGAs is the Partial Reconfiguration (PR), which consists in reconfiguring one or more parts of the FPGA after the start-up configuration [3]. Several modern SRAM-based FPGAs (i.e., manufactured by Altera and Xilinx) support partial reconfiguration allowing the user to select, during

© Springer International Publishing AG, part of Springer Nature 2018
N. Voros et al. (Eds.): ARC 2018, LNCS 10824, pp. 319–330, 2018.
https://doi.org/10.1007/978-3-319-78890-6_26

the design phase, the area of the device that can be configured at run-time, while the other device portion remain unchanged. Due to the growing availability of partially reconfigurable FPGAs, different configuration interfaces were deployed to load the partial bitstream from a non-volatile memory into the FPGA's configuration memory. Typical interfaces are the Serial Configuration Mode and JTAG Partial Reconfiguration, which have a slow transmission speed due to the interfaces hardware characteristics. Faster interfaces are the parallel port configuration interfaces (i.e., Xilinx SelectMAP) and the FPGA internal configuration approach, which exploits the available Internal Configuration Access Port (ICAP) [4, 5].

Several techniques were developed to manage reconfiguration considering that the reconfiguration time is directly proportional to the number of downloaded frames. Scrubbing is the classic method adopted when the whole FPGA needs to be reconfigured; in this case, all the configuration memory frames are re-written. On the other hand, the typical partial reconfiguration approach allows configuring only the configuration frames belonging to the target Reconfigurable Region (RR). On both cases, all the configuration frames are transmitted into the FPGA's configuration memory independently from their content: thus, even empty frames are downloaded. A Capillary (C) approach has been proposed [9] in order to download exclusively the used frames, reducing the reconfiguration time. A recent approach [6] proposed an implementation flow capable to reduce the programmed FPGA interconnection network thus reducing the overall programmed area.

In this paper, we propose a novel approach to reduce the reconfiguration time by acting on the configuration bitstream frame coding relative to the FPGA interconnection network. The approach is based on a routing algorithm that routes a circuit selecting the interconnections that minimize the total number of configured frames. To achieve this result, we implemented a tool to decode the FPGA Programmable Interconnect Points (PIPs) bitstream coding and we generated a database containing the identification of the configuration memory frames and bits used to identify each PIP in a given coordinate of the FPGA. Then, we developed a routing algorithm able to select the interconnections having overlapping frames coding, thus minimizing the total number of programmed frames.

The main scientific innovation of the paper relies on realizing the first frame-driven routing algorithm. In details, the developed routing algorithm routes a net adopting a typical pathfinder method [7] interpolated with the routing segment frame coding to minimize the frames usage. Thus, each PIP is selected not only by timing and congestion minimization goals but also by minimizing number of programmed frames.

We experimentally evaluated our approach comparing the reconfiguration time of five different benchmark circuits using the internal configuration mechanism. We observed a reduction of 40% of the used frames on the average, and we measured a reduction of the reconfiguration time of 35%.

The paper organization is the following: Sect. 2 describes the background on the FPGA topology and configuration memory; Sect. 3 describes the configuration memory decoding method and Sect. 4 presents the developed frame-driven routing algorithm. Experimental results are presented in Sect. 5 while Conclusions and Future works are shown in Sect. 6.

2   Background on the FPGA Configuration Memory

The content of the configuration memory of a SRAM-based FPGA is generated by synthesis and implementation tools and it is coded in a binary file called bitstream, which is loaded inside the FPGA configuration memory at the first programming phase. The bitstream is organized in a regular structure of various bit arrays [8] spanning in vertical the whole device area. Configuration memory bits are arranged in frames that are tiled about the device. The frames are the smallest addressable configuration memory segment for reconfiguration.

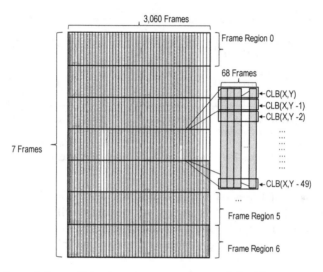

Fig. 1. Overview of the configuration memory structure of the Kintex7-XC7K325T Xilinx SRAM-based FPGA.

As illustrated in Fig. 1, the configuration memory is a rectangular array of bits, organized into several rectangular sub-regions, corresponding to a given Configurable Logic Blocks (CLBs) within the FPGA array. The regular organization of the resources inside the FPGA array is directly translated in the configuration memory structure, which shows the same regularity.

When the Xilinx Kintex-7 XC7K325T is considered, the CLB array is organized in a matrix of 45 × 350 tiles, while the configuration memory is composed of 101 32-bit words (3,232 bits in total) organized in 3,060 frames on the X-axis of the devices and 14 frames regions on the Y-axis. The resources controlled by the configuration memory bits are related to the bitstream physical position. Thus, in every array other fixed sub-regions corresponding to a given type of resource can be identified. In fact, the position of the bits that control the storage, the logic elements and interconnection resources is almost periodic inside the configuration memory. The architectural portion of the logic and interconnection structure is illustrated in Fig. 2, where it is described the FPGA basic unit having on the sides left and right routing matrices of PIPs and in the middle the CLBs containing the hardwired logic, LUTs and Flip-Flops (FFs).

Kintex-7 Basic Unit: Interconnection Tiles (Left & Right) their relative LUTs Slices:

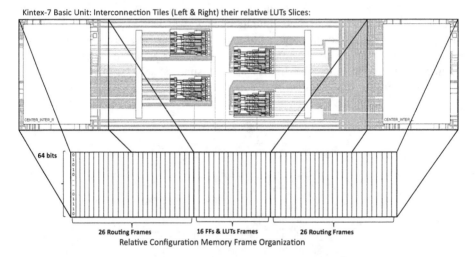

Fig. 2. Xilinx Kintex-7 slice topology and configuration memory overview.

The entire basic unit uses 64 bits in vertical that span over 68 frames along the horizontal axes. In details, 52 frames are used for the routing PIPs while the remaining 16 for LUTs and Control Logic. Thus, considering the 3,232 bits of each frame, it is possible to deduce that each frame is crossing 50 basic units along the same Y-axes.

3 Bitstream and Frame Decoding

The implementation of an enhanced reconfiguration mechanism to reduce the number of frames downloaded into the FPGA configuration memory requires a detailed knowledge of the bitstream format. Unfortunately, the lack of information from the vendors about the details of their FPGA configuration memory and the overall FPGA architecture is still high. Thus, in order to achieve this information, an in-depth analysis of the Xilinx bitstream format has been performed.

Starting from the available documentation from Xilinx and from some custom assumptions about the bitstream format a database to map bitstream has been built [9].

A previously developed approach to decipher the bitstream adopted a physical native description methodology to extract the configuration memory location coordinates of the used SRAM-based FPGA [10], however this methodology is not applicable to state of the art architecture embedding reconfigurable features such as Xilinx Virtex-5 and Kintex-7 families since it is not anymore supported by vendor tools. Other approaches are based on the Xilinx Description Language (XDL) [11] and cross-correlation algorithm to reconstruct the Xilinx bitstream provide good results but also an extremely high computational effort [8].

The methodology we developed is based on the flow diagram shown in Fig. 3. It starts extracting from the target FPGA architecture all the Logic and Programmable Interconnect Points (PIPs) labels, which are contained within the Xilinx Design Language Routing and CLB file (XDLRC) generated by Xilinx vendor tools. The obtained PIP list contains all the interconnection points of the FPGA architecture and it cannot be directly processed since the elaboration time will be impracticable. Since the PIP list contains several replicas of the same PIP but in different FPGA array positions and the configuration memory architecture is regular, the All PIPs list is pruned generating the Essential PIPs (i.e., a Xilinx Kintex-7 XC7K325T device contains about 124 million PIPs, while after pruning it consists of 21,081 PIPs) [5]. The generation of the reference PIP configuration memory coordinate database is then performed by the decoding task, which consists of a set of TCL scripts executed within the vendor tool environment. This task sequentially elaborates each essential PIP generating a configuration memory bitstream where a unique PIP is programmed and extracting the reference configuration memory coordinates in terms of complete Frame Address Register (FAR) information.

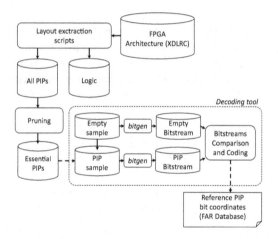

Fig. 3. Overview of the flow diagram used to generate the Frame Address Register (FAR) database of the reference PIP coordinates.

4   The Proposed Method

The main idea behind our approach is to reduce the reconfiguration time of the partial reconfiguration process on SRAM-based FPGAs by exploiting a frame routing policy in order to reroute FPGA connections using the minimum number of frames. In this section, we first describe the key concept, which relies on an in-depth analysis of the bitstream database with respect to the routing resources. Later, we detail the developed frame-driven router presenting the main algorithm routines.

4.1 Frame Routing Policy

After an in-depth analysis of the bitstream database we found out that the bits used to configure each routing resources belong to a variable number of frames and these frames are often shared between different resources, as it is shown in the examples in Fig. 4.

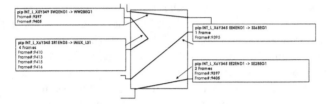

Fig. 4. The three main types of Programmable Interconnect Points (PIPs) of a routing switch matrix: 1, 2 or 4 programmed frames.

In general, the number of bits used to manage the configuration of a PIP it is not fixed. For each PIP, these bits are distributed on 1 up to 5 different frames of the 26 used to configure a given switch matrix. Considering that each frame spans in vertical on 50 CLBs for each *Frame Region*, a PIP can share frames both with PIPs of the same switch matrix and with PIPs of the other switch matrices, which belong to the same Frame Region.

Starting from this key concept, we observed that it is possible to reduce the number of frames to be configured by locally changing the routing topology of a circuit nets and maintaining the original placement of other physical resources (e.g., LUTs, FFs and IOs).

Considering these backgrounds, we identify three possible optimizations rules that can be applied during the routing algorithm phase:

- **Optimization A** occurs when there are no used frames in the current switch matrix or in the whole *Frame Region*. In this situation, the optimization relies on the choice of the PIP that uses the minimum number of frames in absolute. In Fig. 5, on the left, it is provided an example of two PIPs having the same behavior since both of them are connecting a wire coming from the switch matrix of one position south with the *IMUX_L14* of the current switch matrix. Their only difference between the two PIPs resides in the number of frames used to be configured. Thus, selecting *pip INT_L_0Y349 NN2END3 - > IMUX_L14,* it is possible to save two frames. We labeled *Absolute Routing Policy* the selection of a PIP made only considering the number of frame.
- **Optimization B** occurs when two or more PIPs in the same net belong to the same Frame Region. This happens when the switch matrices they belong to are on the same X coordinate and the Y position is instead part of the same Frame Region. In this situation is highly probable that there are resources in the same net that share at least one frame. In the best case some resources can even share all the frames, as in

the example of Fig. 5, right side. In this situation, to select the PIP with respect to the shared frames will be used what we labeled the *Relative Routing Policy*.

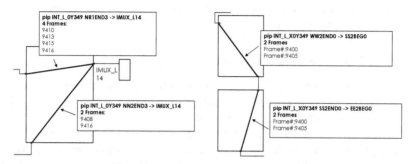

Fig. 5. Left: Optimization A: the frames are not used in prior routing phases. A PIP is selected with the absolute minimal number of frames. Right: Optimization B: two PIPs localized on the same X coordinate and within the same Frame Region. A PIP is selected in order to overlap the previously used frames.

- **Optimization C** occurs when the current switch matrix has not shared frames with any resources of a considered net but there are already programmed frames within the same Frame Region used by previously routed nets of the design. If the resources belong to the same switch matrix, they can even share several bits of the same frame, as in the example in Fig. 6. In this situation, to select the PIP and minimizing the overall number of programmed frames, will be used again the *Relative Routing Policy*.

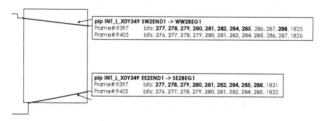

Fig. 6. Optimization C: two PIPs localized on the same X and Y coordinates. PIPs are selected overlapping used frames.

Please consider that, nevertheless optimizations A, B and C are conceptually different, from the practical point of view they can be managed in the same way, since every time a new PIP has to be selected by the router, the algorithm in any case minimize the overall number of frames in the Frame Region. Therefore, the developed frame-driven routing algorithm performs the same computation for both the routing policies:

- *Absolute Routing Policy*: among all the available PIPs with the same behavior, the one that uses less frames is selected.
- *Relative Routing Policy*: among all the available PIPs with the same behavior and considering the used frames in the same Frame region on the same X coordinate, the PIP using less additional frames is selected.

4.2   Frame-Driven Routing Algorithm

The goal of the frame-driven routing algorithm is to complete all the routing of a circuit while minimizing the number of programmed frames among the SRAM-based FPGA *Frame Regions*. The algorithm starts by reading a placement solution (P_{sol}) of the circuit generated by available commercial tools (i.e., Xilinx Vivado toolchain) consisting in logic nodes, their interconnections and the Input/Output pins. The placement information are extracted from Vivado using TCL scripts and transaleted in a format suitable for our Frame-driven Router. The Vivado Placement solution is taken as starting point in order to exploit as much as possible the optimizations performed by the vendor tool. In this manner, the routing frame optimization will not introduce any modification in the topology of the circuit, minimizing its impact on the design performances achieved with vendor tool implementation policies.

The main core of the algorithm relies on a pathfinder router interpolated with a frame filtering optimization process.

The frame-driven router algorithm consists in five phases, as illustrated in Fig. 7.

```
Psol = Placement Solution
//1.Initialization Phase
Rsol = {0};
∀ X,G ∈{MAX_X,MAX_G} → Vfid (X,G)[fSM] = {0};
//2.Nets Extraction Phase
∀ net ∈ Psol → list [net];
//3.Routing
for n ∈ net : Ve(S,D) = listSD[net]{
    for D ∈ E(S,D) : (S,Di){
        STMP = S;
        DTMP = S;
        while (DTMP ≠ Di){
DTMP = pathfinder(STMP, D);
setPIP = list(STMP, DTMP);
//4.Frame Filtering Optimizations
Wmax = fSM;
∀ PIP ∈ setPIP do{
    VfID_TMP[fSM] = VfID (XStmp,GStmp) or VDB_PIP(PIP);
            H = card(VfID_TMP[fSM] xor VfID(XStmp,GStmp));
            if (H < Wmax){
                Wmax = H;
                VfID_BEST = VfID_TMP[fSM];
                PIPBEST = PIP;
            }
        }
        //5.Update Routes and Frames
        Rsol = update_route (PIPBEST);
        VfID(XStmp,GStmp)[fSM] = VfID_BEST;
        STMP = DTMP;
        }// PIPi is routed
    }// S-Di is routed
}// Net is routed
// Circuit is routed
```

Fig. 7. The Frame-driven routing algorithm for programmed frames minimization.

At the initialization phase, the algorithm initializes the storage array of the elaboration, which consists in the Routing Solution (R_{sol}) as an empty graph, and the Flag Frame Identifier Vector (V_{fid}) as null flag for each location. In details, the Flag Frame Identifier Vector, is a vector of logic flags that labels the usage (*1*) or not usage (*0*) of the corresponding frame in the configuration memory. For this reason, the V_{fid} is dimensioned to contain a flag for each unique frame of the FPGA's configuration memory related to the routing resources (X, G: X is the coordinate of the frame along the *x* axes and G is the coordinate along the *y* axes of the configuration memory).

The second phase consists in the extraction of the `list[net]` of all the nets of the circuit. Each net is defined by means of its source S and its destinations D_i since both single and multi-drain nets are considered.

The third phase consists in the routing of each couple (S,D_i) of a given net. The routing is based on a classical pathfinder method [12]: the path between S and (D_i) is reached step by step, considering at each iteration a set of intermediate destinations D_{TMP}, which are the ones that can be reached exploiting a single routing resource available in S. When a D_{TMP} is validated it became the new source S for the next iteration.

At each iteration the function `pathfinder()` returns a temporary destination (D_{TMP}). The function `list()` generates then a list of available routing PIPs that connect S_{TMP} and D_{TMP} Once the list set_{PIP} is generated, the fourth phase starts. The PIP that minimizes the number of frames will be the one that have the lower weight in terms of additional frames needed to be programmed. Thus, at the beginning of each Frame Filtering Optimization phase, the weight (W_{max}) is initialized at the maximum value f_{SM}, which is equal to 26 (i.e. the total number of frames in each switch matrix).

The PIP selection is performed with the following steps. At first, for each PIP extracted from set_{PIP} the vector V_{fID_TMP} is obtained as the logic *or* between the vector storing the current utilization of the frame region the PIP belongs ($V_{fID}(X_s, G_s)$) and the vector storing the frame utilization relative to the PIP itself (V_{fPIP}). The logic *xor* between VfID_TMP and $V_{fID}(X_s, G_s)$ is computed and the number (H) of additional frames introduced by the usage of the PIP under evaluation is obtained as the cardinality `card()` of *xor* result. If this value H is lower than the current W_{MAX}, it became the new W_{MAX} and the current PIP is saved as the temporary best solution. It is important to notice that from the algorithm point of view, the weight H is calculated in the same manner for both *Absolute Routing Policy* and *Relative Routing Policy*. Frame Filtering Optimization phase is summarized with an example in Fig. 8. Once all the PIPs are analyzed, the PIP stored in PIP_{BEST} and its relative frame coding (stored in V_{fID_BEST}) will be the ones that minimize the number of frame for the current set_{PIP}.

In the fifth and last phase of the algorithm the selection performed in the previous phase is validated and added to the global Routing Solution with the function `update_route()`. The V_{fid} flag vector is updated with the new programmed frames. Phase 3, 4 and 5 will be repeated until the circuit is fully routed.

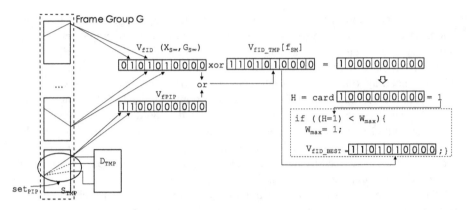

Fig. 8. An example of the Frame-driven routing algorithm. In details, the execution of the frame filtering optimization phase.

5 Experimental Results

The proposed frame-driven routing algorithm has been developed as a software tool integrated with the Xilinx Vivado IDE 2017.2 and capable to elaborate the configuration memory bitstream of the Xilinx Kintex7 XC7K325T device. In order to verify the effectiveness and the capability of our approach, we evaluated it on five different benchmark circuits implemented on the Kintex-7 XC7K325T device. The five circuits correspond to three ITC'99 benchmarks [13], the miniMIPS processor and a Cordic Core. The characteristics of the circuits implemented on the Kintex-7 device are illustrated in Table 1. The circuits have been implemented using a timing constraints of 100 MHz, which corresponds to the working frequency provided by our Kintex-7 evaluation board.

Table 1. Benchmark circuits characteristics implemented with Xilinx Vivado 2017.02.

Circuit	LUTs [#]	FFs [#]	Nets [#]	PIPs [#]	IOs [#]
b05	84	34	110	1,596	39
b12	223	119	242	3,776	13
b14	2,123	219	2,103	29,083	88
Cordic_r2p	949	1,001	1,120	29,163	74
miniMIPS	2,712	2,000	4,797	72,987	175

The circuits have been also re-routed using the proposed approach in order to compare the routing frames used, the overall reconfiguration time and resource distribution (i.e. topology of the implemented circuit) maintain the same clock frequency.

The results of the circuits re-routed with our approach are illustrated in Table 2. It is possible to notice a slight increasing of the number of programmed PIPs but it can be considered negligible, since it do not introduce a modification on the working

Table 2. Percentage of saved frames, PIPs and working frequency of our Frame-driven routing approach

Circuit	Saved frames [%]	PIPs [#]
b05	38.3	1,654
b12	38.8	3,884
b14	37.2	28,054
Cordic_r2p	41.3	29,245
miniMIPS	35.3	73,105

frequency. This is coherent with the fact that the placement constraints are the one set with Vivado and, thus, the Frame-driven routing do not modify circuit topology. It is possible to notice that the average of additional PIPs introduced by our routing policy it is around 100. This amount became almost infinitesimal for bigger circuits: for mini-MIPS it represents 0.16% of routing resources. Supposing these resources do not belongs to critical paths, the performance of the rerouted circuits can be totally equivalent to the original ones.

The re-routed circuits benefit of a high average percentage of frame saving that ranges from 35% to 41%, while number of LUTs, FFs, Nets and IOs remain clearly unchanged.

Finally, we evaluated the overall reconfiguration time characteristics using an ad-hoc reconfigurable core implemented on the K7XC325T device and using the internal reconfiguration with four different approaches: Scrubbing technique, Recon-figurable Region (RR) Reconfiguration, Capillary Approach and the Frame-driven Approach. In the Table 3, the comparison between the reconfiguration time required for each approach is reported confirming again the efficiency of the developed Frame-driven solution.

Table 3. Reconfiguration time comparison [ms].

Circuit	Scrubbing	RR	C approach	Our approach
b05	43.27	0.32	0.18	0.11
b12	43.27	0.27	0.24	0.15
b14	43.27	3.67	1.81	1.14
Cord_r2c	43.27	1.26	0.71	0.42
miniMIPS	43.27	12.60	2.57	1.66

6 Conclusions and Future Works

In this paper, we developed a novel approach to reduce the partial reconfiguration time by reducing the number of configured frames of the FPGA interconnection network. To reach this goal, we were able to decode the configuration memory frames and to develop a new frame-driven routing algorithm. The algorithm routes a circuit selecting the interconnections that minimize the number of globally configured frames that are downloaded within the FPGA configuration memory during the partial reconfiguration process. Experimental results on a various set of circuit benchmarks demonstrate the feasibility of our approach, showing a reduction of the reconfiguration time around 35% on the average with respect to traditional Reconfigurable Regions approach without any impact on the constrained frequency.

As future work, we plan to investigate the performances of larger circuit to confirm the hypothesis that the frames saving is directly proportional to the number of frames in the design. Then we will investigate different placement solutions and different timing constraints to further characterize design routing congestion.

References

1. El-Ghazawi, T., El-Araby, E., Huang, M., Gaj, K., Kindratenko, V., Buell, D.: The promise of high-performance reconfigurable computing. Computer **41**(2), 67–76 (2008)
2. Pham, H.-M., Pillement, S., Piestrak, S.J.: Low-overhead fault-tolerance technique for a dynamically reconfigurable softcore processor. IEEE Trans. Comput. **62**(6), 1179–1192 (2013)
3. Ichinomiya, Y., Usagawa, S., Amagasaki, M., Iida, M., Kuga, M., Sueyoshi, T.: Designing flexible reconfigurable regions to relocate partial bitstreams. In: IEEE 20th International Symposium on Field-Programmable Custom Computing Machines, pp. 241–241 (2012)
4. Xilinx INC: Virtex-5 FPGA Configuration User Guide (UG191) (2012)
5. Heiner, J., Collins, N., Wirthlin, M.: Fault tolerant ICAP controller for high-reliable internal scrubbing. In: IEEE Aerospace Conference, pp. 1–10 (2008)
6. Vansteenkiste, E., Al Farisi, B., Brunee, K., Stroobandt, D.: TPaR: place and route tools for the dynamic reconfiguration of the FPGA's interconnect network. IEEE Trans. Comput. - Aided Des. Integr. Circ. Syst. **33**(3), 370–383 (2014)
7. Cong, J., Kahng, A.B., Leung, K.S.: Efficient algorithms for the minimum shortest part Steiner arborescence problem with applications to VLSI physical design. IEEE Trans. Comput. -Aided Des. Integr. Circ. Syst. **17**(1), 24–39 (1998)
8. Pham, K.D., Horta, E., Koch, D.: BITMAN: a tool and API for FPGA bitstream manipulations. In: IEEE Design, Automation and Test in Europe, pp. 894–897 (2017)
9. Xilinx User Guide: 7 Series FPGAs Configuration. UG470, v1.11, pp. 1–176, 27 September 2016
10. Wang, X.-F., Si, S.-H., Gao, C., Huang, J.: A method of FPGA interconnect resources testing by using XDL-based configuration. In: IEEE Prognostics and System Health Management Conference, pp. 203–207 (2014)
11. Beckhoff, C., Koch, D., Torresen, J.: The Xilinx Design Language (XDL): tutorial and use cases. In: 6th International Workshop on Reconfigurable Communication-Centric Systems-on-Chip (ReCoSoC), pp. 1–8 (2011)
12. McMurchie, L., Ebeling, C.: PathFinder: a negotiation-based performance-driven router for FPGAs. In: ACM Symposium on Field-Programmable Gate Arrays (1995)
13. ITC 1999: ITC 1999 benchmark home page. http://www.cerc.utecas.edulitc99-benchmark slbench.html

A Dynamic Partial Reconfigurable Overlay Framework for Python

Benedikt Janßen$^{(\boxtimes)}$ ⓘ, Florian Kästner, Tim Wingender, and Michael Huebner

Chair for Embedded Systems for Information Technology,
Ruhr-University Bochum, Bochum, Germany
{benedikt.janssen,florian.kaestner,tim.wingender,michael.huebner}@rub.de
https://www.esit.ruhr-uni-bochum.de

Abstract. Dynamic Partial Reconfigurable (DPR) systems enable the exchange of system modules during runtime, and thus, an application-specific optimization of the system. However, the development of these systems, their modules, and the integration is a complex task. In this paper, we present our framework for DPR overlays. With our approach we enable a description of the overlay, and thus the hardware, via software. Based on the software description, our framework assembles the overlay in the field. Therefore, pre-implemented processing modules are loaded into reconfigurable partitions via DPR. The concept of DPR overlays is similar to pre-compiled libraries in the software domain, which dynamically loaded into memory during runtime. The framework is based on PYNQ, and a Yocto-based tool-flow. For the evaluation of our framework, we show the implementation of an artificial neural network.

Keywords: Dynamic Partial Reconfiguration · FPGA · Overlays
Python

1 Introduction

With Field-Programmable Gate Arrays (FPGAs) it becomes possible to optimize application execution in the field by adapting system components during runtime. Application execution based on application-specific hardware accelerators on FPGAs can improve computational performance, as well as the performance per watt ratio. FPGA overlays are an approach of the FPGA community to overcome the complex development of application-specific hardware accelerators. An overlay is a FPGA configuration that is tailored for a limited family of applications and often programmable up to a certain degree. Thereby, it becomes possible to increase the flexibility and support a larger set of applications. However, the flexibility comes with drawbacks that depend on the application, as well as the overlay implementation.

In order to benefit from highly optimized hardware implementations, we propose to assemble overlays in the field, thus a dynamic generation. Therefore, the flexibility depends on the available resources the overlay is assembled from,

© Springer International Publishing AG, part of Springer Nature 2018
N. Voros et al. (Eds.): ARC 2018, LNCS 10824, pp. 331–342, 2018.
https://doi.org/10.1007/978-3-319-78890-6_27

rather than the degree of programmability. For the assembly, we use Dynamic Partial Reconfiguration (DPR) which enables a Reconfigurable Partition (RP) based exchange of hardware accelerators. Within the flow these DPR hardware accelerators are often entitled as Reconfigurable Module (RM). Therefore, partial bitstreams, targeting RPs, define the overlay functionality. In comparison with the software domain, our approach is similar to highly optimized pre-compiled libraries, written by experts to use specific processor features.

This work is based on the work presented in [1]. Our new framework enables hardware developers to package different versions of DPR designs, not supporting a specific application, but a set of related applications. Moreover, our framework enables software developers to define the functionality of these DPR overlays inside their software application. From the perspective of a hardware developer it complements the traditional, and HLS-based, development flow. From the perspective of a software developer it is a counter draft to HLS-based development flows, that moves the requirement hardware knowledge to the hardware developer.

In the following Sect. 2 we present our concept, as well as an overview of our implementation. A more detailed view onto the implementation is given in Sect. 3. We present the results of our evaluation in Sect. 4, and list the related work in Sect. 5. Finally, Sect. 6 concludes this article and gives an outlook to future work.

2   Concept

Our framework concept is based on the Xilinx PYNQ project [8] (PYNQ). Therefore, we target a Python-based hardware/software codesign on a Xilinx Zynq-7000. All Zynq devices consists of an ARM-A9-based hard-core processing system (PS), and an FPGA, called Programmable Logic (PL). The goal of our framework is to provide an interface between software and hardware developers. Software developers are enabled to execute functions in hardware, by selecting functions for acceleration, as well as mark these functions as being pipelined. In contrast to static overlays and overlays based on programmable processing elements, we propose DPR overlays. With DPR we enable assembling the overlay in the field, according to the software developer's application.

To overcome the compatibility issue between the static design, as well as the RMs, we propose to package pre-implemented soft-core processing modules from a common application domain and common resource requirements into a Python package. For instance, image filters from the video processing domain. This approach is similar to pre-compiled shared libraries from the software domain and has two main advantages. First, the concept of packages is already existing within the Python software environment, and it is possible to create hybrid Python packages consisting of software and hardware. Second, the hardware developer creates an overlay with different configurations all depending on the same static design. Thereby, we enable hybrid Python packages with hardware accelerators that can be applied to a specific type or set of problems. At the same time, the development of the static design is simplified as all hardware modules have similar requirements, and the number of partial bitstreams is kept lowered compared to a "one DPR overlay fits all" approach.

On the software side, the applications are executed by the CPython interpreter, running inside a Linux operating system on the PS. On the hardware side, the applications are accelerated by hardware modules, residing inside RPs in the PL, connected via Direct Memory Access (DMA) to the global memory. By the time this article was written, PYNQ supports only the PYNQ-Z1 board officially. As a first step to generalize our framework and loosen the dependency on PYNQ, we created a Yocto-based Linux system. Thereby, we enable a recipe-based build process of the Linux system, that can target different boards. The internal communication between the system components is built around the main memory. The data resides in the global DDR-SDRAM in physical contiguous arrays. Within our hardware architecture, dedicated DMA cores transport the data to and from the hardware accelerators. These hardware accelerators are implemented as RM, residing inside the RPs. An overview of the system architecture is given in Fig. 1. The depicted hardware and software architecture are explained in more detail in the following sections.

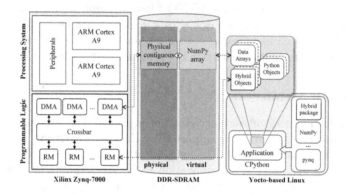

Fig. 1. Framework hardware/software architecture overview.

3   Framework Implementation

Figure 1 gives an overview of the framework hardware and software architecture. The communication is memory-mapped and large chunks of data are exchanged via the global DDR-SDRAM. The hardware architecture is built around DMA and AXI Stream crossbar IP cores. The DMA cores handle data transfers between the RMs and the memory. Through the crossbar, a flexible routing of the data between DMA cores and RM is enabled. Thereby, we can map batched software functions more efficient in hardware. The software architecture is based on a Linux system that itself is based on the Yocto Project [9] (Yocto). The Linux system contains the CPython interpreter, as well as the essential components of the PYNQ's Python package, and Jupyter Notebook. The interface between the software and the hardware domain is based on PYNQ's Python package 'pynq'.

3.1   Linux System

The core components of Yocto that are used to build the Linux system are 'Bit-Bake', 'OpenEmbedded-Core' and 'Poky'. BitBake schedules the tasks that are specified in a format called recipes, which define how the Linux system is build. OpenEmbedded-Core provides commonly used recipes and other configuration data, grouped in layers. Poky provides the environment to build Yocto's reference distribution. It provides necessary tools, such as BitBake, layers, and other components to build a Linux distribution.

In order to implement the Linux system with Yocto, we implemented multiple layers, and recipes. For instance, with the meta-pynq layer, we integrate the essential components of the pynq Python package, used for the basic hardware interaction and DMA access into our Linux system. Therefore, the sources are fetched from the official repository, within this work on the 'image_2017_01' branch, and some minor patches are applied. Other layers and recipes integrate the remaining components, such as the CPython interpreter, and Jupyter Notebook. Similar to the original PYNQ Linux system, we support the physically Contiguous Memory Allocator with a memory size of 128 MB. Thereby, we remove the requirement for a scatter-gather engine, and thus, reduce the resource overhead for data movement by using Xilinx Simple DMA IP core.

3.2   Software Architecture

The overall framework software architecture is depicted in Fig. 2. Our Python package pyhwacc is meant to be imported by the hybrid Python package bundled by the hardware developer. The hybrid Python package is required to setup the hardware if necessary. The application to be accelerated can then use the methods provided in pyhwacc to mark functions for hardware acceleration and pipelining. The memory allocation can be done via pynq's Xlnk class. A more detailed description of the pyhwacc package can be found in the following Subsect. 3.3.

3.3   Python Package Pyhwacc

All classes of the framework, used to manage the hardware, are implemented in the pyhwacc Python package. Moreover, it contains the software developer interface methods.

Mark Function for Hardware Acceleration. To mark a function to be hardware accelerated, the decorator design pattern is used. In our framework the decorator creates a wrapper function that substitutes the original supported function. If the function is not supported, the wrapper is not created, and an error message is returned. The function support depends on the hardware device,

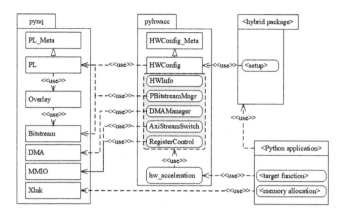

Fig. 2. Framework software architecture.

the function name and the type of the passed arguments. The decorator's and wrapper's execution flow is depicted in Fig. 3. Since Python is a dynamically typed language, the passed arguments' type needs to be checked in every call. Currently, we support keyword-only arguments of type NumPy Array with physically contiguous memory. Our template wrapper function supports an infinite number of passed input arrays, and one output array. Thus, hardware developers have to modify the template wrapper and integrate their own wrapper in case the implementation requires other or additional arguments. We chose NumPy Arrays because of its versatility and performance. Moreover, an implementation with physically contiguous memory is provided within the pynq package. Since our hardware design utilizes DMA cores, it requires sequential chunks of data. An example decorator call is shown in Listing 1.1.

Listing (1.1). Python decorator hw_acceleration usage.

```
@hw_acceleration
def hiddenLayer(src: np.ndarray, src2:np.ndarray, dest: np.ndarray):
    #function implementation
```

Mark Functions for Pipelining. To mark functions as being pipelined, the class HWConfig implements the method 'PipelineFunctions'. The syntax of its arguments is shown in Listing 1.2. In case the input is an array provided by a DMA core, the input is marked as 'dma'. The amount of input arrays is not limited by our software. Moreover, the number of outputs for intermediate functions is not limited. However, in the current version of our framework, only one output array is expected.

An example PipelineFunctions call is shown in Listing 1.3. First, Pipeline-Functions checks, if the passed functions are supported and their argument types match. Afterwards, the hardware is prepared by checking whether the RM is present in the PL. If a required RM is not available, a RP is reconfigured with the corresponding partial bitstream from the imported hybrid Python package. In case all RP are occupied, RM are replaced based on a first-in-first-out strategy.

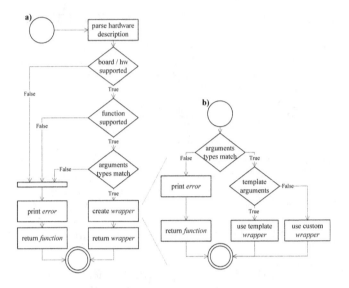

Fig. 3. Control flow of the *@hw_acceleration* decorator call.

Moreover, we implemented a least-recently-used replacement policy to evaluate their effects in performance and power. After the RMs are prepared, the AXI Stream crossbar is configured according to the assignment of functions to RP, and their described connections. In the final step, the DMA cores are prepared, and the data transfer is started. This procedure is depicted in Fig. 4.

Listing (1.2). General syntax of HWConfig.PipelineFunctions().

```
HWConfig.PipelineFunction(
    [1. function, [1. input of 1. function, 2. input of 1. function, ...]],
    [2. function, [1. input of 2. function, 2. input of 2. function, ...]],
    ...,
    src=1. input array, src2= 2. input array, ... dest=output array)
```

Listing (1.3). Pipeling of funA fed by a DMA core, funB fed by funA, and funC fed by funB, the result is passed to a DMA core, see Figure 5(b).

```
HWConfig.PipelineFunctions(
    [funA, ['dma']],
    [funB,[(('funA',0),0)]],
    [funC,[(('funB',0),0)]],
    src=in1, dest=out)
```

It is possible to instantiate a function multiple times in hardware, if supported by the overlay. Therefore, functions are indexed, as indicated by the first '0' in Listing 1.3. Moreover, it is necessary to specify to which output port of the previous hardware accelerator the input is connected to, since intermediate accelerators are allowed to have multiple outputs. This port is indicated by the second '0' in Listing 1.3.

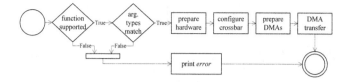

Fig. 4. Control flow of the *HWConfig.PipelineFunctions()* function call.

Through our hardware function we enable different pipeline configurations. The most basic case are two consecutive functions, sharing data over a common intermediate memory area, see Fig. 5(a). In order to remove the expensive memory access, we enable a direct routing of the data from the first RM to the second RM, see Fig. 5(b). Moreover, the framework has native support for RM with two inputs, see Fig. 5(c). Also for these functions it is possible to apply pipelining if supported by the RMs, see Fig. 5(d). Finally, all of the mentioned configurations can be combined, and, described with the previous example, intermediate RM are allowed to have more than one output. Through this pipelining methods we are able to save several expensive memory accesses for intermediate results.

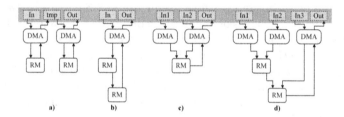

Fig. 5. Data flow configurations supported in our Python package.

3.4   Usability

For a hardware developer using our framework to package an overlay, it is necessary to provide a setup function for the software developer. This can be done via methods in the HWConfig class. Moreover, a description of the hardware is needed. It contains the supported hardware devices and functions, and is expected to be stored in a file named 'hw-info.json'. An example for the evaluation overlay is shown in Listing 1.4. The overlay is called 'MLP' with version 1.01, supporting the Pynq-Z1, and containing the hardware function 'sum', compatible with RP 'RP0'. Section 'DMA_info' contains information about DMA cores and the connection to the crossbar. Section 'Switch' contains the crossbar switch configuration. If the configuration register space is compatible to the Vivado HLS configuration, the provided wrapper template can be used. Thus, there is no need to create an interface. This is especially the case for accelerators implemented with Vivado HLS and AXI Stream data ports.

Listing (1.4). Example hw-info.json file.

```
{ "Overlayname": "MLP",
    "Version": "1.01",
    "supported_Hw": ["Pynq−Z1"],
    "supported_Ft": {
        "sum":{ "Parameters":{ "src": "<class_'numpy.ndarray'>",
                               "dest": "<class_'int'>",
                               "num_elements": "<class_'int'>"}},
        ... },
    "DMA_info": { "dma_in1":{ "Address":"0x40400000", "direction":"in",
                             "switch_ports":{"in":−1, "out":[0]}},
        ... },
    "Switch":{ "Name":"AXISwitch", "Address":"0x43C00000", "in_ports":11,
              "out_ports":11},
    "pblocks": { "RP0":{"Address":"0x43C10000","Functions":
                    ["sum"], "switch_ports":{"in":[1,2],"out":[6]}},
        ... }
}
```

4   Evaluation

The framework evaluation was done within the ongoing development of a hardware/software codesign for data processing based on a Multi-layer Perceptron (MLP), a type of neural network. For evaluation purposes, we focus on the implementation of an image classification for the MNIST image database [11], containing 28×28 pixel images of handwritten digits, with Theano [2]. Therefore, we developed a DPR overlay, wrapped in a Python package that contains the pre-implemented static, as well as partial bitstreams. The hardware implementation of the MLP algorithm was done via Vivado HLS. With this setup, we are able to explore the forward path acceleration of different network configurations, with a purely Python-based flow. The software structure and its mapping to the PL via our DPR overlay is shown in Fig. 6.

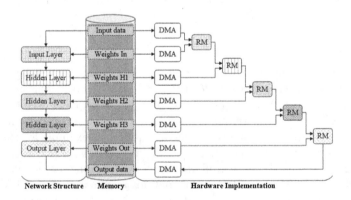

Fig. 6. Mapping of Multi-layer Perceptron onto hardware architecture.

4.1   Results

The static overlay hardware architecture, consisting of seven DMA cores and an
11 × 11 AXI Stream crossbar, consumes 11596 LUT, 13633 FF, and 7 DSP48E
resources, see Table 1. Five DMA cores deliver data to the MLP network, and one
DMA cores delivers data to the memory. A list of resources used by the framework's components can be found in Table 1. All overlay resources are clocked at
125 MHz.

Table 1. Resource usage of framework components, and framework overhead for the
evaluation, compared to available resource on Zynq ZC7020.

Resource	ZC7020	DMA Core		AXI Stream crossbar					Evaluation
	(Available)	To MLP	To memory	2 × 2	4 × 4	8 × 8	11 × 11	16 × 16	(in total)
LUT	53200	553	992	203	624	1911	3288	4733	11596
FF	106400	754	1326	568	926	1698	2287	3274	13633
DSP48E	220	0	0	0	0	0	0	0	0
BRAM tiles	280	1	1	0	0	0	0	0	7

Figure 7 shows an execution time comparison between hardware and software,
as well as the execution time in hardware with and without the configuration
overhead. For this evaluation, the number of layers was kept constant, and the
number of neurons per layer is varying. The point of intercept lies between a
network with 700 and 1000 neurons per layer. The first four layers of the MLP
are equal. They are implemented as summation of the matrix multiplication
result between weights and input, followed by the addition of a bias and the
application of the activation function. For the activation function we evaluated
the tangens hyperbolicus, as well as the ramp function (ReLu). An influence on
the execution time could not be measured. The last layer is implemented with
the softmax function.

For the execution of a MLP with $4 \times 1000 + 10$ neurons, an overall execution
time of 157.1 ms was achieved. Since the last layer outputs the result of the digits
(0 to 9) classification probability, it has ten neurons. Without the pipelining of
the layers, enabled by the HWConfig.PipelineFucntios method, the execution
time increases to 203.2 ms. When executing the same MLP network in Python
via a NumPy implementation, we achieved an execution time of 163.0 ms. As can
be seen on the right side of Fig. 7, the hardware configuration time is constant.
It is based on the configuration parameters to the DMA cores, as well as to the
RM, which is not influenced by the payload data size, and thus the layer size.

Although the execution time is not influenced by the two activation functions,
there is a difference in resource usage. The size of the RP, as well as the RM
is shown in Table 2. For the implementation with Vivado HLS we explored the
pipelining and unroll directive. A combination of the two directives results in
a maximum frequency of only 62 MHz, without a significant improvement in
latency. When comparing the unrolling and pipelining directive, the solutions

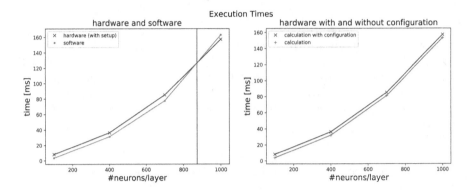

Fig. 7. Execution time evaluation of the MLP network.

generated with the pipeling directive lead to a lower latency. Therefore, we chose the loop-pipelining directive for the evaluation implementation.

The hardware setup time mainly depends on the configuration of the RP. In the case of the evaluation, we measured 23.0 ms to download the bitstream from within the Python application. The bitstream size was 528.2 kB. These values are close the results in [10]. Since the overlay is configured once for the evaluated application, the setup overhead is not included in the execution time.

Table 2. Comparison of resources in layers with tangens hyperbolicus (tanh), ramp function (max), and softmax activation function, to RP size.

Resource	Layer tanh	Layer max	Layer softmax	RP
LUT	3500	704	2553	3600
FF	2539	746	2144	7200
DSP48E	34	5	12	40
BRAM tiles	1	1	6	10

4.2   Discussion

The main goal of the evaluation was the exploration of the capabilities to define hardware from Python. As shown in the previous Subsect. 4.1, we were able to map the MLP to hardware by using our framework's interface. Thereby, we enable an offloading of computations onto efficient application-specific hardware accelerators. Moreover, we were able to achieve a moderate speedup for larger MLPs through hardware acceleration.

With our evaluation, we explored a worst-case scenario. The computations are of low complexity, and only moderate parallelization through pipelining of accelerator cores, as well as in their implementation could been explored. Therefore, the PS is in favor, as its clock frequency is about 5x higher. In addition, the application is highly communication intensive, since every operation requires the transmission of two input operands. When comparing the MLP network with more suitable types of neural networks, as for instance convolutional neural networks (CNNs), the advantage could be much higher. In a CNN, the same weights are used for multiple operations. Thus, the communication workload is lower. Moreover, a higher parallelization is possible, since input values are also used multiple times in the two-dimensional convolution.

5   Related Work

Within this work, we extended the DPR overlay concept presented in [1] with comprehensive hardware/software framework and a Yocto-based build flow. The goal is to increase the accessibility of FPGAs from software by hiding the development complexity. A similar idea drives the research around virtual FPGA architectures. In [7], Wiersema et al. describe their work on combining ReconOS, an operating system for reconfigurable systems in combination with a hardware architecture, and ZUMA, a virtual FPGA architecture with development toolflow. With their work, they enabled a multi-threaded programming model with support for hardware threads, based on a pthread-like interface. The resource overhead of the ReconOS hardware architecture is reported with 3270 LUT for one hardware accelerator. For our overlay, the utilization corresponds to a configuration with two inputs and one output DMA core, as well as a 4×4 crossbar.

Wang et al. present 'SODA', a hardware accelerator for FPGAs that can be defined by software [5]. With their approach they want to close the gap between high-level and hardware developers. In comparison to our framework, their resource usage is within the same magnitude. However, the accelerator cannot be exchanged without downloading a complete bitstream.

In [4], Andrews and Platzner describe the integration of reconfigurable manycore systems into the common software development environment as one of the key components for their future success. In comparison to their works on Hthreads and ReconOS, our approach focuses more on the ability to shape the hardware architecture through a software-like description.

Logaras et al. developed a Python-based approach for system description and verification [3]. Their tool, 'SysPy', enables the generation of implementation and verification scripts based on a description of the system architecture. Another approach, enabling the description of a complete application-specific system is described by the authors of [6] within the FlexTiles project. In comparison to this work, special development environments are necessary for the developer to implement the system. Similar to our work, these works enable a software-based implementation of hardware. In contrast to these works, our goal was to use pre-implemented bitstreams to mitigate the implementation time.

6   Conclusion and Outlook

In this article we presented our work on a DPR overlay framework for Python based on the PYNQ project. Our framework enables a Python-based description of the hardware architecture, assembled during runtime via DPR. Thereby, we enable hardware developers to provide their work to a larger group of software developers. Moreover, we enable software developers to benefit from application-specific hardware accelerators, without the use of Vivado HLS or static overlays.

We evaluated our work with a DPR overlay for MLP in an image classification application, and showed how to use the hardware acceleration and the pipelining of hardware accelerators. This work is meant to be the foundation for following research projects. Therefore, we plan to extend the overlay with other types of neural network layers, as well as a further exploration of the runtime management, and the automation of the application partitioning. Moreover, we are looking for other types of DPR overlays to be implemented and are open for collaboration.

Acknowledgment. This work was supported by the BMWi project MiMEP (03ET1 314A), and by the Ruhr University Research School PLUS, funded by Germany's Excellence Initiative [DFG GSC 98/3].

References

1. Janßen, B., Zimprich, P., Hübner, M.: A dynamic partial reconfigurable overlay concept for PYNQ. In: Proceedings of the 27th International Conference on Field Programmable Logic and Applications (2017)
2. Theano Development Team: Theano: a Python framework for fast computation of mathematical expressions. arXiv e-prints, vol. abs/1605.02688 (2016)
3. Logaras, E., Koutsouradis, E., Manolakos, E.S.: Python facilitates the rapid prototyping and HW/SW verification of processor centric SoCs for FPGAs. In: The Proceedings of the 2016 International Symposium on Circuits and Systems (2016)
4. Andrews, D., Platzner, M.: Programming models for reconfigurable manycore systems. In: The Proceedings of the 11th International Symposium on Reconfigurable Communication-centric Systems-on-Chip (2016)
5. Wang, C., Li, X., Zhou, X.: SODA: software defined FPGA based accelerators for big data. In: Proceedings of the 2015 Design, Automation Test in Europe Conference Exhibition (2015)
6. Janßen, B., et al.: Designing applications for heterogeneous many-core architectures with the FlexTiles Platform. In: Proceedings of the 2015 International Conference on Embedded Computer Systems: Architectures, Modeling, and Simulation (2015)
7. Wiersema, T., Bockhorn, A., Platzner, M.: Embedding FPGA overlays into configurable systems-on-chip: ReconOS meets ZUMA. In: Proceedings of the 2014 International Conference on ReConFigurable Computing and FPGAs (2014)
8. Xilinx Inc.: PYNQ: Python productivity for Zynq. http://www.pynq.io/ (2018). Accessed 18 Jan 2018
9. Yocto Project: Yocto Project - a Linux Foundation collaborative project. https://www.yoctoproject.org/ (2018). Accessed 18 Jan 2018
10. Al Kadi, M., Rudolph, P., Gohringer, D., Hubner, M.: Dynamic and partial reconfiguration of Zynq 7000 under Linux. In: Proceedings of the 2014 International Conference on ReConFigurable Computing and FPGAs (2013, 2018)
11. Deng, L.: The MNIST database of handwritten digit images for machine learning research. IEEE Sig. Process. Mag. **29**(6), 141–142 (2012)

Runtime Adaptive Cache for the LEON3 Processor

Osvaldo Navarro$^{(\boxtimes)}$ and Michael Huebner

Chair of Embedded Systems of Information Technologies,
Ruhr-Universität Bochum, 44801 Bochum, Germany
{Osvaldo.NavarroGuzman,Michael.Huebner}@rub.de

Abstract. Cache memories are a key component of computing systems because they minimize latency between the processor and the main memory. However, they require a large amount of the total energy consumption of the system. This energy demand depends on the application's behavior. Thus, reconfiguring the cache to fit to every application's memory requirements with the minimum resources would save a significant amount of energy. This paper presents an architecture that enables the reconfiguration of the cache associativity during runtime, in order to fit the cache to the executing application. The architecture combines the cache ways using a small amount of logic, maintaining the cache entire capacity. We implemented our architecture in a LEON3 processor model and evaluated it using a Xilinx ZC702 FPGA. Our experiments show that the proposed architecture improves upon a way-shutdown approach in terms of energy savings and execution time.

1 Introduction

One of the key research targets of the embedded systems design area is minimizing energy consumption. Among the best candidate components for such optimization is the cache memory. This component is a prominent part of a processing system, since it is one of the main solutions to the memory wall problem. Nevertheless, the cache can consume a large proportion of a system's energy consumption. For example, the survey in [1] reports that the cache memory in the Alpha2124 processor accounts for approximately 16% of the total power, 30% in the case of the StrongARM processor and 24% in the case of the L2 cache of the Niagara and Niagara-2 processors. In the case of embedded systems, the consumption of the cache is more prominent. For example, the cache memories in processors of Personal Mobile Devices (PMDs) can account from 25% to 50% of the system's total energy consumption [2]. Furthermore, the efficacy of the cache changes with the application. For example, if the memory access patterns of an application exhibit a high temporal locality, a cache memory large enough to hold these frequently accessed values would save both energy and execution time. Nevertheless, using a large cache while running an application, which memory access patterns have a low locality of reference, would not exploit the cache capacity efficiently. The cache would hold all the data needed by the

© Springer International Publishing AG, part of Springer Nature 2018
N. Voros et al. (Eds.): ARC 2018, LNCS 10824, pp. 343–354, 2018.
https://doi.org/10.1007/978-3-319-78890-6_28

application, but power would be consumed needlessly since the cache would be larger than needed. Therefore, these characteristics make the cache memory a suitable candidate for dynamic reconfiguration. This means, that modifying the cache dimensions and/or behavior to hold the application's working load with the minimum resources would yield significant energy savings.

There have been several works that add adaptability to cache memories. Most of these approaches have been implemented on a simulator and their energy consumption has been estimated using mathematical models. Only a few approaches have been implemented in hardware. In one of these approaches, Silva et al. [3] proposed a method to disable the data cache ways by manipulating the *enable* signal of the block RAMs that implement the cache memory in a LEON3 processor [4]. This approach is based on an approach implemented on a simulator [5]. The idea behind this mechanism is to disable the cache ways that are not needed by the application, in order to save power. However, this approach loses part of the cache's capacity every time a cache way is disabled, which may cause an increase in capacity or conflict misses, if the application's data has to compete for a smaller space in the cache later in the execution. Thus, a way to tackle this problem would be a mechanism that reconfigures the cache's associativity but keeps its original capacity, since it could adapt to the application's spatial locality while still being able to store the same amount of data.

In this paper we present a dynamic cache reconfiguration approach that reconfigures the cache associativity during runtime. Our implementation concatenates the cache ways instead of shutting them down, in order to reconfigure the cache while keeping its capacity available to the application. This architecture is based on the work proposed in [6]. We developed our approach as an extension of the LEON3 processor model and implemented it on an FPGA with real power measurement capabilities. Our experimental results show that our approach achieves significant energy savings in comparison with a system running with a static cache and the work of [3]. The contributions of this paper are summarized as follows:

- A dynamic cache reconfiguration mechanism implemented on real hardware, that reconfigures the cache associativity of both data and instruction caches during runtime.
- A comparison with a state of the art hardware implementation that enables/disables the cache ways during runtime.
- An evaluation on an FPGA showing experimental results regarding performance, area and real power and energy consumption measurements.

This paper is structured as follows: on Sect. 2 we provide a brief review of the recent cache reconfiguration approaches. On Sect. 3 we present our proposed approach. The tools and configuration used in our experiments are described on Sect. 4. Next, the results obtained are presented and discussed on Sect. 5. Finally, we conclude our paper with a few remarks and ideas for future work on Sect. 6.

2   Related Work

There have been many efforts to add flexibility and adaptability to the cache memory. These efforts focus mainly on an architecture that enables the reconfiguration of the cache [5–7] or on an algorithm that decides when and what cache configuration to choose [8–15]. Furthermore, these approaches target not only single processor systems, but multicore systems as well, focusing mainly on adapting the Last Level Cache (LLC) [7,8,16]. There have been as well approaches for soft real-time systems [10,13], that have to handle the additional constraint of the applications' deadlines when reconfiguring the cache, in order to minimize deadline misses.

Most of these approaches have been implemented on a simulation platform [5,8–15] and only a few implement a small part of the approach on hardware [6,17]. These approaches are evaluated by combining the estimations provided by the simulators and mathematical models to estimate the energy consumption of the system. One of the most cited approaches was proposed in [5]. In this work, an approach to enable and disable cache ways was proposed, to shut down the uneeded ways and save energy. Moreover, in [6] an approach to reconfigure the cache associavity is proposed. Unlike the work of [5], this approach keeps the entire cache capacity available, and only combines the cache ways as desired.

One of the few dynamic cache reconfiguration approaches implemented on hardware is [3]. This implementation is based on the work of [5], and extends the data cache controller of the LEON3 processor with a mechanism to enable/disable the cache ways during runtime. This approach has the disadvantage of losing part of the cache capacity when decreasing the cache associativity. This can lead to an increase in capacity misses and power consumption, if the running application frequently accesses a set of data larger than the cache's capacity. In our proposed approach, we overcome this limitation by implementing a small circuit that combines the cache ways instead of disabling/enabling them. In this way, the cache's associativity can be reconfigured during runtime while maintaining the cache's original size.

3   Way Concatenation

Figure 1 shows a general diagram of our implementation. We extended the cache controller of the data and instruction caches with 2 1-bit registers for each cache (depicted as the *Cache Config.* block in Fig. 1), that indicate the current cache configuration. The available configurations are: 4 way associativity, 2 way associativity and direct-mapped (1 way available). Moreover, we also added 4 registers that store the current number of hits and misses for the data and instruction caches. The way-concatenation mechanism was implemented in the cache controllers as well. Figure 2 shows a diagram of this mechanism. In the figure, the mechanism for only one of the caches is depicted. In every cache access, the value of the configuration registers (depicted as $reg0$ and $reg1$) are combined with the first 2 bits from the tag address to produce 4 signals ($w0$, $w1$, $w2$ and

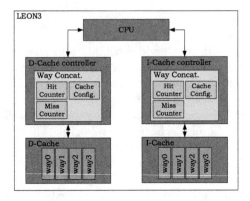

Fig. 1. General diagram of our implementation.

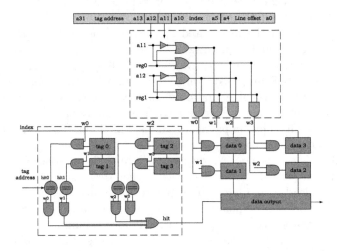

Fig. 2. Diagram of the way concatenation approach, based on the work of Zhang et al. [6].

$w3$), one for each way. These signals indicate which cache ways can be accessed by the current address. More specifically, when $reg0 = 0$ and $reg1 = 0$, only one of the signals $w0$, $w1$, $w2$ and $w3$ would be 1 and the cache would behave like a direct-mapped cache. When $reg0 = 1$ and $reg1 = 0$ or vice versa, only two of the signals $w0$, $w1$, $w2$ and $w3$ would be 1 and the cache would operate like a 2-way associativity cache. Finally, when $reg0 = 1$ and $reg1 = 1$ all the signals $w0$, $w1$, $w2$ and $w3$ would be 1 and the cache would behave as a 4-way associativity cache. It is important to notice that these 4 signals do not disable the cache ways, but rather indicate which cache ways can be used by the current address.

To decide what cache configuration should be chosen, we implemented the *dynamic way-shutdown* Algorithm that was proposed in [3]. A pseudocode of the algorithm is shown in Algorithm 1 and works as follows: the algorithm takes as input the number of hits and misses, a threshold for the difference between the current and previous miss rate, and the current cache configuration. As a first step, the algorithm calculates the current miss rate, and then it calculates the difference between the current miss rate and the previous miss rate. Then, if the current miss rate is lower than the previous one, the algorithm decreases the associativity (line 7). On the other hand, if the current miss rate is higher then the previous one and if the difference between them is higher than the threshold, the algorithm increases the associativity (line 5).

Algorithm 1. Dynamic Way-shutdown algorithm [3].

Input: The threshold for the difference in miss rates, diffThreshold, the number of cache hits, cacheHits, the number of cache misses, cacheMisses and the current cache configuration currentCache.

Output: A new cache configuration newCache.

1 currentMissRate ← cacheMisses / (cacheHits + cacheMisses);
2 missRateDiff ← currentMissRate − previousMissRate;
3 **if** currentMissRate > previousMissRate **then**
4   **if** missRateDiff > diffThreshold **then**
           /* If the current miss rate is higher than the previous one and the difference between them is larger than a threshold, increase the cache associativity. */
5   newCache ← currentCache.increaseAssociativity ( );
6 **else**
       /* If the current miss rate is lower than the previous one, the cache's associativity is decreased.   */
7   newCache ← currentCache.decreaseAssociativity ( );
8 previousMissRate ← currentMissRate;

---

4 Experimental Setup

We implemented our architecture by extending the data and instruction cache controllers of the LEON3 processor model (version grlib-gpl-1.5.0-b4164) [4]. The architecture was evaluated using a Xilinx ZC702 evaluation board [18], running at 52 MHz, to measure execution time, area and power consumption. Furthermore, we loaded applications into the LEON3 using GRMON2 Evaluation/Academic version [19]. To measure the power consumption of the architecture directly from the FPGA, we used a TI USB Adapter and the TI Fusion Digital Power Designer v7.0.11 tool [20]. We used applications from the MiBench benchmark suite [21] (*basicmath, stringsearch, bitcount, dijkstra, patricia, fft, fft_inverse*) as well as the breadth-first search application, *bfs*, obtained from the source code of an implementation of [3] on [22]. Finally, the resource utilization measures were obtained with Vivado 2017.2. We compared our approach, called *way − concatenation*, against an implementation of [3], called *wayshut − down*, and against a fixed cache approach. The cache configuration of this approach was set to: 2-way associativity, line size 32 B, cache size of 128 kB for the data cache and 64 kB for the instruction cache. The available parameter values used for the reconfiguration are as follows: for the data cache size: 64, 128 and 256 kB; for the instruction cache size: 32, 64 and 128 kB; for the associativity of both caches: direct-mapped, 2-way and 4-way. The initial cache configurations used by both *wayshut − down* and *way − concatenation* approaches are: 64 kB of cache size and direct-mapped associativity for the data cache, and 32 kB of cache size and direct-mapped associativity for the instruction cache. Furthermore, the frequency of the evaluation of the miss rate (see line 1 in Algorithm 1) can be configured. If the frequency is too high, the overhead of the reconfiguration will exceed any performance improvements obtained by the new cache configuration. On the other hand, if the frequency is too low, the application might be executed for a long time using a non suitable cache configuration. After several tests, we set the this period to 280 ms, which generated the best results for both approaches. Similarly, we had to set a value for the threshold for the difference between the current and previous miss rate used by the dynamic way-shut down algorithm (see line 4 of Algorithm 1). A too large threshold would cause fewer reconfigurations and might cause that the application runs longer with an unsuitable cache configuration. On the other hand, a very small threshold might cause an excessive amount reconfigurations, which would delay the execution. After several tries, we set this threshold to 1%, which offered the best results for both approaches.

We present results obtained from reconfiguring the data and instruction caches separately. When reconfiguring one of the caches, the other one was fixed to the same configuration of that cache in the fixed cache approach.

5   Results and Discussion

Figures 3 and 4 show a comparison of the energy consumed by the processor using the way shut-down approach and our proposed architecture, applied to the data cache and instruction cache, respectively. These results appear normalized to the energy consumption obtained with the fixed cache approach. In the case of the data cache, in 8 out of 9 cases our proposed approach yields energy savings in comparison with the fixed cache approach, achieving up to an 85% of energy savings in the case of the *bitcount* application. Furthermore, our approach obtained similar results as the way shut-down approach in most of the cases, with the exception of the *bitcount* application, where the way shut-down obtained less energy savings (approx. 47%). In the case of the instruction cache, our approach also obtained significant energy savings, reaching up to 82% energy savings in the case of the *bitcount* application. In the case of the *dijkstra* and *bfs* applications, our approach also yielded notable energy savings, 78% and 80%, respectively. In comparison with the way shut-down approach, our approach obtained similar results, obtaining higher energy savings in 5 out of 9 cases and lower in 3 cases.

In general, the applications that exhibit a high spatial locality benefited more from the way-concatenation approach. This is because more data that is consecutively accessed can be stored in the cache, in comparison with a cache with less capacity, as can be the case using the fixed cache or the way shut-down approach. This was the case with applications such as *bfs*, *bitcount*, *dijkstra*, *fft* and *fft_inverse*. The *bitcount* application benefited the most from the way-concatenation approach among the applications tested. This application consists of a group of functions that calculate the number of bits used to represent a long number. Thus, a cache with large enough ways would store more data used during the iterations and yield fewer conflict misses that would otherwise occur in caches with the same associativity but less capacity, as can be the case with the shut-down approach (which generated only 47% energy savings in comparison).

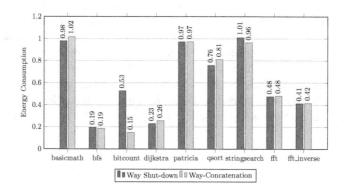

Fig. 3. Comparison of energy consumption between the shut-down architecture and the proposed approach, for the data cache.

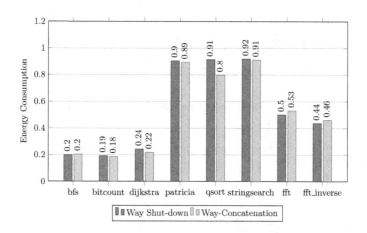

Fig. 4. Comparison of energy consumption between the shut-down architecture and the proposed approach, for the instruction cache.

Moreover, Figs. 5 and 6 show a comparison of the speedups with respect to the fixed cache approach, when reconfiguring the data and instruction caches, respectively. In the case of the data cache, our approach yielded a shorter execution time than the fixed cache approach in all cases. The application where the execution time was improved the most was *bitcount*, where our approach obtained a speedup of 8.99x, followed by the *bfs* and *dijkstra* applications, with speedups 7.25x and 4.85x, respectively. In comparison with the way shut-down approach, our proposed approach obtained better execution times in 5 out of 9 cases, and equivalent execution times in the rest of the cases.

In the case of the instruction cache, our proposed approach obtained shorter execution times in 7 out of 9 cases. The way-concatenation approach performed the best also in the case of the *bitcount* application, with a 7.07x speedup. In comparison with the way shut-down approach, our approach performed slightly better in 5 out of 9 cases. Similarly to the results on energy consumption (Figs. 3 and 4), the applications that obtained a larger speedup were the ones that exhibit high spatial locality (*bfs*, *bitcount*, *dijkstra*, *fft*, *fft_inverse*).

Furthermore, Figs. 7 and 8 show a comparison of the miss rates of the test applications with the way shut-down and the way concatenation approaches for the data and instruction caches, respectively. These results appear normalized to

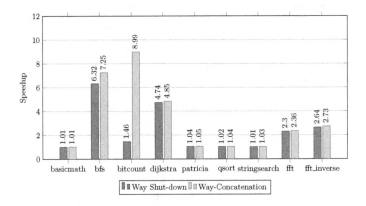

Fig. 5. Comparison of speedup between the shut-down architecture and the proposed approach, for the data cache.

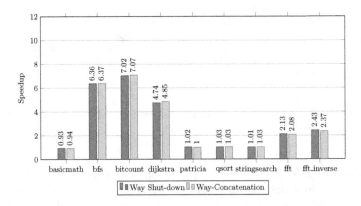

Fig. 6. Comparison of speedup between the shut-down architecture and the proposed approach, for the instruction cache.

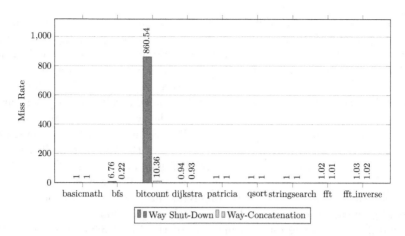

Fig. 7. Comparison of miss rates between the shut-down architecture and the proposed approach, for the data cache.

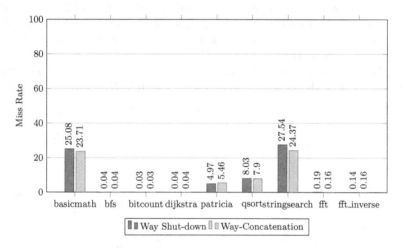

Fig. 8. Comparison of miss rate between shut-down architecture and the proposed approach, for the instruction cache.

the miss rates obtained with the fixed cache approach. In 2 out of 9 applications, *bfs* and *dijkstra*, the proposed approach generated a better miss rate than the fixed cache approach, with 78% and 7% lower miss rates, respectively. In 4 out of 9 cases, the proposed approach did not generate a significantly different miss rate than the fixed cache approach. In the case of the *bitcount* application, the proposed approach obtained a 10.36% higher miss rate than the fixed cache approach. Moreover, the way shut-down approach performed much worse in this case, generating a 860.54% higher miss rate. In the case of the instruction cache, the proposed approached obtained lower miss rates than the fixed cache approach in 5 out of 9 applications. The best case was with the *bitcount* application, where a 97% lower miss rate was obtained. In 4 cases, however, both reconfigurable approaches increased the miss rate significantly, reaching up to a 27.54% increase in the case of the way shut-down approach with the *stringsearch* application.

The increases in the miss rates of some of the applications are mainly due to two reasons: an increase on compulsory misses created by the cache flushes during the reconfiguration process and a suboptimal cache configuration for a particular application. Furthermore, in some cases the way-concatenation approach performed better when reconfiguring the data cache than when reconfiguring the instruction cache, and vice versa. In the case of the *bitcount* application, for instance, even though the proposed approach generated an increase of 10.36% on the miss rate on the data cache, a decrease of 97% was generated on the instruction cache. This suggests that different tuning algorithms should be used to reconfigure each cache, tailored to their specific behaviors.

Figure 9 shows the resource utilization of the LEON3 processor using the fixed cache, the way shut-down and the proposed way concatenation approaches, respectively. The way shut-down approach shows an increase of 18.31% on LUT utilization, an increase of 12.3% on FF utilization and a 39.29% increase in memory utilization. This is due to the additional registers required to count the hits and misses and to store the cache configuration, as well as the additional logic to enable/disable the cache ways. The way-concatenation approach required almost the same resources. As shown in the figure, it requires the same amount of memory than with the way shut-down approach, 0.15% less LUTs and 0.03 less FF.

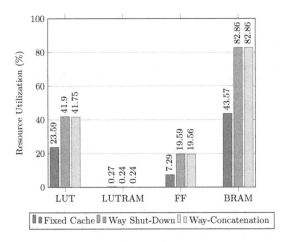

Fig. 9. Comparison of resource utilization by all the evaluated approaches.

6   Concluding Remarks

In this paper we propose a dynamic cache reconfiguration approach, that changes the cache associativity during runtime. Our implementation combines the ways of the cache memory while maintaining the cache's original capacity, as opposed to a shut-down ways approach [3] that disables/enables the block rams that form the cache memory. We implemented our approach on real hardware, extending the LEON3 processor, and evaluated it using an Xilinx ZC702 FPGA. Our results show that our approach obtains significant energy savings in comparison with a fixed cache approach and the shut-down ways approach. As future work, we will extend our approach to change other parameters of the cache memory, such as the line size and the replacement policy, as well as an algorithm that reconfigures the cache on an application-phase basis.

Acknowledgment. The authors of this paper would like to thank CONACyT (grant number 359472) for its support.

References

1. Mittal, S.: A survey of architectural techniques for improving cache power efficiency. Sustain. Comput. Inf. Syst. **4**(1), 33–43 (2014)
2. Hennessy, J.L., Patterson, D.A.: Computer Architecture: A Quantitative Approach. Elsevier, Amsterdam (2011)
3. Silva, B.A., Cuminato, L.A., Bonato, V., Diniz, P.C.: Run-time cache configuration for the LEON-3 embedded processor. In: Proceedings of the 28th Symposium on Integrated Circuits and Systems Design, SBCCI 2015, pp. 42:1–42:6. ACM, New York (2015). https://doi.org/10.1145/2800986.2801026
4. LEON3's download webpage. grlib-gpl-2017.2-b4164.tar.gz, August 2017. http://www.gaisler.com/index.php/downloads/leongrlib
5. Albonesi, D.H.: Selective cache ways: on-demand cache resource allocation. In: 1999 Proceedings of 32nd Annual International Symposium on Microarchitecture, MICRO-32, pp. 248–259. IEEE (1999)
6. Zhang, C., Vahid, F., Najjar, W.: A highly configurable cache architecture for embedded systems. In: 2003 Proceedings of 30th Annual International Symposium on Computer Architecture, pp. 136–146. IEEE (2003)
7. Gupta, S., Gao, H., Zhou, H.: Adaptive cache bypassing for inclusive last level-caches. In: 2013 IEEE 27th International Symposium on Parallel and Distributed Processing (IPDPS), pp. 1243–1253. IEEE (2013)
8. Mittal, S., Cao, Y., Zhang, Z.: Master: a multicore cache energy-saving technique using dynamic cache reconfiguration. IEEE Trans. Very Large Scale Integr. (VLSI) Syst. **22**(8), 1653–1665 (2014)
9. Gordon-Ross, A., Vahid, F., Dutt, N.D.: Fast configurable-cache tuning with a unified second-level cache. IEEE Trans. Very Large Scale Integr. (VLSI) Syst. **17**(1), 80–91 (2009)
10. Wang, W., Mishra, P., Gordon-Ross, A.: Dynamic cache reconfiguration for soft real-time systems. ACM Trans. Embed. Comput. Syst. (TECS) **11**(2), 28 (2012)
11. Navarro, O., Hübner, M.: An adaptive victim cache scheme. In: 2014 International Conference on ReConFigurable Computing and FPGAs (ReConFig), pp. 1–4. IEEE (2014)
12. Navarro, O., Leiding, T., Hübner, M.: Configurable cache tuning with a victim cache. In: 2015 10th International Symposium on Reconfigurable Communication-centric Systems-on-Chip (ReCoSoC), pp. 1–6. IEEE (2015)

13. Navarro, O., Leiding, T., Hübner, M.: A dynamic cache reconfiguration platform for soft real-time systems. In: 2016 IEEE International Conference on Electronics, Circuits and Systems (ICECS), pp. 388–391. IEEE (2016)
14. Navarro, O., Mori, J., Hoffmann, J., Stuckmann, F., Hübner, M.: A machine learning methodology for cache recommendation. In: Wong, S., Beck, A.C., Bertels, K., Carro, L. (eds.) ARC 2017. LNCS, vol. 10216, pp. 311–322. Springer, Cham (2017). https://doi.org/10.1007/978-3-319-56258-2_27
15. Gianelli, S., Adegbija, T.: PACT: priority-aware phase-based cache tuning for embedded systems. In: 2017 IEEE Computer Society Annual Symposium on VLSI (ISVLSI), pp. 403–408. IEEE (2017)
16. Kaseridis, D., Iqbal, M.F., John, L.K.: Cache friendliness-aware managementof shared last-level caches for highperformance multi-core systems. IEEE Trans. Comput. **63**(4), 874–887 (2014)
17. Zhang, C., Vahid, F., Lysecky, R.: A self-tuning cache architecture for embedded systems. ACM Trans. Embed. Comput. Syst. (TECS) **3**(2), 407–425 (2004)
18. Xilinx zynq-7000 all programmable soc zc702 evaluation kit's webpage, August 2017. https://www.xilinx.com/products/boards-and-kits/ek-z7-zc702-g.html
19. GRMON2's webpage, August 2017. http://www.gaisler.com/index.php/downloads/debug-tools
20. Fusion digital power designer's webpage, August 2017. http://www.ti.com/tool/fusion_digital_power_designer
21. Mibench benchmark suite's webpage, August 2017. http://vhosts.eecs.umich.edu/mibench//
22. Baseline source files (2017). https://www.dropbox.com/sh/2a73k3j5cxzavxw/IBz513-Gk6

Exploiting Partial Reconfiguration on a Dynamic Coarse Grained Reconfigurable Architecture

Rafael Fão de Moura[1], Michael Guilherme Jordan[1],
Antonio Carlos Schneider Beck[2(✉)], and Mateus Beck Rutzig[1]

[1] Departamento de Eletrônica e Computação,
Universidade Federal de Santa Maria, Santa Maria, Brazil
{rafael.moura,michael.jordan,mateus}@ecomp.ufsm.br
[2] Instituto de Informática, Universidade Federal do Rio Grande do Sul,
Porto Alegre, Brazil
caco@inf.ufrgs.br

Abstract. Coarse Grained Reconfigurable Architectures (CGRA) have been widely used with General Purpose Processors (GPP) to boost performance of applications by exploiting Instruction Level Parallelism. However, to sustain high performance levels, a great number of functional units must be available, which results in long contexts to represent each configuration. Most CGRA employ dedicated memory structures to store such contexts, in which the memory port width is proportional to the context length. This reduces the reconfiguration time but increases energy consumption. In this work, we propose a Partial Reconfiguration (PR) Technique that focuses on decreasing the energy consumption by storing CGRA contexts in the GPP cache memory hierarchy. This is done by splitting each context into multiple parts (partial contexts), which have the same size as the cache memory block width. Results show that the proposed strategy maintains the performance of the original approach providing, on average, 29 times of energy savings.

Keywords: Partial reconfiguration · Reconfigurable architectures
Multicore

1 Introduction

Even in the era of Multiprocessing Systems, Instruction Level Parallelism (ILP) has been increasing exploited to meet the performance requirements of non-TLP oriented applications. However, the last improvements on superscalar processors to boost ILP gains have no longer provide a positive performance-per-watt.

Reconfigurable Architectures, due to their resources replication ideology, have been widely employed to speedup applications. Fine Grained Reconfigurable Architectures (FGRA), such as FPGAs, are mostly used as an accelerator by transforming application kernels to an equivalent hardware logic function. Since it is based on fine grained programmable logic blocks, FPGAs rely on long contexts and huge reconfiguration time which narrow their code coverage.

© Springer International Publishing AG, part of Springer Nature 2018
N. Voros et al. (Eds.): ARC 2018, LNCS 10824, pp. 355–366, 2018.
https://doi.org/10.1007/978-3-319-78890-6_29

Coarse Grained Reconfigurable Architectures (CGRA) have been emerged as an alternative to boost performance of applications by exploiting ILP into programmable logic based on replication of regular functional units, such as ALU, shifters, multipliers. Since CGRA could be implemented at the same abstraction level of General Purpose Processor, both would work tightly coupled which decreases the configuration time shown in FGRA. However, although CGRA provides smaller contexts than the FGRA, performance improvements rely on high FU replication degree which results on significant number of bits to configure the fabric.

The major concerns about the RA contexts are about storage and energy access costs. The former has been softened due to the advancing of logic integration over the last decades. However, since the energy spent per access increases exponentially with the increasing on the memory port size, researches have been focusing on reducing the number of configuration bits by: optimizing the routing algorithms [1, 2]; compressing the bitstream [3, 4]; or even using partial reconfiguration [5, 6].

Most Partial Reconfiguration (PR) techniques are focused on FGRA optimization. Such approaches aim to enhance the utilization rate of FPGAs resources by sharing the reconfigurable fabric over multiple logic functions. Studies on PR over CGRA also focus on fabric utilization to boost performance mainly to exploit ILP and TLP [7]. However, none of them consider that there is design space exploration over PR that concerns the tradeoff between performance improvements achieved by RA and the energy spent to fetch configuration bits from the storage structure.

Moreover, considering coarse grained reconfigurable architectures, besides the context memory, they employ a cache memory hierarchy to store regular instructions which, somehow, causes a needless redundancy [8–10, 14–16]. Prior work proposes a demand-based allocation cache memory, which joins regular instructions and contexts in a single memory structure sharing dynamically the number of blocks available for each type of information [11]. However, the size of the cache memory port relies on the entire RA context length which limits ILP gains due to the restricted FU replication.

In this work, we extend [11] by proposing a novel Partial Reconfiguration technique for a Dynamic Coarse Grained Reconfigurable Architecture. Besides taking advantage of the demand-based allocation cache memory by storing regular instructions and contexts in a single memory structure, the proposed approach splits the CGRA context in parts, named as partial contexts, that represents the size of the traditional memory block. Performance and energy are benefited since the proposed approach breaks the limit of FU replication and reduces the memory port size of prior work.

This work is organized as follows. Section 2 presents the Related Work. Section 3 shows how the partial reconfiguration technique works. Section 4 presents the results. Finally, conclusion and future works are shown in Sect. 6.

2   Related Work

Several researches explore partial reconfiguration to decrease reconfiguration time and save memory. Most of them explore such an approach over fine grained reconfigurable architectures. In 2004, Xilinx proposes two firsts PR fashions: Different-based PR which is useful when small changes should be done in the current FPGA configuration, such as changing on few LUTs equations; Module-based configures large blocks which relies on longer reconfiguration time than the former approach. Later, Xilinx improves reconfiguration time by proposing the Early-Access Partial Reconfiguration (EAPR) approach that allows communication crossing through PR-modules without execution interruption. In addition, EAPR shows that the mechanism can reduce the size of the bitstream from 512 KB to 12 KB when reconfiguring a scenario composed of a Gray Counter and a Johnson Counter design in a Virtex4-FX12 FPGA [12].

Considering coarse-grained RA, Garp Architecture combines an FPGA, similar to Virtex 4 series, to a MIPS processor to speedup specific kernels of the applications. The smallest configuration block is a row that consumes 192 bytes each and it is reported that at least 32 rows should be used to achieve performance improvements. However, since not every configuration uses all available rows, a per-row-based partial reconfiguration mechanism is proposed. Thus, supposing a 128-bit bus, it is necessary 384 external memory accesses to fetch configuration bits of 32 rows [9]. Using the same approach of Garp, Chiamera couples an FPGA to a MIPS Processor and employs a partial reconfiguration to decrease reconfiguration time. The authors report that, even using PR, the reconfiguration time can be significant, thus techniques such as prefetching, cache algorithms and hierarchy have been implemented, but no details about how they work are shown.

MT-ADRES [7] is a coarse-grained RA approach that employs partial reconfiguration by dividing an array in multiple smaller arrays to execute threads concurrently. The partition can be changed dynamically depending on the ILP and TLP degree of the application providing more flexibility than a traditional multi-core system. Micro-Task Processing [13] maps computational threads via pipelined configuration technique into available physical reconfigurable hardware resources. It proposes a partial reconfiguration which enables the processor cells to be partially configured using Time Division Multiple Access (TDMA) by fetching custom instruction from the main memory.

In this work, we propose a Partial Reconfiguration Technique for a dynamic coarse-grained RA that, different of previous approaches that aims to increase the resource utilization without concerning about energy costs of memory accesses, focuses on decreasing the energy consumption on distributing partial contexts and regular instructions over the regular memory hierarchy. The RA contexts are broken in multiple parts, sized by the cache memory block, so the length of cache memory port is reduced drastically. Such partial contexts are organized as a linked list and fetched from the cache hierarchy reconfiguring the fabric on demand. Since partial contexts are independent, even if the linked list were broken due to a cache miss, the fabric still speeding up the application with the already fetched partial contexts.

As regular instructions and partial context are mixed in the cache hierarchy, the cache replacement algorithm has been modified to follow the pattern memory access of a coarse-grained RA coupled to a GPP. At the beginning of the application execution the system performs a lot more regular instruction accesses than partial contexts, that behavior changes over the application execution due to the increasing RA utilization.

3   The Proposed Approach

3.1   Overview

Figure 1 depicts three coarse grained reconfigurable systems distinguished by memory hierarchy organization. Traditional RA (1) employs a Context Cache (C$) dedicated to hold context bits and an instruction cache (I$) to store regular instructions. The C$ port size relies on the number of bits needed to configure the entire fabric. The I$ port size, usually smaller than the IC$ size, is related to the degree of spatial locality explored by the cache. Prior work (2) proposes merging regular instructions and contexts in a single structure, named instruction-context cache (IC$), where the number of blocks available for each information is managed at runtime by a modified block replacement policy [11]. Similar to the C$, the IC$ port size relies on the number of bits needed to configure the fabric. The proposed PR technique (3) breaks the relationship between the IC$ port size and the context length by splitting up context in multiple parts that configures independent blocks of the fabric. In this way, one can balance the port size and its energy consumption depending on the required spatial locality (considering the regular instructions) and the degree of FU replication (considering the RA contexts).

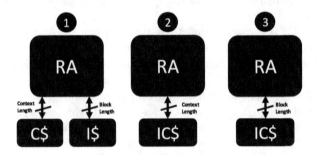

Fig. 1. RA platforms

3.2   Platform

Custom Reconfigurable Arrays for Multiprocessing System (CReAMS) is a platform used to implement the proposed partial reconfiguration mechanism. CReAMS is a multiprocessor system composed of replication of Dynamic Adaptive Processors (DAP). As shown in Fig. 2, each DAP contains a 5 stage SparcV8-based pipeline (IF-ID-EX-M-WB), a coarse grained reconfigurable fabric (RF) and a 4-stage binary translation hardware (ID-DV-RA-UT), named as Dynamic Instruction Merging (DIM) [10], which is responsible for translating, at runtime, SparcV8 instruction to RF contexts. Contexts are indexed, in the cache memory, by the address of the first translated instruction. As shown in Fig. 2, the RF is composed of arithmetic and logic units, memory access units, multipliers and floating pointing units. Such coarse-grained units are organized in levels, which have the same delay of the SparcV8 pipeline stage. A context of CReAMS is composed of different information which can be classified as: Input and Output context bits that store which operands should be fetched and written back from/to the SparcV8 Register File; execution bits (named as Level in Fig. 3) which represent the information to control functional units operation and the multiplexers to route operands to the functional units and results to the output context.

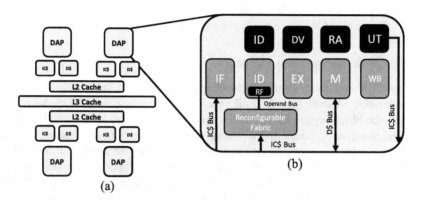

Fig. 2. (a) CReAMS platform (b) DAP blocks

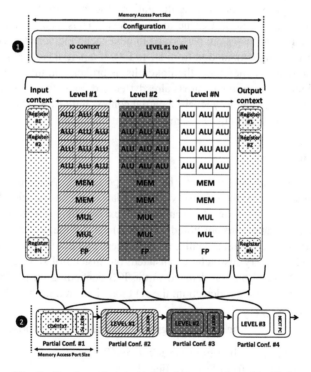

Fig. 3. Configuration strategies of the reconfigurable fabric

Considering the memory hierarchy, the original version of CReAMS, couples on each DAP an unique cache structure, named as IC$, to store regular instructions and context being the size of the IC$ port also dependent on the number of bits to reconfigure the entire RF (Configuration Strategy 1 shown in the upper side of Fig. 3). In addition, as shown in Fig. 2, the platform employs unified L2 and L3 caches shared among N/2 and N DAPs, respectively, being N the total number of DAPs.

3.3 Partial Reconfiguration Mechanism

The proposed Partial Reconfiguration Mechanism is presented in bottom side of Fig. 3 as Configuration Methodology 2. Unlike the original Configuration Methodology that disregards the block organization and configures the entire fabric in a single memory access, the proposed approach divides the configuration bits in blocks, named as partial context, and organizes them as a linked list to configure the fabric on demand. As shown in Fig. 3, the first partial context block contains the Input and Output bits and a field that store the memory address of the first instruction allocated in Level #1. The next memory access should consider such address to fetch the partial context #2 from the IC$ that contains the bits to configure the FUs operations and to route the operands in Level #1. The same process is repeated for the remaining levels.

Different from [11] that just store contexts in the first memory cache level (refer to IC$ of Fig. 2), the proposed partial reconfiguration strategy merges regular instructions and partial context up to the last cache memory level. Thus, if a partial context miss occurs in the L1 IC$, accesses are performed in next cache memory levels (in the case of current CReAMS implementation from L1 to L3). If a partial context is not found in the whole cache memory hierarchy, the linked list is broken and the context would be executed considering the partial contexts already fetched. In addition, as partial context is stored in shared cache memory levels, a partial context built by a DAP can be fetched for another DAP that is running the same code portion.

3.4 Detection Process

The context detection process was modified to support the proposed partial reconfiguration. As shown in Fig. 4, the original version updates the configuration bits on every instruction translated and verifies if the current context building process is completed. If so, the whole configuration bits are stored within a single IC$ memory access. Similar to the original version, the partial reconfiguration process updates the level block bits and the IO block bits on every instruction translated, but instead of storing a context as a whole, it stores the level bits on demand in the IC$ depending on its detection completion. By the end of context detection, the IO block is stored in the IC$ memory.

Reconfiguration Process

Algorithm 1 presents the original reconfiguration process that comprises four steps:

(1) fetching configuration bits from the IC$ (Line 2);
(2) getting the operands from Register File (Line 4);
(3) triggering the execution of the entire context (from line 5 to 7);
(4) writing back the results to Register File (from line 8 to 10);

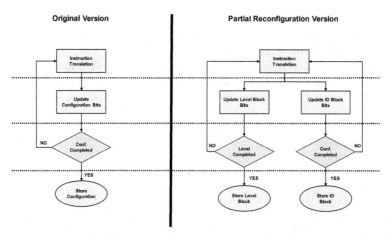

Fig. 4. Detection process: (a) Original version (b) Partial reconfiguration version

Since all configuration bits are fetched in a single IC$, the entire fabric configuration is also performed in a single clock cycle. However, the number of clock cycles of operand fetch and write back processes depend on the number of Register File ports and the number of operands involved in the context execution.

Algorithm 1. Original Reconfiguration Process

```
1:    procedure Reconfiguration()
2:        conf_bits_fetched =fetch_from_IC$(context);
3:        for all clock_cycle do
4:            all_ops_fetched = get_operands_from_RF(context);
5:            if (conf_bits_fetched and all_ops_fetched)
6:                all_level_executed = execute_context(context);
7:            end if
8:            if (all_level_executed)
9:                all_ops_written_back=write_back_ops_context(context);
10:           end if
11:           if (all_ops_written_back)
12:               done();
13:           end if
14:       end for
15:   end procedure
```

Algorithm 2 shows the partial reconfiguration process that comprises five steps:

(1) fetching the IO block from the cache memory hierarchy (line 5);
(2) getting the operands from Register File (line 7);
(3) fetching a level block from the memory hierarchy (line 8)
(4) triggering the execution of the level ready to be executed (from line 9 to 12)
(5) writing back the results to Register File (line 16 to 24).

Unlike the original version, the first step fetches the IO blocks from the entire cache memory levels (in the case of current CReAMS implementation from L1 to L3) aiming to enable getting the operands from the Register File (Step 2). The fetching of level blocks is performed in parallel with the operands getting process. As the number of operands to get from the register file is usually similar or greater to the number of levels, the level execution is triggered when the operands involved in such level are in the input context. Similar to original version, the write back process starts in the cycle after finishing the whole execution.

Algorithm 2. Partial Reconfiguration Process

```
1:    level_to_wb = 0;
2:    level_to_fetch = 0;
3:    level_to_execute = 0;
4:    procedure Reconfiguration ()
5:        fetch_from_IC$ (IO_block);
6:        for all clock_cycle do
7:            level[level_to_execute].all_ops_fetched = get_operands_from_RF(level[level_to_execute]);
8:            level[level_to_fetch].conf_bits_fetched = fetch_from_IC$(level[level_to_fetch]);
9:            if (level[level_to_execute].conf_bits_fetched and level[level_to_execute].all_ops_fetched)
10:               execute_level(level[level_to_execute]);
11:               level_to_execute++;
12:           end if
13:           if (level[level_to_fetch].conf_bits_fetched)
14:               level_to_fetch++;
15:           end if
16:           if (level_to_execute == total_levels)
17:               level[level_to_wb].all_ops_written_back = write_back_ops_level(level[level_to_wb].operands);
18:               if (level[level_to_wb].all_ops_written_back)
19:                   level_to_wb++;
20:               end if
21:               if (level_to_wb == total_levels)
22:                   done();
23:               end if
24:           end if
25:       end for
26:   end procedure
```

4   Experimental Results

4.1   Methodology

The partial reconfiguration mechanism was implemented over CReAMS platform that is described in a System C and VHDL. Eight benchmarks from MiBench, Parsec and Splash 2 suites were selected to evaluate the proposed approach. Cadence RTL compiler was used to gather power results of CReAMS coupled to the partial reconfiguration mechanism using a CMOS 90 nm technology. CACTI tool was used to gather power and operating frequency of cache memories.

As shown in Fig. 3, CReAMS couples three cache memory levels. For all experiments we have used 64 KB L1, 512 KB L2 and 8 MB L3. All memories are 8 way set associative caches and implement Least Recently Used (LRU) block replacement policy. In all scenarios, we have assembled a reconfigurable fabric level composed of

63 arithmetic and logic units, 3 multipliers, 2 memory accesses units and 4 floating pointing units. In our experiments, we have changed the size of reconfigurable fabric from 1 to 6 levels.

4.2 Cache Memory and Configuration Strategies Analysis

Table 1(a) presents the instruction distribution ratio among the reconfigurable fabric levels. As it can be noticed, all benchmarks, but susan_c and Jacobi, have a non-uniform distribution holding more instructions in the firsts RF levels. The more heterogenous is the distribution, the higher is the instruction level parallelism exploited by the reconfigurable fabric in the firsts RF levels. For instance, most performance gains of patricia come from the three first level since 86% of their instructions are allocated in the first two levels. As the partial reconfiguration strategy performs cache memory accesses in a granularity of a level block, if the context linked list broken due to cache miss after the third level, performance would not be drastically affected.

Table 1. (a) Instruction distribution over RF levels (b) cache statistics (c) context hits

Instruction Distribution over RF Levels						
Benchmarks/Levels	1	2	3	4	5	6
fft	30%	17%	16%	12%	12%	12%
lu	38%	21%	14%	16%	10%	2%
md	45%	18%	17%	7%	7%	7%
susan_c	19%	17%	18%	16%	15%	15%
susan_e	20%	17%	18%	18%	15%	14%
patricia	69%	17%	13%	1%	0%	0%
jacobi	17%	17%	17%	17%	17%	17%
susan_s	23%	22%	11%	11%	22%	11%

(a)

Cache Statistics		
Original Configuration Strategy		
RF Levels	Block Size (Bytes)	Access Latency (Cycles)	Energy (nJ)
1	128	2	2,77
2	256	2	14,91
3	256	2	14,91
4	512	4	57,17
5	512	4	57,17
6	512	4	57,17
Partial Configuration Strategy		
	Block Size (Bytes)	Access Latency (Cycles)	Energy (nJ)
IO/Level	64	2	0,21

(b)

Configuration Hits					
Levels	1	2	3	4	5	6
Partial vs Original	1,62	1,01	1,83	1,66	2,86	2,49

(c)

Table 1(b) presents cache statistics, in terms of access time and energy consumption, for the original and partial configuration strategies. As it can be noticed, as the original approach fetches a context in a single access, the cache memory block size increases as the number of level increases as well. For instance, a 2-level context has 256 bytes while a 6-level has 512 bytes. Unlike the original strategy, the partial reconfiguration has a fixed block size that has 64 bytes to configure the level setup specified in the Methodology section.

The increasing in the block size affects the access latency and energy consumption. For instance, supposing a fetching of a 6-level context, the partial configuration would perform seven memory accesses (one to fetch IO block and six to fetch level blocks) of 2 clock cycles each (total 14 cycles) while the original strategy just performs one memory access of 4 cycles. However, as shown in Algorithm 2, the processes of level block fetching and getting operands are done in parallel which decreases the total reconfiguration time. In addition, as the energy spent to perform a single memory access for a 6-level RF is 267 times higher than a single partial context block, there is a great opportunity to the partial configuration strategy achieving energy savings.

4.3   Partial Reconfiguration Strategy – Performance and Energy Results

Table 2(a) shows performance improvements of Partial Reconfiguration Strategy over the Original Reconfiguration considering different number of reconfigurable fabric levels. As it can be noticed, considering all number of levels, except in case of two levels, the partial reconfiguration mechanism maintains the same performance of the original approach. Such behavior is supported by Table 1(c) that shows the improvements in number of context hits in the IC$ of the proposed reconfiguration strategy over the original approach.

Table 2. (a) Performance improvements (a) and energy savings of the proposed approach over the original configuration strategy

Performance						
Bench/Levels	1	2	3	4	5	6
fft	0,91	0,74	1,03	0,97	0,96	0,95
lu	1,15	0,78	1,19	1,11	1,13	1,10
md	1,13	0,74	1,06	1,01	1,05	1,05
susan_c	1,14	0,74	0,93	0,92	0,88	0,91
susan_e	1,12	1,05	0,93	0,92	1,03	0,99
patricia	1,01	0,74	1,13	1,11	1,06	1,08
jacobi	1,02	0,75	0,88	0,88	0,76	0,76
susan_s	1,37	0,84	0,83	0,80	0,85	0,85
Average	1,11	0,80	1,00	0,97	0,97	0,96

(a)

Energy Consumption						
Bench/Levels	1	2	3	4	5	6
fft	6,88	15,09	41,07	37,19	37,89	39,24
lu	6,59	17,01	43,78	40,41	38,27	36,59
md	8,83	14,96	51,37	47,49	46,23	45,15
susan_c	12,93	15,56	24,32	23,86	23,77	25,08
susan_e	8,74	36,93	24,74	26,12	26,06	24,92
patricia	7,69	20,52	57,98	53,43	53,37	56,14
jacobi	8,15	17,69	34,35	30,56	30,26	29,00
susan_s	8,96	30,77	39,89	32,85	32,43	39,82
Average	8,60	21,07	39,69	36,49	36,04	36,99

(b)

For instance, considering a 5-level reconfigurable fabric, the partial reconfiguration strategy context has 386 bytes (6 blocks of 64-bytes each) while the original approach has 512-bytes (refer to Table 1(b)), so more contexts can be stored in the IC$ which increases the number of hits in 2.8 times speeding up more application code. Even speeding up more code, such performance improvements is diluted by the higher reconfiguration time provided by the partial reconfiguration strategy. The proposed approach spends 6 IC$ accesses of 2 cycles while the original reconfiguration spends 1 IC$ access of 4 cycles. At the other hand, considering the 2-level reconfigurable fabric, as the partial reconfiguration spent more time to reconfigure the fabric than the original approach (3 memory accesses × 2 clock cycles against 1 memory access × 2 clock cycles) and the context hit ratio are the same (refer to Table 1(c)) performance losses of 20%, on average, are shown.

Table 2(b) shows the energy savings of partial reconfiguration strategy over the original approach. In all RF levels the proposed approach shows energy savings that increases as the number of levels increases as well. Most energy consumption is spent on memory access which, as shown in Table 1(b), significantly increases with the increasing on the block size. As the partial reconfiguration performs multiple memory accesses of a fixed 64-bytes block size against a single memory access of a greater block size of the original approach, energy savings can be achieved. For instance, comparing the energy consumption of a 4-level partial reconfiguration against original approach, the former performs 5 memory accesses of 0.21nJ against a single memory access that consumes 57.17nJ, energy savings of up to 54 times (ideal scenario) can be achieved. In such comparison scenario, the partial reconfiguration strategy shows 36 times of energy savings over the original approach. Considering all scenarios, energy savings of 29 times, on average, are achieved by the proposed approach maintaining the same performance of the original strategy.

5 Conclusion and Future Work

In this work, we have proposed a partial reconfiguration strategy for a coarse-grained reconfigurable architecture aiming to decrease energy consumption of loading configuration bits from memory. Results suggest that partial reconfiguration: is mandatory to achieve an energy-efficient coarse grained reconfigurable fabric; can achieve the same performance of original approach by decreasing the block size and exploiting concurrent reconfiguration tasks. As future work, we intend to explore the impact of the proposed approach over heterogeneous organization multiprocessing system by sharing level blocks among cores coupled to reconfigurable fabric with different number of levels.

References

1. Ferreira, R.S., Cardoso, J.M.P., Damiany, A., Vendramini, J., Teixeira, T.: Fast placement and routing by extending coarse-grained reconfigurable arrays with Omega Networks. J. Syst. Archit. **57**(8), 761–777 (2011)
2. Alexander, M.J., Robins, G.: New performance-driven FPGA routing algorithms. IEEE Trans. Comput. Aided Des. Integr. Circuits Syst. **15**(12), 1505–1517 (1996)
3. Sandeep, P.M., Manikandababu, C.S.: Compression and decompression of FPGA bitstreams. In: 2013 International Conference on Computer Communication and Informatics, Coimbatore, pp. 1–4 (2013)
4. Beckhoff, C., Koch, D., Torresen, J.: Portable module relocation and bitstream compression for Xilinx FPGAs. In: Field Programmable Logic and Applications, pp. 1–8 (2014)
5. Mao, F., Zhang, W., He, B.: Towards automatic partial reconfiguration in FPGAs. In: International Conference on Field-Programmable Technology, pp. 286–287 (2014)
6. Kamaleldin, A., Ahmed, I., Obeid, A.M., Shalash, A., Ismail, Y., Mostafa, H.: A cost-effective dynamic partial reconfiguration implementation flow for Xilinx FPGA. In: 2017 New Generation of CAS (NGCAS), Genova, pp. 281–284 (2017)
7. Wu, K., Kanstein, A., Madsen, J., Berekovic, M.: MT-ADRES: multithreading on coarse-grained reconfigurable architecture. In: Diniz, P.C., Marques, E., Bertels, K., Fernandes, M.M., Cardoso, J.M.P. (eds.) ARC 2007. LNCS, vol. 4419, pp. 26–38. Springer, Heidelberg (2007). https://doi.org/10.1007/978-3-540-71431-6_3
8. Goldstein, S.C., Schmit, H., Budiu, M., Cadambi, S., Moe, M., Taylor, R.R.: PipeRench: a reconfigurable architecture and compiler. Computer **33**(4), 70–77 (2000)

9. Hauser, J. R., Wawrzynek, J.: Garp: a MIPS processor with a reconfigurable coprocessor. In: Proceedings of the 5th Annual IEEE Symposium on Field-Programmable Custom Computing Machines Cat. No. 97TB100186, Napa Valley, CA, pp. 12–21 (1997)

10. Beck, A.C.S., Rutzig, M.B., Gaydadjiev, G., Carro, L.: Transparent reconfigurable acceleration for heterogeneous embedded applications. In: Proceedings of the Conference on Design, Automation and Test in Europe (DATE 2008), pp. 1208–1213. ACM, New York, (2008)

11. Biazus, T.B., Rutzig, M.B.: Reducing storage costs of reconfiguration contexts by sharing instruction memory cache blocks. In: Sano, K., Soudris, D., Hübner, M., Diniz, P.C. (eds.) ARC 2015. LNCS, vol. 9040, pp. 3–14. Springer, Cham (2015). https://doi.org/10.1007/978-3-319-16214-0_1

12. Lie, W., Feng-yan, W.: Dynamic partial reconfiguration in FPGAs. In: Proceedings of the 3rd International Conference on Intelligent Information Technology Application, Series, IITA 2009, pp. 445–448. IEEE Press, Piscataway (2009)

13. Wallner, S.: Micro-task processing in heterogeneous reconfigurable systems. J. Comput. Sci. Technol. **20**(5), 624–634 (2005)

14. Ló, T.B., Beck, A. C. S., Rutzig M.B., Carro, L.: A low-energy approach for context memory in reconfigurable systems. In: IEEE International Symposium on Parallel and Distributed Processing, Workshops and PHd Forum (IPDPSW), pp. 1–8 (2010)

15. Souza, J.D., Carro, L., Rutzig, M.B., Beck, A.C.S.: A reconfigurable heterogeneous multicore with a homogeneous ISA. In: Design, Automation and Test in Europe Conference and Exhibition (DATE), Dresden, pp. 1598–1603 (2016)

16. Beck, A.C.S., Carro, L.: Dynamic Reconfigurable Architectures and Transparent Optimization Techniques. Springer, Heidelberg (2010). https://doi.org/10.1007/978-90-481-3913-2

DIM-VEX: Exploiting Design Time Configurability and Runtime Reconfigurability

Jeckson Dellagostin Souza[1]($\boxtimes$) , Anderson L. Sartor[1] , Luigi Carro[1] ,
Mateus Beck Rutzig[2], Stephan Wong[3], and Antonio C. S. Beck[1]

[1] Instituto de Informática, Universidade Federal do Rio Grande do Sul (UFRGS),
Porto Alegre, Brazil
{jeckson.souza,alsartor,carro,caco}@inf.ufrgs.br
[2] Departamento de Eletrônica e Computação,
Universidade Federal de Santa Maria (UFSM), Santa Maria, Brazil
mateus@inf.ufsm.br
[3] Computer Engineering Laboratory, Delft University of Technology,
Delft, The Netherlands
j.s.s.m.wong@tudelft.nl

Abstract. Embedded processors must efficiently deliver performance
at low energy consumption. Both configurable and reconfigurable techniques can be used to fulfill such constraints, although applied in different
situations. In this work, we propose DIM-VEX, a configurable processor
coupled with a reconfigurable fabric, which can leverage both design time
configurability and runtime reconfigurability. We show that, on average,
such system can improve performance by up to 1.41X and reduce energy
by up to 60% when compared to a configurable processor at the cost of
additional area.

Keywords: Reconfigurable accelerator · Configurable processor
Binary translation · Binary compatibility

1 Introduction

For the past decades, embedded processors gained a vast market share. These
processors can be found in devices ranging from mobiles to IoT nodes. They
must meet (sometimes conflicting) requirements such as high performance, low
energy consumption, and be small in size. One way of achieving such trade-offs
is through configurable processors. A processor is configurable when it allows the
design of different versions of the same processor, varying a significant number
of features, such as the number of instructions it can issue, the size of its register
file, special or customized instructions, and so on. It is done before deployment
and gives the designer enough flexibility to build the processor according to a
given set of constraints (e.g.: area and power) and the applications it will execute.

An example of a configurable processor is the ρ-VEX Very Long Instruction Word (VLIW) [14]. It is based on the VEX Instruction Set Architecture

© Springer International Publishing AG, part of Springer Nature 2018
N. Voros et al. (Eds.): ARC 2018, LNCS 10824, pp. 367–378, 2018.
https://doi.org/10.1007/978-3-319-78890-6_30

(ISA) with extended reconfigurable custom instructions. ρ-VEX also allows the parameterization of several hardware modules, such as the issue-width, register file size, type and amount of functional units (FUs), and memory buses, allowing a huge design space exploration, not only for performance and energy, but also for other requirements such as fault tolerance [10].

However, this flexibility may not always be enough to meet system requirements. Reconfigurable organizations emerge as an alternative since they can be coupled to processors to boost performance and save energy [3]. These systems can adapt themselves to the application at hand, reconfiguring their datapaths to maximize Instruction-Level Parallelism (ILP) exploitation and improve execution times [1] over classic processors. A particular advantage of such systems is: as it is highly regular, it is possible to couple multiple simple ALUs (Arithmetic and Logic Units) in sequence to execute several dependent operations in one processor cycle, without reducing the operating frequency [2].

In this work, we propose to leverage the advantages of reconfigurable hardware to expand the ILP exploitation capabilities of configurable processors even further, using the ρ-VEX as a case study. To maintain binary compatibility with the VEX ISA, we also use a binary translation system capable of identifying hotspots in the application code and dynamically creating configurations to be executed on the reconfigurable fabric at runtime. Therefore, we created a system which can be parameterized (configurable) during design time - not only the processor features but also the reconfigurable fabric - and reconfigurable during runtime as well, named as DIM-VEX (Dynamic Instruction Merging for VEX).

We show a diverse analysis of systems composed of differently sized reconfigurable fabrics and distinct ρ-VEX processors. Our results show that, while the DIM-VEX may require a considerable additional amount of area, it is possible to increase the performance and reduce the energy consumption of the configurable processors in many scenarios. On average, it is possible to achieve speedups of 1.41X and reduce energy consumption by up to 60% when using a reconfigurable fabric.

The remaining of this paper is organized as follows. Section 2 discusses the background of reconfigurable computing and the state-of-the-art. Section 3 describes the proposed DIM-VEX architecture. Section 4 explains the methodology used in this work, while Sect. 5 presents the results and analysis of the tested systems. Finally, Sect. 6 draws conclusions and future works.

2   Background and Related Work

Reconfigurable systems can adapt themselves to provide acceleration for specific applications. This is achieved through an additional circuit that offers reconfigurability, like a Field-Programmable Gate Array (FPGA) or a reconfigurable array of functional units. These organizations provide performance gains and energy savings over General Purpose Processors (GPP), at the cost of extra area. The reconfigurable logic can be classified by how it is connected to the main processor as follows [3]:

- loosely connected to the processor as an I/O peripheral (communication done through the main memory);
- attached as a coprocessor (using specific protocols for communication);
- tightly coupled as a functional unit (reconfigurable logic is inside the processor and share its resources, like its register file).

Furthermore, the granularity of the reconfigurable logic determines its level of data manipulation. A fine-grained logic is implemented at bit level (like Look-Up Tables in FPGAs) while a coarse-grained logic implements word level circuits (like ALUs and multipliers) [1]. Current implementations of reconfigurable systems usually favor coarse-grain reconfigurable arrays (CGRAs), as they present the following advantages:

- they can be tightly coupled to the main processor, avoiding significant penalties in communication;
- as configuration is applied at word level, the size of the contexts holding configuration bits is much smaller than those from fine-grained architectures;
- they have smaller reconfiguration latencies than fine-grained (e.g., FPGAs) fabrics, even when one considers only partial reconfiguration in the latter [1].

It is possible to use CGRAs as a generic accelerator by providing tools to dynamically analyze and translate regions of code for execution on the array. To achieve this, it is common to combine reconfigurable architectures with dynamic Binary Translation (BT) [6] techniques - in which the system is responsible for monitoring and transforming parts of the binary code, at runtime, in order to accelerate it; and Trace Reuse [4], which relies on the idea that a sequence of instructions will execute repeatedly using the same operands during the application execution. By associating these strategies, one can maintain the binary compatibility between the main processor and the reconfigurable fabric, while avoiding re-translating repetitive instruction block. An extensive characterization and classification study on reconfigurable architectures is presented in [1,3], and we discuss next a variety of works using reconfigurable architectures with dynamic binary translation.

Early studies on dynamically reconfigurable processors include the Warp Processor [9]. This system is based on a complex System-on-a-Chip (SoC), composed of a microprocessor that executes the regular application, a second microprocessor responsible for running simplified CAD algorithms, local memory, and an FPGA fabric. A profiler monitors the execution of the application to detect hotspots. Subsequently, the CAD software decompiles the application code into a control flow graph and synthesizes a circuit to execute the hotspot flow into the FPGA. Finally, the original binary code is modified to use the synthesized circuit. KAHRISMA [8] is an example of a completely heterogeneous architecture. It supports multiple instruction sets (RISC, 2- 4- and 6-issue VLIW, and EPIC) and fine and coarse-grained reconfigurable arrays. Software compilation, ISA partitioning, custom instructions selection, and thread scheduling are made by a design-time tool that decides, for each part of the application code, which assembly code will be generated, considering its dominant type of parallelism and resources availability. A run-time system is responsible for code binding and for avoiding execution collisions in the available resources. Although both systems are dynamic and software compatible, they are heavily dependent on compilers and CAD tools, which increase software deployment time and the execution overhead.

More recent works have been proposed such as the DIM [2], HARTMP [12] and DORA [13]. DIM is a coarse-grained reconfigurable array (CGRA) tightly coupled to a RISC processor and a dynamic BT system. The BT executes parallel to the RISC pipeline, monitoring hotspots and its data dependencies, and allocating instructions to run in parallel inside the array. When the hotspot is re-executed, the RISC pipeline is stalled and execution is transferred to the reconfigurable fabric. DIM supports speculation and the execution of multiple ALU operations in the same cycle, which significantly increases the IPC of the processor. HARTMP is based on a similar strategy as DIM. However, it uses multicore systems with individual arrays for each core. The arrays are dimensioned distinctly to create heterogeneous environments, in which applications can schedule less demanding workloads on energy efficient arrays. DORA is a BT system coupled with a GPP and a CGRA (based on the DySER [5] system). The BT is realized through a microprocessor, which is responsible not only to transform hotspots for the reconfigurable fabric but also to use dynamic optimizations on the parts of application code that run on the GPP. Both the code transformation and optimization are saved for reuse.

Differently from previous works, which use reconfigurable systems to accelerate either RISC or superscalar processors, our work proposes to accelerate configurable VLIW processors and exploit the available design space offered by this configurability. For that, we have adapted the DIM CGRA to work together with the ρ-VEX, creating the DIM-VEX. As already mentioned, the advantage of using ρ-VEX for this work is its ability to parameterize its FUs, issue-width, memory and register file. We use the parameterizable issue-width to create multiple configurations for design space exploration. As for the DIM, its ability to execute various dependent ALU operations in the same cycle perfectly exploits the low frequencies of VLIW processors, as more of these FUs can be nested in sequence. In this work, we create a variety of systems composed of different ρ-VEX configurations and different DIM-VEX versions. We show how a dynamic CGRA can further expand the ILP exploitation of VLIW processors and analyze the impact on performance, energy, and area of such systems.

3   The Proposed Architecture

A general overview of the proposed architecture is given in the Fig. 1, which is an adaptation of the original DIM system proposed in [2]. Initial data flow is exactly the same as the original ρ-VEX: instructions are fetched, decoded and executed in the pipelanes of the processor. However, in the DIM-VEX system, instructions are also translated and saved for future execution on the CGRA. Block 1 in Fig. 1 shows the structure of the reconfigurable datapath. It is composed of registers for input and output context and a matrix of functional units. The matrix is a combinational block with ALUs (Arithmetic and Logic Units), Multipliers, Memory access ports and multiplexers. The matrix is composed of levels that

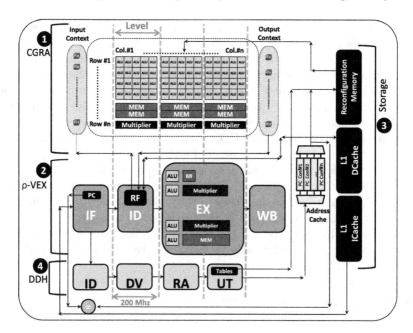

Fig. 1. DIM-VEX: a VLIW processor tightly coupled to a reconfigurable logic and a binary translator.

run in parallel with the VLIW pipeline (block 2). Each level has columns and rows. The columns have units that can run in parallel, executing instructions that do not have data dependency. As the multiplier and load operations stand as the critical path of the level, it is possible to align multiple ALUs in each row and keep the base frequency of the processor unchanged. In the given example, each ALU row has five columns and can execute five data dependent ALU instructions in the same level. During the reconfiguration process, a basic block is mapped to the matrix, to execute the whole block in a combinational fashion.

Block 2 shows the configurable processor coupled with the matrix. In this work, we use different ρ-VEX configurations all running at 200 MHz. This processor has a five-stage pipeline, in which the execution stage needs two cycles for the multiplication and load operations. We have also considered this same latency for multiplications and loads inside the CGRA. In block 3, the necessary storage components are illustrated. Apart from the usual L1 caches, two other memories are used. The address cache holds the address for each basic block decoded by the dynamic detection hardware (block 4) and is used as an index (and to check existence) for the datapath configurations. The reconfiguration memory holds the bits necessary to reconfigure the datapath into a basic block indexed by the address cache.

The Dynamic Detection Hardware (DDH), represented in block 4, does the binary translation and data dependency check of the instructions in a basic block. DDH is a four-stage pipelined circuit that runs in parallel to ρ-VEX, and thus being out of the critical path of the system. The Instruction Decode (ID) stage is responsible for decoding the operands in the base processor instruction to datapath code, while the Dependence Verification (DV) checks if these operands have any dependency with the instructions already stored in the configuration being built. The Resource Allocation (RA) stage uses the DV analysis to determine the optimal functional unit for the given operation inside the array. Finally, the Update Tables (UT) phase saves the new allocation in the reconfiguration memory for future use. Every time a branch or an incompatible instruction is detected, a new configuration is started by the DDH, and a new entry is created in the address cache. Moreover, the DDH can also manage speculation for branch instructions to increase the matrix usage. Further details of the DDH and how it interacts with the reconfigurable array can be found in [2].

During the Instruction Fetch (IF) stage of the base processor, the Program Counter (PC) is compared to the values in the address cache. A hit in this cache means that the following sequence of instructions was already translated to a configuration. In this case, the processors pipeline is stalled, and the configuration is executed in the reconfigurable datapath, greatly exploiting the ILP of the application.

4   Methodology

We have designed three different configurations of the ρ-VEX processor, each using a specific issue-width (2, 4 and 8). Subsequently, we use these same ρ-VEX configurations to attach DIM components and create DIM-VEX platforms. We also vary the sizes of the CGRA to explore a wider design space. In our early experiments, we tested the ρ-VEX with different FUs as well; however, results showed negligible variation in cycle count. Details on the tested configurations, DIM-VEX and ρ-VEX standalone, are shown in Tables 1 and 2, respectively.

Table 1. Configurations for DIM-VEX. Columns include ρ-VEX issue width, levels in the CGRA, number of parallel ALUs in each level, number of sequential ALU in each row level and number of multipliers and memory access in each level

Config	VLIW issues	Levels	ALUs	Seq ALUs	MULs	MEMs
DIM-VEX1	2	3	4	5	1	2
DIM-VEX2	4	3	4	5	1	2
DIM-VEX3	8	3	4	5	1	2
DIM-VEX4	2	6	4	5	1	2
DIM-VEX5	2	9	2	5	1	2

To extract power dissipation and area occupation of DIM-VEX, we have implemented the circuits of ρ-VEX and the FUs of the CGRA in VHDL and synthesized to CMOS 65 nm cells using a library from STMicroelectronics on the Cadence Encounter RTL compiler. The operation frequency of the ρ-VEX was set for 200 MHz. We were able to synthesize ALUs that run at 1/5 of the ρ-VEX cycle time; thus five of these units are nested in sequence to run in one clock

Table 2. Configurations for the ρ-VEX standalone. Columns include the issue width, number of pipelanes that contain an ALU, a multiplier and a memory port and number of registers in the RF.

Config	VLIW issues	ALUs	MULs	MEMs	RF
ρ-VEX1	2	2	2	1	64
ρ-VEX2	4	4	4	1	64
ρ-VEX3	8	8	4	1	64

cycle inside the reconfigurable fabric of DIM-VEX, as shown in the column Seq ALUs in Table 1.

This work uses instruction traces generated directly from the VHDL simulation to feed an in-house cycle accurate simulator for the proposed architecture. We use this tool to reduce the simulation time of the applications and give us flexibility to analyze and parameterize the CGRA. The simulator emulates the behavior of the DIM algorithm, allocating instructions to be accelerated into configurations of the CGRA. With the configurations built, the simulator estimates power and performance of the application, while considering a realistic overhead for the CGRA reconfiguration time. We consider that the CGRA can perform power-gating of its functional units (a state of near 0 energy consumption) when they are not in use. We also consider both static power - the power dissipated by the circuit when it is on but not in use - and dynamic power - the power dissipated when the circuit is active - for energy consumption. When the CGRA is not in use, the system power is equal to the total power (static + dynamic power) of the ρ-VEX processor. While the CGRA is active, the energy of all its functional units in use is accounted for along with the static energy of the ρ-VEX processor (which is stalled). The energy consumption and area are evaluated for the whole DIM-VEX, which is composed of the ρ-VEX, DDH, and CGRA, without the caches and main memory. Even though this methodology simplifies the analysis, it may bias results in energy in favor of the ρ-VEX processor without the CGRA, since it hides an important source of energy savings in the DIM-VEX system: when the CGRA is active in, all instruction fetches are stalled. Therefore, the DIM-VEX reduces the pressure on the instruction memory (cache), while keeping the same access rate to the data memories.

The benchmark set is composed of a subset of 15 applications from the WCET [7] and Powerstone [11] benchmark suites: ADPCM, CJPEG, CRC, DFT, Engine, Expint, FIR, JPEG, LUDCMP, Matrix Multiplication, NDES, POCSAG, QURT, Sums (recursively executes multiple additions on an array), and x264. All benchmarks are compiled using the HP VEX compiler.

5   Results and Analysis

We present the results for performance, energy and Energy-Delay Product (EDP) of all benchmarks in our proposed system and the standalone ρ-VEX. All the data presented in the charts are normalized by the ρ-VEX3 configuration, which is the 8-issue ρ-VEX processor. We chose this configuration as the baseline because it has the best performance among the standalone ρ-VEX systems. We also present the area overhead of each of the analyzed systems.

5.1 Performance

Figure 2 shows the normalized speedup for the tested benchmarks. Bars with values above 1 mean that the configuration improved performance; while for those under 1, performance slowed down. As expected, the ρ-VEX1 and ρ-VEX2 configurations have worse performance than the baseline (ρ-VEX3), as they work with smaller issue-widths. However, when we include DIM, most of the benchmarks show speedups, even when the ρ-VEX processor to which it is coupled to has fewer pipelanes. For instance, for the benchmarks DFT, Engine, Expint and x264, the best configuration for performance is the DIM-VEX5, which consists of a 2-issue processor coupled with a 9-levels array. For the benchmarks ADPCM, CRC, matrix multiplication, NDES, POCSAG and QURT, the best configuration is DIM-VEX2, a 4-issue processor. On the other hand, coupling the array with an 8-issue processor (DIM-VEX3) can still increase its capabilities for exploiting ILP. On average, configuration DIM-VEX3 has an speedup of 1.38X.

Table 3 shows the cycles and resource utilization for the benchmarks. Due to space constraints, we show these data only for configurations DIM-VEX1 and DIM-VEX5, which represent the most contrasting CGRA configurations (with the least and the most levels). We restrain into showing just ALU usage, as this is what impacts acceleration the most in the CGRA. We also position the benchmarks DFT, Expint, CJPEG, and x264 on top of the table for easy visualization, as we use them as examples for explanation.

In Fig. 2, DFT shows a reduction in cycle counts over the baseline for both configurations DIM-VEX1 and DIM-VEX5. In fact, the benchmarks show speedups of 1.21X and 1.78X, respectively. As presented in Table 3, most of the instructions executed by DFT are performed inside the CGRA (80.88% and 83.49%), spread along 12 basic blocks in DIM-VEX1 and 7 in DIM-VEX5, which explains such speedups. A similar behavior is observed in Expint, which executes 92.14% of its instructions on the CGRA in DIM-VEX1, and 87.75% in DIM-VEX5. However, the cycle reduction in Expint is much higher, achieving speedups of near to 2.5x in DIM-VEX1 and 3.5x in DIM-VEX5 with respect to

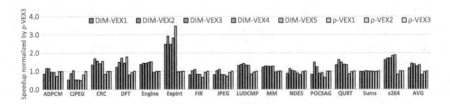

Fig. 2. Execution cycles for each benchmark normalized by the baseline (ρ-VEX3). Bars under 1 represent faster executions than baseline, while bars above 1 represent slower execution.

Table 3. Cycles and resource usage for the CGRA on all benchmarks. Cycles in CGRA is the total number of cycles executed inside the reconfigurable fabric (along with the ratio over the entire system). Significant BB shows the number of basic blocks which execute a meaningful part of the application and the average ALU usage on the reconfigurable fabric for these basic blocks.

	DIM-VEX1				DIM-VEX5			
	Cycles	Cycles in CGRA	Significant BB		Cycles	Cycles in CGRA	Significant BB	
DFT	26841	21708 (80.88%)	Number	Avg ALU usage	18238	15226 (83.49%)	Number	Avg ALU usage
			12	12.36%			7	17.08%
Expint	3677	3388 (92.14%)	6	44.72%	2620	2299 (87.75%)	2	92.78%
CJPEG	773	228 (29.5%)	6	12.21%	764	349 (45.68%)	6	8.89%
x264	9362	8135 (86.89%)	3	17.22%	8029	7827 (97.48%)	3	15.55%
ADPCM	659	254 (38.54%)	5	21.50%	604	179 (29.64%)	3	27.86%
CRC	9866	6003 (60.85%)	4	25.42%	8591	4722 (54.96%)	2	35.56%
Engine	505871	244005 (48.23%)	17	32.26%	455695	206498 (45.31%)	9	44.45%
FIR	139520	44745 (32.07%)	6	33.20%	135464	40479 (29.88%)	4	32.47%
JPEG	1800718	525662 (29.19%)	16	7.81%	1794808	566096 (31.54%)	14	6.52%
LUDCMP	34281	20091 (58.61%)	20	17.51%	33925	20891 (61.58%)	20	9.99%
MM	90848	62241 (68.51%)	9	18.29%	87275	63046 (72.24%)	8	14.98%
NDES	31301	16069 (51.34%)	6	12.48%	30789	17803 (57.82%)	7	8.96%
POCSAG	22890	15616 (68.22%)	4	25.42%	20788	13330 (64.12%)	3	43.71%
QURT	13426	7607 (56.66%)	14	19.93%	13356	7546 (56.50%)	17	28.08%
Sums	328	40 (12.20%)	2	0.80%	325	101 (31.08%)	2	6.11%

the baseline. These speedups are due to the high usage of the CGRA functional units, mostly caused by the large number of ALU operations in the basic blocks. DIM-VEX5 is able to best use the ALU resources (92.78% against 44.72% in DIM-VEX1) because it has only two rows of ALUs executing in parallel, which is a perfect match for this application. In DIM-VEX1, there are four rows, but two of them are mostly not used during the application execution. Nevertheless, executing most of the code on the CGRA does not necessarily translates into high speedups. In the x264 application, almost the whole application is executed in the CGRA, but speedup is of only 1.61X in DIM-VEX1 and 1.88X in DIM-VEX5 when compared to the baseline. The x264 is composed of few (3) and small significant BBs with low ALU usage, which translates into lower speedups. The CJPEG is an example of an application in which the CGRA cannot provide better execution time than the 8-issue ρ-VEX. That is, the CGRA configurations are small and do not support speculation - they are constantly broken by unsupported instructions instead of branch operations -, which limits the acceleration of such application.

5.2 Energy

Figure 3 shows the normalized energy consumption for the tested systems in all benchmarks. In this chart, bars above 1 represent higher energy consumption and bars under 1 lower energy consumption than the baseline. The 8-issue ρ-VEX (ρ-VEX3) processor operates at a higher power usage than its 2- and 4-issue counterparts. This reflects into the results, with ρ-VEX2 reducing energy by half (49.4%)

and ρ-VEX1 reducing energy by 70.4% when compared to the baseline. When the CGRA is added, many new components are integrated to the system, highly increasing its power consumption. However, the CGRA also provides speedups, reducing the time needed to execute the application. As the energy depends on the execution time as well as power, most of the CGRA configurations can provide lower energy consumption than the 8-issue processor alone. The only exception is the DIM-VEX5 configuration running the POCSAG application. Under this scenario, a 2-issue processor is coupled with a big CGRA, but no speedups are obtained. As can be seen in Table 3, POCSAG activates the array in 64.12% of its instructions with a usage of 43.71% of the CGRA ALUs. This results in a power hungry system that cannot provide any speedups, increasing the energy consumption without giving any improvements. On average, the best energy configuration is the ρ-VEX1 (70.4% energy reduction), as it is an extremely low power processor. Among the DIM-VEX systems, DIM-VEX1 presents the best energy consumption, reducing it by 60% with respect to the baseline.

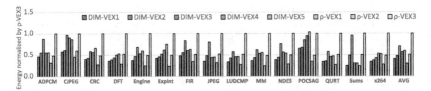

Fig. 3. Energy consumption for each benchmark normalized by the baseline (ρ-VEX3). Bars under 1 represent lower energy consumption than baseline, while bars above 1 represent higher consumption.

Table 3 can also be used to explain the energy results. For example in the Expint benchmark, the speedups for the application are huge in DIM-VEX5 (almost 3.5x); nonetheless, the energy reductions are much more restrained: only 25%. This small reduction is also explained by the usage of the CGRA resources. DIM-VEX5 executes 87.75% of its instructions in the CGRA using an average of 92.78% of its ALUs. This represents an average usage of 83 ALUs (see Table 1 for ALUs per configuration) during 87.75% of the execution time, which results in a considerable power consumption for the system. Resource usage also explains the reason DIM-VEX configurations can still provide energy gains for the CJPEG application, even when such systems provide slowdowns for the applications (DIM-VEX1, DIM-VEX2, DIM-VEX4 and DIM-VEX4 cases). Apart from these configurations using processors that are less power hungry than the baseline (2- and 4-issue ρ-VEX), when the CGRA is active in the CJPEG application, only a few resources are used. The combination of these two conditions results in a much low power environment than the ρ-VEX3 processor.

5.3   Energy and Performance Trade-Off

Figure 4 shows the normalized Energy-Delay Product (EDP) for the benchmarks in all the tested systems. As in the energy chart, bars above 1 represent higher

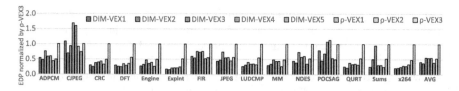

Fig. 4. EDP for each benchmark normalized by the baseline (ρ-VEX3). Bars under 1 represent worst EDP than baseline, while bars above 1 represent better EDP.

EDP and bars under 1 lower EDP than the baseline. The EDP is the product of the energy spent by the system and the execution time of an application. It is used to measure the trade-off between energy and performance (if a system fails to deliver performance, it can still show good results in energy). As can be seen in the Fig. 4, almost all of the benchmarks show better EDP than the baseline. The cases that the baseline is better are when the performance is too highly affected (CJPEG in DIM-VEX1, DIM-VEX4 and DIM-VEX5), or when both performance and energy cannot reach acceptable levels (POCSAG in DIM-VEX4 and DIM-VEX5). On average, the best trade-off between systems comes with DIM-VEX2, reducing EDP by 62.6%, closely followed by ρ-VEX1 (60.8%) and DIM-VEX1 (58.6%).

5.4   Area Analysis

Finally, we analyze the impact in area that is added by the CGRA on our systems. In the Fig. 5, the total area of each of the evaluated systems is presented. In the DIM-VEX configurations, the area is divided between the ρ-VEX processor area and the CGRA. It is clear that all the extra resources in the CGRA can occupy a high amount of space that may be prohibitive in some environments. However, if one considers the configuration DIM-VEX2, it is possible to reach better energy consumption and better performance in all, but one (Sums), of the benchmarks, at the price of an extra 84% in area.

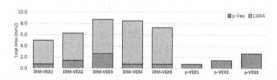

Fig. 5. Total area occupied by the evaluated systems. Bars in DIM-VEX configurations are split in the area occupied by the ρ-VEX processor and the CGRA.

6   Conclusions and Future Work

In this work we have proposed a design time configurable system that is also reconfigurable at runtime (DIM-VEX). By designing a set of configurable processors coupled with reconfigurable logic, we have shown that it is possible to further expand the ILP capabilities of multiple issue processors. Our system is also able to save energy in many scenarios, while keeping the superior performance. All these advantages come at the price of extra area.

Acknowledgments. This work was produced under grant from the Brazilian agencies FAPERGS, CAPES and CNPQ and the European Network HiPEAC.

References

1. Beck, A.C.S., Lang Lisbôa, C.A., Carro, L.: Adaptable Embedded Systems, 1st edn. Springer, New York (2013). https://doi.org/10.1007/978-1-4614-1746-0
2. Beck, A.C.S., Rutzig, M.B., Carro, L.: A transparent and adaptive reconfigurable system. Microprocess. Microsyst. **38**(5), 509–524 (2014)
3. Compton, K., Hauck, S.: Reconfigurable computing: a survey of systems and software. ACM Comput. Surv. **34**(2), 171–210 (2002)
4. Gonzalez, A., Tubella, J., Molina, C.: Trace-level reuse. In: Proceedings of the 1999 International Conference on Parallel Processing, pp. 30–37. IEEE Computer Society (1999)
5. Govindaraju, V., Ho, C.H., Nowatzki, T., Chhugani, J., Satish, N., Sankaralingam, K., Kim, C.: DySER: unifying functionality and parallelism specialization for energy-efficient computing. IEEE Micro **32**(5), 38–51 (2012)
6. Gschwind, M., Altman, E., Sathaye, S., Ledak, P., Appenzeller, D.: Dynamic and transparent binary translation. Computer **33**(3), 54–59 (2000)
7. Gustafsson, J., Betts, A., Ermedahl, A., Lisper, B.: The Mälardalen WCET benchmarks: past, present and future. In: WCET, vol. 15, pp. 136–146 (2010)
8. Koenig, R., Bauer, L., Stripf, T., Shafique, M., Ahmed, W., Becker, J., Henkel, J.: KAHRISMA: a novel hypermorphic reconfigurable-instruction-set multi-grained-array architecture. In: 2010 Design, Automation & Test in Europe Conference & Exhibition (DATE 2010), pp. 819–824. IEEE, March 2010
9. Lysecky, R., Stitt, G., Vahid, F.: Warp processors. ACM Trans. Des. Autom. Electron. Syst. **11**(3), 659–681 (2006)
10. Sartor, A.L., Becker, P., Hoozemans, J., Wong, S., Beck, A.C.S.: Dynamic trade-off among fault tolerance, energy consumption, and performance on a multiple-issue VLIW processor. IEEE Trans. Multi-Scale Comput. Syst. (2017)
11. Scott, J., Lee, L.H., Arends, J., Moyer, B.: Designing the low-power M•CORE™ architecture. In: Power Driven Microarchitecture Workshop, pp. 145–150 (1998)
12. Souza, J.D., Carro, L., Rutzig, M.B., Beck, A.C.S.: A reconfigurable heterogeneous multicore with a homogeneous ISA. In: Proceedings of the 2016 Conference on Design, Automation & Test in Europe, DATE 2016, pp. 1598–1603 (2016)
13. Watkins, M.A., Nowatzki, T., Carno, A.: Software transparent dynamic binary translation for coarse-grain reconfigurable architectures. In: 2016 IEEE International Symposium on High Performance Computer Architecture (HPCA), pp. 138–150. IEEE, March 2016
14. Wong, S., van As, T., Brown, G.: ρ-VEX: a reconfigurable and extensible soft-core VLIW processor. In: 2008 International Conference on Field-Programmable Technology, pp. 369–372. IEEE, December 2008

The Use of HACP+SBT Lossless Compression in Optimizing Memory Bandwidth Requirement for Hardware Implementation of Background Modelling Algorithms

Kamil Piszczek, Piotr Janus, and Tomasz Kryjak[✉][iD]

AGH University of Science and Technology, Al. Mickiewicza 30, Kraków, Poland
k4mil.piszczek@gmail.com, {piojanus,tomasz.kryjak}@agh.edu.pl

Abstract. In this paper the issue of optimizing memory bandwidth to external RAM in FPGA hardware implementation of foreground object segmentation methods is discussed. Three representative background modelling algorithms: Running Average (RA), Gaussian Mixture Model (GMM) and Pixel Based Adaptive Segmenter (PBAS) and three lossless compression methods: Run Length Encoding (RLE), Huffman coding and Hierarchical Average and Copy Prediction (HACP) with Significant Bit Truncation (SBT) coding were considered. After initial simulations in a software model, it was decided to implement the HACP+SBT approach in hardware. In addition, the possibility of using the proposed solution for ultra high-definition video stream processing was evaluated.

Keywords: Foreground object segmentation · Background modelling
FPGA · Lossless compression · HACP · SBT

1 Introduction

Foreground object segmentation is one of the most important components of many advanced video surveillance systems (AVSS). It is a key step in applications like abandoned luggage, forbidden zone or wrong movement direction detection. Moreover, it is also used in many tracking and human behaviour analysis systems.

With the constant technological progress, more and more often high-definition surveillance cameras are used. They resolution range from 1280×720 (HD), 1920×1080 (FHD) to even 3840×2160 (4K, UHD). Their advantages are better image quality, larger area coverage and the ability to detect more distant objects. However, the higher the resolution, the more data needs to be processed, analysed, send to the control centre and stored. One solution of the above mentioned problems is the use of the *smart camera* approach. In this case, the video stream is analysed immediately after acquisition. This reduces the need for bandwidth – the video stream send to the control centre can be compressed or less

© Springer International Publishing AG, part of Springer Nature 2018
N. Voros et al. (Eds.): ARC 2018, LNCS 10824, pp. 379–391, 2018.
https://doi.org/10.1007/978-3-319-78890-6_31

frequently sampled. In addition, with the miniaturization and cost reduction of non-volatile memory modules, archiving can also be carried out locally.

In the case of smart cameras, the choice of a suitable computing platform is very important. It should enable real-time video stream processing capabilities, as well as energy efficiency and flexibility (understood as the ability to update or redesign the used algorithms). Among the available solutions, worth mentioning are: general purpose processors (GPP), application specific integrated circuits (ASICs), field programmable gate arrays (FPGAs), and heterogeneous system on chips (SoC), which are composed of an ARM processor, reprogrammable logic and even GPU (e.g. Zynq UltraScale+ from Xilinx).

This article discusses the challenges of accessing external RAM in FPGA implementations of foreground object segregation algorithms for high definition video stream systems. The main contributions are:

– analysis of the possibility of using different lossless compression methods to optimize the size of the background model for foreground segmentation algorithms. The following compression methods: Run Length Encoding, Huffman coding and HACP (Hierarchical Average and Copy Prediction) prediction with SBT (Significant Bit Truncation) coding and background modelling algorithms: Running Average [12], Gaussian Mixture Models [10] and Pixel Based Adaptive Segmenter [2] were considered.
– FPGA hardware implementation of a compression/decompression module using the HACP prediction with SBT [7,8] (according to authors' knowledge is the first implementation in FPGA of this algorithm).
– analysis of the possibility of using the HACP+SBT method in an embedded system for foreground object segmentation for different video stream resolutions.

The rest of this paper is organized as follows. In Sect. 2 the issue of external memory transfer in FPGA implementation of background modelling algorithms is outlined. In Sect. 3 the considered lossless compression and foreground segmentation methods are briefly discussed. Results of conduced simulations are presented in Sect. 4. The designed hardware module is shown in Sect. 5. The paper ends with a conclusion and possible further research directions.

2   The External Memory Transfer Issue in FPGA Implementation of Background Algorithms

FPGA (*Field Programmable Gate Array*) devices are often used in real-time vision systems. Due to pipelining and fine-grain parallelism, it is possible to achieve significantly higher performance than with general purpose processors. Moreover, almost all common used foreground segmentation algorithms based on background modelling can be very effectively implemented in reconfigurable systems. Examples include Gaussian Mixture Models (GMM) [1] and the Pixel Based Adaptive Segmenter (PBAS) [6]. However, it should be noted that

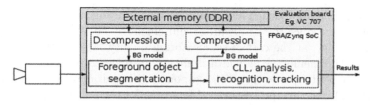

Fig. 1. Concept of the proposed foreground object segmentation system with included compression and decompression of the background model

although the implementation on computation modules (i.e. foreground segmentation and background model update) is relatively simple, a significant limitation is the communication with external RAM memory, where the model has to be stored (FPGA internal memory resources are insufficient). For example, for the popular GMM in RGB using 5 Gaussian distributions, the background model has a size of 560 bits for each pixel, giving 61 MB for HD resolution (1280×720), 138 MB for FHD (1920×1080) and 554 MB for 4K (3840×2160), respectively.

In addition, if a 60 frame per second video stream is processed, the required data transfer reaches 7.2 GB/s, 16.2 GB/s and 64.8 GB/s, respectively. These values can be combined with the external RAM memory parameters available on the popular Xilinx evaluation boards: VC 707 (Virtex 7) – 1 GB DDR3 memory – 12.5 GB/s, VC 709 (Virtex 7) – 2×4 GB DDR3 memory – 25 GB/s and Zynq UltraScale+ – 2×4 GB DDR4 – 21 GB/s. Wherein, in the case of dynamic memory, it is impossible to obtain the maximum values, because of the necessity of refreshing and accessing individual banks and columns. Moreover, for the last platform, one of the memory banks is connected to the ARM processor system part, which further reduces the maximum transfer rate. This exemplary values show, that implementing the GMM algorithm for FHD resolution is challenging, although possible and for 4K very difficult.

One possibility of limiting the transfer to external RAM is to use a background model compression/decompression scheme. Schematically, this is illustrated in Fig. 1. This approach has several advantages. First, it reduces the cost of designing and producing a hardware platform equipped with many high-speed memory modules. Second, it allows to lower power consumption, as the most common used dynamic RAM memory modules require rather high clock frequencies, which negatively affects power consumption. Third, for a given platform it allows to run more complex algorithms, improve algorithm parameters (grayscale vs. RGB, add more distributions in GMM) and run the system for a higher resolution. Finally, due to the use of lossless compression, the quality of segmentation is not deteriorated. Moreover, using this type of compression allows the compatibility with most foreground segmentation algorithms, even those with complex and "non-image" based model.

The topic of using background model compression in case of FPGA implementation was described in few publications. For example, in papers [3–5] the same research group proposed for the GMM method, a spatial similarity based lossy compression approach. This, combined with limiting the model representation, allowed to reduce the bandwidth requirement by 50–70%. However, as the authors point out, at the cost of segmentation quality. Also, authors of [1] pay attention to the memory bandwidth limit and use very careful selection of the background model representation (fixed-point). Without data compression they obtained FHD real-time processing (91 fps) on a Virtex 6 device.

3   The Analysed Compression and Background Modelling Algorithms

3.1   Lossless Compression Methods

Run Length Encoding. One of the basic techniques for lossless compression is the RLE *Run Length Encoding* algorithm [9]. It is based on the premise that if the data sample d is repeated n times in the input stream, then its n repetitions can be replaced by a dn pair. For example, for the following input: $A B B B B B B B B B B C C D E F B$, the compressed string $A1B9C2D1E1F1B1$ will be obtained (compression rate equals 75%).

Huffman Coding. In this approach, the input symbols are converted to variable length codes [9]. The most frequent symbols are assigned to the shortest code words. This method is an example of a statistical compression method. It should be noted that the use of this type of algorithms to compress the background model is cumbersome. Before the proper coding, it is necessary to create some statistics (e.g. histogram of pixel values), which can also vary for different scenes. This introduces an additional delay. In addition, the so-called Huffman's tree, which describes the coding, should be stored along with the compressed data.

HACP+SBT. The algorithm consists of two phases: prediction using the Hierarchical Average and Copy Prediction (HACP) and error (residues) coding of the results using the Significant Bit Truncation (SBT) method.

In the first step the input image is divided into 8×8 blocks. Then, for each block the HACP predictor is applied. It consists of three levels $L = 1, 2, 3$ starting with $L3$. This is illustrated in Fig. 2. Pixels indicated by the two arrows are estimated as the average of two pixels and by one arrow as a neighbours copy. Thus, four types of prediction can be distinguished: Horizontal Average Prediction (HAP) – Eq. (1), Vertical Average Prediction (VAP) – Eq. (2), Horizontal Copy Prediction (HCP) – Eq. (4), Vertical Copy Prediction (VCP) – Eq. (3).

The prediction process for a sample 8×8 block is shown in Fig. 3. In the first step, according to the diagram shown in Fig. 2, the predicted 8×8 values are determined and then the prediction errors (residues) computed. In the second step, these residues are grouped (details in [7] – Fig. 2) and then encoded by the Significant Bit Truncation (SBT) method. It involves the omission of the most significant bits that are repeated in a given group. Thus the length of a code word in a given group equals the length of the code word of the largest error. If this value exceeds 7 bits, then no encoding in performed and the input value are stored. The size of the code word is written in the heading of the group and marked BLH (Bit Length Header). Finally, the result of compression of a single block is a vector consisting of a DC value (8 bit), 8 BLH ($8 \times 4 = 32$ bits) and a variable size part with encoded residues.

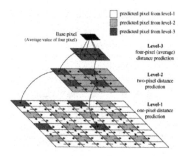

$$x_{i,j} = p_{i,j} - \lfloor \frac{p_{i-d,j} + p_{i+d,j} + 1}{2} \rfloor \quad (1)$$

$$x_{i,j} = p_{i,j} - \lfloor \frac{p_{i,j-d} + p_{i,j+d} + 1}{2} \rfloor \quad (2)$$

$$x_{i,j} = p_{i,j} - p_{i-d,j} \quad (3)$$

$$x_{i,j} = p_{i,j} - p_{i,j-d} \quad (4)$$

where:

Fig. 2. HACP predictor for a 8×8 block. Pixels from the lower level are predicted by those from the higher one. The base pixel is the average of 4 pixels from L3 (the most dark ones'). Image taken from [8]

- $x_{i,j}$ – prediction error for pixel with i (horizontal) and j (vertical) coordinates,
- $p_{i,j}$ – input pixel value,
- d – distance from the input to target pixel – depends on the prediction level $d = 2^{L-1}$.

3.2 Background Modelling Methods

Several foreground object segmentation methods with different degree of background model complexity were used to evaluate the usefulness of the previously described lossless compression methods. The first is the simple running average (RA) [12]. In this case, the background model consists only of grayscale or colour components – it is an image. However, due to the update procedure, the representation has to be fractional. If 16 bits per colour component are used, then the size of the model is 48 bits per single pixel.

The second is Gaussian Mixture Models [10], which is one of the most commonly used background modelling methods. In this approach, each pixel is represented by k Gaussian distributions, which are characterized by three numbers – ω (weight of the Gaussian distribution), μ (mean value) and σ (standard deviation or covariance). The process of foreground object classification and model updating is quite complex and goes beyond the scope of this paper. For the proposed application only the size and structure of the background model is important. It depends on the k parameter and number of bits assigned for particular parameters of a single distribution (fixed-point representation). For example, for $k = 5$ and assuming 112 bits for a single Gaussian distribution model (1 x weight, 3 x mean and 3 x standard deviation, 16 bits each) the size of the model for a single pixel equals 560 bits.

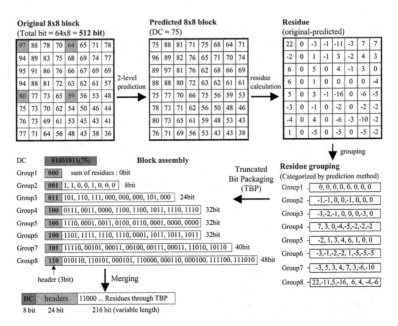

Fig. 3. Scheme of the HACP prediction and SBT coding – image taken from [7]

The last considered algorithm is Pixel Based Adaptive Segmenter (PBAS) [2]. In this case, the background model consists of stored pixels samples (i.e. 8-bit grayscale or 24-bit RGB). The algorithm itself is quite complex and its detailed description goes beyond this work. Like previously, only the structure of the background model is important. In addition to pixel values – samples (B), the corresponding set of distances (D) is also used. During each iteration, the distance between the current pixel and the closest sample is saved at an appropriate position in the D set. Moreover, each pixel has an individual decision threshold R and a update probability parameter T. For an exemplary background model with 20 samples and R and T parameters represented by 16 bits, we obtain: $20 \cdot (8 + 8) + 16 + 16 = 352$ bits. Thus, for the RGB colour space, the model for a single pixel has $3 \cdot 338 = 1056$ bits.

4   Software Simulation Results

In the first step, the usefulness of the described lossless compression methods was evaluated in a software simulation. For this purpose, compression and background modelling algorithms were implemented in Python. The `changedetection` [11] dataset was used as test sequences.

The experiments were divided into two stages: preliminary and extended. In the first case a 128×128 patch from the *highway* sequence was used. It was also limited to 200 frames – one car was moving through the scene.

The CR (Compression Ratio), i.e. the ratio of data size after to size before compression, was used to evaluate the efficiency (all presented results are given in percentages).

For the RLE method, it was decided to perform compression in each row of the image. During initial tests it turned out, that the fractional parts in the RA and GMM models cause a significant problem. A more detailed analysis of integer and fractional parts histograms revealed, that in the later case repetition of values was very rare. Therefore, the compression was limited only to the integer part. Unfortunately, the results were far from satisfactory – for RA the CR was 97%. The RLE method has the potential of a high compression ratio for data that has a large number of neighbouring elements of equal value. Unfortunately, for real video, this situation is very rare (e.g. due to slight sensor noise). Therefore, RLE is not a suitable solution in the proposed compression system.

For the Huffman method, two experiments were conducted. At first, the statistics for the entire background model were collected and then compression was performed. For the RA method a CR of 92% was obtained. Then, the model was split into smaller patches (e.g. 64×64, 8×8), etc. This allowed for an improvement in the CR parameter, e.g. up to 80% for 8×8. However, this solution is not well suited for the considered application. For each patch, the statistics has to be computed, then the codewords assigned and finally the so-called Huffman tree stored along with compressed data. Taking into account the above drawbacks, it was not decided to use this method in the considerate system.

The last of the analysed lossless compression methods was HACP+SBT. For the RA algorithm and integer part compression only, the average CR was 72% (the fractional part was stored uncompressed). It is worth pointing out that for the integer part a 44% CR was obtained. For the GMM method, a CR of 67% was estimated – assuming that the integer part of all colour components were compressed. For the PBAS method, four tests were performed – full compression of the background model, compression excluding fractional R and T parameters, compression without R and T parameters, and compression of sample values only (B). In the first three cases the results were 41–42%, in the last 80%.

In this initial experiment, background models were arranged in a $8 \times 8 \times 2 \times N$ matrix (N – number of samples in the model – $B + D$, R and T are omitted). The input to the encoding module is therefore $2 \times N \times 8 \times 8$ blocks. This is shown schematically in Fig. 4a. This arrangement is the most obvious realization of the HACP+SBT coding for the PBAS algorithm and is a direct transfer of the approach from the compression of a video stream. However, it should be noted that samples in particular blocks, due to the random factor in the method, do not have to create a "coherent" image, as they could be registered at different moments in time.

In the case of hardware implementation designed for real-time processing, it is quite cumbersome to gather a $2 \times N \times 8 \times 8$ context, as it requires many internal block RAM resources. In addition, this solution involves the use of $2 \times N$ HACP+SBT compression/decompression modules, which requires large logic resources.

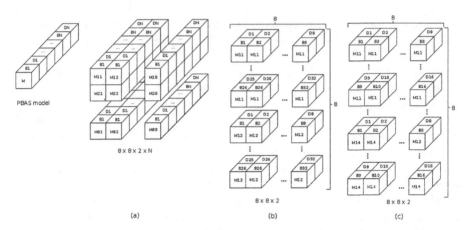

Fig. 4. Possible arrangements of the PBAS background model into an 8×8 data block. (a) spatial context (64 PBAS single pixel models), (b) grouping two consecutive PBAS models into an array ($N = 32$ samples each), (c) grouping four consecutive PBAS models into an array ($N = 16$ samples each)

In case of the PBAS algorithm, a sample based context could be used. For simplicity, let's assume that is consist of $N = 16$ or $N = 32$ samples ($N \times B$ and $N \times D$ values). Two possible grouping schemes are presented in Fig. 4b and c. In this cases, it is not necessary to accumulate a large spatial context, since in only two (1×2) or four (1×4) neighbouring background models are compressed. In addition, only two HACP+SBT compression and decompression modules are needed. The experimental results show that for these solutions the average compression ratio is about 50–55% and 60–65% respectively for 32 samples (two neighbours) and 16 samples (four neighbours). This is about 10% worse that the spatial approach, but compensated by N-times less compression/decompression modules usage and much simpler 8×8 block generation.

Due to promising initial results, for the HACP+SBT method additional tests on four sequences from the `changedetection.net` set: *highway, office, pedestrians* and *PETS2006* were performed. Their results are presented in Table 1 and confirm earlier observations that the best CR values can be obtained for the PBAS method (50–70%).

Based on preliminary and extended test results, it was decided to focus on the HACP+SBT method in combination with the PBAS algorithm. The following factors were considered:

- the PBAS method does not require the use of fractional numbers, whose lossless compression is not effective (they are not repeatable),
- there is no need for statistics computing, as in the Huffman method,
- hardware implementation of the HACP+SBT compression and decompression is quite simple and effective.

Table 1. Mean CR values for the HACP+SBT compression for the analysed background generation methods

Sequence	RA	GMM	PBAS 8×8	PBAS $2 \times 32 - 1 \times 2$	PBAS $4 \times 16 - 1 \times 4$
Highway	80.7%	80.3%	50.906%	62.4%	68.5%
Office	74.4%	63.6%	43.865%	62.2%	68.7%
Pedestrians	73.9%	70.7%	44.469%	62.4%	67.7%
PETS2006	73.7%	77.8%	44.469%	60.1%	66.3%

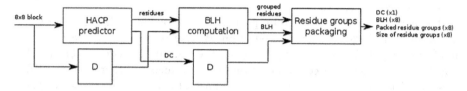

Fig. 5. Scheme of the HACP+SBT compression module. D – synchronization delay.

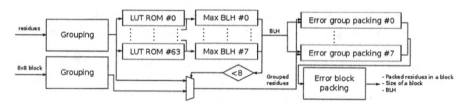

Fig. 6. Scheme of the BLH computation module

5   Hardware Implementation of the HACP+SBT Algorithm

The proposed hardware architecture can be divided into three parts. The first is responsible for reformatting the input data stream into a 8×8 block. It depends on the selected data formatting scheme. The second, for block compression and third for formatting the data send to the memory. In the case of decompression, the order is reversed. In the following section, the compression and decompression modules are described, because the format of the data strictly depends on the algorithm being considered and the solution adopted.

Compression of a Single Block. Scheme of the compression module is shown in Fig. 5. The input is a 8×8 data block. First, the HACP predictor is applied. The analysis of formulas (1)–(4) shows that only addition, subtraction and division by power od 2 (bit shift) operations are required. The output are residues (predictive errors) – 9-bit numbers written in two's complement format and an additional DC value (the average of pixels in the 3'rd compression layer – cf. Fig. 2).

The next steps are BLH computation and residue packaging. The scheme of this module is shown in Fig. 6. The input are 8×8 residue and input value matrices (the later used when compression of the group is not profitable). The first step involves grouping of both matrices (details in [7], Fig. 2). In FPGA this is realised by proper signal routing. Then, for all errors from the residues groups, BLH values are determined. A LUT approach was used. The respective residue values were assigned the corresponding BLH sizes. In the next step, the maximum BLH value was determined and it became the header for the whole group. If BLH was equal 8, then the input values were used instead of residues (multiplexer in the scheme).

The next step was residue group packing. Based on the BLH values for samples from a given group, a SBT operation was performed to remove the most significant bits. This was done in parallel for the 8 groups considered. The results were then combined in a common residue block, which together with the BLH constituted the output from the module. The total latency is 22 clock cycles (HACP prediction – 2, BHL computing – 4, residue group packing – 16).

Decompression of a Single Block. The decompression process is a reverse operation to the compression described above. The input to the module is a DC value, BLH and packaged residue groups. The first step is to unpack the residue groups, which involves adding 0 or 1 (depending on the sign and BLH value). The values are then re-grouped within the block i.e. set at their original locations.

The last stage is the reconstruction of the HACP. Its implementation is more complex than prediction because relationships between data exists. According to the diagram in Fig. 2, the first step was to recreate the value of L3 based on the DC value. Then VAP/VCP reconstruction from level 2, HAP/HCP from L2, VAP/VCP from L1 and finally HAP/HCP from L1. The total latency is 26 (16 ticks for unpacking residue groups and 9 ticks for HACP reconstruction).

Implementation Results. As outlined above, the basic advantage of the HCAP+SBT method is the simplicity of hardware implementation – including FPGAs. The module only involves addition and subtraction operations, LUTs, comparisons, and re-groupings. After synthesis in Xilinx Vivado 2017.2 the following results were obtained. For the compression module: 5264 LUT (including 1035 as memory) and 3815 FF were used – this is about 1.75% of target device i.e. Virtex 7 (XC7VX485T-2FFG1761C). For the decompression module respectively: 3158 LUT (including 18 as memory) and 3957 FF – about 1.05% of target device. Therefore, the compression/decompression chain for a 8×8 block of 8-bit values involves about 3% of the logic resources.

Combining this result with the concepts presented in Fig. 4 it can be concluded that for the PBAS algorithm, the realization of the first approach – $2 \times N \times 8 \times 8$ for "reasonable" values of N (e.g. 16) is impossible due to the excessive use of logic resources. It is much better to re-arrange the background model into a 8×8 block (Fig. 4b or c).

Table 2. Effect of the proposed compression on the greyscale version of the PBAS algorithm parameters. N – the maximum number of samples in the model

Resolution	Bits/pixel	PBAS uncompressed (N)	PBAS compressed (N)
1280 × 720	950	57	88
1920 × 1080	420	24	37
3840 × 2160	106	4	7

The designed compression and decompression modules were tested in Vivado simulations and then evaluated in hardware on the VC 707 development board form Xilinx. As a test case, a 720p colour video stream was compressed and than decompressed.

Practical Application. Finally, it is also worth analysing how the proposed compression scheme could influence the real-time implementation of the PBAS algorithm. For the VC 707 board, the maximum transfer rate to external RAM is 12.5 GB/s. If we assume that the target is a 60 fps video stream, there is about 210 MB of data per frame (105 MB write and 105 MB reading). On this basis, the number of bits per pixel can be determined. The results are summarized in Table 2. The *PBAS uncompressed (N)* column presents the maximal number of samples (N) for the greyscale version of the algorithms. For the *PBAS compressed (N)* column an average CR of 65% was assumed.

In the case of a practical application of the described external RAM access optimization scheme, a situation where for some specific data the compression ratio increases above the assumed value should be considered. Then, due to the upper transfer limit, data loss or the problems with synchronizing the pixel and the background model stream may occur. One possible solution involves the implementation of a compression rate monitoring module. In the case of exceeding the assumed CR, the number of samples (PBAS) or Gaussian distributions (GMM) for a part of the image could be reduced. In the next iteration, these data should be re-initialized. This approach should not have a significant impact on the segmentation performance.

The presented results indicate that using the HACP+SBT method should allow to run a colour PBAS model for 720p and 1080p resolutions. Using the GMM and PBAS algorithms, even in grayscale, for 4K resolution is a challenge and would require an improvement of the compression ratio. However, in the case of GMM and estimated compression rate 80% (which increases the supported word length from 106 to 132 bits), it should be possible to run at least a greyscale model and also a colour one with reduced precision.

6   Summary

In this paper, a discussion concerning using lossless compression methods in hardware implementations of foreground segmentation algorithms was presented.

The obtained results prove that the HACP+SBT approach provides the best efficiency. Additionally, during experiments it was noticed that the compression rate of the fractional part in RA and GMM models was very low due to their low repeatability. Therefore, the proposed approach is mostly suited for segmentation methods with integer-only pixel values like ViBE and PBAS.

The proposed research is the first step towards implementing in FPGA foreground object segmentation algorithms in 4K resolution. In this case, the necessary throughput to external memory is four times bigger than for FHD. Therefore, for more advanced background models, some sort of compression is unavoidable. Moreover, proposing a "general" solution – for GMM, PBAS and other method seems very unlikely. To obtain the required CR, the compression method must be precisely adjusted to the considered background model. The proposed framework could be improved by a more detailed analysis of different possible data groupings for particular methods (spatial and model based). Furthermore, the implementation of the HACP+SBT module could to improved and the resource usage limited. Finally, hardware experiments for different methods should be conducted.

Acknowledgements. The work presented in this paper was supported by the National Science Centre project no. 2016/23/D/ST6/01389.

References

1. Genovese, M., Napoli, E.: ASIC and FPGA implementation of the Gaussian mixture model algorithm for real-time segmentation of high definition video. IEEE Trans. Very Large Scale Integr. VLSI Syst. **22**(3), 537–547 (2014)
2. Hoffman, M., Tiefenbacher, P., Rigoll, G.: Background segmentation with feedback: the pixel-based adaptive segmenter. In: 2012 IEEE Computer Society Conference on Computer Vision and Pattern Recognition Workshops, pp. 35–47 (2012)
3. Jiang, H., Öwall, V., Ardo, H.: Real-time video segmentation with VGA resolution and memory bandwidth reduction. In: International Conference on Video and Signal Based Surveillance, p. 104 (2006)
4. Jiang, H., Ardo, H., Owall, V.: A hardware architecture for real-time video segmentation utilizing memory reduction techniques. IEEE Trans. Circuits Syst. Video Technol. **19**(2), 226–236 (2009)
5. Kristensen, F., Hedberg, H., Jiang, H., Nilsson, P., Öwall, V.: An embedded real-time surveillance system: implementation and evaluation. J. Sig. Process. Syst. **52**(1), 75–94 (2008)
6. Kryjak, T., Komorkiewicz, M., Gorgon, M.: Hardware implementation of the PBAS foreground detection method in FPGA. In: 2013 Proceedings of the 20th International Conference Mixed Design of Integrated Circuits and Systems (MIXDES), pp. 479–484 (2013)
7. Kim, J., Kim, J., Kyung, C.: A lossless embedded compression algorithm for high definition video coding. In: 2009 IEEE International Conference on Multimedia and Expo, pp. 193–196 (2009)
8. Kim, J., Kyung, C.: A lossless embedded compression using significant bit truncation for HD video coding. IEEE Trans. Circuits Syst. Video Technol. **20**(6), 848–860 (2010)

9. Salomon, D., Motta, G.: Handbook of Data Compression. Springer, London (2010). https://doi.org/10.1007/978-1-84882-903-9
10. Stauffer, C., Grimson, W.E.L.: Adaptive background mixture models for real-time tracking. In: Proceedings of IEEE Computer Society Conference on Computer Vision and Pattern Recognition, pp. 246–252 (1999)
11. Wang, Y., Jodoin, P., Konrad, J., Benezeth, Y., Ishwar, P.: CDnet 2014: an expanded change detection benchmark dataset. In: 2014 IEEE Conference on Computer Vision and Pattern Recognition Workshops, pp. 393–400 (2014)
12. Wren, C.R., Azarbayejani, A., Darrell, T., Pentland, A.P.: Pfinder: real-time tracking of the human body. IEEE Trans. Pattern Anal. Mach. Intell. **19**(7), 780–785 (1997)

A Reconfigurable PID Controller

Sikandar Khan[1], Kyprianos Papadimitriou[2,3]([⊠]) [iD], Giorgio Buttazzo[1],
and Kostas Kalaitzakis[2]

[1] Scuola Superiore Sant'Anna, Pisa, Italy
[2] Technical University of Crete, Chania, Greece
kpapadim@mhl.tuc.gr
[3] Technological Educational Institute of Crete, Heraklion, Greece

Abstract. We survey the Proportional-Integral-Derivative (PID) controller variants and we switch them in runtime via reconfiguration, as the control requirements change. Depending on the PID variant, e.g. P, I, PI, PD, PID, PI-PD, the involved computations to produce the control output are different. We rely on a previous published design to shorten the execution cycle of each controller variant, by increasing the number of arithmetic units operating concurrently. Furthermore, we incorporate a design based on multiplexers that allows for eliminating frequent reconfigurations, which were required in the previous work. Finally, we evaluate our approach in terms of resource utilization and reconfiguration time.

1 Introduction

The PID algorithm has been widely adopted by the industry due to its simplicity of design and implementation. An old work [1] surveying over $11,000$ controllers in process industries, reports that more than 97% of regulatory controllers utilize PID. Although designing a PID controller is conceptually intuitive, it is hard in practice, if multiple and often conflicting objectives such as fast transient response and high stability requirements are to be met. Therefore, different PID controller variants have been suggested, each one serving better different control scenarios. These controllers, e.g. P-only, I-only, PI, PD, PID, PI-PD, generate a control output of different nature, ranging from more robust to more stable or accurate [2]. In the present work, we are switching the controller variants via reconfiguration, aiming at achieving a control response that integrates the best feature of all these variants depending on the requirements. The computations required to produce the control output differ, thus we are adjusting them at run-time. Our contributions are:

- the controller type is reconfigured instead of implementing statically all controllers and multiplexing their outputs. This accounts for latency reduction in delivering controller's output, and for resource savings;
- given a number of multipliers and adders, we are examining the overlapped computations so as to parallelize them, while respecting the dependencies and

© Springer International Publishing AG, part of Springer Nature 2018
N. Voros et al. (Eds.): ARC 2018, LNCS 10824, pp. 392–403, 2018.
https://doi.org/10.1007/978-3-319-78890-6_32

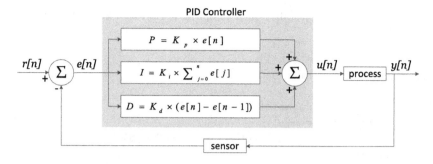

Fig. 1. A PID controller in a feedback loop. $r[n]$ is the desired value.

the delay added from the registers holding the intermediate results in each computational unit;

– we propose a design relying on multiplexers built in each reconfigurable module. This allows for avoiding frequent reconfiguration of the coefficients, i.e. gain parameters, of the controllers, yet respecting their dynamic characteristics.

The rest of the paper is organized as follows. In Sect. 2 we briefly discuss the PID controller and its variants, and in Sect. 3 the adaptive controllers. Section 4 presents our approach for switching the controllers. Section 5 has the implementation details along with its evaluation. Section 6 concludes the paper.

2 The PID Controller and Its Variants

A PID controller is used in industrial applications for regulating processes as part of a control loop. It receives a setpoint request from the user, e.g. vehicle's desired speed when activating cruise control, and compares it to a measured feedback, e.g. vehicle's current speed. The difference between the setpoint and feedback values is termed error, and the job of the controller is to eliminate it. This process takes place continuously during which the PID controller performs computations to generate an output for eliminating the error. Figure 1 illustrates a generic PID controller. Mathematically it is expressed with Eq. 1,

$$u[n] = K_p \times e[n] + K_i \times \sum_{j=0}^{n} e[j] + K_d \times (e[n] - e[n-1]) \tag{1}$$

where $e[n]$ represent the nth sample of the instantaneous error obtained as a difference between the setpoint value $r[n]$, and the measured output of the process $y[n]$ for some physical variable under control, such that $e[n] = r[n] - y[n]$. The PID controller takes the error $e[n]$ as an input and computes its control output $u[n]$ based on its proportional K_p, integral K_i, and derivative K_d gains - termed also coefficients - such that $u[n] = P + I + D$, where P, I, and D refer to the proportional, the integral, and the derivative term, respectively. A closed-loop is inserted in which the process output, $y[n]$, is observed by a sensor, to calculate the instantaneous error $e[n]$ after each sampling period T. The PID pseudo-code is given below.

```
Em = 0            #Em = e[n-1]
SumEm = 0         #SumEm = e[0]+e[1]+...+e[n-1]
LOOP
wait (T)          #1 execution cycle
    En = error    #En = e[n]
    Un = (Kp*En) + (Ki*(En+SumEm)) + (Kd*(En-Em))
    SumEm = En+SumEm
    Em = En
end LOOP
```

A PID controller can be used in different combinations to achieve a control response of different nature. The work in [3] analyzes the different control structures. The P controller has fast system response (robust), and decreases system's steady state error (SSE). However, beyond a certain value of the SSE reduction, a further increase in the proportional gain leads to an overshoot of the system response that causes oscillation and leads to instability. Moreover, P controller never eliminates SSE, so it is suitable for systems that can tolerate a constant SSE. On the other hand, the PI controller eliminates the SSE, but it is characterized by slow response (sluggish); the integral term responds to accumulated errors from the past, thus it can cause the present value to overshoot beyond the setpoint, causing instability. The PD controller prevents sudden changes occurring in the control output resulting from sudden changes in the error signal and has good stability. The downside is that the derivative factor directly amplifies the noise. The PID controller has the optimum control dynamics, however, tuning its parameters to respond to different conditions is challenging. For instance, if a PID controller for motor is tuned without load, it will not perform optimally when the load changes. This is why most often a set of parameters is chosen that is working satisfactory in all cases and not necessarily best for any particular case [4]. The control response of PID variants are summarized in Table 1; their advantages can be grasped by contemplating their differences side-by-side.

Table 1. Response characteristics of different controllers.

Parameter	Controller type			
	P	PI	PD	PID
Rise time	Decreases	Minor decrease	No effect	Minor decrease
Overshoot	Increases	Increases	Decrease	Minor decrease
Settling time	Small change	Increases	Decrease	Minor decrease
Steady state error	Decreases	Eliminates	No effect	Minor decrease
Stability	Degrades	Degrades	Good	Good for small K_d

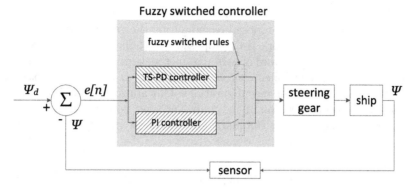

Fig. 2. The proper controller is activated depending on whether faster response or steady accuracy is required.

3 Adaptive Controllers

Non-linear or adaptive controllers operate efficiently in dynamic environments and cover a sufficiently large operating range. Adaptivity is achieved either by combining different controllers and switching amongst them based on their individual operating regime, or, by changing the gain parameters of a single controller as control requirements change.

3.1 Switching Controllers

The concept of dividing the operating envelope of any control process into operating regimes was proposed in [5]. Using this concept, the authors of [6] presented a performance-oriented ship track auto-control that combines the advantages of a fuzzy PD controller and a conventional PI controller. The PD controller is active in the transient regime to deliver fast response, and the PI controller is activated in the steady regime to achieve greater accuracy. The switching decision is based on the rudder angle Ψ of the ship, which is small during straight course (steady regime) but would change by large scale during a course change (transient regime). Figure 2 illustrates the concept of switching the controllers. Other earlier works combining different controllers to integrate both robustness and stability were published in [7,8]. Similarly, [9] proposes switching amongst multiple co-existing PID controllers in an electrostatic micro-actuator system.

3.2 Reconfigurable Controllers

FPGA technology offers good-closed performance and its suitability in control applications has been reviewed in [10], which highlights its advantages of speed and low-cost development, flexibility, and limited power consumption. In addition, reconfiguration has been used to modify the control parameters to a new set of values according to the run-time requirements. To the best of our knowledge, only a few works have proposed reconfiguring the gain parameters [11–13]. The authors of an earlier work [14], proposed a reconfigurable circuit for controlling the passing of the values of gain parameters kept in registers, depending on whether the PID controller executes the P, I or D stage of its execution cycle; this results in frequent reconfigurations. Our approach is different in that it allows partial reconfiguration of the controller type, contrary to changing the gain parameters only. Table 2 summarizes the main attributes of our approach in contrast to previous ones.

Table 2. Static and reconfigurable resources in the proposed controllers. In our design the values of gain parameters are kept in registers that can be changed with a "write" command.

Reference	Static	Reconfigurable
[11–13]	Controller type	Gain parameters
	Tpe of operations	
	# operations	
[14]	Controller type	Switching of operands
	Type of operations	
	# operations	
	Gain parameters	
Present design	Gain parameters	Controller type
		Type of operations
		# operations

4   Designing Effectively the Controller Variants

We are combining both the foregoing adaptive strategies to model a reconfigurable PID controller that can be flexible and fast. Figure 3 illustrates our approach. We are using as vehicle the architecture in [14], and initially we are studying the way it supports all controller variants. We then show how we have parallelized the computations, i.e. multiplications and additions, taking into account the delay introduced by the registers holding the intermediate results in each computational unit. Finally, we show that for switching the gain parameters - depending on the stage of the execution cycle -, we use multiplexers as opposed to frequently partially reconfiguring the fabric, as was done in [14].

4.1   Overlapped and Dependent Computations

In the original architecture [14], 1 multiplication and 1 addition are carried out in each stage of the execution cycle of the PID controller. The gain parameters are stored in registers and depending on the stage of the execution cycle, they

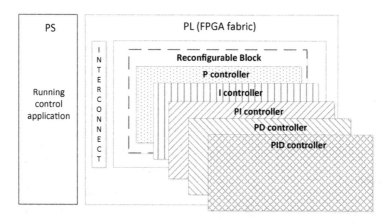

Fig. 3. The partially reconfigurable area is programmed with a different controller depending on the run-time control requirements.

are passed for computation to the PRODUCT and ADDITION blocks via reconfiguring a circuit. We use this original architecture to study its performance for designing other controller variants. Table 3 shows the actual number and type of computations to carry out one complete execution cycle, i.e. generate one control output, along with the dependencies between the computations. In Fig. 4(a), we are analyzing the number of stages per execution cycle for the different variants, assuming they are implemented with the original architecture. In Fig. 4 we have considered the dependencies of the terms inside the involved computations as well as the cycle delay added from the registers in each computational unit.

Table 3. Number and type of computations carried out in 1 period (T) of execution for the different controllers. Table exposes also the dependencies between the computations.

Controller type	# computations	Involved multiplications	Involved additions
P	1	$K_p \times En = P$	0
PI	4	$K_p \times En = P$	$En + SumEm$
		$K_i \times (En + SumEm) = I$	$P + I$
PD	5	$K_p \times En = P$	$En - Em$
		$-1 \times Em$	
		$K_d \times (En - Em) = D$	$P + D$
PID	8	$K_p \times En = P$	$En + SumEm$
		$-1 \times Em$	$En - Em$
		$K_i \times (En + SumEm) = I$	$P + I$
		$K_d \times (En - Em) = D$	$P + I + D$

P controller :

←1 ex. cycle→

product	K_p x En (P)
addition	

no change here : 1 stage is needed also with our design for completing 1 execution cycle

PI controller :

←———1 execution cycle———→

product	K_p x En (P)		K_i x (En+SumEm) (I)	K_p x En (P)
addition	P+I	En+SumEm		P+I

←———1 execution cycle———→

product	K_p x En (P)	K_i x (En+SumEm) (I)	K_p x En (P)
addition	En+SumEm		En+SumEm
addition	P+I		P+I

PD controller :

←————————1 execution cycle————————→

product	K_p x En (P)	-1 x Em		K_d x (En-Em) (D)	K_p x En (P)
addition	P+D		En-Em		P+D

←————————1 execution cycle————————→

product	K_p x En (P)		K_d x (En-Em) (D)	K_p x En (P)
product	-1 x Em			-1 x Em
addition	P+D	En-Em		P+D

PID controller :

←————————1 execution cycle————————→

product	K_p x En (P)	-1 x Em	K_i x (En+SumEm) (I)	K_d x (En-Em) (D)	K_p x En (P)
addition	P+I+D	En+SumEm	En-Em	P+I	P+I+D

←————————1 execution cycle————————→

product	K_p x En (P)	K_i x (En+SumEm) (I)	K_d x (En-Em) (D)	K_p x En (P)
product	-1 x Em			-1 x Em
addition	En+SumEm	En-Em	P+I	En+SumEm
addition	P+I+D			P+I+D

(a) design based on [14] : # stages per execution cycle when 1 multiplier and 1 adder are available

(b) our design : # stages per execution cycle, when the number of multipliers and adders is customized

Fig. 4. Comparison of [14] VS. our design in terms of the number of stages per execution cycle. At the end of every execution cycle the output $u[n]$ is computed. Fewer stages can result in smaller latency.

4.2 Reducing the Number of Stages per Execution Cycle

We parallelize the arithmetic operations by incorporating additional multipliers and adders; the number of additional computational units differs amongst the controllers. This allows for shortening their execution cycle, which accounts for smaller latency and faster responsiveness. This is a typical requirement in real-time domains. The way the controller variants operate now is shown in Fig. 4(b). It illustrates that in almost all cases 1 stage can be eliminated, e.g. for the PD and the PID controllers the original design [14] completes the execution cycle in 4 stages, while our design completes in 3 stages. In the near future, we will study in-depth the trade-offs in terms of the latency from the incorporation of registers in the computational units, i.e. for pipelining and registering their inputs/outputs.

4.3 Switching the Gain Parameters via Multiplexers

In the original design, one reconfiguration occurs in every stage of the execution cycle, e.g. 4 reconfigurations for the PID. If the sampling period (T) for some control variable is 100 ms, roughly speaking, a reconfiguration occurs every 25 ms. We instead create partial bitstreams in which the design for each variant incorporates a fixed set of multiplexers that allow for switching amongst the gain parameters, depending on the stage of the execution cycle. Figure 5 illustrates our design, and its output depending on the stage. A Finite State Machine (FSM) is also implemented in each bitstream for controlling the "SEL" signals of the multiplexers. Depending on the stage of the execution cycle, the FSM enters a different state driving accordingly the "SEL" signals. The operation of the FSM is simple and further details remain out of the scope of this paper. This additional hardware increases the bitstream size, but eliminates reconfiguration in every stage.

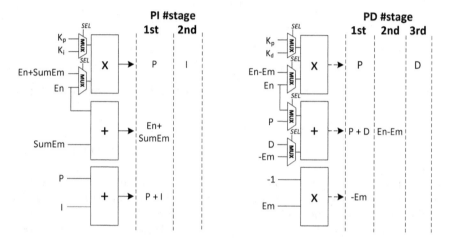

Fig. 5. A fixed number of multiplexers in each RM allows for eliminating partial reconfiguration of the gain parameters, i.e. coefficients, in every stage of the execution cycle.

5   Implementation of a Reconfigurable Arithmetic Block

To demonstrate our approach, we implemented a reconfigurable arithmetic block in the Programmable Logic (PL) of a Zybo platform. We also developed code for the Processor System (PS), which is responsible for I/O data handling, reconfiguration of the block, and runs the control application. This experimental setup is shown in Fig. 6. The functionality of the block PL can be altered by loading the corresponding partial bitstream from a DDR memory into a Reconfigurable Partition (RP) via the PCAP configuration port [15]. One Reconfigurable Partition (RP) in the block can host one Reconfigurable Module (RM) at a time, performing a fixed set of 32-bit wide simultaneous operations. A number of RMs have been predesigned and stored in DDR that implement the arithmetic operations of the different variants. The operands to be processed and the results

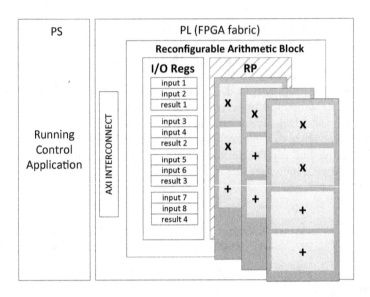

Fig. 6. The proposed reconfigurable arithmetic block, and the experimental setup for testing it.

are stored in a fixed set of register array, accessible to the PS through an AXI interface.

In each RM, adders are implemented in LUTs, and multiplications in DSP slices. The DSP slice, shown in Fig. 7, consists of a fundamental 25 × 18-bit multiplier with pipelining and extension capabilities [16]. A total of 80 DSP slices are available in the PL of Zybo (Z-7010), distributed equally across 4 Clock Regions (CRs) [15, 16]. It should be noted here that according to Xilinx, restricting modules to one CR accounts for reaching high clock frequencies. To support wider multiplications the DSP slices need to be cascaded. This affects the total number of multiplications than can be created within each CR; in

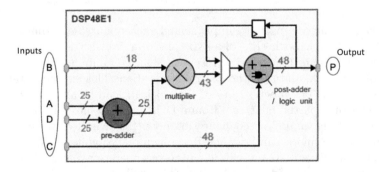

Fig. 7. Xilinx's fundamental DSP48E1 slice [16]

our case the number of multiplications was reduced from 20 (*of* 25 × 18-bit each) down to 16 (*of* 32 × 32-bit each). Such trade-offs between the number of simultaneous multiplications and data widths of the operands must be taken into account when designing any system that involves wider multiplications than the width of the fundamental multiplier. Cascading DSP units also demands more area to be annexed within each Reconfigurable Region (RR). This is why to implement our largest RM - it performs up to 15 simultaneous multiplications with 32 × 32-bit width - we annexed the entire X0Y1 CR in floorplanning the RP of our design. This region is illustrated with the large Pblock on the left side of Fig. 8. However, for the case of the PID controller, a smaller region is required that can implement up to 4 arithmetic units. This is shown on the right side of Fig. 8.

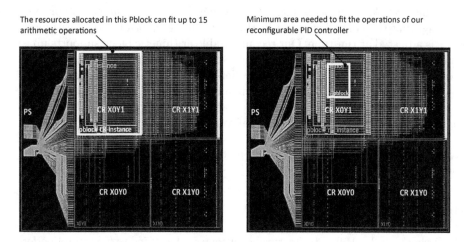

Fig. 8. The large Pblock on the left accommodates up to 15 arithmetic operations. The small Pblock on the right fits the arithmetic operations of the most resource-consuming controller, i.e. PID.

In terms of resource utilization within the Pblock, we obtained that our design is DSP-consuming mainly, while the requirements in flip-flops and LUTs are low. Table 4 summarizes the resource utilization in the larger Pblock of Fig. 8, for different Reconfigurable Modules (RMs). Floorplanning to the region indicated by the large Pblock of Fig. 8, creates partial bitstreams of 192, 343 bytes each. However, by restricting the floorplanning to the smaller region in Fig. 8, which has enough resources to implement the required computations for any variant - 4 is the maximum, in the case of the PID controller - the size of partial bitstream created for each PID variant becomes 55, 727 bytes. Considering the maximum reconfiguration speed of 400 MBps for the latest Xilinx devices, a total of 132.8 μs are needed to load the partial bitstream into the fabric via PCAP configuration port. Future versions can be built using the ICAP configuration port, accessed by a fast hardware reconfiguration engine [17].

Table 4. Resource utilization in the large Pblock of Fig. 8, for different RMs. Each one implements a different number of arithmetic operations. Results are from Xilinx Z-7010 device.

# arithmetic units in the RM	# flip-flops (%)	# LUTs (%)	# DSPs (%)
5	160/5,696 (2.80%)	161/2,848 (5.65%)	5/16 (31.25%)
10	320/5,696 (5.60%)	321/2,848 (11.27%)	10/16 (62.50%)
15	480/5,696 (8.43%)	461/2,848 (16.89%)	15/16 (93.75%)

6   Conclusions

While most works were focused on reconfiguring the gain parameters, we propose reconfiguring the controller type. In this way, the number of active arithmetic units is adjusted at run-time. Our reconfigurable arithmetic block supports up to a max of 15 simultaneous operations (of 32×32-bit each), and we envision its use in adaptive state-space MIMO controllers such as Linear-Quadratic-Gaussian (LQG) control. These controllers have high computational and storage demands as they require several linear algebraic operations including matrix multiplication that needs to store and process more information.

Acknowledgement. This research was partly funded by the EU FP7/2007-2013, under grant agreement no. 610640, DREAMS project.

References

1. Desborough, L., Miller, R.: Increasing customer value of industrial control performance monitoring - honeywell's experience. In: AIChE Symposium Series (2002)
2. Ang, K.H., Chong, G., Li, Y.: PID control system analysis, design, and technology. IEEE Trans. Control Syst. Technol. **13**(4), 559–576 (2005)
3. Hang, C.C., Åström, K.J., Persson, P., Ho, W.K.: Towards intelligent PID control. Automatica **28**(1), 1–9 (1992)
4. Mikkilineni, I., Patel, S., Tai, C.-H.: Optimizing a PID controller for simulated single-joint arm dynamics. Technical report, Integrated Systems Neuroengineering Laboratory, University of California San Diego, San Diego, US, November 2014. http://isn.ucsd.edu/classes/beng221/problems/2014
5. Johansen, T.A.: Operating regime based process modeling and identification. Ph.D. thesis, University of Trondheim (1994)
6. Jia, B., Cao, H., Ma, J.: Design and stability analysis of fuzzy switched PID controller for ship track-keeping. J. Transp. Technol. **2**(4), 334–338 (2012)
7. Jia, B., Ren, G., Long, G.: Design and stability analysis of fuzzy switching PID controller. In: IEEE World Congress on Intelligent Control and Automation (WCICA) (2006)
8. Otsubo, A., Hayashi, K., Murakami, S., Maeda, M.: Fuzzy hybrid control using simplified indirect inference method. Fuzzy Sets Syst. **99**(3), 265–272 (1998)

9. Vagia, M., Nikolakopoulos, G., Tzes, A.: Design of a robust PID-control switching scheme for an electrostatic micro-actuator. Control Eng. Pract. **16**(11), 1321–1328 (2008)
10. Monmasson, E., Idkhajine, L., Cirstea, M.N., Bahri, I., Tisan, A., Naouar, M.W.: FPGAs in industrial control applications. IEEE Trans. Ind. Inform. **7**(2), 224–243 (2011)
11. Economakos, G., Economakos, C.: A run-time reconfigurable fuzzy PID controller based on modern FPGA devices. In: Mediterranean Conference on Control and Automation (MED), June 2007
12. le Roux, R., van Schoor, G., van Vuuren, P.: Block RAM implementation of a reconfigurable real-time PID controller. In: IEEE International Conference on High Performance Computing and Communication and IEEE International Conference on Embedded Software and Systems (HPCC-ICESS), October 2012
13. Pelc, M.: Self-tuning run-time reconfigurable PID controller. Arch. Control Sci. **21**(2), 189–205 (2011)
14. Fons, M., Fons, F., Canto, E.: Custom-made design of a digital PID control system. In: IEEE International Conference on Acoustics, Speech and Signal Processing (ICASSP), May 2006
15. Xilinx: Vivado design suite user guide - partial reconfiguration, UG909 (v2017.1). Technical report, April 2017. http://www.xilinx.com/
16. Crockett, L.H., Elliot, R.A., Enderwitz, M.A., Stewart, R.W.: The Zynq Book Embedded Processing with the Arm Cortex-A9 on the Xilinx Zynq-7000 All Programmable SoC. Technical report, Department of Electronic and Electrical Engineering, University of Strathclyde, Glasgow, Scotland, UK, July 2014. http://www.zynqbook.com/
17. Hansen, S.G., Koch, D., Tørresen, J.: High speed partial run-time reconfiguration using enhanced ICAP hard macro. In: Reconfigurable Architectures Workshop (RAW) co-located with IEEE International Parallel and Distributed Processing (IPDPS), pp. 174–180, May 2011

Design Methods and Fast Prototyping

High-Level Synthesis of Software-Defined MPSoCs

Jens Rettkowski[1(✉)] and Diana Goehringer[2]

[1] Embedded Systems of Information Technology (ESIT),
Ruhr-University Bochum, Bochum, Germany
`jens.rettkowski@rub.de`
[2] Adaptive Dynamic Systems (ADS), Technische Universität Dresden,
Dresden, Germany

Abstract. The end of Dennard scaling led to the use of heterogeneous Multiprocessor Systems-on-Chip (MPSoCs) for a wide variety of applications such as image and signal processing. However, the complexity of programming and designing increases tremendously for heterogeneous MPSoCs. Besides high application requirements in terms of performance, area and energy consumption, short time-to-market is essential for the industry. As a result, a software productivity gap emerges. This paper presents an automatic development environment for heterogeneous MPSoCs that decreases the software productivity gap. Based on an MPI program, a heterogeneous MPSoC for FPGAs consisting of several MicroBlaze processors and accelerators is generated. The accelerators are developed by synthesizing functions using Vivado HLS that are marked with pragmas in the MPI program. To evaluate the environment in terms of performance and area, several use cases have been implemented on a Xilinx Zynq SoC. The design development phase and programming of heterogeneous MPSoCs are significantly simplified by the automatic development environment.

1 Introduction

The end of Dennard scaling led to the use of heterogeneous Multiprocessor Systems-on-Chip (MPSoCs) instead of scalar systems. Heterogeneous MPSoCs provide a high efficiency in performance related to energy, since they benefit from the distinct features of different processing elements (PE). The evolution of MPSoCs shows an increasing number of PEs enabling massively parallel computation power. Nevertheless, the high number of PEs requires a scalable communication infrastructure that has a high throughput as well. Networks-onChip (NoCs) have emerged as the most promising communication infrastructure for MPSoCs. NoCs consist of routers connected by channels and arranged in a topology such as Ring, Torus and Mesh. In comparison to a bus, a NoC provides better throughput and scalability for MPSoCs.

Nowadays, complete heterogeneous MPSoCs [1,2] can be implemented in modern FPGAs that provide the possibility for fast and low-cost prototyping as

© Springer International Publishing AG, part of Springer Nature 2018
N. Voros et al. (Eds.): ARC 2018, LNCS 10824, pp. 407–419, 2018.
https://doi.org/10.1007/978-3-319-78890-6_33

well as high flexibility. However, the design of these platforms might be expensive and complicated using a hardware description language such as VHDL and Verilog. High-level synthesis enables the development of FPGA designs using a high-level programming language. Consequently, the productivity in designing FPGAs increases, since less hardware expertise is necessary. In addition to the rising design complexity, the programming complexity is tremendously increased by the heterogeneity and the rising number of PEs. There are several parallel programming models such as OpenCL, OpenMP and Message Passing Interface (MPI) in common use. These standards are used on top of the underlying hardware architecture and separated from the hardware design. Hardware optimizations for an application are performed independently from the software point of view. On the other hand, short time-to-market is required in industry due to economic reasons and thus, a software productivity gap emerges.

The main contribution of this paper is a development environment for heterogeneous MPSoCs that minimizes the software productivity gap. This environment consists of an automatic flow which analyzes an MPI-based program. MPI is used to define different processes in a single program file. Every process of the MPI program is executed by a MicroBlaze (MB) processor. The MB processors exchange data through a 2D-Mesh Network-on-Chip (NoC) providing a scalable communication infrastructure. Furthermore, each MB processor can be equipped with a application-specific hardware module to improve performance. Functions defined in the MPI program can be marked by pragmas. These functions are synthesized using Vivado HLS for the application-specific hardware modules. A MB processor with a hardware module executes a program that has automatically integrated wrapper functions. A wrapper function handles the data transfer between MB processors and a hardware module. The flow is automated by Python scripts, which generate TCL scripts for the MPSoC and the hardware modules as well as the programs for the MB processors. In this manner, the programming and design are significantly simplified resulting in a shorter development time. The system is evaluated by a benchmark consisting of 6 use cases: RGB to grayscale conversion, sobel filter, magnitude operation, threshold operation, neural network and monte carlo computation. The results show a maximum speedup of 7.6x for an MPSoC with hardware modules compared to an MPSoC without hardware modules. In contrast to a single MB processor, a speedup of 20.4x has been achieved.

The remainder of this paper is organized as follows: Sect. 2 presents and compares related work. Section 3 explains the high-level synthesis of software-defined MPSoCs. The results are presented in Sect. 4. Finally, a conclusion and outlook are presented in Sect. 5.

2   Related Work

Different high-level synthesis tools are explored and compared to the approach presented in this paper. A corresponding taxonomy is defined in Table 1 which divides tools based on the number of hardware modules and processors that

Table 1. A taxonomy for high-level synthesis based on system complexity

		Number of Processors		
		None	Single	Multiple
Number of Hardware Modules	Single			
	Multiple			

they support. The number of processors ranges from none over single to multiple processors. The number of hardware modules ranges from single to multiple. The first column of Table 1 presents the transformation of a high-level language into a hardware description. The step from a single hardware module to multiple modules is not far apart. Different hardware modules must be clearly separated in software.

Most of the high-level synthesis tools such as Bambu [3] and Vivado HLS [4] support the synthesis of a single hardware block. Bambu [3] is a high-level synthesis tool that transforms most of C constructs into hardware. A C program containing a behavioral description of the synthesizable function is transformed to an HDL description of the corresponding Register Transfer Level (RTL) implementation. This HDL description is compatible with commercial synthesis tools. Vivado HLS [4] is a commercial high-level synthesis tool from Xilinx supporting C, C++ and SystemC. It synthesizes a software program into an RTL description, which can be implemented in FPGAs. Several optimizations such as pipelining and loop unrolling can be programmed by inserting pragmas. Another high-level synthesis tool named LegUp is presented in [5]. LegUp which is open-source can transform a C program into a hardware description. The C program is not allowed to contain recursive structures and dynamic memory allocation. Additionally to C, it supports OpenMP and Pthreads and synthesizes them into parallel hardware structures.

A high-level synthesis tool which generates multiple hardware modules is presented in [6]. Mori et al. propose a method, which reduces the design time of high-level synthesis. In order to achieve this, a database of hardware modules is necessary. A C program is analyzed to generate a task graph that has a finite number of nodes. In this regards, a node can be clearly separated by function calls. An optimization algorithm in terms of design constraints determines which hardware module is mapped to a node. If a node is not available in the database, other high-level synthesis tools can be used to synthesize this node. The pre-synthesized database speeds-up the design time. The second column of Table 1 presents high-level synthesis of a program written in a high-level language into single or multiple hardware modules connected to a single processor. For this purpose, parts of the program are synthesized in hardware, while the remaining part is compiled for a processor. The communication between the processor and hardware modules is automatically managed. LegUp can be additionally used to generate a MIPS processor or an ARM processor connected to a single hardware module. The hardware module can be described by a function definition. Alteras memory mapped on-chip bus is used as a communication infrastructure between the processor and accelerator. A commercial tool from Xilinx is SDSoC [7]. It uses Vivado HLS to synthesize functions of a C/C++ program. The remaining program is compiled for an ARM processor which communicates through AXI bus to the hardware modules. It supports Linux as operating system for the ARM processor as well as bare-metal projects. All optimizations from Vivado HLS can be also applied to SDSoC. Furthermore, the number of hardware modules is only limited by the resources of the FPGA. As the system-on-chip evolves to multi-core systems, the high-level synthesis from a single processor with hardware module evolves to a multiprocessor system as well. The number of hardware modules can range from single to multiple. Since SDSoC supports operating systems, a program implemented by a high-level language can contain multiple threads or processes. The ARM processor is a dualcore Cortex-A9 processor containing two cores which can be used to concurrently run threads or processes. However, the ARM processor is limited to these two cores. In [8], a methodology is proposed that uses an RVC-CAL dataflow program for high-level synthesis to a heterogeneous MPSoC. The architecture and the constraints of the application are defined separately apart from the RVC-CAL program. A compiler called Orcc translates the RVC-CAL program into source code for different targets. Vivado HLS is used to synthesize the hardware modules of a heterogeneous platform. Our approach synthesizes an MPI-based program into an MPSoC. The MPSoC consists of MB processors with optional specialized hardware modules. The MB processors communicate through a NoC. Although the main focus of this work is the high-level synthesis of heterogeneous MPSoCs, a single MB processor can also be implemented with hardware modules.

Taking the previously mentioned approaches into account, this work and SDSoC are the only approaches that cover high-level synthesis of one or more processors with hardware modules. SDSoC is limited to the Zynq [9] and Ultra-scale+ [10] SoCs. Both SoCs consists of ARM processors besides an FPGA. Since the ARM processors are not FPGA-based, the scalability regarding the number of processors is limited. Furthermore, a lot of applications such as [11–13] only require a MB processor due to the design constraints. In contrast to SDSoC, our work supports the integration of MB processors to any FPGA supported by the Vivado tools. In addition, it is more scalable than the ARM processor, since the number of MB processors is configurable and only limited by the FPGA resources.

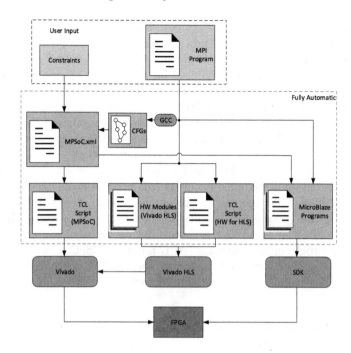

Fig. 1. Overview of the high-level synthesis flow

3   High-Level Synthesis of Software-Defined MPSoCs

A diagram that shows the complete flow is given by Fig. 1. The only user inputs
are constrains for the MPSoC design and the MPI-based application program
implemented in C. The program uses a subset of MPI to specify processes that
are executed by the MB processors. The user determines the MPSoC size and
the FPGA using the constraints. Specialized hardware modules are defined using
pragmas above a function. The constraints and the program are automatically
analyzed by Python scripts. The scripts produce program files for each MB
processor, high-level synthesizable C files for each hardware module with TCL
scripts for Vivado HLS and TCL scripts for Vivado to build the MPSoC. Internally, control flow graphs (cfgs) are created using GCC to identify which MB
processor requires a hardware module. Based on the cfgs, constraints and the
MPI program, an XML file is created that describes the construction of the
MPSoC.

3.1   MPI-Based Program

A lightweight software library that only consumes 1.85 KB is developed for the
MPSoC. This library defines MPI-based functions supporting the initialization
and releasing of MPI communication as well as sending and receiving between
processes. Each process has a unique id which is used to distinguish between

the processes. Using these ids, the system can be programmed in an SPMD manner (Single Program Multiple Data). Since a single MB processor executes one process, the number of processes must be less or equal to the number of MB processors. Multiple threads that run on a single MB processor cannot be implemented using the developed subset of MPI. Nevertheless, libraries such as Xilkernel can be included in the MPI program to provide multiple threads running on a single MB processor. Multiple threads running on the same MB processor can access different hardware accelerators. Multiple threads that access the same accelerator can cause a conflict in communication.

Listing 1.1 shows an example of an MPI-based program with more than one process. This program is compiled for every MB processor and executed in parallel by them. Each MB processor performs one process, hence, the number of MB processors must be greater or equal to the number of processes defined in the MPI program. The lightweight software library included in line 1 provides an application programming interface (API) for the MPSoC. Every process has a unique id that can be identified using the function `MPI_Comm_rank()`. Conditional expressions based on the id enables different operations in different MB processors.

Listing 1.1. Example of an MPI-based program with hardware modules

```
1          #include ."mpi.h"
2          #pragma mb_acc AXISin=in AXISout=out
3          void hw(int in[10], int out[10]){
4                  //program code of function hw
5          }
6          int main(int argc, char *argv[]){
7              MPI_Init(&argc, &argv);
8              int rank;
9              MPI_Comm_rank(MPI_COMM_WORLD, &rank);
10             if (rank == 0){
11                     //process 0
12             }else{
13                     //All processes except process 0
14                 hw(a, b);
15             }
16             MPI_Finalize();
17         }
```

3.2 Hardware Description Using XML Format

The constraints given by the user contain the size of the MPSoC and the FPGA type for synthesis and implementation. Since the scripts are developed for Vivado 2017.2, all Xilinx FPGAs supported by this Vivado version can be used. The size of the MPSoC is specified by two numbers that are representing the dimensions of a 2D-mesh NoC. The XML file contains elements for the NoC and every MB processor. The element that represents the NoC provides the size of each dimension given by the constraints. The total number of MB processors is computed by the product of these dimensions.

Since every MB processor is represented by another element in the XML file, the elements are labeled using a unique address. Furthermore, each element describes all hardware modules that are used by the corresponding MB processor. The hardware modules are consecutively numbered based on the MPI program. Nevertheless, the element provides the name of the of the hardware module according to the function implemented in the MPI-based program for a neatly arranged hierarchy. Every argument of the function is indicated as an AXI stream input or output port. In addition, it gives the corresponding AXI stream port number of the MB processor which has up to 15 AXI stream ports for hardware modules and one port connected to the NoC.

The TCL scripts are generated based on the XML file. In order to identify a hardware module of a MB processor, the MPI program is analyzed. GCC is used to generate a control flow graph for every process by calling GCC with option `-fdump-tree-cfg`. The control flow graphs show all executed function calls. These calls are compared to functions that are marked by pragmas for high-level synthesis. If a marked function occurs in a control flow graph, the corresponding MB processor requires a hardware module.

3.3 MicroBlaze Programs

The MPI-based program is parsed by a Python script that creates C programs for each MB processor. The Python script includes in each MB program a unique process id, which is respectively included in the MPI header file. Functions that are marked by pragmas are exchanged by wrapper functions. Instead of processing data as defined in the original function, the wrapper function manages the data transfers between the MB processors and hardware modules. The hardware description of the XML file gives the information which MB processor has a hardware module. Accordingly, only the functions that are implemented as hardware modules are exchanged with wrapper functions. A wrapper function starts with data transfers to the hardware module and ends with data transfers from the hardware module. The wrapper function blocks the execution of the process until all data has been transferred. This simplified the synchronization between hardware module and MB processor. As mentioned, the generation of the MB programs including the wrapper functions is automated.

3.4 Hardware Modules and TCL Scripts for Vivado HLS

Void functions that are defined in the MPI program can be synthesized to hardware modules using Vivado HLS 2017.2. A non-void function returns a value which cannot be read by a MB processor due to a missing interface. Pragmas are used above a function to port them to Vivado HLS as shown in Listing 1. Every argument of the function is implemented by an AXI stream interface. Accordingly, the arguments can be defined as an array of any data type

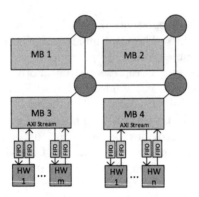

Fig. 2. MPSoC consisting of 4 MB processors with hardware modules (HW)

supported by Vivado HLS. The development environment searches for pragmas that contain the term mb_acc. As a consequence, other pragmas from Vivado HLS can be used without influencing the presented development environment. Each argument can be implemented either as an AXI stream input port or an AXI stream output port of the MB processor. This is also defined within the pragma using the terms AXISin for an input port and AXISout for an output port as presented in Listing 1.1. A hardware module can have up to 15 input or output streams. This is due to the fact that a MB processor provides 16 AXI stream interfaces and one AXI stream interface is used to send and receive data from the NoC. The input and output arguments support the same datatypes as Vivado HLS does.

The development environment automatically extracts the functions marked by pragmas for Vivado HLS. For each hardware module, a source file containing the function is generated with a corresponding TCL script. The TCL script can be launched by Vivado HLS to create an IP Core based on the function.

3.5   TCL Script for MPSoC

Four TCL scripts are automatically generated to build the heterogeneous MPSoC. An example of an MPSoC consisting of 4 MB processors is shown in Fig. 2. The first script creates a new Vivado project by setting the FPGA type and the project name. The 2D-mesh NoC uses routers based on [14] to transfer a message. These routers are defined in the IP-XACT format as cores to integrate them into the project. Moreover, the IP cores for the hardware modules are also integrated into the project. The first script calls consecutively the three remaining scripts. The second script builds the 2D-mesh NoC. The routers have five input and output ports. Routers located at the edges or corners have accordingly fewer ports. The routing of a message is locally computed to determine the output port. In this work, the XY routing algorithm, a fixed priority arbiter and wormhole routing [15] are used. In contrast to other routing algorithms, the XY routing algorithm can be efficiently implemented in FPGA-based NoCs due to its simplicity. A message consists of several flits such as a header flit that contains the address of the destination, payload flits that contain the data and a tail flit that determines the end of a message. Initially, a router analyzes the header flit to forward it to the respective output port, while reserving the input buffer for every following flit corresponding to this message. The payload flits are forwarded to the same output port that has been passed by the header flit. The tail flit releases the reservation for other incoming messages. The buffer of a router can store a single flit. A handshake protocol between routers is implemented to store data inside the buffers without data loss. The bit width of ports is set to 32 bits. The third script generates MB processors for each router. The MB processors are configured with the default configuration of Vivado 2017.2. However, the configuration can be adapted to the application by modifying the TCL scripts, since the configuration is saved in variables. The routers are connected to the first AXI stream port of the MB processor. Other processors with a C compiler such as an ARM processor from Xilinx Zynq can be integrated into the tool. Nevertheless, an MPI library as well as network interfaces must be developed. The fourth script connects the hardware modules to MB processors using AXI stream ports. These ports are consecutively connected to the input and output ports of the hardware modules. The assignment of these ports to hardware modules is defined in the XML file. Any MB processor can be equipped with any number of specialized hardware modules. For instance, MB processor 3 is connected to m hardware modules (HW) and MB processor 4 is connected to n hardware modules in Fig. 2. Furthermore, FIFOs are connected between the MB processor and hardware modules. The FIFOs support a depth to power of two starting with 16 up to 32768. The script set the depth to the next highest value of the array length. This enables that a MB processor can begin with all data transfers to the hardware module and afterwards, receives all data from the hardware module. Otherwise, a hardware module can block further execution, when it is not able to receive new data.

4   Evaluation

The development environment is evaluated using a benchmark consisting of 6 use cases. Four of them process an image with a size of 640×480 pixels. The first algorithm is pixel conversion from RGB to grayscale (RGB2GRAY). The grayscale value g is computed using the RGB values r, g and b as presented in Eq. 1.

$$g = 0.21r + 0.72g + 0.07b \tag{1}$$

It is the default method to convert from RGB to grayscale format in GIMP. The second algorithm is shown in Eq. 2. It is a magnitude computation (MAG) calculating the squareroot out of the sum of two squared values.

$$magnitude = \sqrt{x^2 + y^2} \tag{2}$$

The third algorithm (THRES) creates a binary image using a threshold operation. The fourth algorithm (SOBEL) is edge detection based on the sobel filter for horizontal edges. The fifth use case (MLP) is a multilayer perceptron network consisting of 1 hidden-layer with 10 neurons. It has 400 inputs and 9 output neurons. The activation function of the MLP is an approximated sigmoid function. Such an MLP network can be trained to classify 9 handwritten digits. The sixth use case (MonteCarlo) is the calculation of PI using the Monte Carlo method with 999 particles. According to these algorithms, 6 MPSoCs are implemented using the presented development environment. These MPSoCs consists of 4 MB processors. One of them distributes data to the remaining three MB processors that perform the respective algorithm and gathers the processed data at the end. The three MB processors are equipped with a respective hardware module according to the algorithm. The hardware modules are synthesized and packaged by Vivado HLS 2017.2 without any additional pragmas such as unrolling and pipelining for optimizations. The MPSoC performing the Monte Carlo method uses the MB processors to randomly generate the 999 particles. In the remaining use cases, the MB processors are used to transfer the data from the Network to the hardware module that executes the application-specific function. As a reference, a single MB processor performs all use cases. To evaluate area overhead and performance, an MPSoC without hardware modules is created. Both MPSoCs are built by Vivado 2017.2 on an xc7020clg484-1 FPGA from the

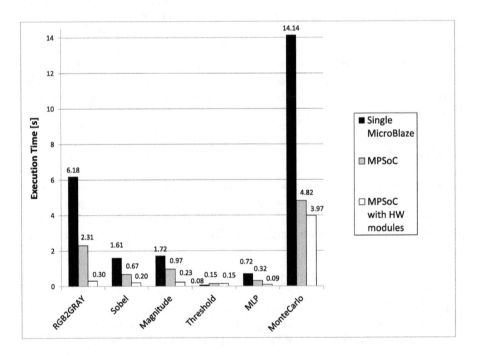

Fig. 3. Execution times of six use cases

Table 2. Resource utilization after place & route for an xc7z020clg484-1 Xilinx FPGA

	LUT	LUTRAM	FF	BRAM	DSP
Single MB	1119 (2.0%)	64 (0.4%)	984 (0.9%)	0 (0 %)	0 (0%)
MPSoC	7188 (13.5%)	660 (3.8%)	6051 (5.7%)	70 (50%)	0 (0%)
RGB2GRAY	11920 (22.4%)	736 (4.2%)	11472 (10.8%)	70 (50%)	75 (34%)
MAG	14395 (27.1%)	662 (3.8%)	12723 (12%)	70 (50%)	3 (1.36%)
THRES	7702 (14.5%)	694 (4.0%)	6381 (6%)	70 (50%)	0 (0%)
SOBEL	11544 (21.7%)	722 (4.1%)	8772 (8.2%)	70 (50%)	0 (0%)
NN	12643 (23.8%)	1015 (5.8%)	12465 (11.7%)	70 (50%)	15 (6.8%)
MC	8479 (15.9%)	900 (5.2%)	7980 (7.5%)	70 (50%)	24 (10.9%)

ZedBoard. The frequency of the MPSoCs is 100 MHz. The MB processors are configured with 64 KB data and instruction memory. The execution times of each algorithm shown in Fig. 3 are measured by a timer that is added to the MB processor. Excluding the threshold operator, all applications are accelerated by the presented approach. The threshold operation is slower, since the communication overhead exceeds the gain of parallelism. The threshold operator is a conditional assignment which can be efficiently executed by a MB processor. The RGB2GRAY application provides the highest speedup of 7.6x compared to an MPSoC without HW modules and 20.3x compared to a single MB processor. That is because the RGB2GRAY operation performs three multiplications that the MicroBlaze cannot execute as fast as specialized hardware. The MPSoCs generated for the presented algorithms are application-specific. Nevertheless, the development process of new applications has been significantly simplified resulting in reduced development time. Table 2 presents the resource utilization of all benchmarks implemented on a Xilinx xc7020clg484-1 FPGA. Besides a single MB processor and an MPSoC without hardware modules, the utilizations of the respective MPSoC containing the application-specific hardware modules are given (RGB2GRAY, MAG, THRES, SOBEL, Neural Network and Monte Carlo). BRAM resources are the most limiting factor. However, the size of the memory can be adapted.

5   Conclusion

In this work, a high-level synthesis approach that significantly simplifies the design and programming of heterogeneous MPSoCs is presented. Based on a program that uses a subset of MPI, TCL scripts are generated for Vivado to build an MPSoC with MP processors. Each MB processor can be equipped with hardware modules that are defined by software functions. Pragmas are used above the functions to specify the hardware modules. The presented approach automatically extracts these functions and ports them to Vivado HLS. Six different use cases are implemented on an xc7z020clg484-1 FPGA. The results show a maximum speedup of 7.6x for an MPSoC with hardware modules compared to an MPSoC without hardware modules. In contrast to a single MB processor, a speedup of 20.4x has been achieved. The design and programming process is essentially simplified due to the automatic flow. In future work, the system will be extended by providing a direct connection between NoC and hardware module.

References

1. Nouri, S., Hussain, W., Nurmi, J.: Implementation of IEEE-802.11a/g receiver blocks on a coarse-grained reconfigurable array. In: 2015 Conference on Design and Architectures for Signal and Image Processing (DASIP), Krakow, pp. 1–8 (2015)
2. Wang, C., Li, X., Chen, Y., Zhang, Y., Diessel, O., Zhou, X.: Service-oriented architecture on FPGA-based MPSoC. IEEE Trans. Parallel Distrib. Syst. **28**(10), 2993–3006 (2017)
3. Pilato, C., Ferrandi, F.: Bambu: a modular framework for the high level synthesis of memory-intensive applications. In: Proceedings of 23rd International Conference on Field programmable Logic and Applications, Porto, pp. 1–4 (2013)
4. Xilinx: Vivado Design Suite User Guide - High Level Synthesis. UG902 (v2017.1) (2017). www.xilinx.com
5. Canis, A., et al.: LegUp high-level synthesis. In: Koch, D., Hannig, F., Ziener, D. (eds.) FPGAs for Software Programmers. Springer, Cham (2016). https://doi.org/10.1007/978-3-319-26408-0_10
6. Mori, J.Y., Werner, A., Fricke, F., Hübner, M.: A rapid prototyping method to reduce the design time in commercial high-level synthesis tools. In: Proceedings of International Parallel and Distributed Symposium, Workshops (2016)
7. Xilinx: SDSoC Development Environment - User Guide. UG1027 (v2017.1) (2017). www.xilinx.com
8. Bezati, E., Casale-Brunet, S., Mattavelli, M., Janneck, J.W.: High-level synthesis of dynamic dataflow programs on heterogeneous MPSoC platforms. In: 2016 International Conference on Embedded Computer Systems: Architectures, Modeling and Simulation (SAMOS), pp. 227–234 (2016)
9. Xilinx: Zynq-7000 All Programmable SoC Technical Reference Manual. UG585 (v1.11) (2017). www.xilinx.com
10. Xilinx: Zynq Ultrascale+ MPSoC Technical Reference Manual. UG1085 (v1.5) (2017). www.xilinx.com
11. Suneeta, Srinivasan, R., RamSagar: SoC implementation of three phase BLDC motor using Microblaze soft IP core. In: 2017 International Conference on Computer, Communications and Electronics (Comptelix), Jaipur, pp. 360–364 (2017)
12. Farhat, W., Faiedh, H., Souani, C., Besbes, K.: Embedded system for road sign detection using MicroBlaze. In: 2015 IEEE 12th International Multi-Conference on Systems, Signals & Devices (SSD15), Mahdia, pp. 1–5 (2015)
13. Khanzadi, H., Savaria, Y., David, J.P.: A data driven CGRA overlay architecture with embedded processors. In: 2017 15th IEEE International New Circuits and Systems Conference (NEWCAS), Strasbourg, pp. 269–272 (2017)

14. Rettkowski, J., Goehringer, D.: Application-specific processing using high-level synthesis for networks-on-chip. In: 2017 International Conference on Reconfigurable Computing and FPGAs (ReConFig), Cancun (2017)
15. Peh, L., Dally, W.J.: Flit-reservation flow control. In: Proceedings of Sixth International Symposium on High-Performance Computer Architecture. HPCA-6 (Cat. No. PR00550), Toulouse, pp. 73–84 (2000)

Improved High-Level Synthesis
for Complex CellML Models

Björn Liebig[1]([⊠]), Julian Oppermann[1], Oliver Sinnen[2], and Andreas Koch[1]

[1] Embedded Systems and Applications, Technische Universität Darmstadt,
Darmstadt, Germany
{liebig,oppermann,koch}@esa.informatik.tu-darmstadt.de
[2] Parallel and Reconfigurable Computing, University of Auckland,
Auckland, New Zealand
o.sinnen@auckland.ac.nz

Abstract. In this work, we present the use of a new high-level synthesis engine capable of generating resource-shared compute accelerators, even from very complex double-precision codes, for cell biology simulations. From the domain-specific CellML description, the compilation pipeline is able to generate hardware that is shown to achieve a performance similar to or exceeding current generation desktop CPUs, and has energy savings of up to 96% even for a single accelerator, which requires just 25–30% area on a mid-sized FPGA.

Keywords: High-level synthesis · CellML · FPGA · Floating-point

1 Introduction

For the simulation of biological systems at the cell level, CellML [1] has proven to be a useful domain-specific representation, from which simulation models for a number of execution platforms can be created. Since experiments commonly require a multitude of simulation runs with different input data, achieving energy efficiency has become an objective in addition to raw simulation performance. To this end, automatic generation of FPGA-based simulation accelerators from CellML descriptions has already been successfully investigated [2,3]. However, the purely throughput-oriented spatial architectures of prior art cannot compile more complex cell descriptions due to chip size constraints, and then only provide single-precision floating point accuracy.

We present the use of a new high-level synthesis engine capable of generating resource-shared compute accelerators even for very complex double-precision simulation codes, for use in a domain-specific CellML-to-accelerator compilation pipeline.

The key contributions presented in this paper are (1) a source-to-source transformation that enables more efficient high-level synthesis of the intermediate C used in the CellML compilation pipeline, (2) adaptions of a high-level synthesis engine for CellML compilation, and (3) a case study using the developed tool flow

N. Voros et al. (Eds.): ARC 2018, LNCS 10824, pp. 420–432, 2018.
https://doi.org/10.1007/978-3-319-78890-6_34

Listing 1.1. Exerpt from CCGS output for [5], reformatted for readability

```
void computeRates(double VOI, double* CONSTANTS, double* RATES, double* STATES, double* ALGEBRAIC) {
    RATES[0]     = CONSTANTS[2] * STATES[2] * STATES[3] * (1.0 - STATES[0]) - CONSTANTS[3] * STATES[0];
    ALGEBRAIC[0] = 1.0 / (1.0 + exp(CONSTANTS[5] * (STATES[1] - CONSTANTS[6])));
    RATES[2]     = (ALGEBRAIC[0] - STATES[2]) / CONSTANTS[687];
    ALGEBRAIC[9] = CONSTANTS[116] / (1.0 + pow(CONSTANTS[119] / STATES[10], CONSTANTS[117]));
    ...
}
```

to accelerate five of the largest CellML models on the Xilinx Zynq platform in double-precision. These models could not be translated using prior approaches, as their fully spatial realization exceeds the FPGA size. We demonstrate significant performance gains compared to CPU execution, and better energy efficiency than a GPU implementation.

2   Related Work

2.1   CellML-Based Simulation

A CellML model is an XML-based description of a cell comprised of interconnected components, and expressed as a system of ordinary differential equations (ODE). OpenCMISS [4] is a simulation workbench where instances of cell models are used as the data points in larger grids (or other spatial arrangements), e.g., to simulate a piece of ventricular tissue. Roughly, the simulation approach is as follows: The interactions between the neighboring grid cells are computed at discrete *macro* time steps. In order to progress the state of each cell from the current to the next macro time step, numerical integration of the ODE system is used. The simulation accuracy depends on the granularity of the integration steps: the more *micro* time steps are used to discretize the time between two macro time steps, the better the approximation. As the integration phase is done for each cell independently, the resulting potential for acceleration on parallel architectures is huge [2, 4]. Note that this observation has a direct impact on us aiming for smaller accelerators: Even though we concentrate here on single-accelerator performance, we could tile the entire FPGA with independent processing elements, as the accelerators are not bottlenecked by memory bandwidth. This use of MIMD computation structures also allows FPGA-based systems to scale beyond the SIMD/SIMT-approach used by GPUs.

While it would be possible to build a front-end to parse and interpret CellML directly, we instead rely on the "C Code Generation Service" (CCGS) [6], which infers a sequential execution order for the underlying initial-value problem. We use the generated highly idiomatic C code as a domain-specific IR for the rest of the compile flow. Listing 1.1 shows an excerpt from the translation of a model by Faville et al. [5]. One execution of the function `computeRates` corresponds to one micro time step in the numerical integration. `VOI` is the "variable of integration", which is usually the time. `CONSTANTS` is a read-only array that contains model parameters. The current state of each component in the model is passed as the read-only array `STATES`. Intermediate values are stored in the array `ALGEBRAIC`.

Its elements are always written before read. Finally, the values in the output-only array RATES represent the rates of change of the components for the next micro time step. All arrays use the C type double, have statically known sizes and are accessed by literal indices. Each statement in the equation-evaluation code is an assignment to one of the aforementioned arrays.

2.2   CellML-Specific HLS with ODoST

The vast potential for parallel processing motivated ODoST [2,3], a high-level synthesis system custom-made to construct accelerators for the numerical integration phase. ODoST reads the C code derived from a CellML model, generates a *fully-spatial* datapath for the computeRates function and handles hardware synthesis for the accelerator. Internally, floating-point (FP) operators generated by FloPoCo [7] are used.

The proposed architecture is deeply pipelined and favors throughput instead of latency: while the computation of subsequent micro-time steps for a *single* cell cannot be pipelined, the accelerator can begin to compute a micro-time step for a *different* cell in every cycle. The fully-spatial design does achieve the optimum throughput of one result per clock cycle, but may have excessive hardware requirements for larger models, even after applying additional standard and domain-specific compiler optimizations [8].

In contrast, our approach constructs latency-optimized, non-pipelined micro-time step accelerators for even the largest CellML models. It leverages the intelligent resource-sharing and fast FP operators proposed by Liebig and Koch [9], and allows us to flexibly trade-off parallelism (number of function units) with area limits.

2.3   Generic HLS with Nymble

As the base for our CellML-specific work described here, we build on the Nymble [10] HLS framework with the Nymble-RS extensions [9] for resource-shared micro-architectures.

Nymble [10] itself uses the LLVM compiler framework as front-end and for target-independent optimization. It can translate just parts of functions to hardware, and even exclude sections within that area, moving them back to software, as required. The generated hardware kernels and software parts execute together in a shared memory architecture in the same address space (allowing transparent passing of pointers between software and hardware). Nymble has already been used as base for research in domain-specific compilation [11] and the synthesis of advanced micro-architectures [12,13].

Nymble-RS allows the area-efficient high-level synthesis of complex irregular codes having unstructured non-vectorizable FP computations in large loop bodies. It uses numerous techniques, such as hierarchical microcode, schedule-sensitive tree height optimization, and multiple mechanisms for intermediate value storage, to tightly control the area of the generated accelerator. As it targets scientific HPC, it also includes highly optimized double precision operators faster than the ones offered by FloPoCo [7].

2.4 Industrial and Academic HLS Systems

Many other academic and industrial HLS tools are capable of translating (often differing) subsets of C into synthesizable RTL HDL code [14].

Most industrial tools such as Vivado HLS [15] or Mentor Catapult [16] focus only on the hardware synthesis itself. They do not support hardware/software-co-execution and interface synthesis in a heterogeneous system. This restriction also applies to the academic compilers Bambu [17] and DWARV [18]. For FP, DWARV does not support typical maths functions [18], while Synphony C and Catapult do not support FP at all [14]. Bambu does supports FP operations using the FloPoCo-Library [7]. However, it lacks the floor operation which is required in many CellML models.

The academic tool LegUp [19] has seen widespread use and much development, which led to its recent commercialization as an industrial software product. LegUp also leverages the LLVM compiler framework and supports a large C subset as input, including FP operations. The tool supports hardware-software co-synthesis in a heterogeneous system, which makes it another interesting candidate for CellML synthesis.

3 Proposed Compilation Flow

Figure 1 shows the compilation flow from an XML-based CellML model to the FPGA hardware design. CCGS [6] is used to translate the actual CellML descriptions from the CellML repository [20] to idiomatic C code. This code, representing the equation systems, is optimized by CellML-opt [8] using the "z" flow, which leads to the optimizations of LLVM's aggressive size optimization preset "-Oz" being applied before the actual hardware synthesis. At this stage, no unsafe FP transformations are performed.

In addition, CellML-opt was modified in this work to use actual local variables for intermediate values, instead of storing them in arrays. This removal of memory operations allows the actual HLS to more flexibly select between multiple storage mechanisms for intermediate values, and also enables, e.g., schedule-sensitive tree height optimization.

The output of the HLS tool consists of Verilog RTL, which is

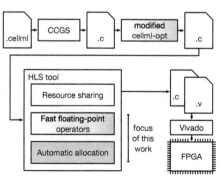

Fig. 1. CellML-to-accelerator compilation flow

then fed for actual logic synthesis into the vendor tools (Xilinx Vivado, in our case). As the Nymble framework is a true hardware-software-co-compilation system, it also performs interface synthesis to access the newly generated accelerator from the software. For evaluation purposes, we use a short software program here that performs only the numerical integration step using the accelerators, instead of the full-scale OpenCMISS [4] simulation framework.

3.1   Additional FP Operators for CellML Models

While Nymble-RS does already support a number of high-performance double precision FP operations (dmul, dadd, dsub, ddiv), it needed to be extended with the additional operations log, exp, floor and pow required by CellML simulation models. In this initial prototype of the flow, these have not yet been optimized to the same degree as the four basic operations, but instead are based on existing implementations. In all cases, we aim for an $f_{\max}$ of 200 MHz on Xilinx Virtex 7-level technology.

The *log* function is realized by an instance of the Xilinx CoreGen log core. For the target frequency, the core was configured to use 34 cycles, which ensures operation above 200 MHz. For the *exp* function, we use the FloPoCo exp core [21]. However, since FloPoCo is using a non-IEEE754 conformant number format, input and output must be converted from and to IEEE754 format. 200 MHz operation thus requires a pipeline depth of 26, with an additional two cycles required for the format conversion.

Since no realization for the *floor/ceil* functions was available to us, a custom implementation was developed. As shown in Fig. 2, it operates as follows: The number of *mantissa* bits to the right of the binary point is computed from the exponent in the first cycle. The second cycle clears the required number of mantissa bits, but tracks if any of these were '1' before. This latter information is used in the third cycle to conditionally increment the mantissa. Each of these operations has only a small delay and allows operation faster than 200 MHz. The first stage has an even shorter delay, and can be chained with a preceding multiplexer in resource-shared architectures.

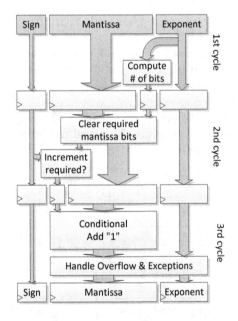

Fig. 2. Newly developed *floor* operator

The final function required for CellML models, *pow(x,y)*, is realized as *exp(log(x) * y)*. While this introduces a larger error (discussed in Sect. 4.3) and is thus not fully IEEE754-compliant, it allows resource-sharing with other exp, log and dmul operations and serves to fulfill our aim of generating area-efficient hardware.

3.2 Heuristic for Automatic Allocation

Despite being generated from CellML descriptions in an idiomatic manner, the actual operation mix varies wildly between different simulation models and should be reflected in the accelerator micro-architecture, specifically the number of FP operators for each operation type.

We extended Nymble-RS with the following heuristic to enable the HLS tool to automatically make a sensible, though not necessarily optimal choice. The only user-set constraint is the total number of FP units to be used, which serves as a limit on the hardware area required by the accelerator.

The simple heuristic aims to reflect the mix of FP operations in the model with the mix FP operators in the hardware, subject to the constraint that at least one FP operator is available for the required operation types. The initial minimum number of FP operators of each type is computed by determining the fraction for each operation type of the total user-set number of FP operators, based on the relative frequency these operation types occur in the model, and rounding down. The initial solution is then incrementally refined by determining the operators farthest away from their ideal ratio, and adding another operator of this type. This happens until the user-set upper bound on the total number of FP operators is reached.

While this heuristic already delivers good performance and energy efficiency (see Sect. 4), it could serve as a initial solution for more intelligent iterative refinement, e.g., by simulated annealing, which could then also consider individual operator areas.

4 Experimental Results

4.1 Test Setup

For ease of integration, we target the Xilinx Zynq XC7Z045 FPGA on the ZC706 evaluation board, running Xilinx "bare metal" software environment. The generated accelerators are accessed from the ARM Cores by using the AXI GP0 port,

Table 1. Examples from CellML repository [20]

Model	# operations										Source
	+ -	*	/	pow	exp	log	⌊ ⌋	other	total	
A	615	687	290	160	36	20	0	11	1819	[5]
B	310	386	133	42	57	6	1	29	964	[22]
C	452	411	0	0	0	0	0	30	893	[23]
D	342	456	106	11	45	3	1	12	976	[24]
E	330	448	98	8	45	3	1	11	944	[25]

while the hardware can access the main memory and second level cache using the AXI ACP port. We used a version of the Nymble-RS tools based on LLVM 3.3 as front-end and for machine-independent optimization.

As our approach targets the translation of large CellML problems, five of the largest models from the CellML repository [20] (at the time of writing) are used as test cases in this evaluation. Table 1 lists the models with the number of their FP operations.

In all tests and for all compilers, we allow inexact mathematical optimizations. For Nymble-RS, this includes the use of faithful rounding FP units. If not stated otherwise, simulations are run on 10 cells, with 1 million micro-step iterations each.

4.2 Design Space Evaluation

Table 2 shows the results when generating accelerators with an increasing number of FP operator units (and thus growing hardware area). Since it gave better results than more recent versions, we used Vivado 2014.1 for synthesis. All timing and area results shown are post-place-and-route.

Table 2. Design space exploration. II = Initiation interval, WCT = Wall clock time

Test case	# FP units	# FFs	# LUTs	# BRAMs	# DSPs	Schedule length	II	f_{max} (MHz)	WCT (s)
A	12	27647 (6%)	46335 (21%)	36 (3%)	92 (10%)	319	305	193	15.803
	16	33973 (8%)	56610 (26%)	50 (5%)	134 (15%)	238	229	184	12.446
	20	36620 (8%)	65826 (30%)	56 (5%)	144 (16%)	231	204	164	12.439
	24	38834 (9%)	68752 (31%)	60 (6%)	169 (19%)	226	215	169	12.722
B	12	27713 (6%)	42383 (19%)	27 (2%)	77 (9%)	224	202	202	10.000
	16	30310 (7%)	47743 (22%)	31 (3%)	102 (11%)	212	192	199	9.648
	20	33615 (8%)	52579 (24%)	38 (3%)	121 (13%)	191	179	188	9.521
	24	33532 (8%)	57144 (26%)	37 (3%)	131 (15%)	191	179	182	9.835
C	12	21895 (5%)	37186 (17%)	21 (2%)	30 (3%)	202	186	203	9.163
	16	24101 (6%)	43513 (20%)	24 (2%)	40 (4%)	177	161	204	7.892
	20	27207 (6%)	52324 (24%)	25 (2%)	45 (5%)	158	142	191	7.435
	24	28671 (7%)	55580 (25%)	32 (3%)	55 (6%)	148	132	191	6.911
D	12	27763 (6%)	42814 (20%)	28 (3%)	77 (9%)	179	167	200	8.350
	16	29360 (7%)	46705 (21%)	30 (3%)	87 (10%)	169	158	202	7.822
	20	31269 (7%)	51069 (23%)	29 (3%)	97 (11%)	161	150	190	7.895
	24	33798 (8%)	56588 (26%)	32 (3%)	127 (14%)	158	149	173	8.613
E	12	27650 (6%)	42393 (19%)	34 (3%)	77 (9%)	179	163	201	8.109
	16	29264 (7%)	47269 (22%)	29 (3%)	87 (10%)	166	155	196	7.908
	20	31188 (7%)	50596 (23%)	32 (3%)	97 (11%)	157	147	188	7.819
	24	33586 (8%)	54845 (25%)	32 (3%)	127 (14%)	156	148	188	7.872

As can be seen, increasing the number of FP units generally carries an $f_{\max}$ penalty, often due to slower wiring. Thus, the fastest accelerator will not necessarily be the largest one.

In general, using ca. 25...30% of the Zynq Z7045 device (a mid-sized chip) per accelerator achieves the best execution time. As discussed in Sect. 2.1, the total simulation performance will ideally scale linearly by employing multiple accelerators, so the remaining FPGA area can be put to good use.

4.3   Computation Accuracy

Table 3 compares the average and maximum relative error introduced by single precision arithmetic (as used in ODoST) to the error introduced by our approach. The errors shown here are computed relative to a IEEE745-compliant reference software execution using double precision and compiled without -ffast-math.

The error introduced by single precision becomes rather large when one million (or more) iterations are used for integration. Depending on the required simulation accuracy, single precision may not suffice, whereas our double-precision based approach carries a much smaller average error.

Table 3. Average relative error

	Average relative error		Maximum relative error	
	Single-precision	Our approach	Single-precision	Our approach
A	5.67E−02	2.22E−14	1.37E−00	6.74E−13
B	2.62E−04	1.16E−14	4.78E−03	1.46E−13
C	3.09E−03	1.78E−14	1.75E−02	6.96E−14
E	6.06E−03	3.04E−14	4.09E−02	1.82E−13
D	7.12E−02	9.43E−15	2.93E−01	4.79E−14

4.4   Comparison to State-of-the-Art HLS Tools

In order to evaluate the performance of our tool, we attempted to compare it against other state-of-the-art HLS systems, both academic and industrial.

LegUp: With LegUp being the most prominent academic C-based HLS tool in recent years, it is a natural reference. However, with its recent commercialization, the license terms for LegUp 5.1 prohibit comparative benchmarking, thus limiting our evaluation to the latest open-source version 4.0, which does not carry that restriction. Since LegUp 4.0 does not fully support Xilinx devices, we target the Altera Cyclone V family of chips for comparison.

Unfortunately, a number of issues caused this attempt to fail: The use of the *floor* function often leads to crashes during HLS. To get around this, we temporarily removed the *floor*-calls and were able to proceed to logic synthesis using the Altera Quartus II vendor tools. Here we ran into the problem that Quartus prohibits the use of exp as a module name, which was present in the Verilog RTL generated by LegUp. Manually renaming then leads to multiple "module signcopy not found" error messages. As this module does not seem to have been distributed with the virtual machine image the LegUp authors kindly have made available for experimentation, we gave up here.

Industrial tool: We cannot publish the name of the industrial HLS tool we used as a reference here due to license restrictions. For these experiments, we employed a recent version of a C-based HLS tool targeting Xilinx devices. Logic synthesis was performed using Xilinx Vivado 2017.2, all numbers reported are post-place-and-route.

As before, we manually explored multiple combinations of inlining, unrolling, and pipelining for the input C-code, all expressed using the tool's directives, and report only the best (=fastest) results here. For comparability, we set the upper bound on the number of FP units for each operation type identically to that our own tool uses, computed as discussed in Sect. 3.2, with an upper bound of a total of 20 FP units. In addition, we permitted the industrial tool the use of one dedicated pow operator, which our tool emulates using log and exp. However, for unknown reasons, the industrial tool exceeded this restriction (by using 2 or 3 pow units instead) for the test cases marked in Table 4 with an asterisk.

In contrast to LegUp, the industrial tool was actually able to compile the code for all of the models. However, for the largest model (case A, Faville), place-and-route failed due to congestion. Attempts to alleviate this by using specific anti-congestion settings in the Vivado tools failed. When the mapping process did succeed, the generated accelerators where all larger and slower (sometimes by an order of magnitude) than those of our system.

Table 4. Accelerators created by industrial HLS tool, relative to our approach

	FFs	LUTs	DSPs	BRAM	II	f_{max}	WCT (s)
A	85K	134K	494	22	413	P+R failed	
	233%	204%	343%	39%	202%		
B*	80K	84K	578	68	121	84.2	14.3
	237%	160%	478%	179%	68%	45%	151%
C	55K	76K	135	0	169	153.3	11.0
	201%	144%	300%	0%	119%	80%	148%
D*	69K	80K	404	23	1933	84.6	228.5
	222%	156%	416%	79%	1289%	45%	2894%
E*	70K	79K	404	23	1230	83.1	148.0
	224%	156%	416%	72%	837%	44%	1893%

4.5 Performance/Energy Relative to CPU

To evaluate the performance and energy efficiency of our approach relative to a fast CPU, we proceeded as follows: We use a fast desktop-class Intel Core i7 6700K CPU running at 4.2 GHz and compile with gcc 5.3.1 with -O3 -ffast-math. On the FPGA side, we employ a Xilinx ZC706 Zynq 7045-based prototyping board. We concentrate on single-core performance, since both the CPU and the FPGA could easily scale to run multiple threads/accelerators in parallel.

We measure the execution time of simulating 10 cells with 1 million iterations each. For the FPGA, we use the 20 FP unit variant of each accelerator, executing at its specific maximum f_{max}. As before, we report wall-clock time for the complete execution, including overhead for HW-SW interfaces.

Power measurements on the Intel CPU are performed using the Running Average Power Limit (RAPL) performance counters. On the FPGA, voltage and current measurements are obtained by directly querying Channel 1 of the on-board Voltage Regulator Module (VRM), which covers the Zynq's programmable logic and the ARM cores (both of which sleep here). In both cases, I/O power consumption is not included. Afterwards, the total amount of energy used for the computation is calculated by multiplying run time with average power consumption. The results are shown in Table 5.

Table 5. Execution wall-clock-time (10 cells, 1M iterations each), power and energy consumption (FPGA vs CPU)

Test case	A	B	C	D	E
WCT i7 6700K (s)	60.17	10.50	1.45	9.67	8.10
WCT XC7Z045 (s)	12.44	9.52	6.91	7.82	7.82
Speed-Up	4.84x	1.10x	0.21x	1.24x	1.04x
Power i7 6700K (W)	19.1	20.4	22.4	20.0	20.2
Power XC7Z045 (W)	3.6	3.0	3.0	3.1	3.2
Energy i7 6700K (J)	1149.8	214.2	32.5	193.6	163.7
Energy XC7Z045 (J)	44.9	28.9	22.1	24.4	24.7
Energy reduction	96%	87%	32%	87%	85%

Our FPGA-based accelerators are significantly more energy-efficient than the CPU, in the largest model A saving 96% of energy. On the performance side, the FPGA-based accelerators are generally faster than the CPU, for the large model A by almost 5x. The outlier here is model C, which is significantly faster on the CPU than on the FPGA. A closer examination of its code reveals an anomaly: Most of the simulation models have a very *irregular* code structure (e.g., large loop bodies with many different computations). But model C has very similar computations (three multiplications and a subtraction) in more than half of its lines of code. We assume that this code structure did allow the software compiler to perform autovectorization (which is included in -O3), and thus achieves a much higher performance.

4.6   Performance/Energy Relative to GPU

We also compare our FPGA result to a GPU implementation. For that implementation, the C-code was used to create a CUDA Kernel. Note that we used the C code generated by cellml-opt, as these optimizations improve the CUDA performance as well. We simulate 100k cells to determine the average rate of cells-computed-per-second on a single NVidia Tesla K80 GK210 GPU. The power is measured using nvidia-smi. These results are shown in Table 6. While our approach has better latency, the Tesla-GPU produces more results per second (as

Table 6. Single FPGA kernel vs GK210 GPU

Test case	Latency [s] for one cell	Throughput [cells per second]	Power [W]	Energy per cell [J]
A on FPGA	1.2	0.81	3.6	4.48
A on GPU	322.3	12.1	138.4	11.46
B on FPGA	1.0	1.05	3.0	2.89
B on GPU	91.3	38.69	131.6	3.41
C on FPGA	0.7	1.35	3.0	2.21
C on GPU	23.9	34.60	132.5	3.83
D on FPGA	7.9	1.27	3.1	2.44
D on GPU	72.0	39.64	145.7	3.67
E on FPGA	7.8	1.28	3.2	2.47
E on GPU	75.3	42.98	147.0	3.42

expected for a throughput-architecture such as a GPU). However, the FPGA is more energy efficient (in terms of Joules per cell).

5   Conclusion and Future Work

We presented a new approach for hardware synthesis of larger CellML models that offers superior latency and energy efficiency compared to CPU and GPU. Furthermore, our specialized HLS tool significantly exceeds the quality-of-results of a state-of-the-art industrial HLS system. The performance and size of the accelerators created by our approach can be flexibly scaled, achieving significant speed-ups in most cases even when dedicating just a quarter of a mid-size FPGA to the accelerator circuit.

To extrapolate the power of our approach beyond the Virtex 7-class devices, which were introduced in 2010, to current generation FPGAs, we have performed an initial experiment compiling and mapping model A to a modern XCVU13P-3 UltraScale+ FPGA. We used a total 16 FP units and achieved an f_{max} of 316 MHz, which would yield a speed-up of *8.3x* relative to the desktop class CPU in single-accelerator performance. As each accelerator requires only 2.9% of that FPGA's area, an *additional* speed-up could be achieved by tiling accelerators, e.g. 8 accelerators implemented in parallel still reach 282 MHz. This huge potential makes further research on reconfigurable computing for cell simulation highly promising.

References

1. Cuellar, A.A., Lloyd, C.M., Nielsen, P.M.F., et al.: An overview of CellML 1.1, a biological model description language. Simulation **79**(12), 740–747 (2003)
2. Yu, T., Bradley, C., Sinnen, O.: ODoST: automatic hardware acceleration for biomedical model integration. TRETS **9**(4), 27:1–27:24 (2016)
3. Yu, T., Oppermann, J., Bradley, C., Sinnen, O.: Performance optimisation strategies for automatically generated FPGA accelerators for biomedical models. Concurrency Comput.: Practice Experience **28**(5), 1480–1506 (2016)
4. Bradley, C., Bowery, A., Britten, R., et al.: OpenCMISS: a multi-physics & multi-scale computational infrastructure for the VPH/Physiome project. Progress Biophys. Mol. Biol. **107**(1), 32–47 (2011). Experimental and Computational Model Interactions in Bio-Research: State of the Art
5. Faville, R.A., Pullan, A.J., Sanders, K.M., et al.: Biophysically based mathematical modeling of interstitial cells of Cajal slow wave activity generated from a discrete unitary potential basis (2009). CellML file: faville_model_2008.cellml (Catherine Lloyd)
6. Miller, A.K., Marsh, J., Reeve, A., et al.: An overview of the CellML API and its implementation. BMC Bioinform. **11**, 178 (2010)
7. de Dinechin, F., Pasca, B.: Designing custom arithmetic data paths with FloPoCo. IEEE Des. Test Comput. **28**(4), 18–27 (2011)
8. Oppermann, J., Koch, A., Yu, T., Sinnen, O.: Domain-specific optimisation for the high-level synthesis of CellML-based simulation accelerators. In: 25th International Conference on Field Programmable Logic and Applications, FPL 2015, London, United Kingdom, 2–4 September 2015, pp. 1–7. IEEE (2015)
9. Liebig, B., Koch, A.: High-level synthesis of resource-shared microarchitectures from irregular complex c-code. In: 2016 International Conference on Field-Programmable Technology (FPT), pp. 133–140. IEEE (2016)
10. Huthmann, J., Liebig, B., Oppermann, J., Koch, A.: Hardware/software co-compilation with the Nymble system. In: 8th International Workshop on Reconfigurable and Communication-Centric Systems-on-Chip, pp. 1–8. IEEE, July 2013
11. Huthmann, J., Mller, P., Stock, F., Hildenbrand, D., Koch, A.: Accelerating high-level engineering computations by automatic compilation of geometric algebra to hardware accelerators. In: 2010 International Conference on Embedded Computer Systems: Architectures, Modeling and Simulation, pp. 216–222, July 2010
12. Thielmann, B., Huthmann, J., Koch, A.: Precore - a token-based speculation architecture for high-level language to hardware compilation. In: 2011 21st International Conference on Field Programmable Logic and Applications, pp. 123–129. September 2011
13. Huthmann, J., Oppermann, J., Koch, A.: Automatic high-level synthesis of multi-threaded hardware accelerators. In: 2014 24th International Conference on Field Programmable Logic and Applications (FPL), pp. 1–4, September 2014
14. Nane, R., Sima, V.M., Pilato, C., et al.: A survey and evaluation of FPGA high-level synthesis tools. IEEE Trans. Comput.-Aided Des. Integr. Circuits Syst. **35**(10), 1591–1604 (2016)
15. Xilinx, Inc.: Vivado Design Suite User Guide - High-Level Synthesis (2012)
16. Fingeroff, M., Bollaert, T.: High-Level Synthesis Blue Book. Mentor Graphics Corporation, Wilsonville (2010)
17. Pilato, C., Ferrandi, F.: Bambu: a modular framework for the high level synthesis of memory-intensive applications. In: 2013 23rd International Conference on Field Programmable Logic and Applications (FPL), pp. 1–4. IEEE (2013)

18. Nane, R., Sima, V.M., Olivier, B., et al.: DWARV 2.0: a CoSy-based C-to-VHDL hardware compiler. In: 2012 22nd International Conference on Field Programmable Logic and Applications (FPL), pp. 619–622. IEEE (2012)
19. Canis, A., Choi, J., Aldham, M., et al.: LegUp: high-level synthesis for FPGA-based processor/accelerator systems. In: Proceedings of International Symposium on Field Programmable Gate Arrays (FPGA), pp. 33–36 (2011)
20. Lloyd, C.M., Lawson, J.R., Hunter, P.J., et al.: The CellML model repository. Bioinformatics **24**(18), 2122–2123 (2008)
21. Detrey, J., de Dinechin, F.: Parameterized floating-point logarithm and exponential functions for FPGAs. Microprocess. Microsyst. Spec. Issue FPGA-based Reconfigurable Comput. **31**(8), 537–545 (2007)
22. Grandi, E., Pasqualini, F.S., Bers, D.M.: A novel computational model of the human ventricular action potential and Ca transient (2010). CellML file: grandi_pasqualini_bers_2010_flat.cellml (Geoffrey Nunns)
23. Hornberg, J.J., Binder, B., Bruggeman, F.J., et al.: Control of MAPK signalling: from complexity to what really matters (2005). CellML file: hornberg_binder_brugge-man_schoeberl_heinrich_westerhoff_2005.cellml (Catherine Lloyd)
24. Iyer, V., Hajjar, R.J., Armoundas, A.A.: Mechanisms of abnormal calcium homeostasis in mutations responsible for catecholaminergic polymorphic ventricular tachycardia (2007). CellML file: iyer_2007_ss.cellml (Penny Noble)
25. Iyer, V., Mazhari, R., Winslow, R.L.: A computational model of the human left-ventricular epicardial myocyte (2004). CellML file: iyer_mazhari_winslow_2004.cellml (Steven Niederer)

An Intrusive Dynamic Reconfigurable Cycle-Accurate Debugging System for Embedded Processors

Habib ul Hasan Khan$^{(\boxtimes)}$, Ahmed Kamal, and Diana Goehringer

Technische Universitaet Dresden (TUD), Dresden, Germany
{habib.khan,ahmed.kamal,
diana.goehringer}@tu-dresden.de

Abstract. This paper presents a dynamic partial reconfigurable debugging system for embedded processors based upon a device start and stop (DSAS) approach [1]. Using this approach, a cycle-accurate debugging system can be dynamically configured to any embedded processor-based design at runtime. The debugging system offers lossless debugging because the design is stopped during data transfer to prevent the loss of data. The data can be transferred by any available data communication interface such as Ethernet or UART and can be viewed by open-source waveform viewers. The technique offers debugging without the need to re-synthesize the design by using the dynamic partial reconfiguration.

Keywords: FPGA · Debugging · Simulation · Device start and stop
DSAS · Device under test · Dynamic partial reconfiguration

1 Introduction

The debugging process of current embedded designs is becoming cumbersome because of increasing design complexities. It is revealed that 35 to 45% of the total development effort is spent on verification [2] and this fraction is likely to grow. Moreover, these studies reveal that debugging constitutes about 60% of the total verification efforts. This is due to the fact that FPGA-based designs have lower visibility.

On-chip visibility normally can be enhanced by instrumentation of the design [3] before implementation. These instruments called integrated logic analyzers (ILA) can be used to save a predetermined window of a subset of signal data into memory blocks for offline analysis. However, because of resource limitation, the signals have to be selected before compilation. Hence a new set of data can only be observed after the circuit has been recompiled, a process that can take hours [4]. Moreover, such trace based embedded design solutions operate mainly on the design before place and route (PAR). These tools instrument the original user circuit with trace buffers and their connections before mapping, making fewer resources available for the original design. Insertion of debug circuitry can alter the place and route of the design and hence can prove hazardous for the design in many ways such as the embedded design may no longer fit in the FPGA device, or timing issues may arise because of the debugging circuitry.

© Springer International Publishing AG, part of Springer Nature 2018
N. Voros et al. (Eds.): ARC 2018, LNCS 10824, pp. 433–445, 2018.
https://doi.org/10.1007/978-3-319-78890-6_35

With the advent of Dynamic Partial Reconfiguration (DPR) [5], the time consuming recompilation step can be avoided. Since reconfiguration of an embedded design is very fast compared to recompilation (tens of milliseconds versus minutes to hours), by taking advantage of DPR, the debug-cycle can be sped up.

This paper presents a DPR-based debugging system for embedded processors using a device start and stop (DSAS) approach. In this methodology, the debugging system is present on the dynamic partition and is configured at runtime. Then the debugging system starts and stops the Device Under Test (DUT) which is the static design and saves the data to external memory without any debug window limitation hence providing a continuous, lossless stream of data without any limitation. Moreover, as the debugging system is configured for the design under test through DPR at runtime therefore re-compilation of the design is no longer required. Furthermore, the debugging data stored on the external devices can be viewed based on open source waveform viewers like GTKwave.

The rest of the paper is organized as follows. Section 2 presents related work and provides background information. Section 3 discusses the design methodology of the proposed design. In Sect. 4 the results are discussed. The paper is concluded in Sect. 5.

2   Related Work

Commercial signal capture tools offered by the two major FPGA vendors: Xilinx's ChipScope Pro and Altera's SignalTap II are based upon embedded logic analyzer IP which is instantiated into the user-circuit during regular compilation. A device-neutral product is offered by Synopsys as Identify, offering similar functionality. It is possible to modify the trigger conditions at runtime, but not the signal sets. Hence changing the signals under observation requires FPGA recompilation. Furthermore, instrumentation is normally done after a failure is observed, hence requiring an iteration of the development process. Another tool called Certus by Mentor, allows pre-instrumentation of a large set of interesting signals in the FPGA prior to compilation. Then, during debugging, a small subset of signals can be selected for observation. This may provide more runtime flexibility to designers than in other tools, but it still requires a set of signals to be preselected for observation before any information about possible bugs is available.

A design-level scan was proposed [6] to connect memory elements such as Flip-Flops (FFs) and embedded RAMs in sequence by using the FPGA resources. However, the main drawback of the technique is its high area overhead because FPGA resources are used to implement the scan-chains in the design. In [7], the authors proposed to pre-insert trace buffers into the design in advance, and then perform low level bitstream modification using incremental techniques for connecting the trace buffers to the desired signals. However, this technique still requires pre-reservation of FPGA resources, making them unavailable to the original design. Furthermore, once the debugging process is complete, the trace buffers need to be removed which may alter the place and route of the design.

A virtual overlay network was introduced in [8] which multiplexes the signals into the trace buffers instantiated into the free FPGA resources to avoid unnecessary re-spins. However, this technique requires spare resources which is not always the case.

A framework called Dynamic Modular Development (DMD) [9] used the Xilinx Partial reconfiguration flow for accelerating the embedded design process by partitioning the design modules into separate partially reconfigurable regions and automatically merging embedded modules which are not required to be modified anymore into the surrounding static region. Consequently, rapid turnaround times can be achieved by partitioning frequently modified modules into separate partial reconfigurable regions [10].

A bitstream modification technique was presented in [11] which allows to modify the bitstream after PAR process. The embedded logic analyzer is instantiated to the design prior to netlisting. The signals of interest can be connected to the embedded design by changing the partial bitstream hence reducing the time spent in PAR process. But, when the set of signals for tracing is changed, re-routing needs to be performed which can significantly affect the design's time to market. Furthermore, logic analyzer needs to be removed from the design after design validation which can affect design response of the validated design. Software-like debug features such as watchpoints and breakpoints to enhance debug capability in reconfigurable platforms was presented in [12]. But changing the watchpoints or breakpoints required recompilation of designs.

A new methodology based upon reconfigurability of FPGA was proposed [13] which permits to monitor a large number of internal signals for an arbitrary number of clock cycles by using only limited external pins and hence eliminating the need for repeated iterations of the re-synthesis, placement and routing processes. A multiplexer (MUX) is instantiated into the design with the MUX inputs being all the potential signals required to trace. Different signals can then be selected by reconfiguring the bitstream for select signals of the MUX. The main disadvantage of this methodology is that the contents of the registers need to be shifted within one clock cycle which greatly affects the maximum frequency (F_{max}) of the design.

A design-for-debug infrastructure namely distributed reconfigurable fabric was proposed [14] whose components can be distributed widely in the FPGA and can debug a large number of signals. The reconfigurable logic is programmed to implement various debug paradigms, such as assertions, signal capture and what-if analysis which can accelerate the debugging process. However, still the design needs to be synthesized and implemented after placement of the debug architecture and also needs significant hardware resources. A programmable logic core based debugging system [15] comprising an access network was introduced which can be controlled by the PLC to select the signals required to be debugged.

In some intrusive debugging works [16, 17], the clock of the embedded design was controlled to get debugging data however these works required breakpoints to stop the clock and hence system state, very close to the breakpoint, could be monitored. An intrusive debug approach [18] based upon stopping the clock by monitoring the occupancy of trace buffers was proposed. However, the approach needs a lot of scarce FPGA resources (1 MB RAM), emulation hardware, and also requires external intervention for data handling. In our previous work [1], we introduced a debugging solution which required only 4 KB RAM for saving the data hence even small FPGAs can be equipped with the debugging system with automated data saving process. However, the debugging system is required to be instantiated before synthesis and PAR process which in some case require a lot of time.

From the above discussion, it is evident that clock management in response to memory occupancy can be used to get a continuous, cycle accurate stream of debugging data. The above methodology can be augmented with DPR to save the time spent on the iterative process of synthesis and PAR.

The main contributions of the work are:

- An access network associated device start and stop approach for complete debugging of microprocessors.
- Using DPR technique to employ our debugging system as a reconfigurable module to the embedded design on requirement basis to reduce the time spent on iterative PAR process of traditional debugging solutions.

3   Debugging Methodology

In this section, we will describe our methodology for a dynamic partial reconfigurable debugging system for embedded processors based upon a device start and stop (DSAS) approach. In this methodology, the device under test (DUT) is the static partition and the debugging system is configured as the dynamic reconfigurable part. The embedded processor can keep on performing the desired task without the debugging system if not required. However, once required, the debugging system is dynamically configured to the design using partial bitstream, then it clocks the DUT present on the static partition and performs data logging to the trace buffers. Once the trace buffers are full, the debugging system stops the clock so that no data is lost and saves the data to external memory during the intermediate period and once done it starts clocking the DUT again. Hence providing a continuous, lossless, stream of data with effectively unlimited debug window. Moreover, since the debugging system is installed to the design under test (DUT) through a partial bitstream hence re-implementation of the design is not required. Furthermore, the debugging data can be sent to the terminal using a UART or Ethernet interface which is saved in a log file on the external devices can be used for debugging based on open source waveform viewers like GTKWave. A block diagram of the debugging methodology is shown in Fig. 1.

The main benefits of the proposed technique are debugging of embedded processors due to no loss of debugging data, re-utilization of the same FPGA resources for

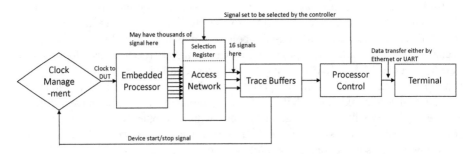

Fig. 1. Debugging methodology

other applications thanks to DPR, no requirement of any specific data acquisition interface (even a UART can be used) and no requirement of an external emulation system.

Furthermore, open-source waveform viewers are used subsequently removing the dependency to use proprietary software. Hence, a cost-effective solution is presented.

3.1   Device Under Test (DUT)

The debugging solution is generic and can be used for any embedded design. However, the methodology is ideally suited for complex embedded microprocessors where it is difficult to identify bugs in the absence of a continuous stream of lossless data. The methodology has been validated by using two different embedded microprocessors as DUT. The embedded processor is treated as a Blackbox and all the interfaces originating from the processor are monitored continuously hence providing a complete picture of the embedded processor activities. The details of the two processors are described below.

3.1.1. The first embedded processor is Xilinx Microblaze [19]. Microblaze is debugged by connecting its interfaces to the debugging system. AXI interconnects can also be connected. Microblaze has already been equipped with a special debugging port (Trace port) which can provide debugging data including the status of the internal registers.

The proposed debugging system can be connected to the Trace port for a continuous stream of data without any loss. The trace port also provides access to some inner registers which are not available on other Microblaze interfaces. In order to debug Microblaze by trace port, a debugging solution was provided by Lauterbach [20] which required an external hardware needed to be connected to the trace port hence required extra cost. By utilizing our proposed debugging system, any interfaces (not limited to trace port) can be debugged without extra overhead cost.

3.1.2. We have chosen an embedded processor based upon RISC-V architecture to highlight the usability of our proposed debugging system. The microprocessor (ORCA developed by Vectorblox) [21] is an open source core based upon RV32IM architecture. Software compilation can be carried out through the available RISC-V cross compiler toolchain. The core was chosen because of its low hardware utilization and hence is suitable for small FPGAs [22]. However, the core doesn't have a debugging solution and hence is hard to debug. The proposed debugging system can be used for complete debugging of the core.

We used the black box approach for debugging of the microprocessor. Hence all the exposed interfaces (including AXI interfaces) are connected to the debugging system for monitoring. The microprocessor fetches the instructions from the memory which are decoded and then executed. The execution of the instruction can result in either saving the data to the memory or the data is used for processing the next instruction. In the first case, once the data is being written to the memory, the data can be acquired by the debugging system. In the second case, data after processing will be saved to the memory. Since in our methodology, there is a continuous lossless stream of data, therefore, monitoring the interfaces results in debugging of the microprocessors. The internal registers can also be debugged by making them visible to the debugging system. One important feature of the processor is that it can be stalled by writing to a Control and Status Register CSR (0x800).

3.2 Clock Management

When the trace buffer is full, the microprocessor needs to be halted so that the data can be sent to the terminal without data loss. Halting the microprocessor is a necessity for debugging the microprocessor at runtime because the data communication is not fast enough to ensure the completeness of data. As already mentioned, the processor can be stalled by writing to a specific register but we didn't choose to stall the processor by writing to the register but by managing the clock. In order to halt the processor, a custom-made clock manager is developed which can stop the clocking of the embedded processor once the connected trace buffers are full.

However, another solution is available for Xilinx FPGAs. The power down pin available at the clocking wizard Xilinx IP [23] can also be used for stopping the clock. Xilinx provided the power down function for power gating but the same function can be used for debugging without the need to develop any custom made IP. However, if the design contains any logic which gets resets upon the absence of clock, that specific logic need to be removed. Otherwise, it will not be possible to get the continuous stream of debugging data from the embedded processor (Fig. 2).

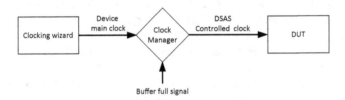

Fig. 2. Clock management

3.3 Concentration Network

In order to have low resource utilization, our proposed debugging system has been configured to debug 16 signals simultaneously. However, the embedded designs may contain large number of nodes need to be debugged. In order to have provision for connecting a large number of nodes, a concentration network can be used. A concentration network has more number of inputs than outputs. The controlling processor can select any output set from the input nodes of the concentration network by just changing the parameter of the concentration network by writing to a selection register without the need to synthesize the block. A concentration network proposed in [24] can be used to connect the DUT with the debugging system. The concentration network can increase the observability of the embedded design at the expense of some logic resources.

3.4   Microprocessor Interfacing

Since the design was verified on the Zedboard, ARM processor has been used in the design as the main controller for data transfer. However, an embedded processor can also be used instead of the ARM processor to make the design independent of any specific processor. Hence, the debugging approach remains valid not only for Xilinx Zynq SoCs but also for other FPGA families without ARM processor. Furthermore, the data can be transmitted by either an Ethernet interface or a UART (whichever is available). Data transmission through Ethernet is faster than UART and hence it is preferred. However, since the processor is not being clocked in either case, no data is lost.

The data is received in a log file in *.txt format. First, a de-multiplexing operation has been performed and then the data has been converted to the Value Change Dump (VCD). Since *.txt format is not directly convertible to VCD format, an application has been created for this conversion so that the design can be monitored by any open source HDL simulator like GTKWave.

3.5   Dynamic Partial Reconfiguration

Dynamic Partial Reconfiguration (DPR) is the ability to reconfigure a portion of the FPGA at run-time while the rest of FPGA remains active [25]. DPR offers the flexibility to change a part of the system's hardware components to reconfigure it to another mode of operation reusing the same hardware resources on the FPGA without halting the rest of the system. In current research work, DPR is used to load the proposed Debugging System (DS) to debug the embedded microprocessors at runtime without the need to repeat the FPGA design flow to add the DS with DUT and re-implement the whole system again on the FPGA. Furthermore, an added advantage is to reuse the same hardware resources consumed by the DS for another Reconfigurable Modules (RM) at runtime after the debugging phase is ended as shown in Fig. 3.

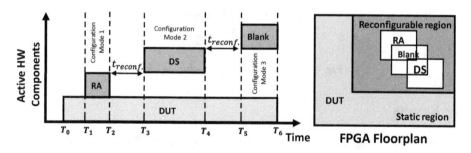

Fig. 3. Using DPR to load the Debugging System (DS)

Xilinx DPR design flow [25] is used for our proposed debugging system. The DPR design flow requires the partitioning of the system into a static region and a Reconfigurable Region (RR). In our case, the static region is the DUT that will not change during the runtime and the RR is allocated for the DS or any RM that will be configured at the same RR after the debugging phase is over. The Hardware Description

Language (HDL) files of the different constituents of the DUT and debugging system were used as input for DPR design flow. Floorplanning was carried out to ensure efficient utilization of the hardware resources. Time of reconfiguration $t_{reconf.}$ is the time consumed to switch to a new operation mode. As $t_{reconf.}$ depends on the size of the RR (Fig. 3), the size of the RR should be optimized to host the largest RM.

In Fig. 3, the proposed reconfigurable system has three RMs (DS, Blank and Reconfigurable Application (RA) for another application). The RR on the FPGA is dynamically reconfigured with one of these RMs according to the time slot. A full configuration mode is the DUT with one of the RMs. The output of the DPR flow is a set of partial bitstream files for each RM of the system and a set of full bitstream files for each configuration mode.

In the proposed DPR-based debugging system, it is possible to load other RMs for another application to reuse the same allocated resources on the reconfigurable region when the DS is not activated (Fig. 3). Therefore, routing or interconnections between the DUT on the static region and DS or any other RMs on the RR should be changed according to the mode of configuration. Hence, to maintain the validation of data flow between the DUT and the RM, a reconfigurable re-routing technique should be used as shown in Fig. 4. In a previous work [26], a proposed re-routing technique is presented to reconfigure the interconnections between the static region and RR for DPR design at runtime.

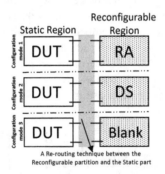

Fig. 4. Routing between the static and RR.

4 Results

The proposed methodology has been tested on the Digilent Zedboard, which has an XC7Z020-484 FPGA We used Xilinx Vivado 2017.1 for the design process carried out on Intel Core i7-6700 CPU running at 3.4 GHz and having 16 GB of RAM. The time taken by the design process when the debugging circuitry is synthesized as a reconfigurable module was about 23 min in comparison to the traditional flow without DPR which took 17 min. It is evident that the difference in synthesis time between the two methodologies is negligible. The main advantage of the presented methodology is the capability of dynamic reconfiguration. The DPR-based debugging system provides the flexibility to load debugging circuitry to the DUT at runtime without the need to repeat the design flow as in the traditional debug flow. Hence, it reduces the design time required for instantiating the debugging circuitry with the DUT in traditional flow. Furthermore; every time the signal set is changed in traditional flow, it requires re-compilation of the design iteratively. But due to the presence of the concentration network in our design, re-compilation of the design is not required. Also the proposed methodology offers the re-usability of the same hardware, allocated to the debugging circuitry, to other applications when the debugging is not required.

4.1   Simulation Results

Once the debugging circuitry has been configured, we can get a continuous stream of data without any discontinuity. In order to display the functionality of the debugging system we made a small data management application. The application performs data handling but when an interrupt is faced, it can leave its normal function and then it carries out a data printing task. In order to debug ORCA, we connected our debugging probes to the data bus so that we can monitor the data read and written from the memory. The results are shown in Fig. 5.

In Fig. 5, RDATA and WDATA are the data read and written respectively. Moreover, ARADDR and AWADDR are the read and write addresses. It must be noted that it is possible to have millions of continuous samples of data for every metric. However, in Fig. 5, 18000 samples of each metric has been plotted to make the figure clearer.

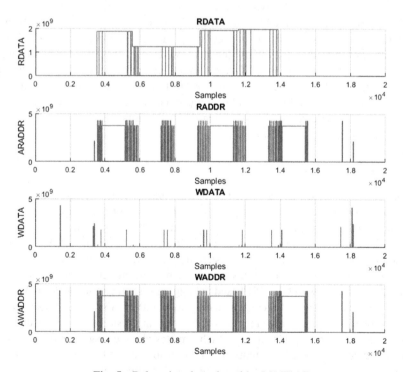

Fig. 5. Debugging data plotted by MATLAB

Since the methodology provides a continuous stream of data, the debugging data can be used for software reconstruction of the microprocessors which can then be used for software debugging. However, the software reconstruction will be explored more in our future work.

4.2 Resource Utilization

Resource utilization of the presented debugging methodology is shown in Fig. 5. The debugging system is synthesized with a sample window of 64 and 1024. 16 signals are monitored with a maximum data width of 32 bits. It can be seen that the resource utilization of the presented debugging system is growing with an increase in debug window, because more BRAM blocks are required as trace buffers. Debugging with a larger window is better for debugging of processors because in one iteration we are getting more data and hence it is faster. However, there is no difference in the quality of data because in any configuration the completeness of data is guaranteed. We have also compared our resource utilization with our previous work (DSAS with a sample window of 64) [1]. At the expense of a minor increase in LUTs and registers utilization, we have been able to reduce the BRAM utilization significantly (10%). It must be noted that the resource utilization for "Window 1024" is approximately equal to DSAS (previous version with sample window 64). Hence using the same resources as the previous version, debugging data can be retrieved more quickly.

Furthermore, as already mentioned that because of DPR, the debugging system is applied only if required. If the debugging system is not required, the resources can be used by any other reconfigurable modules. Another aspect of the proposed DPR based debugging methodology is that the debugging system is not an integral part of the static design like in the traditional FPGA design flow. Hence, the DPR-based debugging system can be removed from the FPGA after qualification of DUT located on the static partition without affecting the routing in the DUT; because both partitions are completely isolated at the level of internal routing. In contrast, for traditional design flow, once the ILA is removed from the design, clock errors arising due to re-routing between resources may occur (Fig. 6).

4.3 Power Utilization

Another benefit of the technique is the low power consumption. Managing the clock for data dispensation imitates clock gating for the embedded design and hence helps in power reduction. It has been noticed that our debugging methodology provides a power saving solution. The static power consumption by Zedboard (including PS+PL), i.e. without programming the FPGA with the DUT bitstream is 2.4 W. As shown in Table 1, the DUT consumed about 3.3 W of power (as measured by current sense J21 jumper on the Zedboard). The DUT with the DPR-based debugging system consumed 3.36 W. Hence the proposed debugging system consumed only about 0.06 W (3.36–3.3). The reason for such low power consumption by the proposed debugging system (0.06 W) is due to the use of clock start and stop technique, which imitates clock gating phenomenon that is known to reduce the power consumption. In order to analyze the effect of clock management carried out by our debug methodology, we removed the debugging system from

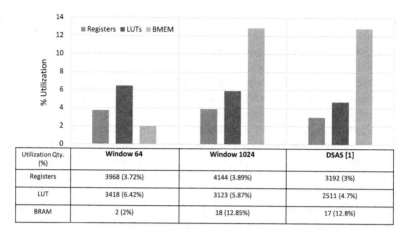

Fig. 6. Resource utilization

Table 1. Power utilization

	Design description	Total consumed power (including PS+PL)
1	ORCA	3.3 W
2	ORCA with DPR-based debug methodology	3.36 W
3	ORCA with clock gating	3.24 W

the design and modified the clocking of the DUT in the same way as was performed by the DPR-based debugging system. It was found out that ORCA with clock gating consumed 3.24 W. It can be seen that 0.06 W (3.30–3.24) of power has been spared by the clock management methodology which provides the cushion for power consumption in the DPR-based debugging system.

4.4 Deployment Time

Using DPR technique to employ our debugging system consumed 260 ms, this is the time of reconfiguration t_{reconf} needed to reconfigure the FPGA at run-time using the JTAG mode of configuration. In contrast the traditional flow requires minutes to hours depending upon the complexity of the DUT. Furthermore, any change in signal set requires to repeat the PAR process again putting a time overhead because of the iterative nature of the traditional debug flow.

5 Conclusions

When an error is encountered in an embedded design, debugging process needs to be followed which requires to first identify potential error-prone signal set and instantiate the debugging system with the DUT. Then a PAR process is followed. The iterative process needs to be repeated until the DUT is verified. These processes require hardware and time resources. Furthermore, the debug core needs to be removed from the design after verification which may change time response of the design and may require further analysis.

In this research work, we presented a DPR based debugging system for embedded processors based upon a device start and stop (DSAS) approach. It has been found that the methodology can be used to troubleshoot bugs in complex SoCs where it is difficult to identify issues in the absence of a continuous stream of lossless data. Moreover, our DPR based debugging methodology employs the debugging system to the design at runtime eliminating the need to go through the PAR process. Furthermore, other applications can use the resources reserved for the debugging system when it is not required.

Since the debugging system provides a continuous stream of data without loss, the work will be extended for software reconstruction in future.

Acknowledgements. This work is funded by German Research Foundation (DFG) via project SFB/TRR 196 "MARIE" through project S05.

References

1. Khan, H., Göhringer, D.: FPGA debugging by a device start and stop approach. In: IEEE International Conference on ReConFigurable Computing and FPGAs (ReConFig) (2016)
2. Abramovici, M., Bradley, P., Dwarakanath, K.: A reconfigurable design-for-debug infrastructure for SoCs. In: 2006 43rd ACM/IEEE Design Automation Conference (2006)
3. Herrmann, A., Nugent, G.: Embedded logic analyzer for a programmable logic device. U.S. Patent No. 6,389,558, 14 May 2002
4. Wrighton, M.G., DeHon, A.M.: Hardware-assisted simulated annealing with application for fast FPGA placement. In: Proceedings of the 2003 ACM/SIGDA Eleventh International Symposium on Field Programmable Gate Arrays, pp. 33–42. ACM (2003)
5. Lie, W., Wu, F.-Y.: Dynamic partial reconfiguration in FPGAs. In: Third International Symposium on Intelligent Information Technology Application, IITA 2009, vol. 2. IEEE (2009)
6. Wheeler, T., Graham, P., Nelson, B., Hutchings, B.: Using design-level scan to improve FPGA design observability and controllability for functional verification. In: Brebner, G., Woods, R. (eds.) FPL 2001. LNCS, vol. 2147, pp. 483–492. Springer, Heidelberg (2001). https://doi.org/10.1007/3-540-44687-7_50
7. Hung, E., Wilton, S.J.E.: Accelerating FPGA debug: increasing visibility using a runtime reconfigurable observation and triggering network. ACM Trans. Des. Autom. Electron. Syst. (TODAES) 19(2), 14 (2014)
8. Hung, E., Wilton, S.J.E.: Towards simulator-like observability for FPGAs: a virtual overlay network for trace-buffers. In: Proceedings of the ACM/SIGDA International Symposium on Field Programmable Gate Arrays. ACM (2013)
9. Iskander, Y., Cameron, D., Patterson, D., Craven, S.D.: Improved abstractions and turnaround time for FPGA design validation and debug. In: 21st International Conference on Field Programmable Logic and Applications. IEEE (2011)

10. Chandrasekharan, A., et al.: Accelerating FPGA development through the automatic parallel application of standard implementation tools. In: 2010 International Conference on Field-Programmable Technology (FPT). IEEE (2010)
11. Graham, P., Nelson, B., Hutchings, B.: Instrumenting bitstreams for debugging FPGA circuits. In: The 9th Annual IEEE Symposium on Field-Programmable Custom Computing Machines, FCCM 2001. IEEE (2001)
12. Lagadec, L., Picard, D.: Software-like debugging methodology for reconfigurable platforms. In: IEEE International Symposium on Parallel & Distributed Processing, IPDPS 2009. IEEE (2009)
13. Poulos, Z., Yang, Y.S., Anderson, J., Veneris, A., Le, B.: Leveraging reconfigurability to raise productivity in FPGA functional debug. In: Design, Automation & Test in Europe Conference & Exhibition (DATE), pp. 292–295. IEEE, March 2012
14. Abramovici, M., Bradley, P., Dwarakanath, K., Levin, P., Memmi, G., Miller, D.: A reconfigurable design-for-debug infrastructure for SoCs. In: Proceedings of the 43rd Annual Design Automation Conference, pp. 7–12. ACM, July 2006
15. Quinton, B., Wilton, S.: Programmable logic core based post-silicon debug for SoCs. In: 4th IEEE Silicon Debug and Diagnosis Workshop, May 2007
16. Kudlugi, M., Hassoun, S., Selvidge, C., Pryor, D.: A transaction-based unified simulation/emulation architecture for functional verification. In: Design Automation Conference Proceedings, pp. 623–628. IEEE, June 2001
17. Vermeulen, B.: Functional debug techniques for embedded systems. IEEE Des. Test Comput. **25**(3) (2008)
18. Panjkov, Z., Wasserbauer, A., Ostermann, T., Hagelauer, R.: Hybrid FPGA debug approach. In: 2015 25th International Conference on Field Programmable Logic and Applications (FPL), pp. 1–8. IEEE, September 2015
19. https://www.xilinx.com/support/documentation/sw_manuals/.../mb_ref_guide.pdf
20. http://www.lauterbach.com
21. VectorBlox Computing Inc.: VectorBlox/risc-v. https://github.com/VectorBlox/risc-v
22. Ng, H.-C., Liu, C., So, H.K.H.: A soft processor overlay with tightly-coupled FPGA accelerator. arXiv preprint arXiv:1606.06483 (2016)
23. https://www.xilinx.com/support/documentation/ip_documentation/clk_wiz/v5_3/pg065-clk-wiz.pdf
24. Khan, H., Grimm, T., Hübner, M., Göhringer, D.: Access network generation for efficient debugging of FPGAs. In: International Symposium on Highly Efficient Accelerators and Reconfigurable Technologies, HEART 2017 (2017)
25. Xilinx Inc.: Partial Reconfiguration User Guide UG909 v2017.1 (2017)
26. Kamaleldin, A., Ahmed, I., Obeid, A.M., Shalash, A., Ismail, Y., Mostafa, H.: A cost-effective dynamic partial reconfiguration implementation flow for Xilinx FPGA. In: New Generation CAS (NGCAS) 2017, pp. 281–284. IEEE, September 2017

Rapid Prototyping and Verification of Hardware Modules Generated Using HLS

Julián Caba$^{1(\boxtimes)}$ ⓘ, João M. P. Cardoso$^{2(\boxtimes)}$ ⓘ, Fernando Rincón$^{1(\boxtimes)}$ ⓘ,
Julio Dondo$^{1(\boxtimes)}$ ⓘ, and Juan Carlos López$^{1(\boxtimes)}$ ⓘ

^{1} University of Castilla-La Mancha, 13071 Ciudad Real, Spain
julian.caba@uclm.es
^{2} Faculty of Engineering, University of Porto, 4200-465 Porto, Portugal
jmpc@fe.up.pt

Abstract. Most modern design suites include HLS tools that rise the design abstraction level and provide a fast and direct flow to programmable devices, getting rid of manually coding at the RTL. While HLS greatly reduces the design productivity gap, non-negligible problems arise. For instance, the co-simulation strategy may not provide trustworthy results due to the variable accuracy of simulation, especially when considering dynamic reconfiguration and access to system busses. This work proposes mechanisms aimed at improving the verification accuracy using a real device and a testing framework. One of the mechanisms is the inclusion of physical configuration macros (e.g., clock rate configuration macro) and test assertions based on physical parameters in the verification environment (e.g., timing assertions). In addition it is possible to change some of those parameters, such as clock speed rate, and check the behavior of a hardware component into an overclocking or underclocking scenario. Our on-board testing flow allows faster FPGA iterations to ensure the design intent and the hardware-design behavior match. This flow uses a real device to carry out the verification process and synthesizes only the DUT generating its partial bitstream in a few minutes.

Keywords: FPGA · Verification · High-level synthesis · Co-simulation

1 Introduction

High-Level Synthesis (HLS) tools are focused on reducing the design gap, as well as the complexity of hardware digital design [1]. Ultimately, using this kind of tools software engineers would be able to accelerate their applications with reconfigurable hardware. In addition, with HLS hardware engineers can work at higher abstraction levels when requirements can be fulfilled without the low-level manual hardware design. Thus, high-level programming languages, such as C or C++, are becoming widespread to describe and speed up user algorithms providing some

© Springer International Publishing AG, part of Springer Nature 2018
N. Voros et al. (Eds.): ARC 2018, LNCS 10824, pp. 446–458, 2018.
https://doi.org/10.1007/978-3-319-78890-6_36

goodness such as adaptability to changes or shorter *time-to-market* [2]. As a consequence, engineers are able to build different versions of their hardware modules in a short time according to the requirements of the project.

Although the use of HLS tools has boosted hardware design productivity, they entail some issues which have not been solved yet. (1) Most HLS tools include a co-simulation strategy in order to check the correctness of hardware designs described in a high-level programming language, reusing the software test into a co-simulation environment (software tests + simulator tool). However, when one synthesizes the generated RTL and runs these tests in a real device, the behavior may not match the expected results and tests may fail. This is because the co-simulation environment does not take into account some physical aspects (e.g., routing paths, resource locations). (2) Performing in-hardware testing using a real device is a hard task and typically implies the conversion of tests according to the deployment platform. Moreover, the engineer has to build a custom hardware platform, which entails an important development time, so the product's *time-to-market* may be affected. (3) The report given by HLS tools is not fully accurate, since it always reports the worst case. Sometimes that worst case is not present in practice and designs could work with higher clock frequencies, for example. (4) Although HLS vendors provide some techniques, such as pragmas, in order to drive the translation process, engineers loss control over generated designs. Engineer's experience plays an important role to generate desired designs. In addition, the visibility is lower when one works at higher abstraction levels.

Because of these limitations, current HLS tools and design flows are not enough to fully verify and perform accurate design space exploration of designs. Tests must be re-written and a handmade verification platform must be built for each hardware design. In addition, simulations close to real scenarios would be desirable in order to ensure the correctness of the hardware design generated from a high-level programming language, both considering the effect of physical parameters and reducing the limitations imposed by HLS tools.

The main contribution of this work is an approach to extend HLS verification, based on software testing techniques, but including design deployment on real hardware as part of the process. Besides the verification of the correctness of the design, the methodology can be used to explore the different physical constraints, and its behavior under different conditions than those used as restrictions during the synthesis process. To achieve our main objective our approach provides the following aspects:

- A *testing framework* to check Design Under Test (DUT) behavior following the point of view of software testing frameworks and using macro assertions.
- Bring *physical parameters* into verification, tests support the configuration of certain physical parameters to obtain results from a real scenario. For instance, tests may configure the clock rate in accordance with the profiling of HLS tools or overclocking the solution generated by these tools.
- An *on-board platform* to handle the verification process on real hardware, providing real timing results, and able to configure the clock rate using software

instructions in order to observe the design behavior under overclocking/under-clocking conditions. This platform is remotely accessible and should decouple the testing framework from the hardware prototype.

This paper is organized as follows. Section 2 describes the current progress in hardware verification. Section 3 describes the proposed development flow, which is implemented on the architecture presented in Sect. 4. In Sect. 5, we present some results using our approach in the context of a case study. Finally, Sect. 6 summarizes this paper and proposes directions for future work.

2   Related Work

During the last decade, FPGA vendors have introduced new HLS tools in order to reduce the complexity of hardware design, thus allowing engineers to work at higher abstraction levels. However, problems arise when engineers try to check the correctness of their designs. The accuracy of the simulation depends on the different levels of abstraction used during the modelling of a SoC [3]. The highest simulation effort is required at High-Level Modelling, but it usually results in inaccuracies. On the other hand, the prototype is the perfect environment to carry out the verification process, but it usually is very hard and costly.

One of the advantages of working at high levels of abstraction is that verification tasks, such as writing Non-Regression Tests (NRT), can be performed much easier (see, e.g., [4]), and can benefit from the use of higher productivity tools such as testing frameworks. Some research efforts (see, e.g., [5,6]) propose formal methodologies, such as UVM (Universal Verification Methodology) [8]. As this methodology entails a complex and hard effort, researchers have focused on techniques to make it simpler and reduce the effort needed [5,6]. As randomized stimuli are considered to be undesirable and difficult for inexperienced engineers, authors [7] propose to reuse the C test cases in the UVM environment. Thus, tests are kept over all the verification levels. Nevertheless, high abstraction techniques are focused on testing the functional behavior of a design, applying a verification methodology or not, into a particular scenario because most of those tests do not take physical parameters into account.

On the other hand, other approaches propose the use of real devices for verifying hardware designs. For instance, [9] introduces a hardware verification platform in order to overcome RTCA/DO-254 verification challenges. However, their solution requires the synthesis of the whole system. Conversely, [10] includes partial reconfiguration and validates synthesized hardware designs with the original model, using a black-box verification approach. In the same context, [11] proposes a verification framework to verify hardware designs directly in an FPGA instead of using simulations. They do not consider the synthesis process and use a *Network Storage* which contains the bitstreams, the input test vectors and the golden reference. It is clear that using a real device for the verification and exploration of the performance of a design entails new challenges, such as building a platform, its synthesis, or communication between the test framework and the DUT, among others.

Indeed, from high-level simulation to in-hardware simulation there is an important gap. In order to narrow that gap, some efforts provide intermediate approaches overcoming several physical parameters from HLS tools. The authors in [12] consider multi-cycling in HLS contexts and use software profiling to guide multi-cycling optimizations. In [13], they perform multi-cycle optimization on chained functional operations. Their approach couples HLS and logic synthesis synergistically so multi-cycle paths can be identified and optimized coherently across both behavioral and logic levels.

Our approach relies on a mixture of high abstraction levels with low ones to ensure the correctness of hardware designs generated from a high-level programming language through HLS, allowing physical modifications, such as clock rate and check the design with overclocking/underclocking configurations.

3   On-Board Testing Flow

Our proposed testing flow is based on the three typical steps. The flow starts from C or C++ code written by the user, plus some functional tests. In the **software domain**, including embedded systems, testing frameworks to verify the software artifacts are very widespread, so we propose the use of *Unity* testing framework [14]. *Unity* can easily be expanded building new macros. Most frameworks have a variety of assertions which are meant to be placed in the test to verify the production code. For instance, the TEST_ASSERT_EQUAL(expected, value) macro checks the equality between the expected value and the one returned.

Once the module is tested in a purely software domain, we consider that an HLS tool is used to translate the high-level code into an RTL description. Although the flow could be easily adapted to any other tools such as LegUp [1] or AUGH [11], in this work we use Vivado HLS from Xilinx [15]. At this stage, we can run the tests again without any change (**co-simulation stage**).

The third step generates the configuration file (partial bitstream) and deploys it to the **on-board** platform. In order to carry out an in-hardware testing process, our platform contains a dynamic area and we use Dynamic Partial Reconfiguration (DPR). Hence, we provide a reference synthesized platform with some checkpoints in order to synthesize only the logic that is programmed into the dynamic area. For this, we include a TCL script following the Xilinx approach for the overall generation process management. This TCL script imports a reference platform and adds RTL description files, customizing a new configuration. Summarising, our TCL scripts automate the partial bitstream generation process from high-level descriptions. Thus, developers do not have to build a new platform or regenerate their IPs, moreover, our approach allows testing designs in a real devices in few minutes (FPGA iterations) as our case study shows.

This stage introduces testing novelities, the tests can be modified to annotate the physical parameters, such as the clock rate to be used or the number of cycles the clock enable must be set active (lines 4 and 5 of Listing 1.1). To carry out these tasks we have extended the *Unity* testing framework with the inclusion of a number of configuration macros (see Table 1). In addition, to ensure that

Table 1. Configuration macros of *Unity* extension.

Macro	Description
`UNITY_RESET`	Sends a reset signal to the DUT (dynamic area)
`UNITY_START`	Enables the dynamic area during the cycles depicted in `CONFIGURE_UNITY_CLK_EN` macro
`CONFIGURE_UNITY_HW_ADDR(addr)`	Configures the hardware address where is mapped the *Hardware Manager* component. By default 0x41000000
`CONFIGURE_UNITY_IGNORE_INPUT(words)`	Configures the input 32-bit words that should be ignored. By default 1
`CONFIGURE_UNITY_IGNORE_OUTPUT(words)`	Configures the output 32-bit words that should be ignored. By default 1
`CONFIGURE_UNITY_CLK_EN(cycles)`	Configures the number of cycles that the `clken` signal is active-high. 0 means that the `clken` signal is always active-high
`CONFIGURE_UNITY_CLK_RATE(clk)`	Configures the clock frequency. Allowed inputs are: 33, 66, 100, 200 and 400. By default 100 MHz

sequential processes of our DUT starts in a known state, we add a special macro that resets the whole module (DUT) before exercising it (line 6 of Listing 1.1).

On-board verification entails another important problem: the communication between different domains. As in this case the module is running in a real device, our approach includes a special function for the transfer of stimuli between the testing environment and the hardware module, the input and output sizes are 16 32-bit words in accordance with a 4×4 window (line 7 of Listing 1.1). Following the testing framework philosophy, we have also added new macros to measure the time in clock cycles spent by the module (line 8 of Listing 1.1). Therefore, Unity extension keeps the same testing technology independently of the module abstraction level, and therefore, the development status. Indeed, macros are added to tests when one wants to check or configure some physical parameters.

Listing 1.1. Example of on-board test with *Unity* extension

```
1   void
2   test_module(){
3   #ifdef HW_TEST
4     CONFIGURE_UNITY_CLK_EN(200); // 200 cycles active-high
5     CONFIGURE_UNITY_CLK_RATE(100); // 100MHz
6     UNITY_RESET(); // Reset Module
7     result = moduleDUT(stimuli)
8     TEST_ASSERT_TIME_LT(50); // Checking time
9   #else
10    result = moduleDUT(stimuli);
11  #endif
12    for(int i=0; i!=16; i++)
13      TEST_ASSERT_EQ(reference[i], result[i]);
14  }
```

4   Architecture Overview

One of our goals is to provide an on-board platform for testing the modules generated by HLS tools, and improve the static analysis provided by them. Our on-board platform relies on a SoC platform which integrates an FPGA and a hardcore-processor in the same device. In our case, we use a Zedboard from Xilinx [16].

This platform allows an easy communication between the hardcore-processor and the logic part. In addition, the Zedboard is connected to a computer network via Ethernet in order to communicate with the workstation where hardware modules have been developed using HLS tools. The testing framework is remote too, thus an FPGA plays the role of a remote service.

4.1   Hardware Architecture

Figure 1 shows the Processing Logic (PL) architecture layout of our on-board platform environment in the Zedboard. The module to verify, the DUT, is programmed in this side and its communication with the Processing System (PS) side is done through two FIFO channels connected to an AXI interface. This AXI bus connects both PS and PL sides, tunneling a master-slave communication, where PL is the master and the components programmed in PL area are slaves.

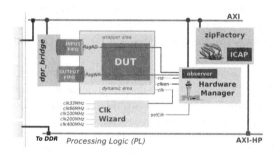

Fig. 1. Processing logic architecture layout

The PL side is divided into two parts, a static one which contains those components that do not change independently of the Design Under Test (DUT), and the DUT, which could be a part of an image filter, a cypher algorithm, etc. The DUT is also deployed into a dynamic reconfigurable area, while the rest of the layout does not change. One of the advantages of the use of DPR is that it reduces the synthesis process and improves synthesis tasks [17] due to working with partial bitstreams. Another benefit motivated by DPR is the fact that engineers can dynamically insert new functionality without redesigning the whole system or moving to a bigger device. Furthermore, it is possible to adapt an FPGA to different scenarios, by just modifying the functionality or the performance of some related tasks [17].

The *zipFactory* component programs (physically deploys) a partial bitstream into the dynamic area available in our on-board platform without the microprocessor intervention. It retrieves bitstream data from the DDR which would have been previously stored into a memory location. This component is able to recognize a desynchronization bitstream word, so it stops reading at that moment. The retrieved data is stored into an internal small buffer, handling them as batched data. The ICAP bandwidth is 32-bits, which matches the internal buffer width. The component knows the type of 32-bit word sent to the ICAP at each transaction, thus when the 32-bit word is the desynchronization word the reconfiguration process is finished, although we attach some NOPs to flush the command pipeline properly.

As we mentioned above, the DUT is connected to an AXI bus through two FIFO channels. This is a typical configuration of most accelerators where they read a stream of input data and produce an output data stream. Anyway, this interface could be replaced by another protocol/interface such as *AXI-Stream* or *AXI-Lite*, or we could even add our own protocol over a streaming channel. The current platform bridges the AXI data whose hardware address matches with the address where the *dpr_bridge* component is mapped, thus the data is stored into an input FIFO when the operation is a write. On the other side, when the operation is a read, the *dpr_bridge* component retrieves data from the output FIFO and sends it through the AXI bus. Besides, a clock enable signal has been added in the dynamic area interface in order to manage when the DUT should be active. This enable signal does not affect the *dpr_bridge* component, so it is able to carry out its tasks independently: fill the input FIFO and empty the output FIFO. Indeed, a *start macro* is executed during the *moduleDUT* function to enable the DUT.

The *Hardware Manager* component carries out the following hardware tasks (each task is controlled from the test using the macros mentioned in the previous section) that would not be feasible or would result in a poor accuracy when performed in the software testing environment.

- It resets the dynamic area in order to assure that internal signals of our DUT start from a well-known state. In addition, one can send a reset in the middle of a DUTs operation in order to know its behavior in that scenario.
- It sets active-high the clock enable signal during the cycles related to the configuration of the test (e.g., line 5 of Listing 1.1). It is active-low until the macro UNITY_START() is called upon. Engineers can set the number of cycles that the clock enable must be active-high using the CONFIGURE_UNITY_CLOCK_EN(cycles) macro.
- It sets the clock rate of the dynamic part and those static modules that interact with it at runtime, such as *clk_rd* of input FIFO. The available clock speed rates are: 33 MHz, 66 MHz, 100 MHz, 200 MHz and 400 MHz. Thus, engineers have only to indicate which clock rate will be used through the CONFIGURE_UNITY_CLK_RATE(clk) macro. This feature provides a flexible environment in which engineers do not need to build a new platform or modify a previous one for the verification of their designs.

– It measures the time elapsed by the tasks performed by a DUT. The *Hard-ware Manager* component observes transactions between the input/output FIFOs and the dynamic part as a spy. Thus, this component is able to know how many transactions take place between both parts and when they happen. It works increasing an internal counter which plays the role of a chronome-ter. This chronometer is triggered by transactions that take place between the input FIFO and the DUT (input transactions), whereas it is stopped by transactions that take place between the DUT and the output FIFO (output transactions). The extension of *Unity* testing framework allows us to config-ure the number of input transactions and output transactions that may be ignored. Therefore, the *Hardware Manager* component must be configured from the test denoting the number of 32-bit words to be ignored during input transactions and, on the other side, the number of 32-bit words of output transactions which must also be ignored. By default, both values are one and we can explicitly configure them in the test source code, e.g., Listing 1.1, the following two configuration macros CONFIGURE_UNITY_IGNORE_INPUT(words) and CONFIGURE_UNITY_IGNORE_OUT PUT(words).

In order to spy the transactions between both FIFOs and the DUT, our platform adds two special signals: *flagRD* and *flagWR*. In our case study both are connected to the input FIFO and output FIFO, respectively. However, both signals can be connected to another sources, modifying the wrapper which adapts the dynamic area interface to the DUT interface.

4.2   Software Architecture

Figure 2 shows the PS architecture of our on-board platform, the developer's workstation side and the communication between them. Messages are sent through a computer network using the zeroC Ice communication middleware [18].

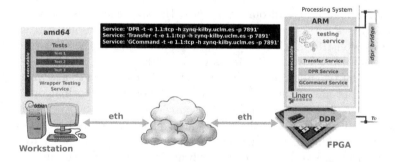

Fig. 2. Communication overview

On the FPGA side, the PS contains an ARM processor which runs an embed-ded operating system (in the experiments we use an OS based on Linaro Ubuntu distribution from a SD card). Over this OS, we deploy three services that enables the use of internal hardware components from outside. For instance, when the partial bitstream is ready we can send it to the FPGA. We choose the network as the channel to carry out this task since the FPGA can be a shared resource, thus we provide the mechanism to share transparently a hardware resource, increasing its availability and accessibility. In addition our reconfiguration engine (*zipFactory* component) is faster than other proposals as shown in the results section. Hence, to send a partial bitstream we may use the *transfer* service, that stores the data sent into a default memory address. Then we may trigger a reconfiguration process through the *DPR* service. Finally, we may run the test on-board mode (step 3 of flow proposed), in this case the *GCommand* service translates the communication messages into AXI messages whose hardware address matches that of the DUT.

In the engineer's workstation, one may use software wrappers of these three services in order to marshall and unmarshall the messages. These services are shown as functions from the testing framework point of view. Indeed, the `moduleDUT` function in Listing 1.1 serializes stimuli into zeroC Ice messages. In addition, `moduleDUT` function deserializes data retrieved from the FPGA too. Note that *stimuli* and *result* are streaming data that will be retrieved and stored from the input FIFO and to the output FIFO respectively.

5   Use Case

Our approach has been developed under a GNU/Linux environment, and has been implemented on a Xilinx Zedboard platform. We use here a case study based on the histogram of oriented gradients (HOG). By default, the platform works at 100 MHz, but the dynamic area and other components can modify this clock speed rate at runtime. The HOG is a feature descriptor used in computer vision and image processing for object detection, particularly suited for human detection in images. The algorithm implementation is divided into different steps: gamma and color normalization, gradient computation, block normalization among other. In our case study, the step chosen is the vector normalization block with several normalization factors and solutions, e.g., single or double precision [19]. Each solution has been developed in the C programming language and using Vivado HLS in its version 2015.4.

We consider two block normalization factors: l^2-*norm* and l^2-*hys* with a 4×4 window as input and output. Thus, the input and output of both algorithms are 16 pixels. Table 2 shows the hardware resource comparison between the results reported by Vivado HLS and the results after place and route process for both algorithms. In addition, we considered some improvements in order to achieve higher performance without a high hardware resource cost. For instance, the difference between *original* and *improved* versions are not very far in hardware resources, whereas the latency is much lower in the second version. The *improved* solution contains some *pragma* in order to pipeline and unroll the solution. Moreover, we consider implementations with single and double floating-point precisions.

Table 2. Comparison between Vivado HLS and after Place and Route reports

	Solution	HLS report				P&R report			
		BRAMs[2]	DSPs	FFs	LUTs	BRAMs[2]	DSPs	FFs	LUTs
l^2-norm 32b[1]	Original	0	5	1904	2628	0	5	1710	1764
	Improved (II=1, Factor=2)	6	5	2039	2777	6	5	1942	1886
l^2-norm 64b[1]	Original	4	14	6403	8123	4	14	6124	5942
	Improved (II=1, Factor=2)	10	14	6834	8415	6	14	6758	6373
l^2-hys 32b[1]	Original	0	5	2129	3160	0	5	1851	2040
	Improved (II=1, Factor=2)	4	5	2334	3416	2	5	2144	2320
l^2-hys 64b[1]	Original	6	14	6828	9149	6	14	6343	6312
	Improved (II=1, Factor=2)	12	14	7460	9685	8	14	7250	7036

[1]Float-Point precision.   [2]BRAM18K.

Table 3 timing and frequency summary of each solution that Table 2 shows. The table compares the HLS report with the on-board report. The maximum frequency is controlled using the UNITY_TIME_CLK_RATE macro, while the latency, throughput and execution time are measured from the *flagRD* and *flagWR* signals which are connected to FIFO channels and are activated when the first transaction happens. All versions are tested with the same hardware platform, generating each partial bitstream, sending them through the network using the services deployed in the FPGA where, they finally are exercised. Contrasting the results in Tables 2 and 3, we can observe some differences between the results provided by the HLS tool and the real results provided by our platform.

Table 3. Summary of latencies, execution times and throughput

	Solution	HLS		On-board				Exec Time/ Freq. Used
		Latency[2]	Max. Freq.[3]	Freq. Used[3]	Latency 1st Output[2]	Latency[2]	Throughput[2]	
l^2-norm 32b[1]	Original	329	122	200	295	385	385	1925
	Improved (II=1, Factor=2)	141	114	200	111	171	155	855
l^2-norm 64b[1]	Original	507	116	200	457	577	577	2887
	Improved (II=1, Factor=2)	166	60	100	152	242	210	2420
l^2-hys 32b[1]	Original	602	122	200	568	658	658	3290
	Improved (II=1, Factor=2)	234	112	200	219	279	263	1395
l^2-hys 64b[1]	Original	910	122	200	860	980	980	4900
	Improved (II=1, Factor=2)	316	60	100	302	392	360	3920

[1]Float-Point precision.   [2]In clock cycles.   [3]In MHz.

On the other hand, we can change the clock period in the HLS tool in order to force it to fulfill the specified time requirement. Then we can use our platform independently of the clock period target to ensure that the design works, or we can even overclock or underclock the DUT.

Engineers can use our platform and design flow based on TCL scripts to verify their designs, or new design versions modifying the target clock period or adding new optimizations through *pragma* directives, in a real device waiting a few minutes. Any of the solutions of our case study takes about 2 min. and 30 sec. to generate one partial bitstream from its high-level description. In addition, the processes for configuring the FPGA and sending the stimuli take only three seconds. Thus, engineers can make faster FPGA iterations to ensure their designs intention and their hardware-designs behavior match.

Our approach allows measuring the real throughput of streaming designs and the related time of each result. For instance, the l^2-*norm original* solution of our case study for single precision version takes 295 cycles to generate the first result (*execution time*), as shown in Table 2. The output rate of this version is 6 cycles, thus the second pixel is written at cycle 301 and so successively to complete the output window. Therefore, this solution takes 385 cycles to process an input window of 16 pixels (*latency*). In this solution, the *throughput* is 385 cycles because we do not apply any improvement to build a dataflow.

One important part of our platform is the reconfiguration engine. This component enables to run tests very fast since the hardware module may be sent to an FPGA through the network. Comparing our approach with other controllers (e.g., the ones presented by [20–23]) we achieve a configuration rate about 387.59 MB/s, very close to the theoretical (400 MB/s), using the half of resources - *zipFactory* core uses 272 FFs, 586 LUTs and 2 BRAMs - that the best solution [22].

6   Conclusion

In this paper we presented a development flow and on-board platform to provide unit testing to hardware modules, considering both functionality and timing issues. Our approach is well-suited for both software and hardware developers. We propose the use of software macros embedded in test cases to program physical parameters such as operating clock frequency. Hardware modules depicted in a high-level programming language are translated into a programmable file automatically through some TCL scripts. In addition, our proposal provides a remote and transparent dynamic reconfiguration service, offering FPGA as a verification service. Thus, we can exercise a design under test (DUT) remotely, breaking down the test from the hardware prototype.

Engineers only need to add a few physical parameters into their tests in order to check their hardware modules on a real device. Engineers should be able to modify the clock speed rate without a high effort, thus the correctness of their hardware modules can be verified in the context of an overclocking or underclocking environments. This can be very useful as it can test if a design works with a higher speed clock rate than the one reported by HLS tools, especially when all input values to be used do not trigger the worst case. In addition, in our approach the original software tests are kept as much as possible during the development life-cycle of hardware modules based on HLS.

Future work will be targeted to synthesizable hardware assertions, in order to enhance real-time verification capabilities in our platform and raise the visibility of internal signals, which are synthesized by HLS tools and are too difficult to be traced from a simulator.

Acknowledgments. This work is supported in part by Spanish Government under projects REBECCA (TEC2014-58036-C4-1R) and PLATINO (TEC2017-86722-C4-4-R).

References

1. Canis, A., Choi, J., et al.: From software to accelerators with LegUp high-level synthesis. In: International Conference on Compilers, Architecture and Synthesis for Embedded Systems (2013)
2. Cong, J., Liu, B., et al.: High-level synthesis for FPGAs: from prototyping to deployment. Comput.-Aided Des. Integr. Circuits Systems (2011)
3. Gong, L., Diessel, O.: Functional Verification of Dynamically Reconfigurable FPGA-Based Systems. Springer, Heidelberg (2015). https://doi.org/10.1007/978-3-319-06838-1
4. Hoffman, H.: Non-regression test automation. In: PNSQC (2008)
5. Podivinsky, J., Simkova, M., Cekan, O., Kotasek, Z.: FPGA prototyping and accelerated verification of ASIPs. In: International Symposium on Design and Diagnostics of Electronic Circuits Systems (2015)
6. Yun, Y.N., Kim, J.B., Kim, N.D., Min, B.: Beyond UVM for practical SoC verification. In: International SoC Design Conference (2011)
7. Edelman, R., Ardeishar, R.: UVM SchmooVM - I want my c tests!. In: Design and Verification Conference and Exhibition (2014)
8. Accellera Organization: Standard Universal Verification Methodology Class Reference Manual, Release 1.1, Accellera (2011)
9. De Luna, L., Zalewski, Z.: FPGA level in-hardware verification for DO-254 compilance. In: Digital Avionics Systems Conference (DASC) (2011)
10. Iskander, Y., Craven, S., et al.: Using partial reconfiguration and high-level models to accelerate FPGA design validation. In: International Conference on Field-Programmable Technology (2010)
11. Wicaksana, A., Prost-Boucle, A., et al.: On-board non-regression test of HLS tools targeting FPGA. In: International Symposium on Rapid System Prototyping (2016)
12. Hadjis, S., Canis, A., et al.: Profiling-driven multi-cycling in FPGA high-level synthesis. In: Design, Automation, Test in Europe (2015)
13. Zheng, H., Gurumani, S.T., Yang, L., Chen, D., Rupnow, K.: High-level synthesis with behavioral level multi-cycle path analysis. In: FPL 2013 (2013)
14. Karlesky, M., VanderVoord, M., Williams, G.: A simple Unit Test Framework for Embedded C. Unity
15. Xilinx Inc.: Vivado Design Suite User Guide: High-Level Synthesis. Xilinx (2014)
16. AVNET: ZedBoard: Hardware User's Guide, AVNET (2014)
17. Kao, C.: Benefits of partial reconfiguration. Xcell J. Fourth Quart. 65–67 (2005)
18. https://zeroc.com/
19. Dalal, N., Triggs, B.: Histograms of oriented gradients for human detection. In: Computer Vision and Pattern Recognition (CVPR) (2005)

20. Hubner, M., Gohringer, D., et al.: Fast dynamic and partial reconfiguration Data Path with low Hardware overhead on Xilinx FPGAs. In: International Symposium on Parallel & Distributed Processing, Workshops and PHd Forum (2010)
21. Manet, P., Maufroid, D., et al.: An evaluation of dynamic partial reconfiguration for signal and image processing in professional electronics applications. EURASIP J. Embedded Syst. **2008**. https://doi.org/10.1155/2008/367860
22. Vipin, K., Fahmy, S.: A high speed open source controller for FPGA partial reconfiguration. In: International Conference on Field-Programmable Technology (2012)
23. Tarrillo, J., Escobar, F.A., Lima, F., Valderrama, C.: Dynamic partial reconfiguration manager. In: Latin American Symposium on Circuits and Systems (2014)

Comparing C and SystemC Based HLS Methods for Reconfigurable Systems Design

Konstantinos Georgopoulos$^{(\boxtimes)}$, Pavlos Malakonakis, Nikolaos Tampouratzis,
Antonis Nikitakis, Grigorios Chrysos, Apostolos Dollas,
Dionysios Pnevmatikatos, and Ioannis Papaefstathiou

Telecommunication Systems Institute, Campus Kounoupidiana,
Technical University of Crete, Chania, Greece
kgeorgopoulos@isc.tuc.gr

Abstract. This paper provides an extensive analysis of the key characteristics, efficiency and overall user-friendliness that stem from the use of two different input methods for the design of *High-Level Synthesis* (HLS) reconfigurable systems, i.e. *C-based* and *SystemC-based*. Each input language has been used within the context of a separate HLS tool that is especially suitable for the particular input method chosen. The study has been based on the use of key fundamental computational and data processing algorithms, while the outlined observations have been drawn by traversing the full HLS flows. The algorithms address both memory- and compute-intensive modules, which are the main cores for numerous modern applications. In this way, detailed observations are made not only with respect to the performance of each approach individually but also against each other. Hence, this paper provides information on an extensive list of issues of major interest to modern reconfigurable systems design engineers, such as design cycle definition, time for HLS flow completion, implementable features, parallelisation, input model complexity and more importantly design effort/time. Moreover, this work presents detailed results on implementation issues as well as implementation guidelines concerning the presented schemes; these guidelines can certainly be used as a reference for any designer implementing such classes of algorithms.

Keywords: High-Level Synthesis · Reconfigurable hardware · C
SystemC

1 Introduction

The motivation for this work has been the rapidly developing sub-field of Electronic Design Automation (EDA) [1] tools known as *High-Level Synthesis* (HLS) [3], especially since they play a key role in the design of reconfigurable systems. Their importance becomes greater by the day, a fact that is clearly demonstrated

© Springer International Publishing AG, part of Springer Nature 2018
N. Voros et al. (Eds.): ARC 2018, LNCS 10824, pp. 459–470, 2018.
https://doi.org/10.1007/978-3-319-78890-6_37

by the number of different HLS tools that has currently been proposed and/or marketed [4]. The strength of HLS is found in the ability to generate production-quality Register Transfer Level (RTL) [5] implementations from high-level specifications. In reality, this is a task that is constantly performed manually by design engineers and programmers while HLS promises to automate it, thus eliminating the source of many design errors and accelerating the currently very long development cycle. This design cycle is also proving to be highly expensive due to escalating non-recurrent engineering costs.

Additional benefits include a design source that is truly generic and, thus, more versatile and portable. Working with purely functional specifications, details, such as clock frequencies, technology and micro-architecture, are eliminated, allowing for greater and easier reuse and re-targeting of the developed models and functional Intellectual Property (IP) cores.

Two of the most prominent input methods in HLS reconfigurable systems design are based on using *(i)* C or C-based variants and *(ii)* SystemC. They are both extensively used and constitute the focus of this paper which provides evaluation insights that are beneficial to the growing number of designers that resort to their use.

Since the purpose of this study has been to investigate the use of those two types of input languages in the context of HLS design, the main focus has been placed towards selecting algorithms that are not overly complicated and have a fast turnaround in terms of results. The interest here has been to use algorithms that bring forward key observations related to the two input methods and their behaviour within the context of a HLS tool. Hence, the use cases include both compute-intensive problems and memory-intensive ones, namely (i) *Mutual Information* [6], (ii) *Transfer Entropy* [7], (iii) *List Manager* and, finally, (iv) *Memory Allocator* [8]. The first two are characterised as compute-intensive, List Manager is a memory-intensive algorithm and the Memory Allocator constitutes a combination of both memory- and compute-intensive characteristics.

Hence, the contributions of this paper are based on the use of two different HLS input modelling languages and convey information related to (i) development time, (ii) Lines of Code (LoC), (iii) latency/performance, (iv) anticipation for mathematical operations, (v) learning curve for efficient modelling, (vi) robustness of high-level models and, finally, (vii) parallelisation capabilities.

The paper is organised as follows. Section 2 presents the two different design flows along with their respective characteristics. Section 3 presents a brief description of the algorithms used in the context of this work. Section 4 has performance figures and technical information on all RTL designs and for all the memory- and compute-intensive algorithms. Section 5 presents a thorough comparative analysis based on both the technical results as well as on the qualitative authors' experience. Finally, Sect. 6 concludes the paper.

2   Tools' Flows and Characteristics

The main development stages of the two input method flows are shown in Fig. 1, from the initial algorithm description to bitstream generation.

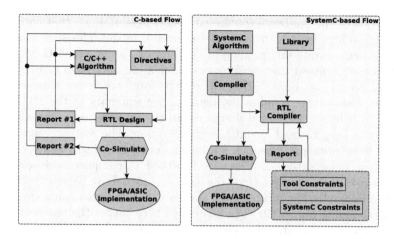

Fig. 1. C-based flow & SystemC-based flow

Note that these two flows do not represent the only way that either a C-based or a SystemC-based HLS design approach can materialise, rather they show the main stages that constitute the design cycle specific to this particular work. The reasons for which these particular flows came about are twofold, *(i)* they empirically settled to be the most efficient means for completing a design cycle, and *(ii)* they were shaped by the nature of the two HLS tools used. However, in order to avoid benchmarking complications, the authors have omitted the names of the tools but are available for clarifications.

In the C-based approach, the process begins with the high-level C code description. Here, the initial software code, most usually untimed C, is subjected to a series of modifications of two major types. The first type refers to the satisfaction of a number of requirements that must be met in order for the high-level model to become compatible with the particular tool's restrictions and characteristics.

The second type of modification is a function of the programmer's/designer's proficiency who develops code optimisations that assist in the extraction of characteristics such as parallelisation and speedup. This is realised in two ways: *(i)* through the use of directives that guide the tool to process certain sections of the code in a certain way and *(ii)* through re-structuring/modifying the initial code in certain ways that will make it easier for the tool to translate the high level model described in C into an efficient low-level equivalent. Consequently, the high-level design description is combined with the user-selected directives in order to generate an RTL model that is accompanied by a detailed report, which points to a number of characteristics of interest, such as, BRAM use, area utilisation, clock speed and others. This information is taken into account in order to re-visit the original high-level model description if desired so.

Alternatively, the process moves onto the stage of co-simulation. Here, the functional and behavioural validation of the RTL-model takes place through the juxtaposition of the hardware simulation results against those that correspond to the original high level description, i.e. untimed C model. This stage also offers significant performance information, in the form of a second report, i.e. Report #2. It should be noted that performance figures are only good estimates and the actual design may have slightly different performance.

Finally, the designer studies the performance summary of the RTL-model and decides whether additional design iterations are required or whether it is now ready to be processed for bitstream generation. The SystemC-based Flow is similar in its principle. The high level model is subjected to a number of user modifications to assist the compiler, as well as the RTL compiler, achieve the best possible low-level RTL model. Here, the high-level model can be potentially complemented by a selection of constraints specific to the targeted hardware located in a corresponding library file. The advantage here is that the implementation constraints are kept separate from the design's functionality, and, therefore, the same high-level model can be re-applied to different end-products with different requirements and process libraries. Potential low-level model optimisations, such as parallelism and pipelining, are triggered by specialised HLS directives that are in effect embedded in the high-level code while they are also imposed by the high-level code itself. At the end of the *RTL Compiler* stage, a fully synthesizable model is produced. Here, the designer gets a report of the key performance criteria. In this way potential additional improvements can be introduced at the high-level SystemC model and the process is repeated until the designer is satisfied. Finally, a co-simulation activity follows, whereby the behavioural operation of the generated RTL model is verified against the desired one.

3   Use Cases

Mutual Information (MI) [6] measures the extent to which the uncertainty about one of the two is reduced through the information known about the other. Subsequently, Transfer Entropy (TE) [7] measures the amount of directed (time-asymmetric) transfer of information between two random processes. Both MI and TE are correlation metrics fundamental in key applications and scientific principles such as biology, astrophysics, image processing, economics and more. A List Manager (LM) is used for linked list organisation in protocols/algorithms, such as the MPI and Portals [9]. It performs three basic list operations, *search*, *insert* and *delete* and each list is implemented by a head and a tail pointer. Finally, the Memory Allocator (MA) [8] provides ways to dynamically allocate portions of memory to programs at their request, as well as free it for reuse when it is no longer needed. The Memory Allocator used here is the *Buddy Memory Allocator* [10].

4   Results

The results of this work have been categorised into three major types, i.e. (i) *Lines of Code (LoC) & Development Time*, (ii) *Latency* and (iii) *Area Utilisation*. Furthermore, the platforms used for evaluation purposes have been

(i) an *Intel Xeon E5620* operating at 2.4 GHz and with 16 GB of RAM for the *software* execution of the original C and SystemC code (single core and single thread) and (ii) the *Virtex-7 XC7VX690T* FPGA as the target reconfigurable *hardware* implementation device in both the C-based and SystemC-based flows. In addition, the Mutual Information (MI) and Transfer Entropy (TE) results are based on a data size of 20K samples and a number of MI and TE iterations of 100 and 10 respectively; these are typical values in order to get results of high accuracy. Finally, the List Manager (LM) and Memory Allocator (MA) analysis has been based on two different testbenches. The LM testbench performs 128K *insert*, 128K *search* and 128K *delete* operations with a 20 byte header size. On the other hand, the MA testbench contains 1,024 allocations and 512 free operations. Finally, all generated RTL models are in Verilog.

4.1 Development Time and Lines of Code (LoC)

This section offers a quantifiable insight on the gains that a designer ought to anticipate when using either of the C-based or SystemC-based flows for reconfigurable system design according to results related to LoC and total development time; two metrics that are indirectly linked to productivity. LoC results are presented in two figures, Fig. 2 for MI and TE and Fig. 3 for LM and MA.

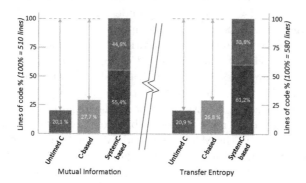

Fig. 2. LoC for Mutual Information (MI) & Transfer Entropy (TE)

The information in both figures refers to the *(i)* original C code, *(ii)* modified HLS C code and *(iii)* HLS SystemC code as percentages with 100% corresponding to the description with the highest LoC number. Hence, Fig. 2 reveals that SystemC requires the longest descriptions for the MI and TE implementations. The reason for this has been twofold, i.e. apart from the necessary SystemC adaptations so that is passes the compiler stage, we also had to account for the support of standard mathematical functions, which are quite common in compute-intensive problems. Hence, the designer has had to not only code-in the description of the target design, but also, develop the code for the mathematical functions required, thereby generating additional code overhead. In terms

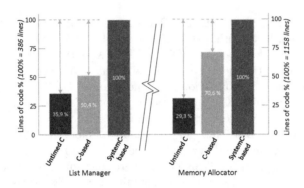

Fig. 3. LoC for List Manager (LM) & Memory Allocator (MA)

of actual numbers, MI requires a SystemC maximum of 510 lines from which 55.4% is the description of the algorithm itself and an additional 44.6% is due to the mathematical function that had to be developed. In contrast, the C-based approach requires 27.7%, i.e. 116 LoC, for a ready-to-be-transformed model. Similarly, the SystemC TE model is described in 580 lines out of which 61.2% is the model itself and 38.8% is the overhead due to the mathematical functions that are missing. Once more, the modified C-based model remains close in size to the original untimed C model thereby underlining a clear advantage of the C-based approach over the SystemC-based approach. Note that even if the additional lines of code for mathematical operations where excluded, SystemC LoC remains greater compared to the C-based description. With respect to LM and MA, Fig. 3, the picture does not change drastically although a distinguishable difference exists. This time, the SystemC approach is not burdened by mathematical function overheads, however, it remains the longest in terms of LoC. For LM, the C-based approach remains noticeably closer to the original untimed C model length, however, in the MA case, C and SystemC are very close and both drift away from the original model's LoC. Finally, although not shown since it has been an anticipated result, the LoC for all developed HLS models is radically, shorter compared to the RTL tool-generated models. In terms of overall development time, results are shown in Table 1 and it becomes apparent that the C-based flow provides the shortest in all four cases. Specifically, it offers synthesisable models for the two compute-intensive algorithms (MI & TE) in less than 1/4 of the time needed by the SystemC model description whereas the difference in the memory-intensive and memory- & compute-intensive algorithms (LM & MA) between the two flows is over 50%. Quite notably, SystemC requires the longest development time even without the need for manually developing mathematical functions for compute-intensive problems, as clearly demonstrated for the memory-intensive cases of LM and MA. Finally, all development times presented have been derived by the same engineers in each use case and the reasoning behind those differences is analytically given in Sect. 5.

Table 1. C-based & SystemC-based design time for all four algorithms

Tool	Algorithm			
	MI	TE	LM	MA
C-based	8 hrs	10 hrs	7 hrs	14 hrs
SystemC-based (math)	20 hrs	20 hrs	-	-
SystemC-based (design)	19 hrs	32 hrs	22 hrs	31 hrs

4.2 Latency

The latency results of this section have been reported in HLS co-simulation using specific reconfigurable hardware specifications that gave the optimal results. Hence, in the case of MI, the best suited Virtex-7 clock frequency for the SystemC-based flow was 115 MHz whereas for the C-based flow was 110 MHz. For TE, the SystemC-based HLS flow clock frequency was 115 MHz whereas for the C-based flow it was 100 MHz, and, finally, for the LM and MA implementations, 303 MHz and 416 MHz, respectively. Table 2 shows the latency for each of the algorithms addressed in this work and presents the corresponding speedup when compared to the software execution on the CPU listed in the beginning of Sect. 4. In addition, the latency/speedup results for LM and MA have been split between the individual operations that each algorithm entails. It is clear that all HLS implementations offer speedups when compared to the latency on a 2.4 GHz CPU, even though the resulting netlists are expected to work at 100 to 400 MHz.

Table 2. Latency results for Intel Xeon (Software), SystemC and C (Hardware)-based approaches

Algorithm		Software (μs)	SystemC (μs)	C (μs)	Speedup	
					SystemC	C
MI		2105	1225	980	1.71x	2.15x
TE		892	857	510	1.04x	1.75x
LM	*Insert*	0.054	0.022	0.035	2.45x	1.54x
	Search	6.877	0.248	0.598	27.7x	11.5x
	Delete	7.169	0.282	0.661	25.42x	10.8x
MA	*Allocation*	12.363	0.371	0.974	33.3x	12.6x
	Free	13.367	0.594	1.605	22.5x	8.32x

The speedup ranges considerably and at the lowest end comes that of SystemC development for MI and TE, which is 1.71x and 1.04x respectively. At the other end of the spectrum, however, SystemC development triggers a speedup for LM and MA which can be up to 33.3x for certain operations. Hence, it becomes obvious that the very vast majority of the HLS implementations significantly over-perform their software counterparts since they are all well above one. Based on the results of this section, two major conclusions can be drawn and are analytically discussed in Sect. 5.

4.3   Area Utilisation

Area utilisation is another important indicator of how the input method used for model description affects the efficiency of the RTL model that an HLS tool will generate. Hence, Table 3 shows how the SystemC-based and C-based modelling methods behave in terms of RTL model area utilisation. These results has been based on the same target FPGA device specified in Sect. 4. The results are split into Look-Up Table (LUT) and DSP utilisation. Subsequently, the C-based flow generates RTL models that utilise the most hardware resources in all four cases. Overall, LUT utilisation is greater for the two compute-intensive algorithms, which also employ DSPs for their mathematical operations. It should be noted that LM and MA, which are memory and compute/memory-intensive algorithms, do not use fixed-point mathematical operations and as a result do not require any DSP processing as part of their implementation.

Table 3. SystemC-based & C-based flow area utilisation

Algorithm	SystemC-based		C-based	
	LUTs	DSPs	LUTs	DSPs
MI	22098	135	33703	134
TE	25063	160	27273	196
LM	1051	0	1324	0
MA	3995	0	4952	0

5   Comparative Analysis

This section offers explanations on why certain aspects of the results came to be the way they did and, also, a concise set of advice as to what the advantages and disadvantages of the two input methods are, from a *qualitative* point-of-view.

5.1   Results-Based

First, the **LoC and latency, i.e. productivity related,** results make a very strong statement that, both in terms of code length as well as overall development time, the **C-based approach always performs better** compared to the SystemC-based input method. This, primarily has to do with the fact that transitioning from an untimed C model to an HLS tool-friendly C model is easier due to the inherent similarity between the two models. This is in contrast to the SystemC-based input method, a C-based language with, nonetheless, significant deviations from standard C, such as template class definitions for all processing functions.

Regarding LoC, it is notable that for **compute-intensive** applications, the **SystemC** high-level description is burdened further by the lack of mathematical operations, which the designer had to develop from scratch. For instance, in the case of MI, what would originally be a 282 (55.4%) LoC description, eventually, increased to 510 due to this disadvantage. Nevertheless, this has been a tool-induced problem and it must not be assumed that this shall always be the case. At any rate, even without the LoC overhead due to the mathematical operations, the SystemC description remained significantly longer compared to the C-based description. Naturally, the original C models are always the shortest compared to the rest of the HLS-friendly models and this is due to the fact that synthesisable C requires a lower level of micro-architecture directives as well as that it does not support certain C features such as pointers. Furthermore, it has been emphatically reaffirmed that the LoC size of both HLS models is always radically shorter than that of their RTL counterparts. This is an anticipated observation, which, however, acquires significance when taking into account published documentation [11,12], which argues that HLS-generated RTL models are comparable (or even shorter) in size to those that can be achieved through a handwritten/handcoded approach.

With regard to the zero mathematical code overhead in the LoC results for LM, this is because it does not use mathematical operations since it is mainly a memory-handling scheme. The MA model also does not have a similar overhead since its computational operations are not fixed-point and can, therefore, be handled as is by the SystemC-based flow's tool. One last remark in regard to the LoC results is that both model descriptions, C-based and SystemC-based, where performed by proficient designers and the difference in the very nature of the two languages meant that no experience from describing one algorithm in C could be brought in its SystemC description or vice versa. This means that the design process for all four algorithms can be thought of as independent since no experience in, for instance, C-based coding for TE could be taken advantage of during its SystemC description to the extent of having an impact in reducing both the LoC or the development time. Subsequently, judging by the **latency** results of Table 2, it becomes apparent that, in addition to the considerable code length reduction over a direct RTL implementation, the **HLS** methodology has the potential for **speedups over a *software* approach** whilst maintaining a comparable code size to the original C code that is executed on a conventional processor. This is something that has been proven in its entirety in this work. In addition, the **compute-intensive applications offer greater speedup** when processed by **the C-based flow** whereas the **memory- and memory and compute-intensive applications are faster** in the case that **the SystemC-based flow** is used. Second, the margin that separates the two approaches differs considerably between the compute-intensive and memory-intensive cases, i.e.

the C-based flow is *slightly* faster compared to the SystemC flow for MI and TE, however, the latter is *significantly* faster compared to the former for LM and MA.

5.2   Qualitative

The information presented in this sub-section is mainly based on the extensive use of the two flows by several experienced hardware designers. First, the HLS tool used in the **SystemC-based flow** offers a characteristic/feature of significant importance. This is the ability to **pre-specify the level and extent of functionality the designer expects to be executed within a given clock cycle**. On the contrary, such feature was not available by the tool of the C-based flow, which, therefore, lost on the ability to define explicitly the design functionality that is to be executed on specific and pre-determined cycle intervals. With this specification, the operations executed at every state of the control flow should be explicitly defined either in source code or in terms of micro-architecture specifications during the scheduling phase. Moreover, the control flow was described by inserting *wait* statements that represent the clock registers separating the combinational logic. Also, each function was triggered during every clock cycle and thus certain signals had to be added in order to mimic the software's control flow such as a 4-phase handshake. Benchmarking reasons forbid the authors to disclose the tools' names, however, they are available to discuss their work further. Subsequently, in the C-based flow, the elimination of functionality specification and 4-phase handshaking leads to an automated transformation from C to RTL code without special intervention from the designer (except from some directives).

A second discernible characteristic that differentiates the two input methods is that of the **level of experience** needed for efficient model descriptions. Here, **the C-based method** is the one with the **shortest time** required to attain a satisfactory level of proficiency in efficient high-level design modelling. On the other hand, **SystemC** is more particular and, therefore, poses a **steeper learning curve** to a designer. A direct consequence of this is that high level description with a C-based flow becomes much more economical, i.e. significantly fewer lines of code, since it is closer to the original untimed-C model of an algorithm, which is almost always the case. Hence, at the early stages of HLS usage, a C-based flow can be considerably faster in completing the process of starting with a high-level model and generating a working low-level RTL equivalent, compared to a SystemC-based flow. The downside for the former, on the other hand, is that what **SystemC** lacks in modelling speed makes it up in thoroughness, making its **models more robust and comprehensive**. Once again, this is due to the level of designer expertise required for high-level modelling when using this language. Hence, as soon as a capable level of expertise has been attained, a SystemC-based flow becomes a much more attractive candidate for HLS reconfigurable systems design. Moreover, it is a risk of some probability, as was in this case, that the **SystemC-based flow's** HLS tool may not offer a library for any kind of **mathematical operation** such as *math.h* in synthesisable code. This

Table 4. SystemC-based & C-based flows

Characteristic	SystemC-based	C-based
Define functionality per cycle	Yes	Not available
Input modelling learning curve	Steep	Smooth
Effort for input model description	Hard	Easy
Level of expected expertise	High	Moderate
Input model modifications	High	Moderate
Input model abstraction level	Medium	High
Math libraries	Weak	Strong
Parallelisation & speed	Linear	Non-Linear
Input model code length	Worse	Better

can be a serious burden in the high-level description of a system and, specifically for the needs of the systems addressed here, the designers had to develop two different mathematical operations from scratch. These have been a fixed-point division and a logarithmic operation on base 2, which is performed with the same latency as in a C++ software implementation, i.e. two cycles. Notably, this has been achieved with the same precision as that met in software. Hence, in the event of selecting this type of input method, the designer must investigate the capabilities of the HLS tool that will be selected as part of the flow. In addition, the **SystemC-based** method required that the model underwent **heavy modifications and adaptations** in order to be compatible with the HLS tool's requirements; for instance, the function of every class must be implemented as a thread and each thread is then executed concurrently which brings up the need for handshaking in order to be able to emulate the function's series of operation.

Another notable observation has to do with parallelisation issues. Specifically, the **SystemC-based** flow is much **more efficient in parallelising a design** and this is a direct consequence of the more detailed description of the SystemC models. Hence, doubling the area of a design lead to half the execution time while this did not apply to the C-based input method. In general, it is always the case that SystemC needs more lines of high-level code compared to a C-based method in order to describe the same design. The significant difference between the two is mainly due to the code inserted for modularity purposes, e.g. template class definitions for all data structure processing functions, wait statements etc. Finally, Table 4 summarises the main points outlined in this sub-section.

6 Conclusions

This paper presents a concise and thorough investigation and comparison between two of the most popular HLS model description input methods, i.e. C-based and SystemC-based, for reconfigurable systems design. This is achieved by analysing the design process for four different compute- and memory-intensive

popular schemes. The paper compares the two methods whilst going through their respective flows, starting from a high-level model description all the way to a low-level RTL equivalent. Finally, this work unfolds an in-depth account on how the two input methods along with their respective design flows compare against one another. This account is based both on the technical results as well as the accumulated experience from their extensive use, thereby creating a foundation on which a designer can base their attempts on transforming popular computing algorithms to their RTL equivalents for rapid prototyping/implementations for reconfigurable systems.

References

1. Birnbaum, M.D.: Essential Electronic Design Automation (EDA). Prentice Hall Modern Semiconductor Design, Upper Saddle River (2004)
2. Whitson, C., Michelsen, M.: The negative flash. J. Fluid Phase Equilib. **35**, 51–71 (1989)
3. Coussy, P., Morawiec, A. (eds.): High-Level Synthesis: From Algorithm to Digital Circuit, vol. 1. Springer, Netherlands (2008). https://doi.org/10.1007/978-1-4020-8588-8
4. Nane, R., Sima, V., Pilato, C., Choi, J., Fort, B., Canis, A., Chen, Y., Hsiao, H., Brown, S., Ferrandi, F., Anderson, J., Bertels, K.: A survey and evaluation of FPGA high-level synthesis tools. Trans. Comput.-Aided Des. Integr. Circuits Syst. **35**(10), 1591–1604 (2016)
5. Thomas, D.E., Lagnese, E.D., Walker, R.A., Nestor, J.A., Rajan, J.V., Blackburn, R.L.: Algorithmic and Register-Transfer Level Synthesis: The System Architect's Workbench. The Kluwer International Series in Engineering and Computer Science, vol. 85, 1st edn. Springer, Boston (1990). https://doi.org/10.1007/978-1-4613-1519-3
6. Cover, T., Thomas, J.: Elements of Information Theory. Wiley-Interscience, New York (1991). ISBN 0-471-06259-6
7. Schreiber, T.: Measuring information transfer. Phys. Rev. Lett. **85**(2), 461–464 (2000)
8. Knowlton, K.: A fast storage allocator. Commun. ACM **8**(10), 623–624 (1965). ISSN 0001-0782
9. Portals 4.0. http://www.cs.sandia.gov/Portals/portals4.html
10. Wikipedia: Buddy memory allocation – Wikipedia, The Free Encyclopedia. https://en.wikipedia.org/w/index.php?title=Buddy_memory_allocation&oldid=653135858. Accessed 21 July 2015
11. Winterstein, F., Bayliss, S., Constantinides, G.: High-level synthesis of dynamic data structures: a case study using Vivado HLS. In: International Conference on Field-Programmable Technology, FPT, pp. 362–365, 9–11 December 2013
12. Karras, K., Blott, M., Kees, A.: High-Level Synthesis Case Study: Implementation of a Memcached Server. CoRR, vol. abs/1408.5387 (2014)

Fast DSE for Automated Parallelization of Embedded Legacy Applications

Kris Heid[(✉)](iD), Jakob Wenzel[(✉)](iD), and Christian Hochberger[(✉)]

Computer Systems Group, Technische Universität Darmstadt, Darmstadt, Germany
{heid,wenzel,hochberger}@rs.tu-darmstadt.de

Abstract. Mapping complex embedded applications to FPGA based SoCs often results in systems consisting of multiple processors to maintain high processing rates. Such systems can be created individually for each application, since FPGAs have very small non-recurring expenses. Thus, the system architecture (including the number of cores and the partitioning and distribution of tasks) must be derived and executed by the developer multiple times. In most cases it is not possible to analytically compute the design performance, so design space exploration comes into play. In this contribution we present a technique leveraging a combination of tools to (1) greatly reduce the effort to create different solutions in the design space and (2) reduce the time required for this design implementation by a factor of three. Compared to similar approaches, we claim to have a highly accurate design point evaluation and loosen the restrictions of the legacy application.

1 Introduction

Field Programmable Gate Arrays (FPGAs) are large enough to implement even complex digital designs. As they can be used without incurring high initial cost, they are attractive implementation platforms for application-specific systems that will be produced in medium or small quantity.

A particular use case for this approach are System-on-Chip (SoC) architectures, where part of the digital design is a software-programmable processor. The overall system functionality is a priori partitioned into a HW and a SW part. The HW part is then implemented using the FPGA's vendor tools and the software part is compiled using the processor-specific software tool chain. The great advantage of this approach is that the selection of peripherals and processor features can be adapted perfectly to the requirements of the application (which is in contrast to off-the-shelf microcontrollers).

As the size of FPGAs is continuously growing, even multi-core SoCs (MPSoCs) can be implemented on FPGAs. In this case, an application-specific interconnect can be defined with respect to the communication requirements of the application. Different communication schemes can be employed (shared memory, distributed shared memory, Network-on-Chip or individual core connectors). The amount of time spent processing SW (parts) within the cores and

© Springer International Publishing AG, part of Springer Nature 2018
N. Voros et al. (Eds.): ARC 2018, LNCS 10824, pp. 471–484, 2018.
https://doi.org/10.1007/978-3-319-78890-6_38

communicating between cores can not accurately be estimated a priori. Thus, analytical approaches to optimize the number of cores and to distribute the workload over the cores are doomed to fail.

The only alternative is to implement different points in the design space and measure their behavior. This is possible, since we can afford to build many different systems on FPGAs without having to pay for manufacturing. While this gives reliable results and thus leads to good design decisions, it comes at the cost of a very long tool runtime. Building individual designs for large FPGAs can easily take hours. Thus, building dozens of designs is very tedious for the developer.

In this paper, we show a methodology to improve the time to explore the design space of MPSoCs. This enables an interactive working style, where a developer starts from an initial solution and modifies this solution until it satisfies the given requirements. Changing the software partitioning and the number of cores can have highly non-linear effects on the runtime and resource consumption of the resulting SoCs. Thus, an explorative way of searching the design space is in many cases inevitable.

The remaining paper is structured as follows: Sect. 2 presents similar approaches and tools. It is followed by a section, where we propose tools that should be used for a fast DSE process. Section 4 discusses the proposed methodology in detail. The results of this methodology are evaluated in Sect. 5 with a typical use case. Finally, a conclusion and outlook onto future work are given.

2   Related Work

Designing hard- and software for multi-core processors or MPSoCs has been researched for many years. Chapter 2 of [1] describes several general strategies for this process. Nevertheless, it tackles the problem more from a constructive angle and also it does not deal with the peculiarities of FPGAs. Since it only targets ASIC based SoCs, it relies on simulation of the potential systems which can be a bottleneck for a serious evaluation of application scenarios.

Some researchers actually target the design space exploration, but with different focus. Their main concern is the optimization of a given HW-SW partitioning to improve goals like power, performance or even thermal distribution. Monchiero et al. [13] manually create a number of different HW instances and map the SW tasks to it. They compare the different architectures with respect to the three criteria mentioned above. No automation of the design space exploration is done.

Heracles [10] improves the design space exploration by providing a tool that allows the user to graphically specify the nature of the MPSoC. The full HW description is generated and can be synthesized to real HW (either an ASIC or FPGA). While this is a good improvement, still the user has to map SW tasks to the individual cores and also, the synthesis time is not affected by this approach.

Koski [8] also tries to model the MPSoC graphically. In contrast to Heracles it does this through a UML design environment where the user models a Kahn-Process-Network (KPN) through state charts. The carried out DSE covers a static, as well as a dynamic exploration through simulation. In contrast to Koski, SystemCoDesigner [9] models the application in SystemC. The user then needs to select desired HW components from a library and manually map the SystemC model to the HW. The behavioral simulation through SystemC enables a fast DSE, but does not deliver directly synthesizable designs. PeaCE [4] requires a dataflow (task graph) and a FSM from which C-code is generated. The DSE consists of resource allocation, task binding, communication overhead calculation and communication system exploration and thus covers HW & SW refinements. The DSE is carried out via co-simulation and is thus fast but also inaccurate. The drawback of the methodologies taken in Koski, SystemCoDesigner and PeaCE is the reformulation/rewriting of legacy applications. This additional step can consume a vast amount of time in the design process and makes these tools impractical for legacy applications.

Daedalus [17] is a tool collection that automatically generates a multi-core HW + SW design from given source-code. Sequential C-code is automatically parallelized through a tool called KPNgen, which constructs a KPN. Afterwards, Sesame does a DSE for finding an optimized mapping of the KPN to the desired target architecture. The automation of this tool set is outstanding, however it can only be applied to source-code formulated as static affine nested loop programs (SANLPs). This limits the tool set to a (not negligible) but smaller subset of multimedia and scientific application domains.

We believe that most environments lack in automated design point creation in terms of SW partitioning for legacy applications. All mentioned programs are either limited to a special program structure or require an application description most likely different from the legacy application to parallelize. Additionally, the used DSE environments are fast but only due to their inaccuracy. The combination of an automated parallelization tool and one to decrease synthesis time could improve on those shortcomings.

3   Fast DSE Tool Selection

As shown in the previous section, existing environments for parallelizing legacy applications have severe drawbacks. We address these drawbacks by a selection of tools, helping the user to: analyze bottlenecks of existing applications, effortless parallelize the application based on the analysis and evaluate a created design point very fast. The following sections shortly evaluate and describe a best fitting tool for each purpose.

3.1   Automatic Embedded Application Analysis

AutoPerf is a simple Cetus-based [3] but quite useful tool, for profiling (embedded) applications. Other well known options like gprof or Intel vTune are rather unsuitable for bare-metal SoCs, since they are either inaccurate and/or demand File-IO or an OS. An applications source code is input to AutoPerf, which inserts calls to record a cycle counter's values. Those calls will be inserted before and after function calls, loops and successive code blocks. By default only the body of the main function will be profiled. With a pragma (`#pragma autoperf`) ahead of another function or inside another functions body the user can profile different parts of the firmware as needed. After running the instrumented code on the device, the cycle counter results are transferred to the PC. The resulting report of AutoPerf contains an exact application profile showing the cycles taken for execution of each source-code line. The report contains a field specifying the location of the measurement, the source code line where the measurement was started in the original source (not in the modified program) and the execution time for this step. The application profile is an important step to choose sections for parallelization of the code.

Enhancements for fast DSE. AutoPerf helps the user to do a fast DSE by carrying out these steps automatically: (1) Instantiation of the cycle counter. (2) Function calls to record the cycle counter before and after every loop, function call and statement block. (3) Printing the measured results with a unique identifier for every measurement point. (4) Creating hardware design for evaluation. Doing these steps manually for an application with several hundred lines of code is a very tedious task.

3.2   (Automated) Parallelization Tools for Embedded SW

Many parallelization tools exist with different application description methodologies, such as APIs, language extensions, domain specific languages or source code annotations. We believe that using source code annotations for parallelizing **legacy** software potentially requires less user expertise, little manual effort and thus allows fast design point creation. A well known annotation based parallelization tool is OpenMP [1]. In OpenMP, the user annotates parallel code sections, but needs to manually take care of task synchronization. OpenStream [15] (an OpenMP extension) and HMPP [16] automatically model task dependencies, but the user still needs to manually specify accessed variables. In ACOTES [14], the only manual effort is to annotate code sections as tasks and task groups. The tool automatically analyzes used variables and handles synchronization. With µStreams [6], a Cetus-based tool was presented that allows the transformation of the source code from a single-threaded application to multi-core streaming pipeline program. Compared to the aforementioned tools, µStreams needs no specification of synchronization variables and makes writing annotations easier by leaving out differentiation between tasks and task groups. Through the construction of a streaming pipeline, µStreams specializes on repetitive tasks whose throughput shall be increased. Thus, this approach is very well applicable for microprocessors running repetitive tasks on bare metal. Instead of trying to run several instances of this application and count on data parallelism, µStreams extracts different steps as dependent tasks of the application,

---

[1] http://openmp.org/.

constructing a data pipeline. However, an additional parallelization like a super-scalar pipeline is still conceivable. The user has to extend the application with few pragma annotations (#pragma microstreams task) to indicate different tasks in the application. Pragmas can be placed before function calls, loops or ordinary statements/statement blocks. The created task's code will reach until the next microstreams task pragma, the end of the scope where the pragma was placed in or until an explicit task end pragma is reached. However, the task end pragma is rarely necessary. A processing pipeline is automatically created from the pragmas if the data dependencies allow it. A communication infrastructure between tasks is automatically created based on the dependency analysis, to exchange the non-exclusive variables. Each task will be mapped to one processing core and a hardware communication infrastructure with simple FIFO buffers is designed. It was demonstrated that this methodology is applicable despite exchanging big data arrays between the tasks in [6]. In addition to the automated firmware splitting, the tool also offers evaluation techniques to help users judge the created design. The tool can create an environment to measure the time spent for task execution and data transmission to the next task with cycle counters. With those measurements, the user can determine if the pipeline stages are balanced and see the communication overhead. The pipeline's processing speed is determined by the longest task's execution time, including communication time.

As output, µStreams delivers several firmware files and a HW system description. Additionally, we showed that µStreams is able to extract used peripherals/hardware from the firmware [5] and add it in the system description. This enables building the required hardware completely based on the underlying firmware with no or little aid from the user.

Enhancements for fast DSE. To sum up, the following steps are automated by µStreams and help the user to do a fast DSE: (1) Split the application at points defined by pragmas and create a processing pipeline. (2) Do a variable dependency analysis between the split code parts. (3) Resolve variable dependencies by adding source code to communicate variable states in between the split parts. (4) Optionally instantiate cycle counters that measure variable receive/send times and program execution time for easy system evaluation. (5) Create a hardware design description to import into the system builder.

While the manual source code splitting is relatively easy, manually analyzing the variable dependency on bigger programs is very tedious and error prone. Depending on the amount of used variables, this step can easily take hours not accounting for errors that are highly likely. Thus, using µStreams allows to create much more design points for evaluation in a shorter amount of time.

3.3 Synthesis Acceleration Tool

Repeatedly synthesizing similar designs performs many tasks over and over. Doing them just once can save a considerable amount of time. HMFlow [11] synthesizes all modules in the design into *hard macros*, which are internally placed and routed. Due to the regularity of FPGAs, they can still be moved, although the use of less frequent primitives (like DSP blocks or RAM blocks) may limit the number of possible locations. It is based on RapidSmith [12], a tool to interface to Xilinx's ISE. HMFlow's input is a Xilinx System Generator design, which is focused on modules as small as individual flip flops or multiplexers and therefore is not particularly suitable for multi-core SoC designs.

RapidSoC [18] employs a similar approach, but is focused on SoC designs. Every module (processor core, peripherals) is separately synthesized, placed and internally routed. All inputs and outputs are connected to FPGA pins. Placement constraints force the modules into a rectangular shape. The resulting design is then loaded by using RapidSmith as well. The pins used in the separate synthesis are then disconnected to get a reusable macro.

Once the user provides a configuration, the corresponding modules are inserted into a single design. The modules are then connected as specified by the system configuration. Afterwards, the placement of modules and the routing between them needs to be calculated. The placement and routing problems that need to be solved contain far fewer items than a regular synthesis. This reduction in problem size allows for a significant speedup. However, the maximum clock frequency is reduced, because the placement is not as optimal as in a regular synthesis flow. If the FPGA's utilization is very high, placement might even fail.

Enhancements for fast DSE. To speed up intermediate synthesis runs, they are done using RapidSoC. Only the final synthesis is performed with the vendor tools. RapidSoC achieves a lower target clock frequency than traditional synthesis, but the number of cycles until the result is computed is the same. Routing time is increased by tight timing constraints. Intermediate synthesis runs are therefore performed with lower operating frequencies than the maximum possible.

The workflow does not require the user to modify any module definitions. This is the best possible case for RapidSoC, because all modules can be created ahead of time.

Using RapidSoC reduces the waiting time to deploy a design point on the FPGA roughly by a factor of three.

3.4   Evaluation Platform

We use the SpartanMC SoC Kit[2] as evaluation platform for convenience, since it is supported by the synthesis acceleration tool as well as the parallelization tool and is freely available. The SpartanMC [7] is a soft-core SoC Kit with an instruction and data width of 18 bit. The 18 bit width makes optimal use of the structure of modern FPGAs, since internal memory blocks and arithmetic blocks are 18 bit wide. It comes with a library of hardware building blocks, a

---

[2] http://spartanmc.de/.

system builder software, a software toolchain consisting of GCC, GNU binutils, GDB and a cycle accurate simulator.

As the processor core and the infrastructure occupy very few resources, it is natural to put more than one core on an FPGA. For this purpose, a set of specialized FIFO based communication peripherals (*core-connectors*) can be used for efficient message exchange.

Each SoC can be tailored in terms of peripherals and processor features to perfectly match the nature of the application. Also, multi-core systems can be employed to improve the response behavior for individual applications. In this case all critical code blocks are executed on a dedicated core. Through spreading the application over several cores, the multi-core systems will improve the overall performance of the system.

4   Methodology for Application Profiling with Fast Design Space Exploration

The goal of the approach is to increase the processing rate of an application, by constructing a processing pipeline. We do not expect the maximum clock frequency to vary much between different pipeline arrangements, because the critical path is inside the processor core and is not affected by its connectivity. Therefore, the number of cycles until the result is computed is a good indicator to compare different systems.

To be able to successfully transform a legacy application to fit new design requirements, the user will go through different steps, as shown in Fig. 1. The steps are described in detail in the following sections.

4.1   Initial Application Profiling

To be able to parallelize an existing application, the user first needs to identify the critical parts of the software. This can be done by: (1) Creating an evaluation environment for the application with AutoPerf. The tool will instantiate cycle counters and inject calls to the cycle counter in the firmware. The tool will measure the cycles to execute each function, loop, and statement block. (2) Finding the system's maximum operating frequency. Since Xilinx's router stops optimizing the design once the target frequency is met, the design needs to be synthesized repeatedly with increasing target frequencies. To this end, a script is provided which uses a binary search to find the absolute maximum frequency. (3) Reading the application profile provided through AutoPerf and match it against the design requirements. If the overall execution time of the application matches the required runtime, the user is done. If the design requirements are not met, the user starts with the parallelization.

4.2   Application Parallelization

Since the timing of the different steps is known from the initial application profiling phase, the developer can start parallelizing the application. If the user

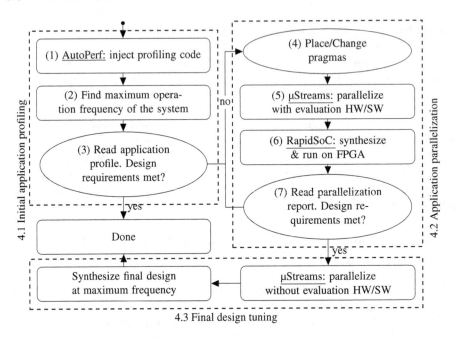

Fig. 1. Workflow: fast DSE for parallelizing legacy applications (manual steps in ellipses, automated steps in boxes)

already has an estimate of how many times faster he wants the application to run, then he already knows into how many tasks the code has to be split at least. In an ideal case if the transmission overhead of the variables is neglected and every pipeline stage has the same execution time, the speedup factor is the number of created tasks. Under normal conditions a splitting into equally long executing tasks is barely possible. The task's execution time might additionally depend on the input data to be processed. In order to meet the timing constraints of the application, the user might run through several iterations of the following process: (4) Add a pragma annotation in the code for each task to be created, while trying to balance task execution times. (5) Parallelize the application with µStreams with evaluation hardware and execution time measurements in the firmware. Read the design into the system builder to instantiate the system. (6) Synthesize the design with RapidSoC and run it on the FPGA. (7) Read the parallelization report of each task. The runtime of the longest pipeline stage defines the speed of the whole pipeline. Check if the processing plus the variables send/receive time meets the timing requirements. If the timing requirement is not met, the amount of tasks should be increased and another parallelization process has to be started with more task pragmas, or a better pragma placement. If the design constraints are met, one can go to the final design tuning.

4.3   Final Design Tuning

After the parallelization report meets the design requirements, one can remove the profiling HW/SW by simply running µStreams again without evaluation options. As a final step, the system is synthesized at its maximum frequency. The parallelized system's maximum frequency should be equal to the single core's frequency.

5   Evaluation

5.1   Use Case

To evaluate our tool and methodology, we use the application of Adaptive Differential Pulse Code Modulation [2] (ADPCM). It is a compression approach used in many places like ITU audio codec G.726 or for signal compression in wireless sensing applications. We focus on the encoding procedure, as it was observed to consume more processing power.

ADPCM is based on differential pulse code modulation, where only the difference between consecutive values is transmitted (together with one initial absolute value). Due to the continuous nature of most signals, this leads to a reduced variance of the transmitted values and thus to smaller codes (given that differences are efficiently encoded, e.g. with Huffman encoding). The overall computation steps of ADPCM can be found in Table 1.

5.2   Evaluation Stages

Profile Source Application. To parallelize the ADPCM application, we first profiled the application as described in Sect. 4.1 with AutoPerf. The measured cycles for each processing step are shown in Table 1 column 2.

1st Parallelization Iteration. Computation steps 1–6 take about as long as steps 7–8. Thus, the first try shall be to put steps 1–6 into one task and 7–8 into another one. This is done by adding a pragma annotation before step 7. After running µStreams with the pragma annotated code and synthesizing the system with RapidSoC, the runtime of the different tasks including the communication overhead can be measured (see Table 1 column 3). In this case, sending and receiving variables (316 cycles) is negligible compared to the calculation time. However, this situation might change if the pragma is set at a different position.

2nd Parallelization Iteration. We assume that the application requirements are not met and the target is to support an input stream at a higher data rate. The processing time of the pipeline stages needs to be decreased. Looking at the application profile in Table 1 column 2, step 7 consumes most processing time, forming the longest pipeline stage. Thus, this step should be optimized. This can be done by splitting the compression loop in step 7 into two smaller loops (7.1

Table 1. Execution time of the different processing steps and the parallelized variants

Processing step	1 Core	2 Cores	3 Cores	4 Cores
	In units of 10^3 cycles			
1: Read input	729	899	**729**	**729**
2: Auto correlation	7		722	171
3: Extract equation system	1			
4: Solve equation system	151			
5: Backsubstitution	9			
6: Write coefficients	1			
7: Compression loop	**1113**	**1205**		552
			653	653
8: Write results	98			

and 7.2), calculating the first and the second half of the samples in separate tasks. This optimization would most certainly reveal the adaptive pass as the longest pipeline stage. Thus, steps 1–6 are also split into two tasks, as shown in Table 1 column 5. After processing the application with µStreams a second time, building and synthesizing the system with RapidSoC, another parallelization report can be read. As shown in Table 1 column 5, it was possible to increase the pipeline processing speed. Let's now assume that the design fulfills the requirements.

Refine/Optimize Parallelization Hardware. However, to further optimize the design it is obvious from Table 1 column 2 that processing step 2–7.1 in total should not take longer than step 1. So steps 2–7.1 can form one task instead of two, as shown in Table 1 column 4. This step saves hardware without decreasing the processing speed of the pipeline.

Further Parallelization. Depending on the application it might get harder and harder for each additional pipeline stage, to find a solution for an balanced workload. Possible ways to increase the pipelines processing speed are either to reformat the application (loop splitting of processing step 1) to have smaller processing steps or to create a superscalar pipeline.

5.3   Results

Synthesis time, maximum clock frequencies and required pipeline execution cycles for each design point are shown in Table 2. Typically the user would perform intermediate synthesis runs with RapidSoC at a low frequency and then final regular synthesis runs to get the maximum frequency. The data generated by those runs is printed in bold. The remaining data serves to evaluate the approach.

Table 2. Synthesis time, maximum clock frequency and required cycles for different pipeline arrangements (Synthesis run on a i7-6700 with 16 GB RAM for XC6SLX45)

Design	Synthesis time (s) @40MHz		Synthesis speedup	Maximum clock frequency (MHz)		Execution time (cycles)
	Regular	RapidSoC		Regular	RapidSoC	
1-Core	77	**27**	2.8	84.8	56	**2012609**
2-Cores	92	**34**	2.7	86.4	54	**1205689**
3-Cores	**124**	**44**	2.8	**87.7**	53	**729424**
4-Cores	167	**53**	3.1	87.7	52	**729424**

As it can be seen, the usefulness of RapidSoC is reflected in the synthesis time speedup. The maximum achievable frequency is about 30 MHz lower than the classically synthesized system. This is not dramatic since in a typical DSE process usually a known working frequency is taken to test the functionality and the maximum operating frequency will be evaluated after the functionality has been thoroughly tested. The maximum operating frequency was evaluated with the tool described in Sect. 4.3. It is the highest result of ten synthesis runs with different seeds.

Looking at the maximum achievable frequencies in Table 2, there are two contradicting phenomena: With regular synthesis, the more cores there are on the FPGA, the higher the maximum achievable frequency gets, because each core needs less memory. When synthesizing with RapidSoC, another effect dominates: More cores on the FPGA result in lower frequencies. The cost function for placement only optimizes for individual net lengths and does not weigh combinatoric paths spanning multiple modules higher. The critical path in multi-core designs spans one more module than in single-core designs, leading to lower clock frequencies.

For getting a rough idea of how much faster our DSE is, we have measured the required manual steps of the DSE process with and without the helper tools. For analyzing the manual source code transformations, we have counted the lines of code that have to be added/deleted/modified and the amount of necessary clicks in the system builder. Table 3 shows the manual steps needed for the application profiling of the ADPCM example and one parallelization iteration into the three-core-design variant. The user only needs four manual steps, instead of 57, to profile the application with the fast design space exploration tools. For a parallelization iteration in fast DSE, 8 user interactions versus 174 interactions are required. It has to be noted that the parallelization iteration with the ADPCM example was executed in total three times. The runtime of all tools except for synthesis and RapidSoC is less than one second and is not noticeably influenced by the input data size. Another important point is that the higher the system is parallelized, the harder and more time consuming an iteration in regular DSE will become, since the hardware design becomes bigger and more variable dependencies have to be resolved.

Table 3. Manual effort comparison DSE vs fast DSE

Step	DSE	Fast DSE
Add cycle counter calls in code	36 code insertions	Tool run: <1 s
Create hardware design	19 clicks in the system builder	Tool run: <1 s
Synthesize & run on FPGA	Tool run: 77 s	Tool run: 27 s
Analyze application profile	Analyze Table 1 column 2	
Manual steps for app. profiling	**57**	**4**
Place pragmas/manually split code	2x copy firmware, 4 code-block deletions	3 code insertions
Resolve variable dependencies	31 code insertions	Tool run: <1 s
Add cycle counters for evaluation	28 code insertions	
Create hardware design	48 clicks in system builder	Tool run: <1 s
Synthesize & run on FPGA	Tool run: 124 s	Tool run: 44 s
Analyze parallelization report	Analyze Table 1 column 4	
Remove evaluation code and HW	Delete 59 code lines	Tool run: <1 s
Manual steps for parallelization	**174**	**8**

To get an idea of the time saved through fast DSE, we have ourselves tried to parallelize the three core variant by hand and it took us roughly 45 min even though exactly knowing what to do. With the usage of the proposed tools we needed less than 2 min.

6   Conclusion and Outlook

In this contribution we have shown that the design space exploration for multi-core embedded systems can be considerably shortened by using tools to firstly speed up the creation of different design points and secondly speed up the implementation of those design points. Additionally, we show that profiling support in the target system can be added automatically. As a result, the pure implementation of the different designs becomes ≈3 times faster. The time saved through the automated parallelization might be much bigger for medium sized designs.

RapidSoC currently only works with Xilinx ISE. We are trying to interface Vivado in a similar way. Unfortunately, first tries like RapidSmith2 exhibit a much higher latency for individual manipulations compared to RapidSmith.

Although µStreams already greatly relieves the user, more automation can be envisioned. E.g. it would be helpful if µStreams automatically suggests split points depending on the users design requirements. Also, in some cases a replication of critical tasks could be used to reduce the processing time of one stage. Finally, splitting loops is necessary in some cases to achieve the required processing rate of a application. It would be very supportive if µStreams could perform this modification on its own.

References

1. Abdallah, A.B.: Multicore Systems On-Chip: Practical Software/Hardware Design. Atlantis Press, Amsterdam (2013). https://doi.org/10.2991/978-94-91216-92-3
2. Cummiskey, P., Jayant, N., Flanagan, J.: Adaptive quantization in differential PCM coding of speech. Bell Syst. Techn. J. **52**, 1105–1118 (1973)
3. Dave, C., Bae, H., Min, S.J., Lee, S., Eigenmann, R., Midkiff, S.: Cetus: a source-to-source compiler infrastructure for multicores. Computer **42**, 36–42 (2009)
4. Ha, S., Lee, C., Yi, Y., Kwon, S., Joo, Y.P.: Hardware-software codesign of multimedia embedded systems: the peace approach. In: RTCSA (2006)
5. Heid, K., Wirsch, R., Hochberger, C.: Automated inference of SoC configuration through firmware source code analysis. In: FPGAs for Software Programmers (FSP), pp. 1–9 (2016)
6. Heid, K., Weber, J., Hochberger, C.: μStreams: a tool for automated streaming pipeline generation on soft-core processors. In: FPGAs for General Purpose Computing (2016)
7. Hempel, G., Hochberger, C.: A resource optimized SoC kit for FPGAs. In: International Conference on Field Programmable Logic and Applications, pp. 761–764 (2007)
8. Kangas, T., Kukkala, P., Orsila, H., Salminen, E., Hännikäinen, M., Hämäläinen, T., Riihimäki, J., Kuusilinna, K.: UML-based MPSoC design framework. ACM TECS **5**, 281–320 (2006)
9. Keinert, J., Streubhr, M., Schlichter, T., Falk, J., Gladigau, J., Haubelt, C., Teich, J., Meredith, M.: SystemCoDesigner - an automatic ESL synthesis approach by design space exploration and behavioral synthesis for streaming applications. ACM TODAES **14**, 1:1–1:23 (2009)
10. Kinsy, M.A., Pellauer, M., Devadas, S.: Heracles: a tool for fast RTL-based design space exploration of multicore processors. In: ACM/SIGDA FPGA, pp. 125–134 (2013)
11. Lavin, C., Padilla, M., Lamprecht, J., Lundrigan, P., Nelson, B., Hutchings, B.: HMFlow: accelerating FPGA compilation with hard macros for rapid prototyping. In: Field-Programmable Custom Computing Machines (FCCM), pp. 117–124 (2011)
12. Lavin, C., Padilla, M., Lundrigan, P., Nelson, B., Hutchings, B.: Rapid prototyping tools for FPGA designs: RapidSmith. In: FPT, pp. 353–356 (2010)
13. Monchiero, M., Canal, R., González, A.: Design space exploration for multicore architectures: a power/performance/thermal view. In: ICS, pp. 177–186 (2006)
14. Munk, H., Ayguadé, E., Bastoul, C., Carpenter, P., Chamski, Z., Cohen, A., Cornero, M., Dumont, P., Duranton, M., Fellahi, M., Ferrer, R., Ladelsky, R., Lindwer, M., Martorell, X., Miranda, C., Nuzman, D., Ornstein, A., Pop, A., Pop, S., Pouchet, L.N., Ramírez, A., Ródenas, D., Rohou, E., Rosen, I., Shvadron, U., Trifunović, K., Zaks, A.: ACOTES project: advanced compiler technologies for embedded streaming. Int. J. Parallel Program. **39**, 397–450 (2010)
15. Pop, A., Cohen, A.: OpenStream: expressiveness and data-flow compilation of OpenMP streaming programs. ACM TACO **9**, 53 (2013)
16. Dolbeau, R., Bihan, S., Bodin, F.: HMPP: a hybrid multi-core parallel programming environment. In: Workshop on General Purpose Processing on GPU (2007)

17. Thompson, M., Nikolov, H., Stefanov, T., Pimentel, A.D., Erbas, C., Polstra, S., Deprettere, E.F.: A framework for rapid system-level exploration, synthesis, and programming of multimedia MP-SoCs. In: IEEE/ACM/IFIP CODES+ISSS, pp. 9–14 (2007)
18. Wenzel, J., Hochberger, C.: RapidSoC: short turnaround creation of FPGA based SoCs. In: International Symposium on Rapid System Prototyping, pp. 86–92 (2016)

Control Flow Analysis for Embedded Multi-core Hybrid Systems

Augusto W. Hoppe[1,2](✉) ⓘD, Fernanda Lima Kastensmidt[2], and Jürgen Becker[1]

[1] Institute for Information Processing Technologies (ITIV) KIT, Karlsruhe, Germany
{augusto.hoppe,becker}@kit.edu
[2] Instituto de Informática – PGMICRO,
Universidade Federal do Rio Grande do Sul (UFRGS), Porto Alegre, Brazil
fglima@inf.ufrgs.br

Abstract. The use of program tracing subsystems is already ubiquitous during the validation phase of an application's life-cycle. However, these functionalities are also extremely useful in the domain of embedded fault tolerance. In this paper we explore the ARM CoreSight Debug and Trace architecture as a new tool for fault diagnosis and control flow assurance. The CoreSight is a dedicated ARM architecture that provides support for Program Flow Tracing without overhead costs for the running application. New FPGA integrated System-on-Chips (SoCs) enable the implementation of Hardware modules with direct access to system peripherals, bypassing the use of external control interfaces such as JTAG or Serial Wire Debug (SWD). We show here a new implementation for an integrated configurable hardware controller that can collect and send program trace data for a ARM Cortex-A9 integrated FPGA SoC. We also propose the use of this interface to measure hang latency, the time between the occurrence of a fault and failure detection.

Keywords: ARM CoreSight · Online trace · Fault injection · FPGA
Soft-error · Control flow

1 Introduction

Real-time embedded systems are in the spotlight of current fault-tolerance research. Safety-critical applications show a clear and still increasing demand for digital processing power, *e.g.*, for automated driving and interconnected intelligent systems with real-time requirements. The usage of multi-core technologies is an imperative for embedded systems in the near future. The ARAMIS-II project [1] aims at the development of processes, tools and platforms for the efficient use of multi-core architectures in such safety-critical domains. New fault tolerant and fault safe techniques must be implemented to work with high performance systems. The project focuses on three major domains related to critical systems, Automotive, Avionic and Industrial applications. Safety standards related to such domains recommend extensive branch coverage and conditional execution

© Springer International Publishing AG, part of Springer Nature 2018
N. Voros et al. (Eds.): ARC 2018, LNCS 10824, pp. 485–496, 2018.
https://doi.org/10.1007/978-3-319-78890-6_39

for their most critical system safety levels, *e.g.* DO-178B/C, IEC 61508, ISO 26262. It is thus important to use trace data effectively, both during the validation phase of critical systems and as a tool to detect failures from randomly occurring events like ionizing radiation or other environmental effects.

Control flow checking (CFC) is an effective and well-researched fault tolerance method that can be used successfully to secure embedded applications. In Sect. 4 we show that a high percentage of system failures come from PC related faults, or control flow errors (CFE). In the literature, CFC techniques have been implemented both through software algorithms and through external hardware modules that access the embedded trace system. Normal software techniques modify the compiled code through different sets of rules and use this extra information during runtime to detect and possibly correct eventual faults [4]. They require no extra hardware but can add considerable overhead to the application in terms of performance and memory usage and are limited in regards to multi-core architecture usage.

Hardware CFC implementations normally require the use of a trace systems to collect control flow information during runtime. Previous work has shown how tracing can be extended in different architectures to enable some form of control flow analysis, *e.g.* PowerPC 5xx [6], and Leon3/Sparc-V8 and miniMIPS [5]. The use of the trace information in Commercial Off-The Shelf (COTS) processors is restricted by the available interfaces in the device. For ASIC devices, the only option is the use of an external JTAG or Serial Wire Debug (SWD) interface. In [5], soft-core processors were configured in an FPGA, this enabled the implementation of a CFC module directly connected to the processor's trace and debug output port. New COTS devices such as Zynq-7000 and Zynq-Ultrascale+ [9,10], provide an integrated FPGA directly connected to powerful multi-core processors such as ARM's Cortex-A9 and Cortex-A53. This new type of architecture provides the flexibility to easily access and process trace information, with all the advantages of a high-end multi-core ASIC processor.

In this paper we implement a novel trace acquisition module for such systems. We also propose a new use of the program flow trace, taking advantage of its cycle accurate branching information to calculate the Hang Latency, or Fault to Failure Time of applications under fault injection. Section 2 explores the CoreSight architecture present in both Cortex-A9 and Cortex-A53, and how it can be used for online fault detection purposes. In Sect. 3 we show our fault injection setup and how we measure the Hang Latency of our test case benchmarks. Finally, in Sect. 4 we present our latency measurements and fault injection campaign results. In Sect. 5 we conclude and elaborate on extensions for this work.

2   Architecture Overview and Implementation

To test and evaluate our trace capture system, we used the ZedBoard, Zynq-7000 evaluation and development board. Figure 1 shows the internal elements of the CoreSight architecture as implemented in the Zynq-7000 [9]. Components of the CoreSight platform can be classified as: Control Components, Trace Sources,

Trace Links, Trace Sinks, or Debug Access Ports [2]. To enable non-invasive trace generation for a selected Processor Unit, we must configure the corresponding Trace Macrocell, *i.e.* the Trace Source, and route it through the Trace Port Interface Unit (TPIU), *i.e.* the Trace Sink. The modules used by our implementation are shown highlighted in the figure. One Program Trace Macrocell (PTM) is available for each CPU core. The PTM monitors the behaviour of the core through a dedicated interface and performs real-time instruction flow tracing. The generated trace packets are routed through the Trace Funnel and a Source ID is added to the packet if multiple Trace Sources are enabled. We then send the packets trough the TPIU directly to our FPGA implemented module.

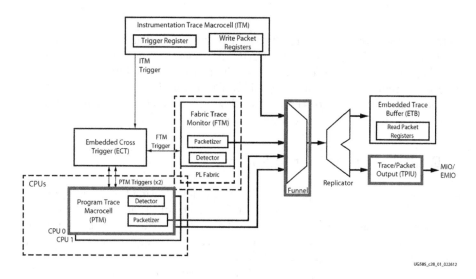

Fig. 1. Internal CoreSight system block diagram for the Zynq-7000 [9].

The Cortex-A9 PTM provides visibility to all code branches, synchronization operations and CPU state changes. It can be configured to enable CPU cycle accurate timing information, which provides trace packets with *cycle count* data informing how many CPU cycles have passed since the last captured packet. By combining all cycle counts throughout the program's execution we can calculate the time between any two flow decision points. It is this information that we use to determine the time between inserted fault and detected failure.

The instructions that generate each packet are called *Waypoints*. They include conditional and direct branches, return from exceptions, arithmetic and memory-related operations that have the Program Counter (PC) register as a destination, and synchronization barriers for instruction fetch, data and memory operations. Figure 2 shows a diagram of our system. Our capture device is responsible for configuring the CoreSight subsystem by accessing its memory mapped registers through a dedicated AXI interface. It then reads and parses

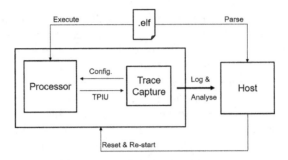

Fig. 2. Diagram for trace capture flow and injection control.

the trace packets from a 32 bit parallel TPIU connection and sends the data to our Host system through a 1 Mbps UART interface, where they are later analysed. The applications are compiled and the generated *.elf* binary is parsed by the Host system to identify all Waypoints. By correlating Waypoint and packet sequences, we can re-create the control flow graph (CFG) for each execution, calculating the delays from one branch to the next.

3   Fault Injection Methodology

We assume a Single Event Upset (SEU) fault model affecting the general purpose registers of a single core of the processor. For each injection, exactly one bit is flipped during a randomly chosen point of the program's execution. The SEUs are generated through a specific injection interruption routine. A timer is configured and used to generate an interruption that will modify the registers saved inside the program stack. At the beginning of the Interruption Service Routine (ISR), registers R0 through R12 are saved in the stack together with the Link Register (LR). By modifying LR, we can simulate Program Counter (PC) faults. When the interruption ends, the modified stack values are re-loaded to the physical registers and the benchmark resumes from exactly the same context, if not for the injected fault (see Fig. 3). When the program starts, before the execution of the benchmark function, three random values are generated: the timer's timeout, the register number to be injected, and the mask value to choose which bit to flip. These values are logged on the Host and used to correlate results extracted from trace with the register affected.

3.1   Fault Classification

Once the fault is injected, the resulting errors are classified. The injected bits can be defined as one of the following [7]: Architecturally Correct Execution (ACE) bits or unACE bits. ACE bits are those strictly required for the correct execution of the system. A transient fault in a ACE bit will by definition corrupt the program and generate an error. unACE bits on the other hand are not required

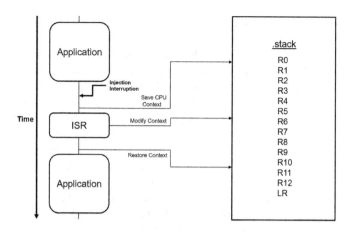

Fig. 3. Injection interruption scheme showing the use of the stack.

for the system to function correctly. They may be secondary configurations that are not used by the application, logically redundant values, or control flows that do not affect the correct execution of the program at a point in time. The errors generated by ACE bit faults can be separated in Silent Data Corruption (SDC) or Hangs. If the application finished normally but its outputs differ from the expected value, it is classified as an SDC. If the application did not finish in time or was aborted due to an internal error, it is classified as a Hang. Hangs are further classified in *Timeouts* and *Hardware Aborts*.

Timeouts are defined as all cases where the application did not finish its computation and had to be stopped by the host. Hardware Aborts are internal errors flagged by the processor that generate a hardware exception interruption. The Cortex-A9 generates exceptions for: *Undefined Instructions*, for when the CPU tries to decode an invalid Opcode; *Data Aborts*, flagged by the Memory Management Unit (MMU) when a data transfer instruction attempts to load or store data at an illegal address; and *Prefetch Aborts*, also thrown by the MMU when the system attempts to execute an instruction prefetched from an illegal address.

We define *Hang Latency*, or *Fault-to-Failure Time*, as the time in clock-cycles from the moment a bit-flip occurs until a failure is detected. The only failures we are currently able to detect are those flagged by the CPU as Hardware Aborts. The interruption that we use for our fault injection and the interruption generated by the CPU in case of a failure are both easily identifiable in the trace stream collected from the program's execution. Each interruption serves as a marker that makes it possible to calculate the time the fault remained latent in the system. Our benchmarks run in an OS-Free, or bare-metal environment. Experiments were performed to validate our trace acquisition module and latency measurements. These measurements can be used as a baseline for comparing with other system configurations in the future.

4   Experimental Results

We performed 2000 fault injections for each of our two test-case applications. The first application is a simple Dijkstra shortest path algorithm. The input for our algorithm was a random connected graph encoded in a 100 by 100 adjacency matrix. The second application is the LZO Compression algorithm [8], using the same matrix as raw input data. Each application was compiled with optimization flag -*O0*, *i.e.* without any optimizations. To generate the final *.elf* file, both programs were linked to the same driver library package provided by Xilinx in its SDK. The execution times for both applications were measured as 27.73 ms and 17.64 ms respectively. In Fig. 4 we show the rate of register usage, other than the PC, for all assembler instructions in our benchmarks while Fig. 5 shows the percent of injections done in each register for the whole campaign. The injection rate was roughly uniform (around 7.7%) but the usage rate shows the influence of the compiler optimization option. In both applications, the most used registers were R3, R11 and PC.

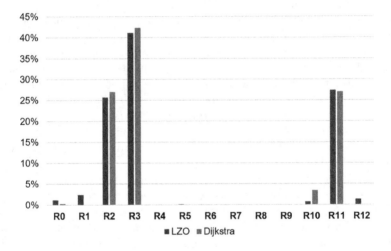

Fig. 4. Register usage rates.

According to the "ARM Architecture Procedure Calling Standard (AAPCS)" [3], registers R0 to R3 are caller-save registers, used to hold temporary values that need not be preserved across calls. While R0–R2 are the preferred registers to hold arguments through function calls, R3 is the preferred working register. The standard also states that while not enforced, R11 is set as the default Frame Pointer (FP). The FP is responsible for pointing to the section of the stack allocated to the currently executing function.

Without any optimization, the compiler will choose the simplest method for memory access and data handling, *i.e.* it will use R3 and FP to read from and write values to the Stack, avoiding the use of other registers to keep intermediary

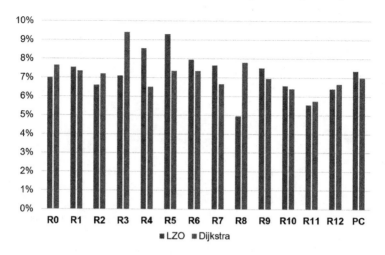

Fig. 5. Register injection rates.

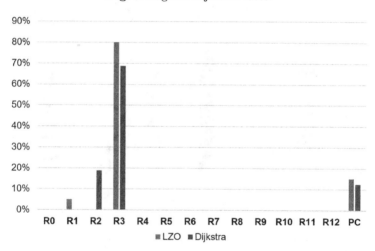

Fig. 6. Rate of register injections that caused SDCs.

values. Figures 6 and 7 show the error rates for each register from our injection campaigns. In Fig. 6 we can see that 70–80% of injections on the R3 register caused SDCs. While Hangs where proportionally distributed between R11/FP and PC (Fig. 7). This validates what we would expect given the functionalities associated with each register, R3 keeps the working data while FP stores the addresses used to access application memory.

In Fig. 8 we observe the proportion of Hangs in each application. In both cases, we only observed Hardware exceptions related to Data Aborts and Undefined Instructions. The number of undetected failures, or Timeouts, stayed roughly equal to the number of invalid Data Aborts. While the MMU raised

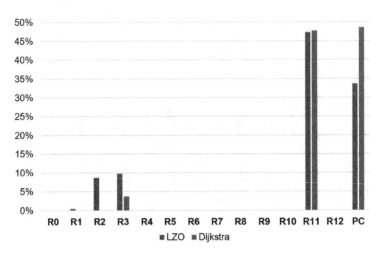

Fig. 7. Rate of register injections that caused Hangs.

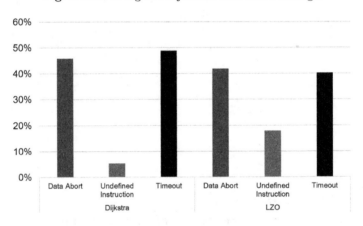

Fig. 8. Distribution of Hangs according to type of failure (see Subsect. 3.1).

exceptions for invalid data accesses, no Preftech Aborts were flagged. We latter confirmed that the default MMU memory configuration available on Xilinx's drivers only defines the *access rights* to the different memory sections, but does not manage their *execution rights*. The whole memory can then be executed by the processor and be interpreted as containing valid instructions. The different types of Hangs were not distributed equally among FP and PC registers. Table 1 shows the proportion of Aborts and Timeouts for both registers in each application. We can see that while faults to the FP resulted understandably in memory access failures, in both applications, 100% of Undefined Instruction failures occurred from faults to the PC, as well as most of the Timeout failures.

Table 1. Distribution of Hang types according to affected register.

	Dijkstra		LZO	
Hang type	PC	FP	PC	FP
Timeouts	72%	23%	58%	4%
Data Aborts	4%	92%	0%	99%
Undef. Instr.	100%	0%	100%	0%

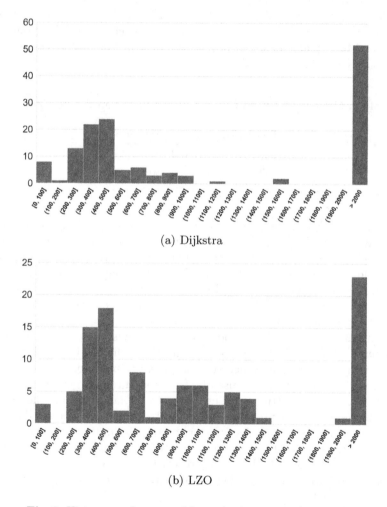

(a) Dijkstra

(b) LZO

Fig. 9. Histogram of measured latencies in groups of 100 cycles.

Figure 9 presents the measured latency distribution for the Aborts identified. The histogram shows the number of latencies measured between 0 and 2000 cycles. Due to the wide range of measured values, the 2000 cycle point is set as a cut-off, with 63% percent of measurements being smaller than it for the Dijkstra benchmark and 78% for the LZO. Measured time is presented in CPU clock cycles, with each clock cycle corresponding to 1.5 ns for the core running at 660 MHz. The values are grouped in classes of 100 clock cycles for visibility. From all the data collected, we observed interesting phenomena such as latencies agglomerating around certain groups of values. Table 2 shows some measures for the distribution that exemplify the behaviour observed. The table shows the mean, the average over all detected latencies, and the median, the middle sample point of our data sets. The presence of very large outliers, greater than 5 Million cycles for Dijkstra and 2 Million cycles for LZO, skewed the averages but we can see that most latencies stayed below the 1000 cycle mark. The grouping of values could be explained as sets of failure modes, or failure behaviours, which are constantly stimulated in different injections.

Table 2. Mean and median values in clock cycles for latency distributions.

Benchmark	Mean	Median
Dijkstra	688 051	595
LZO	335 761	801

From the values collected, one of our first hypothesis was that most of the big latencies came from PC jumps to other memory sections that eventually reached trash values, prompting an Undefined Instruction exception. The default MMU page size for the Cortex-A9 is of 1MB. This means that bits [31:20] of address words encode the memory page address and all faults occurring on these bits inside the PC will cause jumps to unprotected memory regions outside of the range of the program's page.

We analyse in Fig. 10 all injections to the PC register, according to the bit they affected. We see that for both applications, the MMU page bits caused Timeout failures instead of generating any measurable latency. The memory pages outside of the current one used by the program never generated the execution of an incorrect instruction. This is due to the faults leading the program to jump to empty memory regions, whose "instructions" are evaluated as *nops*. Faults to the middle bits of the register, corresponding to the same memory section, were the ones that caused all measured Hang Latencies from PC faults. The latency for PC-related Aborts stayed relatively high, around 60k cycles for the Dijkstra and 670k cycles for the LZO algorithms, but all of the largest values were related to Data Abort exceptions.

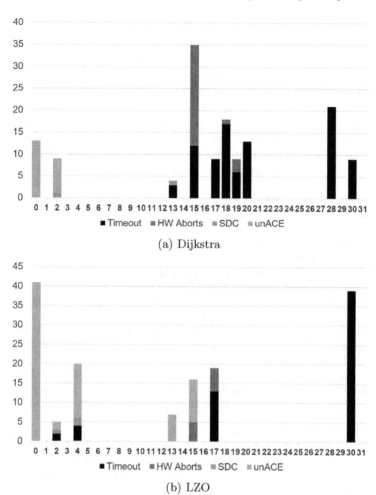

(a) Dijkstra

(b) LZO

Fig. 10. Total number of injections for each PC bit. Injections outcomes are labelled.

5   Conclusions and Future Work

In Sect. 4 we showed that PC errors are more strongly associated to Timeouts than HW Aborts, with all jumps to different memory sections generating Time-outs. We argue that while such errors can be detected by re-configuring the MMU, we were still able to see many errors generated by jumps inside the same memory section that would not be detected. It is worth noting that all PC-related Aborts were faults in bits that left it still pointing to the program's own memory section. The implementation of a CFC module can thus quickly detect problems and return the system to a functioning state.

We also note that the biggest contributor for our latency measurements came from faults to the FP, generating Data Aborts. This shows that many faults stay latent in the system for a long time before they prompt access to an invalid memory region. During this time, several valid target addresses are possibly being corrupted, extending the damage caused by the fault. By detecting such faults early, we can avoid fault propagation and isolate the damage caused. Our compiler optimization strongly influenced the outcomes of our tests, as most memory accesses relied on using only registers R3 and FP. We must verify how different compiler parameters and low-level function call/memory access standards can influence the outcome of errors in the system. After validating our trace acquisition system we plan to implement a full online CFC module on both Zynq-7000 and Zynq-Ultrascale+ devices.

References

1. ARAMIS-II: ARAMIS-II Project Homepage. https://www.aramis2.com/. Accessed 12 Nov 2017
2. ARM: ARM CoreSight Architecture Specification v2.0
3. ARM: Procedure Call Standard for the ARM Architecture
4. Chielle, E., Rosa, F., Rodrigues, G.S., Tambara, L.A., Tonfat, J., Macchione, E., Aguirre, F., Added, N., Medina, N., Aguiar, V., Silveira, M.A.G., Ost, L., Reis, R., Cuenca-Asensi, S., Kastensmidt, F.L.: Reliability on ARM processors against soft errors through SIHFT techniques. IEEE Trans. Nucl. Sci. **63**, 1–9 (2016). https://doi.org/10.1109/tns.2016.2525735
5. Du, B., Reorda, M.S., Sterpone, L., Parra, L., Portela-Garcia, M., Lindoso, A., Entrena, L.: Online test of control flow errors: a new debug interface-based approach. IEEE Trans. Comput. **65**(6), 1846–1855 (2016). https://doi.org/10.1109/tc.2015.2456014
6. Fazeli, M., Farivar, R., Miremadi, S.: A software-based concurrent error detection technique for power PC processor-based embedded systems. In: 20th IEEE International Symposium on Defect and Fault Tolerance in VLSI Systems (DFT 2005). IEEE Computer Society (2005). https://doi.org/10.1109/dftvs.2005.14
7. Mukherjee, S., et al.: A systematic methodology to compute the architectural vulnerability factors for a high-performance microprocessor. In: 22nd Digital Avionics Systems Conference. IEEE (2003)
8. Oberhumer: LZO Compression Library. http://www.oberhumer.com/opensource/lzo/. Accessed 12 Nov 2017
9. Xilinx: Zynq-7000 All Programmable SoC - Technical Reference Manual (2017)
10. Xilinx: Zynq UltraScale+ Device - Technical Reference Manual (2017)

FPGA-Based Design and Applications

A Low-Cost BRAM-Based Function Reuse for Configurable Soft-Core Processors in FPGAs

Pedro H. Exenberger Becker[1]([✉]) , Anderson L. Sartor[1] ,
Marcelo Brandalero[1] , Tiago Trevisan Jost[1] , Stephan Wong[2],
Luigi Carro[1] , and Antonio C. Beck[1]

[1] Institute of Informatics, Universidade Federal do Rio Grande do Sul,
Porto Alegre, Brazil
{phebecker,alsartor,mbrandalero,ttjost,carro,caco}@inf.ufrgs.br
[2] Computer Engineering Laboratory,
Delft University of Technology, Delft, The Netherlands
J.S.S.M.Wong@tudelft.nl

Abstract. Many modern FPGA-based soft-processor designs must include dedicated hardware modules to satisfy the requirements of a wide range of applications. Not seldom they all do not fit in the FPGA target, so their functionalities must be mapped into the much slower software domain. However, many complex soft-core processors usually underuse the available Block RAMs (BRAMs) when comparing to LUTs and registers. By taking advantage of this fact, we propose a generic low-cost BRAM-based function reuse mechanism (the BRAM-FR) that can be easily configured for precise or approximate modes to accelerate execution. The BRAM-FR was implemented in HDL and coupled to a configurable 4-issue VLIW processor. It was used to optimize different applications that use a soft-float library to emulate a Floating-Point Unit (FPU), and an image processing filter that tolerates a certain level of error. We show that our technique can accelerate the former by 1.23x and the latter by 1.52x, with a Reuse Table that fits in the BRAMs (that would otherwise be idle) of five tested FPGA targets with a marginal increase in the number of slice registers and LUTs.

Keywords: FPGAs · Soft-core processors · Function reuse
Approximate

1 Introduction

The implementation of soft-core processors in Field-Programmable Gate Arrays(FPGA) has known benefits such as architecture customization, hardware acceleration, and obsolescence mitigation [1]. These processors have gained space in solutions to specific purpose problems: by using modules that can be configured at synthesis time, they combine the ease of high-level programming for end

© Springer International Publishing AG, part of Springer Nature 2018
N. Voros et al. (Eds.): ARC 2018, LNCS 10824, pp. 499–510, 2018.
https://doi.org/10.1007/978-3-319-78890-6_40

users with performance gains in dedicated tasks. Because many of them require high performance for a wide range of applications, specific hardware like Floating Point Units(FPUs), security and cryptography modules, and coders/decoders for multimedia commonly surround the processor (e.g., Multiprocessor Systems on Chip(MPSoCs)) [2]. However, FPGA designs require more area and energy compared to Application Specific Integrated Circuits(ASICs) [3]. Therefore, in many cases, the resources available in an FPGA will be a limiting factor. In case specific hardware cannot fit inside the FPGA, its functionality must be mapped into the software domain, which is significantly slower.

However, there is one class of resources in FPGAs that is often underutilized when implementing complex logic driven designs: Block Random Access Memories(BRAMs). For instance, in the *OpenSparc T1* (a single-issue, six-stage pipeline that supports up to four concurrent threads), BRAMs are not utilized in the same proportion as registers and Look-Up Tables(LUTs). This comes from the observation that BRAMs usually present a limited number of ports (in most cases, two for reading and one for writing). This feature may forbid many possible uses for BRAMs: for example, the register file in multiple-issue processors usually need multiple read ports to feed all the available functional units adequately [4]. Hence, BRAMs are typically used only to implement moderately sized caches, common in the scope of soft-cores running in embedded environments.

Considering this scenario, this paper proposes BRAM-FR: a function reuse-based technique that leverages those idle BRAMs, resulting in a low-cost and generic hardware solution to speed up specific software parts without the need for implementing dedicated hardware components. Each time a function executes, its results are dynamically stored in a BRAM Reuse Table (RT) and, when the same function with the same input arguments is called again, the output can be directly fetched, avoiding re-calculation and improving performance. Going one step further, we also show that, by tuning how the RT is accessed, it is possible to gracefully switch, by using the same hardware structure, from precise to approximate reuse, which can significantly increase reuse rates and performance at an expense of output quality in some specific classes of applications. Therefore, the proposed reuse mechanism exploits BRAMs that would otherwise be idle to optimize the execution of any given software library, avoiding its ASICs counterpart implementation, which results in significant savings in design time, LUTs and registers.

BRAM-FR was coupled to a complex configurable 4-issue Very Long Instruction Word (VLIW) soft-core at Hardware Description Language (HDL). We investigate six applications that process a significant amount of Floating Point (FP) operations in different scenarios, including one where implementing a FPU in hardware would prevent the inclusion of any new dedicated hardware because of the limited amount of available resources. In this case, BRAM-FR is used to optimize a soft-float library that uses integer units to emulate double precision FP operations. We also evaluate an image processing filter software that tolerates a certain error level, showing that one can switch to approximate mode and trade-off performance and quality.

We demonstrate that an average speedup of 1.23x in the precise mode and 1.52x in the approximate one is achieved when considering an RT that fits in five different test targets. For targets with larger BRAMs, this number can be as high as 1.38x and 2.97x, respectively. Meanwhile, the usage of slice registers and slice LUTs by our generic reuse mechanism increases by 17% and 3% respectively, compared to 140% and 48% for an FPU or 11% and 13% for a dedicated Sobel filter. It is important to note that BRAM-FR is generic, so its cost in registers and LUTs is fixed regardless the number of different applications that it can optimize.

The upcoming sections are organized as follows. Related work about different reuse approaches is covered in Sect. 2. Section 3 discusses the implementation and the particularities of BRAM-FR. Results are presented and discussed in Sect. 4. Section 5 states conclusions and future work.

2   Related Work

Many works have discussed reuse of computation [5]. Implementations vary from software (also known as memoization [6]) to hardware-based solutions, covering different granularities of code. In [7], dynamic instruction reuse is presented with execution-driven simulation. The goal is to avoid re-execution of instructions in an out-of-order processor. In this case, instructions' source registers are the inputs, and its result is the output. Authors in [8] proposed the reuse of FP instructions focusing on multimedia applications, considering only those that take more than one cycle to execute. Average speedup between 1.08x and 1.22x is achieved. Despite a hardware scheme being discussed, the results are taken from an instruction-level simulator.

Going a step further, [9] considers reuse of basic blocks, simulating with SimpleScalar. The source operands (registers or memory) of each instruction inside a basic block are considered as part of the input, while the values written to any register or memory location are considered as part of the output. Their work shows performance improvements of up to 1.14x. A similar system is proposed at trace level (a set of sequential basic blocks) in [10]. In this case, less reusability is found compared to instruction reuse, but more speedup is obtained since larger chunks of code are involved.

The authors in [11] introduced the concept of dynamic function reuse. In this case, only pure functions (which do not use global variables and make no I/O operations, so the global state of the program is not altered) can be reused, so that the return value depends only on the function's input parameters. The study presented 10% to 67% of reusability on a variety of applications. Finally, the authors in [12] implemented function reuse with a mechanism that intercepts calls to the dynamically linked math library. This modified library verifies reusability and returns the respective output value by reuse when available (otherwise, the original math library is called to solve the function).

A few works have explored the concept of approximate function reuse under distinct names. In [13], fuzzy memoization of FP instructions is presented. Similarly to the work developed in [8], only multiplication and division operations are saved in the table due to their high latency, and multimedia applications are used for evaluation. Approximation is achieved by discarding some Least Significant Bits(LSBs) from the input FP value's mantissa, causing close enough values to be grouped into the same table entry. The authors claim that 4x more energy can be saved by using fuzzy memoization compared to the precise reuse approach. Work in [14] presents the clumsy value cache, an instruction/block-level reuse technique targeting (GPUs) fragment shaders. The authors investigate the potential of dropping input bits to increase instruction reuse rates and show that by doing so is the only viable way to implement block reuse. No speedup results are presented in the work, but the technique reduces the amount of instructions executed, on average, by 13.5%. Dropping input bits is also assessed with approximate function reuse in software [15], where the authors achieve 50% reuse rate with less than 10% quality degradation in image benchmarks. The authors in [16] use memoization to accelerate application-specific circuits synthesized for FPGA using High-Level Synthesis(HLS), and show that it can achieve 20% energy savings with less than 5% of area overhead.

Differently from previous works, BRAM-FR specifically considers FPGAs and configurable soft-cores, taking into account their unique components, design constraints and intrinsic characteristics, such as the fact that BRAMs are usually underused. It can provide a generic solution for both precise and approximate computation, delivering a low-cost and flexible technique so the design requirements can be achieved with the FPGA at hand. To the best of our knowledge, this is the first hardware implementation of such technique targeted towards soft-core processors. Through this, this work provides an in-depth analysis of the area/resources consumption of the mechanism, and a level of accuracy that only actual implementations can provide. Our hardware implementation is free of any abstraction layers, leading to a solution independent of user space or operating systems, which are unavailable in bare metal designs. By presenting function reuse in FPGA for configurable soft-core processors, we open new possibilities for design space exploration and new tradeoffs for HW/SW co-design in such devices. For instance, low-price FPGAs may regain space in project decision, since our approach provides performance gains with low overhead in LUTs, occupying, instead, BRAMs that would otherwise be idle.

3   Implementation

BRAM-FR is implemented through a function Reuse Unit (RU) composed of the following:

- *Reuse Table (RT)*: a direct mapped table implemented in BRAM that stores dynamic information of *reusable functions* (frequently executed, likely-to-be-reused pure functions defined at design time). Each entry (Fig. 1) contains the function's address and the input (or a tag, in case it is approximate, as it will be further explained) and output contexts. Its size is defined at design time.

– *Functions Table*: a small (one entry per reusable function) and fully associative table with static information on the reusable functions. Each entry
contains the function's address, execution mode (precise or approximate),
number of parameters of the function, and number of the input bits for quality control (in the case it is configured to be approximate).
– *Reuse mechanism*: implements the process of accessing the reuse table, which
involves the index calculation (using a hash); checking whether the entry in
the RT is valid or not; and reusing it, if it is the case.

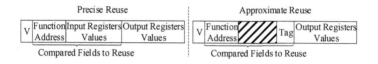

Fig. 1. Difference in RT structure between precise and approximate modes.

The RU is generic (can potentially be used with any application containing pure functions) and can switch between modes at runtime to perform both
precise and approximate reuse.

3.1 Baseline Processor

BRAM-FR was coupled to the ρ-VEX VLIW soft-core processor [17] (a 32-bit
five-stage pipeline, compatible with the VEX Instruction Set Architecture (ISA)
[18], described in VHDL and configurable at design time), even though there are
no restrictions whatsoever that would prevent its implementation to any other
soft-core processor. In this work, we used the default 4-issue version consisting
of 4 ALUs, 2 multipliers, 1 memory unit, and 1 branch unit (as shown in Fig. 2)
and $8 + 8$ KB instruction and data caches. The VEX ISA defines that argument
and return values for function calls are passed through registers *R3* to *R10*.
If more than eight input or output registers are required, the memory is used.
BRAM-FR considers only the first case (up to eight parameters) since we have
found that the number of functions that do not fit in this case is not significant.

3.2 Reuse Mechanism

Figure 2 details the ρ-VEX organization integrated with the RU. Three phases
are highlighted and correspond to (1) how the RU collects reuse information,
(2) verifies and stores reuse information, (3) and applies reuse (when possible).
Precise and approximate reuse use the very same hardware structure and differ
only in the way they access the RT during Phase 2. Algorithm 1 details the three
phases above implemented by the RU, which will be further discussed next.

Phase 1: When the pipeline decodes a *call*, the function and return addresses
are captured by the RU, which checks in the *Functions Table* if the function is
defined as *reusable* (*l. 3–5* in Algorithm 1). If so, it also fetches reuse information

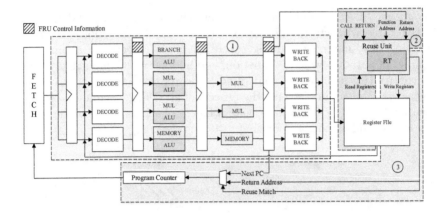

Fig. 2. Organization of a 4-issue ρ-VEX with a Reuse Unit.

(i.e., which input/output registers, whether the function was flagged for precise or approximate reuse, and the number of input bits) and goes to Phase 2. If the function is *not reusable*, the processor continues its regular operation.

Phase 2: In this phase, the current function's input parameters (the input context *ctx*) are collected by accessing the register file. The behaviour depends on whether the function was flagged for *precise* or *approximate* reuse in the *Functions Table*. In the former case, the RU generates a hash key (*l. 11–12*) by *XORing* every 16-bit of data in the current input context and function address, similarly to the approach in [12]. The resulting key's LSBs are used as the RT index to fetch a table entry (*l. 13–15*), which contains the fields shown in Fig. 1. In case the fetched entry is valid, the entry's function address and input parameters are compared with those of the current call (*l. 22–23*). If the comparisons match, there is an RT hit and phase (3) starts.

If the function was flagged for approximate reuse, the process of generating the hash key is almost the same, with one difference: some LSBs (given by the *fun.drop* field) is dropped before computing the hash to group close enough values (*l. 8–9*). With the resulting key generated, an entry in the RT is fetched (see Fig. 1). Then, the current call's function address and hash key are compared against the function address and hash key (tag) of the fetched RT entry (*l. 29–30*). The trade-off between reuse rates and quality can be easily tuned by changing the number of input bits to be discarded (*l. 9*).

For both cases (precise or approximate), a reuse miss happens if the valid bit of the current entry is not set or if the function address and inputs/tag do not match. In these cases, the RU waits for the function to execute regularly and then, with the input context (or hash value, if approximate) and outputs captured from the register file, stores a new entry (if the valid bit was not set, *l. 16–21*) or replace an entry in the RT (in case of data mismatch, *l. 26–28* and *33–35*). Therefore, the RT is dynamically filled as the program executes.

It is important to highlight that the same hardware, controlled only by a small set of multiplexers, and the same table (but with a slight change in how its data is structured) are used for both precise and approximate implementations. The way how RU is accessed from the Functions Table is what defines the mode, so both are available during the execution.

Phase 3: A match was detected in the previous phase, so the result of the whole function is available in the fetched RT entry. Therefore, the RU writes it to the register file, skipping the actual execution (*l. 24 and 31*), and notifies the reuse detection to the processor. Then, the instructions in the pipeline are flushed, and the return address (captured by the RU in Phase 1) is written to the program counter (*l. 25 and 32*). Since reusability can be checked before the pipeline commits any instruction, no rollback mechanism is required.

The register file was modified with the addition of extra reading ports (with marginal area impact, as our results will show). With this modification, there are no stalls in the pipeline when fetching the input parameters or the output values. The number of additional ports can be tuned according to the target functions: the more parameters, the more ports are needed to ensure no pipeline stalls (in our implementation, four reading ports were added). As already mentioned, when the reuse is applied, the pipeline is flushed, and the result of the function is written to the register file. The RU exploits the fact that the write ports of the register file would be idle due to the pipeline flush and uses them to perform this operation, so no additional write ports are necessary.

Algorithm 1. Algorithm Implemented by the Reuse Unit.

Require: Function address (*addr*), return address (*raddr*), function context (*ctx*).

1: **while** program is executing **do**
2:   **if** function CALL instruction **then**
3:     $fun \leftarrow FunctionsTable.srch(addr)$
4:     **if** $fun.reusable$=**false then**
5:       **continue**
6:     **if** $fun.precise$ **then**
7:       $ictx \leftarrow ctx$
8:     **else if** $fun.approx$ **then**
9:       $ictx \leftarrow ctx$, dropping $fun.drop$ LSBs
10:     $h \leftarrow 0$
11:     **foreach** 16-bit words w **in** $\{addr,ictx\}$ **do**
12:       $h \leftarrow h \oplus w$
13:     $n \leftarrow \log_2(RT.size)$
14:     $i \leftarrow h[n-1:0]$
15:     $e \leftarrow RT.fetch(i)$

16:     **if** $e.valid = $**false then**
17:       $octx \leftarrow Execute(fun)$
18:       **if** $fun.precise$ **then**
19:         $RT.update(fun, i, ictx, octx)$
20:       **else if** $fun.approx$ **then**
21:         $RT.update(fun, i, h, octx)$
22:     **else if** $fun.precise$ **then**
23:       **if** $e.addr$=$addr$ **and** $e.ictx$=$ictx$ **then**
24:         $ReuseFunction(fun, e)$
25:         $WritePC(raddr)$
26:       **else**
27:         $octx \leftarrow Execute(fun)$
28:         $RT.update(fun, i, ictx, octx)$
29:     **else if** $fun.approximate$ **then**
30:       **if** $e.addr$=$addr$ **and** $e.h$=h **then**
31:         $ReuseFunction(fun, e)$
32:         $WritePC(raddr)$
33:       **else**
34:         $octx \leftarrow Execute(fun)$
35:         $RT.update(fun, i, h, octx)$

---

4 Results

4.1 Methodology

The soft-float library (case-study for precise function reuse), which emulates FP operations using integer hardware, was statically linked at compile time. We considered the four basic operations (add, sub, mult, div) in double FP precision as the *reusable functions* and evaluated the speedup of six benchmarks: five from the WCET benchmark suite [19]: *lms, ludcmp, minver, qurt, st*; and one from the Powerstone suite [20]: *fir*. The *sobel* image-processing filter (case-study for approximate function reuse) from the AxBench suite [21] was evaluated using 30 distinct images. In this case, only the convolutional kernel was considered as reusable. The benchmarks were compiled with LLVM [22] using the -O3 flag and cycle-accurate simulations were carried out using Mentor Graphics Modelsim 10. To measure performance, we compared the execution cycles of the benchmarks on ρ-VEX with and without the RU (either in precise or approximate mode), experimenting with RT sizes varying from two to 32K lines. We collected FPGA resource usage and timing information after synthesizing and mapping the VHDL of the processor to five FPGA targets from Virtex 4 (xc4vlx40; xc4vsx55), 5 (xc5vsx50t; xc5vsx95t), and 7 (xc7vx690t) Series, optimizing for area and using Xilinx ISE 14.7. Adding BRAM-FR to the design caused no changes in the critical path. Finally, the error metric used to assess the sobel benchmark's output quality was the root-mean-squared (RMS) pixel difference between the original and approximated computations, normalized to the range 0–100%, as defined in the AxBench suite [21].

4.2   Performance

Precise Reuse - Soft-Float: Figure 3 presents the reusability of the soft-float functions. Due to space limitations, we show only a subset of all RT sizes evaluated, including extrapolated results for the best case (when the RT is increased to a point when no replacements take place).

Grouped by benchmark, each column depicts the stacked RT hit rate of *add, sub, mul,* and *div* functions, according to the number of RT lines (x-axis). Naturally, reusability increases with the RT size, since more reuse information is available so a match attempt succeeds. Cases with significant reusability of *div* (e.g., *fir*) and *mul* (e.g., *lms* and *minver*) have more potential for improving performance, since these operations take longer than *add* or *sub*. For these

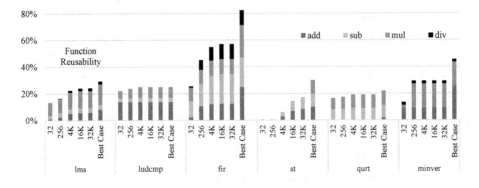

Fig. 3. Reusability of FP functions.

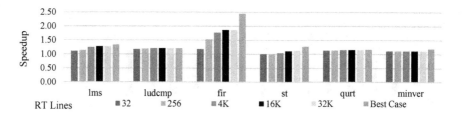

Fig. 4. Speedup for different RT sizes compared to the baseline.

benchmarks, reusability can vary from almost none (*st* with 32 lines) to more than 80% (*fir* in the best case).

Figure 4 depicts the speedup for different RT sizes, also grouped by benchmark. For the largest RT tested (32K lines) significant speedups are achieved: in *ludcmp* (1.21x), *lms* (1.28x) and *fir* (1.86x); and even in the worst cases (*minver*, 1.12x and *st*, 1.13x). When the RT is reduced to only 32 lines, five out of six benchmarks still improve by more than 1.1x (the only exception is *st*, given its small reuse rates). Also, for most benchmarks, note how a 16K or even a 4K-line RT already improves performance near to the theoretical maximum (the *best case*) of the technique. Comparing to a 4K-line RT, for example, the best case brings no improvement in *ludcmp*, and increases *qurt* and *lms* performance only marginally, by 2% and 7%, respectively. This fact highlights that function arguments very often repeat during execution and present limited variability. The exception is *fir*, in which the reuse rates increase significantly with larger table sizes. In the best case, its performance improves by 2.44x compared to the baseline (and 67% more than the 4K-line RT).

Considering the geomean speedup for the six benchmarks, considerable gains in performance can be achieved with low resource overhead. For example, 32-line and 256-line RTs can provide speedups of 1.12x and 1.18x, respectively. A 4K-line RT, which still fits in all five tested FPGAs (which will be discussed in subsection Resource Usage) provides speedups of 1.23x.

Therefore, even resource-limited FPGAs can benefit from the BRAM-FR. When it comes to high-end FPGA, the available BRAMs can be used to increase even more the RT size and consequently get closer to the maximum speedup possible for applications with high reusability rates.

Approximate Reuse - Sobel Image Filter: Figure 5 shows geomean speedup and error rate considering 30 distinct images, in an approximation scenario where 4 LSBs are dropped from the inputs values in the *sobel* benchmark. Modifying this value leads to distinct performance-error trade-offs, so we constrained ourselves to only one representative spot in the vast design space available, chosen after comprehensive experimentation.

The great benefit from approximate reuse is that speedup is achieved more easily than with precise reuse. Note that a 2-line RT, in this case, improves performance by 1.33x, with only 3% error. Error remains under 10% (common error threshold for approximate *sobel* benchmark [21]) for every table up to 4K

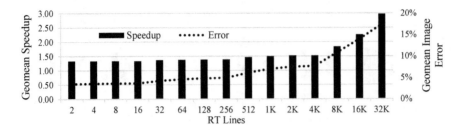

Fig. 5. Speedup for approximate sobel image filter.

lines, where 8% error meets 1.52x speedup. Since higher speedups mean that more reuse was possible, it also means that more errors will appear (since exact values will be exchanged for approximated ones). If higher error rates can be tolerated, the speedup can reach 2.25x with 14% of error (for a 16K line RT), or even 2.97x with 17% of error (32K line RT).

Resource Usage: We collected the usage of BRAM, Slice Registers, and Slice LUTs in four scenarios: baseline (ρ-VEX), ρ-VEX with RU, ρ-VEX with a double precision FPU [23], and ρ-VEX with a hardware sobel filter. They all were synthesized following the methodology explained before, with exception of the hardware implementation of Sobel, which data was taken from [24], covering Virtex 5 FPGAs only. Table 1 presents the comparison in the four scenarios with distinct targets using the largest RT that fits in each design. For example, the Virtex 5 - xc5vsx50t supports a maximum of 16K lines. Smaller tables, yet measured, were omitted. Although each table line for approximate reuse needs less information (a tag instead of all the input values, see Fig. 1) the results consider the size needed for the implementation of both modes (i.e., it considers the size for precise reuse), since it is possible to switch between them at run-time.

All targets can support an RT with at least 4K lines. In the Virtex 4 FPGA (the smallest available device), using the 4-issue ρ-VEX processor with an FPU would occupy nearly all FPGA resources (97% of the available Slice LUTs) and

Table 1. Usage of resources for different designs and targets

Series	Model	Design	Used Slice Registers	% Used Slice Registers	Used Slice LUTs	% Used Slice LUTs	Used BRAM	% Used BRAM
Virtex 7	xc7vx690t	ρ-Vex	3,015	0%	14,675	3%	16	1%
		ρ-Vex + RU (32K lines)	3,494	0%	15,176	4%	242	16%
		ρ-Vex + FPU	7,275	1%	19,926	5%	16	1%
ex 5	xc5vsx95t	ρ-Vex	3,012	5%	15,200	26%	16	7%
		ρ-Vex + RU (32K lines)	3,516	6%	15,717	27%	242	99%
		ρ-Vex + FPU	7,061	12%	23,349	40%	16	7%
		ρ-Vex + Sobel	3,351	6%	17,127	29%	16	7%
	xc5vsx50t	ρ-Vex	3,012	9%	15,200	47%	16	12%
		ρ-Vex + RU (16K lines)	3,516	11%	15,717	48%	129	98%
		ρ-Vex + FPU	7,061	22%	23,349	72%	16	12%
		ρ-Vex + Sobel	3,351	10%	17,127	52%	16	12%
Virtex 4	xc4vsx55	ρ-Vex	3,008	6%	23,986	49%	32	10%
		ρ-Vex + RU (16K lines)	3,511	7%	24,820	50%	258	81%
		ρ-Vex + FPU	7,403	15%	35,888	73%	32	10%
	xc4vlx40	ρ-Vex	3,008	8%	23,986	65%	32	33%
		ρ-Vex + RU (4K lines)	3,511	10%	24,820	67%	89	93%
		ρ-Vex + FPU	7,403	20%	35,888	97%	32	33%

restrict the addition of other hardware accelerators or even the modification of the issue-width (e.g., increase to the 8-issue version). As the original ρ-VEX uses a minimal amount of the available BRAMs, the RT can occupy the remaining ones as much as possible, leveraging these idle components which neither the FPU nor the Sobel hardware could exploit. In some cases, even an RT larger than 3K lines could be used (e.g., it only occupies 15% of the Virtex 7's BRAMs).

As for the logic resources that are usually scarce (slice registers and LUTs), we introduce a small overhead of 17% and 3%, respectively. In contrast, adding an FPU to ρ-VEX more than doubles the number of registers (140% overhead) and significantly increases LUTs usage (48%). The sobel hardware, likewise, increases by 11% the slice registers and 13% the slice LUTs. However, while these units are application-specific and are incremental in terms of resources (i.e. more LUTs and registers are necessary for each new application-specific hardware that is integrated), the overhead in LUTs and registers of our generic design is fixed, being only the RT variable (and thus BRAM usage). Therefore, costs can be amortized as the BRAM-FR encompasses more system features, enabling performance gains when any new robust hardware module does not fit.

Therefore, BRAM-FR can benefit both low and high-end FPGAs: in the former, the reuse mechanism allows performance improvements with minimum hardware overhead. In the latter, not only more hardware accelerators but also extra processors could be integrated into the system. For instance, three cores of the ρ-VEX processor could be instantiated alongside the RU in the Virtex 5 - xc5vsx95t. This would not be possible if a FPU was implemented in hardware.

5   Conclusions and Future Work

This work proposed a new function reuse approach as an alternative to logic-costly specific hardware in soft-core designs. We showed that it is possible to improve software libraries that substitute specialized hardware, using highly available BRAMs. Our scheme is able to perform precise and approximate reuse using much less logic than specific hardware, making low-cost targets to regain space in the design space. As future work, we will consider a multi-core environment, providing reusability for multiple programs at similar hardware cost.

Acknowledgments. This work was supported in part by CNPq, CAPES and FAPERGS.

References

1. Fletcher, B.H.: FPGA embedded processors. In: Embedded Systems Conference. p. 18 (2005)
2. Beck, A.C.S., Lisbôa, C.A.L., Carro, L.: Adaptable Embedded Systems. Springer, New York (2012). Springer-Link: Bücher
3. Kuon, I., Rose, J.: Measuring the gap between FPGAs and ASICs. IEEE Trans. Comput. Aided Des. Integr. Circ. Syst. **26**(2), 203–2015 (2007)

4. Xilinx, Inc.: 7 Series FPGAs Memory Resources User Guide (UG473) (2016)
5. Sastry, S.S., Bodik, R., Smith, J.E.: Characterizing coarse-grained reuse of computation. In: Feedback Directed and Dynamic Optimization, pp. 16–18 (2000)
6. Hall, M., McNamee, J.P.: Improving software performance with automatic memoization. Johns Hopkins APL Tech. Dig. **18**(2), 255 (1997)
7. Sodani, A., Sohi, G.S.: Dynamic instruction reuse. In: Proceedings of 24th Symposium on Computer Architecture (ISCA), vol. 25, no. 2, pp. 194–205 (1997)
8. Citron, D., Feitelson, D., Rudolph, L.: Accelerating multi-media processing by implementing memoing in multiplication and division units. ACM SIGPLAN Not. **33**(11), 252–261 (1998)
9. Huang, J., Lilja, D.J.: Exploiting basic block value locality with block reuse. In: Proceeedings of Symposium on High-Performance Computer Architecture, pp. 106–114. IEEE (1999)
10. González, A., Tubella, J., Molina, C.: Trace-level reuse. In: International Conference on Parallel Processing, pp. 30–37. IEEE (1999)
11. Kavi, K.M., Chen, P.: Dynamic function result reuse. In: Proceedings of Conference on Advanced Computing, pp. 17–20 (2003)
12. Suresh, A., Swamy, B.N., Rohou, E., Seznec, A.: Intercepting functions for memoization: a case study using transcendental functions. ACM Trans. Archit. Code Optim. (TACO) **12**(2), 18 (2015)
13. Alvarez, C., Corbal, J., Valero, M.: Fuzzy memoization for floating-point multimedia applications. IEEE Trans. Comput. **54**(7), 922–927 (2005)
14. Keramidas, G., Kokkala, C., Stamoulis, I.: Clumsy value cache: an approximate memoization technique for mobile GPU fragment shaders. In: Workshop On Approximate Computing, P. 6 (2015)
15. Brandalero, M., da Silveira, L.A., Souza, J.D., Beck, A.C.S.: Accelerating error-tolerant applications with approximate function reuse. Sci. Comput. Program. (2017)
16. Sinha, S., Zhang, W.: Low-power FPGA design using memoization-based approximate computing. IEEE Trans. Very Large Scale Integr. (VLSI) Syst. **24**(8), 2665–2678 (2016)
17. Wong, S., van As, T., Brown, G.: ρ-VEX: a reconfigurable and extensible softcore VLIW processor. In: Conference on Field-Programmable Technology, pp. 369–372 (2008)
18. Hewlett-Packard Laboratories: VEX Toolchain (2009)
19. Gustafsson, J., Betts, A., Ermedahl, A., Lisper, B.: The Mälardalen WCET benchmarks: past, present and future. In: WCET, vol. 15, pp. 136–146 (2010)
20. Scott, J., Lee, L.H., Arends, J., Moyer, B.: Designing the low-power M•CORE™ architecture. In: Power Driven Microarchitecture Workshop, pp. 145–150 (1998)
21. Yazdanbakhsh, A., Mahajan, D., Esmaeilzadeh, H., Lotfi-Kamran, P.: AxBench: a multiplatform benchmark suite for approximate computing. IEEE Des. Test **34**(2), 60–68 (2017)
22. Lattner, C., Adve, V.: LLVM: a compilation framework for lifelong program analysis & transformation. In: Proceedings of Symposium Code Generation and Optimization: Feedback-Directed and Runtime Optimization, p. 75. IEEE Computer Society (2004)
23. Lungdren, D.: FPU Double VHDL (2014)
24. Chaple, G., Daruwala, R.D.: Design of Sobel operator based image edge detection algorithm on FPGA. In: International Conference on Communications and Signal Processing, pp. 788–792. IEEE (2014)

A Parallel-Pipelined OFDM Baseband Modulator with Dynamic Frequency Scaling for 5G Systems

Mário Lopes Ferreira[1]($\boxtimes$) ⓘ, João Canas Ferreira[1] ⓘ, and Michael Huebner[2] ⓘ

[1] Faculty of Engineering, INESC TEC, University of Porto,
Rua Dr. Roberto Frias, s/n, 4200-465 Porto, Portugal
{mario.l.ferreira,joao.c.ferreira}@inesctec.pt
[2] Embedded Systems for Information Technology, Ruhr-University Bochum,
Bochum, Germany
michael.huebner@rub.de

Abstract. 5G heterogeneity will cover a huge diversity of use cases, ranging from enhanced-broadband to low-throughput and low-power communications. To address such requirements variety, this paper proposes a parallel-pipelined architecture for an OFDM baseband modulator with clock frequency run-time adaptation through dynamic frequency scaling (DFS). It supports a set of OFDM numerologies recently proposed for 5G communication systems. The parallel-pipelined architecture can achieve high throughputs at low clock frequencies (up to 520.3 MSamples/s at 160 MHz) and DFS allows for the adjustment of baseband processing clock frequency according to immediate throughput demands. The application of DFS increases the system's power efficiency by allowing power savings up to 62.5%; the resource and latency overhead is negligible.

Keywords: OFDM modulator · 5G · Baseband processing · FPGA
Parallel-pipelined architecture · Dynamic frequency scaling

1 Introduction

The fifth generation of cellular communications (5G) intends to provide an unprecedented range of services to an ever increasing number of users. To do so, 5G will definitely surpass previous generations in terms of data bandwidth, latency requirements, system capacity, energy consumption and spectrum efficiency. However, it will also be necessary to support many low-rate connections

This work is financed by the ERDF - European Regional Development Fund through the Operational Programme for Competitiveness and Internationalisation - COMPETE 2020 Programme within project *POCI-01-0145-FEDER-006961*, by National Funds through the FCT - Fundação para a Ciência e a Tecnologia (Portuguese Foundation for Science and Technology), through the Ph.D. Grant *PD/BD/105860/2014* and the Supplementary Training Grant *CRM:0067654*.

© Springer International Publishing AG, part of Springer Nature 2018
N. Voros et al. (Eds.): ARC 2018, LNCS 10824, pp. 511–522, 2018.
https://doi.org/10.1007/978-3-319-78890-6_41

and to smoothly integrate previous generation communication standards [1]. Consequently, a 5G communication environment should fulfill the needs of thousands of interconnected users with different requirements regarding data rates, latencies, energy consumption and other quality-of-service (QoS) factors [10].

Waveform design and numerology (i.e. waveform parametrization based on communication requirements and channel conditions) are the base for the physical layer (PHY) design of 5G radio access technology. Despite the recent proposal of several alternative waveforms, Orthogonal Frequency Division Multiplexing (OFDM) remains a strong and viable 5G waveform candidate because of its high flexibility, MIMO compatibility, reasonable baseband complexity and easy integration with current OFDM-based standards (e.g. LTE and WiFi) [1]. Due to the great variety of 5G communication system requirements, new and flexible OFDM numerologies must be studied and proposed. This flexibility should also be reflected in the design of digital hardware infrastructures for future wireless devices, such that they can operate using different standards and under changing communication conditions.

The parallelism and flexibility of FPGAs makes them a good hardware platform for the design of wireless baseband processing infrastructures, in particular for base stations [13]. However, for high-performance 5G scenarios, the throughput requirements may approach or surpass the clock rates provided by current FPGA technology. Moreover, pushing the FPGA clock frequency to its limits has a negative impact on power consumption. To reach these hard real-time signal processing requirements while maintaining reasonable clock frequencies, baseband processors should be able to receive multiple samples of the same input data sequence in a single clock cycle and process them in parallel [10]. On the other hand, another concern in future wireless devices is energy efficiency [1]. As high-throughput processing will not always be required, run-time clock frequency adaptation would contribute to a more power-efficient system.

This paper presents a power efficient, FPGA-based, parallel-pipelined architecture for an OFDM baseband modulator supporting 5G numerologies. Our approach starts from the analysis of the OFDM modulator datapath structure and dependencies to propose an architecture that receives the data needed to produce an OFDM symbol via four parallel inputs, processes it by four parallel pipelines and provides the resulting OFDM symbol on four parallel outputs. In a real-case scenario, the higher layers of the communication system would provide every D data subcarriers divided in four parallel input data streams. Then, the four modulator output data streams would be fed to a higher-frequency Digital-to-Analog converter (DAC) or to a set of lower-frequency interleaved DACs [10]. Through Dynamic Frequency Scaling (DFS) the design can adapt the clock frequency for baseband processing at run-time according to communication throughput demands. The system was implemented on a Xilinx xc7z045-2ffg900c device and shows a throughput performance compatible with recently proposed OFDM numerologies for 5G systems. The results also highlight the power savings achieved through DFS techniques.

After this introductory section, Sect. 2 presents fundamental background about OFDM modulation, as well as new 5G numerologies and lists related work on FPGA-based implementations for OFDM modulators. Section 3 introduces our proposed OFDM modulator architecture which is later evaluated in Sect. 4. Finally, Sect. 5 concludes the paper.

2   Fundamental Background and Related Work

OFDM is a Discrete Fourier Transform-based multicarrier modulation technique whose hardware realization is efficiently performed with FFT and Inverse FFT (IFFT) modules. For this reason, it is used in several applications such as digital audio and video broadcast, digital subscriber lines and wireless local area networks. The basic sequence of operations carried out by the an OFDM modulator is depicted in Fig. 1.

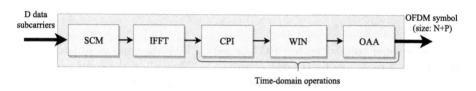

Fig. 1. OFDM modulation datapath structure

First, a stream of D data subcarriers is mapped into an array of N subcarriers (where $N > D$) and a null DC component is inserted - *subcarrier mapping* (SCM). The OFDM waveform synthesis is actually performed through an N-point IFFT operation, which is the operation with higher computational and arithmetic complexity in the datapath. The IFFT operation converts data from the frequency to the time domain and produces a simple OFDM symbol. Then, to increase OFDM spectral selectivity, a cyclic prefix (CP) extension of length P, whose content is part of the symbol's final samples, is prepended to the OFDM symbol produced by the IFFT block - *cyclic prefix insertion* (CPI). Finally, time-domain windowing (WIN) and adjacent symbols overlap-and-add (OAA) are combined - weighted overlap-and-add (WOLA) - to suppress out-of-band leakage. The WOLA operation comprises the multiplication of both symbol head and tail by a raised-cosine window of length W and the addition of a symbol's tail to the head of the following symbol. The modulator input and output data symbols have different sizes: taking D values on the input, the modulator produces a symbol with $N + P$ complex samples.

Regarding new OFDM numerologies for 5G, some effort has been made to provide waveform parametrization for the utilization of previous unused spectrum bands (e.g. millimeter-wave band) [8,14]. Nevertheless, to cover all types of 5G services, new numerologies should be flexible rather than focused on a specific set of use cases. Zaidi et al. [19] picked the LTE numerology as the base to design a family of OFDM numerologies for 5G services and requirements. Table 1 presents several modes of operation included in this numerology family, which range from sub-6 GHz to over-40 GHz spectrum bands. These numerologies are easy to implement, as switching between them only requires the sampling clock frequency scaling, without changing parameters like IFFT size or CP length.

Table 1. OFDM numerologies for 5G services and requirements proposed in [19]. The IFFT size (N) is 4096 and the CP length (P) is 288.

Spectrum band	up to 6 GHz	up to 20 GHz	up to 40 GHz	above 40 GHz
Subcarrier spacing (kHz)	15	30	60	120
Clock frequency (MHz)	61.44	122.88	245.76	491.52
Symbol duration (µs)	66.77	33.33	16.67	8.34
CP duration (µs)	4.69	2.35	1.17	0.58

Conventional approaches to FPGA-based OFDM baseband modulators usually follow a simple pipelined architecture [4,6]. They allow the continuous flow of data using a reasonable amount of resources and, in steady-state operation, are able to produce one sample per clock cycle. Running at clock frequencies below 100 MHz, these architectures satisfy the throughput requirements for 3G/4G. In particular, the transmitter architecture proposed in [6] supports three different 3G/4G standards and explores DFS to change the clock frequency according to the standard in use. The system is implemented on a Xilinx Virtex-5 FPGA device and the Digital Clock Manager output frequency is reconfigured via the FPGA dynamic reconfiguration port. However, the benefit of DFS in terms of power consumption is not evaluated.

These simple pipelined architectures can perform well for the lower clock frequencies from Table 1. However, despite the claims about high-speed radio FPGA design from [15], it is very challenging to design FPGA systems for complex DSP processing that operate at clock frequencies near or above 500 MHz. Furthermore, such a high performance design is not needed for every use case, leading to system over-optimization. There is also the high power consumption associated with high clock rates. So, the proposal of alternative high-throughput architectures that can operate at lower clock frequencies is relevant.

Meyer et al. [11] presented an alternative multiprocessor System on Chip architecture for a software-defined, high-speed OFDM modulator and implemented it on a Xilinx Virtex-6 FPGA device. From a high level perspective, the architecture has a control system connected via an asynchronous bus bridge to a signal processing system (SPS) that performs OFDM baseband operations. The SPS consists of multiple processors specialized in several baseband processing operations (e.g. IFFT or constellation mapping), as well as Block RAM structures connected by a bus system. The SPS is configured to implement four independent and parallel OFDM modulators that produce two samples per clock cycle each (parallelism level of $4 \times 2 = 8$). Running at a clock frequency of 125 MHz, the system achieves a throughput of 720 MSample/s. The OFDM modulator considered is simplified and does not include operations like subcarrier mapping or WOLA. This architecture is convenient when multiple independent data sequences have to be processed and baseband processors can simply be replicated to increase data throughput. This is the case for multiple-input multiple-output (MIMO) communication scenarios.

On the other hand, *parallel-pipelined architectures* are used when multiple chunks of the same input data sequence have to be simultaneously processed in a combined way. Garrido et al. [5] studied and proposed this type of architecture for IFFT/FFT cores to achieve high throughputs with lower clock frequencies.

Our design extends the design principle of parallel-pipelined architectures to the OFDM modulator datapath illustrated in Fig. 1. In contrast with [11], we attempt to parallelize the processing of each individual OFDM symbol instead of replicating OFDM processing datapath to process independent symbols in parallel. To our best knowledge, an extension of parallel-pipelined architectures to all OFDM baseband modulation hasn't been presented yet. In addition, we also evaluate DFS impact on power consumption.

3   Parallel-Pipelined OFDM Modulator Design

A parallel-pipelined architecture with run-time clock frequency adaptation for an OFDM baseband modulator was designed and implemented on an FPGA. In this architecture, the data samples to produce an OFDM symbol are received via s parallel input streams and the modulator considers data dependencies between these s streams to process them in parallel. The output time-domain OFDM symbols are divided in s chunks transmitted via s parallel output streams. In this work, we consider four pipelined streams ($s = 4$), but the extension for other of powers-of-two values of s is straight-forward.

For system validation purposes, we have considered the numerologies presented in Table 1. So the IFFT size (N) is 4096 and the cyclic prefix length (P) is 288. We also assume that the input data consists of 16-QAM modulated complex values. The number of data subcarriers per OFDM symbol (D) is 2552 and, for the WOLA operation, the time-domain raised cosine window has a size (W) of 32 samples. The baseband processing datapath is 16-bit wide and the arithmetic operations are done in fixed-point precision (Q5.11 format for real and imaginary parts). Next, the parallel-pipelined architecture for the OFDM modulator and the adopted dynamic frequency scaling mechanism are described.

The proposed parallel-pipelined architecture is based on the parallelization of the datapath operations involved in the OFDM modulation (Fig. 1), which were briefly introduced in Sect. 2. Throughout this section, the sizes of the input/output streams of each module refer to the amount of data samples required to process and produce one OFDM symbol.

The task of the *subcarrier mapping* module (SCM) is to build a frequency-domain symbol to be processed by the IFFT core. This symbol is composed of

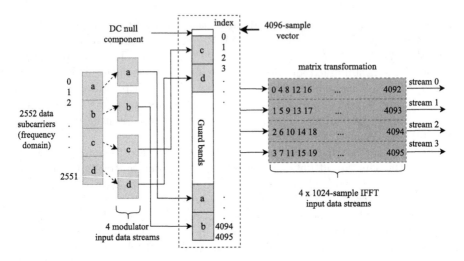

Fig. 2. Basic operation of the parallel-pipelined *subcarrier mapping* module

data subcarriers and guard bands. We assume that the SCM module receives each set of 2552 (D) data subcarriers divided in four contiguous blocks of size 638 ($D/4$). These blocks are simultaneously mapped into a 4096-sample (N-sample) vector to form a frequency-domain symbol, according to the scheme illustrated in Fig. 2. To parallelize the processing of this frequency domain symbol, its samples are rearranged into a 4×1024 ($4 \times N/4$) matrix, following the index transformations from [12]. Each 1024-element row corresponds to an IFFT input stream. Due to this IFFT input reordering, the output IFFT streams will correspond to contiguous time-domain chunks of the overall OFDM symbol. This facilitates the subsequent time-domain datapath operations: cyclic prefix insertion, windowing and overlap-and-add. In pipeline operation, the SCM module receives four input samples and produces four output samples per clock cycle. This requires four write and read operations on the 4096-sample array. Thus, this array is implemented with a BRAM-based quad-port memory. Additionally, control engines to manage write/read operations on the BRAM-based quad-port memory are included in the SCM module.

The four 1024-sample output streams provided by the SCM module are fed to the IFFT module, which has the highest computational and arithmetic complexity within the datapath. Following the divide-and-conquer FFT algorithm proposed by Cooley and Tukey [2], an N-point FFT can be recursively decomposed into smaller size FFTs. Considering the factorization $4096 = 1024 \times 4$, a 4096-FFT core can be implemented with four 1024-FFT cores followed by one 4-FFT core. The algorithm also requires the complex rotation of each 1024-FFT output by twiddle factors before feeding them to the final 4-FFT core. In turn, an IFFT core can be obtained from an FFT core simply by swapping the real and imaginary parts of the inputs and outputs. For each OFDM symbol, the IFFT module receives and outputs four 1024-sample streams.

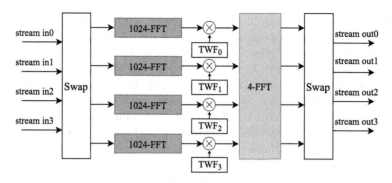

Fig. 3. Internal structure of the parallel-pipelined IFFT module

The architecture adopted for the 4096-IFFT core is depicted in Fig. 3. The four parallel 1024-FFT cores follow the Radix-2^2 Single-Delay Feedback pipelined architecture proposed in [7] and the 4-FFT core structure was derived from the direct implementation of Radix-4 butterfly expressions [9]. Due to the input index arrangement adopted in the SCM module, the IFFT output streams 0 and 3 correspond to the beginning and end of the time-domain OFDM symbol, respectively. This correspondence holds for the subsequent datapath modules.

As previously mentioned, the time-domain operations after the IFFT module are simplified by the natural order of the IFFT output streams. In fact, the *cyclic prefix insertion* (CPI), *windowing* (WIN) and *overlap-and-add* (OAA) operations (Fig. 4) only involve the beginning (IFFT output stream 0) and the end (IFFT output stream 3) of the OFDM symbol. Thus, IFFT output streams 1 and 2 remain unchanged through the CPI, WIN and OAA modules. Yet, registers and other storage structures are used to keep these streams synchronized with streams 0 and 3.

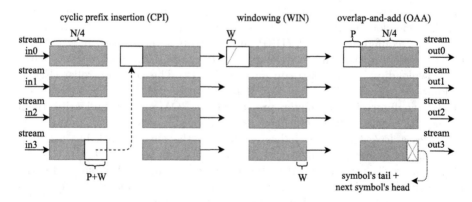

Fig. 4. Basic functioning of the time-domain operations: *cyclic prefix insertion, windowing* and *overlap-and-add*

Apart from inserting a cyclic prefix extension, the CPI module also creates room for the windowing operation. In our parallel-pipelined architecture, it is necessary to copy the last $P + W$ samples of the input stream 3 and prepend them to the input stream 0. Consequently, the size of the output stream 0 is 1344 $(N/4 + P + W)$, while the other three output streams keep the 1024-sample size $(N/4)$. BRAMs are used to store the incoming data streams and a finite state machine (FSM) controls the BRAM write/read operations.

For the WIN module, the OFDM symbol's head and tail are weighted (multiplied) by raised-cosine window coefficients. Only the first 32 (W) samples of the input stream 0 and the last 32 samples of the input stream 3 are affected. This module is implemented using two 16-bit real multipliers (to weight both real and imaginary part separately), one ROM storing 32 16-bit window coefficients, multiplexer structures and a control FSM to manage ROM addressing and the data flow through the module. The output stream size for all streams is the same of the corresponding input streams: 1344 for stream 0 and 1024 for the other three streams.

The OAA is the last module in the OFDM modulator datapath. Its function is to overlap the tail of a time-domain OFDM symbol with the head of the next symbol. Both 32 samples of the head and tail were previously weighted in the WIN module. The OAA operation reduces the size of the stream 0, as its first 32 samples are extracted and overlapped with the last 32 samples of the previous symbol. Thus, on the output side of the OFDM modulator, the stream 0 has a size of 1312 $(N/4 + P)$ and the streams 1–3 have a size of 1024 $(N/4)$. So, the size of a whole OFDM symbol produced by the parallel-pipelined architecture proposed is $N + P$, which corresponds to the OFDM time-domain symbol size mentioned in Sect. 2. The constituent elements of the OAA module are a 16-bit adder to perform the head-tail addition, mux-/demux-structures to correctly forward the data samples to be overlapped and an FSM to control and synchronize the whole module operation.

Dynamic Frequency Scaling is implemented following the method presented in [16]. It allows the dynamic adaptation of the output clock frequency of the mixed-mode clock managers (MMCMs) in Xilinx 7-series FPGAs. Through the dynamic reconfiguration port (DRP) in the MMCM primitives, it is possible to write configuration bits to dynamically change MMCM clock outputs without downloading a new bitstream into the FPGA. The DFS controller (Fig. 5) includes an instantiation of an MMCM primitive, as well as an FSM that reads MMCM configuration parameters pre-stored in a ROM memory and writes them to the DRP. Apart from generating a user-configurable output clock, the MMCM generates a *locked* flag that indicates whether the output clock has achieved phase and frequency alignment with the reference input clock (*clk_in*).

In this work, we considered a 100 MHz reference input clock signal for the DFS controller and we defined MMCM configuration parameters for four output clock modes corresponding to four baseband processing clock frequencies (f_{clkBB}): 20 MHz (mode 0), 40 MHz (mode 1), 80 MHz (mode 2) and 160 MHz

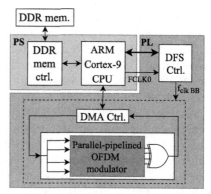

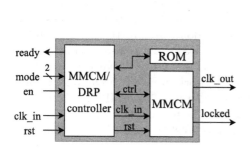

Fig. 5. Dynamic frequency scaling controller structure

Fig. 6. Overall system architecture

(mode 3). To change f_{clkBB}, the DFS controller input signal *en* must be enabled and the desired mode of operation should be given through the *mode* port.

4 Evaluation and Discussion

The architecture previously presented was implemented on a Xilinx xc7z045-2ffg900c Zynq device which is comprised of a Processing System (PS) and a Programmable Logic (PL) section. The OFDM modulator and the DFS controller are implemented on the PL section. The PS is used to setup data transfers between the DDR memory (that stores the data to be processed) and the OFDM modulator. It also issues clock frequency adaptation commands to the DFS controller. A simplified wrapper structure was implemented in the PL section to evaluate system performance. The overall system structure is depicted on Fig. 6.

To take advantage of the proposed architecture, the wrapper includes a DMA controller to accelerate the data transfers to the OFDM modulator. For sake of simplicity, the wrapper fetches a chunk of data from the DDR that is replicated and provided to the four parallel inputs of the OFDM modulator. To allow for continuous processing of data, the 4 data inputs and outputs of the OFDM modulator were implemented as 32-bit AXI4-Stream interfaces. On the output side of the modulator, the wrapper structure picks the four produced output streams and XORs them into a single output stream. As we intend to focus our analysis on the OFDM baseband modulator, the wrapper structure is simplified. It serves the purpose of providing an evaluation environment for the OFDM modulator with a low resource complexity and node activity, such that its share of resource usage and power consumption is reduced. The 100 MHz reference input clock signal for the DFS controller (FCLK0) is one of the four frequency-programmable clocks provided by the PS to the PL [17]. In turn, the OFDM modulator clock signal is the dynamically configurable clock output produced by the MMCM primitive - f_{clkBB}.

Through the comparison with a Matlab model, the functional correctness of the implemented OFDM modulator architecture was validated. The resource utilization for the OFDM modulator, DFS controller and wrapper structure are presented in Table 2. The biggest share of hardware resources is associated to the OFDM modulator, whose resource usage is dominated by the IFFT module. This module not only consumes most LUT and DSPs, but is also responsible for the majority of DSPs and BRAMs used in the system. It is hard to do a fair comparison between our architecture and the work from [11] because it simply replicates independent OFDM modulators and uses a small IFFT size (128), which deeply impacts the resource utilization. The parallel-pipelined 4096-IFFT core from [5] uses more slices and less DSPs (2388 slices; 60 DSPs) than our 4096-IFFT (2248 slices; 76 DSPs).

Table 2. Post-place and route resource utilization

Resource	Available (xc7z045)	Wrapper structure	DFS controller	OFDM modulator					
				SCM	IFFT	CPI	WIN	OAA	Total for the modulator
LUTs	218600	3576	70	350	5432	61	364	1226	7434 (3.4%)
FFs	437200	4783	79	327	6959	233	298	2545	11706 (2.7%)
BRAMs	545	2	0	16	39	4	0	0	59 (10.8%)
DSPs	900	0	0	0	76	0	2	0	78 (8.7%)

The resources used by the DFS controller are below 100 lookup tables (LUT) and flip-flops (FF). So, the DFS feature resource overhead is almost negligible. In our design, the clock frequency adaptation takes on average 2350 clock cycles, which represents a latency of 23.5 µs, considering a 100 MHz input clock signal for the DFS controller. As timing parameters for dynamic frequency selection in spectrum agile radios [3] are in the range of seconds, this latency is acceptable. Under continuous and real-time system operation scenarios, FIFO structures can be used to temporarily store incoming data during DFS procedures.

The proposed OFDM modulator architecture has a latency of 4484 clock cycles to produce the first output sample. For this reason, the achieved throughputs are slightly less than four times the f_{clkBB} values. Then, it enters steady-state operation and is able to produce four output samples per clock cycle. The modulator processing throughput and average power consumption for each considered f_{clkBB} value is presented in Table 3. The achieved throughputs satisfy the requirements from Table 1, even if the modulator operates at a clock frequency that is around a third of the sampling frequencies required.

The xc7z045-2ffg900c device is part of a ZC706 board which features a PMBus port. Using a Texas Instruments (TI) USB adapter attached to the PMBus port and the TI Fusion Digital Power Designer software, it is possible to measure and monitor the power consumption. The parameter monitored was

Table 3. OFDM modulator processing throughput, average power consumption and energy per sample versus clock frequency

f_{clkBB} (MHz)	20	40	80	160
Throughput (MSa/s)	65.1	130.1	260.2	520.3
Avg. power (W)	0.335	0.428	0.587	0.893
Energy per sample (mJ/MSa)	5.15	3.29	2.26	1.72

the output power of the VCCINT power rail, which is the PL internal supply providing an operating voltage of 1 V [18]. Power consumption was measured while the OFDM modulator was continuously receiving data from DDR and processing it. The experience was repeated for every f_{clkBB} considered in this work: 20, 40, 80 and 160 MHz. During all experiments, the room temperature was kept around 23 °C. Although the power consumption does not scale linearly with f_{clkBB}, it is still advantageous to adapt according to the communication requirements. When operating under low-throughput requirements, the adaptation of the OFDM modulator to a low-throughput mode can bring power reductions between 21.7% (changing from 40 to 20 MHz) to 62.5% (changing from 160 to 20 MHz). The lower processing times and energy per sample associated with higher f_{clkBB} values may suggest that it is advantageous to perform signal processing as fast as possible in any situation. However, in a communication environment where devices have different performance capabilities, low-throughput devices won't be able to follow the data rates imposed by high-throughput devices. Under these circumstances, faster devices can improve their power efficiency by downscaling their clock frequency without compromising the quality of service.

5   Conclusions

This paper proposes a parallel-pipelined architecture for an OFDM baseband modulator implemented on a xc7z045 FPGA device. The parallelization of the OFDM modulation datapath operations into multiple combined pipeline structures, achieves high processing throughputs at low clock frequencies. The proposed system employs dynamic frequency scaling to adapt the clock frequency for baseband processing, according to the different throughput requirements defined in a family of OFDM numerologies proposed for 5G systems. The achieved processing throughputs range from 65.1 MSample/s (at 20 MHz clock frequency) to 520 MSample/s (at 160 MHz clock frequency). Dynamic frequency scaling has a negligible resource overhead and the switching between clock frequency modes introduces a latency that is tolerable in wireless communications: 23.5 µs on average. In our system, the clock frequency adaptation can reduce power consumption by up to 62.5%, thus improving the system's power efficiency.

References

1. Andrews, J., Buzzi, S., Choi, W., Hanly, S., Lozano, A., Soong, A., Zhang, J.: What will 5G be? IEEE J. Sel. Areas Commun. **32**(6), 1065–1082 (2014)
2. Cooley, J.W., Tukey, J.W.: An algorithm for the machine calculation of complex Fourier series. Math. Comput. **19**(90), 297–301 (1965). http://www.jstor.org/stable/2003354
3. ETSI: 5 GHz RLAN; Harmonised Standard covering the essential requirements of article 3.2 of Directive 2014/53/EU. Technical report, Draft ETSI EN 301 893 v2.1.1, ETSI, May 2017. http://www.etsi.org/standards
4. Ferreira, M.L., Barahimi, A., Ferreira, J.C.: Dynamically reconfigurable LTE-compliant OFDM modulator for downlink transmission. In: 2016 Conference on Design of Circuits and Integrated Systems, November 2016
5. Garrido, M., Grajal, J., Sanchez, M.A., Gustafsson, O.: Pipelined radix-2^k feedforward FFT architectures. IEEE Trans. Very Large Scale Integr. Syst. **21**(1), 23–32 (2013)
6. He, K., Crockett, L., Stewart, R.: Dynamic reconfiguration technologies based on FPGA in software defined radio system. J. Sig. Process. Syst. **69**(1), 75–85 (2011)
7. He, S., Torkelson, M.: A new approach to pipeline FFT processor. In: Proceedings of IPPS 1996, The 10th International Parallel Processing Symposium, April 1996
8. Huang, L., Wang, Y., Shi, Z., Wen, R.: Radio parameter design for OFDM-based millimeter-wave systems. In: 2016 IEEE 27th Annual International Symposium on Personal, Indoor, and Mobile Radio Communications, September 2016
9. Lin, S.J., Chung, W.H.: The split-radix fast Fourier transforms with radix-4 butterfly units. In: 2013 Asia-Pacific Signal and Information Processing Association Annual Summit and Conference, October 2013
10. Luo, F., Zhang, C.: Signal Processing for 5G: Algorithms and Implementations. Wiley - IEEE, Indianapolis (2016)
11. Meyer, J., Dreschmann, M., Karnick, D., Schindler, P.C., Freude, W., Leuthold, J., Becker, J.: A novel system on chip for software-defined, high-speed OFDM signal processing. In: 26th Symposium on Integrated Circuits and Systems Design, September 2013
12. Meyer-Baese, U.: Digital Signal Processing with Field Programmable Gate Arrays. Springer, Heidelberg (2004). https://doi.org/10.1007/978-3-540-72613-5
13. Moy, C., Palicot, J.: Software radio: a catalyst for wireless innovation. IEEE Commun. Mag. **53**(9), 24–30 (2015)
14. Nokia: White Paper - The 5G mmWave revolution. Technical report. SR1610000323EN, Nokia Corporation (2016). https://resources.ext.nokia.com/asset/200779
15. Pecot, M.: Enabling High-Speed Radio Designs with Xilinx All Programmable FPGAs and SoCs. Technical report. WP445, Xilinx Inc., January 2014. v1.0
16. Tatsukawa, J.: XAPP888 - MMCM and PLL Dynamic Reconfiguration. Xilinx Inc., v1.7
17. Xilinx Inc.: UG585 - Zynq-7000 Technical Reference Manual, v1.11
18. Xilinx Inc.: UG954 - ZC706 Evaluation Board for the Zynq-7000 XC7Z045 All Programmable SoC User Guide, v1.6
19. Zaidi, A.A., Baldemair, R., Tullberg, H., Bjorkegren, H., Sundstrom, L., Medbo, J., Kilinc, C., Silva, I.D.: Waveform and numerology to support 5G services and requirements. IEEE Commun. Mag. **54**(11), 90–98 (2016)

Area-Energy Aware Dataflow Optimisation of Visual Tracking Systems

Paulo Garcia[1], Deepayan Bhowmik[2(✉)], Andrew Wallace[1], Robert Stewart[3], and Greg Michaelson[3]

[1] School of Engineering and Physical Sciences,
Heriot-Watt University, Edinburgh EH14 4AS, UK
{p.garcia,a.m.wallace}@hw.ac.uk
[2] Department of Computing, Sheffield Hallam University, Sheffield S1 1WB, UK
deepayan.bhowmik@shu.ac.uk
[3] School of Mathematical and Computer Sciences,
Heriot-Watt University, Edinburgh EH14 4AS, UK
{r.stewart,g.michaelson}@hw.ac.uk

Abstract. This paper presents an orderly dataflow-optimisation approach suitable for area-energy aware computer vision applications on FPGAs. Vision systems are increasingly being deployed in power constrained scenarios, where the dataflow model of computation has become popular for describing complex algorithms. Dataflow model allows processing datapaths comprised of several independent and well defined computations. However, compilers are often unsuccessful in identifying domain-specific optimisation opportunities resulting in wasted resources and power consumption. We present a methodology for the optimisation of dataflow networks, according to patterns often found in computer vision systems, focusing on identifying optimisations which are not discovered automatically by an optimising compiler. Code transformation using profiling and refactoring provides opportunities to optimise the design, targeting FPGA implementations and focusing on area and power abatement. Our refactoring methodology, applying transformations to a complex algorithm for visual tracking resulted in significant reduction in power consumption and resource usage.

1 Introduction

The dataflow model of computation has become popular in the image processing/computer vision domain for describing complex algorithms [14]. Currently, several different languages and compilers exist for myriad implementation platforms, *e.g.*, processor architectures, GPUs and FPGAs [6], as well as heterogeneous combinations. The computation model, *i.e.*, independent, parallel actors encapsulating computations, connected to form a dataflow network, is ideal for separation of concerns, computational composition and code re-use. In computer vision, where several low level image processing patterns are frequently re-used [13], a dataflow model allows expressing an algorithm as a processing datapath comprised of several independent and well defined computations.

© Springer International Publishing AG, part of Springer Nature 2018
N. Voros et al. (Eds.): ARC 2018, LNCS 10824, pp. 523–536, 2018.
https://doi.org/10.1007/978-3-319-78890-6_42

When implementing *simple* algorithms, where *simple* means static complexity, stateless computations, predictable runtimes and no feedback loops, it is straightforward for a dataflow compiler to analyse the code and identify optimisation opportunities [16]; and refactoring the dataflow network in order to optimise particular metric(s), *e.g.*, area, power, performance. However, contemporary computer vision algorithms are, more often than not, dynamic in complexity, stateful, variable in runtime and result in dataflow networks with feedback loops [15]; thus, they exhibit properties which hinder compiler optimisations [11]: it is left to the designer to manually optimise for the given metrics, which is a non-trivial task in the lack of a formally defined methodology.

Literature suggests generic dataflow specific optimizations that are often non-domain specific and hence do not consider any common patterns in related algorithms. For example, Hueske *et al.* [5] leverage static code analysis to extract information from Map-Reduce-style user-defined functions where the approach is only applicable to Map-Reduce-style code. Based on the post-processing of dataflow execution traces, Brunet *et al.* [2] present a methodology that enables designers to make principled choices in the design space focusing solely on buffer sizes. Schulte *et al.* [12] have identified the problem of power optimizations in dataflow and researched the use of genetic optimization algorithms for software implementations, but did not consider hardware implementations. Kim *et al.* [7] presented a framework for algorithm acceleration from the dataflow to synthesized HDL design, but do not consider size or power.

In this paper, we describe a methodology for the optimisation of dataflow networks, according to patterns often found in computer vision systems. This methodology and associated techniques will be of use for computer vision algorithm designers who must optimise their implementations to meet some metric budget; particularly relevant in remote or mobile applications, where size and power are first class concerns. We demonstrate and evaluate our refinements using a popular complex dynamic computer vision algorithm, mean shift object tracking [3], targeting FPGAs, which are becoming increasingly ubiquitous deployment platforms for remote/mobile computer vision. To the best of our knowledge, such an approach towards area-energy aware domain specific dataflow optimisation is first of its kind.

2   Background

Vision systems are increasingly being deployed in power constrained scenarios, such as automotive, robotics or remote sensing. Whilst deployment on CPU/GPU combinations has been the norm in the past few years, the constrained power budget has motivated the adoption of FPGAs as standard deployment platforms [9]. Softcore solutions for image processing have emerged and the research zeitgeist is the development of novel low-power techniques [18]. In this paper, we target power and size constraints in dataflow based design flows of image processing/computer vision systems.

2.1 Dataflow

A dataflow graph models a program as a directed graph. The model is depicted in Fig. 1. *Tokens* move between asynchronously communicating stateful and well defined functional blocks called *actors*. They transform input streams into output streams via *ports*, connected with *wires*. Inside an actor is a series of fireable sequences of instructions. These instructions are encapsulated within *actions*, and the steps an actor takes determines which ports tokens are consumed and emitted and also which state-modifying instructions are executed. The conceptual dataflow model of explicit data streaming and functional units maps well onto FPGA design comprising explicit wires and basic building blocks [17].

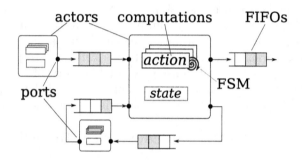

Fig. 1. The dataflow process model

Our dataflow transformations are implemented into Orcc [19] that compiles CAL, a Dataflow Process Network (DPN) [8] language implementation with dynamic properties: *e.g.*, *guards* can be attached to an action to predicate its firing not only on the availability of a token on a given port, but also on its value; explicit *finite state machine* (FSM) transitions between actions, an implicit predication on firing actions as only actions reachable within one transition in the FSM declaration are fireable; *priority* statements declare an inequality between two actions.

2.2 Power on FPGAs

Power consumption on FPGAs consists of *(a)* *static power*, which is directly proportional to the amount of used logic, technology & transistor types; and *(b)* *dynamic power*, which is a weighted sum of several components (these include clock signal propagation power, proportional to clock frequency; signals power, proportional to signal switching rates, among others). Power consumption minimization techniques can be broadly classified in: *(1)* computation independent and *(2)* computation dependent. *Computation independent* techniques neither alter the behavior nor the results of a system which include clock/power/input gating of unused sub-systems [10], dynamic frequency scaling according to load [4] and different implementation strategies (*e.g.*, BRAMs or LUTs) of the given algorithmic.

Computation dependent techniques modify the behavior and/or the results of a system, minimizing power consumption at the expense of performance or accuracy. These include *(1) stored data bit width*: by minimizing the number of bits stored, both static and dynamic power can be reduced as a consequence of smaller required data structures (BRAMs or LUTs). For example, it is possible to discard several least significant bits in image pixels either evenly across color channels; *(2) computation bit width*: by minimizing bit widths of signals used for computations, smaller datapaths (eliminating least significant bits) or range (eliminating most significant bits using saturated arithmetic) can be realized; *(3) arithmetic approximations*: performing calculations on integers rather than floating point numbers consumes less power. Numerical approximations, *e.g.*, square root, trigonometric functions, can be quantized to require less logic; *(4) iterations*: upper limits on algorithm convergence criteria directly impact the number of computations perform (also relates to numerical approximations); and *(5) data access ordering*: when using external memory, high spatial locality greatly contributes to reducing power consumption. All of these optimizations are realizable at the expense of an acceptable reduction in algorithmic accuracy.

3   Area-Energy Aware Implementation Refinements

Our methodology consists of a profiling-refactoring loop, where profiling identifies optimization opportunities and refactoring applies code transformations to optimize the design. Profiling is performed in an orderly fashion considering three major domain specific power-area optimization criteria, observed in computer vision algorithms: *(a)* streamlined memory usage, *(b)* back-propagation of bit width requirements and *(c)* dataflow actor fusion. Profiling is done through simulations, aided by automated tools, and focuses on identifying optimizations which are not discovered automatically by a general purpose non-domain specific optimizing compiler due to nuances in dataflow semantics. To show the effectiveness of our method, we present a case study (implemented in Orcc-CAL dataflow language) of a popular mean shift visual tracking algorithm. However, the proposed methods are portable across other vision algorithms. Because we target FPGA implementations, we focus our analysis on area and power optimizations, rather than performance which has been already addressed in details by related work [15].

3.1   Streamlined Memory Usage

Dataflow actors are independent computational units and every actor's internal memory requirements are eventually mapped to FPGA logic (*i.e.*, LUTs or BRAMs) and consume precious space and power. Hence, it is essential to minimize memory requirements without jeopardizing the algorithm. Our analysis of open-source code repositories[1] reveals several cases where actors can be

---

[1] https://github.com/orcc/orc-apps.

refactored to minimize memory usage: a recurring design pattern is the use of unnecessary local arrays. Consider the following code example, which calculates the mean value of an array of pixels:

Listing 1.1. Unnecessary array for pixel mean calculation

```
int  buffer[100];
int  count := 0;
getValues: action  Stream:[value]  ==>
do
          buffer[count]  := value;
          count := count + 1;
end
filter: action ==> mean:[val]
var int val
do
          val := buffer[0] + buffer[1] +...
          val := val/100;
end
```

This is a typical design pattern, where required values are read from input sources, stored in local arrays, then processed (action scheduling logic is not depicted). Now consider the following refactored code:

Listing 1.2. Pixel mean calculation with streamlined memory usage

```
filter: action  Stream:[values]  repeat 100
                 ==> mean:[(val[0]+val[1]=...)/100]
do
end
```

In this version, the number of required input data and the output data dependencies are explicit in the action declaration, removing the need for local arrays. Data is instead stored in the communication FIFOs used to link actors (*i.e.*, input stream). This optimisation is not automatically applied by optimising compilers because in the first version, the same data is used for read and write in two different actions. Automatic refactoring cannot be safely applied, unless the compiler is capable of determining that: (1) action firing order is temporaly consistent; (2) no other actions use this data; (3) the output calculation can be re-written in a (syntactically/semantically valid) single line. Precisely ensuring these conditions is still beyond compilers' static analysis capabilities, for languages with such varied semantics such as CAL.

3.2   Back-Propagation of Bit Width Requirements

A pervasive pattern in several image processing operations is quantisation, where values (typically pixel color/luminosity components or processed data such as histograms) are scaled down for normalization or other purposes. When values are quantized, lower resolution components (*i.e.*, least significant bits) are not

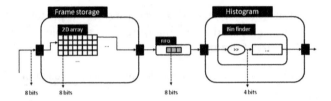

Fig. 2. Actor composition (frame storage and histogram) with bit width usage highlighted.

used for subsequent operations. Optimising compilers can reduce data dimensionality locally, *i.e.*, within a function or an actor, but are not capable of extrapolating these optimisations to broaden the range of optimised areas. This is especially prevalent in the dataflow paradigm, where quantization is performed in one actor, whilst the optimization opportunities are present in another; because communication between actors is performed through FIFO channels which establish data size, the compiler fails to infer the optimization. Figure 2 presents a depiction of this pattern, where the second actor (histogram) performs the following computation to determine the histogram bin:

Listing 1.3. Histogram computation

```
// uint (size=8)
procedure findBin(uint R, uint G, uint B)
var int r, int g, int b
begin
  r := R >> 4;
  g := G >> 4;
  b := B >> 4;
  binValue := r + (g << 4) + (b << 8);
end
```

In our approach, we identify code sections where unnecessary resolution is used, and we trace the flow of data across the network to determine where to reduce bit widths. In the previous histogram bin finding function, the lowest 4 bits of each datum are not required for computation and can be removed. Back propagating new width requirements, the network can be refactored into the one depicted in Fig. 3.

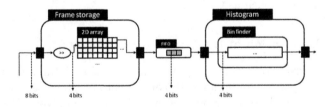

Fig. 3. Actor composition after bit width requirements back-propagation.

Again this optimisation is not automatically applied by optimising compilers because data dependencies are not calculated outside actors' boundaries. Safely applying this optimisation would require a compiler to statically determine that: (1) data sources are not used in any other calculation; (2) the communication channel is not used for any other data, and; (3) the shifting operation could safely be applied before data storage.

3.3 Actor Fusion

Another pervasive pattern in image processing, especially when composing systems using third-party code components, is that separation of concerns (*i.e.*, dedicating actors to specific tasks) leads to over-optimizations. Consider the example depicted in Fig. 4(a), where pipeline consists of an actor performing a smoothing filter operation followed by an actor performing binary thresholding. This sequential composition of operations results in a processing pipeline which is not necessarily balanced in function of data throughput. Consider the smoothing filter requires S time units for operation and the binary threshold requires T time units for operation. If latency between sequential data arrival is greater than $S + T$ time units, temporal parallelism offered by the pipeline does not offer any performance improvement. Instead, both actors can be fused in one that takes $S + T$ time units to compute, decreasing space and power costs (refer Fig. 4(b)).

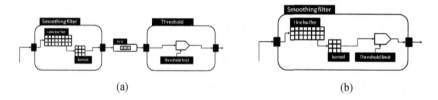

(a)   (b)

Fig. 4. (a) Over-optimised pipeline resulting in area/energy costs. (b) Optimised pipeline after actor fusion.

This optimisation is not automatically applied by optimising compilers because it requires some sort of profiling to determine execution times and throughputs, which cannot be performed automatically at compile time. Furthermore, even after profiling, a compiler would have to be able to ensure that: (1) profiled execution times would remain constant for any data input, and; (2) merging the two actors would not break the intended behaviour. If any of the two actors possessed additional ports, automatic optimisation would be further complicated, as the compiler would have to ensure that other functionalities remained unaffected by actor fusion.

Fig. 5. Example of single target mean shift visual tracking.

4   Case Study: Mean Shift Visual Tracking

We use a popular Mean shift tracking algorithm [3] as a use case for applying our methodologies. Mean shift tracking is an object tracking algorithm; given an object's initial position is the first frame, it tracks the object's position in subsequent frames. We use a benchmark data sets (http://www.cvg.reading.ac.uk/PETS2009/a.html) in our experiments, and have implemented the complete algorithm on a Xilinx Zedboard, connected to an external camera.

Mean shift [3] is a feature-space analysis technique for locating the maxima of a density function. An example of applying mean shift to image processing for visual tracking is shown in Fig. 5. The target is successfully tracked from the initial frame on the left, to the final frame on the right. The algorithm is a kernel based method normally applied using a symmetric Epanechnikov kernel within a pre-defined elliptical or rectangular window. The target region of an initial image is modelled with a probability density function (a colour histogram) and identifies a candidate position in the next image by finding the minimum distance between models using an iterative procedure. A summary is given in Algorithm 1.

Mean shift tracking exhibits several of the properties of computer vision that hinder automatic optimisations. It is a dynamic algorithm, *i.e.*, only worst case estimations of the time require for execution per frame can be performed, due to iterative loops with non-trivial termination conditions. It consists of several different components, each with very different levels of complexity. It is implemented as a network with feedback loops for recursion. Figure 6 depicts the full algorithm, implemented in CAL (https://goo.gl/TKpN7e).

Our implementation targets low-power FPGA implementations, and has been prototyped on a Xilinx Zedboard (https://goo.gl/tsqg1a). Only integer calculations are performed, and our prototype uses 320×240 frames supplied by an external camera. Software on the attached processor, which is used to feed the video from the FPGA to a remote computer over Ethernet, supplies the initial position (*i.e.*, which object to track) to the mean shift implementation.

Algorithm 1. Summary of Mean-shift visual tracking

Input: Target position y_0 on 1st frame;

1 Compute Epanechnikov kernel;

2 Calculate *target* color model $q_u(y_0)$ (*e.g.*, using RGB color histogram);

3 **repeat**

    Input: Receive next frame;

4   Calculate *target candidate* color model: $p_u(y_0)$;

5   Compute similarity function $\rho(y)$ between $q_u(y_0)$ & $p_u(y_0)$;

6   **repeat**

7   Derive the weights ω_i for each pixel in *target candidate* window;

8   Compute new target displacement y_1;

9   Compute new candidate colour model $q_u(y_1)$;

10   Evaluate similarity function $\rho(y)$ between $q_u(y_0)$ & $p_u(y_1)$;

11   **while** $\rho(y_1) < \rho(y_0)$ **do**

12   Do $y_1 \leftarrow 0.5(y_0 + y_1)$;

13   Evaluate $\rho(y)$ between $q_u(y_0)$ & $p_u(y_1)$;

14   **end**

15   **until** $|y_1 - y_0| < \epsilon$ *(near zero displacement)*;

    Output: y_1 *(Target position for current frame)*;

16   Set $y_0 \leftarrow y_1$ for next frame;

17 **until** *end of sequence*;

4.1 Meanshift Transformations

Our initial implementation of Meanshift did not consider any premature optimisations; rather, we attempted to be as faithful to the algorithmic description in Algorithm 1 as possible, following the dataflow paradigm; *i.e.*, each aspect of computations is performed by parallel actors. The *CAL_bin* actor depicted in Fig. 6 is the largest (both in code length and in FPGA resource usage) for two reasons: apart from computations, it also stores the current frame (hence, has the biggest memory requirements in the network) and is responsible for managing network state (*e.g.*, is it processing the first or subsequent frames).

We inspected compilation logs (both for CPU and FPGA backends) to ensure that no optimisations could be applied by the dataflow compiler. Subsequently, we applied our optimisation methodology and iteratively refined the implementation. At each iteration, we measured power consumption and performance (details are described in Sect. 5). We do not show detailed code/block diagram examples from Mean shift in this section, as the examples depicted in Sect. 3 are either identical or sufficiently similar to provide the reader with the necessary understanding.

The first optimisation was the actor fusion transformation (Sect. 3.3). We observed that the actor responsible for storing the Epanechnikov kernel and providing the results to *CAL_mModel* actor, *K_Array* (no longer depicted in the final version in Fig. 6) performed with the same speed and latency as the following actor (*CAL_mModel*), at a processing speed superior to the rate of

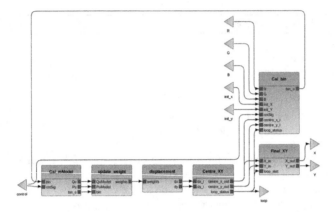

Fig. 6. Meanshift Tracking CAL dataflow process network (final optimised version).

data availability. Hence, we clearly identified an over-optimised pipeline which could be fused to reduce size and power.

The second optimisation applied was the transformation described in Sect. 3.1: streamlined memory usage. We observed that one of the computations in the *update_weight* actor read data from input sources, stored them in local arrays, then processed outputs. After refinement, the number of required input data and the output data dependencies became explicit in the action declaration (*i.e.*, performing a "pure" computation), removing the need for local arrays.

The final optimisation applied was the transformation described in Sect. 3.2: back-propagation of bit width requirements, and the one with the most substantial power/size gains. In the original un-optimised version, the *CAL_bin* actor stored the complete current frame; 3 times 320×240 8 bit values (one per RGB colour channel). These values were passed to a *histogram* actor which binned them according to value, performing the "Calculate *target candidate* color model: $p_u(y_0)$" step in the algorithm. After the transformation, previously depicted in Fig. 3, current frame storage required only 4 bits per value. Actors were subsequently fused.

5   Experimental Results and Discussions

At each iteration in our optimisation methodology, we characterized performance at both actor and network level using RTL simulation in Xilinx Vivado Design suite. We also calculated power consumption, at actor granularity, using Xilinx Power Analyzer embedded in the Vivado suite, reporting high confidence level. Simulation results were verified through physical implementation on a Xilinx Zedboard. Table 1 depicts approximate power and resource usage results for the examples described in Sect. 3. Because the impact of optimisations is highly dependent on their coverage, *i.e.*, what percentage of an actor is affected by the transformation, it is hard to accurately quantify transformation impact without

Table 1. Micro benchmarks results

Refinement	Power (W)		Usage	
	Original	Refined	Original	Refined
Streamlined memory usage	0.008	0.006	783/2012 (FF/LUTs)	648/1593 (FF/LUTs)
Bit width back-propagation	0.125	0.096	84 BRAMs	62 BRAMs
Actor fusion	0.017	0.016	190/690 (FF/LUTs)	170/511 (FF/LUTs)

Table 2. Meanshift power consumption. All reported numbers are in Watt.

	Total	Static	Dynamic	Clocks	Signals	Logic	BRAMS	DSP	I/O
V1	0.461	0.129	0.331	0.112	0.028	0.015	0.172	0.001	0.002
V2	0.356	0.128	0.228	0.070	0.022	0.011	0.123	0.000	0.002
V3	0.321	0.127	0.194	0.070	0.020	0.011	0.091	0.000	0.002

applying them to a large collection of benchmark programs, which is not feasible without automating refactoring. However, the results in Table 1 should suffice as proof of concept of the proposed transformations' impact.

To provide context to transformation results, Table 2 depicts power consumption for Mean shift versions after successive refinements applications and Table 3 depicts FPGA resource usage. In both tables V1, V2, V3 signifies *(V1)* original un-optimised version (baseline), *(V2)* after actor fusion and streamlined memory usage & *(V3)* after actor fusion, streamlined memory usage and back-propagation of bit width requirements, respectively. Peak performance (maximum clock frequency and achievable frames per second) were unaltered by transformations, at 81 MHz and 145 fps, respectively. These results provide designers with a quantitative view of how the aforementioned transformations can contribute to decrease resource usage and power consumption.

Table 3. Meanshift FPGA usage on Xilinx Zedboard (Zynq 7020).

	Registers	LUTs	BRAM	DSP
V1	3792 (3.00%)	9603 (18.00%)	111 (79.00%)	22 (10.00%)
V2	2189 (2.00%)	4679 (8.00%)	124 (88.00%)	8 (3.60%)
V3	2490 (2.34%)	4066 (7.64%)	67 (48.00%)	8 (3.60%)

Our results show that several optimisations which affect power consumption and resource usage can be applied, without compromising functionality or performance: this is certainly desirable for the design of power/size constrained vision systems. However, these cannot be automatically applied by optimising compilers. Two main insights are gained from our experiments: firstly, concerned designers must be aware of manual or semi-automated refactoring methodologies, beyond what is freely given by the compiler. Secondly, compiler optimisation technology, despite great advances in recent years, must still benefit from improvements.

Domain-specific refactoring can be applied by simulation-refinement loops, where performance estimation can expose over-optimised sub-systems, consuming unnecessary power and resources (*e.g.*, actor fusion example). Manual code inspection can reveal refactoring opportunities which minimize resource usage, either through local code optimisation (*e.g.*, streamlined memory usage example) or through cross sub-system code optimisation (*e.g.*, back propagation example). Both of these can be aided by automated profilers (*e.g.*, the CAL-Orcc framework supplies Turnus [1]) and by static code analysers. The methodologies and transformations we have presented should act as a guide for image processing engineers to perform such optimisations on their systems.

Optimisation passes in contemporary compilers are limited by language semantics. Static dataflow (*i.e.*, without loops, stateless) is far simpler to analyse and subsequently optimise than dynamic dataflow (*e.g.*, CAL). However, most real-world code relies heavily on dynamic features and is typically composed from third-party sub-systems. Hence, it is necessary to extend optimisation passes with more sophisticated static analysis capabilities that can infer memory waste and cross sub-system optimisations. The methodologies and transformations we have presented should aid compiler designers in identifying optimisation bottlenecks and possible solutions.

On Mean shift tracking, a complex algorithm exhibiting several design properties which inhibit automated compiler optimisations, our transformations resulted in 31% power consumption reduction, from 0.461 to 0.321 W, and a reduction of 10.36%, 31% and 6.4 % points in LUTs, BRAMs and DSPs resources usage, respectively.

6   Conclusions

We have described a methodology for the optimisation of dataflow networks, according to patterns often found in computer vision systems. The proposed methodology will be of use for computer vision algorithm designers who must optimise their implementations to meet some metric budget and for compiler designers in identifying optimisation bottlenecks and possible solutions. Our refactoring methodology, applying transformations to a complex algorithm, resulted in 31% power consumption reduction and a reduction of 10.36%, 31% & 6.4% in LUTs, BRAMs and DSPs resources usage, respectively. We also identified which design/language features were responsible for hindering automated optimisation. Our current work focuses on developing new static analysis technologies and refactoring tools; in future work, we hope to integrate these static refactoring tools into the Orcc framework and extend the optimisation methodologies so they are applicable to other compilers and language paradigms.

Acknowledgement. We acknowledge the support of the Engineering and Physical Research Council, grant references EP/K009931/1 (Programmable embedded platforms for remote and compute intensive image processing applications), EP/K014277/1 (MOD University Defence Research Collaboration in Signal Processing).

References

1. Brunei, S.C., Mattavelli, M., Janneck, J.W.: Turnus: a design exploration framework for dataflow system design. In: International Symposium on Circuits and Systems (ISCAS), p. 654 (2013)
2. Brunet, S.C., Mattavelli, M., Janneck, J.W.: Buffer optimization based on critical path analysis of a dataflow program design. In: International Symposium on Circuits and Systems (ISCAS), pp. 1384–1387 (2013)
3. Comaniciu, D., Ramesh, V., Meer, P.: Kernel-based object tracking. IEEE Trans. Pattern Anal. Mach. Intell. **25**(5), 564–577 (2003)
4. Ge, R., Vogt, R., Majumder, J., Alam, A., Burtscher, M., Zong, Z.: Effects of dynamic voltage and frequency scaling on a k20 GPU. In: 42nd International Conference on Parallel Processing, pp. 826–833 (2013)
5. Hueske, F., Peters, M., Krettek, A., Ringwald, M., Tzoumas, K., Markl, V., Freytag, J.C.: Peeking into the optimization of data flow programs with MapReduce-style UDFs. In: International Conference on Data Engineering (ICDE), pp. 1292–1295 (2013)
6. Janneck, J.W., Miller, I.D., Parlour, D.B., Roquier, G., Wipliez, M., Raulet, M.: Synthesizing hardware from dataflow programs: an MPEG-4 simple profile decoder case study. In: IEEE Workshop on Signal Processing Systems (SiPS), pp. 287–292 (2008)
7. Kim, Y., Jadhav, S., Gloster, C.S.: Dataflow to hardware synthesis framework on FPGAs. In: International Symposium on Computer Architecture and High Performance Computing Workshops (SBAC-PADW), pp. 91–96 (2016)
8. Lee, E.A., Parks, T.M.: Dataflow process networks. Proc. IEEE **83**(5), 773–801 (1995)
9. Malik, M., Farahmand, F., Otto, P., Akhlaghi, N., Mohsenin, T., Sikdar, S., Homayoun, H.: Architecture exploration for energy-efficient embedded vision applications: from general purpose processor to domain specific accelerator. In: IEEE Computer Society Annual Symposium on VLSI (ISVLSI), pp. 559–564 (2016)
10. Pandey, B., Yadav, J., Pattanaik, M., Rajoria, N.: Clock gating based energy efficient ALU design and implementation on FPGA. In: International Conference on Energy Efficient Technologies for Sustainability (ICEETS), pp. 93–97 (2013)
11. Rheinländer, A., Leser, U., Graefe, G.: Optimization of complex dataflows with user-defined functions. ACM Comput. Surv. **50**(3), 38:1–38:39 (2017)
12. Schulte, E., Dorn, J., Harding, S., Forrest, S., Weimer, W.: Post-compiler software optimization for reducing energy. SIGARCH Comput. Archit. News **42**(1), 639–652 (2014)
13. Seinstra, F.J., Koelma, D.: The lazy programmer's approach to building a parallel image processing library. In: Proceedings 15th International Parallel and Distributed Processing Symposium (IPDPS), pp. 1169–1176 (2001)
14. Sérot, J., Berry, F., Bourrasset, C.: High-level dataflow programming for real-time image processing on smart cameras. J. Real-Time Image Process. **12**(4), 635–647 (2016)

15. Stewart, R., Bhowmik, D., Wallace, A., Michaelson, G.: Profile guided dataflow transformation for FPGAs and CPUs. J. Sig. Process. Syst. **87**(1), 3–20 (2017)
16. Stewart, R., Michaelson, G., Bhowmik, D., Garcia, P., Wallace, A.: A dataflow IR for memory efficient RIPL compilation to FPGAs. In: International Conference on Algorithms and Architectures for Parallel Processing, pp. 174–188 (2016)
17. Teifel, J., Manohar, R.: An asynchronous dataflow FPGA architecture. IEEE Trans. Comput. **53**(11), 1376–1392 (2004)
18. Turcza, P., Duplaga, M.: Hardware-efficient low-power image processing system for wireless capsule endoscopy. IEEE J. Biomed. Health inform. **17**(6), 1046–1056 (2013)
19. Yviquel, H., Lorence, A., Jerbi, K., Cocherel, G., Sanchez, A., Raulet, M.: Orcc: Multimedia development made easy. In: Proceedings of the 21st ACM International Conference on Multimedia, pp. 863–866 (2013)

Fast Carry Chain Based Architectures for Two's Complement to CSD Recoding on FPGAs

Ayan Palchaudhuri$^{(\boxtimes)}$(iD) and Anindya Sundar Dhar

Department of Electronics and Electrical Communication Engineering,
Indian Institute of Technology Kharagpur, Kharagpur 721302, West Bengal, India
ayanpalchaudhuri@gmail.com, asd@ece.iitkgp.ernet.in

Abstract. Canonic signed digit (CSD) representation is a popular choice for realization of high speed, area efficient VLSI architectures in digital signal processing (DSP). In this paper, we address efficient FPGA based architectures for high speed two's complement to CSD recoding using serial and look-ahead based circuitry. We have also demonstrated the feasibility of a scan based design approach integrated into the original design to facilitate fault localization. The generation of the circuit descriptions have been automated making it an attractive option for commercial viability of such a design approach.

Keywords: CSD · FPGA · Look-up table · Carry chain
Primitive instantiation · Fault localization · Placement · Pipelining

1 Introduction

Canonic signed digit (CSD) representation ensures no adjacent non-zero digits, leading to high speed VLSI implementations of digital signal processing (DSP), neural networks and pattern recognition algorithms [1]. This has fuelled significant research towards designing efficient VLSI architectures that can perform CSD recoding [2–7] targeted towards ASIC or static CMOS based implementation. However, special design considerations are necessary for a compact, high speed FPGA implementation of a CSD recoding architecture, which has perhaps not been very poignantly addressed in previous literature.

Present day FPGAs owing to extensive downscaling of technology node dimensions and complex photolithographic techniques, suffer from reliability hazards such as electromigration, hot carrier injection, bias temperature instability and dielectric breakdown, thereby causing permanent hard errors during the lifetime of the chip [8–10]. This has propelled significant research efforts towards realizing fault aware toolchains, and devising other strategies of fault detection, fault localization and fault tolerance in FPGA based designs [11–16].

In this paper, we propose serial and look-ahead (LA) circuitry for two's complement to CSD recoding on FPGAs taking the target state-of-the-art FPGA

© Springer International Publishing AG, part of Springer Nature 2018
N. Voros et al. (Eds.): ARC 2018, LNCS 10824, pp. 537–550, 2018.
https://doi.org/10.1007/978-3-319-78890-6_43

fabric architecture into account. The proposed architectures come with an additional support to aid fault localization using a scan based design approach. This is done through a further design space exploration by appropriately re-designing the configured, yet under-utilized logic elements which realize the original functionality of CSD recoding. The designs have been configured through selection of appropriate high level language constructs to achieve target FPGA specific primitive instantiation [17,18] for superior synthesis results and technology dependent mapping. This is coupled with generating placement constraints for mapping the instantiated primitives on designated slice coordinates, so as to directly configure the FPGA logic slices for a high speed, compact implementation. The primary contributions in this paper are as follows:

– We have presented pipelined high speed serial and LA based FPGA fabric aware architectures for CSD recoding of two's complement numbers.
– We have realized fault localization circuitry in the form of scan based design built into the original proposed circuitry without any logic overhead.
– The circuit descriptions are very regular in their grammar, thereby making it feasible to write C programs for automated generation of the Hardware Description Language (HDL) code in Verilog and placement directives.

The organization of the rest of the paper is as follows. In Sect. 2, we introduce Xilinx Virtex-7 FPGA fabric. The proposed architectures are presented in Sect. 3. The implementation results are discussed in Sect. 4. The principles of design flow and automation are presented in Sect. 5. We conclude in Sect. 6.

2   Architecture of Target FPGA Platform

The 7-series of FPGAs are amongst the state-of-the-art. Each Virtex-7 FPGA slice contains four LUTs which can realize any arbitrary six-input single output or five-input dual output combinational functions [19]. The LUT outputs drive the inputs of the carry chain which comprises of a cascade of four multiplexers as shown in Fig. 1. The carry chain serves as a dedicated, hardwired path to facilitate fast signal propagation between adjacent logic elements, thereby speeding up the critical path. Eight flip-flops (FFs) are available in every slice, which can register the outputs of the LUTs and carry chain, thereby facilitating realization of compact pipelined architectures. Any expression c_4 of the form:

$$\begin{aligned}
c_4 &= \overline{s_3}d_3 + s_3[c_3] = \overline{s_3}d_3 + s_3[\overline{s_2}d_2 + s_2(c_2)] \\
&= \overline{s_3}d_3 + s_3[\overline{s_2}d_2 + s_2(\overline{s_1}d_1 + s_1\{c_1\})] \\
&= \overline{s_3}d_3 + s_3[\overline{s_2}d_2 + s_2(\overline{s_1}d_1 + s_1\{\overline{s_0}d_0 + s_0c_0\})]
\end{aligned} \tag{1}$$

can be mapped on to the carry chain (see Fig. 1), where s_i is the $O6$ LUT output and d_i is either an $O5$ LUT output or a bypass slice input (AX/BX/CX/DX).

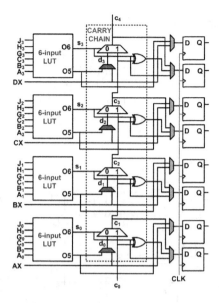

Fig. 1. A simplified Virtex-7 slice architecture.

3   Proposed Architectures

In all our proposed CSD recoding architectures, X is assumed to be the two's complement input and Y is the CSD output.

3.1   Two's Complement to CSD Recoding

Serial Architecture. For CSD recoding, the encoding scheme $Y_i = \{Y_i^d, Y_i^s\} =$ "00" for '0', "01" for '1' and "10" for '−1' is followed. The algorithm replaces a string of 1's ranging from bit index i to $(i+j-1)$ with a "1" at index $(i+j)$ and a $\bar{1}$ at index i. This calls for a recursive based computing. Going by the truth table governing the same functionality [20], a carry-out signal is computed in the first logic level as $c_{i+1} = X_i X_{i+1} + (X_i \oplus X_{i+1})c_i = X_{i+1}(\overline{X_i \oplus X_{i+1}}) + (X_i \oplus X_{i+1})c_i$ which is amenable to carry chain based mapping. The CSD recoded bits may be next computed as three variable functions, such as $Y_i^d = \overline{X_{i+1}}(X_i \oplus c_i)$ and $Y_i^s = X_{i+1}(X_i \oplus c_i)$ in the second logic level. Pipeline registers are inserted across the logic level boundaries. Pipelining often necessitates introduction of staging delays of the newly arriving inputs at subsequent pipelined stages. Hence, it is desirable to keep such an overhead to its minimum value. Thus, instead of directly sending the carry output c_i (after registering) as input to the second logic level, we EX-OR the carry output c_i with the LUT output $(X_{i+1} \oplus X_i)$ using the XOR gate of the carry chain as shown in Fig. 2. This output $(X_i \oplus X_{i+1} \oplus c_i)$ is now registered using FFs within the same slice of the carry chain prior to sending it as input to the second stage. Such a design practice reduces unit FF consumption per bit slice, which otherwise would have been required to delay the

X_i bits explicitly for computing the CSD recoded bits. Hence, the second logic level stage computes $Y_i^d = \overline{X_{i+1}}(X_{i+1} \oplus (X_i \oplus X_{i+1} \oplus c_i)) = \overline{X_{i+1}}(X_i \oplus c_i)$ and $Y_i^s = X_{i+1}((X_i \oplus X_{i+1} \oplus c_i) \oplus X_{i+1}) = X_{i+1}(X_i \oplus c_i)$ using LUTs configured in the dual output mode. The outputs Y_i^d and Y_i^s for a given index i are computed using a single LUT, with the dual outputs registered using FFs available in the same slice as that of the LUTs. The circuit realization guarantees maximal possible utilization of combinational and sequential elements in each slice.

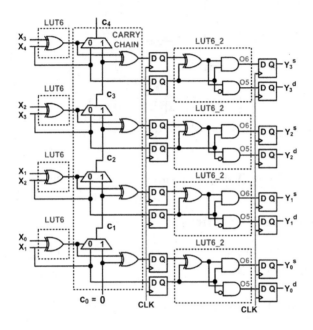

Fig. 2. Pipelined serial architecture for CSD recoding of a two's complement input.

Look-Ahead Based Architecture. The LUTs of the architecture shown in Fig. 2 have only two of its inputs utilized. This leaves a scope for implementation of a LA mode of operation to enable accelerated computation of the cascading signal c_i. LA technique for addition in FPGAs have been previously proposed in [21,22]. A generic LA technique is shown in Fig. 3(a), where the CSD recoder circuit is partitioned into two equal halves, with the lower and upper half accepting inputs from the lower and upper significant bit indices. LA accepts inputs from the lower half word. The CSD recoder accepting the upper significant bit inputs accepts its carry input from the LA output to significantly speed up the recursive based computation of c_i. For designing the LA generator of the CSD recoder circuit, it may be verified that $c_1 = (\overline{X_1 \oplus X_0})X_0 + (X_1 \oplus X_0)c_0 = X_1 X_0 + (X_1 \oplus X_0)c_0$. Hence, $c_2 = (\overline{X_2 \oplus X_1})X_1 + (X_2 \oplus X_1)c_1 = X_2 X_1 + (X_2 \oplus X_1)(X_1 X_0 + (X_1 \oplus X_0)c_0) = X_2 X_1 + \overline{X_2}X_1 X_0 + (X_2 \oplus X_1)(X_1 \oplus X_0)c_0 = X_2 X_1 + X_1 X_0 + (X_2 \oplus X_1)(X_1 \oplus X_0)c_0 = X_2 X_1(\overline{X_0}+1) + X_1 X_0(\overline{X_2}+1) + (X_2 \oplus X_1)(X_1 \oplus X_0)c_0 = X_0 X_1 \overline{X_2} + X_0 X_1 + X_2 X_1 + X_2 X_1 \overline{X_0} + (X_2 \oplus X_1)(X_1 \oplus X_0)c_0 =$

$X_0X_1(\overline{X_2 \oplus X_1}) + X_0X_1(\overline{X_1 \oplus X_0}) + X_2X_1(\overline{X_2 \oplus X_1}) + X_2X_1(\overline{X_1 \oplus X_0}) + (X_2 \oplus X_1)(X_1 \oplus X_0)c_0 = (X_2X_1 + X_1X_0)((\overline{X_2 \oplus X_1}) + (\overline{X_1 \oplus X_0})) + (X_2 \oplus X_1)(X_1 \oplus X_0)c_0 = (\overline{X_2 \oplus X_1})(\overline{X_1 \oplus X_0})(X_2X_1 + X_1X_0) + (X_2 \oplus X_1)(X_1 \oplus X_0)c_0$. Similarly, $c_3 = X_3X_2 + (X_3 \oplus X_2)(X_2X_1 + X_1X_0) + (X_3 \oplus X_2)(X_2 \oplus X_1)(X_1 \oplus X_0)c_0 = \overline{(X_3 \oplus X_2)(X_2 \oplus X_1)(X_1 \oplus X_0)}(X_3X_2 + X_2X_1 + X_3X_1X_0) + (X_3 \oplus X_2)(X_2 \oplus X_1)(X_1 \oplus X_0)c_0$. Hence, $c_4 = X_4X_3 + (X_4 \oplus X_3)(X_3X_2 + X_2X_1 + X_3X_1X_0) + (X_4 \oplus X_3)(X_3 \oplus X_2)(X_2 \oplus X_1)(X_1 \oplus X_0)c_0 = \overline{(X_4 \oplus X_3)(X_3 \oplus X_2)(X_2 \oplus X_1)(X_1 \oplus X_0)}(X_4(X_3 + X_2X_1) + X_3(X_2 + X_1X_0)) + (X_4 \oplus X_3)(X_3 \oplus X_2)(X_2 \oplus X_1)(X_1 \oplus X_0)c_0$. Hence, c_4 may be computed from c_0 using a single LUT and a single multiplexer of the carry chain as shown in Fig. 3(b), and c_{16} may be computed from c_0 using a single slice with four LUTs and a single carry chain, as the governing Boolean logic may be shown to conform to the form suggested in (1) for feasibility of carry chain implementation. If $P_i = X_{i+1} \oplus X_i$ and $G_i = X_{i+1}X_i$, we can define a *group-generate* signal $G_{i:j}$ and *group-propagate* signal $P_{i:j}$ as

$$P_{i:j} = \begin{cases} P_i, & \text{if } i = j. \\ P_iP_{i-1:j} & \text{if } i \geq j. \end{cases} \tag{2}$$

$$G_{i:j} = \begin{cases} G_i, & \text{if } i = j. \\ G_i + P_iG_{i-1:j} & \text{if } i \geq j. \end{cases} \tag{3}$$

The composite *propagate* signal spanning over $(k + 1)$ bit indices starting from LSB may be defined as $P = (X_k \oplus X_{k-1})(X_{k-1} \oplus X_{k-2}) \cdots (X_1 \oplus X_0)$. The corresponding composite *generate* signal may be defined as $G = X_k(X_{k-1} + X_{k-2}(\cdots + X_1X_0) \cdots) + X_{k-1}(X_{k-2} + X_{k-3}(\cdots + X_2X_1) \cdots)$ if k is even, and the positional index $(k - w) > 0$, considering $w > 0$. Similarly when k is odd, $G = X_k(X_{k-1} + X_{k-2}(\cdots + X_2X_1) \cdots) + X_{k-1}(X_{k-2} + X_{k-3}(\cdots + X_1X_0) \cdots)$. $X_{k-w} = 0$ if $(k - w) < 0$.

3.2 Two's Complement to CSD Recoding with Fault Localization Support Using Scan Based Design

Modification of FF state or introducing a known state are essential for debugging and functional verification in a scan based design [23,24]. Though it was believed that scan insertion is not an essential requirement of FPGA testing [25] as all gate level I/O nodes may be accessed, the various reliability issues mentioned in Sect. 1 leading to permanent hard errors during the lifetime of an FPGA chip makes scan based design an attractive solution [14,26]. We shall also demonstrate the architectural feasibility of realizing scan based fault localization circuitry.

Serial Architecture. The original FPGA based two's complement to CSD recoding architecture presented in Fig. 2 have only two inputs in each configured LUT utilized. The vacant inputs are now deployed to realize the scan based design. The proposed architectures can operate in two modes in a time multiplexed fashion: the *normal* mode and the *test* mode. In the *normal* mode

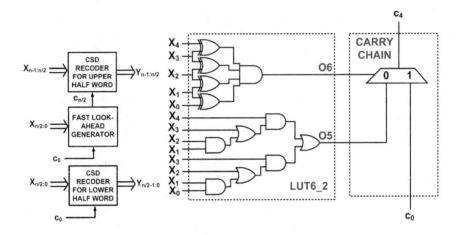

(a) LA scheme   (b) Single LA block slice of CSD recoder

Fig. 3. Look-ahead based configuration of CSD recoder

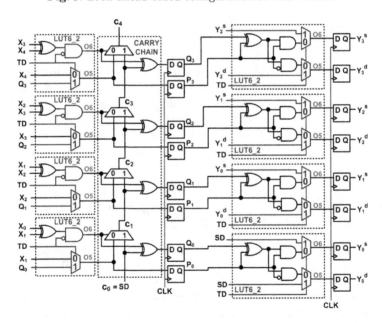

Fig. 4. Scan based pipelined, serial architecture of two's complement to CSD recoding.

$(TD = 0)$, the circuit functions as per the original functionality of two's complement to CSD recoding. In the *test* mode $(TD = 1)$, the FFs are stitched together in the form of a shift register using a multiplexer based realization. $c_0 = SD = 0$ in the *normal* mode of operation, whereas during the *test* mode, c_0 accepts serial data input SD preferably from a finite state machine. This multiplexing arrangement is encapsulated within the same LUT realizing the original CSD recoding circuitry as shown in Fig. 4. The additional control input TD and the serial data input obtained from previous FF output are fed into the configured LUTs using their vacant inputs. The first pipeline stage of the CSD recoding circuitry in Fig. 2 establishes its scan path via LUTs and carry chain. To encapsulate the scan based logic into dual output LUTs of the first pipeline stage, a minimum of 40% under-utilized inputs are required, a criterion which is comfortably satisfied in our proposed original architecture. For the subsequent pipelined stage logic, the dual outputs of each LUT are registered. Thus, in order to establish the scan path, a *test* mode input and two serial data inputs need to be driven using the vacant LUT inputs (minimum of 60% under-utilized inputs) to avoid logic overhead, a criterion which is satisfied for our proposed architecture. Multi-scan path arrangement is also feasible for our design by replacing any of the serial data inputs to each LUT with an external serial data input SD. Such an arrangement optimizes the test time and increases the granularity of fault localization (Fig. 5).

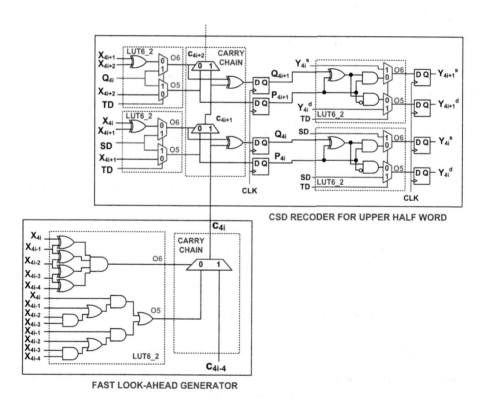

Fig. 5. Scan based pipelined, LA architecture of two's complement to CSD recoding.

Look-Ahead Based Architecture. For the scan based LA architecture, the CSD recoder for lower half word is identical to that shown in Fig. 4. The CSD recoder for the upper half word, which accepts its carry input from the fast LA generator undergoes slight modification in its LUT configuration, as the initial carry chain multiplexer data input is no longer directly controllable. Hence the LUT in the CSD recoder for the upper half word acts as the input source of the new serial scan data input. It may be noticed that the scan based approach does not apply for the fast LA generator as there are no FFs attached to it. Instead, the carry chain response may be verified by applying the appropriate test vectors. Each successive LUT accepts inputs $X_{4i:4i-4}$, $X_{4i-4:4i-8}$, $X_{4i-8:4i-12}$ and so on. Hence, every LUT shares a common input e.g., X_{4i-8}, with the preceeding LUT, and another common input, e.g., X_{4i-4}, with its successive LUT. Thus, tying the common inputs to logic zero (low), $c_{4i+4} = c_{4i}$ if $\{c_{4i}, x_{4i-1:4i-3}\} = \{00XX, 010X, 1101, 111X\}$; and $c_{4i+4} \neq c_{4i}$ if $\{c_{4i}, x_{4i-1:4i-3}\} = \{011X, 10XX, 1100\}$. Similarly, tying the common inputs to logic one (high), $c_{4i+4} = c_{4i}$ if $\{c_{4i}, x_{4i-1:4i-3}\} = \{000X, 0010, 101X, 11XX\}$; and $c_{4i+4} \neq c_{4i}$ if $\{c_{4i}, x_{4i-1:4i-3}\} = \{0011, 01XX, 100X\}$.

4   Results and Discussions

Virtex-7 FPGAs with device family, package and speed grade being XC7VX330T, FFG1157 and -2 respectively are chosen as the Xilinx platform settings using ISE 14.7 and post place and route results have been reported. Our proposed two's complement to CSD recoding architecture is compared with a previously proposed binary to CSD recoder [2] (Table 1), where it was mentioned that every proposed processing element fits into one slice of a Virtex-4 FPGA comprising of two LUTs. The Virtex-4 platform is now several generations out of date, but the noteworthy point remains that the "bypass" signal [2] generation logic and its subsequent cascadable design is not amenable for carry chain based implementation. In the process, the circuit is mapped solely using LUTs and relies upon the relatively slower programmable routing fabric instead of the fast, dedicated, hardwired routing fabric of the carry chain to route the bypass signal, leading to a slow speed realization. Additionally, the circuit of [2] is not amenable to forward path pipelining in a manner similar to our proposed architectures. We have registered the inputs and outputs of the circuit proposed in [2] and mapped it onto Virtex-7 FPGA to estimate its delay, whose results have been tabulated in Table 1, and compared with our proposed serial and LA based designs. Both the serial and LA based designs outperform the previously proposed CSD encoder [2] in speed. To the best of our knowledge, there are no other FPGA amenable CSD recoders available in literature. Our proposed serial and LA based CSD recoders exploits the carry chain fabric to achieve higher speed. The LA based design further accelerates the computation of the carry signal four times as faster as compared to the serial design for the lower half word with a nominal logic overhead of 6.25%. For an n-digit output wordlength, the proposed serial design occupies $4n$ FFs, $2n$ LUTs and $\lceil \frac{n}{2} \rceil$ slices. Similarly,

Table 1. Implementation results for two's complement to CSD converter

Operand width	Design style	#FF	#LUT	#Slice	#Pipeline stages	Frequency (MHz)/Delay (ns)
32	Behavioral realization of [2]	–	46	29	Non-pipelined	[a]401.77/2.489
	Proposed serial design	**128**	**64**	**16**	**2**	**852.51/1.173**
	Proposed LA design	**128**	**68**	**17**	**2**	**987.17/1.013**
64	Behavioral realization of [2]	–	94	61	Non-pipelined	[a]292.48/3.419
	Proposed serial design	**256**	**128**	**32**	**2**	**624.22/1.602**
	Proposed LA design	**256**	**136**	**34**	**2**	**781.25/1.280**
96	Behavioral realization of [2]	–	142	85	Non-pipelined	[a]278.78/3.587
	Proposed serial design	**384**	**192**	**48**	**2**	**491.64/2.034**
	Proposed LA design	**384**	**204**	**51**	**2**	**645.99/1.548**
128	Behavioral realization of [2]	–	190	112	Non-pipelined	[a]223.26/4.479
	Proposed serial design	**512**	**256**	**64**	**2**	**402.41/2.485**
	Proposed LA design	**512**	**272**	**68**	**2**	**550.36/1.817**
160	Behavioral realization of [2]	–	238	142	Non-pipelined	[a]204.46/4.891
	Proposed serial design	**640**	**320**	**80**	**2**	**344.47/2.903**
	Proposed LA design	**640**	**340**	**85**	**2**	**478.93/2.088**

[a]The behavioral designs are essentially combinational circuits. The delay and the frequency of operation were obtained by inserting FFs at the primary input and output ports of the circuits.

Table 2. Implementation results for scan based two's complement to CSD converter

Operand width	Design style	#FF	#LUT	#Slice	#Scan paths	Frequency (MHz)/Delay (ns)
32	Serial scan	128	64	16	1	782.47/1.278
	LA scan	128	68	17	2	931.10/1.074
64	Serial scan	256	128	32	1	585.82/1.707
		256	128	32	2	585.82/1.707
	LA scan	256	136	34	2	777.00/1.287
96	Serial scan	384	192	48	1	467.51/2.139
		384	192	48	2	467.51/2.139
		384	192	48	3	467.51/2.139
	LA scan	384	204	51	2	665.78/1.502
128	Serial scan	512	256	64	1	386.10/2.590
		512	256	64	2	386.10/2.590
		512	256	64	4	386.10/2.590
	LA scan	512	272	68	2	581.73/1.719
		512	272	68	4	581.73/1.719
160	Serial scan	640	320	80	1	313.48/3.190
		640	320	80	2	313.48/3.190
		640	320	80	4	313.48/3.190
	LA scan	640	340	85	2	514.67/1.943
		640	340	85	4	514.67/1.943

for an n-digit output wordlength, the proposed LA design occupies $4n$ FFs, $(2n + \lceil \frac{n}{8} \rceil)$ LUTs and $(\lceil \frac{n}{2} \rceil + \lceil \frac{n}{32} \rceil)$ slices.

Table 2 shows the implementation results for the scan based design of two's complement to CSD recoding for both the serial and LA based design. The scan based architectures do not consume additional logic in comparison to the original designs. However some minor differences in the delay amongst the original and the scan based architectures may be possibly attributed owing to routing of the additional signals to establish the scan path. The architectures with multi-scan path arrangements have identical performance metrics compared to their single scan path equivalent. The area consumption for the original and their equivalent scan based designs are also the same. The scan paths of the LA based CSD recoder for the lower and the upper half word are kept separate, hence the minimum number of scan paths in the LA design as tabulated in Table 2 is two.

5   Design Flow and Automation

All the architectures have been conceived following the art of primitive instantiation and the placement directives to map the primitives on designated slice

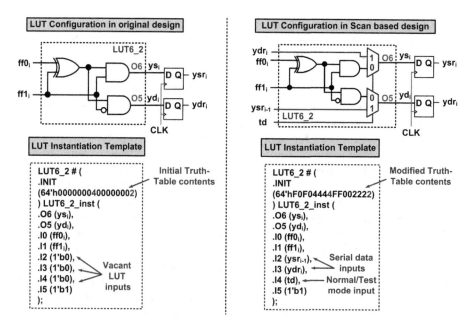

Fig. 6. Highlighted changes in the LUT instantiation templates to facilitate scan insertion into the original design

coordinates often dictated by the proximity of the bit indices or successive stages of logic. The structural regularity of the circuits aids in design automation for generating the circuit descriptions by writing simple C programs with computational complexity $O(n)$ where n is the output digit size. Consider the LUT instantiation template for the configured LUTs in the second stage of pipelining shown in Fig. 6. The unused inputs of the configured LUT have been grounded by attaching logic zero ($1'b0$) to them. For the scan based design, the vacant inputs are used to drive the serial data inputs and the mode input, and necessary alteration of the truth-table contents for the new function is taken care of as shown in Fig. 6. The C programs for the original and scan based design may be generated independently, or one may be generated from the other.

For fault localization, the first faulty bit response (if any) from the scanned out bit-stream during the *test* mode is noted, where the FFs are pre-initialized with a known string in the *normal* mode. If each FPGA slice generates r output bits, and the circuit is mapped starting from the slice located at X_iY_j in a columnar fashion and the total number of FFs in the scan chain is x, the LUT or FF located at the $S = (mod\ (x - p, r) + 1)$-th position in the slice situated at the $X_iY_{j-1+\lceil \frac{x-p}{r} \rceil}$ coordinate may be the faulty candidate. For example, consider "101001010110001010101110", a scanned out bit-stream from a single scan path, with the bold red (underlined) "1" at position $p = 15$ from right as the first faulty response. If the circuit is mapped starting from the X_iY_j coordinate in a columnar fashion, with the rightmost bit (0) of the above string being the first scanned out element, and total number of FFs in the scan chain is x ($x = 24$), the LUT or FF located at position $S = mod\ (24 - 15, 4) + 1 = 2$ may be deemed faulty. Thus, the second LUT or the second FF present within a slice located at the coordinate $X_i Y_{j-1+\lceil \frac{x-p}{r} \rceil} = X_i Y_{j+2}$ may be the faulty candidate. Such defective slices may be bypassed by providing Xilinx proprietary PROHIBIT constraints and a new set of slice coordinates for the circuit may be generated by re-running the automation machinery, that accepts the CSD output digit size and the initial slice coordinates for mapping the circuit as its inputs. This practice enables real-time detection of any newly generated FPGA defects without any expensive test-bed set up or expertise in testing. A multi-scan path arrangement in such cases increase the granularity of fault localization, as it searches for the faulty logic element within a smaller radius of neighbourhood.

The scan path cannot solely decide upon the fault coverage. The designer shall now formulate the test vectors to achieve the desired percentage of fault coverage. We have only provided for the hardware support in the form of designing the scan paths without logic overhead, and spelt out the control bit specifications for run-time reconfiguration to *test* mode. However, we have performed post-route simulations by emulating certain faults in the FPGA and have been able to localize the area from which the fault has emanated.

6   Conclusion

In this paper, we have proposed high speed, compact CSD recoding circuits on FPGAs, by properly exploiting the carry chain fabric. The proposed bit-sliced circuits are amenable to forward path pipelining, and comfortably outperforms another state-of-the-art circuit proposed for FPGAs in [2] with respect to speed. The feasibility of automating the circuit descriptions makes it attractive for commercial viability. The placement directives generated ensured a compact architecture and maximum resource utilization in every configured slice. The circuit descriptions are backward compatible for realization on Virtex-6 FPGAs and scalable for other 6 and 7 series of FPGAs.

References

1. Parhi, K.K.: VLSI Digital Signal Processing Systems: Design and Implementation. Wiley India Pvt. Limited, Delhi (2007)
2. Faust, M., Gustafsson, O., Chang, C.-H.: Fast and VLSI efficient binary-to-CSD encoder using bypass signal. Electron. Lett. **47**(1), 18–20 (2011)
3. Ruiz, G.A., Granda, M.: Efficient canonic signed digit recoding. Microelectron. J. **42**(9), 1090–1097 (2011)
4. Herrfeld, A., Hentschke, S.: Look-ahead circuit for CSD-code carry determination. Electron. Lett. **31**(6), 434–435 (1995)
5. Koç, Ç.K.: Parallel canonical recoding. Electron. Lett. **32**(22), 2063–2065 (1996)

6. He, Y., Ma, B., Li, J., Zhen, S., Luo, P., Li, Q.: A fast and energy efficient binary-to-pseudo CSD converter. In: 2015 IEEE International Symposium on Circuits and Systems (ISCAS), pp. 838–841 (2015)
7. Tanaka, Y.: Efficient signed-digit-to-canonical-signed-digit recoding circuits. Microelectron. J. **57**, 21–25 (2016)
8. Modi, H., Athanas, P.: In-system testing of Xilinx 7-series FPGAs: part 1-logic. In: IEEE International Conference for Military Communications (MILCOM), pp. 477–482 (2015)
9. Naouss, M., Marc, F.: Modelling delay degradation due to NBTI in FPGA look-up tables. In: 26th International Conference on Field Programmable Logic and Applications (FPL), pp. 1–4 (2016)
10. Naouss, M., Marc, F.: FPGA LUT delay degradation due to HCI: experiment and simulation result. Microelectron. Reliab. **64**(C), 31–35 (2016)
11. Gupte, A., Vyas, S., Jones, P.H.: A fault-aware toolchain approach for FPGA fault tolerance. ACM Trans. Design Autom. Electron. Syst. **20**(2), 32:1–32:22 (2015)
12. Kyriakoulakos, K., Pnevmatikatos, D.: A novel SRAM-based FPGA architecture for efficient TMR fault tolerance support. In: 19th International Conference on Field Programmable Logic and Applications (FPL), pp. 193–198 (2009)
13. Nazar, G.L., Carro, L.: Fast error detection through efficient use of hardwired resources in FPGAs. In: 17th IEEE European Test Symposium (ETS), pp. 1–6 (2012)
14. Palchaudhuri, A., Dhar, A.S.: Efficient implementation of scan register insertion on integer arithmetic cores for FPGAs. In: 29th International Conference on VLSI Design, pp. 433–438 (2016)
15. Basha, B.C., Pillement, S., Piestrak, S.J.: Fault-aware configurable logic block for reliable reconfigurable FPGAs, In: IEEE International Symposium on Circuits and Systems (ISCAS). pp. 2732–2735 (2015)
16. Wheeler, T., Graham, P., Nelson, B., Hutchings, B.: Using design-level scan to improve FPGA design observability and controllability for functional verification. In: Brebner, G., Woods, R. (eds.) FPL 2001. LNCS, vol. 2147, pp. 483–492. Springer, Heidelberg (2001). https://doi.org/10.1007/3-540-44687-7_50
17. Ehliar, A.: Optimizing Xilinx designs through primitive instantiation. In: Proceedings of the 7th FPGAworld Conference, FPGAworld 2010, pp. 20–27. ACM, New York (2010)
18. Palchaudhuri, A., Chakraborty, R.S.: High Performance Integer Arithmetic Circuit Design on FPGA: Architecture Implementation and Design Automation. Springer India, New Delhi (2016). https://doi.org/10.1007/978-81-322-2520-1
19. Xilinx Inc.: 7 Series FPGAs Configurable Logic Block User Guide UG474 (v1.8) 27 Sep 2016. https://www.xilinx.com/support/documentation/user_guides/ug474_7Series_CLB.pdf
20. Hwang, K.: Computer Arithmetic: Principles Architecture and Design. Wiley, Hoboken (1979)
21. Zicari, P., Perri, S.: A fast carry chain adder for Virtex-5 FPGAs. In: 15th IEEE Mediterranean Electrotechnical Conference (MELECON), pp. 304–308 (2010)
22. Källström, P., Gustafsson, O.: Fast and area efficient adder for wide data in recent Xilinx FPGAs. In: 26th International Conference on Field Programmable Logic and Applications (FPL), pp. 1–4 (2016)
23. Wheeler, T.B.: Improving design observability and controllability for functional verification of FPGA-based circuits using design-level scan techniques. Master's thesis. Brigham Young University (2001)

24. Wheeler, T., Graham, P., Nelson, B., Hutchings, B.: Using design-level scan to improve FPGA design observability and controllability for functional verification. In: Brebner, G., Woods, R. (eds.) FPL 2001. LNCS, vol. 2147, pp. 483–492. Springer, Heidelberg (2001). https://doi.org/10.1007/3-540-44687-7_50
25. Toutounchi, S., Lai, A.: FPGA test and coverage. In: International Test Conference, pp. 599–607 (2002)
26. Palchaudhuri, A., Amresh, A.A., Dhar, A.S.: Efficient automated implementation of testable cellular automata based pseudorandom generator circuits on FPGAs. J. Cell. Autom. **12**(3–4), 217–247 (2017)

Exploring Functional Acceleration of OpenCL on FPGAs and GPUs Through Platform-Independent Optimizations

Umar Ibrahim Minhas[✉] , Roger Woods , and George Karakonstantis

Queens University Belfast, Belfast, UK
u.minhas@qub.ac.uk

Abstract. OpenCL has been proposed as a means of accelerating functional computation using FPGA and GPU accelerators. Although it provides ease of programmability and code portability, questions remain about the performance portability and underlying vendor's compiler capabilities to generate efficient implementations without user-defined, platform specific optimizations. In this work, we systematically evaluate this by formalizing a design space exploration strategy using platform-independent micro-architectural and application-specific optimizations only. The optimizations are then applied across Altera FPGA, NVIDIA GPU and ARM Mali GPU platforms for three computing examples, namely matrix-matrix multiplication, binomial-tree option pricing and 3-dimensional finite difference time domain. Our strategy enables a fair comparison across platforms in terms of throughput and energy efficiency by using the same design effort. Our results indicate that FPGA provides better performance portability in terms of achieved percentage of device's peak performance (68%) compared to NVIDIA GPU (20%) and also achieves better energy efficiency (up to 1.4×) for some of the considered cases without requiring in-depth hardware design expertise.

1 Introduction

The rapidly increasing use of heterogeneous accelerators such as Graphic Processing Unit (GPU) and Field Programmable Gate Array (FPGA) in data centres necessitates the adoption of a unified programming environment that also maintains better throughput and energy efficiency [1]. This is hard to achieve, however, due to widely varied architectures and technologies, which have been traditionally programmed via specialized languages e.g. VHDL for FPGAs and CUDA for NVIDIA GPUs, using detailed knowledge of underlying hardware. In addition to programming inefficiency, this hinders fair comparison of achieved performance and design cost across the different accelerating technologies.

To address this challenge, the Open Computing Language (OpenCL) [2] has been introduced as a C-based platform-independent language, to allow parallelism to be expressed explicitly regardless of the underlying hardware. OpenCL is now supported by a range of programmable accelerators including GPUs and

© Springer International Publishing AG, part of Springer Nature 2018
N. Voros et al. (Eds.): ARC 2018, LNCS 10824, pp. 551–563, 2018.
https://doi.org/10.1007/978-3-319-78890-6_44

FPGAs. However, OpenCL only provides functional portability and the application implementation needs to be optimized by the underlying accelerator vendor compilers. Under such a reality, the question remains about performance portability of OpenCL applications on various accelerators. That is, how much performance an application can achieve across various platforms and how to gauge the efficiency of the vendor-specific compilers to map OpenCL source code to the targeted device with minimum or even no user-defined platform-specific optimizations. Also, it is questionable if FPGAs still require more in-depth knowledge of underlying hardware compared to other technologies.

Achieving performance portability and fair evaluation is becoming extremely important with increased usage of accelerators in data centres and cloud environments [3]. Researchers have approached these challenges from two angles. On one hand some studies compare programming languages such as a hardware descriptive language (HDL) and Compute Unified Device Architecture (CUDA) with OpenCL on the same platform, e.g. FPGAs [4] and GPUs [5]. On the other hand there is portability evaluation of the same language e.g. OpenCL across multiple platforms i.e. NVIDIA GPU, AMD GPU, Intel CPU and Sony/Toshiba/IBM Cell Broadband Engine [6]. These works conclude that although platform independent language can lead to better portability, additional effort is required for tuning kernels to each device to achieve comparable performance.

An architectural and programming model study on fractal video compression involving optimization of OpenCL on FPGA has been presented in [7] and provides a series of FPGA-based optimizations on FPGA before comparing the results with CPU and GPU for an optimized kernel. In [8], six benchmarks of the Rodinia suite are evaluated using OpenCL and FPGA-specific optimizations are performed on kernels optimized for GPU-like devices, achieving up to 3.4x better energy efficiency compared to GPUs. However, this work requires platform-specific optimizations, which partially nullifies the motivation behind a software-based approach via a unified programming environment. In addition, they compare the output with already-optimized implementations on other platforms and do not discussed performance portability.

In this paper, we develop and apply a systematic approach to gauging performance portability and fair evaluation. We apply a set of uniform microarchitectural optimizations for fair porting, optimization and evaluation of applications across platforms using OpenCL. The optimizations are based on carefully selected common micro-architectural features that can be easily parametrized via the OpenCL model. Initially, we take C source code of kernels for 3 accelerated computing applications, namely matrix-matrix multiplication (SGEMM), Binomial-tree Option Pricing (BOP) and 3 dimensional Finite Difference Time Domain (FDTD) and port them to OpenCL as base kernels before applying the platform-independent optimizations.

We then evaluate these optimisations on 3, state-of-the art, platforms namely Altera FPGA, a high performance NVIDIA GPU and a low power ARM Mali GPU. In doing so, we analyse the underlying compilers' job in generating an optimized implementation. We also compare the achieved performance to the theoretical peak throughput and platform-specific implementations. To the best of our knowledge, this is the first work to discuss platform-independent, design space exploration across FPGA and GPU and use the same optimization efforts, programming environment and runtime for a fair comparison of heterogeneous accelerators for throughput and energy efficiency.

In brief the key contributions of this paper include:

- A micro-architectural optimization and design space exploration approach based on platform-independent parameters of OpenCL model.
- Implementation of three applications from linear algebra (SGEMM), financial computation (BOP) and electromagnetic modelling (FDTD) on heterogeneous accelerators while analysing the architectural and algorithmic challenges using OpenCL.
- Fair comparison of the implementations of the above applications on state-of-art FPGA and GPUs in terms of application-specific metrics for throughput and energy efficiency while trying to keep the design efforts the same.
- Comparison of achieved performance through platform-independent optimizations with theoretical peak and platform-specific optimizations.

The rest of the paper is organized as follows. Section 2 describes the design environment by reviewing OpenCL programming model, the tested use cases and experimental platforms. Section 3 summarizes the optimization and design space exploration methodology and its application to the use cases. Sections 4 and 5 then analyse the throughput and energy efficiency optimizations on each of the platforms. Finally, Sect. 6 concludes the presented work.

2   Design Environment

2.1   Overview of OpenCL

OpenCL is a cross platform open standard for heterogeneous parallel programming that defines platform-independent APIs for abstraction of parallelism. A serial OpenCL program runs on a host CPU with parallel compute intensive tasks being offloaded via a kernel definition and OpenCL runtime onto a compute device. A compute device contains one or more compute units (CU) each of which has one or more processing elements (PE) (Fig. 1).

A complete application is usually divided into smaller tasks, work-groups, with each running independently on a CU. A work-group has further 3 dimensional parallel work-items, which run on a PE. Memory types of OpenCL based on latency are high-latency *global* memory accessible to a whole kernel and fast *local* memory shared within a work-group.

2.2   Use Cases

We take three different use cases from linear algebra, financial computation and electromagnetic modelling; their computation range offers diverse testing of micro-architecture, as summarized in Table 1. These are briefly explained below.

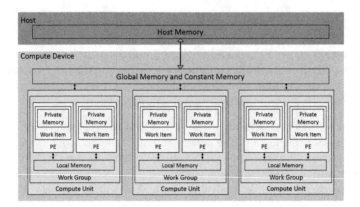

Fig. 1. OpenCL architecture

Table 1. Use cases characteristics

Characteristic	SGEMM	BOP	FDTD
Domain	Linear algebra	Finance	Modelling
Evaluated data points	Up to 32K	Up to 4K	105M
Data dimensions	1	2	3
Data access pattern	Regular	1 Regular, 1 Irregular	Regular
Architecture	SIMD	Iterative	Sliding window
Data reuse	Order of matrix	2	$Radius^2$

Matrix-Matrix Multiply: SGEMM of two square matrices, A and B, of order n results in a matrix C of order n where each ij^{th} element of C is the dot product of ith row of A and j^{th} column of B. SGEMM is a main component of various libraries and benchmarks (such as LAPACK) used in dense linear algebra algorithms and for benchmarking purposes.

Binomial-Tree Option Pricing: BOP is a key model in finance that offers a generalized method for option valuation and can be applied for more exotic options with complex features. It calculates the value of the option at the final nodes of a binomial tree. The next, computationally complex step involves walking backwards up the tree calculating the price of all nodes at each time step sequentially, until the first node is reached. Each node, n, in a vertical column at a time step, t, is dependent on two nodes, n and $n+1$, in the time step, $t+1$.

3 Dimensional Finite Difference Time Domain: FDTD is an important numerical method in electromagnetic numerical modelling which builds a model space and stores it in memory. The calculation of electric and magnetic field progression in 3D space, $dimx \times dimy \times dimz$, is conducted in a sliding window fashion, where window is a sphere of set radius. Apart from the computational needs, another reason for selecting this algorithm for comparison is due to the availability of fine tuned implementations from vendors, Altera and NVIDIA.

2.3 Platforms

We evaluate 3 typical state-of-the art platforms, based on the same technology, from Altera, NVIDIA and ARM (Table 2). In terms of architecture, both GPUs share similarities with fixed micro-architecture consisting of processing cores and cache. The main differentiation factor lies in the device scale and non-availability of separate local memory for CUs in Mali. In comparison, FPGA offers a reconfigurable architecture with variable precision Digital Signal Processors (DSPs), a common large local memory for all DSPs and non-availability of cache.

Table 2. Key platforms characteristics

Characteristic	Altera	NVIDIA	MALI
Board	Nallatech 385	GTX 980	ODROID XU-3
Chip	5SGXA7	GM204	T628
Technology (nm)	28	28	28
Frequency	Variable	1216 MHz	600 MHz
Compute units	Variable	16	4
Floating point units	256	2048	16
Local memory	6.25 MB	256 KB	Virtual
Cache	-	2 MB	256 KB
Work-items	Single preferred	$1024 \times 1024 \times 64$	$256 \times 256 \times 256$

3 Platform-Independent, Application-Specific Optimizations

Here we define a platform-independent micro-architecture optimization flow and apply along with application-specific optimizations applied to various use cases.

3.1 Platform-Independent Optimizations

Irrespective of underlying hardware, we target the following optimizations based on general principles of parallel computing and the OpenCL model (Fig. 2):

Explicit Parallelism: The first step is to define parallelism explicitly using the OpenCL model of work-items and work-groups. This requires a general understanding of the application to explicitly divide each task into fine-grained multiple parallel units, forming the base kernel.

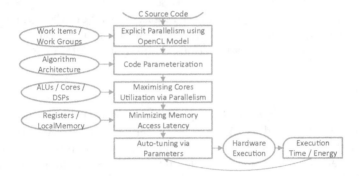

Fig. 2. Formalized micro-architecture optimization flow

Cores: The second step is to implement core-level optimizations in two ways: firstly, by providing enough parallel work-items and data to enable maximum cores utilization in time and secondly, exploiting vector operations in a single core, if available, using OpenCL vector data types for maximizing spatial usage.

Memory: The third step optimizes memory access for reduced latency by hiding the main memory access latency. This is achieved by memory coalescing and also by maximising the use of high speed, local memories in OpenCL.

Auto-tuning: Finally, auto-tuning using an iterative approach, where the tunable parameters are scaled from minimum to maximum in power of two, is essential to maximise workload balancing and resource utilization. In our context, this involves varying OpenCL parameters such as number of work-items, work-groups, loop unrolling, etc., via argument passing to compiler, to find the optimum combination.

Next, we consider these optimizations in addition to application-specific optimizations that are applicable to all platforms.

3.2 Application-Specific Optimizations

We start by applying the steps of optimization flow on SGEMM and then briefly summarize the applied optimizations on BOP.

Matrix-Matrix Multiply: 4 different implementations of SGEMM kernels have been investigated. Let us consider the pseudo code for the kernel as:

```
for (i in range n)
   for (j in range m)
      acc = 0
      for (k in range p)
         acc += A(i,k) * B(k,j);
      C(i,j) = acc;
```

Then each kernel optimizes the pseudo code as follows:

Kernel 1 , the basic implementation, distributes the first two outer loops into parallel work-items such that each work-item computes one element of C. There is plenty of parallelism but no explicit use of data locality.

Kernel 2 exploits on-chip, fast memory by loading smaller blocks of data on local memory and maximally utilizing it before being replaced by new data from global memory.

Kernel 3 builds on kernel 2 to exploit the fastest memory, registers. Using the same local memory of the OpenCL model, the inner-most loop is divided into sub-blocks, targeting data-locality equal to the size of the registers.

Kernel 4 exploits high bandwidth memory operations as well as parallel arithmetic operations, if supported by hardware units. This is achieved by processing vector of values in SIMD fashion using vector data types of OpenCL.

Furthermore, block size for kernels 2–4 is chosen to make maximum use of local memory and data-locality. All devices benefit from memory coalescing when consecutive work-items access data from consecutive memory locations. Finally, auto-tuning for SGEMM is simple, as each work-item works in a single instruction multiple data (SIMD) fashion on elements and data size is large enough to keep resource usage to maximum.

Binomial Option Pricing: The BOP computation is not as inherently parallel as SGEMM as the iterations over number of steps during backwards walk have loop carried dependences. Within each step, there is anti-dependence due to each value being used in two backward nodes calculation. The later can be removed by using two buffers. Parallelism can also be achieved by pricing multiple options in a work-group.

Targeting the defined flow, the first basic implementation included definition of kernel's parallelism via work-groups and work-items. From the top level, the number of options in a work-group can be varied with each work-group running on an individual CU. To maximise local memory usage, maximum number of options are selected such that all intermediate values are stored on local memory.

Similarly, multiple work-items per option operate on different nodes at a single time step in parallel and thus balance cores usage. However, increasing number of options per work-group or number of work-items per option put constraints on local memory bandwidth as work-items share local memory. Work-items also need to synchronize before moving on to next step in backward walk due to true dependence and the penalty for that increases with increasing number of work-items. In addition, fewer work-items limits the parallelism available to maximise compute resource usage. The optimum point is achieved with auto-tuning as explained in Sect. 4.1. Vector processing is also evaluated.

Finite Difference Time Domain: FDTD kernels from vendor optimized libraries were only auto tuned for each device to maximise local memory and cores usage.

4   Throughput Analysis

In this section, we analyse the achieved throughput computed via kernel processing time on the 3 targeted accelerators using the defined optimization flow.

4.1   Throughput Variations

SGEMM: We observe varying trends for all devices for SGEMM kernels 1–4 (Fig. 3). For kernel 1, the FPGA performs the worst compared to GPUs. This can be partially attributed to more mature GPU compilers allowing them to scale out significant performance from basic definition of explicit parallelism. More importantly, although no local memory usage is defined for any device, the cache in GPUs is able to improve memory latency whilst FPGAs suffer due to non-availability of cache.

Throughputs for kernel 2 improve for all platforms. However, FPGA benefits the most of this optimization due to large local memory of FPGA and its explicit description compensating for lack of cache. For kernel 3, both the GPUs perform better than the 2nd kernel, making use of the registers. For FPGA, the performance degrades as explained later. For kernel 4, only the Mali GPU is able to exploit vectorization. For Altera and NVIDIA, the additional control instructions provide overhead and perform worse than kernel 2 and 3, respectively.

SGEMM - FPGA Analysis: We take a more detailed look at various SGEMM kernels mapping on hardware to better understand the variation of the throughput on FPGA. Looking at Table 3, kernel 1 offers reasonable parallelism, defined by loop unrolling, and a decent operating frequency. However, the actual throughput is lower than expected due to global memory latency.

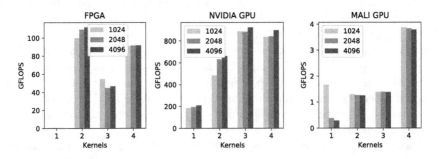

Fig. 3. SGEMM throughput variations on devices for square matrices of various sizes mentioned in legend

Table 3. SGEMM synthesis results on FPGA

Resource	Kernel 1	Kernel 2	Kernel 3	Kernel 4
Logical elements (%)	28.87	41.41	36.11	45.59
Flip flops (%)	22.61	30.43	26.31	38.43
RAMs (%)	62.38	49.80	33.55	60.66
DSPs (%)	39.06	100	84.37	100
Frequency (MHz)	210.7	236.23	201.93	179.14
Parallelism	32	256	192	256
GFLOPS	0.37	111.65	46.43	91.66

Kernel 2 achieves maximum parallelism and full utilization of DSPs. Using only two nested loops results in lower overhead and the highest synthesized frequency. The theoretical performance after synthesis is about 120 GFLOPs compared to actual 111 GFLOPs which is due to higher global memory latency.

Kernel 3 is interesting since, unlike GPUs, it degrades throughput. This is due to lower frequency owing to the additional overhead of 3rd nested loops over the sub-blocks. In FPGAs, the compiler should use registers for 3rd loop elements, however, the OpenCL memory architecture does not support a different memory type for registers and the Altera compiler is not able to do it automatically. Also the structure of kernel 3 made full utilization of DSPs difficult, resulting in 192 way parallelism only.

Finally, an extra processing dimension in kernel 4 due to two way vectorization of elements in matrices A and B resulted in the lowest frequency. This requires a loop to go over the width of vector with each iteration multiplying a vector element from A with a sub-vector element (selected via switch statement) of vector B. However, it offers improvement in memory latency owing to vectorized access and achieves the same performance as predicted after synthesis.

Surprisingly, Altera, NVIDIA and Mali perform the best for Kernels 2, 3 and 4 and show up to 298×, 4.4× and 13× improvement over their worst implementation, respectively.

BOP: As described earlier, after the parametrized implementation of the BOP kernel, auto-tuning is needed to optimize number of work-items in a work-group. For all devices, the throughput followed a similar trend and increased when the work-items were increased by power of two starting at 4. Taking 2048 steps as an example, the best throughput for NVIDIA, FPGA and Mali GPUs was seen at 128, 128 and 64 work-items, respectively. After that it started increasing again for higher number of work-items due to resources contention.

Vectorization performed worse for Altera and NVIDIA while for Mali the 4-way vectorisation improved the throughput by more than 3×. Using more number of options per work-group reduced performance owing to increased local memory bandwidth contentions. Even if all other optimizations are ignored,

Altera, NVIDIA and Mali showed 2.8×, 3.5× and 2× improvement over worst case via balancing of work-items.

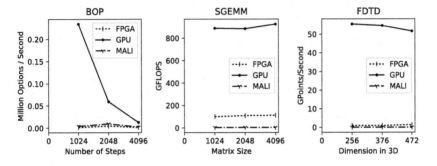

Fig. 4. Throughput comparison across devices.

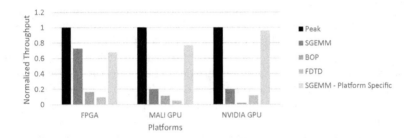

Fig. 5. Normalized peak vs achieved throughput for various devices

4.2 Throughput Comparison

The absolute throughputs for varying data sizes are shown in Fig. 4. We chose the best throughputs for each device which were measured using OpenCL's clGetEventProfilingInfo. As expected, the NVIDIA GPU performs the best by up to 8×, 17× and 56× over Altera FPGA for BOP, SGEMM and FDTD respectively. The FPGA performs up to 56×, 5.5× and 16× better than Mali GPU. The overall performance on all devices can be related to the size of each device.

4.3 Theoretical vs Achieved Throughput

Compiler efficiency can be estimated by analysing their ability to achieve high throughput compared to the theoretical peak performance on each platform. The theoretical peak throughput for NVIDIA GPU is 4612 GFLOPS computed as number of $cores \times Frequency \times 2(ArithmeticPipelinesPerCore)\ FLOPS$. As the Stratix V has 256 of 27×27 and 512 of 18×18 multipliers and a floating point unit uses 2 of 27×27 or 4 of 18×18 multipliers with 2 FLOPs per cycle with a peak operating frequency of 300 MHz [9], the peak throughput can be calculated as $256 \times 300 \times 2 = 153.6 \ GFLOPS$. For Mali GPU, the peak is estimated using $cores \times Frequency \times 2(ArithmeticPipelinesPerCore) \times 4(way-vectorization) \ FLOPS$ as $19.2 \ GFLOPS$.

For SGEMM the FLOPs are calculated as $2 \times n^3$ where n is the size of square matrices. For BOP, the total FLOPs are given by $3 \times n(n+1)/2$, where n is number of steps. For FDTD, we used a radius of 4 for calculating the new field values. A radius of 4 constitutes 25 points and thus 49 FLOPs per point. The total number of FLOPs are then $dimx \times dimy \times dimz \times 49$.

We have also included figures for achieved performance using platform-specific optimizations for SGEMM on each platform. For FPGA and MALI GPU, figures are projected estimates from implementations in [10,11], respectively, on similar devices while NVIDIA figures are of execution via CuBLAS library [12]. The normalized peak throughputs are shown in Fig. 5. It shows that for our used methodology, FPGA performs the best and even though GPU is supposed to be the preferred candidate for OpenCL, it requires more optimization effort utilizing platform-specific characteristics to achieve maximum throughput.

5 Energy Efficiency Analysis

To focus only on energy consumed in computing, we measured the dynamic power, i.e. the power utilized on top of static power during computation, using on-board sensors and looked at how it varied for different use cases.

5.1 Energy Efficiency Variations

SGEMM: Although the energy efficiencies of all devices for SGEMM followed a similar pattern to the throughput as both depend on resource usage, they are not exactly proportional. For example, kernel 4 outperforms kernel 3 for NVIDIA GPU, kernel 3 is better than kernel 4 for FPGA while kernel 2 is better than kernel 3 for Mali GPU whereas it was vice versa for throughput. In addition, although FPGA has the best peak performance, NVIDIA is better than FPGA for kernels 1 and 3 highlighting the importance of the platform-independent optimizations. Overall, the optimization methodology improves energy efficiency of FPGA, NVIDIA and Mali by 24× (Kernel 2), 5.8× (Kernel 3) and 14× (Kernel 4), respectively, compared to the worst performing points.

BOP: The achieved energy efficiency trend for 2048 steps (Fig. 6) is different from throughput with a maxima of 64 and 256 work-items for NVIDIA and Mali GPU, respectively. Interestingly, the energy efficiency curves cross over at multiple points for all platforms. Overall, the methodology improves energy efficiency of Altera, NVIDIA and Mali by up to 2.8×, 2.7× and 2.7×, respectively.

5.2 Energy Efficiency Comparison

As with throughput analysis, we choose the best energy efficiency points for each device which may not have the best throughputs. The graphs shown in

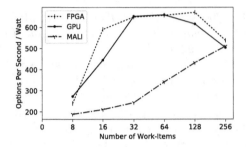

Fig. 6. BOP energy efficiency variation with number of work-items

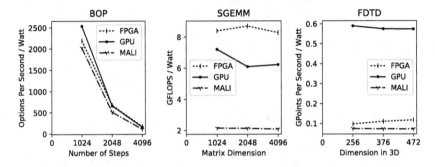

Fig. 7. Energy efficiency comparison across devices

Fig. 7 against application-specific metrics are self explanatory to characterize the accelerators based on energy efficiency. For BOP, Altera performs 1.15× worse than NVIDIA for a smaller problem size but performs up to 1.02× better for higher step sizes. For SGEMM and FDTD, Altera and NVIDIA perform the best by up to 1.4× and 6×, respectively. Mali performs the worst for all cases.

6   Conclusion

This work develops a design space exploration based on OpenCL and the identification of platform independent optimization that are applied on a variety of accelerators. To evaluate the energy efficiency and performance of the considered accelerators we mapped three popular application kernels. The results show that although GPUs outperform FPGA in terms of throughput, FPGA is able to achieve better energy efficiency for some of the tested cases whilst not requiring traditional hardware design expertise. On the other hand GPU requires more platform-specific optimizations utilizing in-depth knowledge of hardware to achieve high performance.

Acknowledgment. The work was supported by the European Commission under European Horizon 2020 Programme, grant number 6876281 (VINEYARD).

References

1. Schadt, E.E., et al.: Computational solutions to large-scale data management and analysis. Nat. Rev. Genet. **11**(9), 647–657 (2010)
2. Stone, J.E., Gohara, D., Shi, G.: OpenCL - a parallel programming standard for heterogeneous computing systems. Comput. Sci. Eng. **12**(3), 66–73 (2010)
3. Barr, J.: Developer preview – EC2 instances (F1) with programmable hardware. Amazon Web Services (2016)
4. Hill, K., et al.: Comparative analysis of OpenCL vs. HDL with image-processing kernels on Stratix-V FPGA. In: IEEE International Conference on ASAP (2015)
5. Fang, J., Varbanescu, A.L., Sips, H.: A comprehensive performance comparison of CUDA and OpenCL. In: IEEE ICPP (2011)
6. Rul, S., et al.: An experimental study on performance portability of OpenCL kernels. In: Symposium on Application Accelerators in High Performance Computing (2010)
7. Chen, D., Singh, D.: Fractal video compression in OpenCL: an evaluation of CPUs, GPUs, and FPGAs as acceleration platforms. In: ASP-DAC. IEEE (2013)
8. Zohouri, H.R., et al.: Evaluating and optimizing OpenCL kernels for high performance computing with FPGAs. In: Proceedings of IEEE/ACM Supercomputing Conference (2016)
9. Berkeley Design Technology, Inc.: Floating-point DSP design flow and performance on Altera 28-nm FPGAs. In: Independent Analysis (2012)
10. Giefers, H., Polig, R., Hagleitner, C.: Analyzing the energy-efficiency of dense linear algebra kernels by power-profiling a hybrid CPU/FPGA system. In: 25th International Conference on Application-Specific Systems, Architectures and Processors. IEEE (2014)
11. Gronqvist, J., Lokhmotov, A.: Optimising OpenCL kernels for the ARM Mali-T600 GPUs. In: GPU Pro 5: Advanced Rendering Techniques, p. 327 (2014)
12. NVIDIA, CUDA: Basic Linear Algebra Subroutines (cuBLAS) library (2013)

ReneGENE-Novo: Co-designed Algorithm-Architecture for Accelerated Preprocessing and Assembly of Genomic Short Reads

Santhi Natarajan[1]([⊠]) ⓘ, N. KrishnaKumar[1]ⓘ, H. V. Anuchan[2], Debnath Pal[1], and S. K. Nandy[1]

[1] Indian Institute of Science, Bangalore 560012, India
santhi@cadl.iisc.ernet.in
[2] National Institute of Technology Karnataka, Surathkal 575025, India

Abstract. Sufficiently long genome strings, permitting adequate overlaps, is key to producing a quality genome assembly with minimal error rates and high coverage. Next Generation Sequencing (NGS) platforms produce large volumes (tera bytes) of short-sized raw genomic strings or reads (150–600 genomic alphabets or bases) with minimal error rates. If we are able to increase the read lengths of raw short reads computationally before assembly, then the full potential of short reads from NGS and *de novo* assembly can be harvested. The large data redundancy offered by billions of such raw reads, compounded by the target genome length of billions of bases, requires a complex big data engineering solution. This paper presents a co-designed algorithm-architecture model for ReneGENE *de novo* assembly (part of a larger ReneGENE-GI Genome Informatics pipeline). This module takes randomly presented short reads from NGS platforms and extends them iteratively to an appropriate length by identifying overlaps among them, aiding high-coverage assembly with minimal error rates. This task is parallelized across multiple processes, to allow parallel read assembly with performance scalability. Supported by parallel algorithms, multi-dimensional data structures and fine-grain synchronization, the module realises irregular computing for *de novo* assembly. A single FPGA realization of this model with 128 *de novo* compute elements, shows a 48.69x improvement in performance when compared to an 8-core implementation on a standard workstation based on Intel Core i7-4770 processors.

1 Introduction

The genome of an organism encompasses the complete set of genetic instructions for its growth and existence. Algorithmically, the genome is represented as a long string (human genome is typically 3 billion characters long) made up of the genomic alphabet set $\Sigma = \{A,\ C,\ G,\ T\}$. Currently, genomes are being sequenced through Next Generation Sequencing platforms where short genomic

N. Voros et al. (Eds.): ARC 2018, LNCS 10824, pp. 564–577, 2018.
https://doi.org/10.1007/978-3-319-78890-6_45

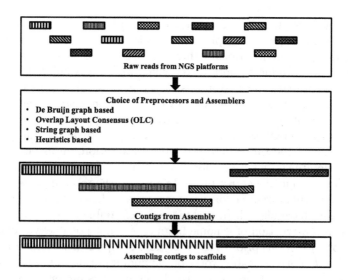

Fig. 1. *de novo* assembly workflow

segments or substrings ranging from 30 to a few kilo bases (genomic alphabets) are determined from biological samples, with high throughput [1]. Genome sequence assembly is a classical approximate string computation problem of identifying the right order of these short reads (typically amounting to tera bytes in data size), derived with high redundancy and coverage depth from NGS platforms, and hence come up with the most accurate representation of the genome.

1.1 *de Novo* Assembly: A Complex Big-Data Engineering Problem

The *de novo* assembly [2] workflow is captured in Fig. 1. In the absence of a template genome for the sample under consideration, the short reads are ordered, merged and reordered *de novo* by the assembly tool to reconstruct the target genome. The assembly generates larger fragments, called contigs or contiguous sequence fragments, from the short reads. These contigs are further reordered and reoriented to form scaffolds, while allowing sufficient gaps or regions of uncertainty among the contigs.

While attempting to produce intact genome assemblies, the following factors decide the quality of the assembly:

1. Nature of the reads and read lengths
2. Throughput and redundancy at which reads are generated
3. Error profile of the NGS platform
4. Availability of a template reference genome
5. Strategy adopted to sequence repetitive regions (sequence segments repeated in an almost identical order) in a genome
6. Rate of read assembly that leads to early coverage of a major portion of the target genome.

The assembly is guided by the amount of similarity among the short read substrings, which helps in grouping reads with sufficient neighbourhood and originating from nearby locations within the target genome. However, a repeat region sequencing produces short reads which are very similar, but originate from highly separated repeat locations in the genome. The presence of short reads from genomic repeats provides an exponential increase in the number of possible overlaps of short reads to form contigs, compounded by an exponential increase in the number of contig re-arrangements involving similar contigs, at each location of the target repeat region. In addition, an assembler cannot accurately generate contigs from short reads that are from NGS platforms with sufficiently large sequencing error rates. As a result, the resultant contigs diverge more from the actual target genome segments than what the assembler's heuristics alone would have offered. In presence of such ambiguous inputs, a reliable and efficient reconstruction of genome fragments is not possible without involving read-error corrections prior to assembly and computational heuristics during assembly. The *de novo* assembly works on random input data, irregular memory access patterns and spontaneous growth of contigs, thus presenting an irregular computing pattern.

The choice of an assembler [3], defines the throughput and performance of the *de novo* assembly pipeline. Sequence assemblers are chosen predominantly based on the short read characteristics. Highly accurate short reads of smaller length (<200 bases) are typically assembled using the de Bruijn graph based approaches [4,5]. As the short reads get longer and data is loaded with sequencing errors, overlap-based approaches like Overlap Layout Consensus (OLC) [6] and string-graphs [7,8] are preferred. To apply de Bruijn graphs for longer reads, a pre-processing stage is used in the assembly pipeline to correct the errors in sequencing.

The de Bruijn graph based methods avoid the computational complexity of extracting overlaps among billions of short reads and accelerate the assembly process. The OLC and string-graph based methods use highly memory-efficient data structures and compressed storage formats which allow for a highly scalable assembler. Attempts have been made to accelerate various stages of the assembly pipeline on reconfigurable and heterogeneous platforms, with profiling studies and extensive design space exploration of the algorithmic implementations [9,10]. Nevertheless, all these approaches suffer from the need for heuristics-based and ad hoc preprocessing involved in handling longer reads, error correction, memory management and identifying contigs in repeat regions of genome. The large data redundancy observed in billions of raw short read substrings, compounded by the target genome length of billions of bases, requires a complex big data engineering solution.

In this context, we present ReneGENE-Novo, a co-designed algorithm-architecture model for running *de novo* assembly of short reads. Our solution computationally extends the small short reads to more accurate "readtigs" prior to the assembly, as against conventional assemblers that use heuristic and ad hoc corrections for length and errors. This helps in harvesting the full potential

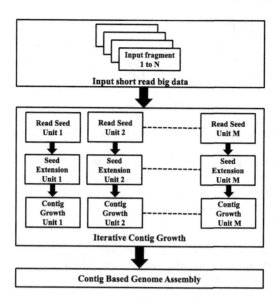

Fig. 2. ReneGENE-Novo workflow

of short reads from NGS and *de novo* assembly. ReneGENE-Novo takes randomly presented short reads from NGS platforms and extends them iteratively and accurately to an appropriate length by identifying overlaps among them, aiding high-coverage assembly with minimal error rates. This task is parallelized across multiple processes, to allow parallel read assembly with performance scalability. Supported by parallel algorithms, multi-dimensional data structures and fine-grain synchronization, the module realises irregular computing for *de novo* assembly. The extended readtigs can then be subjected to normal assembly using conventional assemblers. ReneGENE-Novo also serves to increase the coverage in the comparative genomics pipeline by extending the unaligned reads which were left aside by the short read mapping algorithms while aligning them against a reference genome. The unaligned reads are extended to readtigs alongside the aligned reads, which allows to cover the large gaps for an otherwise poor alignment.

2   ReneGENE-Novo

The ReneGENE-Novo module, shown in Fig. 2, works on the principle of identifying overlap among the incoming reads presented at random, by a novel and parallel scheme, thereby generating readtigs or extended reads in a deterministic number of cycles and operations, as captured in Algorithm 1. An overlap is said to occur, when a seed/partially grown readtig has substrings which are computationally similar to the substrings of the incoming read, over regions spanning the string boundaries. Once an overlap is identified, the non-overlapping

---

Algorithm 1. RENEGENE_NOVO_READTIG()

1: // **Purpose:** *de novo* assembly function to generate readtigs
2: // **Input:** Input short reads R in fastq format
3: // **Output:** Assembled Readtigs C in fastq format
4: -
5: Partition the short reads R into S_n read sets
6: **for** each read set S_i in S_n **do**
7:     Load each M_i in M_n readtig maps with reads from S_i to form readtig seeds
8: **end for**
9: **for** each readtig map M_i in M_n parallel maps **do**
10:     **for** each read r in R in the forward direction **do**
11:         **if** r overlaps with a readtig seed from M_i **then**
12:             Assemble r with the seed
13:         **end if**
14:     **end for**
15:     **for** each read r in R in reverse direction **do**
16:         **if** r overlaps with a readtig seed from M_i **then**
17:             Assemble r with the seed
18:         **end if**
19:     **end for**
20: **end for**
21: **for** each readtig map M_i in M_n **do**
22:     Merge contents to form readtig set C
23: **end for**

---

regions and the overlapped segments are concatenated to enable readtig growth. For example, for the seed AAAATGCA (length = 8) and the incoming read string TGCAGGGG (length = 8), the readtig can be constructed as AAAAT-GCAGGGG (length = 12). The overlap criteria (extent of overlap and mismatches within overlapped string region) across iterations of readtig growth, determines the length of the readtig.

Here, a single read can share a similar overlap relationship with several of its sequence neighbours, resulting in a single seed growing into many tangible readtigs. This is again decided at run time and hence the computations are clearly irregular due to the irregularity in the relationships among the input data sets. To accommodate the readtigs that grow on the fly, the *de novo* assembly module implements dynamically growing multi-dimensional data structures cast in the map-reduce framework, hence allowing a parallel deployment.

The readtigs, coming from the ReneGENE-Novo module, are now accurately extended forms of the short reads, combined with the base quality information of the reads. The accuracy of readtig growth stems from the fact that the two reads are expected to have absolutely matching substrings over the overlap distance. The overlap distance decides the extent and rate of growth during the initial rounds of readtig growth. Once a reasonable number of reads have participated in the initial rounds, an iterative growth among the already formed readtigs and the residual reads would result in a set of final readtigs sufficiently long enough to advance to contig growths. The overlap distance is a function of the read length. This value is provided as a user input, where the user can choose to start from a lower overlap distance and close with a larger one and vice versa.

The final set of readtigs can now be assembled using any conventional read assemblers like Velvet, leading to more accurate contigs and scaffolds. Since the growth of readtigs are independent of each other, this provides a good coverage of the short reads from the repeat region of the genome, thus preventing purging of valid reads that can give rise to contigs for target repeats. While conventional assemblers tend to work only with unique seeds and unique contigs from seeds, ReneGENE-Novo allows every read to hold the status of the seed during the readtig growth stage. This allows all reads to grow to readtigs and hence to contigs that encompass the repeat regions.

3 Prototypes and Results

3.1 Experimental Setup

The prototype for the ReneGENE-Novo was deployed on three different platforms, as detailed in Table 1. The first platform is a workstation, with an Intel Core i7-4770 based 8-core processor and 32 GB of system memory. The second platform is an accelerator platform based on the Intel Xeon E5620 host processor, supported by multiple Xilinx Virtex-6 6vlx550tff1759-2 FPGAs, each capable of hosting a maximum of 256 instances of ReneGENE-Novo hardware models, developed and implemented in Verilog HDL. The inherent parallel nature of the reconfigurable hardware provides additional room for parallelizing the already parallel Novo algorithm. The third platform is Cray XC40, a hybrid

Table 1. ReneGENE-Novo platform details

Feature	P1: Workstation	P2: Reconfigurable Hardware Accelerators (FPGAs)	P3: Cray XC40
Application environment	C++	C++/Verilog HDL	C++
Compilers	GNU 4.8.2	Intel 4.8.1	Intel 16.0.4.258
Library	MPICH 3.1.4	MPICH 3.1.4	Cray MPICH 7.4.3
Processor	Intel Core i7-4770	Intel Xeon E5620	Intel Xeon-Phi Coprocessor 5120D (KNC) and host CPU of Intel Xeon Ivybridge E5-2695 v2
Number of nodes	1	1	24
Memory	32 GB	48 GB	64 GB host memory, 8 GB co-processor memory
Interconnect	Nil	Nil	Proprietary Cray Aries Interconnect with Dragonfly Topology

High Performance Computing (HPC/supercomputing) system, configured with Intel's Xeon-Phi 5120D (KNC) based cards. Each platform comes with its own set of compiler-specific and architecture specifications, which have their effects on the related performance numbers.

3.2   ReneGENE-Novo Test Data

To verify the correctness and analyse the performance scaling of ReneGENE-Novo, we have run experiments on a non-random short read set synthetically derived from the reference genome of the organism E.coli. The reads are derived contiguously at various read lengths, ranging through 32, 64, 128, 256, 512, 1024 and 2048 bases. If the reads are extended accurately, the extended readtigs are expected to grow to the full length of the reference from which the reads are derived, provided an overlap exists for all reads. This check ensures the functional correctness of the algorithm. The choice of the read length is expected to influence the performance of the prototypes. The performance of the module is compared for the various implementations as shown in Table 1.

3.3   ReneGENE-Novo: Measure of Accuracy and Performance on Platform P1

The performance comparison of the prototype for ReneGENE-Novo on platform P1, for various read length options, is compiled in Table 2. As mentioned in Sect. 2, ReneGENE-Novo validates the accuracy of the readtigs by allowing all the reads to become seeds and then grow independently to readtigs. The performance numbers in this paper account for the computations done by ReneGENE-Novo to not only grow the seeds to form readtigs, but to also validate their accuracy. All the seeds in ReneGENE-Novo grow to the same readtig, as the seeds are extracted from contiguous locations of the same genome. This essentially means that we have successfully achieved accurate readtig growth. ReneGENE-Novo generates readtigs of same length and coverage.

Table 2. ReneGENE-Novo performance on P1

Read length	ReneGENE-Novo (single process): time in seconds	ReneGENE-Novo (8 processes): time in seconds	ReneGENE-Novo: number of readtigs
32	3462	1199	9969
64	2575	1205	9937
128	2970	1180	9873
256	2997	1192	9745
512	3971	1220	9489
1024	3978	1202	8977
2048	4065	1252	7953

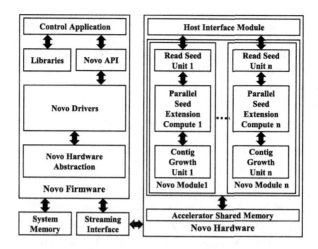

Fig. 3. The ReneGENE-Novo hardware

3.4 ReneGENE-Novo Performance Analysis on Platform P2

The ReneGENE-Novo was implemented on a reconfigurable hardware platform, with multiple FPGAs. The prototype was modelled in Verilog HDL, embedded within the acceleration framework. The application workflow is shown in Fig. 3.

Coded in a multithreaded fashion, the Novo firmware runs on the host system. The firmware implements the *de novo* assembly workflow in Fig. 1, with the support of the accelerator hardware consisting of the Xilinx 6vlx550tff1759-2 Virtex-6 devices. The firmware is built around custom APIs, supported by stand-alone libraries for ReneGENE-Novo. These APIs help in setting up and maintaining a streaming interface with the hardware. The firmware hosts drivers for the scalable Novo hardware on reconfigurable platform. These drivers help in initializing and setting up the hardware, with application and algorithm parameters. The Novo hardware abstraction layer interacts with hardware during configuration, and also participates in control and data transfers during assembly run time.

Table 3. ReneGENE-Novo configuration and occupancy on P2

Feature utilization	8 units	70 units	128 units
Slice registers	27756 out of 687360 (4%)	83137 out of 687360 (4%)	213082 out of 687360 (31%)
Slice LUTs	16247 out of 343680 (4%)	124908 out of 687360 (36%)	292128 out of 687360 (85%)
Bonded IOBs	34 out of 840 (4%)	34 out of 840 (4%)	34 out of 840 (4%)
BRAM/FIFO	63 out of 632 (9%)	63 out of 632 (9%)	63 out of 632 (9%)

As seen in Table 3, three different configurations were realized on the hardware; with 8, 70 and 128 parallel instances of the ReneGENE-Novo module, with each instance growing one seed to a readtig. The growth of one seed to a readtig is totally independent of any other seed or readtig growth. The performance numbers are extracted based on the simulation of the ReneGENE-Novo using Xilinx proprietary simulation tools. The performance parameters for ReneGENE-Novo on P2 is given in Table 4.

Table 4. ReneGENE-Novo scalability and performance parameters on P2

Symbols	Description
L	Short read length
N	Total number of reads
NOP_{read}	Total Novo Operations per seed for a single read, $NOP_{read} = 4 \times L$
τ_{clk}	Operating clock period of the ReneGENE-Novo module, in seconds
T_{config}	Time taken to configure the ReneGENE-Novo module on the hardware, in seconds
$T_{ContigN}$	Time taken in seconds, per seed or novo module, to grow readtigs from N reads, $T_{ContigN} = \tau_{clk} \times (3 \times N + 1)$
T_{Total}	Time taken in seconds, to grow readtigs from N reads for N modules over B iterations (n seeds per iteration), $T_{Total} = B \times T_{ContigN} + T_{config}$
NOP_{Nreads}	Total Novo Operations for N reads, per seed, $NOP_{Nreads} = 3 \times N \times NOP_{read}$
n	Number of Novo instances within the FPGA
NOP_n	Total Novo operations across n parallel modules within the hardware, $NOP_n = n \times NOP_{Nreads}$
B	Number of batches required to cover the reads
$NOP_{nAssembly}$	Total Novo Operations across B Batches, $NOP_{nAssembly} = B \times NOP_n$

The performance of a group of n ReneGENE-novo modules, over a single batch of n seeds, covering readtig growth across N reads per seed, measured in Giga Novo Operations Per Second (GNOPS), is given by:

$$P_{Novo} = \frac{NOP_n}{T_{ContigN} \times 10^9} \tag{1}$$

The performance of a group of n ReneGENE-Novo modules (considering the assembly time only), over a B batches having n seed growth per batch, covering readtig growth across N reads per seed, measured in GNOPS, is given by:

$$P_{NovoAssembly} = \frac{NOP_{nAssembly}}{B \times T_{ContigN} \times 10^9} \tag{2}$$

The performance of a group of n ReneGENE-Novo modules (considering assembly time and configuration time), over a single batch of n seeds, covering readtig growth across N reads, measured in GNOPS, is given by:

$$P_{NovoTotal} = \frac{B \times NOP_n}{T_{Total} \times 10^9} \qquad (3)$$

Table 5 summarizes the performance comparison of ReneGENE-Novo for all the three configurations. Here, we can see that as the number of Novo modules increase, there is a substantial increase in the performance in terms of GNOPS from the parallel ReneGENE-Novo hardware. This is only limited by the maximum number of novo modules that we can accommodate within a single FPGA. Beyond the boundaries of the single FPGA, we can scale the hardware across multiple FPGAs, thereby providing an improved performance.

3.5   ReneGENE-Novo Performance Analysis on Platform P3

ReneGENE-Novo was configured on the Intel Xeon Phi co-processors on the Cray XC40 platform [11]. Cray XC40 has a total of 48 Intel Xeon Phi co-processors, each node is a combination of 12 CPU cores and One Xeon-Phi Co-Processor. The host CPU cores are composed of Intel Xeon Ivybridge E5-2695 v2 12-core processors operating at 2.4 GHz. The Intel Xeon-Phi Co-Processor 5120D (Knights Corner) for each node has 60 cores. There is 64 GB of main memory and 8 GB of device memory available for data handling. The nodes are interconnected through Proprietary Cray Aries Interconnect with Dragonfly Topology.

The results of the experiments conducted on 24 Intel Xeon Phi co-processors on P3 are provided in Table 6. Here, we have considered the short reads from

Table 5. ReneGENE-Novo performance analysis on P2

Feature	8 units	70 units	128 units
Operating frequency F (MHz)	225.202	122.585	120.746
τ_{clk}	4.4 ns	8.16 ns	8.4 ns
L	64	64	64
N	10000	10000	10000
n	8	70	128
P_{Novo} (GNOPS)	461.24	2196.55	3956.4
$P_{NovoAssembly}$ (GNOPS)	461.24	2196.55	3956.4
$P_{NovoTotal}$ (GNOPS)	115.23	143.69	149.45

Table 6. ReneGENE-Novo performance analysis on P3

Feature	Helix	P3
Parallelization	64 processes	288 processes
Heuristics	NIL, accurate overlap	NIL, accurate overlap
Number of reads	596,100	596,100
Time taken	3211 min 13 s	42 min 45 s

E.coli organism (SRR1948068 of the NCBI database), consisting of around 600,000 short reads, each read with 251 bases. We have compared the performance with a workstation named Helix with AMD Opteron(TM) Processor 6284 SE having 64 cores.

We can see that P3 reports a better performance as the irregular computing scales well across the 288 processes in P3 compared to 64 cores in Helix. Though we could not achieve a linear scaling in performance, the parallelization involved at both the algorithmic and architectural levels, along with architecture-specific optimizations, offers a notable improvement in performance.

3.6   ReneGENE-Novo: Effect of Algorithm-Architecture Co-design on Various Platforms

Here, we have compiled the performance of ReneGENE-Novo across the platforms P1, P2 and P3. The results of algorithm-architecture co-design of ReneGENE-Novo, where the algorithm and hardware parameters have together been tailored for individual platforms, have been presented in Table 7. The GNOPS based performance analysis is done on P1, P2 and P3 while varying the number of processes/units for a total number of 76800000000 novo operations to extend all seeds against all reads across all processes/units. The results suggest that the hardware based implementation of ReneGENE-Novo outperforms the single and eight-process variations of P1. The presence of 288 processes in

Table 7. ReneGENE-Novo: analysis of effects of algorithm-architecture co-design on various platforms

Feature	P1: 1 process	P1: 8 processes	P2: 8 units	P2: 70 units	P2: 128 units	P3: 288 processes
1. Number of reads	10000	10000	10000	10000	10000	10000
2. Number of parallel units/processes	1	8	8	70	128	288
3. Number of seeds per process/unit	10000	1250	8	70	128	35
4. Total number of Novo operations to extend single seed against all reads in a single process/unit	7680000	7680000	7680000	7680000	7680000	7680000
5. Time taken (seconds) to extend single seed against all reads in a single process/unit	0.17	0.02	0.000133	0.000244	0.000248	0.000590
6. Time taken (in seconds) to extend all seeds against all reads across all processes/units	1700	25	0.667	0.535	0.520	0.0305
7. ReneGENE-Novo performance for multiple processes/units in GNOPS	0.0452	3.07	115.23	143.69	149.45	2518.38

P3 provides superior performance compared to P2, due to a more optimal and parallel distribution of data, control and synchronization.

There is more scope of parallelism on P2, as we are currently using only a single FPGA. The ReneGENE-Novo is further scalable across multiple FPGAs which shall result in an improved performance. The reconfigurable hardware platforms serve to be an optimal choice for better parallelism and scalability for ReneGENE-Novo deployment. With many reconfigurable HPC platforms available with high-end FPGAs of larger logic capacity from vendors like Xilinx at affordable costs, we can deploy more parallel units of our model with optimal timing and power ratings. Platform P2 offers a more cost effective model when compared with a supercomputing platform like P3, as the power consumption of such deployments are much lesser, along with lesser maintenance and Non-Recurring Engineering (NRE) costs.

4   ReneGENE-Novo Use Case: Deployment for Genome Informatics

The ReneGENE-Novo is currently being used as part of a larger Genome Informatics (GI) pipeline, namely ReneGENE-GI. Fig. 4 illustrates the ReneGENE-GI pipeline, which performs Short Read Mapping (SRM) [12,13]. The short reads are mapped or aligned against a reference genome string through SRM. The novelty of the ReneGENE-GI pipeline lies in the fact that it offers a unique blend of comparative genomics and *de novo* sequence assembly, offering the most precise SRM. The comparative genomics module exploits the parallel Dynamic Programming [14] methodology to accurately map the short reads against the reference genome. The alignment is backed by an accurate indexing and lookup of reads against the reference using the parallel implementation of dynamic Monotonic Minimal Perfect Hashing (MMPH) method [15–17]. The ReneGENE-Novo module generates readtigs as explained in the previous sections. These readtigs

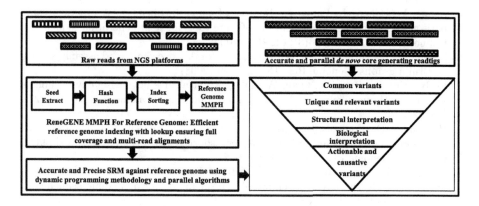

Fig. 4. The ReneGENE-GI pipeline

are further mapped on to the reference genome to encompass the possible insertions and deletions of genetic alphabets at certain locations, thereby widening the map space and coverage accuracy.

5 Conclusion

This paper addresses the fundamental biocomputing problem of short read assembly as a big data engineering problem. We present the algorithm-architecture co-design of ReneGENE-Novo, the short read extender and assembler, that employs multi-dimensional data structures, novel read-extension algorithms and fine grain synchronization techniques to handle tera bytes of randomly presented raw genomic short read strings. The readtigs, extended versions of the short reads with computed overlaps across the associated sets of related reads, form ideal candidates for further assembly using conventional *de novo* assemblers like Velvet. We have analyzed performance of ReneGENE-Novo across three different platforms. We observed a good scalability in performance attributed to the amount of parallelism, compiler-specific and architecture-specific features of each platform. The ReneGENE-GI Genome Informatics pipeline is presented as a use case for ReneGENE-Novo. The pipeline offers a unique blend of comparative genomics and *de novo* sequence assembly, by extending the depth and coverage of an accurate short read mapping using the extended readtigs from ReneGENE-Novo. The prototypes demonstrate the useful implementation of irregular computing which has significant implications for genome assembly.

References

1. Frese, K.S., Katus, H.A., Meder, B.: Next-generation sequencing: from understanding biology to personalized medicine. Biology **2**, 378–398 (2013)
2. Nagarajan, N., Pop, M.: Sequence assembly demystified. Nat. Rev. **14**, 157–167 (2013)
3. Zhang, W., Chen, J., Yang, Y., Tang, Y., Shang, J., Shen, B.: A practical comparison of de novo genome assembly software tools for next-generation sequencing technologies. PLoS ONE **6**(3), e17915 (2011)
4. Zerbino, D.R., Birney, E.: Velvet: algorithms for de novo short read assembly using de Bruijn graphs. Genome Res. **18**, 821–829 (2008)
5. Li, R., Zhu, H., Ruan, J., Qian, W., Fang, X., et al.: De novo assembly of human genomes with massively parallel short read sequencing. Genome Res. **20**, 265–272 (2010)
6. Hernandez, D., Francois, P., Farinelli, L., Osteras, M., Schrenzel, J.: De novo bacterial genome sequencing: millions of very short reads assembled on a desktop computer. Genome Res. **18**, 802–809 (2008)
7. Dohm, J.C., Lottaz, C., Borodina, T., Himmelbauer, H.: SHARCGS, a fast and highly accurate short-read assembly algorithm for de novo genomic sequencing. Genome Res. **17**, 1697–1706 (2007)
8. Bryant Jr., D.W., Wong, W.K., Mockler, T.C.: QSRA: a quality-value guided de novo short read assembler. BMC Bioinform. **10**, 69 (2009)

9. Varma, B.S.C., Paul, K., Balakrishnan, M., Lavenier, D.: Fassem: FPGA based acceleration of de novo genome assembly. In: FCCM 2013, pp. 173–176. IEEE Computer Society, Washington, DC (2013)

10. Varma, B., Paul, K., Balakrishnan, M.: Accelerating genome assembly using hard embedded blocks in FPGAs. In: 27th International Conference on VLSI Design and 13th International Conference on Embedded Systems, pp. 306–311, January 2014

11. Cray Inc.: Cray XC40: Scaling Across the Supercomputer Performance Spectrum. http://www.cray.com/sites/default/files/resources/CrayXC40Brochure.pdf

12. Natarajan, S., KrishnaKumar, N., Pal, D., Nandy, S.K.: AccuRA: accurate alignment of short reads on scalable reconfigurable accelerators. In: Proceedings of IEEE International Conference on Embedded Computer Systems: Architectures, Modeling and Simulation (SAMOS XVI), pp. 79–87, July 2016

13. Natarajan, S., KrishnaKumar, N., Pal, D., Nandy, S.K.: Accurate and accelerated secondary analysis of genomes: implications for genomics. In: Barcelona NGS 2017: Structural Variation and Population Genomics, April 2017

14. Natarajan, S., KrishnaKumar, N., Pavan, M., Pal, D., Nandy, S.K.: ReneGENE-DP: accelerated parallel dynamic programming for genome informatics. In: Accepted at the 2018 International Conference on Electronics, Computing and Communication Technologies (IEEE CONECCT), March 2018

15. Myers, E.: A sublinear algorithm for approximate keyword searching. Algorithmica **12**, 345–374 (1994)

16. Shi, F.: Fast approximate string matching with q-blocks sequences. In: Proceedings of 3rd South American Workshop on String Processing, pp. 257–271 (1996)

17. Ukkonen, E.: Finding approximate patterns in strings. J. Algorithms **6**, 132–137 (1985)

An OpenCL^{TM} Implementation of WebP Accelerator on FPGAs

Zhenhua Guo^(✉), Baoyu Fan, Yaqian Zhao, Xuelei Li, Shixin Wei, and Long Li

State Key Laboratory of High-End Server & Storage Technology
(Inspur Group Company Limited), Jinan 250001, China
{guozhenhua, fanbaoyu, zhaoyaqian, lixuelei, weishixin,
lilong}@inspur.com

Abstract. With the development of cloud computing, the super-large scale of image data has bring severe challenges for the storage cost and network bandwidth in data centers. In order to alleviate the present situation effectively, WebP has replaced the current mainstream image file format due to its better compression efficiency. In this paper, we provide an OpenCL implementation of WebP accelerator on FPGAs to optimize the performance of WebP Lossy Compression Algorithm. Our accelerator makes use of a heavily-pipelined custom hardware implementation to achieve a high throughput ~ 450MPixel/s. The performance-per-watt of our OpenCL implementation on Intel's Arria 10 device is 8.32x better than a highly-tuned CPU implementation on Intel Xeon E5-2690v3 with 24 thread cores. Additionally, the delay time per image can be reduced to $\sim 90\%$ by the data parallelism and macroblock pipelining on FPGAs. Finally, our OpenCL^{TM} implementation of WebP accelerator on FPGAs is more competitive for data centers to achieve higher performance and lower cost.

Keywords: WebP · FPGAs · OpenCL · Accelerator

1 Introduction

In this paper, we study the implementation of WebP lossy compression on FPGAs motivated by its potential application in data centers and communication networks. A recent report stated that the scale of internet data stored in data centers will be expected to reach 915EB by 2020 from 171EB in 2015, and the most of data is generated by pictures and videos [1]. According to the latest statistics, there are more than 8 billion new images stored in datacenter servers every day. It is a serious challenge for storage and bandwidth in data centers. Generally speaking, most of the companies are spending 12% of their IT budget on storage, and more seriously this cost is doubling every two years. This trend motivates the research and development on usefulness of image compression to reduce the size of image data. Additionally, the motivation helps to reduce the associated hardware cost and electrical energy in date centers. Similar with the efficient image compression, time delay also need to be reduced so as to take more advantages of network bandwidth. For the above requirements, high-efficiency image compression is imperative and urgent to achieve better performance for data center servers.

© Springer International Publishing AG, part of Springer Nature 2018
N. Voros et al. (Eds.): ARC 2018, LNCS 10824, pp. 578–589, 2018.
https://doi.org/10.1007/978-3-319-78890-6_46

WebP is a kind of image format supporting both lossy and lossless compression. It was developed by Google based on VP8 technology [2]. WebP lossless image are 26% smaller in size compared to PNGs, and WebP lossy image are 25%–34% smaller than comparable JPEG images at equivalent SSIM quality index [3, 4]. Given the need for high performance implementations to keep up with networks and storage device data rates, there are several works have addressed implementations targeting high image compression ratio. Google is the first to use WebP in data center for YouTube, Gmail and Google Play. Since using WebP for YouTube video thumbnail, the load response speed of web pages has increased 10%. Chrome Play APPs Store can save TBs-level of bandwidth for google by using WebP image format completely to replace the original JPEG and PNG images, and reduce average loading time by 1/3 for webpage. Because of using WebP, Google+ can save 50TBs data space for datacenter every day. Due to high compression capability and the same image quality, there are many other companies trying to use WebP in their applications, such as Tencent, Facebook, E-bay, Taobao, Meituan. But all the implementations above are developed on CPU platform. As a result of higher image compression ratio, it is done at the expense of significantly longer compression time by WebP lossy algorithm.

FPGAs can provide higher performance, lower cost and better flexibility. It has become an attractive alternative for improving the efficiency of data centers [5]. Parallel processing of image pixels can be achieved by mapping applications of the inherent parallelizable nature into the silicon fabric to take advantage of the capabilities of FPGAs [6]. Consequently, custom hardware implementation offers much greater performance. Additionally, the exceptional decrease in algorithm's execution time can be achieved compared to traditional CPUs. Nevertheless, WebP lossy algorithm is rarely studied in the field of performance optimization with FPGAs for data centers, because FPGA implementations traditionally were written using hardware description languages, such as Verilog HDL or VHDL which are akin to assembly language for hardware. This makes FPGA design time-consuming and difficult to be verified. Instead, this paper proposes an OpenCL implementation of WebP lossy algorithm for accelerating data center servers by FPGAs. OpenCL is a C-based language intended for application acceleration on heterogeneous systems [7]. We demonstrate that the use of OpenCL for FPGA implementation enables incredible productivity gains while maintaining high efficiency as prior works.

In the following section we briefly describe the WebP lossy compression algorithm and the design architecture of WebP Accelerator. Section 3 describes the implementation and optimization of WebP on OpenCL. Section 4 outlines our preliminary compression ratio and performance results. Finally, Sects. 5 and 6 is about the related work and conclusion.

2   WebP **Lossy Compression Accelerator**

WebP lossy compression is based on the VP8 video codec with a Resource Interchange File Format (RIFF) container [8]. It uses the same methodology as VP8 for predicting frames, and holds exclusively an 8-bit YUV 4:2:0 image formats. Like any block-based codec, WebP lossy compression is also based on block prediction, and divides the frame into smaller segments called macroblocks, whose Y dimensions are 16×16 and both of U and V dimensions are 8×8.

The steps involved in WebP lossy compression are as follows [9]. First, intra prediction is actually used in the case of image compression, and mostly taken from H.264. The predictive coding only uses the pixels already decoded in the immediate spatial neighborhood of every macroblock, and tries to inpaint the unknown part of them. There are ten intra prediction modes used in WebP lossy compression, including horizontal, vertical, true-motion, horizontal-up, etc. Second, the predictive data is subtracted from the block, and only the difference is left called residual for encoded. After being subjected to a mathematically invertible transform, the famed DCT (Discrete Cosine Transfrom) and WHT (Walsh-Hadamard transformed), the residuals which typically contain many zero values, can be compressed more effectively. The transformation result is then quantized and entropy coded through a non-adaptive arithmetic coder. Loop filtering is used to remove blocking artifacts introduced by quantization of DCT coefficients from block transforms. The only step where bits are lossy discarded is quantization in WebP lossy compression. All the other steps are invertible and lossless. The differentiating features compared to JPEG are circled in red.

WebP uses block quantization and distributes bits adaptively across different image segments: fewer bits for low entropy segments and higher bits for higher entropy segments. The arithmetic entropy encoding used by WebP can achieve better compression compared to the Huffman encoding used in JPEG. In our implementation, the key of WebP lossy compression is implemented by OpenCL kernels for FPGAs, mainly including predictive coding, DCT, WHT, Quantization, inverse-DCT, inverse-Quantization. However, the algorithm is inherently serial (data is compressed block by block and is depended with previous macroblock for predictive coding) and exists many complex data dependencies. Therefore, we need to resolve the dependencies between the adjacent macroblocks, and this is the key to improve the performance of WebP Accelerator.

The WebP lossy compression accelerator is implemented in a heterogeneous system which includes an x86-based system as the host processor and FPGA cards as the accelerator. The overall design architecture is shown as Fig. 1. The host portion of the implementation extracts the YUV data from the other image formats such as JPG, PNG, etc. It also sends the YUV data to FPGA cards for compressing by OpenCL's API functions named *clEnqueueWriteBuffer*. The data to be compressed is stored in DDR memory on the FPGA card. The WebP lossy compression algorithm is designed

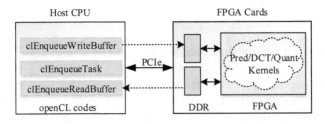

Fig. 1. System architecture of WebP lossy compression

by several kernels including Prediction, DCT, WHT, Quantization and the others. The WebP's IP core is generated automatically by the compiler of Intel FPGA SDK for OpenCL [10]. We can execute the kernel by *clEnqueueTask* in the portion of host, and then the YUV data in DDR memory is loaded by kernels used to lossy compress. When the compression is finished, the compressed image data is transferred to the host side by *clEnqueueReadBuffer*.

The implementation of WebP lossy compression is also extendable to standalone FPGA systems such as the case where YUV data streams in and out of the FPGA through Ethernet cables. In these environments, new generations of FPGAs with embedded hard processors can easily replace the functionality of the x86 host. Additionally, the host code is supporting the process of multi-pictures, which are processed with asynchronous behaviors. It allows to overlap the host-to-device communications and WebP kernel computations among the different pictures. Therefore, this paper only analyzes and evaluates the optimization technology and performance of WebP kernel.

3   Implementation and Optimization

In this section, we discuss implementation details and show how to optimize the procedure of WebP lossy compression algorithm by OpenCL on FPGAs.

3.1   The Architecture of WebP Accelerator

The first step of the WebP lossy compression algorithm is to load image data from global (DDR3) memory to local memory which is stored in on-chip RAM or registers. The image data is divided into three channels, and YUV channels are processed in parallel. Then YUV's data is divided into smaller macroblocks, whose Y dimensions are 16×16 and both of U and V dimensions are 8×8.

Figure 2 shows the architecture of WebP kernels for implementing WebP lossy compression algorithm. The Y and UV data is processed at the same time. There are 12 kernels totally and the nonblocking channel, which can't get blocked without input

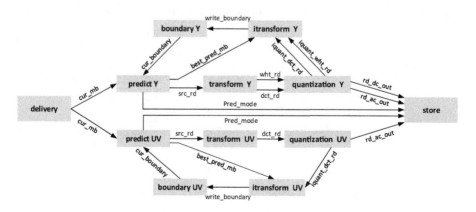

Fig. 2. The architecture of WebP accelerator on OpenCL kernels

data, is used for passing data to kernels and synchronizing. As shown in Fig. 2, the delivery kernel is responsible for loading a new macroblock data from global (DDR) memory, and the loaded data is passed to predict Y or UV kernel. The predict kernel can implement several prediction mode for chroma macroblocks, including horizontal prediction, vertical prediction, DC prediction, and TrueMotion prediction. There are also six additional prediction mode for 4×4 luma blocks. Based on the complicated dependencies, we have simplified the prediction mode. The best prediction mode is selected by calculating the mean variance of the predicted result and the original macroblock data. The residual value of macroblock is passed to transform kernel for DCT/WHT transformation by OpenCL channels. And then, the results of transformation are quantified by quantization kernels and the AC/DC coefficients are generated. The quantitative results and the best prediction mode are stored in global memory. At the same time, the inverse quantization and inverse transformation is running, and the results are used to predict by adjacent macroblocks. All the channels in Fig. 2 are nonblocking, and the overall architecture can process every macroblock pipelined well.

3.2   Inter-macroblock Pipeline

In WebP lossy compression algorithm, the prediction of next macroblock need to use the previous macroblock data which is generated by inverse DCT and quantization. This will lead to strong dependencies among the macroblocks in the process of encoding. Figure 3(a) illustrates the dependencies between macroblocks. This will lead the macroblock to be processed serially, and the performance is limited. To avoid the inter-macroblock dependencies and increase the parallelism among different kernels, we process the images data by zigzag sequence as shown in Fig. 3(b). But the Intel FPGA SDK for OpenCL cannot infer pipelining well for the iterations with an unfixed bounds. The index variables bound of inner loop is depended on the index of outer-loop on the control structure in OpenCL kernel. Due to the report of compilers, this will result that the iteration cannot be pipelined well. To build the well-structured loop in OpenCL kernels, we have to fill each row of macroblocks with zero-values macroblock. As shown in Fig. 3(c), the number of macroblock in every row is the same. Due to the reconstruction of image, we can implement the well-structured

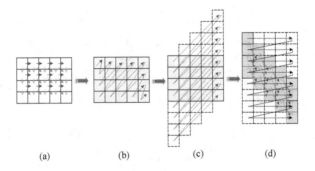

(a)   (b)   (c)   (d)

Fig. 3. Data sufficiency and the rotation of macroblocks

iterations in delivery kernel. Figure 3(d) shows that the structure of macroblock is rebuild and the dependencies between the adjacent macroblocks within one row are eliminated. Meanwhile, the loop can be structured well, and the compiler can perform pipeline parallelism execution in loops for every macroblocks. The report of compilers shows that the loop is pipelined well.

This work is realized in the delivery kernel. The macroblock is loading to local memory from global (DDR) memory in order of Fig. 3(d). And then, the delivery kernel distributes each macroblock to prediction kernels. It can achieve the performance of ∼1300MPixel/s and ensure the providing of data. This can improve the performance of loading data from global memory efficiently.

3.3 Macroblock Prediction

We have implemented four prediction modes in our WebP lossy compression algorithm, including horizontal prediction, vertical prediction, DC prediction, and True-Motion prediction. As shown in Fig. 4, the prediction of macroblock needs the boundaries data of adjacent macroblock. In order to improve the performance of predict kernel, one predict mode can be done in one cycle by unrolling the iteration. The results of prediction need the value of left, top and left_top for TrueMotion predict mode. For vertical prediction and horizontal prediction, the value of left boundary and top boundary are respectively required. Due to the need of WebP decompression, the value of boundary is generated after inversed quantization and DCT.

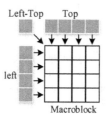

Fig. 4. The prediction of 4 × 4 sub-block

When the delivery kernel has loaded the macroblock data, the macroblock is sent to prediction kernel by OpenCL channel. Four prediction modes are implemented in the predict kernel, including horizontal, vertical, DC mode, and TrueMotion for 4 × 4 sub-block. For each prediction mode, the image similarity with the original block data is calculated based on the mean-squared difference coefficient. Next, as shown in Fig. 5, the best prediction result is selected and the residual data is passed to the next kernel for DCT and WHT.

3.4 DCT and WHT Transformation

In this step, each macroblock, which is the residual data between original and prediction, is send to transform kernels. Each 16 × 16 macroblock is divided into sixteen

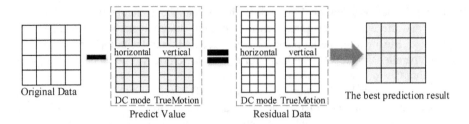

Fig. 5. The process of prediction kernel

4×4 DCT blocks, and is transformed by a bit-exact DCT approximation. The DCT concentrates the most significant coefficients in the top left of the matrix. The first coefficient is known as the DC coefficient in Y 4×4 blocks, which are Walsh-Hadamard transformed (WHT) to further increase entropy in the DCT blocks. The remaining 15 coefficients are known as AC coefficients. For UV blocks, the WHT is not considered.

The OpenCL kernel code of DCT transformation is implemented without floating-point arithmetic. We have used "#pragma unroll" to tell the compiler to coalesce the memory accesses into one wide access of 4 bytes per read/write port. Moreover, the generated on-chip memory supports that width to be able to load/store each pixel in one access. And then, we implement DCT transformation for the columns of 4×4 block using the same way. By this way, the 2D-DCT is implemented to the 4×4 blocks. Due to the well-structured loop code, the compiler can process the iteration pipelined well. Each 4×4 block can be processed in one cycle by loop unrolling .

Among the 16 4×4 blocks within 16×16 macroblock, the 2D-DCT transformation is executed pipelining well. To take advantage of the correlation among the first DC coefficients of the 16 4×4 blocks within one macroblock, the Walsh-Hadamard transform is designed and implemented in the transform_Y kernel. The two-dimensional WHT are implemented as illustrated in Fig. 6. First, each row of 4×4 DC coefficients is transformed by the way of Fig. 6(a). Second, each column of DC block is processed as shown in Fig. 6(b).

The statement of "#pragma unroll" is also used to tell the compiler to replicate the compute units in WHT function. Both of the 2D-DCT and 2D-WHT are executed concurrently within one row or one column.

3.5 Quantization

After the transform kernel creating 16×16 AC coefficients and 4×4 DC coefficients for luma macroblock, and 8×8 AC coefficients for chroma macroblock. These residual coefficient blocks are divided by quantization matrix. The quantization matrix is decided by a quantization parameter in normal WebP lossy compression algorithm. The quantization parameter is chosen for adjusting to match a desired bitrate and quality. We quantize 16 coefficients parallelism in one pipeline stage by using "pragma unroll". Each coefficient is processed at the same time by loop unrolling.

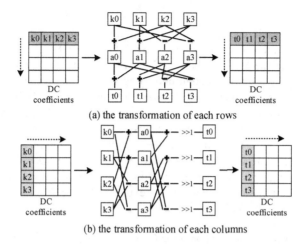

(a) the transformation of each rows

(b) the transformation of each columns

Fig. 6. The process of 2D-WHT for 4×4 DC coefficients

In WebP lossy compression algorithm, the 4×4 coefficients are processed in Zigzag order. But this will lead to inefficient load operation due to the fetch mechanism of Intel FPGA SDK for OpenCL. To improve the quantification efficiency, we reorder the result of quantified by Zigzag after all the coefficient is generated. This method avoids the inefficient using of non-continuous memory access.

When the quantization is done, the macroblock data and prediction mode are stored in the global memory by the store kernel for entropy encoding. Furthermore, the store kernel is also responsible for deleting the zero-values macroblock in the stream of macroblock data and reorganizing the location of macroblock.

4   Results and Comparison

In the following subsections, we focus on comparing Intel's highly tuned CPU and CTACCEL's hand-coded Verilog implementation to better understand the tradeoffs across design platforms (FPGA vs. CPU) and design abstractions (OpenCL vs. Verilog).

4.1   FPGA versus CPU

We compare our OpenCL FPGA implementation to the known CPU implementation of WebP lossy encoder by G. Ginesu. Our implementation uses a 20-nm Intel Arria 10 GX1150 FPGA device (45W) and the chip model is 10AX115H3F34E2SG. The CPU measurement is performed on a 22-nm Intel Xeon E5-2690 v3 processor (135 W) @ 2.60 GHz, which has 12 cores (24 thread cores). Both host system of FPGAs and CPU implementation are based on CentOS 7.1 system.

Performance

Table 1 shows the result of performance, performance-per-watt and compression ratio compared with Intel CPU implementation by MIT-Adobe FiveK Dataset [11] and Kodak Dataset [12]. The MIT-Adobe FiveK Dataset collectes 5000 photographs taken with SLR cameras by a set of different photographers, and the Kodak Dataset is from the Kodak lossless true color image suite. We select about 4 GB images from MIT-Adobe FiveK datasets and Kodak dataset for comparing the performance across the two platforms. The WebP lossy compression implementation presents several parameters that can be used to improve the rate-distortion-complexity tradeoff. The latter parameter (m) controls the tradeoff between the encoding speed, compressed file size and quality. Higher values let the algorithm inspect additional encoding possibilities and decide on the quality gain at the expense of the processing time.

Table 1. Comparison between our OpenCL FPGA implementation and Intel CPU

Implementation	Performance	Performance per Watt	Compression ratio
OpenCL FPGA	464.24MPixel/s	10.32MPixel/J	50.59%
Intel CPU (m = 4)	167.86MPixel/s	1.24MPixel/J	35.64%
Intel CPU (m = 1)	434.36MPixel/s	3.22MPixel/J	50.59%
Gap (m = 4)	2.77x faster	8.32x better	70% weaker
Gap (m = 1)	1.07x faster	3.20x better	On par

The Intel CPU implementation is based on libwebp-0.5.0. The libwebp-0.5.0 code can only process one image every time. Therefore, we have modified the main function to support multithread for encoding batch images. WebP is worked in method = 1 and method = 4(default parameter). Because of more complex computing, libwebp can provide better compression ratio. Due to the resources of Arria 10, the WebP lossy compression algorithm is simplified in our OpenCL implementation. As shown in Table 1, even though the optimized Intel CPU implementation runs at 2.6 GHz and all 24 thread cores are used meanwhile the utilization percentage of CPU is near 99%, our OpenCL FPGA implementation can achieve 2.77X higher throughput, or 8.32X better when normalized to power consumption. We can get almost the same result of geometric mean compression ratio over the yields with the parameter method = 1 implemented by Intel CPU. Notes that our goal is to create a reference design with high throughput, and the compression ratio can be further improved by implementing the macroblock segments and more macroblock prediction mode.

Compression Ratio

To evaluate compression ratio, we test our hardware with the Kodak datasets to be able to compare with WebP Lossy compression implementation results on CPU. In order to reduce the cost of hardware resources in FPGA, we simplify the process of WebP Lossy compression algorithm. As shown in Fig. 7, our OpenCL FPGA implementation can achieve the compression ratio of m = 1 on average. Even though the result is only equal to method = 1, the average 42% compression ratio can also significantly reduce the storage and network bandwidth cost in data center.

4.2 OpenCL versus Verilog

To evaluate the Intel OpenCL compiler, we compared our OpenCL FPGA implementation of WebP Lossy compression to the Verilog implementation of CTACCEL [13] which design architecture is based on Xilinx XCKU060. The Verilog implementation is expected to be somewhat higher performance and efficiency because it is implemented in a low-level language that gives the user very fine control over the design. For the same reason, we expect our OpenCL FPGA implementation to have a much lower design effort and thus higher productivity.

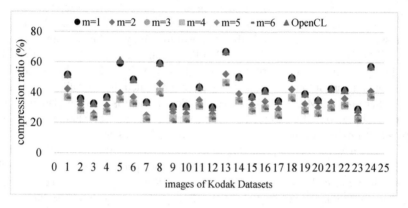

Fig. 7. The compression ratio of Kodak datasets with different methods

We summarize the results in Table 2. Note that the designs are not identical, and our design is a work-in-progress. In addition, we are certain that both performance and efficiency can still be improved. However, we compare the results attained after 4 months on this reference design to be able to evaluate the performance/efficiency vs. productivity tradeoff of OpenCL compared to Verilog.

Table 2. Comparison between OpenCL and Verilog

	Performance	FPGA	Productivity
OpenCL kernel	450MPixel/s	Intel Arria 10 GX1150	High (4 month)
Verilog HDL	195MPixel/s	Xilinx XCKU060	Low

Compared to Verilog, the performance of our OpenCL implementation is increased by 2.3x and even though the resource of FPGA is similar. We believe that the result is determined by our heavily-pipelined architecture of WebP kernels. Through the Zigzag traversal on the macroblock, we can eliminate the dependencies among the adjacent macroblocks, and these macroblocks can be processed pipelined well. With OpenCL, the architecture of WebP lossy compression algorithm can be coded, optimized and verified in several weeks. OpenCL essentially makes hardware design as easy as software design.

5 Related Work

WebP has been widely used in the Internet companies since it is released by google in 2010 [3], includes Tencent, Alibaba, Baidu, Facebook, Youtube. Due to its good compression rate, WebP has alleviated the pressure of these companies server on data storage effectively. But its more complex algorithms bring higher computational costs to these datacenter server. In order to speed up the performance of WebP Lossy Compression Algorithm, Foivos firstly attempted to deploy WebP algorithm on FPGA in 2014 [14]. Through the profiling of WebP, he map the performance bottleneck of WebP Lossy Compression algorithm to the Xilinx Zynq7045 device by Vivado HLS. Because only a part of the algorithm has been implemented, the overall performance is 1.71x higher than ARM Cortex-A9 processor. So far, there is no WebP heterogeneous acceleration based on GPU, so we does not compare our implementation with GPU in this paper. Xilinx has further released the solution of heterogeneous acceleration about WebP based on Vivado HLS [15]. Due to its published performance data, the solution of Xilinx's WebP acceleration can get the throughput performance of 110MPixel/s–180MPixel/s with method = 4 in the platform of AWS-VU9P-F1 instance. As for the others heterogeneous acceleration about WebP, there is no corresponding literature for reference, includes Tencent FPGA Cloud and Alibaba Cloud. We can only find their release information about WebP and their solution is implemented by Verilog HDL/VHDL. Our paper is the first solution to implement the WebP algorithm for FPGAs by OpenCL. On the basis of previous research, we are implementing more complex functions of WebP Lossy Compression algorithm to FPGAs. We need to implement more advanced compression patterns to accommodate more complex application scenarios.

6 Conclusion

This paper focuses on the research of OpenCL-based FPGA development on WebP lossy compression application. It demonstrate that we can provide a high-performance implementation over WebP lossy compression algorithm using a high-level OpenCL language on the FPGA platform. The OpenCL allows fast iterations for various architectures, and allows the user to focus on the algorithm details. We are able to achieve a compression ratio of method = 1 with throughput of 450MPixel/s. Compared to the Intel CPU implementation, OpenCL FPGA performance-per-watt is 8.32x better. Additionally, the delay of per image can be reduced to $\sim 90\%$ by the data parallelism and macroblock pipelining on FPGAs. Finally, our research provides an attractive solution for data centers to improve performance and reduce cost while strengthening their competitiveness.

References

1. Cisco Global Cloud Index: Forecast and Methodology, 2015–2020 (2016)
2. WebP homepage. http://code.google.com/speed/webp/. Accessed 03 Feb 2017
3. Ginesu, G., Pintus, M., Giusto, D.D.: Objective assessment of the WebP image coding algorithm. Image Commun. **27**(8), 867–874 (2012)
4. Si, Z., Shen, K.: Research on the WebP image format. In: Ouyang, Y., Xu, M., Yang, L., Ouyang, Y. (eds.) Advanced Graphic Communications, Packaging Technology and Materials. LNEE, vol. 369, pp. 271–277. Springer, Singapore (2016). https://doi.org/10.1007/978-981-10-0072-0_35
5. Wirbel, L.: Xilinx SDAccel (a unified development environment for tommorrows's data center). Technical report (2014)
6. Chalamalasetti, S.R., Margala, M., Vanderbauwhede, W.: Evaluating FPGA-acceleration for real-time unstructured search. In: IEEE International Symposium on PERFORMANCE Analysis of Systems and Software, New Jersey, USA, pp. 200–209. IEEE (2012)
7. Compiling OpenCL to FPGAs: A Standard and Portable Software Abstraction for System Design. http://www.fpl2012.org/Presentations/Keynote_Deshanand_Singh.pdf. Accessed 03 Feb 2017
8. VP8 Data Format and Decoding Guide. https://datatracker.ietf.org/doc/rfc6386/. Accessed 03 Feb 2017
9. Compression Techniques. https://developers.google.com/speed/webp/docs/compression. Accessed 03 Feb 2017
10. Intel FPGA SDK for OpenCL. https://www.altera.com/products/design-software/embedded-software-developers/opencl/overview.html. Accessed 03 Feb 2017
11. Bychkovsky, V., Paris, S., Chan, E., Durand, F.: Learning photographic global tonal adjustment with a database of input/output image Pairs. In: IEEE Computer Vision and Pattern Recognition (CVPR), June 2011, Colorado Springs, CO (2011)
12. Kodak Lossless True Color Image Suite. http://www.r0k.us/graphics/kodak/. Accessed 03 Feb 2017
13. CTAccel. http://www.ct-accel.com/. Accessed 03 Feb 2017
14. Foivos Anastasopoulos. Implementation of WebP algorithm on FPGA Implementation of WebP algorithm on FPGA. http://dias.library.tuc.gr/view/manf/20213. Accessed 03 Feb 2017
15. WebP Image Compression. https://github.com/Xilinx/Applications/tree/master/webp. Accessed 03 Feb 2017

Efficient Multitasking on FPGA Using HDL-Based Checkpointing

Hoang-Gia Vu[✉], Takashi Nakada, and Yasuhiko Nakashima

Nara Institute of Science and Technology, Takayama, Ikoma, Nara 89165, Japan
{vu.hoang_gia.uw9,nakada,nakashim}@is.naist.jp
http://arch.naist.jp

Abstract. Multitasking on FPGA is a method allowing multiple users to share a reconfigurable fabric, thus improving the flexibility of hardware task management. However, current multitasking schemes bring with it considerable performance degradation and several issues, that can be solved. In this paper, we first present a multitasking scheme based on checkpointing in the hardware description language (HDL) level. The scheme can eliminate the need for reading the bitstream back, thus reducing the task switch latency. We then propose a new HDL-based checkpointing architecture for FPGA computing. Third, we propose a static analysis of the original HDL source code in order to reduce the hardware overhead caused by the checkpointing insertion. Our evaluations show that the proposed architecture with the static analysis can reduce up to 50% of the LUT overhead, compared with the tree-based checkpointing architecture. The checkpointing architecture causes small degradation in maximum clock frequency (1.65% on average), while it consumes low memory footprints. Comparisons with previous multitasking schemes highlight the advantages of our scheme.

Keywords: Checkpointing · FPGA · Task switch · Multitasking

1 Introduction

Thanks to high computational capabilities, reconfigurability, power efficiency, and the advantages of customizing hardware for domain-specific applications, Field Programmable Gate Arrays (FPGAs) are now widely deployed in modern datacenters [1–5]. Similar to the case of CPU-based computing, multitasking is expected to be employed in FPGA-based computing in order to allow multiple users to share a reconfigurable fabric. In this case, task switching is required. Multitasking on FPGA is not a new idea. Previous approaches to multitasking [6–10] using the readback-of-bitstream method for task switching have several serious drawbacks, that can prevent multitasking from being deployed in reconfigurable computing. First, the readback-of-bitstream method cannot ensure that a readback bitstream (a taken snapshot) is consistent with other components. For example, a bitstream, taken while FPGA is accessing off-chip memory, is not

© Springer International Publishing AG, part of Springer Nature 2018
N. Voros et al. (Eds.): ARC 2018, LNCS 10824, pp. 590–602, 2018.
https://doi.org/10.1007/978-3-319-78890-6_47

consistent with the off-chip memory. Thus, the application cannot be resumed correctly on FPGA. Second, the readback bitstream is not enough to resume the normal operation of dedicated blocks, which have outputs delayed compared with inputs [11]. Third, the report in [6] indicated that only less than 8% of the data in the bitstream is useful, thus 92% of readback time is a waste of time.

It is believed that the three drawbacks can be overcome by using HDL-based checkpointing for multitasking. Additional circuits can be inserted into the application circuit at the HDL level in order to checkpoint dedicated blocks, and to manage communication channel states for consistent snapshots [11]. Furthermore, working in the HDL level shows high programmability for checkpointing insertion. The HDL also accounts for the widest use in hardware design. Therefore, we chose HDL-based checkpointing for our multitasking scheme. We also assume that the user hardware operates with a single clock domain.

It is noted that inserting checkpointing circuits always brings with it hardware overhead for the application circuit. However, we believe that there are some rooms to improve the checkpointing architecture. In many cases, hardware resources utilized for normal operation can be also employed for checkpointing functionality in order to reduce the total hardware consumption. Therefore, in this work, we make the following specific contributions. First, we propose a multitasking scheme on FPGA that takes the advantages of HDL-based checkpointing, thus minimizing the task switch latency. Second, we propose CPRflatten - a new checkpointing architecture for FPGA checkpointing that is transparent to applications and portable across hardware platforms. Third, we provide a static analysis of HDL original source code in order to re-use hardware resources for the checkpointing purpose, thus reducing the hardware consumption.

2 Related Work

Related work on multitasking on FPGA using the readback-of-bitstream method for task switching has been highlighted with some serious drawbacks in Sect. 1. In this section, we provide more discussion about related work on FPGA checkpointing. There are several approaches to FPGA checkpointing except the readback-of-bitstream method. The first approach is the netlist-based method. The scan-chain structure was employed in this method [12]. This method used tools to insert scan multiplexers as checkpointing infrastructures at the netlist level. The scan multiplexers were used to connect flip-flops to create scan chains. Although the netlist-based method with scan chains is an attractive option for hardware test and verification, it has two drawbacks when coming to FPGA checkpointing. They are technology dependence and poor programmability.

The second approach is the high-level synthesis based (HLS-based) method. Bourge et al. [13,14] presented a high-level synthesis design flow manipulating the intermediate representation of an HLS tool to insert a scan chain into the initial circuit. The main contribution of this work is checkpoint selection, in which only in some states of a finite state machine, checkpointing can be performed. However, this work did not consider the issue about consistent snapshots

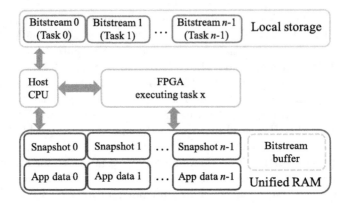

Fig. 1. Multitasking on an FPGA-based computing node

of FPGAs and other components. Once taking it into account, the state that checkpointing can be performed should depend on the state of communication channels between FPGA and others [11]. Therefore, the checkpoint selection may be no longer feasible. Furthermore, the authors limited their benchmarks to using a specific HLS tool, which generates application circuits having a single finite state machine. This constraint may prevent developers from designing complicated applications.

The third approach is the HDL-based method. In [15], the authors provided a context interface to capture/restore registers, FIFOs, and BRAMs without proposing an architecture to deal with the structure of nested HDL module. Our previous work [11] first proposed a reduced set of state-holding elements for the definition of FPGA context. The set can be used to checkpoint dedicated blocks on FPGA. We also proposed a method to guarantee the consistency of snapshots between FPGA and other components. Third, we proposed a tree-based checkpointing architecture on FPGA. In this work, we continue to improve the checkpointing architecture and optimize checkpointing circuits.

3 Multitasking Scheme

3.1 Multitasking Structure

A multitasking system is organized in an FPGA-based computing node as Fig. 1. Initial bitstreams are stored in the local storage. The host CPU will load an initial bitstream and configure FPGA when the corresponding task is required. FPGA can execute only one task at a time. Multiple tasks can share the reconfigurable fabric by using task switching. Each task is allocated a time period to run before being replaced by another task. For task switching, HDL-based checkpointing is employed to capture FPGA context when a task is swapped out, and to restore FPGA context when another task is swapped in. Captured context will be written to the unified memory as a snapshot of the corresponding task at a

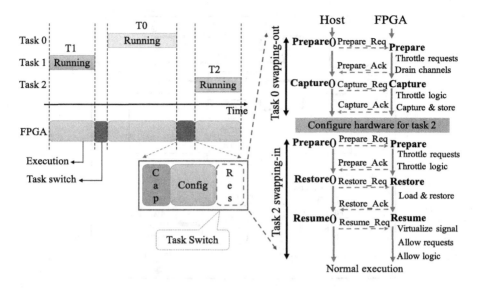

Fig. 2. Task execution and task switch timing diagram

given physical address. Therefore, saving snapshots to the local storage is not required in our scheme. In addition, to reduce the configuration time, a bitstream can be pre-loaded to the unified memory at a given physical address area, called a bitstream buffer, before being written to FPGA.

Multiple tasks running on FPGA require fixed contiguous memory allocation at a given physical address space for both snapshots and application data in the unified memory. This is easy on stand-alone systems, but more complicated on operating systems (OS) using virtual addresses like Linux. For the later, a reserved memory should be created when building the OS so that the kernel and other software applications will not touch the memory space.

3.2 Timing Diagram for Task Execution and Task Switching

Figure 2 shows a timing diagram for three tasks running on FPGA. The tasks can be allocated different time periods (T0, T1, and T2) to run. The cost of multitasking on FPGA consists of performance overhead, hardware overhead, additional footprints on the unified memory, and maximum clock frequency degradation on FPGA when checkpointing functionality is inserted. The performance overhead is the total task switch latency. Since HDL-based checkpointing is employed, no readback of the bitstream as [7] is required. Also, saving snapshots to the local storage as [14] is not required. Therefore, the task switch latency (T_{switch}) is the sum of the context capturing latency (T_{cap}), the bitstream configuration latency (T_{conf}), and the context restoring latency (T_{res}). The restoring latency is not required if the task swapped in runs on FPGA for the first time.

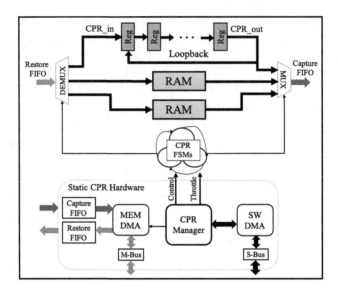

Fig. 3. Ring-based flattened checkpointing architecture

The timing diagram for a switch from task 0 to task 2 includes task 0 swapping-out, bitstream configuration for task 2, and task 2 swapping-in. The host uses API functions [11] *Prepare*() and *Capture*() to swap task 0 out. It also uses *Prepare*(), *Restore*(), and *Resume*() to swap task 2 in. The consistency of snapshots between the FPGA and other components, such as the host CPU and the unified memory, is guaranteed by the *Prepare* procedure on FPGA [11]. Checkpointing of dedicated blocks is also guaranteed by the *Resume* procedure with signal virtualization [11].

4   CPRflatten: A Ring-Based Flattened Checkpointing Achitecture on FPGA

4.1   Overview of CPRflatten

It is assumed that hardware structures are flattened in HDL level. That means two objects can be connected without the need for considering complicated structures of nested modules. Our checkpointing architecture as in Fig. 3 is derived from the idea of removing all connectors between checkpoint/restart (CPR) levels of CPRtree [11]. In this case, Mux-based capturing/restoring circuits and Shift-Reg-based capturing/restoring circuits can no longer be used anymore, and, instead, a shifting matrix of register bits must be employed in register checkpointing. However, the output of the matrix (CPR_out) is looped back to the input of the matrix to make sure that the values of registers after capturing are kept unchanged. Thus, this forms a shifting ring, and this architecture is

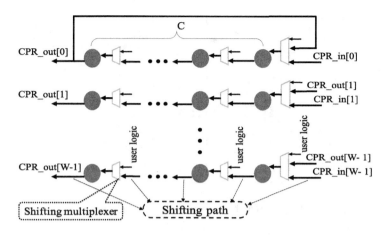

Fig. 4. Shifting ring of register bits

called *ring-based flattened checkpointing architecture* in this paper. In the architecture, the reduced set of state-holding elements [11] is divided into two sets:
register set and RAM set. While capturing/restoring circuits for registers are
configured as a shifting ring, capturing/restoring circuits for RAMs is separated
from each other and is separated from the shifting ring. The proposed architecture can be divided into two parts: *static CPR hardware part* and the rest, called
user-logic-based part. The later includes a shifting ring for register checkpointing, capturing/restoring circuits for RAMs, and two CPR finite state machines
(CPR FSMs) for capturing and restoring.

4.2 Shifting Ring

The shifting ring is formed from the shifting matrix of register bits with outputs
looped back to inputs. Let W be the data width of checkpointing, B be the
number of register bits in the reduced set of state-holding elements, and C be
B/W. If B is not a multiple of W, then a padding register is added to guarantee
a multiple of W. As showed in Fig. 4, the shifting matrix of register bits is a W-
by-C matrix. There are two advantages of using shifting ring in checkpointing.
First, it ensures that the content of registers is kept unchanged after capturing.
Second, the shifting ring can be used for both capturing and restoring processes,
thus saving hardware resources.

However, employing a shifting ring leads to complexity in hardware. In the
worst case, particularly, one more input pattern is added to each register bit, thus
one input is added to the multiplexer in front of the bit. As a result, additional
LUTs may be used for such logic functionality. If the multiplexer is re-structured
including more levels, the degradation of maximum clock frequency will be more
serious due to the increase in the critical path.

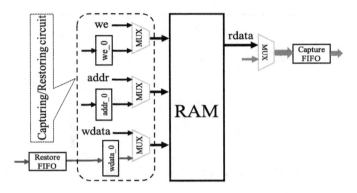

Fig. 5. RAM capturing/restoring circuit

4.3 RAM Capturing/Restoring Circuit

On-chip RAM context can be captured and restored by iterating reading and writing through its whole address space. To keep the inputs and outputs of a RAM unchanged after capturing, multiplexers are employed to separate check-pointing from the normal operation. However, instead of writing the context read from a RAM to the next CPR level when capturing as in CPRtree [11], the context is written directly to Capture FIFO in our architecture as in Fig. 5. Con-versely, when restoring, context is read from Restore FIFO, and then written to the RAM. This implementation is possible by flattening HDL modules for RAM checkpointing. A RAM port includes four signals: write enable (we), address (addr), write data (wdata), and read data (rdata). While the read data signal (output) can be shared between the normal operation and capturing, the other signals (inputs) require multiplexers to be shared between the normal operation and the restoring process. Therefore, three registers: we_0, addr_0, and wdata_0 are added for RAM checkpointing.

5 Static Analysis of Original HDL Source Code

5.1 Fundamentals of Static Analysis

In the shifting ring in Fig. 4, a shifting path may bring with it not only an additional input to the shifting multiplexer in front of each register bit but also cause complexity for the combinational circuit generating select bits. This input may require more LUTs for the multiplexing functionality, whereas the complexity of the combinational circuit may also consume more LUTs. While the complexity cannot be avoided, the additional input will be not required if the shifting path coincides with one of the inputs from the user logic. Such coincidence is achieved when the preceding register bit (F1) in the shifting path

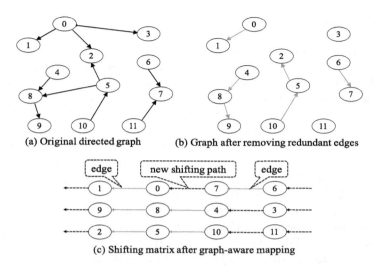

(a) Original directed graph

(b) Graph after removing redundant edges

(c) Shifting matrix after graph-aware mapping

Fig. 6. Static analysis of original HDL source code

is used to determine the value of the register bit (F0) in the next clock cycle. In this case F0 at the time t is a function of F1 at the time t-1, written as F0(t) = f(F1(t-1)). If register bits are considered as vertices of a directed graph, then F0 and F1 are two of the vertices of a graph and there is an edge from F1 to F0. Therefore, we believe that the LUT consumption caused by a shifting ring can be reduced if the shifting ring is designed in such a way that some shifting paths coincide with edges of the graph of register bits.

However, if there are several edges from one vertex, then only one edge can be mapped onto a shifting path. Conversely, if there are several edges to one vertex, then, too, only one edge can be used as a shifting path. Therefore, there are three steps to design a shifting matrix. The first step is to analyze the original HDL source code to identify the graph of register bits. The second step is to find groups of edges to the same vertex, then keep only one edge in each group while removing the rest of the group. The rest is called *redundant edges*. The third step is to map all remaining edges onto shifting paths of the shifting matrix. These three steps are called static analysis of original HDL source code. They are described in an example in Fig. 6. This mapping is called *graph-aware mapping*. The original graph has 12 vertices and 10 directed edges. After removing redundant edges, there are 6 remaining edges. Therefore, after mapping vertices and edges onto the shifting matrix, only 3 additional shifting paths are required. As a result, the graph-aware mapping eliminates 6 shifting paths.

5.2   Algorithms

The Pseudo code to describe how to remove redundant edges and how to map register bits onto a shifting matrix are outlined in Algorithms 1 and 2.

Let *bitSet* be the set of register bits in the module. Let *unvisitedBitSet* define the set of register bits that has not been visited. Let *rightBitSet* of register bit B be the set of register bits used to determine B in the next clock cycle. Let *leftBitSet* of register bit B be the set of register bits that are determined by B in the next clock cycle. Let *preceding* of register bit B define the preceding register bit of B in the shifting path. *preceding* will be None if the shifting path does not coincide with any edge. Let *following* of register bit B be the following register bit of B in the shifting path. *following* will be None if the shifting path does not coincide with any edge. Let *noFollowBitSet* define the set of register bits that have no *following* but have *preceding* in the shifting path. Let *noFollowNoPrecBitSet* be the set of register bits that have no *following* and no *preceding* in the shifting path. Let *matrixBitList* define the list of bits in the shifting matrix. The bit index increases by 1 in the same column and increases by W in the same row. Let *unmappedIndexList* be the list of indexes of bits in *matrixBitList* that has not been mapped onto. Let Nb be the number of register bits in the module.

Algorithm 1 Removing redundant edges

1: unvisitedBitSet ← bitSet
2: **while** unvisitedBitSet **is not** ∅ **do**
3:       min_length ← min{length(B.rightBitSet), B ∈ unvisitedBitSet}
4:       **for all** B ∈ unvisitedBitSet **do**
5:            **if** length(B.rightBitSet) == min_length **then**
6:                 **for** b ∈ B.rightBitSet **do**
7:                      **if** b.following **is None and** b.preceding **is not** B **then**
8:                           B.preceding ← b
9:                           b.following ← B
10:                          **for** C ∈ b.leftBitSet **do**
11:                               C.rightBitSet ← C.rightBitSet − {b}
12:                          **break**
13:                 unvisitedBitSet ← unvisitedBitSet − {B}

In Algorithm 1, register bits are consecutively visited to remove redundant edges (line 4). It is noted that after removing such redundant edges, all edges starting from a register bit can be removed, while one of them is expected to be mapped onto a shifting path. To avoid this case, register bits having a *rightBitSet* with fewer elements should be visited first (line 3, 5). *length(B.rightBitSet)* is the number of elements in the set. After removing the redundant edges of a group, only one edge remains in the group (the edge from b to B). The vertex b cannot be used anymore, thus it is removed from *rightBitSets* (line 10, 11).

Algorithm 2 Graph-aware Mapping Algorithm

1: noFollowBitSet ← {B ∈ bitSet, B.preceding **is not None**, B.following **is None** }
2: noFollowNoPrecBitSet ← {B ∈ bitSet, B.preceding **is None, B.following is None** }
3: **for** all B ∈ noFollowBitSet **do**
4:     k ← unmappedIndexList.Pop()
5:     matrixBitList[k] ← B
6:     B0 ← B
7:     **while** B0.preceding **is not None do**
8:         **if** (k + W) < Nb **then**
9:             matrixBitList[k + W] ← B0.preceding
10:            unmappedIndexList.Remove(k + W)
11:            k ← k + W
12:            B0 ← B0.preceding
13:        **else**
14:            **if** B0.preceding.preceding **is None then**
15:                noFollowNoPrecBitSet ← noFollowNoPrecBitSet ∪ {B0.preceding}
16:            **else**
17:                noFollowBitSet ← noFollowBitSet ∪ {B0.preceding}
18: **for** all B ∈ noFollowNoPrecBitSet **do**
19:     k ← unmappedIndexList.Pop()
20:     matrixBitList[k] ← B

The next step to map register bits and remaining edges onto the shifting matrix is presented in Algorithm 2. Since the register bits with edges must be mapped onto the most left-side column first, the *noFollowBitSet* must be visited first as in line 3. The visit to bits in the *noFollowBitSet* also leads to a visit to bits that have both following and preceding by tracing the preceding on the bit chain (line 7 when B0.*preceding* is not None). It finally leads to a visit to the bits that have *following* but no *preceding* (line 7 when B0.*preceding* is None). After that, it continues to visit the *noFollowNoPrecBitSet* to cover all bits in the *bitSet* (line 18).

Table 1. Experimental setup.

EDA tool	Vivado 2014.4 and ISE 14.7
FPGA	Xilinx Zynq-7000 XC7z020clg484-1
Evaluation board & clock frequency	Zedboard & 100 MHz
Host CPU & operating system	ARM Cortex-A9 & Debian 8.0

6 Evaluation

6.1 Hardware Resource Ultilization

We demonstrate CPRflatten on four realistic applications: - pipelined SIMD matrix multiplication (Mat-Mul), Dijkstra graph processing (Dijkstra), 9-point Stencil Computation (Stencil), and String Search (S-Search). Since the static

CPR hardware part is fixed and transparent to applications, to evaluate the efficiency of checkpointing architectures, only the hardware overhead of the user-logic-based part is considered. Table 2 shows that the hardware overhead is reduced the most from 92.97% (CPRtree) to 29.83% (CPRflatten) in the S-Search application (a decline of 67.91% of LUT overhead). The average decline of 49.25% of LUT overhead shows that the proposed checkpointing architecture (CPRflatten) with the proposed static analysis is much better than CPRtree [11] in terms of hardware overhead.

Table 2. LUT utilization.

Apps	LUTs (original)	Additional LUTs (CPRtree)	Additional LUTs (CPRflatten)	Decline of additional LUTs
Mat-Mul	3323	5339 (160.67%)	2593 (78.03%)	51.43%
Dijkstra	8126	1461 (17.98%)	1020 (12.55%)	30.18%
Stencil	6748	7395 (109.59%)	3883 (57.54%)	47.49%
S-Search	4056	3771 (92.97%)	1210 (29.83%)	67.91%
Mean				49.25%

Table 3. Maximum clock frequency degradation.

Apps	F_{max} (MHz) (original)	F_{max} (MHz) (CPRtree) & degradation	F_{max} (MHz) (CPRflatten) & degradation
Mat-Mul	115.075	103.875 (9.73%)	103.875 (9.73%)
Dijkstra	161.627	161.589 (0.02%)	165.822 (−2.6%)
Stencil	200.844	202.184 (−0.67%)	202.184 (−0.67%)
S-Search	188.929	188.644 (0.15%)	188.644 (0.15%)

6.2   Maximum Clock Frequency Degradation

The synthesis estimation results in Table 3 show that both CPRflatten and CPRtree have negligible impact on the maximum clock frequency. The average degradation is only 2.31% and 1.65%, respectively. The most significant degradation is 9.73% (Mat-Mul). It can be seen that the maximum clock frequencies of Stencil and Dijkstra even increase after inserting checkpointing functionality. This may come from the optimization of the synthesis tool. Particularly, no logic element is inserted into the critical paths, while the physical distance of logic elements may reduce, thus reducing the critical path. These average values are really small compared with the value of around 20% in the scan-chain netlist-based method [16].

Table 4. Context size (data footprint) and task switch latency.

Apps	Register context kbyte	RAM context kbyte	Total context (kbyte)	Capturing latency (ms)	Restoring latency (ms)	Configuration time (ms)
Mat-Mul	0.70	7.31	8.01	0.022	0.023	31.095
Dijkstra	0.20	0.87	1.07	0.005	0.007	31.095
Stencil	1.26	13.06	14.32	0.039	0.04	31.095
S-Search	0.44	2.38	2.82	0.009	0.01	31.095

6.3 Memory Footprint and Task Switch Latency

Table 4 shows the breakdown of the total context size (memory footprint) and the task switch latency. The memory footprints (less than 15 kbyte) are much lower than the memory footprint in the readback-of-bitstream method (4 Mbyte for Zedboard). The capturing latency and the restoring latency depend linearly on the corresponding context size. The FPGA on Zedboard is configured from host programs in C language using processor configuration access port (PCAP). The measured configuration time is stable at 31.095 ms. The task switch latency caused by switching from Mat-Mul to Stencil is 31.157 ms for example. The improvement of our scheme over the previous schemes based on the readback method in terms of the task switch latency is that the readback latency (tens to hundreds of milliseconds [7,8]) is removed and replaced by the capturing latency (less than 0.039 ms).

7 Conclusion

This paper has presented a new multitasking scheme on FPGA using HDL-based checkpointing. The improvements of our scheme over the previous schemes include: (1) It has lower task switch latency, (2) it consumes lower memory foot-prints, (3) it can manage the consistency of taken snapshots for task switching, and (4) it allows task switching between hardware applications containing dedicated blocks. We also proposed a new HDL-based checkpointing architecture on FPGAs that is transparent to applications and portable across hardware plat-forms. We then proposed a static analysis of the original HDL source code to re-use hardware resources for the purpose of checkpointing. Thanks to the proposed architecture and the analysis, the hardware overhead decreases by around 50% on average, compared with CPRtree. Our evaluation shows that checkpointing hardware has an insignificant impact on maximum clock frequency (average degradation of 1.65%). The task switch latency in the proposed scheme is much lower than that of the readback-of-bitstream method since no readback of the bitstream is required in our scheme.

References

1. Putnam, A., et al.: A reconfigurable fabric for accelerating large-scale datacenter services. Commun. ACM **59**(11), 114–122 (2016)
2. Putnam, A.: FPGAs in the datacenter combining the worlds of hardware and software development. In: Proceedings of Great Lakes Symposium on VLSI, p. 5 (2017)
3. Falsafi, B., et al.: FPGAs versus GPUs in data centers. IEEE Micro **37**(1), 60–72 (2017)
4. Tarafdar, N., et al.: Enabling flexible network FPGA clusters in a heterogeneous cloud data center. In: FPGA2017, pp. 237–246 (2017)
5. Caulfield, A., et al.: Configurable clouds. IEEE Micro **37**(3), 52–61 (2017)
6. Kalte, H., Porrmann, M.: Context saving and restoring for multitasking in reconfigurable systems. In: FPL 2005, pp. 223–228 (2005)
7. Simmler, H., Levinson, L., Männer, R.: Multitasking on FPGA coprocessors. In: Hartenstein, R.W., Grünbacher, H. (eds.) FPL 2000. LNCS, vol. 1896, pp. 121–130. Springer, Heidelberg (2000). https://doi.org/10.1007/3-540-44614-1_13
8. Landaker, W.J., Wirthlin, M.J., Hutchings, B.L.: Multitasking hardware on the SLAAC1-V reconfigurable computing system. In: Glesner, M., Zipf, P., Renovell, M. (eds.) FPL 2002. LNCS, vol. 2438, pp. 806–815. Springer, Heidelberg (2002). https://doi.org/10.1007/3-540-46117-5_83
9. Levinson, L., Manner, R., Sessler, M., Simmler, H.: Preemptive multitasking on FPGAs. In: FCCM 2000, pp. 301–302 (2000)
10. Happe, M., Traber, A., Keller, A.: Preemptive hardware multitasking in ReconOS. In: Sano, K., Soudris, D., Hübner, M., Diniz, P.C. (eds.) ARC 2015. LNCS, vol. 9040, pp. 79–90. Springer, Cham (2015). https://doi.org/10.1007/978-3-319-16214-0_7
11. Vu, G., Kajkamhaeng, S., Takamaeda, S., Nakashima, Y.: CPRtree: a tree-based checkpointing architecture for heterogeneous FPGA computing. In: 4th International Symposium on Computing and Networking (CANDAR 2016), pp. 57–66 (2016)
12. Koch, D., Haubelt, C., Teich, J.: Efficient hardware checkpointing - concepts, overhead analysis, and implementation. In: FPGA 2007, pp. 188–196 (2007)
13. Bourge, A., Muller, O., Rousseau, F.: Automatic high-level hardware checkpoint selection for reconfigurable systems. FCCM 2015, pp. 155–158 (2015)
14. Bourge, A., Muller, O., Rousseau, F.: Generating efficient context-switch capable circuits through autonomous design flow. ACM Trans. Reconfigurable Technol. Syst. **10**(1), 9 (2016)
15. Schmidt, A., Huang, B., Sass, R., French, M.: Checkpoint/restart and beyond: resilient high performance computing with FPGAs. FCCM 2011, pp. 162–169 (2011)
16. Mavroidis, I., Papaefstathiou, I.: Accelerating emulation and providing full chip observability and controlability. IEEE Des. Test Comput. **26**, 0740–7475 (2009)

High Level Synthesis Implementation of Object Tracking Algorithm on Reconfigurable Hardware

Uzaif Sharif[(⊠)] and Shahnam Mirzaei

California State University, Northridge, CA 91330, USA
uzaif.sharif.778@my.csun.edu, smirzaei@csun.edu

Abstract. This paper presents a variation of Hough Transform (HT) algorithm implementation for symmetrically shaped object detection in the real-time video systems. The proposed algorithm is implemented on Xilinx ZYNQ-7000 series XC7Z010 SoC using High-Level Synthesis (HLS). The integrated system architecture contains a high definition camera that communicates with the SoC through HDMI interface. The algorithm is efficient in terms of memory space, computational resources, performance and accuracy as it only uses one-dimensional HT space instead of two-dimensional HT space. The proposed algorithm does not require an external memory for storing the HT space and does not require complex computations to detect the object. The experimental results show that only 40 18K BRAMs are used to implement the proposed algorithm at 60 frame per second. The proposed architecture is implemented for the video frame size of 1920 × 1080 pixels, at maximum latency of approximately 2099032 clock cycles, i.e., 14.69 ms for this HD video frame. Our algorithm uses only 26 DSP blocks for radius calculation while the entire video processing design uses 19150 slices of ZYBO SoC.

Keywords: Object detection · Object tracking · ZYBO · Hough-Transform
High-level synthesis

1 Introduction

Video and image processing have a plethora of applications ranging from face detection on smartphones to autonomous vehicles (AVs). In real-time scenarios, detecting or tracking something needs to be done as fast as possible as control signals need to be generated through it. Video processing algorithms are typically computationally intensive as they deal with streaming data. These processes were commonly done in software due to simplicity but had several limitations including long time to process the information as well as processing speed. These factors restrict the video processing algorithms to be implemented on sequential processors. Therefore, the best approach to implement video processing algorithms is using hardware that is parallel in nature unlike software running on the processor. In this regard, FPGAs offer the best way for video processing algorithms because of their low-cost, less time to market and low NRE.

© Springer International Publishing AG, part of Springer Nature 2018
N. Voros et al. (Eds.): ARC 2018, LNCS 10824, pp. 603–614, 2018.
https://doi.org/10.1007/978-3-319-78890-6_48

In the past decade, the use of reconfigurable hardware particularly FPGAs has framatically been extended to implement vision systems. Although hardware implementation requires more development time, the overall performance is from 10 to 100 times faster than the software implementation. Algorithms for tracking objects in the real-time video stream is one of the hottest topics in the computer vision as it has several applications like robot navigation. Due to parallelism, hardware can perform much faster than the software, but still, there are some limitations of utilization. To not go beyond the resources limitation, some techniques to scale down the frame resolution or image size have been used before applying tracking algorithms [1]. Hough Transform (HT) is widely used for detecting lines and circles in the images [2–4].

The Implementation of HT algorithm is really challenging because of the high demand for memory resources. Usually, these implementations use external memory space [5] which restricts the frame size as well as the frame rate. Our proposed algorithm is entirely different from the previously proposed implementations regarding technique and image size. Our algorithm uses one-dimensional arrays as HT space and uses midpoint method likewise [1], but our algorithm is for HD real-time streaming videos not just for still images. It does not require downscaling the frame resolution and can accurately find the centroid and radius (in case of a circle) of the detected object. One-Dimensional Hough Transform (ODHT) is implemented using high level synthesis (HLS) and mapped to ZYNQ SoC [8]. It does not require on-chip memory as much as needed by the algorithms used in [2, 4]. That makes our algorithm scalable and portable across different platforms. Our algorithm is based on midpoints calculations. The implementation includes the morphological processing to extract boundaries followed by the main detection algorithm. Specifically, our algorithm is designed to detect a circular object within the frame size of 1920×1080 pixels at the rate of 30/60 FPS.

The algorithms for HT work on the boundaries obtaining through morphological or edge detection processing. Each boundary point contributes in the voting for all instances of the objects being detected. These votes for all instances of the object require memory to be stored. This memory is called HT space. The location that has maximum votes would be the point of interest. As the circle is defined by three parameters, coordinates of the center and the radius. Therefore, $O(N^3)$ HT space is required, or if we just consider the centroid still $O(N^2)$ HT space is needed which is probably not possible to have in FPGA for the large size of images. Many solutions use 2D HT space like [6], and 1D HT space like [4, 7] have been proposed. The 1D algorithm is proposed for the low-resolution image, not the video. Thus the parallel computation for rows and columns is possible while in case of video it is not possible.

2 System Architecture

The overall design is implemented on ZYNQ All Programmable System-On-Chip (APSOC) and contains several blocks connected with each other to develop a video streaming system. This system architecture consists of DVI to RGB decoder which decodes the HDMI signal from the camera to the RGB signal while RGB to VGA decoder block converts the final RGB signal into VGA. In between these two blocks, all processing blocks including VDMA (Video Direct Memory Access) and ODHT block are connected. The system block diagram of the complete video processing design is shown in Fig. 1.

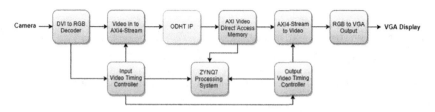

Fig. 1. System block diagram

3 One Dimensional Hough Transform (ODHT) Algorithm

This paper presents an efficient one-dimensional Hough Transform (ODHT) algorithm implementation for the detection symmetrical objects. Our ODHT algorithm includes the following processes:

- **One-Dimensional Hough Transform:** Proposed algorithm only uses five one-dimensional arrays as HT space, thus there is no need for on-chip memory. It just uses few BRAMs and registers.
- **Midpoint Calculations:** Proposed ODHT algorithm is based on midpoint calculation. Hence, there is no need to complex or trigonometric computations which increases the hardware resources usage.
- **Euclidean Distance Arithmetic:** For radius calculations, Euclidean distances are calculated from the detected centroid to those boundary points which are used in the midpoint calculations during the entire process. Euclidean distance is calculated using this formula presented in (III – 1).

$$D = \sqrt{(x_2 - x_1)^2 + (y_2 - y_1)^2} \qquad \text{(III–1)}$$

Figure 2 shows the points involved in Euclidean distances calculations.

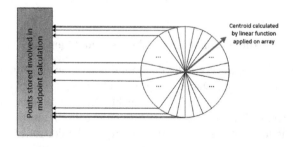

Fig. 2. Euclidean distances

The ODHT IP is primarily developed using high-level synthesis (HLS) flow. The video stream is processed through three stages to detect the circular shaped object. This is shown in Fig. 3 below.

Fig. 3. ODHT detection algorithm functional block diagram

As depicted in above Figures, the video is sourced pixel by pixel to the ODHT IP block and converts into HLS MAT [11] data type then processed further.

3.1 Color Image to Binary Image Conversion

In this stage, the three-channel RGB video is split into separate channels, and an average of them is taken to make a gray-scaled image show in (III − 2).

$$\text{Gray-Scaled Image} = (\text{Red} + \text{Green} + \text{Blue})/3 \qquad \text{(III–2)}$$

To obtain the binary image, first the red components are to be detected only, and this is done by subtracting a gray-scaled image from the Red channel shown in (III − 3).

$$\text{Color-Detected} = \text{Red/Green/Blue} - \text{Grey-Scale Image} \qquad \text{(III–3)}$$

The design is scalable thus any channel can be selected during runtime using switches. The last step of this stage is to make a binary image which is done by the process of thresholding. Thresholding is done by defining a range of color value which is also scalable and can be adjusted according to the brightness of color.

3.2 Boundary Extraction

The second stage is to extract the boundaries of all objects in the image. It is done by a morphological process called Erosion [9]. After, binary image conversion the video frame is duplicated into two streams so that on one stream erosion is applied and subtracted from the second stream. After applying such conversion, all boundaries are obtained.

3.3 Proposed One-Dimensional Hough Transform Algorithm

In a general HT algorithm, every individual point contributes in a circle formation to detect an original circle. For instance, if the algorithm uses 8 values of angles, i.e., 0, 45, 90, 135, 180, 225, 270, and 315. Thus, eight point coordinates are voted in two dimensional HT space. Therefore, after processing the entire frame the point which has maximum votes is the centroid of the original circle to be detected. The radius of the original circle is unknown. Thus, range of radii needs to apply so this is another parameter which increases the computation as number of circles drawn increased because of the radius range.

A general ODHT algorithm is applied in the third stage to detect the circular (symmetrical) object in the frame. This stage mainly works on a pixel by pixel computations. The ODHT algorithm is based on midpoint calculations and uses five arrays, two for storing midpoints, two for storing locations of white pixels, and one is used to store Euclidean distances for radii. A pixel can be entirely white or entirely black having values 255 or 0 respectively. All arrays are flushed to zero after completion of one frame.

The ODHT algorithm processes the pixel values in a scanning pattern, i.e., from top to bottom, left to right. The main components of the ODHT algorithm are condition evaluation and midpoint average calculation. These can be realized using hardware components such as multiplexers, adders, comparators, and shifters. Two variables are used to store index values of the white pixels while two other variables are used to store the values (0 or 255) of the current and previous pixels respectively. x-coordinates of centroid candidates are accumulated as voting midpoints of every two boundary or edge points in each row while y-coordinates of centroid candidates are accumulated as voting midpoints of every two boundary or edge points in each column likewise [4]. Two variables are also used for radii and their indices.

There are six conditions which accumulate arrays with votes. These conditions are based on values of the current pixel, previous pixel, and the variables which are used to store the indices of the pixels which are going to be a part of midpoint for a particular row.

I. The first condition checks if the current and previous pixels are black then it sets the previous pixel to black.

II. The second condition checks if the current pixel is white, the previous pixel is black, and the variable for first location still has zero value then it sets the previous pixel to white and the variable for first location to the current index of the column.

III. The third condition checks if both the current and previous pixels are white then do nothing and left the previous pixel as it was.

IV. The fourth condition checks if the current pixel is white, previous is black and variable for first location has non-zero value then it sets the variable for second location to the current index of the column and previous pixel to white.

V. The fifth condition checks if the current pixel is black previous is white then it checks if the array storing the column votes has value 1, then it calculates the midpoint for row while increments the vote in that array and stores the index value of the row in the array storing the row indices.

VI. To check if the variables for the first and second location are non-zero values. That being the case, it enables the midpoint calculations for columns.

Algorithm starts and sets the variable for first location when the current pixel is black and previous pixel is white. Then, the variable for second location is set when again the white pixel appears. The midpoint point is calculated and voted in an array storing the midpoints of columns and the variable for second location is flushed. Again, the variable for first location is set, and the same thing happens again and again. In this

way, array storing the midpoints of columns is accumulated with all votes in a particular row and the array storing the midpoints of rows is accumulated with all votes for
midpoints for all columns. This is is shown in the Fig. 4 below.

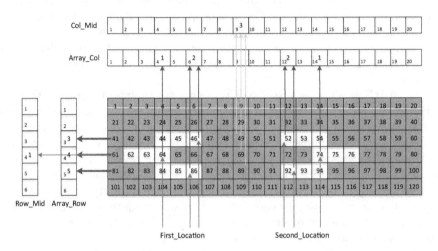

Fig. 4. ODHT detection algorithm illustration (Color figure online)

In Fig. 4, red arrows indicate the first and second locations; blue arrows show how
the votes are increasing in arrays storing votes of rows 'Array_Row' and columns
'Array_Col' while pink arrows show how the votes are stored for the midpoints. The
word 'Vote' is referred as the increment of value by 1. The arrays are initialized with all
zeros so when first and second locations are set then the value of array corresponding to
the index of first and second location increases by 1. The indices are shown in arrays
while the numbers from 1 to 130 represent the pixel numbers.

In Fig. 4, it is depicted that the midpoints in three rows are calculated and voted on
index 9 because the shape is shown as ideally symmetrical. For instance, the third row
has the first location at index 6 and the second location is at index 12 thus the midpoint
is 9 while the fourth array has the first location at index 4 and the second location is at
index 14 thus the midpoint is at index 9. In this way, all three midpoints lie on index 9.
Therefore, votes are increased till three at index 9 in the accumulating array.

As the white pixels appear in rows 3, 4 and 5 thus all indices are stored in an array
storing votes of rows 'Array_Row'. For instance, when the first location is set in row 5
and array for storing votes for columns 'Array_Col' has already value 1 which means
the first location of 3th and 5th rows are same thus midpoint is calculated and voted in
an array storing midpoints of rows 'Row_Mid'.

In this way, all midpoints are voted in both arrays storing midpoints of rows and
colums i.e., 'Col_Mid' and 'Row_Mid.' Therefore, when one frame is over the linear
search filter is applied on both arrays to find where do the maximum votes lie, thus
indices are taken for maximum votes and stored as the centroid of the object. Multiple
objects can also be found through linear search if the indices of maximum votes are
recorded in descending order.

Linear method is applied to the radii calculation, in which Array_Row and Array_Col are used with the calculated centroid values to determine the Euclidean distances. These distances are voted in an array called Distance using the same voting method. Lastly, the same linear filter is applied to find the index of maximum votes and that index is the radius of the circle. In case of other objects the algorithm ideally makes the radius zero. Therefore, the radius value can create a difference between a circle and other symmetrically shaped objects.

4 Implementation of Algorithm Using HLS

4.1 High-Level Synthesis Design Flow

The High-Level Synthesis design flow consists of the algorithm coding using C/C++ as the main body while it needs to be simulated and tested before synthesis, therefore, a design file called Testbench is also coded in C/C++. It may contain the Golden Reference, which is a method of verification of the main design. Therefore, a replica testing function is coded in Testbench which is capable of producing the same results as the original does. In this way, the original design results are matched and verified through Testbench vectors. It is called functional verification. The algorithm is simulated for only one frame.

The next step in the HLS design flow is the synthesis of the design from a high-level language to the RTL level code. For this step, directives and constraints have to be applied to the design. The last step is the C/RTL Cosimulation which is done after the synthesis of design. The RTL design is co-simulated through the same Testbench which is also converted in RTL but possible with not synthesizable functionalities (Fig. 5).

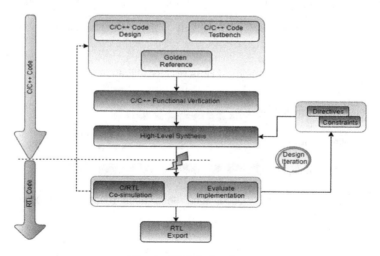

Fig. 5. HLS design flow

4.2 IP Interface Synthesis

During the coding the creation of an IP block in Xilinx® Vivado HLS a lot of challenges were faced. To code any algorithm in C++ is easy but to synthesize this code is a
little bit complicated as it requires the knowledge of interfaces and constraints to be
applied. In this project, the video streams use AXI4 Video Stream interface [10] while
AXI4-Lite interface [10] is used for control signals including handshaking signals as
well.

Our IP block uses two streaming ports for input and output video data while it also
has some ports for IOs including row and column values, centroid, selection of colors
and radius. The input video is converted into HLS MAT data [11] which is not a simple
matrix as its elements cannot accessible as a standard matrix thus, it is converted into
scalar data type for further processing.

4.3 Design Constraints

Constraints are a backbone of the IP without applying them nothing could work. As the
algorithm is developed for high definition video of size 1920 × 1080 pixels, parallelism must have to be involved it is only possible by implementing pipelining. The
designed IP is synthesized with different conditions of pipelining shown in Fig. 6.

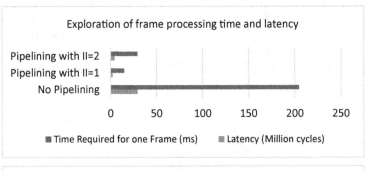

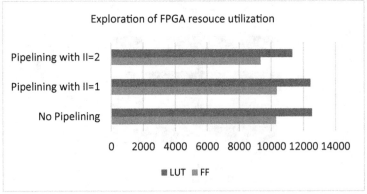

Fig. 6. Applying pipelining to ODHT algorithm

Without applying Pipelining, the latency was too large because of loops. Secondly, Pipelining with Initiation Interval (II = 2) was applied, latency decreased tremendously while resource utilization also decreased in this case. Lastly, Pipelining with (II = 1) is applied that resulted the half of the latency as compare to the previous case while it increases the utilization with some extent. A design constraint called 'HLS PIPELINE' is used for applying pipelinig. The last case is fully optimized as the time required to process a frame became smaller than the refreshing rate at 60 Hz.

The algorithm uses FOR loops to process the pixels. Thus, a constraint called 'HLS LOOPFLATEN OFF' is used to disable the nested loops from flattening. If loop flattening is enabled, then the loops are nested because of that the required frequency cannot be met. Although, applying loop flattening has increased the latency a little bit but the design is optimized with the desired clock frequency of 7 ms.

As the data is coming in the form of a stream, it is not stored anywhere. Thus, it is not possible to hold the data without buffering it. Therefore, a constraint called 'HLS STREAM DEPTH' is also used in the implementation. When the streams are duplicated to two, one stream needs to be buffered till the erosion operation has been done on the other one. The value of depth depends on the length of the stream, and it needs to be taken carefully because it uses registers to buffer the stream. Different values are tried for stream depth finally an optimized value of 4000 is selected. Although, it uses block RAMs but without buffering the data it is not possible to hold the stream for later processing.

5   Related Work

Elhossini and Moussa proposed a memory efficient implementation of HT on reconfigurable hardware [3]. The proposed architecture by [3] detects circles based on Circular Hough Transform (CHT) algorithm and implements the algorithm on reconfigurable hardware using Virtex-4 FPGA. Although this solution was pipelined, it uses HT memory with double buffer structure. This implementation uses arithmetic blocks composed of three stages to compute parameters like centroid coordinates. These arithmetic blocks consist of fixed-point calculations. The overall design was applied to the image of size 800×600 pixels because of memory limitation, and only four specific radii were detected due to the limitations of on-chip memory.

A different implementation for HT was proposed in [4] that uses the one-dimensional HT. The implementation was mapped to Xilinx Virtex-7 FPGA. The proposed architecture was implemented only for images of size 400×400 and work on 181.812 MHz. The input image is stored in block RAM which contains edge pixels in row and column order respectively. Rows and columns are processed simultaneously because image data is stored in the on-chip memory in a non-streaming fashion.

Our proposed architecture is based on one-dimensional Hough Transform similar to [4], but it is implemented for real-time video of frame size 1920×1080 pixels at 30/60 FPS. Unlike the architecture proposed by Elhossini in [3], our detection algorithm does not use any double buffer structure and arithmetic blocks for midpoint calculations. In our proposed system, the video is sourced through the HD camera and centroid is displayed on the detected object via the VGA displaying device.

The frame of size 1920 × 1080 having total 2073600 pixels thus, it requires 2073600 clock cycles latency. Our proposed solution results in 2099032 clock cycle latency that means 25432 clock cycle latency is due to all other operation from the conversion of video stream into HLS MAT to the operations implementing ODHT. Our solution works on 142.85–150 MHz frequency as it uses 7 ns period clock. Thus, for one complete frame, all processing is done in 14.67 ms that is still less than the 16.66 ms frame rate at 60 Hz. Therefore, the object is easily detected for every individual frame in the real-time video of size 1920 × 1080 at 30/60 FPS (Table 1).

Table 1. Comparison of architectures

Architecture	Memory architecture	Frame size	Image/video	Detection	Frame rate	FPGA device
Elhossini and Moussa [3]	2D	800 × 600	Image	Laplacian	30	Virtex 4
Zhou et al. [4]	2D	400 × 400	Image	Edge	30	Virex 7
Our solution	1D	1920 × 1080	Video	Erosion	60	ZYNQ

6 Experimental Results and Performance Evaluation

The proposed design for the circle and symmetrically shaped objects was implemented and evaluated on XC7Z010 ZYNQ SoC. This design only uses 40 18K BRAMs, 26 DSP48E blocks just for implementing the ODHT IP while overall video streaming architectures use 19150 Slices of ZYBO SoC. The proposed architecture works at 142.85 MHz frequency. The memory can be more reduced by decreasing the bit width of the interfaces ports and storing data that depends on the video size. Here, we used integer data type as standard, but HLS offers the selection of bit widths as well. The latency of the overall design is 2099032 clock cycles at the rate of 142.85 MHz or 7 ns period.

There are a lot of proposed solution exist for circle detection using reconfigurable hardware. Therefore, it is a little bit unfair to do an apple to apple comparison as they were proposed for numerous sizes of images, different algorithms, and various hardware devices. However, they were excellent and reliable at their places, but our proposed algorithm is efficient as it doesn't require memory, complex calculations and splendidly implemented for detecting the objects in real time video rather than stored images. It can also detect multiple objects with a little addition of linear filter that identifies the maximum votes in descending order.

Figure 7 shows the reduction of memory in the proposed architecture as compare to the architecture proposed in paper [4].

Figure 8 shows the simulation result followed by real-time implementation results in Fig. 9.

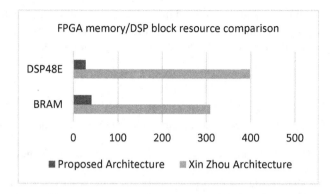

Fig. 7. FPGA resource utilization comparison

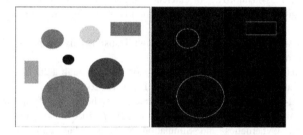

Fig. 8. Simulation test image and result

Fig. 9. Real time implementation result

7   Conclusion and Future Work

We presented an efficient implementation of one-dimensional Hough Transform algorithm for a color based circular and symmetrically shaped object detection in real-time video. Our implementation approach reduces the use of the memory as compare to the memory used in [4] while ameliorates the processing speed. This approach is implemented for high resolution images of size 1920 × 1080 without losing any information contained in the image or downscaling the image.

Future work on this design is expected in some areas including finding the index in the array of the location containing maximum votes and using the exact bit widths of ports and all accumulating arrays for the streaming and storing data respectively.

References

1. Saisudheer, A.: Object tracking system using stratix FPGA. Int. J. Comput. Eng. Sci. **3**(10) (2013)
2. Duda, R.O., Hart, P.E.: Use of the Hough Transformation to detect lines and curves in pictures. Commun. ACM **15**, 11–15 (1972)
3. Elhossini, A., Moussa, M.: A memory efficient FPGA implementation of Hough Transform for line and circle detection. In: 25th IEEE Canadian Conference on Electrical and Computer Engineering (CCECE) (2012)
4. Zhou, X., Ito, Y., Nakano, K.: An efficient implementation of the one-dimensional Hough Transform algorithm for circle detection on the FPGA. In: Second International Symposium on Computing and Networking (2014)
5. Tagzout, S., Achour, K., Djekoune, O.: Hough Transform algorithm for FPGA implementation. Sig. Process. **81**(6), 1295–1301 (2001)
6. Ioannou, D., Huda, W., Laine, A.F.: Circle recognition through a 2D Hough Transform and radius histogramming. Image Vis. Comput. **17**(1), 15–26 (1999)
7. Goneid, A., El-Gindi, S., Sewisy, A.: A method for the hough transform detection of circles and ellipses using a 1-dimensional array. In: 1997 IEEE International Conference on Computational Cybernetics and Simulation Systems, Man, and Cybernetics, vol. 4, pp. 3154–3157. IEEE (1997)
8. ZYBO FPGA Board Reference Manual. https://reference.digilentinc.com/_media/zybo: zybo_rm.pdf
9. Gonzalez, R.C., Woods, R.E.: Digital Image Processing, Chapter 9
10. AXI Reference Guide. https://www.xilinx.com/support/documentation/ip_documentation/axi_ref_guide/v13_4/ug761_axi_reference_guide.pdf
11. HLS MAT. http://www.wiki.xilinx.com/HLS+Mat

Reconfigurable FPGA-Based Channelization Using Polyphase Filter Banks for Quantum Computing Systems

Johannes Pfau$^{(\boxtimes)}$ (ID), Shalina Percy Delicia Figuli (ID), Steffen Bähr (ID),
and Jürgen Becker

Institute for Information Processing Technologies, Karlsruhe Institute of Technology,
Engesserstr. 5, 76131 Karlsruhe, Germany
{johannes.pfau,shalina.ford,steffen.baehr,juergen.becker}@kit.edu

Abstract. Recently proposed quantum systems use frequency multi-plexed qubit technology for readout electronics rather than analog cir-cuitry, to increase cost effectiveness of the system. In order to restore individual channels for further processing, these systems require a demul-tiplexing or channelization approach which can process high data rates with low latency and uses few hardware resources. In this paper, a low latency, adaptable, FPGA-based channelizer using the Polyphase Filter Bank (PFB) signal processing algorithm is presented. As only a single prototype lowpass filter needs to be designed to process all channels, PFBs can be easily adapted to different requirements and further allow for simplified filter design. Due to reutilization of the same filter for each channel they also reduce hardware resource utilization when compared to the traditional Digital Down Conversion approach. The realized sys-tem architecture is extensively generic, allowing the user to select from different numbers of channels, sample bit widths and throughput spec-ifications. For a test setup using a 28 coefficient transpose filter and 4 output channels, the proposed architecture yields a throughput of 12.8 Gb/s with a latency of 7 clock cycles.

Keywords: Quantum computing · FPGA · Signal processing
Channelization

1 Introduction

"Is there a boundary to the never ending, data hungry applications that emerge afresh every day?" is the constant question confronted in the world of science and technology. On one hand, modern applications ranging from data-streaming to video conferencing, high-resolution detectors to quantum computing have the urgency to process a huge amount of data with input frequencies in the range of THz and beyond. On the other hand, Moore's law, the engine that has powered the semiconductor industry is descending towards obsoleteness, as the state-of-the-art Field Programmable Gate Arrays (FPGAs) are struggling to be clocked

© Springer International Publishing AG, part of Springer Nature 2018
N. Voros et al. (Eds.): ARC 2018, LNCS 10824, pp. 615–626, 2018.
https://doi.org/10.1007/978-3-319-78890-6_49

above 1 GHz. Even in the analog domain, although recent Analog to Digital Converters (ADCs) have been pushed to GHz range, dividing the ever-widening multiplexed input spectrum into narrower bandwidths through analog front-ends gets more complicated, requires higher cost, more power and greater area. An alternate method to tackle this problem is to turn the focus towards available channelization techniques which can be further optimized and made scalable to meet our requirements. Channelizers, also known as filter banks, perform the task of processing an input signal with a certain bandwidth into one or multiple derived signals covering a subset of the input signal's bandwidth. Through the lineage of channelization commencing from the latter half of 1970s has its trail all along the way from television receivers to Wi-Fi, the recent, more sophisticated and hot off the fire application cases such as Cryogenic Particle Detectors (CPDs), multi-qubit Quantum Computing (QC) and the like use frequency multiplexed readouts and thereby require a channelizer which can fulfill the following requirements:

1. Allow for high input sampling and data rates required by wide-bandwidth inputs and high-resolution samples.
2. Process data with low latency, as certain applications in QC use feedback loops and therefore limit the highest tolerable latency.
3. Utilize as few resources as possible to fit in state-of-the-art or even low budget FPGAs.
4. Allow scaling for different, and large number of channels to adapt to a variety of application use cases.
5. Allow reconfiguration to allow for rapid development and easy adaption to other applications.

Among the popular channelization techniques available, such as Digital Down Conversion (DDC), Weighted Overlap Add (WOLA) and Pipelined Frequency Transform (PFT) [1], this paper focuses on the implementation of PFBs on FPGAs. PFBs allow scaling with larger number of channels and performing filtering at lower sample rates. Combined with advantages of FPGAs such as reconfigurability, flexibility and fast I/O interfaces, this enables PFBs to meet the aforementioned requirements. The main design scheme of our channelizer is not only a solution for applications with high data throughput but also for the ones in QC where maintaining low latency is crucial. Thereby, the objective is to make appropriate trade-offs between supported sample rate, required resources and filter specification in order to embrace high data rates with lower latency. The rest of the paper is structured as follows: Sect. 2 briefs the available common channelization concepts with Sect. 3 discussing the related work. The proposed channelizer architecture is elaborated in Sect. 4 and its implementation in FPGA technology along with validation results are presented in Sect. 5. Finally, conclusions are summarized in Sect. 6.

2   Common Channelization Concepts

Fast implementations of well-studied Digital Down Conversion systems have been presented by Meyer et al. [2], but one of the limitations of such systems is resource sharing. The components cannot be shared between multiple channels, even though each channel requires the same components for data processing. As shown in Fig. 1a, each channel's input signal has to be multiplied with a heterodyne to shift the desired channel's center frequency to the base band. This is followed by a low pass filter to limit the signal bandwidth to the channel width. The filtered signal is then downsampled to reduce the sample rate for further processing. This same chain of working principle is followed for all the other channels. As the number of channels increases, duplication of heterodyne multiplication and filtering operation also increases proportional to the number of channels and thereby makes this approach cost ineffective. When certain characteristics about the input signal are met, specialized Orthogonal Frequency Division Multiplexing (OFDM) demultiplexing systems are also a valid option [3]. But as our system has to deal with arbitrary input signals, such a solution can not be used here.

Shown in Fig. 1b, the Pipelined Frequency Transform channelizer recursively applies half band filtering to split the current signal into two new signals consisting of the lower and upper half of the original bandwidth. When equal bandwidth channels are desired, the number of channels supported by PFT is limited to powers of two. As the number of channels increases, the hardware resource requirements increase on a logarithmic scale with data processing latency being increased for every added filter stage. The absolute processing latency and resource usage depends largely on the used half band filters. The design of efficient half band filters such as Infinite Impulse Response (IIR) filters depends on output characteristics, for instance on linear phase requirements [4]. As our channelizer needs to be easily adaptable to different applications, approaches such as PFT depending on filters to be manually optimized for each application are not further considered.

In Weighted Overlap Add filter banks, a block of input data is multiplied with a signal processing window and the multiplied data is sliced into multiple buffers. These are then overlapped and added. This summed data is further block processed by a Discrete Fourier Transform (DFT) or Fast Fourier Transform (FFT) block processor as depicted in Fig. 1c. Although arbitrary resampling rates can be adopted for polyphase channelizers as exhibited in [5] and [6], it demands modifications in the channelizer's structure, whereas WOLA channelizers require only a different overlap and therefore no change to the structure is needed [7]. On the other hand, adjusting channel filter characteristics is more straightforward in PFBs, as the filter which shapes individual channels is designed directly, whereas WOLA channelizers require a windowing function which is a more abstract way to describe channel characteristics. As simple reconfigurability for different channel shaping filters is a requirement and arbitrary oversampling is not mandatory for our use case, PFB is chosen over WOLA channelizer.

Polyphase Filter Banks. PFBs are an extension of polyphase filters to process multiple channels in parallel using a single prototype filter. Polyphase filter partitioning is a special structure used to describe FIR filters, leading to new per-

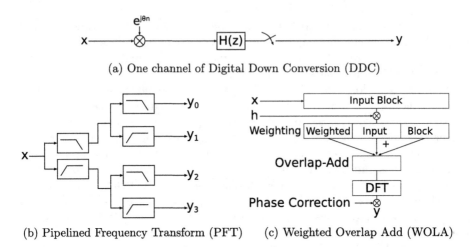

(a) One channel of Digital Down Conversion (DDC)

(b) Pipelined Frequency Transform (PFT)   (c) Weighted Overlap Add (WOLA)

Fig. 1. Block diagrams of various channelizer systems

spectives in signal processing. These structures are possible when an FIR filter is followed by an interpolator or decimator which respectively increases or reduces the sample rate after filtering. Since splitting one wide-band signal into multiple narrow-band signals with lower sampling rates is of interest in this context, only decimating filters are described here. The well-known Finite Impulse Response (FIR) filtering equation is combined with the equation of a downsampler [5] to yield Eqs. (1) to (3) with (1) describing the filter phases p_ρ, (2) illustrating the filter input signals x_ρ and (3) the restructured filtering equation for an M phase polyphase filter. The equations represent a counterclockwise commutator structure, where $h(n)$ represents the FIR filter coefficients and $x(n)$ represents the input signal. Alternatively, equations for the clockwise commutator model can be deduced as well. The models are mathematically equivalent and neither provides an advantage in implementation, but it is important not to mix filter phase signals and filter input signals of the different models.

$$p_\rho(n) = h(nM + \rho) \tag{1}$$
$$x_\rho(n) = x(nM - \rho) \tag{2}$$
$$y(n) = \sum_{\rho=0}^{M-1} p_\rho(n) * x_\rho(n) \tag{3}$$

A block diagram for a two phase polyphase filter ($M = 2$) is shown in Fig. 2. The commutator depicted by a bent arrow takes input signal $x(n)$ to produce filter input signals $x_\rho(n)$ according to (2). The phase filters p_0 and p_1 are standard FIR filters using coefficients as described by (1). The inputs are filtered using the phase filters and are summed at the output according to (3).

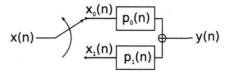

Fig. 2. Block diagram of a polyphase filter

The polyphase channelizer concept extends polyphase filters to form a channelizer. A polyphase lowpass filter produces the downsampled output of the
input spectrum filtered by a lowpass spectrum centered on DC frequency. This
produces a single output channel, whereas a polyphase channelizer duplicates
and shifts the prototype filter's spectrum to generate multiple output channels.
Eq. (4) as derived in [4] describes the output signals of a polyphase channelizer.
In this equation, y_r is the r-th polyphase filter phase output signal and M is the
number of total output signals. When comparing this output equation to the
well-known DFT transform equation, the polyphase channelizer structure can
be deduced as shown in Fig. 3 using a combination of polyphase filter and DFT.
It should be noted that the center frequencies of the channels in a polyphase
channelizer are distributed equidistantly and the distance between adjacent center frequencies is entirely determined by the number of output channels and
the input bandwidth. The center frequencies of the channels can therefore only
be further modified by shifting all the channels simultaneously such as in the
Generalized Discrete Fourier Transform (GDFT) channelizer [5].

$$y(nM, k) = \sum_{r=0}^{M-1} y_r\,(nM)\, e^{j\frac{2\pi}{M}rk} \qquad (4)$$

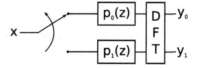

Fig. 3. Block diagram of a polyphase channelizer

3   Related Work

PFBs have been first studied in digital signal processing fields [5] and are often
applied in audio applications for signal processing, composition and decomposition [8]. More recently, PFBs are introduced in the domain of communication
technology, where they are called polyphase channelizers [4], and in the field of
astrophysics [9]. They have also been used as spectrum analyzers, as described
by Fahmy in 2010 [10]. It is interersting to note that in [11] PFBs are combined

with Frequency Response Masking (FRM) filters instead of FIR filters. Wu also described an FPGA based polyphase channelizer with odd or even stacking support and optional oversampling [12]. A polyphase channelizer for many-core CPU systems has been proposed in [13] and Chennamangalam et al. have developed a polyphase channelizer system for astrophysics running on GPUs [14].

Previous work has not been concerned with latency introduced by the channelization process and thereby provides no latency measurements. As our channelizer needs to be used in QC applications, where the channelization output is used as feedback to the system, it needs to have well-defined and well-known latency characteristics. Using polyphase channelizers in such systems has the potential to significantly reduce hardware resource consumption while obeying the latency requirements.

4   Proposed Channelizer Architecture

System Overview. An overview of the proposed channelizer architecture is shown in Fig. 4. The data flow closely follows the channelizer block diagram presented in Fig. 3 with some additional modules for signal processing. As this is a pipelined approach, there is no need for any control signals except for local signals handling data flows between modules. In order to allow combinations of commutator and filter modules to either pass the input data in parallel to polyphase branches or to implement the branches in a single filter and pass the input samples serially, interfacing between the modules is kept generic.

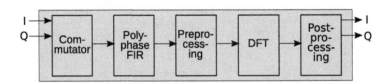

Fig. 4. Overview of modules in the channelizer architecture

The commutator being the first module maps the incoming complex-valued data stream (I and Q) to the polyphase filter phases. If the input data is already available as parallel bitstreams and in the correct format, then the commutator can be skipped with the bitstreams directly given to the respective polyphase filters. These filters are implemented in the polyphase FIR module. In this case, the sample rate of each filter branch is the same as the data rate of a single input bitstream. When the input data is a single bitstream, then the commutator uses a time based demultiplexing approach with the sample rate equal to $(data\,rate/number\,of\,channels)$. For an optimized implementation, FIR filters can be either clocked at a lower frequency or some filters can be combined into a single filter clocked at higher frequency. The FFT module is a standard FFT or DFT component and can be implemented either as a pipelined FFT processing data serially or as a parallel FFT processing data in parallel for achieving maximum throughput. The preprocessing and postprocessing modules are responsible for additional processing at the DFT input and output. They are required only for advanced cases such as oversampled PFBs or GDFT PFBs which are not further discussed in this paper.

Truncation and Scaling of Intermediate Values. As filtering and FFT operations are based on multiple additions and multiplications, the output bit width increases significantly due to fixed point data processing. In order to allow maximum precision in channelizer's result, the output samples are supported with full bit growth. For reduced resource usage, each module can optionally apply truncation and scaling to its output data.

5   Implementation, Test Application and Results

In addition to hardware implementation on Xilinx Virtex-7 VC707 evaluation board, a complete MATLAB model has been developed to pre-evaluate the expected behavior and to serve as a reference for the implemented system.

5.1   FPGA Implementation

Commutator Module. The commutator module splits the incoming bit stream into parallel streams to be processed by the polyphase filter branches using a counter driven demultiplexer. Whenever a valid input sample is processed, the counter is incremented and the next sample is delivered to a different filter branch. When data is transferred from a fast ADC, it is already available as parallel streams. In such cases, if the number of parallel streams and the number of channels (filter branches) match, then the commutator is replaced by a simple pass-through entity. If the input is available as parallel streams but does not match the number of channels, a more advanced remuxing concept has been implemented. Two clock sources have been utilized with the commutator making use of the faster one.

FIR Filter Bank. Each implemented FIR phase filter is structurally equivalent to other filters but with different coefficients. For our use case, the incoming bit stream is split into multiple parallel streams and thereby all the filter branches are processed in parallel. This in turn will increase the hardware requirements especially when the number of channels is very high. In order to reduce resource usage, various filters can be merged into a single hardware filter implementation using time domain multiplexing. When using fully parallel processing, the data rate and clock rate of the individual phase filters are reduced compared to the input signal sample rate. As the filters are built using Digital Signal Processing (DSP) slices, having lower clock frequency will allow for using less pipelining and thereby introduce less latency.

Using a direct form FIR filter is favorable when implementing hardware sharing by using multiple filter coefficient sets with one filter implementation. This kind of filter however requires additional pipelining at the output stage due to the large adder tree. As lower latency is one of the key criteria in QC, a simple transpose FIR filter as shown in Fig. 5 has been implemented using DSP48 slices. In transpose filters, delay registers are not used at the input stage as shift registers, but are instead interposed into the adder chain. This makes the adder chain intrinsically pipelined. By using dedicated routing channels on the FPGA, this structure can be implemented efficiently. Even though increased complexity in realizing multiple filters in such a transpose filter hardware structure is a disadvantage, hardware sharing is not a concern for our fully parallel filter bank. While higher fanout at the circuit driving filter inputs may limit the filter performance, testing shows a simple transpose filter to be a better option for our parallel filter bank implementation.

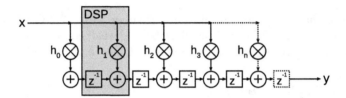

Fig. 5. Transpose form FIR filter

DFT. Considering a four channel configuration in the QC system, an optimized four channel channelizer using the well-known radix-2 Cooley-Tukey decimation algorithm has been employed. Explicit equations for real and imaginary components of each output channel derived from the standard DFT Eq. (5) yield a simple FFT structure, which can be implemented using two stages of adders. In this special case of a four channel DFT, all phase shifts degenerate to multiplications by 1, -1, j or $-j$ which can be interpreted as sign inversion and coupling between real and imaginary channels. Therefore, the need for multipliers can be eliminated. For example, derived equations for channel 0 depicted in (6) and (7) can be directly used to implement a 4-point parallel DFT where the input data samples x_n are passed as two independent values $Re(x_n)$ and $Im(x_n)$.

$$X(k) = \frac{1}{N} \sum_{n=0}^{N-1} x_n e^{-j\frac{2\pi nk}{N}} \tag{5}$$

$$Re\left(X_0\right) = \left(Re\left(x_0\right) + Re\left(x_2\right)\right) + \left(Re\left(x_1\right) + Re\left(x_3\right)\right) \tag{6}$$

$$Im\left(X_0\right) = \left(Im\left(x_0\right) + Im\left(x_2\right)\right) + \left(Im\left(x_1\right) + Im\left(x_3\right)\right) \tag{7}$$

The 4-point DFT equations can therefore be simplified as a signed addition of the outputs of two other signed additions, which results in an adder tree. Though pipelining the adder stages leads to shorter critical paths and thereby higher clock frequencies, it comes at the cost of introduced cycle delays. Consequently, the 4-point FFT has been configured to use zero, one or two pipeline stages and also supports both DSP slices and fabric logic implementation. Although Xilinx synthesis tool sets fabric logic as default, DSP slice implementation has been preferred as their utilization ratio is very small and fabric usage can be minimized by using DSP slices.

5.2   Integration into the Testing System

Although the channelizer is primarily meant to target QC systems, we use a generic, non-application specific test setup to enable testing and evaluation with different system parameters and for different application cases. The channelizer has been integrated into an existing data processing system[1] to test its functionality when the center frequencies of the channel do not exactly match the center frequencies dictated by the PFB structure. The test system needs to channelize two frequencies at $f_1 = 4492.63\,\text{MHz}$ and $f_2 = 4627\,\text{MHz}$ with the input signal being down-mixed using a configurable local oscillator (f_{lo}). The down-mixed signal is given as input to the 500 MHz ADC, which converts it into four parallel input data streams with 16-bit per sample at a sample rate of 125 MHz per channel.

Figure 6a shows the absolute frequencies of the input signals before mixing with the oscillator frequency f_{lo}. By setting $f_{lo} = 4497.315\,\text{MHz}$ the input frequencies f_1 and f_2 are translated to f_1' and f_2' as shown in Fig. 6b. As each channel has a sample rate of 125 MHz, the center frequencies of the channels are placed at multiples of 125 MHz which in turn offsets the input frequencies by 4.685 MHz compared to the channel centers. The prototype filter's bandwidth must be large enough to include these frequencies and therefore, a passband width of 6 MHz with an acceptable passband ripple of 5 dBand a stopband starting at 7.5 MHz with stop band attenuation set to 40 dB are chosen as system parameters. This results in a 337-tap FIR prototype filter.

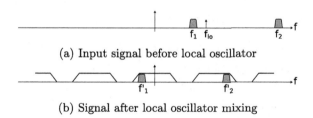

(a) Input signal before local oscillator

(b) Signal after local oscillator mixing

Fig. 6. Input signal and channel filter layout for the test system

[1] Our special thanks to Nick Karcher and Oliver Sander of IPE, KIT for providing the test setup.

Figure 7 shows a block diagram of the integrated system. As the ADC streams out four complex data streams in parallel, the commutator module has been omitted and the channelizer is implemented using only PFB and DFT modules. As the DFT outputs data at the same sampling rate of 125 MHz with 16-bit complex-valued samples, a data rate of 125 MHz $\times$ 16 bit $\times$ 2 $\times$ 4 channels is too demanding for the 10 Gbit/s Ethernet interface. Hence, a simple decimator module has been employed to downsample the output data to a sample rate of 125 MHz / 8 = 15.625 MHz by removing seven out of eight samples. No additional band-limiting filters are required as the bandwidth is sufficiently limited by the PFB. To evaluate the setup, a linear combination of complex phasors fed to a Digital to Analog Converter produced the input signal for the system. Verification of the results is done by examining the output data of the PFB channels using spectrum analysis techniques.

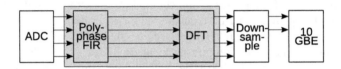

Fig. 7. Block diagram of polyphase channelizer integration

5.3   Results

Latency and Throughput. For hardware utilization analysis, a simpler test setup with only the channelizer has been synthesized using Vivado 2016.2 on a Virtex-7 FPGA platform. The setup uses a 28 coefficient FIR filter with 8 bit sample size and four channels. A single input bitstream with 200 MHz data rate is fed to the commutator. Then each channel transfers data to a prototype filter of length 7.

Table 1. Clock cycle latency

Configuration	FIR	Pre	FFT	Post	Total
Transpose DFT	6	0	1	0	7
Transpose GDFT	7	0	1	1	9
Xilinx serial	-	-	-	-	16–19

As shown in Table 1, transpose DFT configuration requires only 6 clock cyles for FIR filter with $n-1$ stages being fully pipelined, where n denotes filter length and 1 additional clock cycle for FFT module. The GDFT implementation used for odd channel stacking has 1 clock cycle overhead due to the implementation of complex filter coefficients. The Xilinx serial filter is included as a reference serial implementation. It processes the polyphase filter branches using a partially time multiplexed, optimized filter component and our standard, parallel DFT module. Because of some inherent parallelism in the Xilinx filter core combined with serial processing of branches, generating the output for all the n channels requires 16 to 19 clock cycles. The input samples are passed serially, but the output is provided in parallel so measured latency for different channels varies. The tested configuration does not require any preprocessing, so the latency introduced in this module is zero. Latency is calculated as the time required for the first input sample to be available at the output. Depending upon the channelizer's use case, another relevant metric is the group delay depending the FIR filter. It is generally lower than the presented delay metric. The throughput of the system can be calculated as the data input sample rate multiplied by the bit width of the complex samples: $50\,\text{MHz} \times 8\,\text{bit} \times 2 \times 4\,\text{channels}$.

Resource Usage. The resource usage per module has been charted down in Table 2. As expected since GDFT filter banks modulate the filters and therefore require complex filter coefficients, a higher LUT and DSP utilization can be observed for FIR filter in the GDFT configuration.

Table 2. Resource utilization per component

	Configuration	Commutator	FIR	FFT	Post	Other	Total
LUT	Transpose DFT	6	2	0	0	11	19
	Transpose GDFT	6	46	30	18	10	110
Register	Transpose DFT	131	8	1	0	35	175
	Transpose GDFT	131	8	1	35	35	210
DSP	Transpose DFT	0	50	6	0	0	56
	Transpose GDFT	0	67	6	0	0	73

6   Conclusion

The proposed reconfigurable FPGA-based polyphase channelizer has been tested and synthesized using Vivado 2016.2 on a Virtex-7 FPGA platform. The reconfigurability of FPGAs allows for fast development iterations and adaption to changing system requirements. When compared to per-channel approaches like traditional Digital Down Conversion, PFB operates filters at lower clock frequency. This allows PFBs to process large input bandwidths as made available by high throughput data interfaces of modern FPGAs. The PFB can be adapted to different application cases by configuring the number of channels, data width and throughput specifications. Different configurations using transpose filters and DFT or GDFT transforms have been analyzed for a test setup with a 28 coefficient FIR filter and 4 channels. In order to balance latency against throughput, the user has the choice of optional pipelining. Additionally, resource utilization can be balanced against throughput by configuring the hardware parallelism of the FIR filter and DFT. The test results show the transpose PFB with DFT to yield throughput of 12.8 Gb/s with a latency of 7 clock cycles for a sampling frequency of 200 MHz. These results suggest that a PFB may well be used in high-bandwidth, latency critical QC systems. Additionally, the possibility to gauge spectral channel shape, latency and resource requirements is especially useful for these systems.

References

1. Lillington, J.: Comparison of wideband channelisation architectures. In: International Signal Processing Conference (ISPC), Dallas (2003)
2. Meyer, J., et al.: Ultra high speed digital down converter design for Virtex-6 FPGAs. In: 17th International OFDM Workshop 2012 (InOWo 2012), 1–5 (2012)
3. Meyer, J., et al.: A novel system on chip for software-defined, high-speed OFDM signal processing. In: 2013 26th Symposium on Integrated Circuits and Systems Design (SBCCI), 1–6 (2013)
4. Harris, F.J.: Multirate Signal Processing for Communication Systems. Prentice Hall PTR, Upper Saddle River (2004)
5. Crochiere, R.E., Rabiner, L.R.: Multirate Digital Signal Processing. Prentice-Hall, Eaglewood Cliffs (1983)
6. Harris, F.J., Dick, C., Rice, M.: Digital receivers and transmitters using polyphase filter banks for wireless communications. IEEE Trans. Microw. Theory Tech. **51**, 1395–1412 (2003)
7. Wang, H., Lu, Y., Wang, X.: Channelized Receiver with WOLA Filterbank. In: 2006 CIE International Conference on Radar (2006)
8. Löllmann, H.W., Vary, P.: Low delay filter-banks for speech and audio processing. In: Hänsler, E., Schmidt, G. (eds.) Speech and Audio Processing in Adverse Environments. Signals and Communication Technology, pp. 13–61. Springer, Heidelberg (2008). https://doi.org/10.1007/978-3-540-70602-1_2
9. Tuthill, J., Hampson, G., Bunton, J.D., Harris, F.J., Brown, A., Ferris, R., Bateman, T.: Compensating for oversampling effects in polyphase channelizers: a radio astronomy application. In: 2015 IEEE Signal Processing and Signal Processing Education Workshop (SP/SPE), 255–260 (2015)
10. Fahmy, S.A., Doyle, L.: Reconfigurable polyphase filter bank architecture for spectrum sensing. In: Sirisuk, P., Morgan, F., El-Ghazawi, T., Amano, H. (eds.) ARC 2010. LNCS, vol. 5992, pp. 343–350. Springer, Heidelberg (2010). https://doi.org/10.1007/978-3-642-12133-3_32
11. Wu, F., Villing, R.: FPGA based FRM GDFT filter banks. In: 27th Irish Signals and Systems Conference (ISSC) (2016)
12. Wu, F., Palomo-Navarro, Á., Villing, R.: FPGA realization of GDFT-FB based channelizers. In: 26th Irish Signals and Systems Conference (ISSC) (2015)
13. Adámek, K., Novotný, J., Armour, W.: A polyphase filter for many-core architectures. Astron. Comput. **16**, 1–16 (2016)
14. Chennamangalam, J., et al.: A GPU-based wide-band radio spectrometer, vol. 31. Publications of the Astronomical Society of Australia (2014)

Reconfigurable IP-Based Spectral Interference Canceller

Peter Littlewood, Shahnam Mirzaei[✉],
and Krishna Murthy Kattiyan Ramamoorthy

California State University, Northridge, Northridge, CA 91330, USA
plittlew@gmail.com, smirzaei@csun.edu,
krishnamurthy.ramamoorthy.145@my.csun.edu

Abstract. This paper presents a technique to detect and compensate the spurious signals present in a continuous wave (CW) signal which is fixed in frequency and amplitude where the frequency and amplitude of the interfering signal is unknown to the receiver. The interference canceller proposed in this paper is used to detect the presence of standing spurious signals from approximately 0–500 kHz through waveform digitization and processing. This is an alternative solution to the existing analog implementations which function by receiving a certain bandwidth, and creating an out of phase version of the original signal, and then summing the two, cancelling spurs at a specific frequency. The source of these spurs can be internal (ex: self-coupling) or external (ex: nearby transmission stations). As the spur power approaches and exceeds the signal of interest, the receiving system experiences difficulty distinguishing between the intended signal and the spur. To the best of our knowledge, this is the first digital solution to the baseband interference problem. The technique presented in this paper was implemented on ZYNQ-7000 series housed on Xilinx Zedboard development board. The utilization reports show 36% of the Slices, 28% of the LUTs, 43% of the BRAMs, and 36% of the DSP blocks have been used for the complete system. Furthermore, its end-to-end functionality was verified using Xilinx's Integrated Logic Analyzer (ILA) in removing standing spurious signals, while minimizing distortion to the signal(s) of interest.

Keywords: Interference canceler · Digital signal processing
Hilbert Transformation · CORDIC · Fast Fourier transformation

1 Introduction

A set of signals received consists of both the signal(s) of interest and undesired components due to noise and co-located transmission sources, interfering with the receiver's ability to correctly interpret the desired data signaling. It is desired to suppress or remove interfering signals while minimizing impact to the signal of interest. This paper considers detecting CW signals where the frequency and amplitude of the interfering signal is not known to the receiver at the time of hardware synthesis. Therefore, the cancellation system is required to have a flexible architecture allowing identification and removal of interference sources. The proposed design in this paper was developed considering the following minimum criteria: streaming throughput,

© Springer International Publishing AG, part of Springer Nature 2018
N. Voros et al. (Eds.): ARC 2018, LNCS 10824, pp. 627–639, 2018.
https://doi.org/10.1007/978-3-319-78890-6_50

frequency independent recognition, and minimal impact to the signal of interest. Our approach is to perform corrections using frequency domain information as opposed to time domain correction techniques. By building a spectrum image of the input by merging multiple adjacent frames, a correction frame is constructed to play back against incoming data frames, thereby providing a real-time correction.

The major contribution of this paper is to present an alternative digital solution to the existing analog solution for the interference problem in baseband domain. Furthermore, the solution presented by authors is a proper implementation for reconfigurable hardware; the system parameters are simply modified to match systems with different requirement characteristics. To the best of our knowledge, this is the first digital solution to the baseband interference problem.

The rest of this paper is organized as follows: Sect. 2 provides the background to the subject matter and discusses the analog implementation. Section 3 presents the system architecture and implementation. Implementation results, performance, and simulations are presented in Sect. 4 and finally we conclude the paper in Sect. 5.

2 Background

2.1 Interference Cancellation Problem

A simple, direct analog implementation operates on undesired signals by using a phase controlled length of cabling to create a delayed version which is 180° out of phase from the original signal. The magnitude of the delayed signal is balanced, and summed with the original signal to provide frequency-specific cancellation. This is shown by Fig. 1a and b for a single CW tone where no error is considered. Simple simulations show variations in the outputs are on the order of 10^{-15} and can be attributed to small rounding precision error (discarded as an artifact of simulation). This method of cancellation requires precise cuts of cabling matching the desired multiple of the wavelength and filtering. This presents problems in terms of adaptability, and the manual skill/equipment required to accurately tune delays to match phase and magnitude. When errors arise in the tuning, effects such as phase shifting (phase error) occur. Depending on the filtering performed, the re-introduction of a specific bandwidth may produce unintended frequency 'beat' effects; shown in Fig. 1c, stemming from a 5% error in the frequency resulting from the summation of the original signal and its delayed version as described by Eqs. (II-1) and (II-2):

$$A cos(2\pi f_1 t) + A cos(2\pi f_2 t) = 2A \cos(2\pi t \frac{f_1 - f_2}{2} t) \cos(2\pi t \frac{f_1 + f_2}{2} t) \qquad (II-1)$$

$$f_{beat} = |f_1 - f_2| \qquad (II-2)$$

Similarly, if we fix the frequency at an ideal value, and introduce phase error, the new signal created will have a different phase and amplitude described by Eqs. (II-3) and (II-4). The effect of introducing phase error, created by inaccuracy of the summation path, is shown in Fig. 1d.

$$\alpha\cos(2\pi f_1 t) + \beta\sin(2\pi f_1 t + \theta) =$$
$$\sqrt{\alpha^2 + \beta^2 + 2\alpha\beta\,\cos\theta}\,sin(2\pi f_1 t + \tan^{-1}\frac{\beta\,\sin\theta}{\alpha + \beta\,\cos\theta} + \varphi) \qquad (\text{II}-3)$$

Where φ is given by:

$$\varphi = \begin{cases} 0 \ if \ \alpha + \beta cos(\theta) > 0 \\ \pi \ if \ \alpha + \beta cos(\theta) < 0 \end{cases} \qquad (\text{II}-4)$$

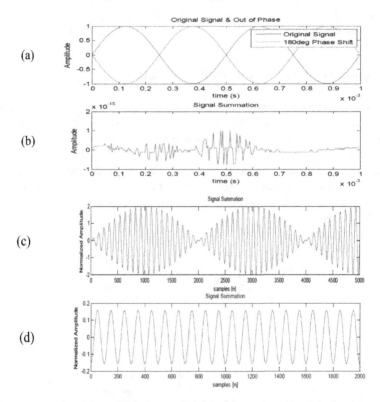

Fig. 1. MATLAB simulation of signal cancellation by summation: (a) original and out of phase signals (b) signal summation (c) frequency difference (d) phase difference

There has been a number of solutions to the baseband interference canceller such as the one presented in [1]. To the best of our knowledge, the implementation presented in this paper is the first to offer a fully digital solution to the problem. A fully analog solution to the interference problem is developed by Radio Sky [2] and it is comprised of potentiometers and a series of phase taps to create the signal, and can be switched over at divisions of the wavelength to select the best cancellation for summation. This solution does suffer from impedance mismatching. While coaxial cabling is being used to create the delay taps, the frequency characteristics of the potentiometers used are not guaranteed.

2.2 Digital Solution to Interference Cancellation Problem

The system proposed in this paper does not require delay taps or specifically tuned filters, as the incorporated digital processing scheme within the design recognizes spurious signals to remove them from the output waveform. Additionally, any arbitrary frequency is considered valid. However, for frequencies above the receiver's bandwidth, additional circuitry is required to bring broadband signals down to baseband. Subsequently, this system would be part of a receiver chain consisting of an analog front end and digital back end. This introduces a higher system cost, however still retains greater flexibility compared against a direct analog solution.

3   System Architecture and Implementation

The block diagram of the overall proposed system is shown in Fig. 2. The stages include signal digitization, DC cancellation, filtering, Fast Fourier Transform (FFT), rectangular to polar coordinate conversion, magnitude correction, polar to rectangular reversion, Inverse Fast Fourier Transform (IFFT), and output reconstruction. By sampling the input, processing, and separating the magnitude and phase of the frequency domain data, information regarding the spectrum can be obtained about what signals are present, and their corresponding power and phase.

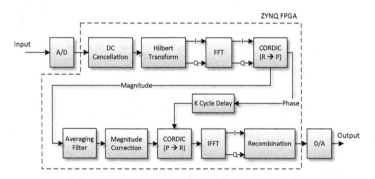

Fig. 2. System block diagram

The correction is built and subsequently applied based on an input start command connected to a push button on the ZedBoard. When applied, the synthesized logic builds an image representing an average magnitude data frame, and subsequently begins applying this image to future data based on the bin indices.

After magnitude correction is applied, the frame is passed through the reverse CORDIC/IFFT and recombined for output to the next processing stage. When a new set of deterministic signals is overlaid on the continuous spurs, these should be passed through, so long as the original spurs remain unmodified. The Xilinx ZYNQ-7000 series XC7Z020 FPGA device was chosen as the hardware platform, housed on the ZedBoard development board [3]. In the following, we will discuss the major blocks of the proposed system.

3.1 DC Cancellation

The ADC output consists of AC and DC components. The undesired DC component has the tendency to offset the signal, which creates hindrances in signal detection and estimation. The DC component artifact of non-zero input signals may be the result of level shifting, or an actual DC component of the signal. The major benefit of cancellation of this DC component is that FFT power spectrum will not be dominated by the DC component. A flexible, lightweight solution offered by Xilinx white paper WP279 [5] is an effective low-pass filter implementation; over a large number of samples produces an approximated DC component of the signal. The DC cancellation can be visualized through simulation, shown in Fig. 3. A periodic signal is applied, comprised of an AC and DC component. At the start of the simulation all register values are zero and the output is equal to the input signal. As cycles accumulate, the filter response rises with the DC component, is fed back, and subtracted from the input until equilibrium is reached. In Fig. 3 due to the large number of points necessary, the signals appear as a solid block instead of a periodic signal.

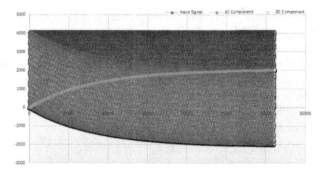

Fig. 3. DC cancellation simulation

3.2 Hilbert Transformation

The ideal Hilbert Transform results in the frequency and impulse response given by Eq. (III-1) shown below (6):

$$H_{HT(e^{jw})} = \begin{cases} -jsgn(\omega)e^{-j\omega\alpha}, & \omega1 < |\omega| < \omega2 \\ 0, & otherwise \end{cases} \qquad (III-1)$$

This indicates that the output of the Hilbert Transform is a 90° phase shifted signal for positive frequencies, and −90° for negative frequencies. An important property that has occurred is the creation of a sine function from a cosine, which can be used to form the in-phase and quadrature vectors. A quantized, causal form of the Hilbert Transform can be implemented with a Finite Impulse Response (FIR) filter, using the architecture in Fig. 4 [7]. Using a Type III filter (antisymmetric, odd), the general difference equation can be shown using Eq. (III-2).

$$y[n] = \sum_{k=0}^{\frac{M}{2}-1} a[k](x[n-k] - x[n-M+k]) \qquad (III-2)$$

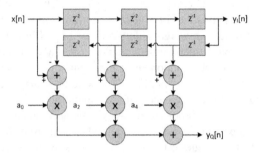

Fig. 4. Hilbert Transformation implementation using FIR structure [6]

Using the antisymmetric property of the difference Eq. (III-2), only even numbered coefficients are required. This results in using half as many hardware multipliers, implemented either by subtractions or negating the value and using the hardware adder chain. The Hilbert FIR structure shown in Fig. 4 is implemented to generate the quadrature signaling. Due to the impulse response of all the positive frequencies, a 90° phase shift will have occurred. This filter operates from approximately 0.05π to 0.95π, with a passband ripple of 2 dB. These are depicted in the MATLAB simulation of the transform shown in Fig. 5.

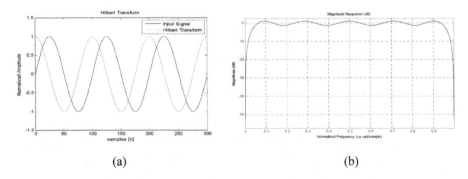

(a)   (b)

Fig. 5. Hilbert Transform MATLAB simulation: (a) phase response (b) magnitude response

3.3   Fast Fourier Transform and Inverse Fast Fourier Transform

The Fast Fourier Transform (FFT) is an efficient implementation of the Discrete Fourier Transform (DFT), requiring a computational complexity of approximately $Nlog_2N$, as opposed to the approximately N^2 complexity of directly computing the DFT. The Xilinx FFT core [10] is used for computing the frequency spectrum in terms of quantized 'bins' of data related to the power spectral density. Given an arbitrary input frame of time domain data, the FFT can be calculated using the Eqs. (III-3) and (III-4).

$$X[k] = \sum_{n=0}^{N-1} x[n] \, e^{\frac{-jnk2\pi}{N}}, \quad k = 0, 1, \ldots, N-1 \qquad (\text{III} - 3)$$

$$\Delta f = \frac{1}{N\Delta t} \qquad (\text{III} - 4)$$

Where Δt is the sampling period that the FFT is being run at. As an example, with a 4096 point FFT implemented, the frequency resolution can be calculated:

$$\Delta f = \frac{1.11 \times 10^6}{4096} = 271 \, \text{Hz}$$

The Xilinx IFFT IP [10] is used for converting the frequency domain data back into the time domain, and can be calculated by the Eq. (III-5) below. The IFFT calculation involves a factor of 1/N that differs from the FFT, however in all other respects is implemented as the FFT IP.

$$x[n] = \frac{1}{N} \sum_{k=0}^{N-1} X[k] \, W_N^{-kn}, \quad n = 0, 1, \ldots, N-1 \qquad (\text{III} - 5)$$

3.4   K-Point Averaging Filter

A general time domain averaging function uses a consecutive series of data samples that are summed and averaged according to the Eq. (III-6). This leads to an efficient implementation in the time domain as a series of shift and add operations.

$$x[n] = \sum_{i=0}^{K-1} \frac{1}{K} x[n-K] \qquad K = 2^L, \, L = 0, 1, 2, \ldots \qquad (\text{III} - 6)$$

Our proposal to save FPGA area is to use RAM blocks to store FFT samples as well as the delay line. Each RAM block can be configured to hold one full FFT transform length, and the inherent cycle delay acts as the shift register. By connecting the FFT frame index as a module input, a ring counter is driven to perform circular shifts whenever the maximum transform length is reached. For example, for K = 4 in this implementation, 001, 010, 100, 001, ... is the sequence used to form a 4-point averaging system as shown in Fig. 6. The read address for each RAM block is tied to the frame index, so that on the next cycle the data will be outputted from the RAM, right shifted by $\log_2 K$ and averaged with incoming data from the current frame. This new average value, corresponding to a one cycle of the FFT transform index, is then stored in the final RAM as the new average transform at a specified index.

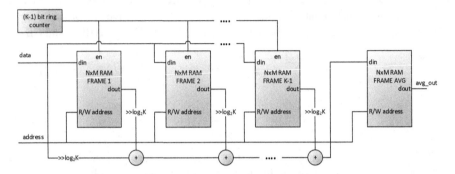

Fig. 6. K-Point averaging filter block diagram

4   System Performance and Results

Table 1 shows the breakdown of device resources for major components of the system. This system was developed on Xilinx Zedboard development board that houses ZYNQ-7000 series XC7Z020 FPGA. The utilization reports show 36% of the Slices, 28% of the LUTs, 43% of the BRAMs, and 36% of the DSP blocks have been used for the complete system. The function of several blocks in this paper is verified using Xilinx ILA debugger IP [4] and oscilloscope in real time while design is operating. These results are shown in Figs. 7, 8, 9, 10, 11 and 12.

Table 1. Device resource utilization

Module	SLICEs	LUTs	BRAMs	DSP blocks
DC cancellation	12	42	0	0
Hilbert Transform	36	104	12	6
FFT	1139	3032	24	45
CORDIC	911	3383	0	0
Averaging filter	29	25	12	0
IFFT	1737	5193	18	30
Total	4825	15192	61	81
Available	13300	53200	140	220

4.1   Hilbert Transformation

The in-phase signal generated by the transform is the same as the input signal matched with the latency of the quadrature signal. The in-phase and quadrature output signals represent just over a 3 dB loss in power. Figure 7 shows the Hilbert FIR ILA real time simulation of in-phase and quadrature outputs, which is being clocked at 100 MHz with a 4.5 MHz input. Comparing with the expected results, there is about 1 dB more loss compared to the MATLAB generated filter parameters, attributable to the quantization error accumulated during construction of the filter.

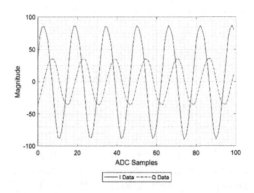

Fig. 7. In-phase and quadrature output ILA verification

4.2 Fast Fourier Transform and CORDIC

The time domain I/Q data needs to be converted to frequency domain for further processing. A 4096 point, single channel, streaming FFT/IFFT is used through Xilinx IP Integrator. Following from the Δf calculation by Eq. (III-4), the appropriate bin ranges for the FFT can be calculated from 0 to NFFT/2 using Eqs. (IV-1):

$$f_{bin\_start} = bin * \Delta f \text{ and } f_{bin\_stop} = bin * (\Delta f + 1) \qquad (IV - 1)$$

As an example, for bins 0, 1, 2, ... the start and stop frequency pairs will be (0, 271), (271, 542), (542, 813), etc. An identical image will occur in the upper half of the bin ranges referenced against sampling frequency, representing a mirror image of the lower bin ranges. For a 50 kHz test tone, the low image side is expected to peak in bin 184 when N < NFFT/2, and bin 3912 when N > NFFT/2 as shown in Fig. 8.

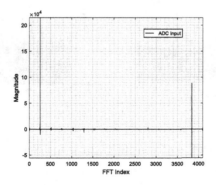

Fig. 8. FFT output verification using ILA for 50 kHz test tone

The FFT and IFFT modules have the advantage that each has a throughput of one value per cycle when implemented as a streaming configuration. At the beginning, there will be a time delay prior to the first frame of IFFT data. Disregarding the delays of other components, a total latency time of approximately 22 ms to the first signal transmission occurs, and after that it will appear to be fully streaming. The latency information are shown in Table 2 for both FFT and IFFT IPs.

Table 2. FFT/IFFT latency

Module	Transform cycles	Latency (ms)
FFT	12446	11.2
IFFT	12444	11.2

It is to be noted that the magnitude of the signal computed after FFT is not the actual magnitude and the actual magnitude and phase vectors are computed by using Coordinate Rotation Digital Computer (CORDIC) [9]. The CORDIC function is able to accomplish its task without hardware multipliers using only simple shifts, addition, and subtraction. In hardware, the output of the magnitude vector of the CORDIC is the signal of interest, as the phase will be simply passed through.

4.3   DC Cancellation

The DC cancellation logic performance is best examined using the frequency domain information. When DC cancellation applied, the ADC data will be fed directly into the Hilbert Transform block, bypassing the DC cancellation. The effects of the cancellation on the FFT spectrum are demonstrated in Fig. 9. As designed, the DC component is intended to always be removed prior to further processing; the ability to use a multiplexor to bypass the module is for demonstration purposes only.

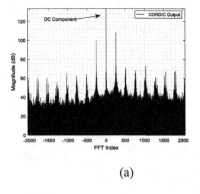 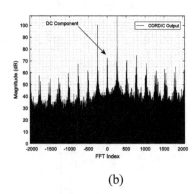

(a)   (b)

Fig. 9. FFT ILA output verification for (a) pre-cancellation (b) post-cancellation

4.4   Averaging

A four-point averaging circuit is used to verify the output of the averaging circuit. The synthesized averaging function contains a total of 16,384 memory locations. Given that the test tone is a CW signal, the frame to frame spectral data is expected to show no significant changes, discounting the random noise being generated. Therefore, the output of the averaging block should be similarly shaped to the translation output, and average out small random spikes that may occur at each FFT frame. Zooming in on the noise floor, the harmonics can be seen at a magnitude of approximately 3% of the primary tone. As expected, the waveform closely follows a delayed version of the CORDIC output as shown in Fig. 10.

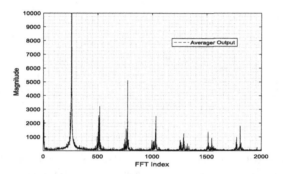

Fig. 10. Averager ILA output verification

4.5   Output Correction

In order to set up our system test, Direct Digital Synthesizer (DDS) [8] IP was used to generate four DDS blocks, each one providing a different frequency within the ADC's bandwidth. Figure 11a shows the four peaks with 150 kHz tone selected to be the desired tone, and all others considered interfering. By disabling the DDS controlling the 150 kHz tone, the communication system has opened up a timeslot for the receiver to build an image of the spectral content shown in Fig. 11b.

(a)   (b)

Fig. 11. Oscilloscope capture of multi-tone signals for (a) multi tone signal (b) interfering test sources

The combined three tones, as seen in the time domain by the ADC, are shown in Fig. 12a. An image of this can now be built during the timeslot, prior to the communication system resuming the 150 kHz CW tone. After the correction, has been applied, the system can begin retransmission, resulting in Fig. 12b.

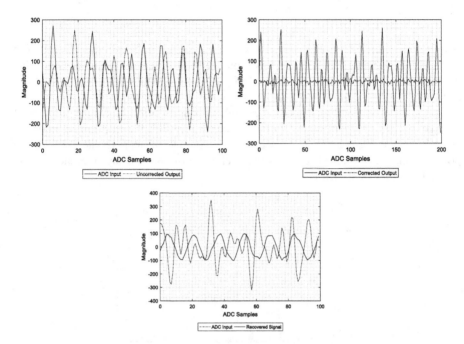

Fig. 12. FPGA ILA output verification for (a) ADC combined input: 70 kHz, 110 kHz, 200 kHz (b) interfering source cancellation (b) input vs. recovered output signal verification

The 150 kHz signal is recovered, with some amount of envelope distortion present (modulation of the amplitude). As long as the interfering sources remain constant, the system will be able to separate out the desired signal from the interference. A final image is shown in Fig. 12c, overlaying the input signal with the recovered output signal.

5   Conclusion

The interference canceller design proposed by this paper meets the objective of removing fixed (CW) signals within the given bandwidth. As long as the interfering sources remain constant, the remaining tone experienced a small envelope modulation. If there is no information being carried on the amplitude of the signal, no loss of information will have occurred; this will depend on the type of communication system used. The system end-to-end functionality was verified using Xilinx's Integrated Logic Analyzer (ILA) in removing standing spurious signals, while minimizing distortion to the signal(s) of interest. Synthesis builds are made with the ILA [4] IPs removed, as they are not necessary for proper operation. To demonstrate multi tone test capability, synthesis is run with four DDS IPs. During normal operation of just the receiver chain, the entire signal generation portion would be eliminated.

References

1. Kaufman, B., et al.: An analog baseband approach for designing full-duplex radios. In: Asilomar Conference on Signals, Systems and Computers, CA, USA (2013)
2. Local RF Interference Canceller (2014). From Radio Sky: http://radiosky.com/cancelit.html. Accessed 7 Jan 2017
3. Zedboard Avnet Inc.: www.zedboard.org, http://zedboard.org/product/zedboard. Accessed 7 Jan 2017
4. Xilinx Inc., DS299: LogiCORE IP Integrated Logic Analyzer, San Jose, USA (2011)
5. Xilinx White paper, WP279. Digitally Removing a DC Offset, San Jose, CA, USA (2008)
6. Manolakis, D.G., Ingle, V.K.: Applied Digital Signal Processing. Cambridge University Press, Cambridge (2011)
7. Xilinx Inc., DS534: LogiCORE FIR Compiler v5.0, San Jose, CA, USA (2011)
8. Xilinx Inc., DS558: LogiCORE DDS Compiler v4.0, San Jose, CA, USA (2011)
9. Xilinx Inc., DS249: LogiCORE IP CORDIC, San Jose, USA (2011)
10. Xilinx Inc., DS260: LogiCORE IP Fast Fourier Transform, San Jose, USA (2011)

FPGA-Assisted Distribution Grid Simulator

Nikolaos Tzanis$^{(\boxtimes)}$ ⓘ, Grigorios Proiskos ⓘ, Michael Birbas ⓘ,
and Alexios Birbas ⓘ

Department of Electrical and Computer Engineering,
University of Patras, 26500 Patras, Greece
ntzanis@ece.upatras.gr

Abstract. The inclusion of multiple Distributed Energy Resources in the modern distribution grid, which are integrated in the grid via high frequency power electronic components, imposes the need to incorporate the transient behavior of those components in the traditional node based simulation of distribution grid. The different simulation time steps associated with this interaction is addressed by incorporating hardware assisted (FPGA) co-simulation platforms. This co-simulation platform can capture simultaneously time-steps of tenths of μs and less than one μs. This is achieved by exploiting the inherent parallelism of FPGAs in combination with customized modeling of power electronic components so as to accurately simulate them. Those simulation models are fed to the node based grid simulation running in the general purpose machine, enabling the capture of all transient phenomena for ensuring operational integrity, monitoring and control of the grid. As proof of concept of our work in progress, the implementation of a one phase PWM full bridge inverter is demonstrated, and results obtained by Matlab/Simulink and FPGA prove the models' validity.

Keywords: FPGA · Simulation · Microgrid

1 Introduction

In recent years, the penetration at a great extent of Distributed Generation (DG) and power electronic devices, has transformed accordingly the structure and nature of power Distribution Network, so that the use of power grid simulators is a necessity. Traditional distribution power grid simulators use a time step of 50 μs or smaller (for 50-/60-Hz power systems), for an adequate detection of grid transients at the system level [1]. Such simulators use node based techniques and can be executed on a general purpose multicore computational platform, even when a large number of nodes exists. However, in the modern distribution grid the various energy resources (DER) and loads are connected to the grid via power electronic systems which employ high-frequency switching circuits. In order to simulate these power electronic system a much smaller time step is required (less than μs) [1, 2]. This is a time-demanding task for a general purpose computer and makes the simulator unsuitable for studying such fast phenomena without sacrificing resolution or speed.

© Springer International Publishing AG, part of Springer Nature 2018
N. Voros et al. (Eds.): ARC 2018, LNCS 10824, pp. 640–646, 2018.
https://doi.org/10.1007/978-3-319-78890-6_51

This paper reports on an on-going work which aims to develop an embedded simulation platform with similar architecture as those reported in literature [1] but which will be mainly focused and customized appropriately so as to address efficiently micro-grid configurations, detecting transients arising from fast switching devices as close to real-time as possible. The approach employed is based on the execution of the system simulation algorithm in an embedded multicore microprocessor for the purpose of avoiding the interconnect latencies during co-simulation. The platform consists of strong embedded μp (e.g. ARM-based) and a number of FPGA devices as co-processing elements (re-configurability provides increased flexibility compared to i.e. GPUs). A general network simulation algorithm similar to these presented in [1] will be executed in the micro-processor for the subset of power network under investigation. The present state of each network node is computed and inserted as input to the algorithm at each simulation step, so that computation of active and reactive power values on each branch of the network is feasible. The needed input of fast switching nodes can be easily retrieved with memory read instructions, since FPGA devices will be configured as memory mapped. A limited number of FPGAs will be enough to simulate a micro-grid.

With this co-simulation procedure we will manage to capture the fast transients of power electronics with the aid of co-processing units acting as hardware accelerators (FPGAs). For this reason, the research on reliable and accurate models of power electronic sub-systems, and especially for models that can take advantage of the FPGA resources [2] is of great importance. In this work this is exploited by proper modeling customization of power electronic device topologies.

The dominant Dommel's EMTP algorithm [3–5] and the Associated Discrete Circuit (ADC) switched model [6] are employed. Implementation is inspired by the work in [2]. All related works [2, 4], present a general implementation of the algorithm, suitable for a wide range of topologies. The proposed implementation instead, is fully customized taking into account the special characteristics of the specific topology, so as to mostly benefit in terms of simulation speed and area resources.

As proof of concept of our work in progress, an indicative implementation of a one phase PWM full bridge inverter is demonstrated here. Firstly, the customized model of the specific topology (full bridge inverter) is formed. It is then implemented in Matlab, and compared against the equivalent solution derived by SimPowerSytem library of Simulink, so as to ensure that our modeling algorithm exhibits adequate accuracy. Having verified that our modeling approach is accurate, an efficient implementation of it, is then demonstrated on an FPGA and a comparison/trade-off in terms of accuracy and speed, is presented.

Section 2 introduces the customized algorithms used for the simulation of power electronic devices. In Sect. 3, the FPGA implementation of the inverter is presented, whereas in Sect. 4, the overall simulation results are illustrated. Finally, in Sect. 5, conclusions are given.

2   Simulation Models of Power Electronic Devices

Regarding the modeling of power electronic devices, Dommel's iterative algorithm [3] is adopted, which is a switch model approach and the nodal equations of the system are extracted. The voltage of every node, for each time-step, is given by Eq. (1).

$$u(t) = Y^{-1}(t)i(t) \tag{1}$$

where u, are the nodal voltages, i are the node injected currents from the independent current sources of the system, and Y is the system's admittance matrix. Our modeling method is based on the ADC switched model [6] where a switch is modeled by a small inductance L/capacitance C when the switch is ON/OFF respectively and a current source that is dependent on the voltage of the previous time-step [4]. The values of L and C are chosen such that:

$$G_s = G_L = G_C \tag{2}$$

without this condition affecting the overall performance [6], thus resulting in the configuration shown in Fig. 1. Since a switch is represented by a fixed conductance G_S, a fixed admittance matrix is in turn constructed. As a result, there is no need to re-calculate the admittance matrix at each time-step and a significant computation reduction is achieved.

Fig. 1.   ADC representation of a switch

With the use of the ADC model, Eq. (1) is transformed to Eq. (3), where $I_{history}$ is the current sources' vector representing past history elements values [3, 4].

$$u(t) = Y^{-1}[i(t) - I_{history}] \tag{3}$$

The modeling customization of our approach and its application to the specific device is given in Sect. 3 along with its FPGA implementation, for clarity reasons.

3   FPGA Implementation of the Power Inverter

In this section the proposed modeling customization is described, followed by its application on the full bridge power inverter (Fig. 2) and the way that this could lead to an efficient FPGA implementation is demonstrated.

The power inverter illustrated in Fig. 2 is transformed to its ADC equivalent circuit. Any of the system's sub-circuits e.g. sub-circuit 1(circled in Fig. 2) can be modeled

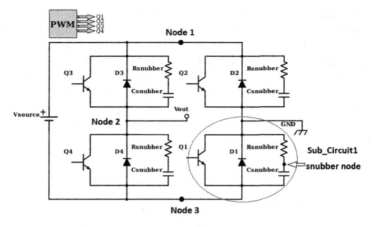

Fig. 2. PWM inverter model

with its ADC equivalent as in Fig. 3a, which is the usual case employed by most methods as e.g. mentioned in [4]. This is a convenient technique for a general simulation method, since information for all sub-circuit nodes is maintained for observability reasons.

In our approach, the internal node information (the snubber node in Fig. 2 in the specific case) is redundant, and it is omitted, since only the node voltages 1, 2 and 3 (Fig. 2) participate in the calculation of $I_{history}$ and via this to the computation of Vout (u(t) in Eq. 3), which is the target parameter for each time-step. By omitting this redundancy, each sub-circuit is transformed to the simplified model illustrated in Fig. 3b. This transformation can be readily applied to any other power switching component.

As a direct result of the simplified model of Fig. 3b, significant node reduction participating in Vout calculation is achieved (e.g. only such 3 nodes are associated with the simplified model instead of 7 nodes associated with the model of Fig. 3a). This in turn, has as effect that the admittance matrix is reduced accordingly. This means that much less computational effort is needed for the calculation of Eq. 3 than the conventional method usually adopted in literature.

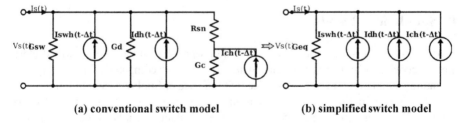

(a) conventional switch model   (b) simplified switch model

Fig. 3. a. Conventional switch model b. Simplified switch model

In order to exploit the inherent parallelism of FPGAs, the flow dependency of the afore-described algorithm is necessary to be studied [2]. This dependency can be briefly derived from Fig. 4. Specifically, a 1st level of parallelism exists (Fig. 4) since node voltages u(t) can be calculated in parallel owed to the fact that each u(t) only depends on the I(t) vector. Moreover, a 2nd level of parallelism is exhibited, in the sense that all the products participating in the final calculation of each node voltage u(t) can be computed in parallel. Finally, a closer look to Fig. 3b, shows that all elements of a sub-circuit share the same voltage. As a result, the history currents of each sub-circuit can be also calculated in parallel.

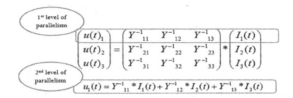

Fig. 4. Parallel computation of node voltages

The design of the full-bridge inverter with all afore described levels of parallelism having taken into account, is implemented in a Xilinx Virtex 6 device (**xc6vlx75t-2-ff484**). Synthesis results are shown in Table 1.

Table 1. Synthesis results

Slice LUTs used	15429	33%
Number of bonded IOBs	70	29%
Number of DSP48E1s	14	4%
Minimum time-step	126 ns	

As shown in Table 1, the minimum time-step is on the order of tenths of nanoseconds, which is close to real-time network constraints.

4   Simulation Results

In order to test the speed and accuracy of the proposed solution, the described algorithm is coded and simulated in Matlab. These results were compared with the output of a Simulink simulation of the same device, with the use of SimPowerSytem library. The next step is to implement the aforementioned algorithm in an FPGA device (Xilinx Virtex 6 3E in our case). Figure 5 illustrates the simulation results (Simulink, Matlab, FPGA) and verifies the functional performance of the design. A slight difference in accuracy shown in this figure is justified from the use of signed fixed point configuration (Q14.20) instead of a floating point one that Simulink adopts and is not due to

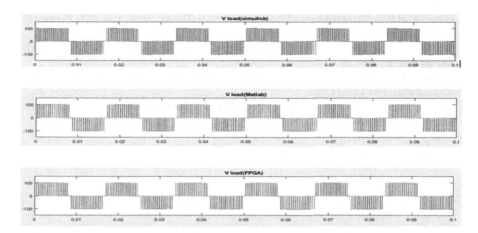

Fig. 5. Simulation results in simulink, Matlab code and FPGA

any kind of deficiency of the modeling algorithm. The desired accuracy can be achieved through the use of a fixed point configuration with higher resolution.This will not affect the computational time, but rather the area utilization.

5 Conclusions

This work presents an efficient FPGA-based simulation of an one-phase power inverter and is part of a generalized distribution grid simulator. It is based on a novel customized modeling of power electronic devices so that to fully exploit the inherent parallelism of FPGA structures. The architecture can scale up from a few FPGAs (micro-grid) to multiple FPGAs or high lever Real Time Simulators (broader grid model). That leads to the accurate simulation of fast switching power electronics and their transient behavior. The validity of our modeling approach was verified by comparing its simulation results with those of Simulink. The enhanced speed gain and the small simulation time-step achieved, prove that FPGAs can be employed as co-processing elements of the embedded (power grid) simulation platform which is the target of our research. The next step, will be the creation of a library of different power electronic FPGA based topologies and their integration with the grid-line simulator.

References

1. Faruque, M.O., Strasser, T., Lauss, G., Jalili-Marandi, V., Forsyth, P., Dufour, C., Dinavahi, V., Monti, A., Kotsampopoulos, P., Martinez, J.A., Strunz, K., Saeedifard, M., Wang, X., Shearer, D., Paolone, M.: Real-time simulation technologies for power systems design, testing, and analysis. IEEE Power Energy Technol. Syst. J. **2**, 63–73 (2015)
2. Matar, M., Bayoumi, A.M.: An FPGA-based real-time simulator for the analysis of electromagnetic transients in electrical power systems (2009)

3. Dommel, H.W.: Electromagnetic Transients Program Theory Book, vol. 483. Bonneville Power Administration, Portland (1986)
4. Watson, N., Arrillaga, J.: Power systems electromagnetic transients simulation. IEE Power Energy Ser. **39**, 449 (2003)
5. Hollman, J.A.: Step by step eigenvalue analysis with EMTP discrete time solutions. New Methodology Test Cases (2006)
6. Hui, S.Y.R., Morrall, S.: Generalised associated discrete circuit model for switching devices. IEE Proc. Sci. Meas. Technol. **141**, 57–64 (1994)

Analyzing the Use of Taylor Series Approximation in Hardware and Embedded Software for Good Cost-Accuracy Tradeoffs

Gennaro S. Rodrigues[1](✉), Ádria Barros de Oliveira[1,2],
Fernanda Lima Kastensmidt[1,2], and Alberto Bosio[2]

[1] Instituto de Informática - PGMICRO,
Universidade Federal do Rio Grande do Sul (UFRGS), Porto Alegre, Brazil
{gsrodrigues,adria.oliveira,fglima}@inf.ufrgs.br
[2] LIRMM - University of Montpellier/CNRS, Montpellier, France
alberto.bosio@lirmm.fr

Abstract. This work proposes a universal method to approximate computational functions. It employs Taylor series to compute approximations and provide results with high accuracy at low cost. A multitude of software and hardware implementation designs are presented and evaluated on a Zynq-7000 APSoC for their area cost, accuracy and time performance. Results show that embedded software approaches tend to provide excellent accuracy at a better cost/accuracy rate, and that hardware projects can save resources costs by slightly relaxing their accuracy requirements.

Keywords: Hardware · Software · Embedded processors
Approximation · Numerical

1 Introduction

Several algorithms can present a *good enough* result even when executing inexact computations. Such is the case of approximative computing techniques [1], which have been used in many scenarios, from big data to scientific applications [2]. Approximate computing has been proposed as an approach to developing energy-efficient systems [3], saving computational resources, and presenting better execution times [4]. Past works even proved that software with approximative nature presents higher intrinsic fault tolerance than conventional algorithms [5].

Systems-on-a-chip (SoC) arise as perfect implementation platforms for approximative computing. Industry-leading companies offer SoC FPGAs, presenting both a programmable logic layer (PL) and an embedded processor. Those Commercial Off-The-Shelf (COTS) devices are intensively used in systems design. Approximative computing projects can profit from the hardware-software

© Springer International Publishing AG, part of Springer Nature 2018
N. Voros et al. (Eds.): ARC 2018, LNCS 10824, pp. 647–658, 2018.
https://doi.org/10.1007/978-3-319-78890-6_52

co-design made available from COTS systems to implement any approximation, or as means of co-processing.

The literature presents a plethora of approximation strategies and techniques. Those can be applied to software or hardware level. The loop perforation technique is an excellent software approximation example, being able to achieve useful outputs while not executing all the iteration of an iterative code [6]. Indeed, the authors claim this approach typically delivers performance increases of over a factor of two while introducing an output deviation of less than 10%. Another approximation technique for software applications consists of reducing the bit-width used for data representation [7], also achieving a better execution speed than their non-approximative counterparts. Hardware-based approximation techniques usually make use of alternative speculative implementations of arithmetic operators. An example of this approach is the implementation of variable approximation modes on operators [8]. Hardware approximation is also present on image processing domain in the form of approximative compressors [9].

Given such an extensive amount of possible approximative computing methods, finding the most suitable strategy for a given application is a significant challenge. Each approximation method presented in the literature is specially developed for a single application, being unscalable and many times even inapplicable for a different purpose or algorithm. Theoretically speaking, one can say that an infinity of applications have still not been approached by approximative computing studies, and never will. For some applications, developing a unique approximative design might be an extreme intellectual work.

This work presents a universal method capable of numerically approximating functions for general purposes. Because mathematical functions can represent any algorithm, the proposed approach can be used to generate an approximative version of any given software. We also show that the same strategy can be used to provide approximated hardware. Both software and hardware implementations are evaluated in a COTS SoC, presenting an FPGA and an embedded ARM Cortex-A9 microprocessor. The main contribution of this work is to provide a theoretical basis for the later development of a tool capable of generating approximated numerical versions of any software or hardware design. This work relies on approximation theory and mathematical analysis to provide mathematically valid approximations.

2   Proposed Method

This work uses Taylor series to numerically approximate functions. Although many numerical techniques for mathematical approximation are available, Taylor series was selected due to its high applicability and simplicity [10]. Another reason to chose it was the fact that its terms can be previously calculated, implying in a performance gain when implemented in software. In particular, Taylor series was chosen instead of Maclaurin series due to its higher usability and generality [11,12]. Maclaurin series is a specific case of Taylor series, and has a smaller applicability due to its constraints.

2.1   Taylor Series Approximation

Taylor series are used in mathematics to represent a function as a sum of previously calculated terms. These terms are generated from the values of the function's derivatives at a given point. The more terms are used, the better the representation. This way, functions are approximated using a finite number of terms in a Taylor series. An infinite number of terms would adequately represent the original function. However, calculating infinite terms is computationally impossible. Equation 1 shows the compact sigma notation for Taylor series, where n stands for the current term (from 0 to N), and a stands for the center point (where the derivatives are calculated), being $f^{(n)}(a)$ the nth derivative of the function f at the point a. When $a = 0$, the Taylor series is called a Maclaurin series.

$$\sum_{n=0}^{N} \frac{f^{(n)}(a)}{n!}(x - a)^n \tag{1}$$

Being an approximation, a Taylor series with finite terms presents an error when compared with the original function. This error is variable depending on the center point used and the number of terms. For some functions, the Taylor series may converge in a given range and diverge when out of its bounds. However, it is possible to estimate this error quantitatively using Taylor's theorem. Functions that contain one or more singularities cannot be represented as Taylor series either. The convergence of a given function using Taylor series approximation needs to be evaluated before its usage. The designer is also accountable to employ a sufficient number of Taylor terms so that the errors do not interfere with the generation of a *good enough* result.

Some of the approximation problems presented by Taylor series can be dealt by the designer during implementation time. For instance, if the range of the input values of a function is known, the designer can evaluate if an approximation by Taylor series is feasible. Also, even when such an approximation shows up as divergent in a critical range, the designer can achieve a good approximation by merely changing the Taylor series center point a (see Eq. 1).

2.2   Numerical Approximation Applicability

Numerical analysis is essential for all branches of science and engineering. In a matter of fact, it is the only way to solve many computation problems, such as derivatives and integrals. Numerical methods are algorithms designed to solve numerical analysis problems. They make use of mathematical properties and numerical analysis theory to approximate their results to the mathematically expected one. Those strategies are also used to assist solving NP and NP-Complete computational problems.

Past works indicate that numerical approximation algorithms are inherently more tolerant to faults than ordinary computation [5]. Therefore, using Taylor series to approximate any given function is expected to improve their fault tolerance as well. Varying the number of Taylor series terms will impact not only resource usage but also tolerance. For those reasons, this study is fundamental for safety-critical system designers willing to implement numerical algorithms.

3   Implementation

This work is implemented in a Zynq-7000 APSoC (XC7Z020-CLG484 package), designed by Xilinx with 28 nm technology. Nevertheless, the proposed method is generic and extendable to other APSoCs. The Zynq board has embedded a high-performance ARM Cortex-A9 processor with two cache levels on the processing system (PS), alongside a programmable logic (PL) layer. The PL presents an FPGA based on the Xilinx 7-Series with approximately 27.7 Mb configuration logic bits, 4.5 Mb Block RAM (BRAM), 85K logic cells, and 220 DSP slices, with a clock frequency of 100 MHz. The dual-core 32-bit ARM Cortex-A9 processor runs at a maximum frequency of 666 MHz. It counts with two L1 caches (data and instruction) per core with 32 KB each, and one L2 cache with 512 KB shared between both cores. A 256 KB on-chip SRAM memory (OCM) is shared between the PS and PL parts, and so is the DDR (external memory interface).

A Taylor series approximations for the exponential function is implemented as benchmark. The algorithm is coded in C, and implemented both in software and hardware. Hardware implementations are generated by High Level Synthesis (HLS) using the very same code, and use the PL part. The HLS is provided by the Vivado Design Suit, by Xilinx. Figure 1 presents the implementation diagram of the approximations. Equation 2 presents the mathematical equation for this Taylor series approximation. The software versions are executed in the PS part of the board, that is, the ARM processor.

$$e^x = \sum_{n=0}^{N} \frac{x^n}{n!} = 1 + x + \frac{x^2}{2!} + \frac{x^3}{3!} + \cdots + \frac{x^N}{N!} \qquad (2)$$

3.1   Hardware Implementation

Two parameters are considered during the hardware implementation: data precision type and the usage of a pipeline. The data precision types evaluated are *double* and *float*. The pipeline is used to accelerate the Taylor series computation loop and is implemented into the algorithm by merely adding a *pragma*

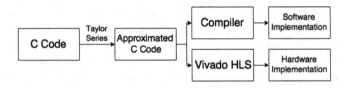

Fig. 1. Taylor series approximations implementation flow

(option from Vivado HLS) in the C code. No particular argument is passed to the HLS pipeline pragma, so by default, it will try to pipeline the loop as much as possible.

Table 1 presents the resource usage for the four implemented Taylor series approximations. It shows the data from the four variants of the approximation for a variety of numbers of Taylor series terms. The double precision variant with pipeline presents data from 3 to 13 terms because it is the maximum number of terms we can implement that fits in the Zynq-7000 FPGA layer. For the same reason, the float precision variant with the pipeline is presented from 3 to 34 terms. Resources usage concerning area is divided into four categories: DSPs, FFs, LUTs and Essential Bits. The last two columns present the data for latency (in clock cycles) and accuracy (in percentage). The accuracy is calculated comparing the output value with the best value obtainable computationally without Taylor series approximation (the exponential function from the *math.h* C library

Table 1. Performance and resource usage analysis from HLS hardware implementation

Precision	Pipe.	Terms	Area				Lat. [c.c.]	Accuracy [%]
			DSPs	FFs	LUTs	Esst. bits		
Double	No	5	14	4761	6250	804046	215	89.28417678
		10	14	4765	6254	824732	430	99.97332604
		25	14	4769	6258	810620	1075	100
		50	14	4773	6263	825134	2150	100
		100	14	4777	6267	806337	4300	100
	Yes	3	28	1797	3518	449824	16	54.70235457
		4	42	5987	8967	1126115	41	76.02448002
		5	67	7264	11400	1409144	47	89.28417678
		8	109	19777	27747	3502632	65	99.58761712
		11	162	29396	41078	5183543	83	99.99410196
		13	190	37738	51976	6618716	95	99.99977405
Float	No	5	5	1648	2361	251843	130	89.28417875
		10	5	1652	2365	255535	260	99.97332926
		25	5	1656	2369	250510	650	99.99998919
		50	5	1660	2374	258650	1300	99.99998919
		100	5	1664	2378	256350	2600	99.99998919
	Yes	3	10	837	1454	168274	12	54.70235538
		4	15	2054	3191	342306	24	76.02448475
		5	23	2646	4255	445723	29	89.28417875
		8	38	6276	9498	991407	44	99.58761582
		16	81	15338	22753	2377350	84	99.99998919
		34	177	35882	52737	5494006	174	99.99998919

for the given data precision). Vivado HLS implementation report provided the estimation of the hardware latency and area resources usage presented at the table. Measuring the latency in another manner would be more laborious and inaccurate.

It becomes clear by the analysis of Table 1 that the usage of pipeline profoundly affects area resources occupation, while the latency slightly increases. On the other hand, the absence of pipeline implies an almost constant hardware area but makes the latency grow with the number of terms. The essential bits are configuration bits on which a bit-flip causes an error. This data is important for safety-critical systems design, where it shall be as low as possible. The table also shows that *double* precision achieves accuracy per number of terms almost at the same rate as *float* precision. Nevertheless, only *double* precision was capable of achieving full accuracy. Another interesting fact is that not many terms are needed to provide good accuracy. In fact, 8 terms seem to be enough to provide accuracy of 99% for any implementation. From that point further, the area and latency costs increase, but the accuracy remains almost the same. The data from Table 1 is analyzed and discussed in Sect. 4.

3.2   Embedded Software Implementation

The same code used at Vivado from the last section was also implemented on Vivado SDK and executed on the ARM processor. The software executed baremetal, i.e., on no operating system. However, in this case, only two versions of the algorithm are presented: one for *double* precision and another for *float* precision. That is because there is no implementation strategy on embedded software that is equivalent to Vivado HLS pipeline.

Table 2 presents the data from the embedded software execution performance. The two columns present the data for execution latency (in clock cycles) and accuracy (in percentage). The accuracy is calculated the same way did on the Sect. 3.1: comparing the output value with the best value obtainable for the given data precision (using the function from the *math.h* library). The execution latency of the embedded software is measured by executing the applications on the Zynq board making use of the *xtime_l.h* C library provided by Xilinx.

As expected, both the execution latency and accuracy increased with the number of Taylor series terms. Table 2 shows that the accuracy increases exponentially with the increase of the number of terms. The latency also increases with the number of Taylor series terms, but not as much. Surprisingly, *float* precision appears as a better choice when using 10 to 15 terms, providing both better accuracy and execution latency. Those behaviors are discussed and analyzed in Sect. 4.

4   Discussion

The data from Tables 1 and 2 arise a multitude of questions. They show that the hardware and software implementations have each its own particularities.

Table 2. Performance analysis from embedded ARM software implementation

Terms	Double		Float	
	Exec. lat. [c.c.]	Accuracy [%]	Exec. lat. [c.c.]	Accuracy [%]
2	230	28.9872284	238	28.98722979
3	202	54.70235457	164	54.70235531
4	252	76.02448002	204	76.02448465
6	348	95.88087592	284	95.88087586
8	444	99.58761712	364	99.58761569
10	540	99.88980474	444	99.97332912
13	684	99.99977405	576	99.99978126
15	780	99.99999351	644	99.99999681
16	828	99.99999986	696	99.99998933
20	1020	100	844	99.99998933

For instance, a comparison between the area resources usage from HLS and embedded software does not make sense, because the area of the ARM processor is constant and not dependable of the program implementation. However, it is possible to compare some data from hardware and software. As an example, the latency of HLS hardware implementations (particularly the ones without pipeline) is comparable with the execution latency of the embedded software implementation. This section discusses the results obtained from Sect. 3 and speculates on their implications.

4.1   Hardware Implementation Analysis

Section 3.1 presented the Vivado HLS implementation details, at Table 1. The usage of pipeline arises as a good alternative for projects that need to rely on a fast execution, and are implemented on boards on which area is not a problem. In fact, using pipeline may even not be costly. For instance, comparing the pipelined version of *double* precision with its counterpart with no pipeline, Table 1 shows that when both achieve an accuracy of more than 99% the pipelined version uses around four times the number of LUTs and FFs but is almost seven times faster. A similar behavior is observed on the *float* precision variants.

Area resource usage can be a problem for some systems. As was explained at Sect. 3.1, the maximum numbers of Taylor series terms that fit in the Zynq board FPGA are 13 and 34 for *double* and *float* precision, respectively. Nevertheless, every benchmark variation shows that the accuracy of Taylor series approximation largely increases following a small number of terms. Because of that, the need for a high number of terms is improbable. Projects in need of high accuracy can also achieve it while saving area by limiting the size of the pipeline, breaking the computation loop into big chunks. This type of implementation strategy is not the focus of this work. Table 1 also shows that increasing the area of the design increases the number of essential bits. This can be seen as problematic for safety-critical systems since it is highly related to the project susceptibility to errors when exposed to radiation [13]. As referenced in Sect. 2.2, the type of approximation presented in this work might improve the fault tolerance of an application. If that is the purpose of the approximation, a designer may choose not to use the pipeline approach.

The accuracy is determined by different factors for each variant of the benchmark. The versions without pipeline implementations have their accuracy determined by their area size. However, the pipelined versions achieve accuracy increasing their latency. A designer shall know which is the better cost to pay: latency or area. The advantage of using implementations with no pipeline is that, despite taking a long time to output, it is always capable of achieving the best accuracy possible. That is because time is a resource not limited by the hardware, but by project constraints. The same can not be said of pipelined implementations: even though they are faster, they have their maximum accuracy limited by the programmable area of the hardware.

Table 1 shows that improving the accuracy of an already accurate version of the algorithm is more costly than enhancing an inaccurate one. As a good example, there is the *double* precision pipelined version. In that case, improving the accuracy from 54.7% to 89.28% is less costly in area than improving it from 99.994% to 99.999%. The same behavior is observed on all versions of the code. It shows that the higher the index of the Taylor series term, the lower is its impact on the final result, thus less critical it is. It also indicates that there is a maximum accuracy attainable by the approximation method, but it is very near 100%. The table proves the importance of a preliminary study to avoid unnecessary or unworthy area usage. For instance, there is no reason to use 100 Taylor terms on the *double* precision without pipeline version because 25 is already enough to achieve an accuracy of 100%.

4.2   Software Implementation Analysis

Section 3.2 presented on Table 2 the performance details from the Taylor series implementation running as a bare-metal application on the ARM A9 processor. The *double* precision variant of the algorithm was the only one capable of achieving an accuracy of 100%. Nevertheless, the *float* precision met good accuracy with low execution latencies.

Contrary to the hardware HLS approach, the only cost for embedded software to acquire accuracy is execution latency. The memory use of the variants is also different, but the absolute value is so small that it has no cost impact. The output is only one 64- or 32-bit variable, for *double* and *float* precision, respectively. Unless a project needs an accuracy of 100%, there seems to be no reason to use *double* precision instead of *float*. Nevertheless, it is important to remember that the accuracy of each algorithm variant is calculated taking as parameter its own best result possible (assuming it to be the *math.h* library result). It means that not only *double* precision provides accuracy, but also a more thorough result. The type of data precision defines how much decimal points the variable can hold. This number may change depending on the target processor architecture or compiler used, but normally *double* precision holds 13 decimal points, while *float* holds 7. For projects that need high exactitude, the 7 decimal points provided by *float* may not be enough. In those cases, *double* precision is a must. However, as Table 2 shows, Taylor series can provide accuracy with almost the same computation execution latency as *float* precision.

4.3   Software and Hardware Comparison

The software implementation achieves accuracy by increasing the number of Taylor series terms, which by its turn increases the execution latency. In the HLS implementations, increasing the number of terms would cause an increase of area and latency (being a higher variation in area for the pipelined variants and higher latency for the ones without pipeline). Because the pipelined hardware sacrifices area to achieve accuracy, and almost no latency, it is not fair to compare it with the software implementations. The hardware implementations without pipeline, however, are comparable with the software implementations, as both achieve accuracy at the same price: latency.

Figure 2 presents the data from software and hardware execution latency for the *double* precision algorithms. The black vertical lines mark some important precision barriers. Following the tendency observed at Tables 1 and 2, the precision increases faster for the first terms, and slower as it gets near 100%. The unexpected result is that the hardware HLS and software (SW) implementations had virtually the same execution in clock cycles.

The comparison between the HLS hardware without pipeline and software implementations with *float* precision regarding execution latency is presented at

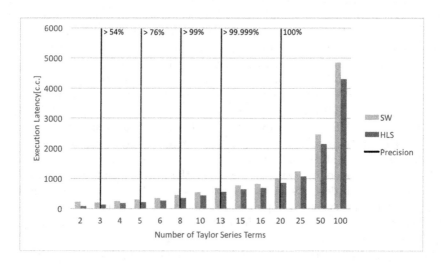

Fig. 2. Execution latency comparison between HLS without pipeline and SW (software) implementations for *double* precision

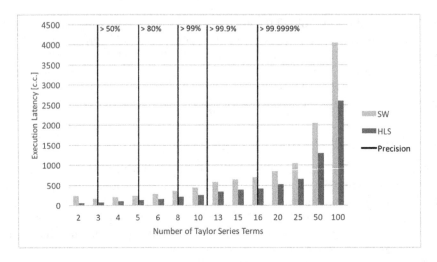

Fig. 3. Execution latency comparison between HLS without pipeline and SW (software) implementations for *float* precision

Fig. 3. In this case, the software implementation takes more clock cycles to finish than the hardware one. The lines progression show that the number of required clock cycles rise exponentially, as well as the difference between their absolute values. It indicates that if a higher number of terms were needed, the software approach would take much more clock cycles to finish the execution than the HLS.

Studying the execution performance only through the number of clock cycles may be misleading. That is because the ARM processor and the PL of the Zynq-7000 APSoC have different frequencies. The embedded ARM processor work with on 666 MHz while the FPGA on the PL runs with a frequency of 100 MHz. It means that a software version of the algorithm may execute faster than an HLS hardware implementation even with a higher clock cycles count.

Figure 4 presents the execution time in seconds of the two data precision variants from HLS hardware (without pipeline) and software implementations. It shows that the software implementations are always faster than a hardware with no pipeline. This is an unexpected result, taking into account that hardware implementations tend to be faster than embedded software. In contrast to Figs. 2 and 3, Fig. 4 shows that a more general and less optimal design (with a higher clock cycles count) can execute faster than an optimal one (with fewer clock cycles). It all depends on the target hardware. It is important to notice, however, that the hardware implementations on Fig. 4 do not take full profit of the parallelization capacity of the FPGA since they are not implementing pipelines and loop unrolling.

The question of whether to use hardware or embedded software to implement approximation through Taylor series seems to have no definite answer. While software arises as a better alternative than low-area hardware, it is still slower

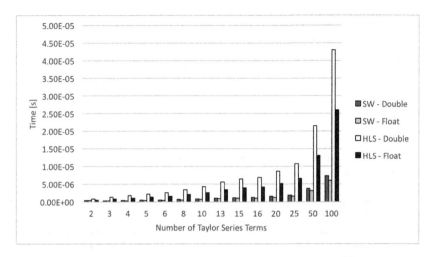

Fig. 4. Time comparison between HLS without pipeline and SW (software) implementations for both data precisions

than an optimal pipelined hardware implementation. However, the high area cost of a pipeline for Taylor series with a high number of terms may prove its implementation unfeasible on smaller FPGAs. A profound evaluation of the alternatives shall be performed before a design decision, since project time and area constraints may vary.

5   Conclusion

Taylor series approximation arises as an excellent approximation technique for both software and hardware. Its implementation on the Zynq-7000 APSoC proved to be uncomplicated. Vivado HLS proved to be a useful tool for generating hardware implementations, as well as providing easy-to-code optimizations in the form of *pragmas*. This work demonstrated that the theoretical and mathematics concepts can be implemented on software and hardware projects with great functionality.

Results show that Taylor series approximation is capable of achieving excellent accuracy with a small number of Taylor series sum terms. The performance and cost of Taylor series approximation depend on the target algorithm accuracy constraints. It proved to be able to provide fast and low-cost approximations for systems with low limitations as well as good approximations (up to 100% accuracy) for those which need it (and can pay for its cost). Hardware implementations appear to be either slower than embedded software or consume too many resources.

On future works, we will explore more profoundly all the optimization options and strategies provided by Vivado HLS and how they affect the system. An in-depth study on the effects of approximative computing on safety-critical systems is also planned. The development of a tool automatically provides the best Taylor series approximation code for given cost and accuracy constraints is in course. The usage of multicore parallelism on embedded software approximation is also currently being studied as a means of acceleration.

References

1. Venkataramani, S., Chakradhar, S.T., Roy, K., Raghunathan, A.: Approximate computing and the quest for computing efficiency. In: Proceedings of 52nd Annual Design Automation Conference. In: DAC 2015, pp. 120:1–120:6. ACM, New York (2015)
2. Nair, R.: Big data needs approximate computing: technical perspective. Commun. ACM **58**(1), 104 (2014)
3. Han, J., Orshansky, M.: Approximate computing: an emerging paradigm for energy-efficient design. In: 2013 18th IEEE European Test Symposium (ETS), pp. 1–6, May 2013
4. Chakradhar, S.T., Raghunathan, A.: Best-effort computing: re-thinking parallel software and hardware. In: Proceedings of 47th Design Automation Conference, DAC 2010, pp. 865–870. ACM, New York (2010)
5. Rodrigues, G.S., Kastensmidt, F.L.: Evaluating the behavior of successive approximation algorithms under soft errors. In: 2017 18th IEEE Latin American Test Symposium (LATS), pp. 1–6, March 2017
6. Sidiroglou-Douskos, S., Misailovic, S., Hoffmann, H., Rinard, M.: Managing performance vs. accuracy trade-offs with loop perforation. In: Proceedings of 19th ACM SIGSOFT Symposium and 13th European Conference on Foundations of Software Engineering, ESEC/FSE 2011, pp. 124–134. ACM, New York (2011)
7. Rubio-González, C., Nguyen, C., Nguyen, H.D., Demmel, J., Kahan, W., Sen, K., Bailey, D.H., Iancu, C., Hough, D.: Precimonious: tuning assistant for floating-point precision. In: Proceedings of International Conference on High Performance Computing, Networking, Storage and Analysis, SC 2013, pp. 27:1–27:12. ACM, New York (2013)
8. Shafique, M., Ahmad, W., Hafiz, R., Henkel, J.: A low latency generic accuracy configurable adder. In: Proceedings of 52nd Annual Design Automation Conference, DAC 2015, pp. 86:1–86:6. ACM, New York (2015)
9. Momeni, A., Han, J., Montuschi, P., Lombardi, F.: Design and analysis of approximate compressors for multiplication. IEEE Trans. Comput. **64**(4), 984–994 (2015)
10. Ren, Y., Zhang, B., Qiao, H.: A simple Taylor-series expansion method for a class of second kind integral equations. J. Comput. Appl. Math. **110**(1), 15–24 (1999)
11. Foy, W.H.: Position-location solutions by Taylor-series estimation. IEEE Trans. Aerosp. Electron. Syst. **AES-12**(2), 187–194 (1976)
12. Moller, T., Machiraju, R., Mueller, K., Yagel, R.: Evaluation and design of filters using a Taylor series expansion. IEEE Trans. Vis. Comput. Graph. **3**(2), 184–199 (1997)
13. Tonfat, J., Tambara, L., Santos, A., Kastensmidt, F.: Method to analyze the susceptibility of HLS designs in SRAM-based FPGAs under soft errors. In: Bonato, V., Bouganis, C., Gorgon, M. (eds.) ARC 2016. LNCS, vol. 9625, pp. 132–143. Springer, Cham (2016). https://doi.org/10.1007/978-3-319-30481-6_11

Special Session: Research Projects

CGRA Tool Flow for Fast Run-Time Reconfiguration

Florian Fricke[✉], André Werner, Keyvan Shahin, and Michael Huebner

Chair for Embedded Systems, Ruhr-University Bochum, 44801 Bochum, Germany
{florian.fricke,andre.werner-w2m,keyvan.shahin,
michael.huebner}@ruhr-uni-bochum.de
http://www.esit.rub.de

Abstract. Coarse-grained reconfigurable hardware reduces reconfiguration effort in terms of bitstream-length and synthesis time, since the configuration-bits target a set of wires or a processing units functionality instead of single connections and LUT-entries. Therefore logic-synthesis can be reduced to mapping and scheduling. In this paper we present a CGRA Tool Flow to (semi-)automatically create VCGRA architectures for numerical computations and the corresponding configurations for these architectures. In our example we achieved run-time reconfiguration times of around 6.5 μs. To additionally reduce area consumption we evaluated the TLUT/TCON tool flow from the University of Ghent as a backend-tool for implementation. Results show up to 75% reduction in LUT utilization.

Keywords: Coarse-grain reconfigurable array · Overlay architecture
Image processing · Dynamic reconfiguration

1 Introduction

Recently, new devices, suited for handling typical data-center workloads and compute intensive tasks have been introduced by FPGA vendors. These FPGA architectures include general-purpose processors as well as programmable logic [1]. The logic itself includes dedicated hardware blocks like DSPs and BRAMs next to the logic cells to speed-up numerical computations. However, development on these platforms still requires a lot of expertise. Functional blocks in hardware can be described in high-level programming languages using High-Level-Synthesis (HLS) tools, but the acceleration of these blocks, as well as the implementation on hardware, still requires a lot of experience in hardware design. The configuration of FPGAs generally requires long bitstreams and therefore needs long synthesis times, depending on the size of the design. For instance, implementing a design on a typical FPGA, takes – depending on the synthesizing platform and the size of the target device – minutes to hours. Implementing a design on a device takes several steps: (1) Synthesizing, (2) Logic Optimization and (3) Packing, Placing and Routing. In general, all these steps are very

© Springer International Publishing AG, part of Springer Nature 2018
N. Voros et al. (Eds.): ARC 2018, LNCS 10824, pp. 661–672, 2018.
https://doi.org/10.1007/978-3-319-78890-6_53

time-consuming and hard to parallelize. The recent research results show a big gap in speed and resource utilization between commercial development tools for FPGA design [2] and commonly used open-source tools like the widespread Verilog-To-Routing (VTR) tool [3]. VTR includes the ODINII Verilog frontend from the University of Toronto [4], a logic optimizer and synthesis-tool called ABC from the University of Berkeley [5] and the Pack, Place and Routing tool VPR [6,7]. There have been efforts done in [8–11] to accelerate the placement stage. However, the degree of parallelization and acceleration is limited and the results show speed-ups of 3.5x when using a hardware-accelerated iterative placer. Considering that some of the designs need synthesis times up to one hour and more, this speed-up will not satisfy our objective of Just-in-Time reconfiguration. Coarse-grained devices reduce reconfiguration effort in terms of bitstream-length and synthesis time since the configuration-bits target a set of wires or a whole processing unit's functionality and logic-synthesis can be reduced to mapping and scheduling. Moreover, computational tasks, depending on the desired accuracy, may require higher bitwidths, in this instances coarse-grained architectures will be beneficial. Of course, a physical implementation of a coarse-grained architecture is limited to its internal bitwidth and the speed benefit decreases if the architecture's bitwidth does not fit the application's one. By using virtual overlay architectures on top of an FPGA architecture the bitwidth can be set depending on the application's requirements. Moreover, by using *reconfigurable* virtual coarse-grained overlays, an overlay design can be chosen specifically to fit a specific application class. This can be very valuable, especially in High-Performance-Computing (HPC) applications, where performance and energy efficiency are of high importance. Furthermore, by addressing overlay architectures, the overlay design benefits from architectural improvements of the underlying hardware when ported to a new hardware-generation. This enables a better reusability of well tested implementations over multiple hardware generations, since the overlay can be implemented on new hardware while the configuration for the overlay will still be used. In this article a tool flow has been presented, which uses a commercial backend as well as the TLUT/TCON tools for the implementation of a virtual overlay architecture on physical or virtual FPGA architectures. Addressing a virtual overlay architecture makes our tool-flow independent from architectural changes and the vendor of the architecture underneath. Moreover, it hides the complexity of the underlying hardware from the user. Domain experts can provide functional blocks which can then be used by a wider user community for realizing specific applications. This solution equips the users with a tool generating tailored hardware/software solutions for their applications.

2 Virtual CGRA Design and Configuration Tool Flow

Overview to the VCGRA Target-Architecture. An example of the architecture presented in this paper is shown in Fig. 1. It consists of processing elements (PE) and virtual channels (vCH) [12]. The array is structured in layers, containing alternately PEs and virtual channels. The input channel, which receives the input data from the processing system, differs from other vCHs regarding its size, which depends on the selected number of the VCGRA's inputs. It is used to add flexibility to the mapping of inputs to the first layer of processing elements. Two configuration-streams are used to parametrize the functionality of a VCGRA. While the *Channel Configuration* controls the data flow among the VCGRA's levels, the *PE Configuration* controls the operation of a PE. The size of the configuration bitstreams is defined by the number of PE operations and the number of PEs within a VCGRA level and is statically determined at design time. A synchronization module is used to synchronize the data processing within the VCGRA with an external processing system (PS). It raises a bit flag after all PEs in the last level are done with their computations. All components of the VCGRA as well as the VCGRA itself are described in VHDL, containing annotations. These annotations are later used by the TLUT/TCON backend, to control its reconfiguration technique, resulting in reduced resource utilization.

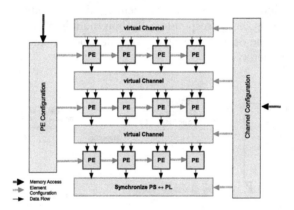

Fig. 1. Example of a virtual CGRA

CGRA-Generator. To create architectures like the ones described above, the generalization techniques provided by VHDL are not sufficient. To facilitate the task of creating architectures several tools have been built, assisting the designer in creating architectures and configurations for them and the implementation of hardware using vendor tool-chains. Within this proposed tool-chain, the CGRA-generator creates architectures. It processes the HDL-description of architectural templates for the components and a definition of the desired target architecture as input and generates the adequate VHDL code and supplemental description files. Those supplemental files are required to allow the mapping of algorithms and the creation of configuration vectors for the generated CGRA. All tools are implemented using Python 3 and directly handle the VHDL code's textual representation. No library for interpreting the VHDL code has been used and the tools are completely based on manual parsing using Python methods for text manipulation and regular expressions. This decision is based on the fact that no suitable up-to-date and well maintained library could be found. The VHDL generator creates the top-level entity and all the corresponding architectural components for the CGRA implementation. The description of the communication infrastructure and the processing elements are provided to the tool as input files. To allow the adaption of the template files for the selected use case, the files hold modified VHDL code, which contains specified strings instead of fixed values for parts that should be modifiable (e.g. *INPUT_DEFINITION_LIST* as placeholder for the definition of the inputs). The virtual channel uses the channel-multiplexer-elements and can be configured by the tool for an arbitrary number of input- and output-processing-elements. The number of required configuration bits is set automatically, depending on the number of input- and output ports. This number is also an output of the tool, which is needed by e.g. the tool for generating the configuration bitstreams for the *VCGRA*. The template for the processing element allows the selection of supported operations and automatically adjusts the number of required configuration bits according to the number of selected operations. All template files mentioned are handled the same way: the content is read by the corresponding Python module; the requested changes are performed and the output is written to a file whose name is determined by the functions parameters.

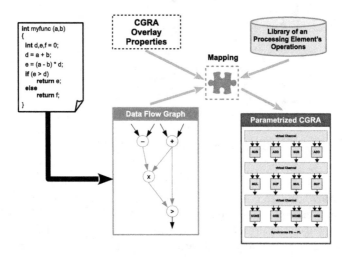

Fig. 2. Mapping overview

CGRA-Configuration-Generator. As an addition to the tools for creating the architectures, the tool described in this section is used for mapping arbitrary algorithms into predefined VCGRA architectures. As the mapping algorithms we want to evaluate are based on graphs, the wide-spread and well-tested software library graph-tool [13] has been selected for implementing the mapping-tool.

This library is a Python frontend for the `Boost::Graph` C++ library, which includes many algorithms for common graph-problems and has an excellent and well-documented Python interface. The mapping tool, which is currently under development, requires two graphs as input. The definitions of the graphs properties are oriented on common data-flow-graphs for the "software-graph" and on the internal description of the VCGRA from the other tools for the "hardware-graph". In a first step, the tool checks whether the software graph entirely fits into the hardware graph, in terms of the VCGRA's size. If it doesn't, a partitioning is performed before the (sub-)graphs are scheduled and placed on the VGCRA architecture. Different algorithms for partitioning the graphs and creating an efficient reconfiguration schedule are currently evaluated. The output of the mapping tool is a schedule for the subgraphs (if applicable), the description of the connection of inputs and outputs between the subgraphs and the VCGRA configurations for all the partitions of the algorithm's data-flow-graph. A schematic overview of the mapping tool is presented in Fig. 2. The design entry can be an algorithm which is represented as data-flow-graph and described in JSON. The conversion from text based programming languages to data-flow-graphs has to be handled by external tools. Other inputs to the mapping tool are the properties of the overlay (e.g. the shape and the number of inputs) and the library of processing elements' operations. All mentioned inputs can be extracted from the hardware-graph-representation in JSON. The format has been defined to serve as input for the VHDL generation tools as well as for the mapping tool. As stated out before, the output is the VCGRA's configuration which can be converted to bitstreams using the configuration generation tool.

3   Application Description

Image processing applications are heavily employed in many kinds of industrial and academic disciplines. Edge detection is a widely used task in image processing that can be realized using convolution filters. Many different filters for detecting edges in images have been proposed [14]. One simple and widespread filter is the *Sobel Filter* or *Sobel Operator*. If the filter's set-point is in the middle of the filter-mask, a pixel in the result image is calculated by the formula:

$$G_x(x,y) = \sum_{i=1}^{3}\sum_{j=1}^{3} I(x+i-a, y+j-a) \cdot S_x(n+1-i, n+1-j) \qquad (1)$$

Where:

- $G_x(x,y)$ is a pixel in the result image of a convolution in vertical or horizontal direction.
- I is the input image. The corresponding pixels underneath the mask are addressed relatively, depending on the filter set-point.
- S_x is a filter in either vertical or horizontal direction. The coefficients for a corresponding input pixel are addressed absolutely – the indexing starts with one.

Accelerated Kernel Code. Equation (1) can be expressed as a set of nested loops. In Listing 1.1 an example of a C/C++ implementation is shown. The first two loops run over all coordinates of the input image and generate the coordinates of the pixel at which the filter's set-point is placed within the input image. The second two loops run over all coordinates within the filter kernel and the kernel-code calculates the weighted sum of the convolution. Afterwards, the algorithm generates an absolute value of the temporary result and calculates the average value over the nine additions. The convolution code for one gradient pixel is marked with *convolute*. If the loops for the convolution are unrolled, they can be shown as a directed-acyclic-graph. Figure 3 shows such a graph, corresponding to the convolution with a Sobel-filter for one output-pixel.

At the top of the graph, circled nodes are inputs. $I(x+a, y+b) \mid a, b \in [-1, 1]$ represents the input pixels of the input image. Input pixels are multiplied (MUL) by the corresponding filter coefficients $S(a, b) \mid a, b \in [0, 2]$ in the second row of the graph. Afterwards, all temporary products are accumulated (ADD) until the sum for one output pixel $G(x, y)$ is calculated. All operational nodes have two inputs and one output. That matches the design of the PEs of the VCGRA architecture, with two inputs and one output.

Listing 1.1. C/C++ Kernel Code for Convolution

```
extern const int16_t sobel[3][3];
void convolute(const uint8_t* inputImage, uint8_t* gradientImage,
  const uint32_t sizeX, const uint32_t sizeY) {
  //temporary variables
  int16_t tempResult{0};
  uint32_t posX, posY;
  // run over all input pixels of input image
  for (uint32_t yIter = 1; yIter < sizeY - 1; ++yIter) {
  for (uint32_t xIter = 1; xIter < sizeX - 1; ++xIter) {
    tempResult = 0;
    posX = xIter - 1;
    posY = yIter - 1;
    //convolute
    for(uint8_t j = 0; j < 3; ++j)
      for(uint8_t i = 0; i < 3; ++i)
        tempResult +=
          ((int16_t) *(inputImage + (((posY + j) * sizeX) + (posX + i))))
          * sobel[2 - j][2 - i];
    // make result absolute
    if (tempResult < 0)
      tempResult *= -1;
    // save pixel in gradient image.
    *(gradientImage + ((yIter*sizeX)+xIter)) = (uint8_t)(tempResult/9);
  }
  }
  return;
}
```

4   VCGRA Implementation

The way of implementation depends on the requirements of the design, like the depth of a graph, number of implemented PE-operations or bitwidth of data paths, and the preferences of the designer e.g. the grade of specialization. If the platform is big enough, the graph-representation can be implemented without any reconfiguration. In this case, the design is fully application specific and the performance is not affected by reconfigurations. The execution time solely depends on the depth – the number of levels of PEs and channels – of the architecture and the execution times of the PE's operations. Timings for data

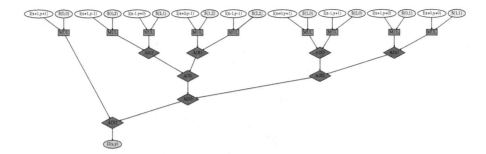

Fig. 3. Directed acyclic graph for the kernel code of a convolution

transfer through the channels are small compared to PE operations. When a partitioning of the graph has to be performed, two effects can lead to a performance reduction: the reconfiguration-time and the communication effort for feeding the outputs from one iteration into the next one as inputs. Both of these effects lead to requirements for the optimization within the partitioning algorithm. The degree of acceleration thus depends heavily on the characteristics of both architecture and application.

Cohesive Design. The most straightforward way of implementing a given data-flow-graph at Fig. 3 is a direct implementation of all graph-nodes as PEs and the direct mapping of the interconnections onto the channels. In this case, the architecture's structure corresponds to the data-flow-graph and the configuration of the elements and channels might be done statically, which means it is fixed during execution. The result will be an application specific implementation with fast connections and a minimal area utilization. However, this static implementation is, as already mentioned, only usable for one specific design. The big advantage is, that the overlay acts as an abstraction layer to decouple the design from the physical hardware underneath. If the configuration is not fixed during design time, the system is flexible as the PE's functionality and the connections can be configured. Though, even in this case, the shape of the array is still fixed and, as already mentioned, a graph has to be partitioned to fit to the structure of the VCGRA's shape. Figure 4 shows a schematic of such a fixed design for our small convolution example. The design requires 20 PEs and 6 vCHs and results in five levels. Additionally, buffers (*BUF*) have to be inserted into the design. This is done automatically and is caused by restrictions of the data-flow-structure. The VCGRA's inputs are always at the top and bypassing of unused levels is not implemented. Therefore, a datum, which is used in a next level of an array, has to be transmitted to the this via a buffer operation.

Clustered Design. The clustered design shown in Fig. 5 needs two reconfigurations for calculating one gradient-image pixel-value and fits onto an array with three levels composed of four PEs and one vCH each. The graph in Fig. 3 is

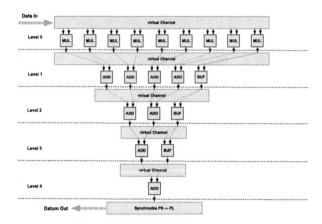

Fig. 4. Schematic of a cohesive design of the convolution example

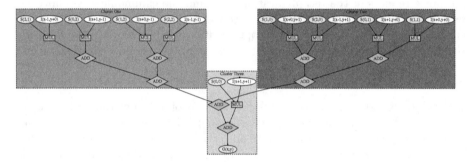

Fig. 5. Direct acyclic graph for the kernel code of a convolution (Clustered)

divided in three parts. Two of them have the same structure – four multipliers and three adders – and are using the configuration from the left hand side of Fig. 6 and the third part covers the rest of the graph and uses the right hand side's configuration. The cluster-colors in Fig. 5 are also used in Fig. 6 for arrows which mark the data transport between the PS and the VCGRA. In comparison to the design mentioned first we were able to reduce the number of PEs and the number of vCHs by 40% and 33%, respectively. Temporary sums of the first two runs are stored at the PS and used in the third – and last – run as additional inputs. PEs which are configured as *NONE* have no impact on the calculation of the results; they stay in an idle stage. Indeed, the communication- and synchronization-overhead increases in this design. For every output pixel-value, data has to be transmitted from the PS to the VCGRA three times, data has to be transmitted back three times and additionally a new configuration needs to be loaded into the VCGRA twice. This example is meant to show the reconfiguration possibilities of our proposed VCGRA. However, the acceleration increases, if the number of transmissions of data (configuration or payload) is reduced.

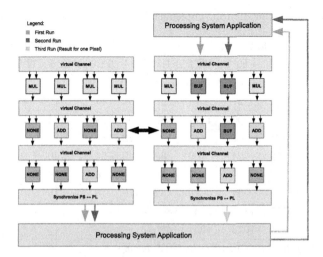

Fig. 6. Schematic of a clustered design of the convolution example

5   Experimental Results

Offline Comparison of Area Utilization. For the comparison both designs mentioned in the previous section have been considered. We used *Vivado 2017.1*, *ISE 14.7* and the current master branch of the TLUT/TCON tool flow [15] to synthesize the designs. For the comparison of the different tools, we synthesized only the PE design from the convolution-example-architecture with all required functions, all channels used in the example as well as the whole VCGRA design. In Vivado we used a Zedboard [16] as target platform while we used the XUPV5-board with a Virtex-V in ISE. Both FPGA devices contain FPGAs with 6-LUTs. Thus, we set the LUT-parameter for the TLUT/TCON virtual target-architecture to six as well for a fair comparison. However, due to some limitations with the TLUT/TCON tool-flow currently it is impossible to implement larger designs e.g. a whole VCGRA architecture. Therefore, we are unable to show results for all complete designs using this tool-set. In Table 1 we outline the logic-utilization estimates for both designs, *cohesive* and *clustered*. **TLUT**-results are using TLUTs and LUTs only, while **TCON** involves tunable connections and tunable LUTs. The results in the tables for both commercial tools (**Vivado 2017.1, ISE 14.2**) are utilization estimates after synthesis. The implementation of a PE uses fewer LUTs in Vivado and ISE compared to the TLUT/TCON tool-flow. This could be caused by better optimizations for numerical operations in commercial tools. Circuits with multiplexers are better optimized using TLUT/TCON tool-flow. Especially tunable connections are heavily used for the implementation of vCH, because multiplexers are well suited for optimizations of shared resources. As can be seen, only tunable connections, which are placed on physical switching resources of an FPGA, are applied together with standard LUTs.

Table 1. Logic utilization for implemented cohesive and clustered designs

Component	Vivado 2017.1		ISE 14.2		TLUT		TCON		
	LUT	FF	LUT	FF	LUT	TLUT	LUT	TLUT	TCON
Logic utilization for implemented cohesive designs									
Proc. element	61	27	74	27	67	14	72	8	12
vCH 18/9	973	306	1171	288	151	703	144	0	2378
vCH 9/5	321	162	361	152	72	180	72	0	640
vCH 5/3	109	94	109	88	40	54	40	0	204
vCH 3/2	37	60	37	56	24	36	24	0	63
vCH 2/1	10	34	19	32	16	18	16	0	18
VCGRA	5117	1861	5941	1861	-	-	-	-	-
VCGRA static	2528	1078	1341	1485					
Logic utilization for implemented clustered designs									
Proc. element	61	27	74	27	67	14	72	8	12
vCH 8/4	145	136	145	128	64	144	64	0	435
vCH 4/4	73	104	73	36	32	72	32	0	224
VCGRA	2528	1076	2971	1078	2724	181	2801	181	1410

On average, a reduction of 9% and 75% in LUT utilization for TLUT and TLUT/TCON implementations compared to Vivado can be obtained in cohesive design. In clustered design, TLUT results are on average 40% worse compared to Vivado, while TLUT/TCON implementations are using 37% less LUT resources. The average results show benefits using TLUTs together with TCONs to dramatically save area on an FPGA. However, currently it is not possible to synthesize a design for a physical FPGA using the TLUT/TCON tool flow. Thus, measurements for reconfiguration times on real hardware could not be obtained.

Online Execution-Timings for a Clustered Parameterizable Design.
Xilinx Vivado has been used for implementing the design on a Zedboard. An AXI-Module to read and write GPIOs of the PS has been added for the synchronization between the PS and the VCGRA. Additionally, a VCGRA wrapper was created with four AXI-lite interfaces to send and receive data and to parameterize the implemented VCGRA. Using this interface, the configuration data can be transferred from the PS to the programmable logic where it is saved locally within configuration registers. Currently, the obtainable performance is limited by the AXI-lite interface, because AXI-lite does not support bursts or data-streaming. Thus, for each data package of four bytes, the overhead of a full AXI-communication sequence is needed [17]. The whole VCGRA-design utilizes 65% of the LUT-logic resources, 3% of available FF and 16% of the DSP48-blocks.

Figure 7 illustrates relative timing-results to generate an output-pixel-value. As one can see, more than half of the whole processing-time is used to transmit data-values and coefficients. Moreover, frequent reconfigurations – as used in this example – are not beneficial for the execution timings.

On average, the current design needs around 160 μs to calculate a single result pixel within the gradient-image. To reconfigure all PEs or all vCHs we need 6.4 μs or 6.5 μs, respectively. To calculate the result for the whole 500 × 500 pixel example-image, current implementation needs around 40 s. The bottleneck in the design is the AXI-Lite interface between the PS and the VCGRA. The amount of data transfer limits the performance. In future an AXI-Stream interface is planned to boost the performance. Moreover, it is planned to adapt our design to provide pipelining to speed up performance but still offering fast reconfiguration flexibility.

Fig. 7. Relative execution timings of a static VCGRA implementation for one output pixel

6   Conclusion and Future Work

The proposed CGRA tool flow approach facilitates the use and the generation of coarse-grained arrays. The overlay design increases usability over multiple hardware generations. A configuration bitstream is automatically generated for an application's kernel code, depending on the features of the CGRA overlay. Additionally, the computations within the VCGRA run in parallel to the PS and synchronization is done by using interrupts. The performance can be improved through pipelining and using a streaming interface for transferring data to the array. Moreover, the interface-generation should be done (semi-)automatically since the characteristics of the interface are dependent on the architecture's parameters.

Acknowledgment. The EXTRA project has received funding from the European Union Horizon 2020 Framework Programme (H2020-EU.1.2.2.) under grant agreement number 671653.

References

1. Xilinx Inc.: Zynq UltraScale+ MPSoC - Product Brief (2016)
2. Murray, K.E., Whitty, S., Liu, S., Luu, J., Betz, V.: Timing-driven titan: enabling large benchmarks and exploring the gap between academic and commercial CAD. ACM Trans. Reconfigurable Technol. Syst. **8**(2), 10:1–10:18 (2015)

3. Luu, J., Goeders, J., Wainberg, M., Somerville, A., Yu, T., Nasartschuk, K., Nasr, M., Wang, S., Liu, T., Ahmed, N., Kent, K.B., Anderson, J., Rose, J., Betz, V.: VTR 7.0: next generation architecture and CAD system for FPGAs. ACM Trans. Reconfigurable Technol. Syst. **7**(2), 6:1–6:30 (2015)
4. Jamieson, P., Kent, K.B., Gharibian, F., Shannon, L.: Odin II - an open-source verilog HDL synthesis tool for CAD research. In: 2010 18th IEEE Annual International Symposium on Field-Programmable Custom Computing Machines, pp. 149–156, May 2010
5. Berkeley Logic Synthesis and Verification Group, Berkley: A System for Sequential Synthesis and Verification (2014). http://www.eecs.berkeley.edu/~alanmi/abc/
6. Betz, V., Rose, J.: VPR: a new packing, placement and routing tool for FPGA research. In: Luk, W., Cheung, P.Y.K., Glesner, M. (eds.) FPL 1997. LNCS, vol. 1304, pp. 213–222. Springer, Heidelberg (1997). https://doi.org/10.1007/3-540-63465-7_226
7. Luu, J., Kuon, I., Jamieson, P., Campbell, T., Ye, A., Fang, W.M., Rose, J.: VPR 5.0: FPGA cad and architecture exploration tools with single-driver routing, heterogeneity and process scaling. In: Proceedings of the ACM/SIGDA International Symposium on Field Programmable Gate Arrays, FPGA 2009, pp. 133–142. ACM, New York (2009)
8. Haldar, M., Nayak, A., Choudhary, A., Banerjee, P.: Parallel algorithms for FPGA placement. In: Proceedings of the 10th Great Lakes Symposium on VLSI, GLSVLSI 2000, pp. 86–94. ACM, New York (2000)
9. Lukowiak, M., Cody, B.: FPGA based accelerator for simulated annealing with greedy perturbations. In: 2007 14th International Conference on Mixed Design of Integrated Circuits and Systems, pp. 274–277, June 2007
10. Sidiropoulos, H., Siozios, K., Figuli, P., Soudris, D., Hubner, M.: On supporting efficient partial reconfiguration with just-in-time compilation. In: 2012 IEEE 26th International Parallel and Distributed Processing Symposium Workshops PhD Forum, pp. 328–335, May 2012
11. An, M., Steffan, J.G., Betz, V.: Speeding up FPGA placement: parallel algorithms and methods. In: 2014 IEEE 22nd Annual International Symposium on Field-Programmable Custom Computing Machines, pp. 178–185, May 2014
12. Kulkarni, A., Stroobandt, D., Werner, A., Fricke, F., Huebner, M.: Pixie: A heterogeneous Virtual Coarse-Grained Reconfigurable Array for high performance image processing applications, February 2017
13. Peixoto, T.P.: The Graph-tool Python Library. figshare (2014)
14. Pratt, W.: Digital Image Processing: PIKS Scientific Inside. Wiley, Hoboken (2007)
15. University Ghent - HES Group: Online Resource of the TCON Tool Flow. https://github.com/UGent-HES/tcon_flow.git. Accessed 17 July 2017
16. AVNET: Zedboard Contributer Homepage. http://zedboard.org/product/zedboard. Accessed 26 July 2017
17. Xilinx Inc.: UG761 - AXI Reference Guide (2011)

Seamless FPGA Deployment over Spark in Cloud Computing: A Use Case on Machine Learning Hardware Acceleration

Christoforos Kachris$^{(\boxtimes)}$, Ioannis Stamelos, Elias Koromilas,
and Dimitrios Soudris

Institute of Computer and Communications Systems (ICCS), Zografou, Greece
kachris@gmail.com

Abstract. Emerging cloud applications like machine learning and data analytics need to process huge amount of data. Typical processor architecture cannot achieve efficient processing of the vast amount of data without consuming excessive amount of energy. Therefore, novel architectures have to be adopted in the future data centers in order to face the increased amount of data that needs to be processed. In this paper, we present a novel scheme for the seamless deployment of FPGAs in the data centers under the Spark framework. The proposed scheme, developed in the VINEYARD project, allows the efficient utilization of FPGAs without the need to change the applications. The performance evaluation is based on the KMeans ML algorithm that is widely used in clustering applications. The proposed scheme has been evaluated in a cluster of heterogeneous MPSoCs. The performance evaluation shows that the utilization of FPGAs can be used to speedup the machine learning applications and reduce significantly the energy consumption.

Keywords: Hardware accelerators · Data centre · Heterogeneous
Big data

1 Introduction

Machine learning, data analytics and Big Data are some of the emerging cloud applications responsible for the significant increases in data-center workloads during the last years. In 2015, the total network traffic of the data centres was around 4.7 Exabytes and it is estimated that by the end of 2018 it will cross the 8.5-Exabyte mark, following a cumulative annual-growth rate (CAGR) of 23% [1]. In response to this scaling in network traffic, data-centre operators have resorted to utilizing more powerful servers. Relying on Moore's law for the extra edge, CPU technologies have scaled in recent years through packing an increasing number of transistors on chip, leading to higher-performance ratings. However, on-chip clock frequencies were unable to follow this upward trend due to strict power-budget constraints. Thus, a few years ago a paradigm shift to

© Springer International Publishing AG, part of Springer Nature 2018
N. Voros et al. (Eds.): ARC 2018, LNCS 10824, pp. 673–684, 2018.
https://doi.org/10.1007/978-3-319-78890-6_54

multicore processors was adopted as an alternative solution for overcoming the problem. With multicore processors one could increase server performance without increasing their clock frequency. Unfortunately, this solution was soon found to scale poorly in the longer term, as well. The performance gains achieved by adding more cores inside a CPU come at the cost of various, rapidly scaling complexities: inter-core communication, memory coherency and, most importantly, power consumption [2].

The failure of Dennard scaling, to which the shift to multicore chips is partially a response, has limited multicore scaling just as single-core scaling has been curtailed. This issue has been identified in the literature as the "dark-silicon" era in which some of the areas in a chip are kept powered down in order to comply with thermal constraints [3].

A solution that can be used to overcome this problem is the use of application-specific accelerators. Specialized multicore processors with application-specific acceleration modules can leverage the underutilized die area to overcome the initial power barrier, delivering significantly higher performance for the same power envelope [4]. The main idea is to use the abundant die area by implementing application-specific accelerators and dynamically powering up only those accelerators suitable for a given workload. This approach can be applied either at fine-grain level (using accelerators inside the chip) or at coarse-grain level (using rack-based accelerators). In the latter case, the accelerators can either be located on the same board with the server processor or in a different blade/rack. The use of highly specialized units designed for specific workloads can greatly enhance server processors and can also increase significantly the performance of data centres subject to a maximum power budget.

The VINEYARD project aims towards the development of an integrated platform for the efficient utilization of hardware accelerators in the data centers. VINEYARD aims to develop an integrated platform for energy-efficient data centers based on programmable hardware accelerators. It also developed a high-level framework for allowing end-users to seamlessly utilize these accelerators in heterogeneous computing systems by using typical data-center programming frameworks (e.g. Spark, etc.).

2   VINEYARD Project

VINEYARDs goal is to develop the technology and the ecosystem that will enable the efficient integration of the hardware acceleration in the data centre applications, seamlessly. The deployment of energy-efficient hardware accelerators will be used to improve significantly the performance of cloud computing applications and reduce the energy consumption in data centres.

VINEYARD is developing an integrated framework for energy-efficient data centres based on programmable hardware accelerators. It is working towards a high-level programming framework that allows end-users to seamlessly utilize these accelerators in heterogeneous computing systems by using typical data-centre cluster frameworks (i.e. Spark). The VINEYARD framework and

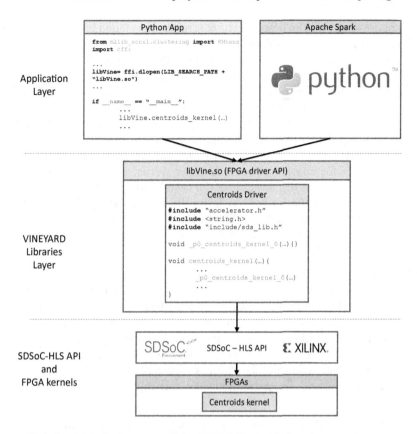

Fig. 1. High-level block diagram of the VINEYARD library for seamless integration with programming frameworks

the required system software hides the programming complexity of the heterogeneous computing system based on hardware accelerators. This programming framework also allows, the hardware accelerators to be swapped in and out of the heterogeneous infrastructure so as to offer both efficient energy use and flexibility. To allow the efficient utilization of the accelerators from several applications, a novel VM appliance model for provisioning of data to shared accelerators has been developed. The enhanced VINEYARD middleware augments the functionality of the resource manager, by enabling more informed allocation of tasks to accelerators.

Figure 1 depicts the high-level overview of the VINEYARD library. Applications that are targeting heterogeneous data centers using traditional servers or micro-servers are programmed using traditional data center frameworks, such as Spark, or more application specific frameworks such as the PyNN framework that is used for neural networks. In these applications, VINEYARD provides the required APIs that enable the utilization of the heterogeneous infrastructures without any other modifications in the source code.

The figure shows all the layers of the controllers developed in VINEYARD for the efficient communication of the FPGAs with the programming frameworks. The controllers that we developed support the Xilinx Zynq platforms. We created a unified software stack, tailored to our new needs, that would be able to support expansions for supporting more platforms or new accelerators. The FPGA driver API is packed in a shared object library and can be used in a transparent way hiding all the low level details. What is more, we implemented top level APIs in Python for standalone and Apache Spark integrated use, that are easy to be used and are also easily maintained since the middle layer, our shared library remains the same for all of the above. In other words, we implemented a 3-tier style software stack. The top level hosts the users' applications, the middle layer hosts our libraries and the lower layer hosts the SDSoC-HLS API which is used to actually invoke the accelerator. This 3-tier scheme has a lot of advantages which we will go through in more detail in the next paragraphs.

Application Layer: This layer hosts users' applications. The applications can run natively using Python. Users are able to perform a plethora of methods (i.e. train(), test(), load() etc.) on their machine learning models. Users already having their machine learning applications running standalone or in an Apache Spark cluster, don't need to change a single line of code except from the imported library. Except from that, changes in the lower layers of our stack won't affect this. This way we are able to make changes, optimize and add stuff or functionality to our libraries and drivers without affecting any top-level applications.

Vineyard Layer: This layer hosts the whole functionality of our framework. The key element of this layer is the implemented shared library (libVine.so). It hosts the FPGA drivers for each application, written in C/C++ and is used to communicate with the SDSoC - HLS API. Each kernel driver (e.g centroids_driver) invokes the corresponding FPGA kernel to perform the requested tasks.

SDSoC-HLS API and FPGA Layer: The bottom layer, that serves as the FPGA runtime, is basically consisted of the SDSoC-HLS library that is provided from Xilinx along with the FPGA itself hosting any implemented kernels.

3   Seamless Deployment of FPGA Under Spark: A Use-Case on KMeans Clustering

In this section we present a use-case for the evaluation of the VINEYARD framework under the Spark framework. Apache Spark [5] is one of the most widely used frameworks for data analytics. Spark has been adopted widely in recent years for big data analysis by providing a fault-tolerant, scalable and easy to use in-memory abstraction.

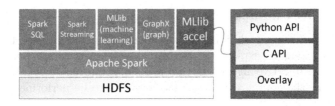

Fig. 2. VINEYARD's library for the deployment of FPGAs in the Spark library

Specifically, Spark provides programmers with an application programming interface centered on a data structure called the resilient distributed dataset (RDD). RDD is a read-only multiset of data items distributed over a cluster of machines, that is maintained in a fault-tolerant way [6]. It was developed in response to limitations in the MapReduce cluster computing framework, which forces a particular linear dataflow structure on distributed programs. MapReduce programs read input data from disk, map a function across the data, reduce the results of the map, and store reduction results on disk.

In the typical case, the Spark application invokes the Spark MLlib and this library utilizes the Breeze library (a numerical processing library for Scala). Breeze library invokes the Netlib Java framework that is a wrapper for low-level linear algebra tools implemented in C or Fortran. Netlib Java is executed through the Java Virtual Machine (JVM) and the actual linear algebra tools (BLAS - Basic Linear Algebra Subprograms) are executed through the Java Native Interface (JNI).

All these layers add significant overhead to the Spark applications. Especially in applications like machine learning, where heavy computations are required, these layers add significant overhead to the computational kernels. Most of the clock cycles are wasted for passing through all these layers.

In this project, we have developed the required APIs for python and C that allows the direct invoking of the hardware accelerators from the python level used in Spark. The Python API is used for each accelerator that is used for the communication with the hardware accelerator. Each Python API is communicating with the C library that serves as the hardware accelerator driver. Therefore, the only modification that is required is the extension of the Python library with the new function calls for the communication with the hardware accelerator.

The utilization of hardware accelerators directly from Spark has two major advantages; firstly, the application in Spark remains as it is and the only modification that is required is the replacement of the machine learning library's function with the function that invokes the hardware accelerator. Secondly the invoking of the hardware accelerators from the Python API eliminates many of the original layers thus making faster the execution of these tasks. The Python API invokes the C API that serves as a hardware acceleration's library (Fig. 2).

3.1   Python API for Spark

Most machine learning techniques have a common characteristic that makes them ideal as means to explore the performance benefits of our heterogeneous cluster. They are iterative algorithms that make multiple passes over the data set, while also allow the computations in each iteration to be performed in parallel on different data chunks.

In KMeans, for example, the computation of the partial sums and counts for each new cluster is performed on the available Workers, and then the Master aggregates the results and calculates the new centroids.

Taking into account and understanding the structure of Sparks MLlib, we developed new libraries for KMeans clustering, that take advantage of the accelerator that is available in the workers. As a result, when a Spark user wants to utilize the hardware accelerator in an existing application, the main change that needs to be made, is the replacement of Sparks mllib library, that is imported, with our mllib_accel one. Therefore, a user can speedup the execution time of a Spark application by simply replacing the library package.

The first approach was to simply replace the mapper functions (*centroids_kernel*) with Python APIs that drive the hardware accelerators. Inside these new functions we used to download the equivalent overlay, create the necessary DMA objects, store the data inside the corresponding buffers, perform the DMA transfers and finally destroy them, free the allocated memory and return the results. After profiling the applications though, we concluded that most of the time (99%) is wasted on writing the train RDD data to the allocated DMAs buffers.

However, since the data remain the same (cached) over the whole execution of the training, we have managed and implemented a novel scheme that allows the persistent storing of the RDD in contiguous memory, avoiding in-memory transfers every time the accelerator is invoked. For this reason, we developed a new mapper function that allocates and fills contiguous memory buffers with the training data, in order to remain there for the rest of the application execution. So when the DMA objects are created in each iteration, there is no need to create new buffers for them and fill them with the corresponding data, they just get assigned the previously created ones. Also, before destructing these DMA objects, their assigned buffers are set to 'None', so that they remain intact and are not freed as it is shown in Fig. 3.

Based on the above, we have created Python APIs which basically consist of three calls:

- **cma** (contiguous memory allocate): This call is used for the creation of the buffers and the further allocation of contiguous memory. Also at this point the overlay is downloaded and the training data is written to the corresponding buffers. Using cma, a new RDD, which contains only information about these buffers (memory addresses, sizes, etc.), is created and persisted.
- **kernel_accel** (centroids): In this call, the DMA objects are created using Xilinxs built-in modules and classes; previously allocated buffers are assigned to DMAs, current weights/centers are written in memory and finally data

are transferred to the programmable logic. Counts and sums are computed in return, buffers are dis-assigned from DMAs and the last ones are destructed.
- **cmf** (contiguous memory free): This call is explicitly used to free all previously allocated buffers.

It is important to note that the above demonstrated APIs are Spark independent and can be used in any python application.

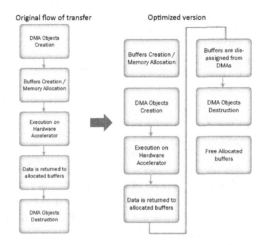

Fig. 3. Flow of the original and optimized method for the DMA transfers to the accelerator

4 Use-Case on Machine Learning Under Spark

To evaluate the proposed framework, we have developed a hardware accelerator for KMeans clustering and more specifically for the computation of the centroids. The hardware accelerator has been implemented using the Xilinx Vivado High-Level Synthesis (HLS) tool. The algorithm have been written in C and has been annotated with HLS *pragmas* for the efficient mapping in reconfigurable logic.

4.1 Algorithmic Approach of KMeans

KMeans is one of the simplest unsupervised learning algorithms that solve the well known clustering problem and is applicable in a variety of disciplines, such as computer vision, biology, and economics. It attempts to group individuals in a population together by similarity, but not driven by a specific purpose.

The procedure follows a simple and easy way to cluster the training data points into a predefined number of clusters (K). The main idea is to define K centroids c, one for each cluster.

Given a set of $numExamples$ (n) observations $\{x^0, x^1, \ldots, x^{n-1}\}$, where each observation is an m-dimensional real vector, KMeans clustering aims to partition the n observations into K $(\leq n)$ sets $\{s^0, s^1, \ldots, s^{K-1}\}$ so as to minimize total intra-cluster variance, or, the squared error function:

$$J = \sum_{k=1}^{K} \sum_{x \in s^k} ||x - c^k||^2$$

The KMeans clustering algorithm is as follows:

---

1 : **procedure** $train(x)$
2 :   initialize c with K random data points
3 :   **while** not converged:
4 : $centroids\_kernel(x, c)$
5 :   **for** every $k = 0, \ldots, K-1$:
6 : $c^k = \frac{1}{|s^k|} \sum_{x \in s^k} x$

7 : **procedure** $centroids\_kernel(x, c)$
8 :   **for** every $k = 0, \ldots, K-1$:
9 : $s^k = \left\{ x : \left\| x - c^k \right\|^2 \leq \left\| x - c^{k'} \right\|^2 \ \forall k', 0 \leq k' \leq K-1 \right\}$

The algorithm as described, starts with a random set of K centroids (c). During each update step, all observations x are assigned to their nearest centroid, while afterwards, these center points are repositioned by calculating the mean of the assigned observations to the respective centroids.

5   Performance Evaluation

As a case study, we built a KMeans clustering model with 784 features and 14 centers, using 40k available training samples, for a handwritten digits recognition problem. The data are provided by Mixed National Institute of Standards and Technology (MNIST) database [7]. To evaluate the performance of the system and to perform a fair comparison we built a cluster of four nodes based on the Zynq platform and we compared it with four Spark worker nodes using the Intel Xeon cores [8]. Table 1 shows the features of each platform.

It is important to note that a single Spark executor JVM process requires most of the available 512 MB RAM on PYNQ-Z1s, placing a restriction on the Spark application, which requires main memory to cache and repeatedly access the working dataset from FPGAs off-chip RAM once read from HDFS. This results in delays during the execution as inevitably are performed transfers between the memory and the swap file, which is stored inside the SD card. This memory restriction is also the reason why we limit the number of Spark executors to 1 ARM core per node, thus preventing both cores from performing Spark tasks simultaneously.

On the other hand, the Xeon system consists of 12 cores with 2 threads each core. The Spark cluster started on this platform allocates 4 out of 24 threads, as worker instances, in order to compare it with the 4 nodes of the Pynq cluster. We also compared the accelerated platform with the software only scenario in

Table 1. Main features of the evaluated processors.

Features	Xeon	Zynq
Vendor	Intel	ARM
Processor	E5-2658	A9
Cores (threads)	12 (24)	2
Architecture	64-bit	32-bit
Instruction Set	CISC	RISC
Process	22 nm	28 nm
Clock frequency	2.2 GHz	667 MHz
Level 1 cache	380 kB	32 kB
Level 2 cache	3 MB	512 kB
Level 3 cache	30 MB	-
TDP	105 W	4 W
Operating system	Ubuntu	Ubuntu

Fig. 4. KMeans speedup versus the number of the iterations (Intel XEON vs Pynq).

which the algorithm is executed only on the ARM cores. Such comparison is valuable as there are applications where only embedded processors can be used and big-core systems like Xeon cannot be supported due to power constraints.

5.1 Latency and Execution Time

Figure 4 depicts the execution time of the KMeans clustering application running on a high-performance x86_64 Intel processor (Xeon E5 2658) clocked at 2.2 GHz and a Pynq cluster which makes use of the Programmable Logic, for an input dataset of 40000 lines splitted in chunks of 5000 lines, for various numbers of iterations. In the PYNQ-Z1 boards the data extraction part, for the KMeans clustering, takes about 80 sec to complete, while every iteration of the algorithm is completed in 0.54 s, since the train input data is already cached into the previously allocated buffers. On the other hand, Xeon CPU reads, transforms and caches the data in only 7.5 s, but every iteration takes approximately 3.3 s. This is the reason why the speedup actually depends on the number of iterations that are performed. For this specific example the LR model converges, and achieves up to 91.5% accuracy, after 100 iterations of the algorithm, in which up to 2x system speedup is achieved compared to the Xeon processor. However, there are cases in which much higher number of iterations is required, until the convergence criteria is met, and thus much higher speedup can be observed.

Table 2 shows the execution time of the main mapper functions which are executed on the worker nodes. In the Xeon platform and the ARM-only case, both the data extraction and the algorithm computations are performed on the CPUs, while in the Pynq workers the data extraction is executed on the ARM core while the algorithmic part is offloaded to the programmable logic. Figure 5 show the speedup of the accelerated execution compared to the software only solution running on the same cluster but using only the ARM processors. In this case, we can achieve up to 31x for KMeans, compared to the software only case, which shows that it is definitely crucial to provide accelerator support for future embedded datacenters.

Table 2. Execution time (sec) of the worker (mapper) functions.

Worker type	Data extraction	KMeans algorithm computations (per iteration)
Intel XEON	7.5	3.3
ARM	80	41.5
Pynq	80 (ARM)	0.54 (FPGA)

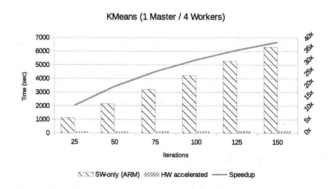

Fig. 5. KMeans speedup versus the number of the iterations (ARM vs Pynq).

5.2   Power and Energy Consumption

To evaluate the energy savings we measured the average power running the algorithm both in the SW-only, and the HW accelerated cases. In order to measure

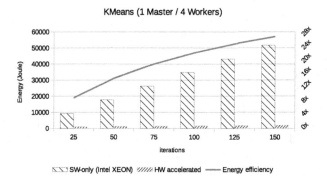

Fig. 6. KMeans energy consumption based on the number of iterations (Intel XEON vs Pynq).

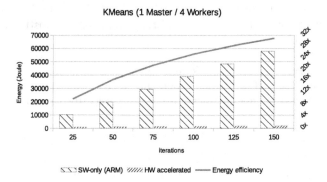

Fig. 7. KMeans energy consumption based on the number of iterations (ARM vs Pynq).

the power consumption of the Xeon server, we used Intels Processor Counter Monitor (PCM) API, which, among others, enables capturing the power consumed by the CPU and DRAM memory for executing an application. We also measured the power consumption in the accelerated case using the ZC702 Evaluation board, which hosts the same Zynq device as the PYNQ-Z1 board, taking advantage of the on-board power controllers.

Figure 6 show the energy consumption of the Xeon processor compared to the Pynq cluster. The average power consumption of the Xeon processor and the DRAMs is 100 W, while a single Pynq node (both the AP SoC and the DRAM) consumes about 2.6 W during the data extraction and 3.2 W during the hardware computations. In that case, we can achieve up to 23x better energy efficiency due to the lower power consumption and the lower execution time.

In Fig. 7 is depicted the energy consumption comparison between the SW-only (ARM) and HW-accelerated execution of the application on the Pynq cluster. It is clear that the average power consumption of the accelerated case is slightly higher than the power consumption of the ARM-only one, because of the need to power supply also the programmable logic. However, due to the significant much higher execution time of the ARM-only solution, eventually, up to 29x lower energy consumption is achieved.

6   Conclusions

The main goal of the VINEYARD project is to develop a new framework for the efficient integration of accelerators into commercial data centres. The VINE-YARD project will not only develop novel accelerator-based servers but will also develop all the required systems (hypervisor, middleware, APIs and libraries) that will allow the users to seamlessly utilize the accelerators as an additional cloud resource. The efficient utilization of accelerators in data centres will significantly improve the overall performance of cloud-based applications and will also reduce the energy consumption in the data centres. Finally, VINEYARD aspires to foster the innovation of soft-IP accelerators in the domain of cloud computing by the promotion of a central repository for the hosting of the relevant accelerators.

Acknowledgment. This project has received funding from the European Union's Horizon 2020 research and innovation programme under grant agreement No. 687628 - VINEYARD: Versatile Integrated Heterogeneous Accelerator-based Data Centers.

References

1. Cisco Visual Networking Index: Global Mobile Data Traffic Forecast Update 2014–2019 White Paper
2. Guz, Z., Bolotin, E., Keidar, I., Kolodny, A., Mendelson, A., Weiser, U.C.: Many-core vs. many-thread machines: stay away from the valley. IEEE Comput. Archit. Lett. **8**(1), 25–28 (2009)
3. Esmaeilzadeh, H., Blem, E., Amant, R.S., Sankaralingam, K., Burger, D.: Dark silicon and the end of multicore scaling. In: Proceedings of the 38th Annual International Symposium on Computer Architecture, ISCA 2011, pp. 365–376. ACM, New York (2011)
4. Hardavellas, N., Ferdman, M., Falsafi, B., Ailamaki, A.: Toward dark silicon in servers. IEEE Micro **31**(4), 6–15 (2011)
5. Apache Spark. http://spark.apache.org/
6. Zaharia, M., Chowdhury, M., Das, T., Dave, A., Ma, J., McCauley, M., Franklin, M.J., Shenker, S., Stoica, I.: Resilient distributed datasets: a fault-tolerant abstraction for in-memory cluster computing. In: Proceedings of the 9th USENIX Conference on Networked Systems Design and Implementation, NSDI 2012, Berkeley, CA, USA, p. 2. USENIX Association (2012)
7. Fatahi, M.: MNIST Handwritten Digits (2014)
8. Kachris, C., Koromilas, E., Stamelos, I., Soudris, D.: FPGA acceleration of spark applications in a PYNQ cluster. In: 2017 27th International Conference on Field Programmable Logic and Applications (FPL), p. 1, September 2017

The ARAMiS Project Initiative

Multicore Systems in Safety- and Mixed-Critical Applications

Jürgen Becker and Falco K. Bapp[✉]

Karlsruhe Institute of Technology (KIT), Karlsruhe, Germany
{becker,bapp}@kit.edu

Abstract. Embedded systems play an ever increasing role in almost any field of daily life, including the mobility domains taking massive benefits from using software in their products. The intense use of software leads to a situation, where electronics is used at the performance limits. Thus, new functionalities and systems have to be implemented using alternative architectures. Multicore technology, being state of the art in standard ICT for a couple of years now, seems to be the most promising way and probably is the key enabler for future systems. However, from a technical perspective challenges arise, which need to be specially addressed for safety critical systems. For this reason, the ARAMiS project initiative was initiated in Germany. This paper gives a high-level overview of the topics that are investigated in the research projects ARAMiS and ARAMiS II.

Keywords: ARAMiS · Multicore · Embedded systems · Functional safety
Mobility domains

1 Motivation

1.1 Multicore Processors in Safety Critical Systems

Electronic components and systems are the key factors for the integration of novel functionality in any technical system. Already today, more than 90% of all innovations in modern vehicles are possible through the use of electronics and software. In consequence, the vast majority of modern technology contains to some extend electronics and very often software running on an embedded processor. The use of embedded software is independent from the devices complexity, which can range from tiny sensing devices' (Internet of Things) up to highly complex technical systems such as vehicles, airplanes, industrial plants and the like.

It is a general observation, that every new generation of a product comes with an increasing amount of software, being executed on processors with additional performance. In fact, it is the only way to master the increased complexity, meet environmental challenges, enhance competitiveness, and to improve cost efficiency. In other words, the performance of next generation's embedded systems will be a key factor for the success of novel applications such as highly automated systems.

© Springer International Publishing AG, part of Springer Nature 2018
N. Voros et al. (Eds.): ARC 2018, LNCS 10824, pp. 685–699, 2018.
https://doi.org/10.1007/978-3-319-78890-6_55

Embedded systems have to fulfill a huge amount of functional and non-functional requirements, which – especially in the case of safety critical systems – go far beyond the standards of best effort driven systems. The most important characteristics can be summarized as follows:

- Real-Time Capabilities
- Performance
- Reliability and Availability
- Functional Safety (Certification/Qualification)
- Robustness against Malicious Attacks
- Energy Efficiency
- Compatibility to existing Concepts (Legacy Code)

Obviously developing embedded systems, which fulfill all the requirements that result from the aforementioned characteristics is a challenging task, not even mentioning the architectural complexity within a product. In fact, embedded systems in automotive, avionics and rail are typically represented by a complex network of ECUs, which is distributed throughout the whole car, plane or train. The central component of these ECUs is a microcontroller chip, which contains a single processing core (singlecore CPU). In the past, integration of new functionality was very often realized by adding another ECU for this novel functionality. Obviously, this is not a scalable approach, as limitations of size, weight, power and costs come into play after a while. Consequently, each existing ECU needs to execute more functionality.

For these reasons singlecore devices as presently used come to their performance limits. Further raising the clock frequency is not an option, because of technical reasons i.e. power dissipation density. Consequently, an alternative approach to singlecore devices is needed. Otherwise, novel functionality might not be realizable, and the limitation of singlecore might turn out to be a major impediment to innovation.

1.2 Multicore Challenge

The singlecore performance limitation is an issue in high-performance computing and standard ICT for several years now. Instead of increasing the performance of the unique core of the processor, it was decided to increase the processors' performance by increasing the number of cores, running at the same or even lower clock frequencies. Theoretically, doubling the number of cores also doubles the performance.

Using multicores is the best known technical solution, allowing to cross the singlecore limitations and providing additional performance. Therefore, it has been widely adopted in standard ICT and data centers. A similar development can be seen in the embedded systems domain, which makes up for more than 90% of all processors worldwide. In fact, almost all smartphones, gaming stations, and others use multicore technology for a couple of years now. The mobility domains automotive, avionics, and rail only make up for a very small share below 10% of all processors. Consequently, these domains are not the drivers of future multicore systems development, but rather have to use Commercial Off The Shelf (COTS) processors from other domains. Hence, architecture development focuses on optimizing the best effort performance.

Looking to the automotive, avionics and railway domains in more detail, similarities in motivation of multicore use can be identified. Any reason hindering the use of multicores in these domains would probably delay or even block innovations. This is noteworthy, because several technical challenges show up, when starting to use commercial of the shelf multicore devices for safety critical applications. These challenges are to a large extent also shared among the application domains:

- **Segregation in space and time:** Concepts are necessary, that allow sharing resources with clear limits in memory space and time to reduce interferences. This affects all kind of resources, including memory, coprocessors or peripherals.
- **Efficient application software distribution:** The distribution of software needs to be efficient and minimize total execution costs (including communication).
- **Legacy Code on multicore:** Concepts and mechanisms are needed, that allow deploying legacy singlecore code on multicore platforms. This also includes parallelization of legacy software.
- **Efficient platform software distribution:** Concepts for the distribution of platform infrastructure software, including operating systems and middleware is necessary.
- **Analysis of multicore platforms and software:** Analysis methodologies and tools are needed that allow detecting potential multicore-specific software errors (e.g., race conditions, WCET).
- **Configuration Complexity:** Multicores have an enormous configuration space that needs to be managed to find valid and robust configurations for safety critical systems.
- **Certifiability/Qualifiability:** Achieving certifiability is a major challenge, due to the multicores complexity and interferences.

2 ARAMiS – Automotive, Railway, Avionics Multicore Systems

2.1 Goals of ARAMiS

Although multicore technology found its way into some application domains, the use in mobility applications is not straightforward due to the challenges introduced in Sect. 1.2. Hence, solutions from other domains are not applicable. On the other hand, existing single core based solutions from these safety critical domains cannot be used as well, because they do not support parallel execution of code and mastering of the complex state space of multicore processors. Consequently, dedicated architectures, methods, and tools need to be adapted for the mobility domains. To face this challenge, companies from three domains joined their forces and started the project Automotive Railway Avionics Multicore Systems - ARAMiS.

It was the primary goal of ARAMiS to develop a fundamental understanding, provide initial and pragmatic solutions and proof the applicability of multicore technology in safety-critical applications in the mobility domains. This way, ARAMiS contributed to the higher level goals of improving safety, efficiency and comfort in the three selected application domains (Fig. 1).

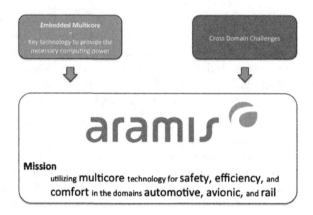

Fig. 1. The ARAMiS project

2.2 Consortium

Within ARAMiS a consortium, including all the stakeholders affected by the multicore development worked together to achieve the goals. The composition of the consortium with partners from leading industry companies and research institutions was one of the key success factors. The consortium was built from the following groups coordinated by KIT:

OEM and System Suppliers
OEMs and system suppliers have to provide products based on multicore technology shortly. Hence, it is also this group with a huge pressure in bringing multicore into applications. Within ARAMiS, the participants of this group provided their knowledge about applications characteristics. Demonstrators were mostly driven by the participants of this group. The group of OEMs consisted of AUDI, BMW, Daimler, Airbus and Siemens.

Semiconductor Vendors
Semiconductor Vendors contributed to the project with in-depth knowledge of hardware architectures, their behavior and limitations in usage. They also provided input to all partners that worked on architectural concepts on the system, hardware and software level. Additionally, semiconductor vendors worked on possible extensions of multicore architectures with respect to the input they received and results achieved in the project. Within the project, Infineon, Intel and Freescale have been contributing.

Tool/Software Providers
The role of software providers in the project was to extend their software platforms for multicore architectures. This includes the extension of operating systems as well as the adoption of hypervisors and virtualization solutions. Similarly, tool providers extended their tooling towards multicore architectures and application scenarios. As representatives, Sysgo, Wind River, AbsInt, Elektrobit, Open Synergy and Symta Vision were part of the project.

Research

Universities and research centers provided their knowledge and were working in all fields including architectures, methodologies, and tools. They supported industrial partners by providing solutions for their challenges. The following research institutions have been contributing: KIT, TUM, OFFIS, fortiss, Fraunhofer, University of Stuttgart, TU Braunschweig, CAU Kiel, TU Kaiserslautern, and University of Paderborn.

2.3   Working Focus and Selected Results

Scenarios and Requirements: Starting point of the project were the scenarios, which have been presented in road-maps (see [1, 2]). Based on the environmental conditions defined in these road-maps, a cross-domain application scenario has been defined. This scenario was the origin of domain specific scenarios, which have been defined for each domain accordingly. System level requirements have then been derived from these specific scenarios.

System: The breakdown of system level requirements down to the level of multicore-specific requirements took more effort than originally expected. Especially OEM and Tier 1 put much domain specific application experience into the deduction of multicore-specific requirements. Based on this, the evaluation of existing system-level approaches started, followed by the development of ARAMiS specific system architectures and methodologies. In the last phase of the project, all hardware and software approaches were revisited on system level. Approaches from the first phase were improved based on the feedback from the hardware and software development.

Hardware: System level requirements and existing hardware architectures were the starting point for the hardware development. ARAMiS was not a hardware project. However, within the project, suggestions for improvements of existing architectures were made in different areas. Especially, improvements and architectural measures in shared resources including support for virtualization were given.

Software: The system requirements were also the input for the work on the software level. Software approaches have been developed on different layers of the system, including hypervisor, operating system, middleware, and application software layer. On the application layer, especially reuse and parallelization of legacy code were of interest. OS and hypervisor extensions rather focus on hiding multicore complexity for applications by providing synchronization and communication mechanisms. As in hardware, resource sharing was another predominant topic from a software point of view.

Methods and Tools: The development of multicore-specific tools and methodologies has been one of the major focuses within ARAMiS. Often, methodologies are specific to certain purposes and architectures. Hence, both have been developed throughout the whole project. However, a holistic approach, which allows integrating the tools and methodologies into one consistent approach, was a challenge on its own.

Demonstrators: The concepts were validated with demonstrators in five different fields (see Fig. 2). Each of the demonstrators took a set of results from the different work packages and demonstrated the feasibility based on pre-defined industrial scenarios. There were two demonstrators from the automotive, two from the avionics and one from the rail domain.

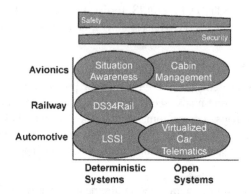

Fig. 2. ARAMiS demonstrators and their working focus

Selected Results and Conclusions from ARAMiS

Electronic components and systems are the key factors for the integration of novel functionality in any technical system. Embedded Electronics, as it is used today is operating at its performance limits, thereby creating the demand for new technologies. Embedded multicore processors are seen as the most promising alternative, which might provide enough computational power for future applications. The benefit of multicore technology has been initially proven in standard ICT (e.g. high performance computing, data-centers, personal computers, etc.). Multicores also found their way into mobile applications such as smart-phones or tablets. The prevalence of multicore architectures in all field of applications seems to be unstoppable.

However, for good reasons multicores are not used in the context of safety-critical applications. Along with the transition from one single to multiple cores several challenges arise, thus elevating the complexity of safety-critical embedded systems development. Especially, parallel code execution together with sharing of resources leads to interference scenarios that have a strong influence on the execution time and eventually behavior of applications. In other words, fulfilment of safety requirements and the proof of correct behavior in all possible system states is hard to achieve.

Interestingly, the multicore challenge is shared among all domains, which have to develop safety-critical or mixed-critical systems. In the course of the project, it turned out, that the diversity of requirements does not allow one single solution approach, neither on hardware, nor on software level. Depending on the respective development purpose an appropriate set of solutions needs to be chosen. The ARAMiS consortium worked hard to provide a comprehensive set of solutions, which can be used in various application domains.

Safety and Certification aspects obviously play an important role in safety-critical and mixed-critical systems. The underlying standards have been analyzed in the project. However, all of them state very little about multicores and the respective measures, which have to be taken into account. Especially in avionics, certification authorities are very reluctant and cautious. Multicore is under intense discussion in different groups such as MCFA, all with the goals to find ways for multicore certification. Within ARAMiS, the multicore challenges were derived, classified and structured. Protection mechanisms were developed throughout the whole project and were eventually reviewed and summarized by the safety activities in the project.

System Architecture Aspects and Deployment: Models on different abstraction levels played an important role in the ARAMiS project. Based on the SPES modeling approach, the relevant abstraction levels for multicore technology have been defined and appropriate logical and technical architecture metamodels have been developed. The models have been used to annotate requirements as well as to show architectures and solutions. In general, system development comprises several important steps, which have to be taken into account, including timing analysis, decomposition, deployment, trade-off analysis and the like.

Application Software Layer: An important aspect that needs to be considered, is the use of legacy code. Also on most modern multicore platforms, existing applications have to run efficiently. Application code typically is platform and hence domain specific. This extends to the necessary steps, taken into account from the application perspective. Here the partners worked on migration, segregation and parallelization/ deployment aspects for applications. Although the results have been summarized per domain, the approaches are likely to be transferable to other domains.

Operating System and Middleware: Obviously middleware and operating systems are affected by the underlying hardware. Within ARAMiS a thorough analysis of typical embedded operating systems has been conducted. Based on the results various improvements have been suggested. Because they are highly integrated into other topics like virtualization or target special configurations, operating system extensions were considered throughout the whole project.

Embedded Virtualization is not directly bound, but strongly related to multicore technology. Within ARAMIS virtualization played a very important role and has been investigated in various ways. Especially the use in real-time systems is new and demands some careful tuning of configurations. The use of virtualization is especially interesting in mixed critical environments, or scenarios, requiring various operating systems. In general, virtualization refers to a full set of different solutions, ranging from micro hypervisors up to full virtualization. ARAMiS examined various solutions and suggested improvements for safety critical systems.

GPU Sharing with Virtualization: Virtualization is especially interesting for infotainment systems. These have to run mixed-critical applications, and typically show results on various displays. Each of the displays also shows a mix of safety-critical and non-critical information. Second must not have any negative influence on the first. Therefore, it is important to add segregation mechanisms. Also the graphical rendering is typically executed on shared graphics processors (GPUs). Within ARAMiS concepts for sharing of this resource have been developed.

Hardware Support for Coprocessors: Not only GPUs but also other coprocessors are in the group of shared devices. Sharing of these units has been analyzed and a hardware sharing concept was developed. In principal, it extends the original interface with additional interfaces and scheduling mechanisms, thereby omitting the need for software virtualization mechanisms. In other words, the resource is not shared from the software perspective. This works for fixed coprocessors as well as for reconfigurable ones.

Hardware Support for Peripherals is also beneficial and has thus been investigated in the project. Again, virtual interfaces play an important role. Various ways of virtualization have been discussed, including software and hardware mechanisms. Eventually, a hardware based approach has been chosen and war prototypically implemented for a CAN bus controller.

Security and Multicore: Ensuring security gains more and more importance in all kinds of systems. Typically, special hardware support is needed, which provides the cryptographic fundamentals for safe and secure software implementations. Several embedded architectures therefore provide a hardware security module (HSM), which again becomes a shared resource in multicore devices. Therefore, in ARAMiS, a multicore capable HSM was developed and the necessary software adaptation in the virtualization layer were conducted.

On-Chip Communication: The central interconnect plays an important role in multicore devices, as any data transport has to pass the communication infrastructure. Within ARAMiS, the interconnect was examined in various work packages, depending on the various use cases. Still some dedicated work on interconnects was conducted, especially focusing on requirements and solutions for future network on chip-based communication.

Methods and Tools are the foundation in multicore discussions. ARAMiS was not a tool driven project, but during the project the need for multicore specific tooling gained more and more awareness. Work on methodologies and tooling were conducted in most of the work packages. In addition, specific work was done to harmonize the tool chain and sketch a coherent tooling framework. This has been especially tailored for the demands in the automotive and avionics domain, but is still configurable, to allow adaptation to other domains.

Right from the beginning ARAMiS focused on the industrial applicability of its solutions. Therefore, industrial partners evaluated ARAMiS approaches in the domain specific demonstrators. It was the primary goal of the demonstrators, to proof the applicability of multicore devices. In total, there were four automotive demonstrators, three avionics demonstrators and one rail demonstrator:

Automotive VCT Platform A/B: The Virtualized Car Telematics (VCT) Demonstrator focused on the use of virtualization in infotainment platforms. Two different platforms have been developed. Platform A primarily focused on heterogeneous multicores with additional virtualization hardware support. Platform B focused on sharing of GPUs and sharing of displays. Platform A was built into a vehicle, whereas B was implemented in a vehicle cockpit mockup.

Automotive LSSI Platform C/D: The Large Scale Software Integration (LSSI) platforms focused on the integration of functionality from different singlecore ECUs onto one multicore ECU. Two different approaches were taken and compared. Platform C examined a non-intrusive approach, where the software stack wasn't adapted but virtualized by means of a micro hypervisor. Platform D used an intrusive approach, where applications were migrated to one AUTOSAR software stack. Platform D is a prototype of a multicore automotive chassis ECU, platform C runs on an evaluation board.

Avionics Situation Awareness: The Situation Awareness Demonstrator focused on the integration of a radar function running on several DSPs onto one multicore chip. A multicore based computer, allowing for dual-lane processing was developed and built. Mechanisms for migration and segregation of the radar application were developed. Additionally, a multicore based flight control demonstrator was developed. Both demonstrators proof the possible use of multicore devices in avionics applications.

Avionics Cabin Management Server: Similarly to the infotainment devices in automotive, avionics investigated the development of a cabin management server, which mainly focuses on mixed-critical applications. Additionally, the security concept played an important role for this platform.

Rail Automation Demonstrator: Eventually, one demonstrator was developed for rail automation. For this demonstrator the use of standard ICT COTS hardware was chosen. On top of the standard hardware runs a special virtualization approach that allows to abstract from the unreliability of the underlying hardware. Reliability is achieved by using several different emulators, executing the same application in parallel. The overall concept has been implemented to show the feasibility. Furthermore, it has been evaluated by certification authorities.

The automotive demonstrators were driven by the automotive OEMs Audi, BMW, Daimler. The Avionics demonstrators were developed by Airbus, Cassidian and Liebherr. The rail demonstrator was developed by Siemens. This way, a high relevance and closeness to series could be ensured and was expressed by project participants and reviewers.

The major challenges identified in the ARAMiS project are temporal and spatial segregation, synchronization, deployment, and complexity-management. All these challenges have been consequently addressed throughout the whole project lifetime and many also highly industrial relevant solutions have been developed in all working fields of the project. It was one of the initial ideas of ARAMiS to find a common multicore architecture for safety critical applications. Up to know, such an architecture does not exist. ARAMiS showed, that the requirements for different applications are too different. Several proposals how current architectures have to change were discussed within the consortium including the semiconductor providers.

Certification and to some extend also qualification demand an in-depth knowledge about the internal behavior of multicore devices. Especially if devices are not designed for safety critical applications, their documentation lacks information. Also the silicon might have more functionality than stated by the manual. There might exist phantom cores, hidden peripherals, hidden registers and the like, which might influence systems behavior, if activated by an erroneous access. Solving interference and synchronization challenges typically demands a tight interaction of hardware and software approaches to be efficient and predictable. Any additional support by hardware reduces the overhead and hence should be used. Interestingly many challenges can be derived from the deployment challenge, which has many aspects that need to be considered. For example, it has spatial (mapping to cores, memories, etc.) as well as temporal (scheduling, access to resources, etc.) aspects, directly leading into interference scenarios and synchronization issues with dependencies. Hence, achieving a feasible and efficient deployment inherently solves many of the questions that have to be asked during systems development. Obviously, tool support would be beneficial. ARAMiS showed that a tooling ecosystem is very important, but not existing yet. Within ARAMiS first steps towards a holistic tooling and methodology view have been made. These can serve as basis for future tools, which can be combined as needed by a specific process. These tools must be able to exchange models and results in a very flexible and compatible way.

It was the mission of the ARAMiS project to utilize multicore technology for safety, efficiency, and comfort in the domains automotive, avionic and rail. The goal was fully achieved and the foundation stone for a structured multicore development was laid.

3   ARAMiS II – Development Processes, Methods and Toos, Plattforms for Safety-Critical Multicore Systems

Future applications in automotive, avionics and railway show an ever-increasing demand of computational processing power and tend to be even more networked and integrated with other systems and services. The same applies to upcoming industry 4.0 applications. Thereby multicore will be the predominant computing architecture in future networked and safety critical applications.

Apart from the great success in fulfilling its objectives, ARAMiS has also revealed major obstacles, which still prevent the efficient use of multicore in the targeted industrial applications (Fig. 3):

- The step from singlecore to multicore in safety critical applications comes along with a huge leap in complexity. The development of multicore systems cannot be managed anymore with isolated state of the art methods and tools. Instead, even stricter systematic and structured development approaches are needed which necessitate interlocked methods and tools.
- A top-down development process is necessary in order to handle the complexity, allow safe-by-design properties and to consider multicore related aspects early and on a higher level of abstraction.
- The well-established platform standards such as AUTOSAR or IMA do not reflect the requirements of multicore solutions regarding segregation, synchronization, and communication mechanisms.

DEVELOPMENT PROCESSES I TOOLS I PLATFORMS
FOR SAFETY-CRITICIAL MULTICORE SYSTEMS

Fig. 3. The ARAMiS II project

The ARAMiS findings as described above directly lead to the objectives of ARAMIS II (Fig. 4):

1. The provision of systematic and structured approaches for the development of multicore software and platforms (or, '**Structured Multicore Development**' as we call it).
2. The development of **methods and tools** for supporting the Structured Multicore Development.
3. The development and extension of established **industrial platform architectures** for multicore requirements.

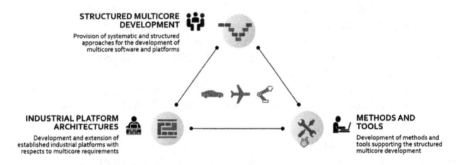

Fig. 4. Objectives of ARAMiS II

Based on these objectives, ARAMiS II is more tool centric from its work focus. However, partners of ARAMiS II are from the following groups coordinated by KIT:

- **OEM and System Suppliers:** AUDI, Airbus, Siemens, GE, Hirschmann, KSB, Diehl, Liebherr, Bosch, Continental, Schaeffler, Denso
- **Tool/Software Providers:** AbsInt, Elektrobit, Accemic, Vector, Sysgo, Opensynergy, Silexica, Symta Vision, Timing Architects
- **Research:** KIT, DLR, TU Braunschweig, fortiss, CAU Kiel, TUM, OFFIS, Fraunhofer, TU Kaiserslautern, University Augsburg, University Lubbeck.

In the following, the work focus and the objectives are described more in detail.

3.1 Processes

As previously mentioned all steps taken within ARAMiS II shall contribute to the top-level goal of a systematic and structured approach for multicore development. For this, the following baseline for the project is defined:

- A primary top-down, but iterative development process avoiding unnecessary loops is preferable.
- Development processes tend to be company specific.
- Introduction of multicore technology should not require a complete revolution of existing processes.
- Existing components shall be reusable, thereby leading to bottom-up parts in development processes.

In order to reach the goal under these boundary conditions, a flexible approach, which can be adapted to individual needs, is required. Methodology frameworks such as the one defined by SPES 2020 can serve as basis.

Still, the SPES 2020 framework is not precise enough on technical level by itself and does not include multicore related aspects by itself. However, it can serve as good basis for extensions. In a development process based on SPES 2020, the functional description is split up into smaller functional parts and finally mapped onto a selected platform. Especially in such a top-down development process, several multicore related design decisions have to be taken. Some of these are listed in the following:

- Granularity and partitioning: When shall a functional description be split up into smaller parts? What is the right granularity for a core mapping?
- Allocation: Which is the most efficient platform for a given application setup?
- Deployment: What is the best mapping of functional components (typically software components) onto cores?
- Scheduling: What is the best scheduling of the mapped multicore components?
- Guarantees: How to ensure certain aspects of the platform (e.g. behavior, timing, segregation)?

Note: The clear split between these tasks is made for the sake of clarity and simplicity. In reality, all these aspects are not independent but strongly influence each other.

3.2   Methods and Tools

In order to implement the Structured Multicore Development, existing tools and methodologies have to be extended on a technical level. A possible exemplary flow is depicted in Fig. 5. Different models of application, middleware and hardware are necessary and hence investigated. These models are needed for the steps, which can for itself be partitioned into different other steps. The results of the distinctive steps are parameters that are used for the configuration of the implementation or noted in the configuration model of the system. Also, specific characteristics can be extracted from the implementation and used to synthesize or to extend the application, middleware or hardware models.

The goal is to achieve the required high performance data processing in combination with real-time behavior in safety-critical mobility systems including their certification/qualification. Therefore, tackling the following topics will lead to an increased productivity in the development of such systems:

- Tooling interoperability
- Design space exploration, partitioning, deployment and scheduling
- Correctness, concurrency and timing
- Parallelization of code.

Additionally, the proof of absence of defectiveness as well as mastering the corresponding complexity of multicores is supported. This includes efficient programmability and efficient implementation of novel innovative applications.

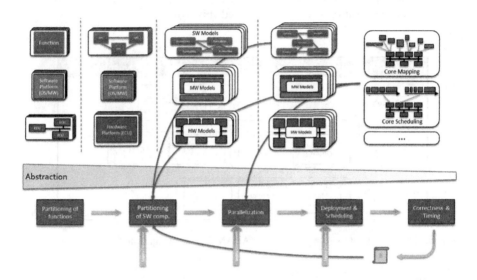

Fig. 5. Scientific and technical approach

3.3 Platforms

Besides the application development process and tooling, the platform aspects play an important role to be addressed. These aspects should include but not be limited to platform software such as hypervisors, operating system, middleware, container-based virtualization, legacy software, application components, and methodologies.

- Platform architecture and distribution pattern
- Synchronization and communication
- Virtualized systems
- 'Fail-Operational' concepts on multicore platforms.

Platform architectures and architectural mechanisms are investigated and developed taking into account the hardware architecture and the newly available fields of application's requirements. Thus, it will range from low-level aspects such as efficient inter-core communication and synchronization to high-level aspects of patterns for application and basic-software distribution. Across the whole range the developed principles and platforms will consider non-functional aspects of safety, security, and availability. Furthermore, it provides specifics for the tool extensions. The developed platform architectures and mechanisms are validated in the use case implementations.

3.4   Evaluation of Results in Industrial Use Cases

In order to validate the developed methodology for the 'structured multicore development', the tools for multicores and the developed platforms, industrial use cases close to production are investigated in the three investigated domains. Based on these use cases, which provide also requirements for the development, the applicability of the methods, tools and platforms are demonstrated (Fig. 6).

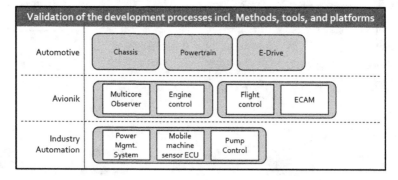

Fig. 6.   Industrial UseCases investigated in ARAMiS II to evaluate and validate the results

4   Summary

Even though, many different domains are using Multicore processors, mobility domains and others with requirements in terms of functional safety have issues using this technology. With the ARAMiS project first steps have been made and a general feasibility of using multicore in safety-critical applications has been shown. However, the lack of a standardized development processes for multicore software, the necessary methods and tools as well as platforms are still open issues. These issues are addressed in the ARAMiS II project to reduce the effort for mastering the complexity and increase the efficiency of multicores in embedded safety-critical systems. Detailed technical information can be found in the contributions that are published. A list of publications can be found in [3, 4].

Acknowledgement.   This work was funded within the project ARAMiS and ARAMiS II by the German Federal Ministry for Education and Research with the funding IDs 01IS11035 & 01IS16025. The responsibility for the content remains with the authors.

References

1. Nationale Roadmap Embedded Systems. ZVEI - Zentralverband Elektrotechnik- und Elektronikindustrie e.V. (2009)
2. Geisberger, E., Broy, M., Cengarle, M.V., Keil, P., Niehaus, J., Thiel, C., Thoennissen-Fries, H.-J.: agendaCPS - Integrierte Forschungsagenda Cyber-Physical Systems. Acatech, Muenchen (2012)
3. The ARAMiS Project. www.projekt-aramis.de
4. The ARAMiS II Project. www.aramis2.de

Mapping and Scheduling Hard Real Time Applications on Multicore Systems - The ARGO Approach

Panayiotis Alefragis[1]([⊠]) [iD], George Theodoridis[2],
Merkourios Katsimpris[2] [iD], Christos Valouxis[2], Christos Gogos[3] [iD],
George Goulas[1], Nikolaos Voros[1], Simon Reder[5] [iD],
Koray Kasnakli[4], Marcus Bednara[4], David Müller[6], Umut Durak[6] [iD],
and Juergen Becker[5]

[1] Technological Educational Institute of Western Greece, Patras, Greece
{alefrag, ggoulas, voros}@teiwest.gr
[2] University of Patras, Patras, Greece
{theodor, katsimpris}@ece.upatras.gr, valouxis@sch.gr
[3] Technological Educational Institute of Epirus, Arta, Greece
cgogos@teiep.gr
[4] Fraunhofer-Institut für Integrierte Schaltungen IIS, Am Wolfsmantel 33,
91058 Erlangen, Germany
{koray.kasnakli, marcus.bednara}@iis.fraunhofer.de
[5] Karlsruhe Institute of Technology, Karlsruhe, Germany
{simon.reder, juergen.becker}@kit.edu
[6] Deutsches Zentrum für Luft- und Raumfahrt e.V. (DLR), Institut für
Flugsystemtechnik, Flugdynamik und Simulation, Lilienthalplatz 7,
38108 Braunschweig, Germany
{david.mueller, umut.durak}@dlr.de

Abstract. Using multi-core architectures for embedded time-critical systems creates a big challenge for developers due to the complexity of the underline mapping and scheduling problem. H2020 ARGO project [2] proposes a tool flow to minimize multi-core applications development time while guaranteeing real-time performance. In this paper, we provide an overview of ARGO tool flow and we focus on the heuristic approach of solving the worst case execution time aware (WCET) mapping and scheduling problem on hierarchical task graphs. Examples from two real applications from the aerospace and image processing domains are presented.

Keywords: Parallel multicore mapping and scheduling · Model based design
Integer linear programming · Heuristics

1 Introduction

Hard real time applications require tight estimation of the worst case execution time (WCET) [12] in order to guarantee that the implemented schedule meets the required completion deadline. The problem becomes more complex with the introduction of

© Springer International Publishing AG, part of Springer Nature 2018
N. Voros et al. (Eds.): ARC 2018, LNCS 10824, pp. 700–711, 2018.
https://doi.org/10.1007/978-3-319-78890-6_56

many core processors, as shared resource usage creates competition between parallel executing tasks. The problem is analogous to the multi-mode resource-constrained project scheduling problem where the execution time of each task is not fixed. To make the problem even more difficult the execution time of each task has a cyclic dependency with the assignment of tasks to processing cores, the sequencing of tasks in each core and the assignment of variables to different memory resources. It is also common that these applications are specified using modelling languages that are support by system simulation environments like Simulink by engineers with little knowledge of parallelization techniques or insufficient time to explore all the possible combinations and the side effects their decisions have in the performance of the application on a specific hardware architecture. The H2020 ARGO project proposes a semi-automated workflow to assist developers reduce time to market while creating high quality parallel applications starting from a high level model specification. In this paper, we make a brief introduction to the ARGO work flow and we present a mathematical model and a heuristic approach to solve the problem. Finally, a brief introduction and experience from the use of the ARGO work flow for two industrial use case applications from the aerospace and the image processing domain are presented.

2 ARGO Work Flow

The ARGO design workflow is presented in Fig. 1 with the optimization component expanded. The main concept in ARGO is that end users describe their applications using dataflow modeling through the open-source Xcos framework enhanced with code fragments expressed in the Scilab programming language, an open source language similar to Matlab. This approach enables end users to use readily made components from the Xcos library and provide applications specific functionality using the Scilab language. The Xcos/Scilab models are translated to an intermediate program representation using a

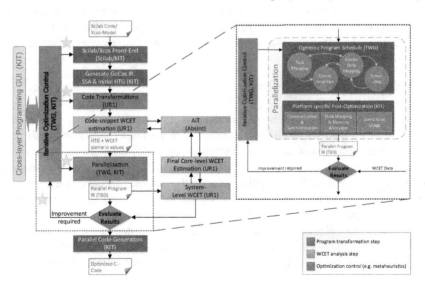

Fig. 1. ARGO tool flow

combination of the ePS translator and the GeCoS [5] source-to-source transformation framework. A similar work flow has been proposed in the past for the average case task scheduling problem for homogeneous architectures [10].

The ARGO intermediate representation uses the Hierarchical Task Graph (HTG) provided by the GeCos compiler framework. In HTG, composite activities with back dependencies like loops, functions etc. are enclosed in a lower hierarchical level subgraph, resulting in a forest of hierarchical trees of directed acyclic task graphs (DAG). Edges represent task dependencies and the information that need to be exchanged between tasks. Nodes represent tasks and have information related to the sequential worst case execution time, the size and the frequency of accessed variables and the potential execution gain for each variable when mapped to faster memory banks. In addition, the target hardware platform characteristics (cores, memory banks, interconnect network, etc.) are described in the ARGO Architecture Description Language (ADL). The ADL follows the principals described in [9] enhanced to support interference between simultaneous accesses to shared resources and inter core message routing policies.

Using the HTG program representation and ADL information as input, the mapping and scheduling algorithms annotate the HTG with high level mapping and scheduling information for tasks, variables and communication placement. Communication exist when two dependent tasks are mapped to different cores. The annotated HTG is then transformed to a parallel program model (PPIR) where synchronization points are inserted and final variable mapping to memory address is performed. Using PPIR, the system-level WCET analyzer can then validate if the generated program meets end user requirements. If the result is positive, the ARGO flow generates WCET aware parallel C code for the spe-cific target platform and then uses target platform tools to generate the executable program. If the results are not acceptable, an semi-automated iterative optimization is performed which allow end users to identify application bottlenecks using a GUI interface and control specific ARGO work flow component parameters to influence the result of the complex parallelization process. Such parameters include code transformations, mapping and sequencing constraints for specific tasks, task clustering, mapping and scheduling algorithms selection, communication placement policies etc.

3   Mapping and Scheduling

The goal of mapping scheduling algorithms is to identify potential parallelization opportunities, estimate the resource interference of parallel tasks and subsequently decide on the optimal allocation of tasks and variables to processing cores. Tasks clustering may also be performed if the mapper estimates that tasks should be treated as sequences assigned to a single core. Data mapping refers to the variables allocation on the available memory banks, which can be private or shared and a number of accesses for each variable is required for each task node in the HTG. There is a cyclic dependency of data mapping with the calculation of WCET of tasks. This is due to the fact that when a variable is accessed by a task, depending on the number of tasks executed in parallel on different cores and the capacity of the communication infrastructure each memory access time is not constant. An iterative process may be implemented to break the cycle or an integrated model that simultaneously takes all decisions can be introduced.

The main motivation of the proposed approach is that there can be no "best" algorithm that will be able to perform well according to all the requirements of the end users. The goal was to create a number of interchangeable and cooperating algorithms with different quality and performance characteristics that are able to operate on a common problem representation. Thus an algorithmic toolbox is created that is able to generate mapping and scheduling solutions. The algorithms are either constructive, i.e. not using a previous solutions as a start, or the can be improving i.e. they will start from a given solution and will try to improve it.

In this paper we present two of the constructive algorithms. An ILP based top down algorithm that is able to generate an "optimal" solution given enough time for relative small HTGs and a bottom up heuristic based approach that is using a WCET aware HEFT extension. In order to solve the problem the following objectives must be fulfilled. First, each task of the HTG should be assigned to at least one core in the MPSoC. This allows the replication of tasks at multiple cores. Second, we must decide the sequence of each task per core and calculate the the start time of each task respecting its dependencies with other tasks. Third, we must decide on the mapping of each variable to a memory bank. Without loss of generality we assume that there is a private fast local memory per core (SPM) and some shared off-chip memory. In the current model, we assume static data assignment, i.e. the variable is assigned to a specific position in memory for the whole program execution.

Figure 2 presents a single layer of an annotated HTG example where colors represent assigned core to task, rectangular task represent composite tasks. Multicolor tasks means that a task is assigned to more than one core at a lower hierarchy level. Variable names inside tasks represent variables that are mapped to the scratchpad memory of the given processor. Timing information inside task represent start and end time on the specific processor. Variables on black arcs represent data dependencies that should be implemented as communication tasks on the specific architecture and the estimated data that should be transferred. Inactive means that a data dependency will require no communication as the source and destinations tasks are mapped on the same processor. Red arcs represent mapping and scheduling decisions due to lack of resources.

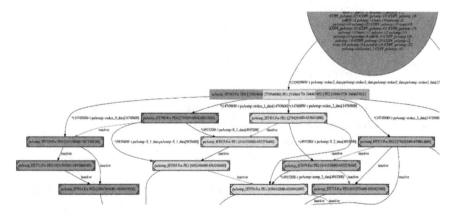

Fig. 2. Annotated HTG example after mapping and scheduling (Color figure online)

3.1 ILP Formulation

An ILP formulation is proposed and its main objective is to provide an optimal solution to the previous described problem. Similar approaches have been used in the past for the average case variant of the problem [3, 4] for heterogeneous systems, memory aware average case scheduling [6] and for the WCET problem for homogeneous architectures [7]. The presented model iteration assumes static allocation of variables and negligible time to copy a variable from the shared memory to the private memory of each core. Let P be the set of processing cores, T the set of all tasks, CT the set of composite tasks, LT the set of leaf tasks, V the set of variables, E the set of the edges, $N_{v,t}$ the number of accesses of variable v from task t and $VAR(t)$ the accessed variables from task t. Let MEM_COST and SPM_COST the cost in cycles for an off-chip memory access and private memory access respectively and M a big number. Finally, let $NC(t)$ the tasks are not either predecessors or successors of task t. The objective function is to minimize the start time of the sink node, thus generating a minimum makespan schedule.

$$\min \, s_{sink}$$

Table 1 presents the variables that are used in the model. The first group of constraints make sure that each task must be mapped to one processor and that precedence order between dependent tasks must be fulfilled. To make the model simpler we assume that each task receives of the required information from other tasks before executing and sends the generated values to dependent tasks at the end of the tasks execution. In the ARGO context, this assumption is refined at a later post processing

Table 1. ILP model variables definitions

Notation	Definition
$x_{t,p}$	1 if task t is assigned to core p
s_t	Start time of task t
$w_{t,p}$	Worst case execution time of task t in processor p
$a_{i,j}$	1 when task i starts before task j
$exec_t$	Execution time of task t in cycles where all the variables are located in the off-chip memory
$z_{v,p}$	1 when the variable v is assigned in the SPM of processor p
$size_v$	Size of the variable v
cap_p	Capacity of the SPM of processor p
$pre(t)$	Task set with all the predecessor of task t
$edges(t)$	Task dependencies in a composite task
$gain_{v,t}$	The execution gain in cycles if the variable v in task t is allocated in SPM
$cost\_mem_{v,t}$	Additional cycles in the execution time of a task t when variable v is allocated in off-chip memory
$cost\_spm_{v,t}$	Additional cycles in the execution time of a task t when variable v is allocated in SPM memory

phase where local optimization of the position of each send receive task is performed. Disjunctive constraints are added to make sure that independent tasks mapped on the same core do not overlap.

$$\sum_{p\in P} x_{t,p} = 1 \; \forall \, t \in T$$

$$s_{receive_t} + exec_{send_{t,p}} \le s_{exec_t} + (1 - x_{t,p})M$$
$$s_{exec_t} + w_{t,p} \le s_{send_t} + (1 - x_{t,p})M \qquad \forall \, t \in T, p \in P$$
$$s_{send_i} + exec_{send_{i,p}} \le s_{receive_j} + (1 - x_{i,p})M \quad \forall \, (i,j) \in E, p \in P$$

$$s_{send_i} + exec_{send_{i,p}} \le s_{receive_j} + (3 - x_{i,p} - x_{j,p} - a_{i,j})M \qquad \begin{matrix} \forall i \in T \\ j \in NC(i), \\ p \in P \end{matrix}$$
$$s_{send_j} + exec_{send_{j,p}} \le s_{receive_i} + (2 - x_{i,p} - x_{j,p} + a_{i,j})M$$

A second group of constraints calculate the worst case execution time according to the data allocation of the variables. In our approach we flatten the hierarchical tasks graph up to a level K from the top level and for each composite task at level K we maintain all nested task with the added constraint that all tasks must be mapped on the same processor. We call these tasks clustered tasks. The edges inside the clustered tasks are control edges and are maintained to calculate the changes in the worst case execution path (WCEP) [8]. The variable $w_{entry,p}$ represent the WCEP length in the composite task and is the WCET of the composite task. Critical path changes based on the variable mapping and the interference of other tasks that execute in parallel.

$$w_{entry,p} = w_{t,p}$$
$$w_{i,p} \ge w_{j,p} + exec_i - \sum_{v\in var(i)} z_{v,p} gain_{v,i} \quad \forall \, (i,j) \in CE(t), \, t \in CT$$
$$w_{sink,p} = 0$$

The third group of constraints guarantee that each variable in the HTG is allocated to one private (SPM) or the off-chip memory. The total size of the allocated variables in the SPM must be less than the SPM capacity.

$$\sum_{p\in P} z_{v,p} \le 1 \; \forall \, v \in V$$
$$\sum_{v\in V} z_{v,p} size_v \le cap_p \; \forall \, v \in V, \, p \in P$$

Finally, a number of constraints that calculate the execution time of receiving and send tasks are added in addition to constraints that the calculate the WCET of composite and leaf tasks depending on the selected variables allocation.

$$exec_{receive_{t,p}} = \sum_{v\in receive\_vars(t)} load^t_{v,p} size_v mem\_cost \; \forall \, t \in T, \, p \in P$$
$$exec_{send_{t,p}} = \sum_{v\in send\_vars(t)} store^t_{v,p} size_v mem\_cost \; \forall \, t \in T, \, p \in P$$
$$w_{t,p} = w_{entry,p} \; \forall \, t \in CT$$

In order to calculate interference between parallel tasks we extend the model using the following. Let $T_1, T_2, ..., T_p$ the p parallel tasks. Each task T_i does $(1 - z_{v,p}) * N_{v,t}$ external memory accesses. If we sort the tasks by the number of memory accesses, where small index indicate smaller or equal number of memory accesses to the external memory and *MEM_COST* is the atomic time needed to access the external memory, the worst-case interference caused, if Round Robin arbitration is considered, can be expressed by

$$w_{t,p} = \text{exec}_t - \sum_{v \in \text{var}(t)} z_{v,p} \text{gain}_{v,t} + \sum_{j=1}^{j \leq i-1} \sum_{v \in \text{var}(t)} (1 - z_{v,p}) * N_{v,t} * MEM\_COST$$
$$+ \sum_{j=i+1}^{j \leq p} \sum_{v \in \text{var}(t)} (1 - z_{v,p}) * N_{v,t} * MEM\_COST \; \forall \, t \in LT$$

3.2   Heuristic Solver

In ARGO, we extended HEFT-LA [1] and CPOP [11] list based heuristics to accommodate the requirements of the WCET problem. The significant difference compared to the literature is that most algorithms perform metrics on the critical path and in WCET the critical path changes. One cause of the critical path changes is due to the fact that the task execution time is a function of the used variables mapping and the interference that is generated by all the tasks that can be executed in parallel and compete to access shared resources. In our approach, we only allow changes to memory state at the beginning of a task. The memory state then remains constant until the task has finished. The problem of mapping variables to memory banks can be modelled as a multiple knapsack problem, where each memory bank represent a

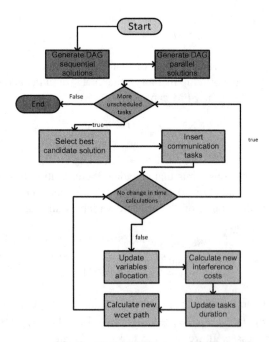

Fig. 3. HTG WCET aware HEFT

knapsack of a given capacity and the size of each variable represent the used space in the knapsack. The gain for each variable can be computed by the usage frequency multiplied by the memory access cost. In addition, the gain is penalized for all variables that are mapped to shared memory banks and is proportional to the usage frequency. The memory state before the execution of the knapsack problem is used to calculate the cost to move variables that are not used to other memory banks to create more space for the specific memory bank, if these variables are used by unscheduled tasks.

Another cause is the interference between communication tasks. In our approach, we model the WCET communication cost using the two values latency and pitch. Compared to the literature where communication cost between tasks are fixed, all algorithms consider the communication costs as dynamic and will use call back functions to calculate the communication cost. Figure 3 presents the execution logic of the WCET aware HEFT heuristic.

4   Use Case Applications

The first use case comes from the aerospace domain. EGPWS is one of various Terrain Awareness and Warning Systems (TAWS) and defines a set of features which aim to prevent uncontrolled flight into the terrain. There are various TAWS options available on the market for various platforms in various configurations. The core feature set of an EGPWS is to create visual and aural warnings between 30 ft to 2450 ft Above Ground Level (AGL) in order to avoid controlled flight into the terrain. The prototype EGPWS that is under development as a test case in the context of ARGO project is developed as Scilab/Xcos models conforming to typical EGPWS logical data interfaces. The ARGO workflow was utilized to generate parallel code from this model that will be deployed on the available ARGO target architectures. The system will be integrated into DLR's full flight simulator, namely Air Vehicle Simulator (AVES), for hardware-in-the-loop testing with piloted flight simulator experiments. Figure 4 presents the top level Xcos model of the EGPWS prototype.

The second use case is a Polarization Image processing System (PIPS) which is comprised of a camera with a novel polarization CMOS sensor and software for camera control, signal processing and visual representation of the polarization information. The system is designed for the inline inspection in industry, such as the measurement of residual stress for a 100% quality control of glass products. The CMOS sensor is designed for capturing the polarization orientation in a single shot image. This requires a division of focal plane architecture and some sophisticated algorithms to reconstruct the entire polarization information from sensor data. In order to obtain an optimal signal quality, the pixel streams have to be preprocessed in several steps. These sensor specific algorithms are the main part of the ARGO test case provided by Fraunhofer IIS. During this preprocessing, the sensor data is prepared for the later computation of application dependent evaluations. For industrial applications like production quality monitoring, there are hard real time constraints applying to the polarization image processing system. For example, no frame drops due to slow image processing

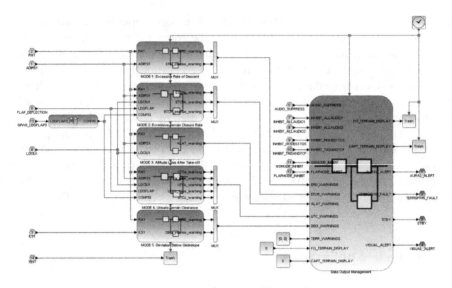

Fig. 4. EGPWS Xcos model description

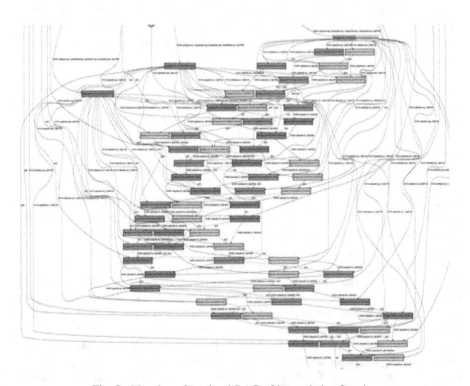

Fig. 5. Mapping of top level DAG of interpolation function

tasks are allowed. So the timing behavior is determined by the sensor resolution, the sensor frame rate (i.e. number of image frames per second), and the complexity of the processing steps.

Due to the size of the generated graphs for the use cases, experimental result have shown that the mathematical model can only be used in practice only as a benchmark for the quality of the generated solutions from the heuristic solvers, given ample execution time. On the other hand, end user estimate that the use of the tool chain can reduce the time to market by more than 60% due the provided automation in generating parallel WCET aware programs. To give the reader a hint of the complexity of the applications, Fig. 5 presents the top level graph of the interpolation function; colors represent core mapping. This is just a single function of the PIPS application while the whole applications has more than 12 similar sized functions, executed possibly in parallel to each other.

5   Current Status and Future Work

In the current iteration of the ARGO tool chain it is possible to generate functionally correct parallel code for the target architecture starting from a high level description of Xcos models and/or Scilab code. Both target platforms are supported by the components of the tool chain through the ADL description of each platform, making the provided components platform agnostic, allowing more platforms to be supported in the future given their ADL description. All ARGO related software and the tool chain components are provided to the users using a docker image that is automatically generated when a new revision of the tool chain is created. The same mechanism is used during automated integration tests accelerating the development effort and allowing a common platform for both developers and end user, independent from the local working environment of the user. This allow easier replication of problems and an effort free installation to the end users.

The current status is in order to the planned work of the project and the current outlook is that the project will be able to provide a functional prototype that will allow the end users to interactively generate and evaluate different parallelization approaches, while estimating the WCET performance of each approach. It is estimated that a reduction of more than 40% in the development time will be realized by the end of the project compared to the baseline development currently followed by the end users. The recent inclusion of the Emmtrix Technologies [13] to the project partners allows results from the project to be further exploited commercially extending the currently provided products to support hard real time applications.

In the immediate plans of the ARGO project is the integration of a parallel system level WCET estimator to evaluate the correctness of the generated solutions and the evaluation of the augmented models of the end user use cases. For the mapping and scheduling of the application work is under development to introduce single path and population based meta-heuristics to further enhance the quality of the generated solutions.

Acknowledgement. This work was funded by the European Union under the Horizon 2020 Framework Program under grant agreement ICT-2015-688131, project "WCET-Aware Parallelization of Model-Based Applications for Heterogeneous Parallel Systems (ARGO)".

References

1. Bittencourt, L.F., Sakellariou, R., Madeira, E.R.M.: DAG scheduling using a lookahead variant of the heterogeneous earliest finish time algorithm. In: 2010 18th Euromicro Conference on Parallel, Distributed Network-Based Processing, pp. 27–34 (2010)
2. Derrien, S., Puaut, I., Alefragis, P., Bednara, M., Bucher, H., David, C., Debray, Y., Durak, U., Fassi, I., Ferdinand, C., Hardy, D., Kritikakou, A., Rauwerda, G., Reder, S., Sicks, M., Stripf, T., Sunesen, K., ter Braak, T., Voros, N., Becker, J.: WCET-aware parallelization of model-based applications for multi-cores: the ARGO approach. In: Design, Automation & Test in Europe Conference & Exhibition (DATE), Lausanne, Switzerland, pp. 286–289. IEEE (2017)
3. Emeretlis, A., Theodoridis, G., Alefragis, P., Voros, N.: A logic-based benders decomposition approach for mapping applications on heterogeneous multicore platforms. ACM Trans. Embed. Comput. Syst. **15**, 1–28 (2016). ACM
4. Emeretlis, A., Theodoridis, G., Alefragis, P., Voros, N.: A hybrid approach for mapping and scheduling on heterogeneous multicore systems. In: 2016 International Conference on Embedded Computer Systems: Architectures, Modeling, and Simulation (SAMOS), Samos, Greece (2016)
5. Floch, A., Yuki, T., Moussawi, A.E., Morvan, A., Martin, K., Naullet, M., Alle, M., L'Hours, L., Simon, N., Derrien, S., Charot, F., Wolinski, C., Sentieys, O.: GeCoS: a framework for prototyping custom hardware design flows. In: Proceedings of the 13th IEEE International Working Conference on Source Code Analysis and Manipulation, SCAM 2013, Eindhoven, Netherlands, 22–23 September 2013, pp. 100–105. IEEE (2013)
6. Jovanovic, O., Kneuper, N., Engel, M., Marwedel, P.: ILP-based memory-aware mapping optimization for MPSoCs. In: 2012 IEEE 15th International Conference on Computational Science and Engineering, pp. 413–420. IEEE (2012)
7. Kelter, T., Borghorst, H., Marwedel, P.: WCET-aware scheduling optimizations for multi-core real-time systems. In: XIVth International Conference on Embedded Computer Systems: Architectures, Modeling, and Simulation, SAMOS 2014, Agios Konstantinos, Samos, Greece, 14–17 July 2014, pp. 67–74 (2014)
8. Kwok, Y.-K., Ahmad, I.: Dynamic critical-path scheduling: an effective technique for allocating task graphs to multiprocessors. IEEE Trans. Parallel Distrib. Syst. **7**(5), 506–521 (1996). IEEE
9. Stripf, T., Oey, O., Bruckschloegl, T., et al.: A compilation - and simulation - oriented architecture description language for multicore systems. In: IEEE Proceedings of 15th IEEE International Conference on Computational Science and Engineering (CSE), pp. 383–390. IEEE (2012). https://doi.org/10.1109/iccse.2012.60. ISBN 978-1-4673-5165-2
10. Stripf, T., Oey, O., Bruckschloegl, T., Becker, J., Rauwerda, G., Sunesen, K., Goulas, G., Alefragis, P., Voros, N.S., Derrien, S., Sentieys, O., Kavvadias, N., Dimitroulakos, G., Masselos, K., Kritharidis, D., Mitas, N., Perschke, T.: Compiling Scilab to high performance embedded multicore systems. Microprocess. Microsyst. **37**, 1033–1049 (2013). Elsevier
11. Topcuoglu, H., Hariri, S., Wu, M.-Y.: Task scheduling algorithms for heterogeneous processors. In: Proceedings of the 8th Heterogeneous Computing Workshop. IEEE (1999). https://doi.org/10.1109/hcw.1999.765092

12. Wilhelm, R., Engblom, J., Ermedahl, A., Holsti, N., Thesing, S., Whalley, D., Bernat, G., Ferdinand, C., Heckmann, R., Mitra, T., Mueller, F., Puaut, I., Puschner, P., Staschulat, J., Stenstrom, P.: The worst-case execution-time problem – overview of methods and survey of tools. ACM Trans. Embed. Comput. Syst. **7**, 36:1–36:53 (2008)
13. https://www.emmtrix.com/

Robots in Assisted Living Environments as an Unobtrusive, Efficient, Reliable and Modular Solution for Independent Ageing: *The RADIO Experience*

Christos Antonopoulos[1]($\boxtimes$), Georgios Keramidas[1],
Nikolaos S. Voros[1], Michael Huebner[2], Fynn Schwiegelshohn[2],
Diana Goehringer[3], Maria Dagioglou[4], Georgios Stavrinos[4],
Stasinos Konstantopoulos[4], and Vangelis Karkaletsis[4]

[1] Technological Educational Institute of Western Greece, Patras, Greece
{cantonopoulos,gkeramidas,voros}@teiwest.gr
[2] Ruhr-Universität Bochum, Bochum, Germany
{Michael.Huebner,Fynn.Schwiegelshohn}@rub.de
[3] Technische Universität Dresden, Dresden, Germany
diana.goehringer@tu-dresden.de
[4] Institute of Informatics and Telecommunications,
NCSR "Demokritos", Agia Paraskevi, Greece
{mdagiogl,gstavrinos,konstant,
vangelis}@iit.demokritos.gr

Abstract. Demographic and epidemiologic transitions have brought a new health care paradigm where life expectancy is increasing as well as the need for long-term care. To meet the resulting challenge, healthcare systems need to take full advantage of new opportunities offered by technical advancements in ICT. The RADIO project explores a novel approach to user acceptance and unobtrusiveness: an integrated smart home/assistant robot system where health monitoring equipment is an obvious and accepted part of the user's daily life. By using the smart home/assistant robot as sensing equipment for health monitoring, we mask the *functionality* of the sensors rather than the sensors themselves. In this manner, sensors do not need to be discrete and cumbersome to install; they do however need to be perceived as a natural component of the smart home/assistant robot functionalities.

1 Introduction

Demographic and epidemiologic transitions have brought a new health care paradigm with the presence of both growing elderly population and chronic diseases [1]. Life expectancy is increasing as well as the need for long-term care. Institutional care for the aged population faces economical struggles with low staffing ratios and consequent quality problems [2, 3].

© Springer International Publishing AG, part of Springer Nature 2018
N. Voros et al. (Eds.): ARC 2018, LNCS 10824, pp. 712–723, 2018.
https://doi.org/10.1007/978-3-319-78890-6_57

Although the aforementioned implications of ageing impose societal challenges, at the same time technical advancements in ICT, including robotics, bring new opportunities for the healthcare systems. The full realization of this potential depends on:

- Concrete evidence for the *benefits for all stakeholders*, including the elderly end-users and their formal and informal care givers (secondary end-users), as well as the health care system
- *Safety of and acceptability by* the end-users
- *Cost-effectiveness* in acquisition and maintenance, *reliability*, and *flexibility* in being able to meet a range of needs and societal expectations
- The provision of functionalities that can *reduce admissions and days spent in care institutions*, and prolong the *time spent living in own home*

RADIO project has adopted and extended the approach of making the sensing devices **obvious and accepted part of the user's daily life.** Specifically, this is accomplished by the introduction of robotic system as an assistive smart home companion to the persons, and not as omnipotent "invisible" platform taking over the person's home environment which would result in increased obtrusiveness and low probability of acceptance. Another critical role of the robot system is that it comprises a central entity with which the persons interact, and thus his/her attention is not distracted by the rest of the sensors/actuators covering the premises and collaborating with the robot. In this way the functionality of the sensors rather the sensors themselves is hidden, allowing the development of complex services of significant added value representing the main objectives of the project as follows:

- To wide range of methods have been developed for detecting the *activities of daily life (ADL)*. Such methods include simple activities, such as rising from the bed, walking, medication intake as well as more complex ones such as meal preparation.
- A highly efficient integration approach is adopted making the robot the central focus of interaction, while it collaborates with multiple heterogeneous wireless sensor technologies. Furthermore, the robot interacts with a novel gateway allowing reliable operation even in cases of communication failure with the backend infrastructure.
- All RADIO platform components are based on off-the-shelf, commercially available solutions.
- Specialized hardware based components are developed and integrated offering ultra-low power, reliable and real-time recognition methods particularly with respect to image and vision processing related ADLs.
- The RADIO platform has gone through three different and rigorous evaluation phases, each one validating ever more advanced prototypes. Evaluation also took place in different countries and in both clinical premises and private homes, thus accurately and objectively highlight advantages, capabilities but also weaknesses in different contexts.
- With respect to the backend infrastructure, two different platforms are offered specifically targeting the end-users, caregivers and technicians. These platforms incorporate and support prominent communication technologies such as MQTT message passing and RestAPI webservices.

The high level conceptual architecture of RADIO is depicted in Fig. 1. In order to achieve its ambitious objectives, the RADIO project addressed challenging issues in several ICT fields. In the remainder of this paper we first frame this research in the context of the RADIO architecture and heterogeneous smart home/robotics environment (Sect. 2), and present integrated sensing and actuation in this environment (Sect. 3), embedded system design (Sect. 4) and communications infrastructure (Sect. 5), and conclude (Sect. 6).

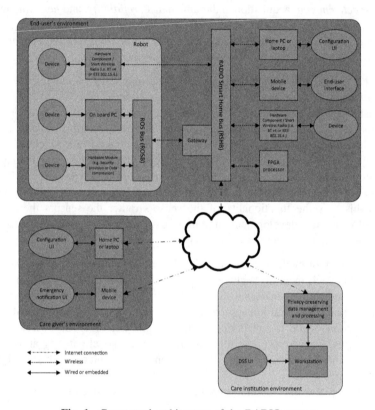

Fig. 1. Conceptual architecture of the RADIO system

2   Unobtrusive Data Collection and Processing

One of the core promises of RADIO was to build an integrated robot and smart home system that primarily serves end user's convenience and assistance while at the same time monitors ADLs. In RADIO, no action is explicitly motivated by health monitoring. On the contrary, monitoring only occurs during interactions with the system initiated by the user and only if, such monitoring is unobtrusive.

The primary end users are elderly people who need assistance in order to maintain their independence and quality of life. *RADIO* offers a number of smart home automation conveniences and a thoroughly integrated *domestic assistant* robot. Besides running errands, such as looking through the house for eyewear or keys or bringing medication, the robot also acts as the contact point for home automation conveniences, such as lights that can be switched on and off, heating that can be turned up or down, etc. It collects and analyses behavioural data in order to attract a doctor's attention when necessary, helping diagnose symptoms early and take timely remedial action. Through its direct involvement in the end-users daily activities, RADIO observes *ADLs*. Such observations, could be exploited to establish ADL patterns and to identify deviations.

RADIO detects ADLs related to *functional status*, such as bed mobility and locomotion, as well as *instrumental ADLs* such as the ability to observe a medication regime. These ADLs were presented in the list of clinical requirements for the RADIO system chosen from interRAI Long-Term Care Facilities (LTCF) and Home Care (HC) instruments. The final selection of ADLs was based on both unobtrusiveness and technological readiness of the monitoring methods criteria.

For each ADL, we considered the level of obtrusiveness to the primary end-user, taking into account several dimensions; physical, usability, privacy, function, human interaction, self-concept, routine and sustainability [4]. These considerations were taken along with the suggested method of monitoring. ADL detection was based on audio, visual, depth, and range data from the robot as well as their fusion with smart home sensor data.

Moreover, for each ADL and suggested monitoring method, the level of abstraction of information needed by clinical staff for proper assessment is considered. After considering all the above, the following ADL monitoring capabilities were developed:

- Bed and chair transfer, using visual data; the duration of the activity is reported to the clinician.
- 4-m walking, using range data; the duration of the activity is reported to the clinician.
- Pill intake, using visual data; confirmation that the activity took place is reported to the clinician.
- Meal preparation, fusing several smart home sensors detecting opening and closing of cupboards and turning kitchen appliances on and off; the time at which the activity took place is reported to the clinician.
- TV watching, fusing smart home sensors detecting turning the TV set on and off and sitting on chairs; the duration of the activity is reported to the clinician.
- Going out of the house, fusing smart home sensors that report and reports time of activity.

To achieve this, an adequate audio-visual processing architecture was developed that integrates the primary audio-visual and range data methods and the secondary methods that use the former's output to make measurements or infer that activities took place. The architecture also established appropriate interconnections and articulation points of the ADL recognition components, based on the principles of moving computation close to the raw data to address privacy and network bandwidth issues and moving computation away from the on-board computer to address battery autonomy and limited computational resources [5].

Both primary and secondary methods are distributed between the robot's on-board CPU and FPGA board and off-board computational resources. Decisions regarding how to best distribute components are based on the "rostune" system [6] which collects and reports statistics about CPU and bandwidth usage.

The inventory of machine perception methods developed in order to instantiate the architecture into the RADIO prototype includes acoustic event detection [7–9], machine vision [10, 11], pattern recognition in range data [12], and localization [13].

3   Integrating Smart Home Systems and Robotics Technology

In the context of RADIO, the smart home service and the robot service are integrated into a unique solution. The data communication between the smart home and the robot is achieved through the smart home controller or the IoT platforms supported. As designed, the components of the RADIO ecosystem are the smart home platform (comprised by heterogeneous WSN technologies), IoT platform, and the robot platform. The smart home platform contains sensors and actuators deployed in the home location and the Smart Home Controller (SHC). The IoT platform is a collection of smart home services outside the boundaries of the smart home that aims to provide more complex automation functionality, such as the request of historical data by the robot.

The integration between the smart home platform and the IoT platform provides the following services:

- Remote management of the sensors and actuators: manage sensor values, mange sensor and actuators status, and download sensor firmware. The SHC is responsible of (i) acquiring data from sensors by using communication protocols such as WiFi, Z-Wave and Bluetooth Low Energy (BLE) (ii) storing the last state/values from the sensors and actuators, and (iii) sending this information to the IoT platform to be stored as historical data when new information arrives.
- Management of the data generated by the sensors.
- Real-time event communication between the IoT platform and the smart home: Two solutions are supported. On one hand service API relies on ASP.NET SignalR technology that provides real-time web functionality in order to support a "server push" feature. On the other hand, an MQTT communication architecture is deployed between the main control and smart home controller enhancing respective flexibilities and capabilities.

Secure communication: Standard security mechanisms such as authentication mechanisms, self-signed certificates and HTTPS protocols have been developed. The integration between the smart home, the IoT platform, and the robot platform enables the addition of new functionalities to the RADIO ecosystem. Finally, the development of this overall integration within the RADIO context enabled the provision of several added value functionalities such as:

- Recognition of a wider number of ADLs by using smart home information.
- Cross platform and cross-WSN data combination: The robot platform will detect activity patterns that will be complemented with data coming from the smart home platform capable of modelling user behaviour based on household energy consumption data.
- Correlation exploration, between the household energy consumption data and a user's wellness. The household energy consumption pattern anomalies represent changes in user behaviour.
- Enhance robot's functionalities, e.g. allowing the control of the smart home actuators by the robot.

4 Embedded Systems Design and Hardware Accelerators

The RADIO robot is outfitted with two processing units: an Intel NUC which is responsible for controlling sensors and actuators and an Avnet PicoZed equipped with Xilinx Zynq-7000 all programmable System on Chip (APSoC). Apart from the FPGA fabric, the Xilinx platform includes also an ARM Cortex A9 processor interfaced with programmable logic. In general, there are two types of data processed in the system:

- *High throughput streaming data* that comes from continually receiving the output of a microphone (audio stream) or a camera (video stream)
- *Event or control-like data* with relatively small size, collected by sensors. Event/measurement data can also be the outcome of streaming data analysis, e.g., processing of video can lead to the generation of an "exit" event.

As noted, the assisted living approach heavily relies on the collection of audio and video streams for recognizing ADLs or the identification of emergency situations, such as the detection of falls. As a result, the main processing engine(s) of the robot are designed as a power-efficient architecture for streaming data processing.

Figure 2 illustrates the streaming data flow through the robot processing elements and their interfaces. Depending on the specific combination of algorithms that get

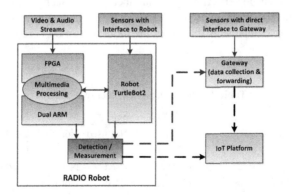

Fig. 2. The main data flow scenario

triggered, the computational tasks may be executed in the (i) NUC, (ii) Zynq ARM processor, or (iii) accelerated by hardware components in the FPGA. To put this into perspective, an example state-diagram of the robot is presented in Fig. 3.

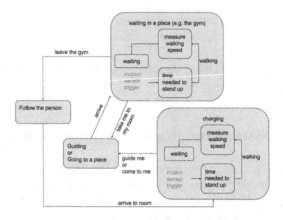

Fig. 3. State diagram highlighting different modes

If all subsystems are always active, the RADIO robot will need to be recharged every few hours, which results in long periods of robot non-availability. As a first step, we had to understand how each subsystem is used and if it indeed needs to be active at each use case. Table 1 provides an overview of the derived states:

- *Waiting:* at this state, the robot is not moving; neither it is processing sensor data. It will be triggered by some external event
- *Moving:* when leading the way or following a person
- *Monitoring:* at this state, the robot is not moving but it is processing sensor input data in order to detect an ADL or understand patient's mood

The energy consumed at each state by each subsystem is not the same. For example, the CPU while waiting can be clocked at lower frequency, drastically reducing the required power. Although a number of such techniques are used, their impact on power consumption is not drastic. To this end, our view is to develop dedicated hardware components that allow the robot to turn-off specific subsystems in some cases.

Table 1. Robot subsystem energy usage

State	CPU	FPGA	Sensors	Motors	Network
Waiting	Used	Not used	Not used	Not used	Used
Moving	Used	Used	Used	Used	Used
Monitoring/Away	Used	Used	Used	Not used	Used
Monitoring/Charging	Used	Used	Used	Not used	Used

4.1   FPGA Hardware Accelerators

In order to reduce the time spent in full operation mode, the PicoZed is connected to an additional camera, the PYTHON FMC camera. The image data from this camera is directly fed to FPGA hardware of the PicoZed. While in this low power mode, only the FPGA part of the system is running, all other components are in sleep mode, thus reducing the energy consumption of the overall system dramatically. The complete PicoZed accelerator architecture can be seen in Fig. 4. The main components of this architecture are the hardware acceleration and the low power operation components, highlighted in red. Table 2 shows the resource utilization of the complete architecture.

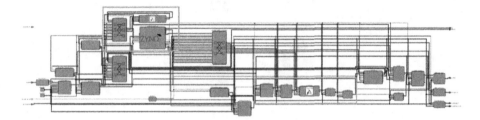

Fig. 4. Complete hardware architecture of the PicoZed SoC (Color figure online)

Table 2. Resource utilization of the PicoZed architecture

Resource	Utilization %	Resource	Utilization %
LUT	35.727444	BRAM	57.14286
LUTRAM	7.695402	DSP	9.090909
FF	24.675753	IO	30.5

The resource utilization of the different resources does not exceed 60%, meaning we have more than enough space to implement more accelerators on hardware. Even if the resource utilization would be higher, we could still support more accelerators because Xilinx FPGAs allow partial dynamic reconfiguration which enables us to map several hardware accelerators onto the same part of the FPGA and load them when it is necessary.

5   Communication Infrastructure

Domestic homes of elderly people pose multiple, multifaceted and important communication challenges. On one hand, a complete plug and play solution is designed integrating all required communication capabilities (both local and remote) assuming insufficient technological infrastructure provided by the home itself. On the other hand, a wide range of diverse communication technologies and sensors are integrated and collaborate. Figure 5 indicates the overall RADIO communication infrastructure consisting of: (i) the local, wireless communication of the components deployed within each RADIO Home and (ii) the backhaul communication between each RADIO Home and remote back-end infrastructure facilitating storage, processing and notification services at the hospital are-givers' facilities.

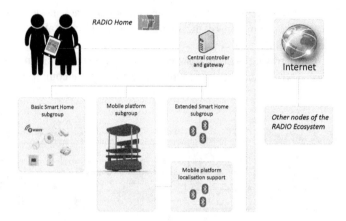

Fig. 5. Architecture of RADIO Home communication channels

Aiming to provide a holistic and of significant added value platform challenges are addressed and extension are proposed in the following subgroups.

Basic smart home: off-the shelf smart home devices. In order to provide long term support and reliability, the *basic smart home* sensor and actuator devices rely on COTS components such as Z-Wave products. Z-Wave is a wireless communication protocol designed for close range sensor and actuator networks. It does not require a coordinator node as it automatically initializes a full mesh network [14]. However, in the context of RADIO, coordinator nodes are used for Z-Wave in order to ensure connection robustness and reliability. However, by contrast to some current smart home architectures, the individual devices do not rely on internet connectivity for their operation. This is due to the privacy requirement that all raw data processing must be carried out within each home and only high-level event logs should be recorded at cloud storage or other remote databases. Even so, the smart home architecture in RADIO has several requirements that need to be fulfilled regarding the back-end infrastructure. In that respect RADIO integrates a smart home solution called enControl™. Respective platform comprised an initial solution for home automation that is adequately enhanced and upgraded complementing other technologies and developments within RADIO offering the final RADIO solution.

Extended smart home: advanced devices, integrating sensing and low-energy processing, as well as the RADIO Home server. Concerning the *extended smart home subgroup various ultra-low power, open communication solutions have been considered. Following an elicitation process* RADIO invested on BLE to connect devices that carry out sensing and local processing in order to offer enhanced services. Benefitting of the hugely successful Classic Bluetooth, BLE shows significant dynamics compared to analogous technologies. Furthermore, it offers high degree of flexibility both concerning implementation approaches and communication approaches. Apart from offering BLE support, RADIO partners have explored the feasibility of mesh networking over BLE providing new capabilities and increasing the IoT functionalities. Therefore, RADIO designs a mesh mechanism integrated in distributed sensor/actuator devices scattered across the RADIO AAL environment covering both *Network Formation* and *Message Forwarding* functionalities.

Robotic platform, integrating sensors and limited computation functionality. Finally, the mobile platform establishes its own internal network in order to integrate its various sensing and processing elements, but also needs to connect to the overall RADIO Home. The platform is outfitted with two interfaces, the BLE and the WiFi interface. BLE connectivity is provided to support direct access to devices of the extended smart home and WiFi connectivity for data transfer requirements.

Finally, envisioning RADIO as a continuously evolving Cyber Physical System (CPS) platform, typically, short range wireless communication protocols enable data aggregation to a central point (indicated as the Gateway). Although a plethora of different communication technologies (mainly originating from WSN research domain) are available, they offer diverse characteristics exhibiting high degree of incompatibility. In that respect a highly efficient gateway has been designed and explored that is able to support the most prominent short range wireless communication technologies such as IEEE 802.15.4 [15], ZigBee [16], Bluetooth [17], BLE [18] and Z-Wave [19]. Also, a critical goal of the design is to facilitate the continuous development and integration of new solutions. Communication complexity however, is also related to efficient data transfer between the gateway and remote installations like service providers, databases, graphical user interfaces etc. Consequently, the presented gateway design supports both HTTP based communication facilitating well-known technologies such as REST, SOAP as well as more contemporary approaches such as message passing communication aiming to support increased communication complexity.

6 Conclusion

The RADIO project provides an integration approach of robotic equipment in the environment of house automation. To achieve the project's objectives multifaceted challenges were tackled whereas a highly flexible and configurable architecture was developed regarding various research and ICT domains. From the algorithmic point of view in order to offer realistic and practical solutions regarding ADLs observation stringent unobtrusiveness requirements had to be met while designing highly efficient and versatile software tools able to support diverse application scenarios. Additionally, such components had to be seamlessly integrated into state-of-art robotic platform comprising the main entity of the whole RADIO platform with which the end-user mainly interact. Envisioning RADIO platform as a continuously evolving system able to be used in an extending range of real life cases, multiple heterogeneous communication technologies had to be supported. In that respect a highly efficient home controller was designed and developed allowing the interaction and collaboration between sensors/actuators supporting different ultra-low power communication protocols. Communication challenges extended beyond the local house area, posing critical requirements regarding reliable and highly configurable backend IoT infrastructures, representing a major concern of the RADIO communication infrastructure. Additionally, configurable hardware based solutions came into play to address processing capabilities limitations as well as scarce energy availability typically encountered in low cost robotic platforms. Finally, multifaceted integration effort was also required so as all developed components are combined into a single robust and reliable platform evaluated in three distinct evaluation phases.

Acknowledgment. The work described here was carried out in the context of the RADIO project. This project has received funding from the European Union's Horizon 2020 research and innovation programme under grant agreement No. 643892. For more details, please visit the RADIO Web site http://www.radio-project.eu.

References

1. Lee, R.: The outlook for population growth. Science **333**, 569–573 (2011)
2. Kash, B.A., Hawes, C., Phillips, C.D.: Comparing staffing levels in the Online Survey Certification and Reporting (OSCAR) system with the medicaid cost report data: are differences systematic? Gerontologist **47**(4), 480–489 (2007)
3. Weech-Maldonado, R., Meret-Hanke, L., Neff, M.C., Mor, V.: Nurse staffing patterns and quality of care in nursing homes. Health Care Manag. Rev. **29**(2), 107–116 (2004)
4. Hensel, B.K., Demiris, G., Courtney, K.L.: Defining obtrusiveness in home telehealth technologies: a conceptual framework. J. Am. Med. Inform. Assoc. **13**(4), 428–431 (2006)
5. Giannakopoulos, T., Konstantopoulos, S., Siantikos, G., Karkaletsis, V.: Design for a system of multimodal interconnected ADL recognition services. In: Keramidas, G., Voros, N., Hübner, M. (eds.) Components and Services for IoT Platforms, pp. 323–333. Springer, Cham (2017). https://doi.org/10.1007/978-3-319-42304-3_16
6. Stavrinos, G., Konstantopoulos, S.: The rostune package: monitoring systems of distributed ROS nodes. In: ROSCon 2017, Vancouver, Canada (2017)
7. Siantikos, G., Giannakopoulos, T., Konstantopoulos, S.: Monitoring activities of daily living using audio analysis and a RaspberryPI: a use case on bathroom activity monitoring. In: Röcker, C., O'Donoghue, J., Ziefle, M., Helfert, M., Molloy, W. (eds.) ICT4AWE 2016. CCIS, vol. 736, pp. 20–32. Springer, Cham (2017). https://doi.org/10.1007/978-3-319-62704-5_2
8. Giannakopoulos, T., Konstantopoulos, S.: Daily activity recognition based on meta-classification of low-level audio events. In: Proceedings of the 3rd International Conference on Information and Communication Technologies for Ageing Well and e-Health (ICT4AWE 2017), Porto, Portugal, 28–29 April 2017 (2017)
9. Giannakopoulos, T., Siantikos, G.: A ROS framework for audio-based activity recognition. In: Proceedings of the 9th ACM International Conference on Pervasive Technologies Related to Assistive Environments (PETRA 2016), Corfu, 29 June–1 July 2016 (2016)
10. Papakostas, M., Giannakopoulos, T., Makedon, F., Karkaletsis, V.: Short-term recognition of human activities using convolutional neural networks. In: Proceedings of the 12th International IEEE Conference on Signal-Image Technology & Internet Based Systems (SITIS 2016), Naples, Italy, 28 November–1 December 2016 (2016)

11. Schwiegelshohn, F., Al Kadi, M., Wehner, P., Smoluk, P., Hübner, M., Göhringer, D.: Accelerating image processing algorithms for the RADIO project's assistant robot system. In: Jasperneite, J., Lohweg, V. (eds.) Kommunikation und Bildverarbeitung in der Automation. TA, pp. 233–245. Springer, Heidelberg (2018). https://doi.org/10.1007/978-3-662-55232-2_18

12. Zamani, K., Stavrinos, G., Konstantopoulos, S.: Detecting and measuring human walking in laser scans. Submitted to the 10th Hellenic Conference on Artificial Intelligence (SETN 2018), Patras, Greece (2018)

13. Schwiegelshohn, F., Wehner, P., Werner, F., Göhringer, D., Hübner, M.: Enabling indoor object localization through bluetooth beacons on the RADIO robot platform. In: Proceedings of the International Conference on Embedded Computer Systems: Architectures, Modeling and Simulation (SAMOS XV), Samos, Greece, 18–21 July 2016. IEEE, January 2017

14. Z-Wave Alliance. http://z-wavealliance.org/. Accessed Aug 2015

15. http://standards.ieee.org/about/get/802/802.15.html

16. Zigbee Specification, January 2008

17. Bluetooth, Specifications (SIG), Version 1.1 (2001)

18. Bluetooth SIG (Hrsg.): Specification of the Bluetooth System: Covered Core Package version: 4.0, June 2010

19. OpenZWave: (n.d.). OpenZWave Google Code. https://code.google.com/p/openzwave/. Accessed June 2013

HLS Algorithmic Explorations for HPC Execution on Reconfigurable Hardware - ECOSCALE

Pavlos Malakonakis, Konstantinos Georgopoulos$^{(\boxtimes)}$, Aggelos Ioannou,
Luciano Lavagno, Ioannis Papaefstathiou, and Iakovos Mavroidis

Telecommunication Systems Institute, Campus Kounoupidiana,
Technical University of Crete, Chania, Greece
kgeorgopoulos@isc.tuc.gr

Abstract. Modern-day High Performance Computing (HPC) trends are shifting towards exascale performance figures in order to satisfy the contemporary needs of many compute-intensive and power-hungry applications. It is in this context that the EU-funded ECOSCALE project came about. It introduces a highly innovative architecture that offers spreading the workload among a number of independent concurrently operating standard and reconfigurable processing elements that execute OpenCL cores as well as minimising the need for data transfers. The particular cores implemented on the ECOSCALE prototype correspond to the project use cases and have been the source of a meticulous exploration process for optimal performance results such as execution time. This paper documents the synthesis process for two ECOSCALE algorithms, i.e. *Hyperbolic* and *Michelsen*. They are both seminal in the calculation of the Rachford-Rice equation used extensively in the field of oil Reservoir Simulation (RS). The two algorithms are first optimised manually by proficient designers in the field using Vivado HLS. Subsequently, additional processing is performed based on a specialised Design Space Exploration (DSE) tool that delivers synthesisable code for reconfigurable logic implementation. Finally, the resulting reconfigurable cores are executed on the ECOSCALE system in order to perform measurements on real data. The evaluation results reveal significant benefits in calculation times over conventional CPU platforms which merits even better considering that they come at a significantly reduced power consumption cost.

Keywords: High-level synthesis · Reconfigurable hardware
OpenCL · Exascale

1 Introduction

In order to sustain the ever-increasing demand for storing, transferring and mainly processing data, HPC servers need to improve their capabilities. Scaling in number of cores alone is not a feasible solution any more due to the

© Springer International Publishing AG, part of Springer Nature 2018
N. Voros et al. (Eds.): ARC 2018, LNCS 10824, pp. 724–736, 2018.
https://doi.org/10.1007/978-3-319-78890-6_58

increasing utility costs and power consumption limitations. While current HPC systems can offer petaflop performance, their architecture limits their capabilities in terms of scalability and energy consumption. To that end, the ECOSCALE [6,10] approach puts forward a scalable programming environment combined with a hardware architecture tailored to the current and future trends of HPC applications. Such an approach can facilitate significant reduction in network traffic as well as energy consumption and execution time. This is due to the reconfigurable technologies for data processing involved in the system, which are economical in energy consumption, memory units spread out across the system as well as the UNILOGIC architecture [6], which allows for efficient sharing of reconfigurable resources in a multi-FPGA system.

Subsequently, at the core of the ECOSCALE system, which consists of multiple interconnected FPGAs, lies a processing element tasked with performing a specific type of calculation. This takes place in the reconfigurable part of the architecture. Hence, those elements are re-programmable and can be reconfigured in order to implement different types of functionality since the corresponding hardware fabric allows it. In ECOSCALE nomenclature, these processing elements are called *accelerator cores* since they are destined to implement functional blocks of popular algorithms involved in HPC applications in a way that delivers results faster than was originally possible.

These cores are implemented using a High-Level Synthesis (HLS) [2] process that starts off with a high-level description of the desired algorithm in OpenCL [9], and finishes with the production of its Register-Transfer Level (RTL) [3] equivalent in the form of an IP block. The key here is for the HLS stage to perform this transformation in a way that produces a functional block that is efficient in terms of important parameters such as performance, latency, power consumption and area.

This paper documents this process for two ECOSCALE use case algorithms, i.e. *Hyperbolic* and *Michelsen*. These two algorithms facilitate the calculation of the Rachford-Rice [1] equation which is effectively responsible for providing insight as to the flow of liquids in the depths of an oil reservoir. They are variations on the Newton-Raphson [5] method that provide results at less iterations and, therefore, in less time.

The two algorithms have gone through a design space exploration process that consists of both a manual and an automated approach. First, ECOSCALE designers meticulously analyse the original high-level OpenCL description of the algorithm of interest in order to perform appropriate code modifications that potentially lead to performance optimisation. Second, a specialised tool, designed within ECOSCALE, uses as basis the description of the manual stage and subjects it to an automatic DSE [4] process in order to perform further optimisations and, therefore, deliver a highly-efficient accelerator IP core.

Finally, the resulting RTL models for both algorithms have been executed on the current ECOSCALE prototype and real measurements have been obtained allowing for key observations to be extracted in relation to important *evaluation criteria* such as execution time, power consumption and resource utilisation.

The paper is organised as follows. Section 2 provides a brief but concise introduction to the ECOSCALE architecture and Sect. 3 provides a short description of RS simulation. Subsequently, Sect. 4 presents the design space exploration activities performed on both algorithms and Sect. 5 unfolds a thorough evaluation analysis on the system's performance based on the cores generated earlier. Finally, Sect. 6 concludes the paper.

2   The ECOSCALE System

ECOSCALE provides a methodology and the corresponding architecture that automatically executes HPC applications on a platform, which, can potentially support thousands or millions of reconfigurable hardware blocks, while taking into account the projected trends and characteristics of HPC applications. Within this context, ECOSCALE aims at introducing FPGA-based acceleration as an integral part of the processing nodes within the system architecture and adapting them to work in an HPC environment.

At the heart of the ECOSCALE system lay several *Workers* communicating through a multi-layer interconnection, Fig. 1. The actual number of Workers inside a single Compute Node depends on the integration capabilities of future technologies. Each Worker is an independent computing node, which runs an Operating System (OS) that can execute, fork, and join tasks or threads of an HPC application in parallel with other Workers. It includes a CPU, a reconfigurable block and an off-chip DRAM memory. The communication and synchronisation between Workers is performed through a multi-layer interconnection, which allows load and store commands, DMA operations, interrupts, and synchronisation between Workers within a Compute Node. Compute Nodes are interconnected in a tree-like structure to form larger Partitioned Global Address Space (PGAS) regions also hierarchically interconnected [6].

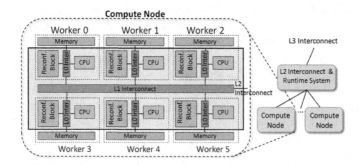

Fig. 1. The Compute Node & its use within the ECOSCALE tree-like structure

3   Use Cases

Reservoir Simulation (RS) is the state-of-the-art technology used to predict oil-field performance under several possible production schemes. It combines the physical laws applying to the oil production process, that is mass and energy conservation, flow in porous media and thermodynamic phase equilibrium together with differential equation numerical solution techniques, in order to come up with a prediction of the future oil and gas production. From a mathematical point of view, the difficulty in treating such problems lies in the fact that they consist of tightly coupled systems of non-linear differential and algebraic equations exhibiting significant spatial and temporal dependency.

Subsequently, the tank reservoir model has been analysed by employing, at different grid points, the Rachford-Rice equation. This is an important equation since it provides insight as to the liquid and vapour elements within the porous material of the rock substrate. The algorithm that solves for the Rachford-Rice equation is the Newton-Raphson method. This is a complicated method that involves multiple iterations at each grid point in order to determine the composition of liquid and vapour elements at each timestep of the simulation.

In this work we describe the implementation of two kernels that are variations of the Newton-Raphson method, specifically tuned for the RS problem. The respective OpenCL kernels used in this work are Hyperbolic and Michelsen and provide a faster convergence in solving the Rachford-Rice equation for oil reservoir simulation.

4   Reconfigurable Cores

The implementation of the reconfigurable cores has occurred in two distinct steps, i.e. a manual process and an ECOSCALE tool-based automated process. Regarding the former, it is common for conventional CPU-targeted software implementations not to be very efficient when directly implemented on FPGAs. Hence, manual code transformations are needed in order to reach efficient hardware implementations. In the Hyperbolic and Michelsen cases, at each grid point, the original OpenCL code is sequential due to a *while* loop, and the aim of the optimisations is to introduce and maximise parallelism. Subsequently, a set of directives have been manually introduced for further optimisation benefits.

Regarding the latter step, the work has been heavily based on Xilinx's Vivado HLS [11]. This is a tool that produces equivalent RTL designs to high-level model descriptions of various algorithms. The Vivado HLS tool offers a set of *Directives* in order to make the respective codes more efficient for FPGA implementation. Therefore, the process has been to start off with an initial set of directives as well as code modifications introduced manually that improve the performance of the OpenCL kernels. Consequently, further exploration steps have been performed automatically using the ECOSCALE *Design Space Exploration* (DSE) tool. The DSE tool provided an additional set of directives for the OpenCL kernels of the manual stage and delivered the final version used in the production of the accelerator core.

```
int a
int b
for (all grid points)
        /*initialization*/
        a=amin
        b=bmin
        operation 3
        ....
        while(optimization
target)
                b=b+1
                a=a+1
                operation 3
                operation 4
                ....
        end while
        operation 1
        ......
        write result
end for
```

```
Buffer data
/*All variables become arrays*/
int a[pipeline_size]
int b[pipeline_size]
while (all problems solved)
        for (n : all grid points)
                if (initialization)
                        /*initialization*/
                        a[n]=amin
                        b[n]=bmin
                        operation 3
                        ....
                end if
                else /*while loop code*/
                        b[n]=b[n]+1
                        a[n]=a[n]+1
                        operation 3
                        operation 4
                        ....
                        If (optimization reached)
                                operation 1
                                ......
                                write result[n]
                                solved++
                        end if
                end else
        end for
end while
```

Fig. 2. Initial RS pseudocode   **Fig. 3.** Optimised RS pseudocode

4.1   Manual Code Optimisation

The manual analysis consisted of carefully investigating the two OpenCL kernels, i.e. Hyperbolic and Michelsen. The main characteristic of the algorithms that could be taken advantage of is that of multiple small *optimisation* problems, which are independent of one another. The suitable way for doing this is by pipelining the process.

The original OpenCL pseudocode of the target application looks like the one shown in Fig. 2. The problem here is that this form of the code description does not allow for the use of a pipeline directive due to the *while* loop, otherwise called *optmisation* loop since the coefficient it produces approximates, to an acceptable level of deviation, a real-life value. This loop is burdened with dependencies as well as being non-statically bounded, thereby making it a sequential process that cannot be pipelined. This would make the FPGA implementation of such algorithms inefficient due to the inherently slow FPGA clock frequency, which results in significant slow downs compared to the equivalent software running on a conventional processor.

Unrolling the *for* loop at the top was also investigated, however, no significant benefits were obtained, hence, this option was rejected. That is because it led to a small speedup at a cost of significantly high area overhead.

Hence, we propose a method for making such cases efficient for implementation on FPGAs. The HLS tools cannot pipeline non-statically bounded *while* loops but they can pipeline statically bounded loops very efficiently. A restriction is that the small optimisation problems have to be independent from one another. Therefore, we had to move the *while* loop to the top of the code and the *for* loop inside it. As such the tool can pipeline the latter which results in significant speedups. Consequently, the pseudocode that represents the modified architecture is shown in Fig. 3. The resulting architecture consumes significantly more resources as it needs a buffer for each variable in order for the processing to be independent between the steps. The two architectures, i.e. *initial* and *optimised* are also graphically depicted in Figs. 4 and 5. Note that both Hyperbolic and Michelsen algorithms have essentially the same pseudocode, hence, they are discussed together.

The improvement of such an approach is that the hardware that would remain unused while each loop is executing is now utilised by another optimisation problem. Each independent problem will have exactly the same amount of iterations inside the *while* loop as it had with the previous code.

The analysis that can show the effectiveness of the method is as follows. For the conventional method the required latency is:

$$total\_latency = init\_time * opt\_problems + while\_latency * avg\_num\_iter * opt\_problems$$

where *init_time* includes the I/O of the data as well as the initialisation before the loop, *while_latency* is the latency of the operations of the *while* loop, *avg_num_iter* the average number of iterations each problem needs, and *opt_problems* the amount of problems that are solved.

Subsequently, the latency of the optimised code that supports pipelining is:

$$total\_latency = input\_time * opt\_problems + pipeline\_latency + avg\_num\_iter * opt\_problems$$

where *input_time* is the I/O time, which is less than the *init_time* as the *init* is in the pipeline, and *pipeline_latency* is the latency of the pipeline within the *for* loop, greater than *while_latency* as it includes the *init* stage counted only once at the start of each calculation as well as the operations needed for the application of the method.

As we can see the *while_latency* is multiplicative over the product between *opt_problems* and *avg_num_iter* on the initial method latency. On the other hand, the optimised code's *pipeline_latency* is additive. The pipelining of the operations allows the completion of one iteration, i.e. *while* iteration, every clock cycle. The expected speedup should be comparable with *while_latency*, as instead of paying the full latency of the *while* loop the same operation is completed every clock cycle.

Finally, as a bridge to the next step of the automated tool-based analysis, an initial set of directives have been added in order to provide Vivado HLS the proper guidelines to produce the expected pipelined architecture.

Fig. 4. Block diagram of initial architecture

4.2   Automated - Tool-Based DSE

Optimising OpenCL code for FPGA implementation by using Vivado HLS requires a significant amount of effort. The task is to guide the compiler to generate optimised compute and memory architectures for each kernel. In other words, the design problem is reversed, from optimising the application for the architecture (on a CPU or GPU) to optimising the architecture for the code (on an FPGA). However, the advantages in terms of energy consumption per kernel execution, and sometimes in terms of performance, more than justify the additional effort.

The Xilinx OpenCL high-level synthesis tool, namely Vivado HLS, is used to optimise the code for execution on the Xilinx FPGAs. It requires significant manual annotations of the code with both standard and Xilinx-specific OpenCL attributes in order to achieve a good level of performance. Hence, the DSE tool has been used to enable automated design space exploration and micro-architecture definition without requiring the designer to specifically know the architectural features of the underlying FPGA.

More specifically The ECOSCALE DSE tool consists of a set of programs and scripts that:

- Take as input an FPGA-neutral OpenCL application, composed of a set of kernels and some host code.
- Parse and analyse the OpenCL code to identify areas of the code whose performance, cost or power consumption can be affected by a judicious usage of synthesis directives.
- Generate a full or partial set of design space exploration options, consisting of legal combinations of those synthesis directives. Of course a partial set ensures faster exploration at the price of some optimality. Currently the designer is in charge of selecting which general areas of optimisation should be explored, e.g. whether loop unrolling should be used at all.
- Execute in a controlled fashion a set of parallel runs of the Vivado HLS synthesis tool, in order to generate a large set of solutions. Parallel execution is essential in order to keep design time limited while exploiting modern multi-core CPUs and multi-CPU compute farms.
- Read back the results, from the synthesis runs in order to (i) Compile a set of Pareto-optimal points, i.e. dominating all other micro-architectures in terms of at least area or performance and (ii) Make decisions about how to prune the design space in case only partial DSE is performed.

Subsequently, DSE was applied to the manually modified kernels of the reservoir simulation, mainly the optimised Hyperbolic kernels. As the Michelsen and Hyperbolic kernels have exactly the same structure and only differ in terms of mathematical operations, the Pareto-optimal solution for the Hyperbolic kernels will be the same with the Michelsen kernels. On the optimised hyperbolic kernel the DSE algorithm explored 256 points in the design space, and found the Pareto-optimal design points shown in Fig. 6. The red dot identifies the best manual design that had been discovered before DSE was applied. Note that in this specific case, only two Pareto points, namely P94 and P153, have sufficiently different performance and area to be considered meaningful. For example, point P132 achieves 2% better performance than P153, but at the cost of 2X the area.

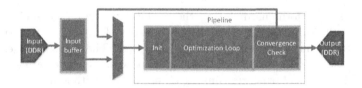

Fig. 5. Block diagram of optimised architecture

4.3   Implementation Summary

The DSE provided the Pareto-optimal points presented above. The manual design (red dot) appears to be sub-optimal because it includes the *pipeline* directive in the main *for* loop. P94 and P153 have excluded this directive, which is expected to provide the highest increase in performance. This was due to the fact that the DSE tool has to perform using small data sets in order to be able to complete in a meaningful amount of time. However, the price to be paid for this faster exploration was an incorrect estimation of the overall performance, and hence of the quality of the solution.

Eventually the optimal solution has been a merging between the manual and P153 points. Hence, the *pipeline* directive was added to the main *for* loop, while the rest of the directives were taken from the P153 point. Also some directives were removed from the *for* loop body as they were overwritten by the previously mentioned *pipeline* directive.

Furthermore, the same set of directives was chosen for the Michelsen kernel as they provided the highest increase in performance after several design tries. For the initial kernels, a manual set of directives was chosen as the appropriate directives were obvious. The main calculations are done inside the unbounded *while* loop body which cannot take any performance oriented directive. The only meaningful performance improvement was achieved by partitioning the temporary input tables which allowed pipelining the smaller *for* loops over the components in the code, including those inside the *while* loop.

5   Evaluation

The generated accelerator cores have been evaluated on the ECOSCALE architecture, using an intermediate prototype that is comprised of two Workers. The cores have been mapped to the reconfigurable fabric of one of the Workers and measurements have been obtained with respect to the execution time of the two algorithms on two data sets of different size, i.e. data for 100K and 200K grid points. Subsequently, the measured times have been compared against those for the identical procedure but on a different execution platform, i.e. i5 Quad-core CPU at 3.1 GHz.

5.1   Implementation Platform

The hardware platform used during the evaluation phase is made up of the current ECOSCALE Worker. This Worker consists of two separate boards, i.e. the TE0808 and the TEBF0808 by Trenz Electronic. The TE0808 [7] features a Xilinx Zynq UltraScale+ (US+) MPSoC device, which includes a 64-bit quad-core ARM Cortex-A53 platform running up to 1.2 GHz with a dual-core Cortex-R5 real-time processor up to 600 MHz. The board also provides 2 GB of DDR4 SDRAM coupled to the US+ device.

Subsequently, the Trenz Electronic TEBF0808 Mini-ITX baseboard [8] has been developed specifically for the TE0808 MPSoC. This is a baseboard that enhances the utilisation potential of the TE0808 by providing a range of different I/O, communication and multimedia ports and storage capabilities.

5.2   Results

The measured results have been obtained under a set of specific conditions and parameters. Specifically, the DSE process resulted in four different accelerator cores, i.e. two for the Hyperbolic algorithm and two for the Michelsen. Multiple sets of such cores can execute the same mathematical algorithm in-parallel and on the same set of data, thereby, taking full advantage of the parallel nature of reconfigurable hardware.

Hence, for measuring the results we utilised different numbers of accelerator cores and the execution of the Hyperbolic and Michelsen algorithms on a data size of 100K grid points using the initial HLS description to generate a core is shown in Fig. 7.

Here, a number of observations can be made. First, the actual execution times are very low. However, the time drops almost linearly up to the mid-point of four cores and from that point onwards the time reduction begins to level-off. That is because the data transfer time begins to play a part, i.e. the cores are not being fed the data needed for performing the calculations fast enough.

Subsequently, the optimised accelerator core results are shown in Fig. 8. This time the number of parallel cores has been up to four. Hence, providing data to the accelerators does not limit significantly the performance since there is an almost entirely linear relationship between execution time versus number of

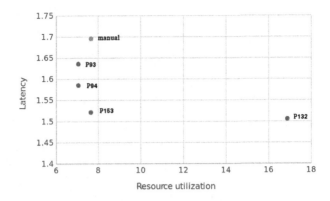

Fig. 6. Automated design space exploration for Reservoir Simulation (Color figure online)

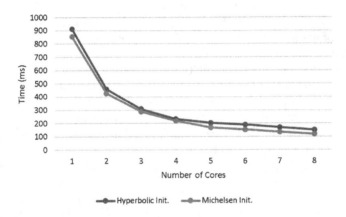

Fig. 7. Execution time (ms) vs. no. of cores - initial

cores. Also, the actual execution times are significantly smaller and are, therefore, indicative of the potential from using such hardware for processing. Also, note that the specific execution times are the result of using a single Worker, i.e. four accelerator cores inside a single Worker, whereas using more Workers would utilise additional accelerators which can lead to additional time reductions.

An additional remark regarding this first set of information has to do with area utilisation. It has been observed that a single US+ FPGA can efficiently accommodate for a maximum of four optimised accelerator cores, whereas it can implement significantly more than eight of the initial ones. However, the latter option would not pay any dividends since the cap imposed by the finite rate at which data can be provided to the cores limits the potential of using many of the initial cores.

Moving on, the execution times achieved by the optimised cores have been compared against those achieved by using conventional processing methods, i.e. a CPU with either a single-thread or a four-thread execution using OpenMP.

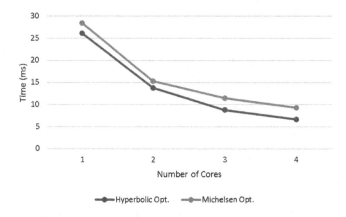

Fig. 8. Execution time (ms) vs. no. of cores - optimised

The best times achieved using these two approaches as well as those achieved by the two sets of implemented cores, i.e. initial and optimised, and on two different data sets have been gathered in Table 1.

It is clear that the execution of the optimised accelerator cores on reconfigurable hardware yields the best performance and this is better displayed in Table 2. First, the optimised cores offer a speedup of 3.8 and 3.1 over single-thread CPU execution for the Hyperbolic and Michelsen algorithms respectively. Even with a four-thread CPU execution a speedup is noted of 1.3 and 1.2 for Hyperbolic and Michelsen respectively.

Moreover, considering that the CPU consumes significantly more power, the advantages of using reconfigurable hardware becomes even more apparent since the CPU comes at a typical cost of 77 Watts of power consumption whereas an average US+ FPGA power consumption is at 7.8 Watts. Hence, this provides an additional order of magnitude in terms of overall energy efficiency for the optimised accelerator cores over that of the four-thread CPU making it 13 and 12 for the Hyperbolic and Michelsen algorithms respectively, as shown in Table 2.

Table 1. Best execution times (ms) between different hardware platforms

Platform	Software			
	CPU		CPU OpenMP (4 thread)	
Data size	100K	200K	100K	200K
Hyperbolic	25.5	50	8.8	17.2
Michelsen	29	56	11.7	22.3
Platform	Hardware			
	Initial 8 core		Optimised 4 core	
Data size	100K	200K	100K	200K
Hyperbolic	151	298	6.7	13.8
Michelsen	117	235	9.3	18

Table 2. Speedup and efficiency attained using HW accelerator cores

	Speedup opt. vs. init	Speedup opt. vs. 4-thread	Speedup opt. vs. 1-thread	Efficiency vs. 4-thread
Hyperbolic opt	22.5	1.3	3.8	13
Michelsen opt	12.5	1.2	3.1	12

6 Conclusions

The ECOSCALE project is a collective effort of European academic and industrial institutions to bring closer the utilisation of reconfigurable technology so as to execute HPC applications at exascale speed. This is achieved through the introduction of a novel architecture, real-time reconfiguration and programming model all integrated into one framework.

This paper demonstrates that by using a combination of manual optimisations together with those achieved by a Design Space Exploration tool implemented within ECOSCALE, we can execute on the ECOSCALE platform mathematical cores very efficiently.

In particular the implemented reconfigurable cores are 20%–30% faster than a state-of-the-art multi-core CPU while consuming an order of magnitude less power.

References

1. Whitson, C., Michelsen, M.: The negative flash. J. Fluid Phase Equilibria **35**, 51–71 (1989)
2. Coussy, P., Morawiec, A.: High-Level Synthesis: From Algorithm to Digital Circuit, 1st edn. Springer Publishing Company, Incorporated, Cham (2008). https://doi.org/10.1007/978-1-4020-8588-8. ISBN 1402085877, 9781402085871
3. Thomas, D., Lagnese, E., Walker, R., Nestor, J., Rajan, J., Blackburn, R.: Algorithmic and Register-Transfer Level Synthesis: The System Architects Workbench. The Kluwer International Series in Engineering and Computer Science, vol. 85, 1st edn. Springer, Boston (1990). https://doi.org/10.1007/978-1-4613-1519-3. ISBN 978-1-4612-8815-2, 978-1-4613-1519-3
4. Kang, E., Jackson, E., Schulte, W.: An approach for effective design space exploration. In: Calinescu, R., Jackson, E. (eds.) Monterey Workshop 2010. LNCS, vol. 6662, pp. 33–54. Springer, Heidelberg (2011). https://doi.org/10.1007/978-3-642-21292-5_3. ISBN 978-3-642-21292-5
5. Milton, A.: Handbook of Mathematical Functions, With Formulas, Graphs, and Mathematical Tables. Dover Publications, Incorporated, New York (1974). ISBN 0486612724
6. Mavroidis, I., Papaefstathiou, I., Lavagno, L., Nikolopoulos, D., Koch, D., Goodacre, J., Sourdis, I., Papaefstathiou, V., Coppola, M., Palomino, M.: ECOSCALE: reconfigurable computing and runtime system for future exascale systems. In: 2016 Design, Automation & Test in Europe Conference & Exhibition, DATE 2016, Dresden, Germany, 14–18 March 2016, pp. 696–701 (2016)

7. TE0808 Overview. http://www.trenz-electronic.de/products/fpga-boards/trenz-electronic/te0808-zynq-ultrascale.html
8. TEBF0808 Overview. https://wiki.trenz-electronic.de/display/PD/TEBF0808
9. OpenCL Overview. https://www.khronos.org/opencl/
10. ECOSCALE Web-Site. http://www.ecoscale.eu/
11. Vivado Design Suite User Guide v2016.2, Xilinx Inc. http://www.xilinx.com/

Supporting Utilities for Heterogeneous Embedded Image Processing Platforms (STHEM): An Overview

Ahmad Sadek[1]([✉])(iD), Ananya Muddukrishna[2], Lester Kalms[1],
Asbjørn Djupdal[2], Ariel Podlubne[1], Antonio Paolillo[3], Diana Goehringer[1](iD),
and Magnus Jahre[2](iD)

[1] TU Dresden, Dresden, Germany
{ahmed.sadek,lester.kalms,ariel.podlubne,diana.goehringer}@tu-dresden.de
[2] Norwegian University of Science and Technology (NTNU), Trondheim, Norway
{ananya.muddukrishna,djupdal,magnus.jahre}@ntnu.no
[3] HIPPEROS S.A., Ottignies-Louvain-la-Neuve, Belgium
antonio.paolillo@hipperos.com

Abstract. The TULIPP project aims to simplify development of embedded vision applications with low-power and real-time requirements by providing a complete image processing system package called the *TULIPP Starter Kit*. To achieve this, the chosen high-performance embedded vision platform needs to be extended with performance analysis and power measurement features. The lack of such features plagues most embedded vision platforms in general and practitioners have adopted ad-hoc methods to circumvent the problem. In this paper, we describe four generic utilities that complement and refine the capabilities of existing platforms for embedded vision applications. Concretely, we describe a novel power measurement and analysis utility, a platform-optimized image processing library, a dynamic partial reconfiguration utility, and an utility providing support for using the real-time OS HIPPEROS within Xilinx SDSoC. Collectively, these utilities enable efficient development of image processing applications on the TULIPP hardware platform. In future work, we will evaluate the relative benefit of these utilities on key embedded image processing metrics such as frame rate and power consumption.

Keywords: Embedded vision · Image processing
Performance analysis · Profiling · Low-power
Dynamic partial reconfiguration

1 Introduction

Image processing is an application domain that deals with image manipulation, transformation and analysis. Images are a diverse class of input data since their width, height and pixel-depth depends strongly on the sensor used to acquire it. The wide variety of sensors and application types makes image processing a

© Springer International Publishing AG, part of Springer Nature 2018
N. Voros et al. (Eds.): ARC 2018, LNCS 10824, pp. 737–749, 2018.
https://doi.org/10.1007/978-3-319-78890-6_59

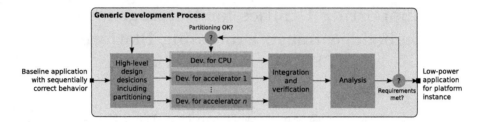

Fig. 1. The generic development process

complex and diverse application domain. Due to the large data volumes, high performance is needed to analyze images in systems with real-time constraints. Furthermore, image processing systems are often deployed in scenarios where power, energy, weight, cost and physical size are first-order constraints. The result is an overwhelming challenge for developers.

The overall objective of the *Towards Ubiquitous Low-power Image Processing Platforms (TULIPP)* project is to reduce the magnitude of this challenge by providing a complete image processing system package that developers can leverage towards their specific embedded application [9]. We refer to this package as the *TULIPP Starter Kit (TSK)* which consists of a reference handbook, project applications and a platform instance. The reference handbook is a high-level best-practice introduction to embedded low-power image processing which is complemented by a collection of concrete, validated guidelines for embedded image processing system design. The project applications are industry-grade examples taken from the medical, automotive and unmanned aerial vehicle domains. Finally, the platform instance consists of a hardware platform, a real-time operating system and a collection of design and analysis tools. In this paper, we focus on the design and analysis tools that we have developed during the first year of the TULIPP project.

The main objective of the TULIPP tools is to contribute to substantially reducing the effort required to implement an image processing solution on selected heterogeneous platforms. The tools guide the developer through step-wise improvements to an image processing implementation and are designed to use the hardware technology and the operating system services developed in TULIPP. The overall development process is based on software optimization best practices by iteratively guiding the developer through successive changes to the code with the aim of achieving real-time performance with maximum energy efficiency. To maximize impact, we leverage existing tools where these are available.

We connect all components of the platform instance – hardware, RTOS, and tools – using an abstraction called the generic development process which is shown in Fig. 1. The generic development process is an iterative process for programmers to implement image processing applications that meet low-power requirements while leveraging the heterogeneous processing resources available on the platform instance. The starting point of the generic development process

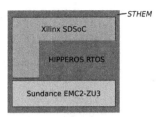

Fig. 2. The TULIPP-PI1 platform instance held together by STHEM to enable the generic development process [8]

is the baseline application that executes with correct sequential behaviour on a modern machine with a general-purpose processor. High-level partitioning decisions decide which baseline functions should be accelerated and how. Partitioning splits off into accelerator-specific development stages that later join to produce an integrated application with the same correct behaviour as the baseline. The performance of the integrated application is checked against requirements. If found lacking, the partitioning and development stages are restarted. In this manner, programmers iteratively refine the baseline application to approach the required low-power and high performance features.

A platform instance can be created using any combination of hardware, RTOS, and development tools. However, support for the generic development process in each platform instance is unlikely to be readily available. For example, all the components of the TULIPP reference platform have independent workflows that partially overlap with the generic development process, and at a more basic level have poor to non-existent support for each other. We build utilities to resolve limitations of components of platform instances to ensure simplified support for the generic development process. Our utilities are collectively called *Supporting uTilities for Heterogeneous EMbedded image processing platforms (STHEM)*. STHEM is designed to be as vendor-independent as possible to simplify implementation for arbitrary platform instances. STHEM includes connecting glue that interfaces independent components together and standalone tools that extend individual components to provide complementary features.

The TULIPP toolchain is a combination of STHEM and existing components of a given platform instance that work together to simplify the generic development process for programmers. Figure 2 shows the TULIPP-PI1 platform instance which is platform instance that the TULIPP consortium is currently focusing most attention on. The reason for the attention is familiarity with the components that make up the platform instance. TULIPP-PI1 consists of the Sundance EMC2-ZU3 carrier board with the Xilinx Zynq UltraScale+ MPSoC processor arranged in a two-board configuration to expose a high degree of parallelism to applications. The hardware is operated seamlessly by the HIPPEROS RTOS. Application development tools in the platform instance are custom adaptations of Xilinx SDSoC and HIPPEROS tools to support multi-board acceleration and real-time requirements.

Table 1. Limitations of TULIPP-PI1 components

Utility	EMC2-ZU3	HIPPEROS	SDSoC
Power Measurement Utility (PMU)	No power measurement hardware	Does not quantify task power consumption	Cannot correlate power consumption with application phases
HIPPEROS & SDSoC (HSCL)		Cannot accelerate tasks on FPGA	No support for HIPPEROS
HW/SW Image Processing Library (IPL)			Few optimized image processing functions

Table 1 lists the limitations of the main TULIPP-PI1 components and how our utilities alleviate these limitations. The current version of STHEM includes the three utilities that are necessary to provide a minimal end-to-end image processing system for the TULIPP-PI1 platform:

- The *Power Measurement Utility (PMU)* provides hardware support for measuring power in the EMC2-ZU3 and enables programmers to correlate instantaneous power samples with concurrent HIPPEROS application tasks and SDSoC's HW/SW traces.
- *HW/SW Image Processing Libraries (IPL)* enables high performance and productivity for commonly used image processing operations.
- *Dynamic Partial Reconfiguration Utility (DPRU)* enables runtime reconfiguration of the FPGA fabric which can be used both within a single image processing algorithm and by the OS to switch accelerators at runtime.
- The *HIPPEROS SDSoC Compatibility Layer (HSCL)* adds HIPPEROS support to SDSoC, enabling programmers to accelerate HIPPEROS application tasks on FPGA accelerators.

The rest of the paper is organized as follows. Section 2 describes the implementation of the PMU, IPL, DPRU and HSCL utilities which is the main contribution of the paper. We conclude the paper and indicate further work in Sect. 3.

2   STHEM Utilities

The STHEM utilities are a set of components that facilitate the development of low power image processing systems, shown in Fig. 2. In the current phase of the project, they integrate different tools and components in a single suite to make them easier to use for developers.

2.1   Power Measurement Utility (PMU)

Improving the power efficiency of embedded applications begins with prudent device selection. For example, choosing FPGAs made with latest FinFET technology [1]. Once the device is fixed, power efficiency is refined to desired levels in successive stages of profiling and optimization. Profiling uses power models during early design phases, and shifts to real-hardware measurements post-implementation. While standard power profiling methods are available for HPC-like systems [16], power profiling in embedded systems remains largely ad-hoc [2, 4, 13, 17, 26].

The Xilinx Zynq-based embedded platform that we have chosen for the applications of the TULIPP project, has poor support for power profiling. Neither hardware nor vendor tools have support for measuring power consumption at runtime. This complicates selection of application phases to direct power optimizations and makes it difficult to judge whether low-power requirements are met. Ultimately, a key contribution of the project – design guidelines for low-power embedded vision – cannot be demonstrated.

To solve this problem, we first looked towards solutions recommended by vendors. Xilinx recommends adding on-board current sensors such as precision shunt resistors to provide current measurements to the XADC [27], a hard-IP block in the FPGA substrate of the Zynq. A better solution, also recommended by Xilinx, is to replace the voltage regulators on the hardware platform with digital power controllers from Texas Instruments (TI) to measure current and voltages supplied to all power planes [24]. Another option is to use special measurement-friendly variants of the embedded platform built by third-parties [23]. While useful, these recommended hardware modifications were prohibitive due to cost reasons. We also deliberated about a model-only approach, i.e., use the Xilinx-provided power model called the *XPE* [26] to refine power efficiency as much as possible during early design phases. However, XPE can at best provide coarse-grained estimates and cannot correlate power problems with application phases.

We decided in the end to build external, cost-effective measurement hardware, complemented by specialized profiling software, to diagnose power problems of TULIPP applications at runtime and, in general, advance the state-of-the-art in power profiling of embedded vision applications.

Power profiling implementation: Our power profiling approach is packaged as the PMU. It essentially consists of an external measurement board that communicates power measurements to profiling tools on the host computer, as shown in Fig. 3. The external measurement board is custom-designed and has multiple current sensors that measure power consumed by individual *units of interest* on the embedded platform, i.e., the EMC2-DP board in TULIPP-PI1. Profiling tools collect additional profiling data from EMC2-DP and analyze it together with power measurements to diagnose problems. Problems are shown on various visualization widgets, some of which are part of existing vendor tools.

We developed an external measurement board which we call *Lynsyn*. Lynsyn uses two INA169 current-shunt monitors [22] from TI to measure and amplify currents across 0.1Ω shunt resistors connected in series with high-side current wires/PCB-tracks that drive units of interest on the EMC2-DP. Measurements from the current-shunt monitors are sampled by a Teensy 3.6 microcontroller [21] using 13-bits and transmitted over USB to the host computer at approximately 12K samples per second. This rate supports measurements of

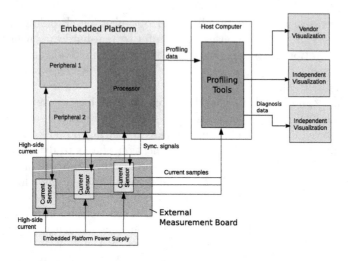

Fig. 3. Overview of power profiling

application tasks with runtime longer than 83 micro-seconds. Synchronization signals are sent over JTAG and LVTTL GPIO ports on the EMC2-DP to the Teensy to control measurements. At present, we consider two units of interest – the Zynq SoM and the FMC port that connects to the camera. Lynsyn can sense currents between 250 mA to 3 A. Measuring currents lower than 250 mA is possible by using larger shunt resistors. The BoM cost of Lynsyn is less than 50 US dollars. A protoboard version of Lynsyn connected to the EMC2 (non-stacked) is shown in Fig. 4.

We validated the current measurements from Lynsyn using the Uni-T UT139C true-RMS digital multimeter as a reference for two hours of continuous operation. Current measurements had negligible differences compared to the reference. Rigorous testing with a constant current load is planned as part of future work.

Lynsyn's design assumes that it is possible to insert shunt resistors in all current-carrying lines of interest. However, not all current-carrying lines are accessible. For example, rails that supply power to the FPGA substrate of the Zynq SoM are buried due to dense packaging constraints. Potential workarounds include using current-mirrors to avoid inserting shunt resistors [13], or using special test fixtures that expose current-carrying lines on top layers [23].

Power visualizations: Current samples sent from Lynsyn to the host computer are converted to power readings assuming a constant supply voltage and stored in the Common Trace Format (CTF) [6] by a profiling tool. CTF is a flexible, high-throughput, binary trace format developed by the Multicore Association. The power traces can be visualized using Trace Compass, an open-source, standalone viewer popularized by the Linux Tracing Toolkit (LTTng) project [14]. Trace Compass enables correlation and filtering of power traces. An example is provided in Fig. 5.

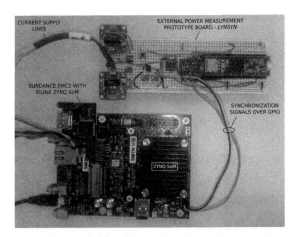

Fig. 4. Lynsyn, the power measurement board connected the EMC2-DP. The current supply wire connects to a current sensor. Synchronization signals are used to start and stop power profiling.

Fig. 5. Inspecting a power trace on Trace Compass

We visualize instantaneous power computed from the current samples on a running line graph as shown in Fig. 6. This helps understand power trends in real-time as the application executes. Abrupt, large changes in power values are flagged on the visualization to alert users.

SDSoC enables users to understand timing of application events in a timeline visualization called the *AXI Trace Viewer* [25]. We extend the AXI Trace Viewer to visualize power traces correlated with application phases as shown in Fig. 7. This enables programmers to conveniently attribute power consumption to concurrent application events and isolate power problems. However, we are not able to refine user interaction in this mode since SDSoC is closed-source software.

Improving the PMU: As part of future work, we intend to profile application-specific data such as the program counter and parallelization events via the JTAG port while collecting power samples. The idea is to analyze this data to

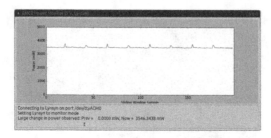

Fig. 6. Power monitor visualization tracks instantaneous power consumption during application execution

Fig. 7. Attributing power consumption to application events on SDSoC's AXI Trace Viewer

pinpoint power problems on high-level semantic visualizations such as control flow graphs and grain graphs [15].

2.2   HW/SW Image Processing Libraries (IPL)

The HW/SW Image Processing Library helps programmers implement accelerated image processing applications. A template-based software library for streaming based applications has been implemented (C++). FPGAs can outperform other hardware architectures, like CPUs and GPUs, for streaming based applications as shown in [11]. The provided functions have been optimized to be accelerated on FPGAs using SDSoC. Furthermore, the library has been optimized for latency, memory throughput and resource usage. The functions follow the OpenVX specification [12], to address a large group of users. OpenVX is an open, royalty-free standard for cross platform acceleration of computer vision applications. Additionally, more data types and auto-vectorization are supported for most functions.

Normally, an image processing function processes one pixel per clock cycle. Using vectorization, it can process one, two, four or even eight pixel per clock cycle. The maximum bit-width of the complete vector is set to 64-bit. Therefore, the maximum vectorization depends on the bit-width of the image data. One advantage of vectorization is the possibility to process higher image resolution.

Another advantage is that the frequency of the design can be reduced. Therefore, the power consumption of applications decreases.

The library contains several compile time optimizations, to reduce inputs from users. For example, the Gaussian kernel coefficients are computed at compile time using the standard deviation and kernel size. They are computed using double precision floating point numbers, then normalized and converted to fixed-point numbers. This computation does not consume extra resources of the FPGA logic. The developer will also get compile time errors if unsupported data types or combinations of them are used, to increase usability. Image data for functions can be in 8-bit, 16-bit or 32-bit fixed-point representation (unsigned/signed).

There are three groups of library functions. The first group consists of all windowed functions. This includes 3×3 Scharr, 3×3 Sobel, 3×3 Median, Box, Gaussian Convolution and Custom Convolution filters. All functions are normalized to avoid overflow (below 1.0 for unsigned and between 0.5 and -0.5 for signed) and optimized in their structure to reduce resource usage. The windowed operations support replicated, constant and undefined border handling.

The second group consists of all pixel-wise functions, which are basically bit-wise and arithmetic operations. This includes: Absolute Difference, Arithmetic Addition, Arithmetic Subtraction, Gradient Magnitude, Pixel-wise Multiplication, Bitwise And, Bitwise Xor, Bitwise Or and Bitwise Not. The arithmetic operations support conversion policies against overflow and different rounding policies if needed.

The last group contains all remaining functions. This includes the Convert Bit Depth, Convert Color, Scale Down, Integral Image, Histogram and Table Lookup functions. The Color Conversion function can convert between the RGB, RGBX and grayscale formats. The Scale Down function supports nearest neighbor and bilinear interpolation.

2.3 Dynamic Partial Reconfiguration Utility (DPRU)

SoCs such as the Xilinx Zynq combine hardened processors with programmable logic which can be used to accelerate application hot-spots. The programmable logic can be partitioned into static and dynamic regions. The dynamic regions can be reconfigured at runtime while the logic in the static region is fixed. The procedure of reconfiguring the dynamic region is called *Dynamic Partial Reconfiguration (DPR)* [3,5]. DPR allows upgrading the design without the need to erase the whole FPGA and saves programming time. Also, it allows more applications to be time-multiplexed onto the same FPGA.

The dynamic partial reconfiguration feature is used in TULIPP to:

- Reduce the need for FPGA-resources by fitting more functionality on the same set of programmable hardware.
- Reduce power consumption by disabling dynamic regions of the FPGA that are not used and re-operating them when they are needed.
- Runtime upgrading which enables more implementation techniques to be deployed at run-time.

DPR is being integrated into the STHEM utilities to allow the TULIPP platform user to update the design freely. Concretely, a set of TCL scripts have been developed to enable DPR within the Xilinx SDSoC high-level workflow [10]. These scripts extend SDSoC functionality for embedded application developments and add more options to the software-hardware partitioning task. In future work, we plan to add optimization logic that analyzes the design to help decide which parts of the application are implemented in static and dynamic regions.

2.4   HIPPEROS SDSoC Compatibility Layer (HSCL)

Xilinx SDSoC is a tool for developing applications for Xilinx System-on-Chip (SoC) architectures and enables the programmer to target its C/C++ code to one of the CPU cores or, through high level synthesis, to the FPGA fabric. HIPPEROS [7] is a multi-core real-time operating system (RTOS) that is adapted for high performance and safety-critical embedded systems applications [8]. The HIPPEROS SDSoC Compatibility Layer is added to Xilinx SDSoC to enable SDSoC to compile applications for HIPPEROS. Previous research work involving the HIPPEROS RTOS includes multi-core micro-kernel design [18], power-aware real-time scheduling [20] and mixed-criticality scheduling [19].

SDSoC is not easily extendable and supports only bare metal, FreeRTOS and Linux applications. Being a closed-source application, it is not possible for a third party to add an additional OS to SDSoC. The approach chosen in this project was to add HIPPEROS support under the disguise of being FreeRTOS.

To achieve this, the following components were necessary:

- *SDSoC platform description:* The SDSoC platform description is used by SDSoC to target a specific hardware platform. In addition to information about the available hardware, it also contains the necessary configuration files and libraries to compile for one of the three supported operating systems. HSCL adds to the platform description by modifying the FreeRTOS configuration files such that HIPPEROS binaries are used instead of FreeRTOS.
- *C library:* Both SDSoC and HIPPEROS need to be initialized correctly when the developed application boots. We cannot modify the SDSoC libraries, so the solution was to put all initialization code into a special C library that automatically gets linked to by the SDSoC toolchain. Additionally, SDSoC requires some specific ABI compilation flags to set for every object file linked within the accelerated program. Therefore, we created a specific HIPPEROS distribution dedicated to the Tulipp platform and the compatibility with SDSoC.
- *Scripts:* Unlike FreeRTOS, HIPPEROS needs an additional step after compilation to package the resulting elf file into an executable binary. The necessary script for doing this is provided and presented to the user in the SDSoC SD-card generation step.
- *Bootloader:* In order to correctly boot a HIPPEROS application, a bootloader is necessary. This is also the case when starting the application from the Xilinx

debugger. It is not sufficient to upload the binary files to memory and jump to the entry address. Therefore, a small bootloader is provided such that debugging and tracing from the SDSoC GUI or command line is possible.

3   Conclusion and Further Work

In this paper, we have presented the underlying philosophy of the analysis and development tools that will be developed during the TULIPP project. Further, we have described the implementation of our first four utilities: a novel power measurement and analysis utility (the PMU), a platform-optimized image processing library (the IPL), a dynamic partial reconfiguration utility (the DPRU), and an utility providing support for using the HIPPEROS RTOS within Xilinx SDSoC (the HSCL).

The work achieved so far forms the basis of the research that will be carried out during the second half of the TULIPP project. We will leverage the developed utilities to provide novel performance analysis and design space exploration tools that specifically focus on embedded image processing systems. In addition, we aim to quantitatively compare our image processing library to other libraries and full-custom FPGA implementations. Finally, we will use the utilities to improve the TULIPP use case applications. The use cases are industry-grade applications within the medical, automotive and unmanned aerial vehicle domains.

Acknowledgement. The work is funded by European Commission under the H2020 Framework Program for Research and Innovation under grant agreement number 688403.

References

1. Abusultan, M., Khatri, S.P.: A comparison of FinFET based FPGA LUT designs. In: Proceedings of the 24th Edition of the Great Lakes Symposium on VLSI, GLSVLSI 2014, pp. 353–358. ACM, New York (2014)
2. Buschhoff, M., Günter, C., Spinczyk, O.: MIMOSA, a highly sensitive and accurate power measurement technique for low-power systems. In: Langendoen, K., Hu, W., Ferrari, F., Zimmerling, M., Mottola, L. (eds.) Real-World Wireless Sensor Networks. LNEE, vol. 281, pp. 139–151. Springer, Cham (2014). https://doi.org/10.1007/978-3-319-03071-5_16
3. Cornil, M., Paolillo, A., Goossens, J., Rodriguez, B.: Research and implementation challenges of RTOS support for heterogeneous computing platforms. In: Heterogeneous Architectures and Real-Time Systems Seminar, May 2017
4. Di Nisio, A., Di Noia, T., Carducci, C.G.C., Spadavecchia, M.: High dynamic range power consumption measurement in microcontroller-based applications. IEEE Trans. Instrum. Meas. **65**(9), 1968–1976 (2016)
5. Dye, D.: Partial reconfiguration of Xilinx FPGAs using ISE design suite, wp374 (v1.2) (2012)
6. EfficiOS: Common Trace Format (CTF) (2017). http://www.efficios.com/ctf
7. HIPPEROS (2017). http://hipperos.com/

8. Jahre, M., Djupdal, A., Kalms, L., Muddukrishna, A.: D4.1: basic tool chain. Technical report, TULIPP Project (2017)
9. Kalb, T., Kalms, L., Göhringer, D., Pons, C., Marty, F., Muddukrishna, A., Jahre, M., Kjeldsberg, P.G., Ruf, B., Schuchert, T., Tchouchenkov, I., Ehrenstrahle, C., Christensen, F., Paolillo, A., Lemer, C., Bernard, G., Duhem, F., Millet, P.: TULIPP: towards ubiquitous low-power image processing platforms. In: 2016 International Conference on Embedded Computer Systems: Architectures, Modeling and Simulation (SAMOS), pp. 306–311, July 2016
10. Kalb, T., Göhringer, D.: Enabling dynamic and partial reconfiguration in Xilinx SDSoC. In: ReConFigurable Computing and FPGAs (ReConFig). IEEE (2016)
11. Kalms, L., Göhringer, D.: Exploration of OpenCL for FPGAs using SDAccel and comparison to GPUs and multicore CPUs. In: 2017 27th International Conference on Field Programmable Logic and Applications (FPL), pp. 1–4, September 2017
12. Khronos Vision Working Group: The OpenVX Specification (2017). https://www.khronos.org/registry/OpenVX/specs/1.2/OpenVX_Specification_1_2.pdf
13. Konstantakos, V., Chatzigeorgiou, A., Nikolaidis, S., Laopoulos, T.: Energy consumption estimation in embedded systems. IEEE Trans. Instrum. Meas. **57**(4), 797–804 (2008)
14. LLTng: Linux Tracing Toolkit Next Generation (2017). http://www.lttng.org
15. Muddukrishna, A., Jonsson, P.A., Podobas, A., Brorsson, M.: Grain graphs: OpenMP performance analysis made easy. In: Proceedings of the 21st ACM SIGPLAN Symposium on Principles and Practice of Parallel Programming (2016)
16. Mukhanov, L., Petoumenos, P., Wang, Z., Parasyris, N., Nikolopoulos, D.S., De Supinski, B.R., Leather, H.: ALEA: a fine-grained energy profiling tool. ACM Trans. Archit. Code Optim. (TACO) **14**(1), 1 (2017)
17. Nakutis, Z.: Embedded systems power consumption measurement methods overview. MATAVIMAI **2**(44), 29–35 (2009)
18. Paolillo, A., Desenfans, O., Svoboda, V., Goossens, J., Rodriguez, B.: A new configurable and parallel embedded real-time micro-kernel for multi-core platforms. In: Proceedings of the ECRTS Workshop on Operating Systems Platforms for Embedded Real-Time applications, July 2015
19. Paolillo, A., Rodriguez, P., Svoboda, V., Desenfans, O., Goossens, J., Rodriguez, B., Girbal, S., Faugère, M., Bonnot, P.: Porting a safety-critical industrial application on a mixed-criticality enabled real-time operating system. In: Proceedings of the 5th Workshop on Mixed-Criticality Systems, December 2017
20. Paolillo, A., Rodriguez, P., Veshchikov, N., Goossens, J., Rodriguez, B.: Quantifying energy consumption for practical fork-join parallelism on an embedded real-time operating system. In: Proceedings of the 24th International Conference on Real-Time Networks and Systems, RTNS 2016, pp. 329–338. ACM (2016)
21. PJRC: Teensy 3.6 (2017). https://www.pjrc.com/store/teensy36.html
22. Texas Instruments: INA169-Q1: Automotive Grade, 60-V, High-Side, High-Speed, Current Output Current Shunt Monitor (2017). http://www.ti.com/product/INA169-Q1/datasheet/detailed_description#SGLS1854308
23. Trenz-Electronic: Test fixture for Zynq UltraScale+ MPSoC (2017). https://wiki.trenz-electronic.de/display/PD/TEBT0808+TRM

24. Xilinx: Measuring ZC702 Power using TI Fusion Power Designer Tech Tip (2014). http://www.wiki.xilinx.com/Zynq-7000+AP+SoC+Low+Power+Techniques+part +2+-+Measuring+ZC702+Power+using+TI+Fusion+Power+Designer+Tech+ Tip
25. Xilinx: Xilinx Environment Tutorial (UG1028) (2016)
26. Xilinx: Xilinx Power Estimator (2017). https://www.xilinx.com/products/ technology/power/xpe.html
27. Xilinx: Xilinx XADC User Guide (2017). https://www.xilinx.com/support/ documentation/user_guides/ug480_7Series_XADC.pdf

Author Index

Printed in the United States
By Bookmasters